Charles Seale-Hayne Library
University of Plymouth
(01752) 588 588
LibraryandITenquiries@plymouth.ac.uk

THE BICKERSTETH FAMILY
WORLD WAR II DIARY

J.B.B.

THE BICKERSTETH FAMILY WORLD WAR II DIARY

Dear Grandmother

Volume I

1939-1942

Edited by

Nick Smart

Studies in British History
Volume 58

The Edwin Mellen Press
Lewiston•Queenston•Lampeter

Library of Congress Cataloging-in-Publication Data

The Bickersteth family World War II diary, dear grandmother / edited by Nick Smart.
    p. cm. -- (Studies in British history ; v. 58)
    Includes index.
    ISBN 0-7734-7904-X (v. 1)
    1. World War, 1939-1945--Great Britain. 2. Great Britain--Social life and Customs--20th century. 3. World War, 1939-1945--Personal narratives, British. 4. Bickersteth family. I. Smart, Nick, 1952- II. Series.

D759 .B55 1999
941.084--dc21   99-046935

This is volume 58 in the continuing series
Studies in British History
Volume 58 ISBN 0-7734-7904-X
SBH Series ISBN 0-88946-450-2

A CIP catalog record for this book is available from the British Library.

Front cover: War Weapons Week in a Country Town, by Michael Ford
              Courtesy of The Imperial War Museum

The Edwin Mellen Press   The Edwin Mellen Press
Box 450   Box 67
Lewiston, New York   Queenston, Ontario
USA 14092-0450   CANADA L0S 1L0

The Edwin Mellen Press, Ltd.
Lampeter, Ceredigion, Wales
UNITED KINGDOM SA48 8LT

Printed in the United States of America

Contents

Acknowledgments			v
Foreword			vii
The Bickersteth Family			ix
		Introduction	xi
	i	The Diarists	xvi
	ii	The Diaries	xxi
		1939 September-December	1
		1940 January-December	57
		1941 January-December	261
		1942 January-April	379
Abbreviations			415
Index			417

Acknowledgments

To recall that the first step in the process of editing this volume of *Dear Grandmother* was a chance encounter with the Bickersteth Second World War diaries in the Churchill College Cambridge archive, is also to remember that without the help of numerous people, publication would not have been possible.

My thanks are due to the Bickersteth family for the *sine die* loan of their set of war diaries. Michael Bickersteth, the owner, and before him his father Edward, who died in 1997, have been most generous in allowing me not merely the privilege of access, but the priceless advantage of being able to work on the manuscript at home. Ursula Bickersteth was most encouraging from the start, but without the constant help of Bishop John Bickersteth it is doubtful whether much of substance would have seen the light of day. His encouragement, tactful liaison work and tireless reading of drafts have been of inestimable value. His prompt return of the buff envelope, always with kindly note, sometimes with more material, and invariably with the script heavy with annotations, became a welcome regular feature of the editing process.

My Faculty's gift of a budget was most welcome, and Simon Rippingale's early assistance in setting-up the computer files proved a lasting asset. More generally, Alex Palmer and Kai Petersen helped in the avoidance of computer problems. Alan Gentle's work with photographs was, as it always is, much appreciated, while the library staff at Exmouth were forever models of cheerful efficiency. Irene Breckon and Frances Keays scarcely realised what they had taken on when they agreed to 'do me a favour' and help print-out the manuscript. Above all, thanks are due to my former colleague, Keith Waddams. The efficient and interested way in which he proof-read the manuscript, transformed what is usually the difficult phase of pre-publication fine-tuning into a stimulating and relatively stress-free exercise.

Being able to work on the material at home was the greatest pleasure because there, in the company of Sara, Katie and Jacob, I could work at an agreeable pace without losing sight of what was important in life.

Exmouth, April 1999

FOREWORD

The Right Reverend John Bickersteth
*Sometime Bishop of Bath and Wells
and Clerk of the Closet to
Her Majesty The Queen*

Editor of *The Bickersteth Diaries, 1914-1918*

How did a West Country academic, quite unknown to our family, come to be tackling the editing of seven volumes of the 1939-1945 Bickersteth War Diary? How has he managed to persevere so far with disentangling who was who in all the ramifications of our large clan, and furthermore seems to be showing every sign of pressing on with the second half of the whole project? I have decided to use Nick Smart's very kind invitation to write a Foreword to his work by offering an answer to those two questions.

Nick only swam into the Bickersteth family's ken as a result of being in Cambridge, at the Churchill College Archive Centre, in the autumn of 1995, when he was doing some work on the papers of people connected with Neville Chamberlain's government. While doing just that, he came across, and was intrigued by, the Bickersteth family papers, in particular the Second World War Diary. He found them there because my late brother, then the owner of the two sets of the same work, had recently given one set to Churchill College, to honour a half-promise, made some years before, to the Cambridge historian Stephen Roskill by Burgon Bickersteth, himself the moving spirit behind the Diary in both wars, that 'one day' this would happen. My brother Ted used the moment of his move into a small house to do this. Thus it came about that the Senior Lecturer in History at the University of Plymouth was actually the first person to write to Ted as follows: 'I would relish the chance to edit towards publication ... I am aware that the 1st World War Diary is about to have an edited version published, in which case the emergence of the 2nd might be appropriate.'

As the launch of *The Bickersteth Diaries 1914-1918*, for which I was responsible, was only a few weeks away, my brother (who only died in 1997) and I decided to invite Dr Smart to it. At Ted's suggestion I brought with me all eighteen volumes of the Diary (eleven of the 1st War, seven of the 2nd) for the 80 or so guests at the launch to see; and afterwards we entrusted the would-be editor with the seven he wanted, asking him to explore possibilities and report back. He duly did, saying that he would be glad to do the work. What you are holding here is the first part of the result of his four-year labour; and I can only say that I have thoroughly enjoyed working with Nick to the extent of reading every word he has written, commenting and correcting on many points of detail as he has sent me his instalments. His perceptive introduction has totally converted me to the rightness of doing what he has so wholeheartedly undertaken, and I am quite certain that these two volumes will prove to be of considerable interest to a generation that continues to be hungry for material on both world wars; and also that the family will be immensely grateful to be reminded in this way of 'the uncles', of whom we were inordinately fond; and indeed to read again the now fifty-year-old letters which many of us wrote to the matriarchal figure whom we knew and loved as 'Dear Grandmother'.

+ John Bickersteth

The branch of the Bickersteth family

Samuel Bickersteth 1857-1937   *m.* 1881   Ella Monier-Williams 1858-1954

| Monier 1882-1976 *m.* Kitty Jelf 1882-1936 | Geoffrey 1884-1974 *m.* Jean Sorley 1893-1976 | Julian 1885-1962 | Burgon 1888-1979 | Morris 1891-1916 | Ralph 1894-1989 *m.(i)* Alison Grafton 1894-1959 |

m. (ii) Frances Pangbourne 1919-

| Kay 1912-1993 *m.* Charles Beveridge | Edward 1915-1997 *m.* Elspeth Cameron | Mary 1918- | John 1921- *m.* Rosemary Cleveland-Stevens |
| 2s. 1d. | 3s. | | 3s. 1d. |

Peter, 1924-
m. 1998
Victoria Macpherson *(i)*
m.
Pauline Poupard *(ii)*

2s. 1d.

| Tony 1920-1948 | Julian 1921-1945 | Elfride 1924- | Ursula 1928- | David 1930- *m.* Joyce Allen |
| | | | | 3s.1d. |

Introduction

In the belief that future generations might be interested in what their forebears did in times judged unproblematically historic, one of the families of the large Bickersteth 'clan' kept diaries for both world wars. The first series, comprising eleven 'fat cloth-bound volumes' of nearly 4,000 typescript pages was the source for the 1995 publication of *The Bickersteth Diaries, 1914-1918*, edited by Bishop John Bickersteth.[1] The second series, a mere 2,300 typed pages forming a 'rather less bulky' collection, provides the subject for this and a subsequent volume of the family's record of the Second World War. Volume I of *Dear Grandmother* is the edited version of the Bickersteth Second World War diaries from the outbreak of hostilities in September 1939 to the spring of 1942. Volume II covers the remainder of the Second World War.

If explanation is needed for the seeming paradox of published output standing in inverse proportion to available material, it needs stressing that while there is nothing more or less intrinsic about claims of interest or relevance attached to memoirs of either World War, both editors set about their tasks in quite different ways and from different generational standpoints. To John Bickersteth, born in 1921, the story of the Great War, as related by friends and relatives, was a feature of his upbringing and attracted his historical imagination in a way that the Second World War, which he had lived through and fought in, could not. In his editing of *The Bickersteth Diaries* he knew the people he was writing about. They were his blood relatives, and it was their memory he wished to celebrate. In contrast, the editor of *Dear Grandmother* is not related to the family, was born in the 1950s, and possesses no instincts beyond those of the historian to discriminate between what is worthy of publication and what is best left out.

That in relative terms more diary material is exposed in *Dear Grandmother* is a function of these differences of editorial position. More does not mean better or worse, just different. The claim that the Bickersteth Second World War diaries are important enough to command widespread interest could scarcely be made by a member of the family, but can be sustained with conviction by an outsider. This being so, the editorial tone and style of interventionism is much changed. In that

---

[1] John Bickersteth (ed.). *The Bickersteth Diaries, 1914-1918* (Leo Cooper, 1995), p. xvii

the balance maintained between respect and affection towards the people concerned cannot be that of a family member, anxieties about maintaining the tempo of excitement are reduced, while the scope for livening up entries with editorial comment or anecdote is diminished. Only a member of the family could have conveyed the kind of fondness for his grandmother and uncles with the confident imagination John Bickersteth deploys, whereas this editor was bound to take a more sober back-seat approach, content to let the epistolary narrative take its time to evolve. Characters, brought vividly to life in *The Bickersteth Diaries*, have, of necessity, been afforded flatter identities in *Dear Grandmother*. They are cast less as people of vibrant personal memory than as actors performing roles. The touch is less personal, the editorial voice is quieter, and an extra generation has, as it were, to be added on. In short, though the form of both series of war diaries is similar, with some of the same principals at their core, two very different histories are produced.

On these grounds there never was any sense of the *The Bickersteth Diaries* constituting an act to follow. From the start it was agreed that a drier, less obviously dramatic kind of work was needed. The differing character of the two World Wars offers further reasons for constructing an alternative treatment. To John Bickersteth it was appropriate to focus on his uncles, the brothers Julian and Burgon, who served on what is remembered as the major theatre of that war, the Western Front. But just as the erosion of the distinction between combatant and civilian in the Second World War meant that neither brother, though too old for active service, was left inactive, other members of the family - old as well as young - were no less directly affected, and merit, therefore, their place in the narrative. Hence the need to accommodate more actors in settings which were at once more domestic and at the same time more varied. Such has been the editorial freedom afforded that the *Dear Grandmother* series is not, nor ever was intended, as a sequel to the book John Bickersteth produced. Indeed, and with his help and encouragement, the project was envisaged more as a comprehensive, wide-ranging and accessible source on the diversity of life lived during the Second World War than as a family history as such.

Editing, it has been said, is a licensed form of reading other people's letters. The fascination lies in equating the historian's knowledge, in broad terms, of what happened next, with the revealed thought-world of sensitive and well-informed people who wrote in response to events as they occurred, and whose spirits rose and fell with the fortunes of war. War news was eagerly devoured and discussed. Some reactions are as we might expect, but there are others which, seen from today's perspective, are surprising. For a family which could count bishops amongst its members and was very much of what later would be called 'the establishment', it is notable how quickly the notion took root that war would sweep away much of the existing social order and usher in a regime of state-led redistributive change. Or again, the speed with which suspicion of the Soviet Union gives way to admiration after the German invasion of Russia in 1941 is, in its way, remarkable. The seemingly unmerited sense of gloom which greeted news of military defeat in Crete reads oddly when set against the tone of positively Micawberish optimism that followed the fall of France. When thoughts turned to the future, predictions were very often wrong. The notion that the public schools would have to radically adapt or perish was, as we now know, exaggerated. Equally the assumption that eventual victory could only consolidate and strengthen the British Empire has not stood the test of time. But that the same people could be wrong on some things and yet make blindingly accurate projections on, say, the power-bloc dominated shape of the post-war world, serves as a reminder that whatever the condescensions of posterity, people at the time were thinking ahead, and that the uncertainties induced by war had not destroyed their powers of reasoned thought and expression.

If a sense of surprise is the reader's constant companion over family reactions to great events, it also extends to coverage of more mundane matters. Though geographically dispersed, the family was kept close-knit by the correspondence that formed the war diary. Amidst the concern for each other's health and safety there is much humour. The stylised cockney 'We can take it' stuff is there, if expressed in more genteel terms, and there is also a good deal of grumbling about the numerous inconveniences and shortages of wartime. The 'People's War' it may have been, but evidently some prejudices died harder than others in the early years of the conflict. If, for example, evacuated schoolchildren were not always regarded as a nuisance, the teachers who accompanied them invariably were. Soldiers, and particularly officers, who sought to make themselves too comfortable in their billeting arrangements were looked down on; and a queer sense of propriety meant that voluntary war work was afforded a status far superior to anything that smacked of compulsion. From the start, just about everything that issued from the Ministry of Information was condemned outright as pernicious propaganda, and, when it came, the conscription of women was bitterly resented. Amidst all this, fear, still less defeatism, scarcely intrudes, although criticism of the way the war was being run was often direct and candid. The Bickersteths were not Evelyn Waugh grotesques adapting with instinctive rearguard defensiveness to some imagined takeover by the great unwashed. Nor, by the same token, were they creatures of J.B. Priestley's imagination, doing their respective bits with cheerful unruffled fortitude. But however strong the historian's instinct to back away from the clichéd images of Britain in wartime - whether as a response to childhood over-exposure to Churchill's speeches or, for that matter, *Dad's Army* episodes - there is a case for saying that the Bickersteths' sense of history came to meet them during the early years of the Second World War. The spectacle fascinated them, and, in their account, the summer of 1940 really was our finest hour. The more threatening the military situation the more enchanting the weather, and the more precious the English countryside. They may have spoken in the assured tones of the middle class, though perhaps at times the optimism they expressed concealed anxieties about the strategic situation and the temper of the people around them. But on one thing there can be no mistake; these were people who would have died in defence of 'our island'.

Of course the family could not be described as typical. Those who rely on kind business friends or relatives to pay for their sons' education at Charterhouse, Marlborough and Rugby as a prelude to their going up to Christ Church, Oxford tend to exclude themselves from that category. Theirs is not the language of subordinacy striving to find a form of words that would adequately convey their thoughts. Their fluency in accepted standard English is both an affirmative statement of what, sociologically, they were and also offers clues as to the kind of codings they used in their correspondence. Some of the these are quite interesting. War, it was understood, meant for-the-duration social disruption. Hence, in much the same way as, when at school, one would submit to being captained in the House XI by someone who was, quite patently, a social inferior, the same calculus could be made to apply in wartime. Part of the pleasure, it seems, of Home Guard duty lay in the carnivalesque inversion of social rank whereby Pte. Bickersteth would suffer dreadful verbal abuse undertaking a Bren gun course and mutely take orders from the Sergeant who, ordinarily, was a local estate agent. Fire-watching and other civil defence activities were also subject to similar would-be egalitarian notions of 'good form'. When the games-playing stopped however, the assumption that war service meant a leadership role for the Bickersteths went unquestioned. That the boys coming of military age should obtain commissions and serve - preferably in a smart regiment - was the ordained correct course in wartime. There was a collective family sigh of relief when Hore-Belisha resigned as Secretary of State for War in January 1940, if only because it was expected - rightly as it turned out - that those 'democratic reforms' of the army he had sponsored would perish with him. Equally the naturalness with which strings were pulled, and connections with powerful and influential figures exploited, was both a source of mobility and confirmation of high status. To mention here that, in this respect, Burgon was a wirepuller and shoulder-rubber *par excellence* is but to make an obvious point. Less obviously but more important is the observation that none of this serves to disqualify. Within the diaries are insights into, and cameo descriptions of, a system. It was one bounded by clubland gossip and élite reputationism whereby, with the minimum of public fuss, important and far-reaching decisions were made. The present-day high-minded might disapprove of the privileging of such entries on the grounds that skewing the narrative away from social history lays too much stress on descriptions of wheel-greasing political insider gossip. But if so, no apology is offered. *Dear Grandmother* makes no pretence at providing a 'from-the-bottom-up' view. To contrive to knead the Bickersteth record of the Second World War so as to conform with some constructed notion of ordinariness would be folly. Yet in saying this, it remains the case what this untypical family records is as richly textured a memoir as any that exists of Britain during the Second World War.

Today's Bickersteths have not sought to interfere with this project. They have been too encouragingly generous to wish to impose a paeanistic sentimental line on the editing process. Content to allow a historian's curiosity free rein and let their grandmother's, their uncles', and even their own record of the Second World War speak for itself, they have allowed themselves to be persuaded that what is 'turgid' or 'old hat' to them is a valid historical record that deserves exposure to a wider public. While the title, *Dear Grandmother*, acknowledges their guardianship of the material, it also conveys some sense of the editor's gratitude towards the grandchildren for allowing themselves to become actors in a narrative not of their moulding. In their kindness they encouraged a 'warts and all' treatment of their uncles Julian and Burgon, both of whom were awarded the Military Cross in the Great War, and each of whom was in his way exceptional. Their not crimping at the emotional range of the entries - negative as well as positive - has made the editorial task all the more stimulating and in its way easier. Their permission to edit was, of course, fundamental. But over and above that, without their active support, neither this volume nor its sequel could have been produced.

Dear Grandmother: the actors

In a formal sense Ella Bickersteth, John Bickersteth's grandmother, was the family diarist for both world wars. It was to her that the majority of the letters that feature in the war diaries were written, and it was she who acted as keeper of the material until it was typed-up and bound. But, well into her eighties at the beginning of the Second World War, a widow, blind and housebound, she was in no position to play a more active role than record items of news from the wireless and receive letters sent to her. In this role, and able only to listen, someone - a maid, a 'companion' or a friend - had to read the letters to her and take dictation. Thus communication was rendered indirect. Moreover, from September 1940 she was moved from her home and familiar surroundings in Canterbury (regarded as being very much in the front line of invasion), staying with her eldest and youngest sons Monier and Ralph, or, more usually, with her third son Julian, who on his own initiative had evacuated his school from Felsted in Essex to Herefordshire. It was not till October 1944 that she was able to return to Canterbury.

Ella Chlora Faithfull Monier-Williams (E.C.F.B.) was the daughter of the Professor of Sanskrit at Oxford. One of the six or seven little Oxford girls who, along with Alice Liddell, was written to and photographed by Lewis Carroll, she married Samuel Bickersteth in 1881. His father, who later became Bishop of Exeter, and his brother, who became Bishop of Tokyo, pointed the way to the extent that Sam was himself ordained in the year of his marriage. He and Ella had six sons, all of whom were grown up by the time the First World War broke out, and two of whom, Monier and Julian, were already ordained. In 1916, the same year as their fifth son, Morris, was killed on the first day of the Battle of the Somme, Sam was appointed Canon Residentiary at Canterbury. This position he held until shortly before his death in 1937.

Monier, the eldest son, was ordained in 1907. After curacies in a number of parishes, and a lifetime's involvement in missionary work, he became Rector of Chiddingstone on the Kent-Sussex border in 1935. If this represented a kind of coming home, the sadness was that his wife, Kitty, died the following year. Of their four children, the eldest, Kay married Charles Beveridge, a Naval Reservist, in 1939. Edward, though engaged to a local girl, was in the Sudan Political Service, while Mary, whose voluntary war work was prodigious, stayed at home. The youngest child was John, the future Bishop of Bath and Wells and editor of *The Bickersteth Diaries, 1914-1918*. He was in his last year at Rugby and in the normal course of events would have gone up to Christ Church, Oxford for the Michaelmas term of 1940. That he decided against this, and worked in forestry after he left school before his call-up for officer's training is but one of the threads to the *Dear Grandmother* narrative.

Geoffrey, the second son, had served in Naval Intelligence in the First World War. He was an academic who had recently left the University of Glasgow to become Professor of English at Aberdeen, though his scholarly interest was devoted to pre-Renaissance Italian poetry, particularly the works of Dante Alighieri. Intellectually formidable and fully equipped to express himself on a wide range of subjects, Geoffrey made his dislike of the idea of a family war diary beginning again clear from the start. Though he wrote regularly to E.C.F.B., he insisted that his views were of little worth and that his letters were not written as entries. There was nothing arch about such modesty, and yet in seeking to distance himself from the Canterbury-centred war diary inspired by his brother Burgon and kept by his mother, Geoffrey placed himself in something of a false position. For his epistolary contributions are among the most interesting - certainly the most belligerent - of all the family's. Never short of an opinion - whether on grand strategy, the foibles of the War Office, or the advice of so-called food experts - Geoffrey's bulletins from Aberdeen pepper the narrative with characteristic multi-claused pungency. The effects are at times comic, yet Geoffrey's war was touched by tragedy. Of his two serving sons, one, [young] Julian was killed in Greece in 1945, aged twenty-three. The other, his dearly beloved Tony, survived a dangerous war fighting with the Gurkhas in Burma, only to be killed in a climbing accident in France in 1948.

Ralph, the youngest son, was a successful London businessman, a director and later chairman, of the City insurance company A.W.Bain. While he became increasingly involved in government business with the Ministry of Food, his wife Alison served for a time at a YMCA canteen on Victoria Station. Of all the family Ralph was best placed to witness and record the devastations of the London Blitz, and was, perhaps, the coolest and most dispassionate contributor to the war diary.

Determined to look always on the bright side, and yet as aware as anybody that there might be no future to look forward to, Ralph's capacity for dry understatement was his distinctive hallmark. But for all his cool-headed ability to take everything in his stride, Ralph's obvious love for and pride in Peter, his only son, is one of the narrative's more touching themes.

To jump from Geoffrey, the second son in the cast list, to Ralph, the youngest, is, of course, a device. It serves to save discussion of *Dear Grandmother*'s principal actors to the end. These are E.C.F.B's third and fourth sons, Julian and Burgon (J.B.B.), the same brothers who feature so prominently in John Bickersteth's *Bickersteth Diaries*.

Julian and Burgon shared much in common. Both had been decorated in the Great War, they were tremendous friends, and both, as it happened, were lifelong bachelors. Each was or had been in his way involved in education in the Dominions; Julian in Australia as a headmaster (he returned to England in 1933 to take up the headship of Felsted) while Burgon's stamping ground was Canada, where from 1921 he had been Warden of Hart House, an institution intended by the Massey family (who paid for its building) as a kind of Oxbridge-type non-residential college within the University of Toronto. With Burgon '[bringing] the stone walls and timber to life,'[1] Hart House became under his stewardship very much the cultural hub of the University.

Burgon's habit was to return to England -or better perhaps Europe - for his long summer leave, and extensive continental touring holidays with his parents and, as often as not with Julian, became the established pattern. Morris's grave near Albert was often visited, but as the 1930s progressed, trips further afield to Italy and Germany were undertaken. It was on the basis of the projected 1936 summer tour that the prime minister, Baldwin, 'snatch[ing] at any chance of a new perspective on the state of Germany',[2] commissioned Burgon to write a report covering a wide range of impressions; the position of the Churches, the stability of the regime, colonial restitution, and attitudes towards Britain. Burgon's seventeen-page-long memorandum, 'Notes on the German Situation', was duly submitted.[3]

---

[1] Massey, V. *What's Past is Prologue* (Macmillan, 1963), p. 57.

[2] Middlemas, K. and Barnes, J. *Baldwin* (Macmillan, 1969), p. 951.

[3] J.B.B.'s copy of this memorandum is in vol. XII of the [First] World War Diary. This, covering the years 1931-39, is a sort of appendix to the previous volumes and consists mainly of itinerary accounts of the annual summer holiday.

At war's beginning, in September 1939, the summer holidays were drawing to a close. Julian had his public school to prepare for the new academic year, and Burgon who had, as usual, taken his annual leave in England, France and Switzerland, set sail for Canada 'feeling more miserable than [he] had ever felt in [his] life', having been persuaded that his place was in Toronto. A day into the voyage he heard Chamberlain broadcast Britain's declaration of war over the wireless, and learned later that the liner *Athenia* had been torpedoed and sunk. He was in Canada during the months of the 'phoney war'. The greater the distance, the fuller the correspondence. One letter writer was Lord Hankey, the former secretary to the Cabinet, and then a member of Chamberlain's War Cabinet. Having struck up a 'warm friendship' as far back as 1927, and knowing J.B.B. was an intimate with the Canadian premier Mackenzie King, Hankey used his friendship to 'keep himself *au courant* with [Canadian] political feelings and political developments.'[1] Euan Wallace, a brother-officer and friend from First World War days, and Minister of Transport until May 1940, was a regular correspondent, as, less regularly, were Stafford Cripps and Tom Jones, the former deputy secretary to the Cabinet, who still kept a finger in a number of pies.[2] If these names provide a taste of the political links Burgon cultivated, his connections with senior figures in the army and the Church of England were as numerous and ran as deep. General Ismay, Churchill's Chief of Staff from May 1940, was an old friend from Charterhouse days. Close contact was kept with General Paget, Commander in Chief Home Forces 1940-42, and, like Julian, Burgon was in frequent touch with Cosmo Gordon Lang, the Archbishop of Canterbury, and others at Lambeth Palace. In the early months of the war, Burgon was kept up-to-date by E.C.F.B. with news of Hewlett Johnson, the 'Red Dean' of Canterbury. Later entries reveal a good deal of mutual warmth in the relationship, but in the winter of 1939-40 Burgon could do little but record the storms of protest that accompanied Hewlett Johnson's book, *The Socialist Sixth of the World*, his efforts to turn the nave of Canterbury Cathedral into an air raid shelter,

---

[1] S. Roskill, *Hankey: Man of Secrets vol. III, 1931-1963* (Collins, 1974), pp. 131 and 137.
[2] Jones's own edited *Diary with Letters (OUP, 1954)* suggest a correspondence with J.B.B. going at least as far back as 1931, and the Bickersteth index entries thereafter imply that letters passed to and fro on a regular basis. It had been T.J. who had introduced J.B.B. to Baldwin in 1936, and, like Hankey, he had evidently come to regard J.B.B. as a useful contact; not least as a sort of listening post on Canadian affairs.

and, notoriously, for his refusal to condemn the Soviet Union's invasion of Finland.

Both brothers, it seems, were men liable to make sudden decisions. In the crisis month of May 1940, Julian reached the quick but firm conclusion that Felsted must be evacuated, while Burgon decided to return to England. He was, as he describes, listening to an evening concert in Hart House but thinking all the while of the German forces sweeping through northern France in their dash for the Channel coast. In an instant he made up his mind that home was where he was needed. Having obtained leave of absence from the University of Toronto authorities, he was back in Canterbury within less than a fortnight ready to join the Home Guard, an organisation which he and other members of the family persisted in calling the Local Defence Volunteers. Whatever the name, from June until September 1940 it is J.B.B.'s accounts of guard duty, drill, alarms over parachutists and fifth columnists, and the threat to the countryside which give the narrative its shape. To say that his descriptions of the Kentish landscape are, in their way, beautiful is also to register that Burgon was probably having the time of his life that summer. Meanwhile, Julian was weighed down with the responsibility of evacuating Felsted School - its staff, its pupils and its portable property - to various hired premises in Herefordshire.

Burgon was not left to linger undisturbed with the Canterbury Home Guard for long. Whether he announced his availability for work in his trips to London over lunch at the Travellers' Club, or whether his friend Vincent Massey, the Canadian High Commissioner in London, exerted influence, he was diverted away from Euan Wallace's recommendation to work with MI6 and, in early September was asked by Sir James Grigg, the Permanent Under-Secretary at the War Office, to serve as educational adviser to Lieut-General McNaughton whose 1st. Canadian Corps was forming in Surrey. Interestingly the person who seems to have recommended Burgon to Grigg, by 'speaking very highly of [his] work in Canada', was the civil servant lately disgraced by too close an association with Neville Chamberlain, Sir Horace Wilson.[1] Whatever, as General McNaughton put it, 'the question of the welfare of the troops this winter and ... the development of opportunities for extra-mural work', had been on his mind for some time. Sure that Burgon, with all his experience at the University of Toronto 'would be able to give

---

[1] Lt-Gen. Brown to J.B.B., 24 August 1940, with holograph note that the meeting Brown suggested took place on 4 September.

us advice of great value', he invited him to join his staff. Thus began Burgon's twenty-month stint as civilian educational adviser to General McNaughton's Canadian forces in England. He held this post until his appointment in April 1942 - by the same James Grigg, now Secretary of State for War - to the War Office as Director of Army Education.

How Burgon fared as Director of Army Education is, properly, the concern of Volume II of *Dear Grandmother*. It is also in the second volume that the theme of wartime social change, at any rate of élite conceptions of the future of social policy, merit full discussion. Certainly Burgon's involvement with the Army Bureau of Current Affairs (ABCA) and his own work in the publication of *British Way and Purpose* (BWP) makes him a figure of central importance in any discussion of the extent to which left-wing ideas or 'Beveridgism' came to dominate political and civil service thinking in the later war years. That Volume I is less concerned with such considerations does not mean they are absent. Burgon's collaboration with W.E.Williams and ABCA, for example, began in the autumn of 1941. His connections with the Council for the Encouragement of Music and the Arts (CEMA) - generally remembered as the forerunner of the Arts Council - began earlier still, thanks to some deft introductory work by Tom Jones. But, while Burgon would probably have agreed with Julian Huxley's 1941 contention that the experience of war 'gave an existential reality to the organic conception of society in a way that had never been achieved by [previous] abstract analysis',[1] his thinking on the achievement of such an end was as yet undeveloped. He worked too hard with the Canadian forces to have the leisure to think beyond the short term. The same could be said of Julian who, until his appointment as Archdeacon of Maidstone in 1943, was too embroiled with the problems of headmastering the evacuated Felsted to raise his sights much beyond the urgencies of the present. Hence an organisational logic as well as a sense of period have driven the decision to edit *Dear Grandmother* into its two-volume form. If the first volume covers that phase of the war when thoughts of national survival were to the fore, and victory was a question of 'if', the passage to that state of assumption where victory became a matter of 'when' provides the context for the second.

---

[1] Julian Huxley, cited by Harris, J. 'The debate on State Welfare', in Smith, H (ed.). *War and Social Change: Britain and the Second World War* (Manchester University Press, 1986) p. 236.

There is always an element of schematic meat-cleaver crudity about editing a narrative into two parts. But just as 400-odd pages seem enough for one volume, the spring of 1942 presents itself as the appropriate moment to make the break. It was the time when Burgon knew he would soon leave his Canadians, and was fretting about his margarine and clothing coupons before taking up his new post in the War Office. It was the time when war reports from the Middle East were not good, and when news from the Far East was unremittingly bad. That Tony, Geoffrey's son, had just arrived with his battalion in that theatre of war was an extra source of anxiety. With the Americans yet to land in Britain in any strength, and with the German army set for a new offensive deep inside Russia, Burgon and Julian witnessed the enthronement of William Temple as Archbishop of Canterbury unsure whether the ceremony marked an end or a beginning. Reflecting that German bombers were stationed less than thirty miles away from the Cathedral in which the ceremony took place, the brothers stumbled their way through the blacked-out Precincts late that night, having stayed up to hear the BBC broadcast of the enthronement in the Deanery while listening to their host, Hewlett Johnson, begin declaiming on the Godlike qualities of the Soviet Union. Pondering what a strange world it was, they made their way home to the small house in New Dover Road, which, though still kept up, had not been lived in for more than a year.

The Diaries

Two cloth-bound sets of the Bickersteth Second World War diaries were made. One lies in the archive of Churchill College, Cambridge, and the other is retained by the family. Each set is of seven volumes comprising some 2,300 closely typed pages. The Churchill College set is in good unmarked condition, while the one retained by the family is heavily scored with Burgon's post-war red and blue pencil margin comments. Interleaved are numerous handwritten letters, pamphlets and newspaper cuttings. Though this editor first encountered the diaries in Cambridge, it has been the family set - most usefully annotated by Burgon - which has been worked on to produce *Dear Grandmother*.

These points carry with them a number of implications. One is that the Bickersteth Second World War diaries are, and have been for the last few years, items of public record. Subject to the normal protocol of any record office they are accessible in Churchill College to anyone who wishes to see them. A second point is that the diaries are heavily mediated; by which is meant that the form in which they exist pushes at the limits of what is generally accepted as primary source material. The romance quotient of the editorial experience has been high, but any notion that, as though in a film, the material was discovered by torchlight inside some rusty long-forgotten trunk in a cobwebbed attic, never applied. In physical form the diaries are not disorganized documents yellowed with age, but a well-cared for, typed-out and bound manuscript already subject to an editing process. Formally Ella was the diarist, but it is clear that during and after the war Burgon did most of the work. His annotations offer clues about his criteria of selection, but it is difficult to know how much, let alone what kind of, material he was prone to cut. It seems likely that family correspondence was typed out pretty much in full, save for the pleasantries of greeting and signing off, while letters from friends were often reduced considerably. Until May 1940 - that is, over the time Burgon was in Canada - Hart House secretaries did the typing, on machines with a surprisingly modern-looking typeface. Thereafter a Miss Linnell of Canterbury handled the copy, presumably conforming to his posted editorial instructions and using good quality carbon paper.

One early decision made in the production of the *Dear Grandmother* volumes was to adopt an interventionist editorial approach. The impulse to be respectful without being reverential meant that the typists' slips were corrected. These were not many; they, and Miss Linnell in particular, were good at their jobs. Abbreviations were adjusted, and acronyms dealt with in acceptable point-dropping modern form (except in headings, O.C.T.U., for example, is rendered OCTU, B.B.C. becomes BBC). On occasion in the diaries places and names are misspelled, and these when traceable have been altered. The contributors' punctuation tended to vary considerably, and, though Miss Linnell's copy-typing kept faith with an individual's style, the editorial policy of *Dear Grandmother* has been to aim for consistency while maintaining sense. Lower-case characters are generally deployed ('government' is generally preferred to 'Government'), and such visible editorial intrusion as there is takes footnote form. These, as often as not, concern the career details of people encountered in the narrative and normally occur at the first instance of entry. This, a time-consuming but enjoyable aspect of the editing process, was not entirely problem-free. The names of those born of or admitted into the ranks of the titled constituted an occupational hazard. Common names too were sometimes a problem. That a certain Major Humphreys should become 'Humphries' before slipping back to the original, or then again, that the name 'Williams' should substitute itself for 'Willans' caused many anxious checks back-and-forth through the narrative with works of reference to hand. Memoirs, biographies and campaign histories were much consulted, but *Who Was Who*, whether in print or CD-ROM form, was an essential editorial companion.

But, with problems there to be solved, the editorial intent was to make the text appear as clean and uncluttered as possible There are no square brackets or references to holograph notes, and italicized elipses are kept to a minimum. The pomposity of [*sic*] has been avoided, and as everything in the diaries is legible the tantalising [*indecipherable*] never appears. Some editors seem positively to rejoice in the problems their material presents. Not this one. To say with gratitude that the Bickersteths of more than fifty years ago made life easy for a future editor is also to acknowledge that any remaining errors are his responsibility, not theirs.

A large number of entries, as stated before, consist of members of the family writing to E.C.F.B. She was, if not the diarist as such, the focal point of correspondence. This meant of course that letters written to her bore her blindness in mind, and were composed to be read, not so much by as to, a doughty, intensely interested, but frail old lady who should not be subject to undue stress. There can be no doubt that all correspondents had a very strong sense of implied readership in mind and were conscious that communication with her was indirect. That they did not wish to disturb, still less depress her is evidenced by the much more candid, perhaps more muscular style in which, say, Tony would write to Burgon or Julian to Geoffrey. But just as had there been no 'Dear Grandmother' there would have been no war diary, it is worthwhile registering that the exercise of writing to E.C.F.B. imposed its own discipline. All letter-writing is a rhetorical activity, and the truths expressed corresponding with one's grandmother are not necessarily less truthful than those which characterize letters to friends, husbands, bank managers, lovers or children. That sense of history or generational continuity which so powerfully colours the entries of the summer of 1940, was no doubt enhanced in the writers' minds by the knowledge that the one who would receive the particular fragment was herself, by definition, an institutionalized relic of the past.

Whereas Burgon tended to group diary entries by theme, *Dear Grandmother* adheres more closely, though not exclusively, to chronological sequence. This is a function of the substantial comb-out involved in the editing process, and a reflection that Burgon was obliged to work less on the basis of when something was written, as when he received it. Quite apart from his own busy work schedule, there were interruptions. His sudden return to England in May 1940 meant that letters chased him back and forth across the Atlantic. The general state of the mails in wartime was, as often as not, the governing factor in determining what Miss Linnell's next batch of material would be. That Burgon was not desk-bound from the Autumn of 1940, and that he and Sanders, his driver, criss-crossed southern England in their little two-seater visiting isolated Canadian units, imposed obvious delays. Paperwork was not regular. Periodically Burgon would receive a tranche of letters from Canada, some of which had been written weeks before, and he was diary-minded enough to be on the look-out for material from friends with particularly vivid stories to tell. Numerous people, the future Lord Bessborough and E.C.F.B.'s doctor among them, were commissioned to write down their accounts of evacuation from Dunkirk and other French ports, as and when they were encountered. Others, whose return to safety took longer, would add their contribution to the diary sometimes months after the event.

Editors are, of course, responsible for the decisions they make. Considerations of length, readership and would-be interest value have jostled with each other continually. And yet for all the editorial interventionism of the *Dear Grandmother* volumes, it has always been borne in mind that with E.C.F.B. as 'keeper' Burgon maintained from the start a conception of the diaries such that he acted as the on-the-spot orchestrator. That he should return to the manuscript after the war and annotate passages, while carefully inserting relevant newspaper cuttings or obituary notices into the family set, convey powerfully the impression that the diaries were of more than casual importance to him. Recognizing this is also to make something of an unscholarly admission; that the interpreting of J.B.B.'s intentions and keeping faith with his war diaries conception became, for this editor, something of an obligation. Historians, they say, are supposed to leave the sentiment out. Nevertheless, trying to do justice to J.B.B.'s accumulated efforts, and making, or trying to make, a fair fist of the kind of record he was putting together have been the most important criteria of editorial decision-making. He could not foretell events. Therein, in large part, lies the diaries' interest. But he also had a sense of context; a notion that background might at times be foregrounded, and an understanding that the dramatic and the commonplace could sometimes work well in combination. Above all he possessed a pronounced investigative instinct. As editor, this was how Burgon worked. As contributor he was careful not to dominate, but he wanted to see things for himself so as to be able to describe, indeed document, his observations and impressions. His longer entries, whether concerned with visits to country churches, military encampments on Salisbury Plain or Bermondsey railway arches turned into shelters, are very much of a documentary nature, and these, juxtaposed with other fragments, also represent something else; his own compositional sense of what the family war diaries should be; a narrative that was broad as well as deep, wherein the long sweep could combine with short sharp rushes.

Having said this, nowhere is there any sense that Burgon was composing/orchestrating with publication in mind. He wrote for E.C.F.B., his mother, and none of the other contributors' entries are self-conscious enough to suggest that anything other than a narrow family readership was ever envisaged. But for all that, the vividness and immediacy of the writing makes the Bickersteth record of the Second World War a compelling testament to life as it was lived then. There is no sex, love-interest or scandal. Family members do not criticize each other, and what grudges there were are heavily muted. But for all its correctness, the Bickersteth family's record is peculiarly close, well-observed and intimate.

The passage of time, the luxury of being able to read the diaries backwards as well as forwards, and, of course, the availability of computers, all serve to simplify the modern editor's task. The problems of insertion and deletion, nightmares to secretaries of old, bound as they were to typewriters, are in modern times reduced to the level of pressing a few buttons. Pagination, page-settings and printing-out are, these days, as easily achieved. Having struck the technological note, it is perhaps worthy of mention that whatever the advent of computers may have done to prose composition, they have at least allowed the footnote (for so long regarded by typists and publishers as the enemy) to make something of a comeback.

* * * *

Hitherto, the characters of *Dear Grandmother* have been referred to as actors. This is useful in that when the play ends and the curtain, so to speak, comes down, the cast withdraws and the audience simply disperses. Editors can exploit the metaphor. In their relations with their subjects they are more akin to capitalist employers than slave owners. In their economy they need have no concern for their charges, their operatives, after their labour power has been extracted. Once the contract is terminated, responsibility ceases. Liquidation is easy. Of course the actors had post-war lives. They were, for the most part and happily, long and prosperous. But of course too, the years have taken their toll. Ella died in 1954, aged ninety-six. Julian died in 1962, while Monier, Geoffrey and Burgon lived into the 1970s. Ralph, well into his nineties, died in 1989, while his beloved Peter outlived him by eleven years. Edward, who wrote his delightful letters from Sudan, and to whom the family set of war diaries belonged, died in December 1997. Editing, the licence to read other people's letters, is, at one level, to rejoice in the voyeurism of the present. More starkly, it is also to catch a glimpse of one's own mortality.

1939

The Holidays interrupted - Everybody returns to their post - the declaration of war - 'Everyone is busy doing something' - The discussion of war aims - Canterbury transformed by war, and the activities of the 'Red Dean' - The arrival of the evacuees - 'London is really a miserable sight' - The Englishamn is no longer his own master' - 'This is a very queer war' - 'All our ages are wrong for active service' - Problems of psychology and morale to contend with - 'No news to speak of and nobdody carries his gasmask' - 'Espionage in England is extensive' - 'Some people strongly resent Winston's truculence, I don't! - 'It is a almost as if we were living on one planet and the war was going on on another'

Introductory Note by Burgon Bickersteth

It was only a few years ago that our family war diary, describing our experiences during the Great War of 1914-1918, was finally closed. And now, almost exactly 25 years after that diary was begun, the outbreak of the second great war on 3 September 1939 calls for some record of how it affected the family. Those of us who were actively engaged a quarter of a century ago are now past the age for active service. Of the younger male generation, none in the immediate family circle except Edward are old enough to serve, and Edward went out to the Sudan to join the political service in December 1938. If the war continues for several years others such as Tony, John and young Julian will be called up but at present it is only indirectly that we are affected. This record, therefore, will in many ways differ from that of the war of 1914-1918. Indeed, even had many members of our family been serving in His Majesty's forces as was the case in 1914, this diary would have been altogether unlike its predecessor because the war itself is so different in character and scope.

The summer of 1939 found me on my usual leave from Hart House. Mother, Julian and I, with Julian's chauffeur Chappell had spent most of August motoring in France and Switzerland, though we had started with some misgiving owing to the growing tension between Germany and Poland and the British guarantee of Poland. Crossing to Calais on 7 August, we slept at Arras and went on the second day via Sedan to Verdun. Having inspected Fort Douaumont and Fort Vaux, we motored on 9 August via St Mihiel and Domrémy to Gerardmer. The following day Julian and I, from the heights of the Grand Ballon, surveyed the Rhine Valley almost from Strasbourg to Basle. On 11 August we motored down through the Col de la Schlucht to Colmar and then to Neuf Briesach and so to Basle along the fortifications of the Maginot Line and in full view of the Siegfried Line on the other side of the Rhine. After spending 10 days in Geneva and St Cergues we left Switzerland on Monday 21 August and slept that night at Saulieu in Burgundy. The news even then was serious but there had been so many false alarms that we took little notice. On Tuesday 22 August, motoring by Avallon, Vezelay, Auxerre and Sens, we arrived about 4 pm at Fontainebleau. The London papers of that day announced the signing of the non-aggression pact between

Germany and Russia.[1] This news determined us to go straight home the following day, which we did. Skirting Paris by Melun and Senlis, we lunched at Amiens and at 5 pm reached Boulogne. Everywhere French troops were on the move, mobilisation having in actual fact begun. With great good fortune we were able to get the car on a cargo boat, several of which had been put on to deal with the hundreds of motors belonging to those, who, like ourselves, were rushing home. We followed at 7.30 pm on the ordinary cross-channel boat.

Rab and Sydney Butler[2] were on board. They had been to the Riviera for a short holiday and Rab, as Under Secretary for Foreign Affairs, had been recalled for the special session of Parliament the following day. We reached Canterbury at 11 pm on Wednesday 23 August. On Thursday evening the BBC news was appallingly serious. A broadcast by the Prime Minister took place that night. On Friday all Germans were leaving England and France, and the English and French were leaving Germany. There were frontier incidents at Danzig and on the German-Polish border. It was clear that only by a miracle could war be avoided. On Saturday it was announced that Sir Neville Henderson,[3] our Ambassador at Berlin, was bringing a personal message from Hitler to Neville Chamberlain.[4] Julian left for Felsted after lunch. There were many problems to claim his attention there; among these was the fact that he had undertaken to open the school to any boys whose parents wished them to return.

Ralph, Alison and Peter had left England on 9 August and were at Locarno a few days later. They did not get news of the Russo-German pact till Wednesday 23 August. They cancelled their plan of going to Italy and on Thursday reached Berne where the Consul-General advised them to make for home as fast as possible. Motoring continuously, they reached Boulogne and then had the greatest

---

[1] Signed by Molotov and Ribbentrop on 22 August 1939.

[2] Richard Austen Butler (1902-82) m. Sydney (1926). MP (Con) Saffron Walden 1929-65; U-Sec. India 1932-37; Perm. Sec. Labour 1937-38; U- Sec. FO 1938-41; Pres. Bd. of Ed. 1941-45; Min. of Lab. 1945; Chanc. of Excheq. 1951-55; Ld. Privy Seal 1955-59; Home Sec. 1957-62; Dep. PM 1962-63; For. Sec. 1963-64; Con. Party Chmn. 1959-61; Chmn. Con. Res. Dept. 1945-64; Master of Trinity College, Cambridge 1965-78; Cr. Baron Butler of Saffron Walden, 1965; KG (1971).

[3] Rt Hon. Sir Neville Meynick Henderson (1882-1942). Entered diplomatic service 1905; Amb. to Berlin 1937-39; Gp. Cdr. Home Guard 1941-42; KCMG (1932), PC (1937).

[4] (Arthur) Neville Chamberlain (1869-1940). MP (Con) Ladywood 1918-29, Edgbaston 1929-40; Postmaster-General 1922-23; Paymaster-General 1923; Min. of Health 1923, 1924-9, 1931; Chanc. of Excheq. 1923-24, 1931-37; Prime Minister 1937-40; Lord Pres. of the Council 1940; Con. Party Chmn. 1930-31.

difficulty in crossing. They reached Canterbury on Sunday 27 August and in the small hours of Monday their car arrived at Dover. Ralph, Alison and I waited hours for it on the quay. At midnight that evening the Admiralty took over Dover harbour. Ralph and Alison went on to London next day. In France they had met many who had seen British troops at coast towns and on the roads. French mobilisation was in full swing.

Monier, John and Mary were at Chiddingstone and planning a holiday in Brittany two weeks later. Kay and Charles Beveridge, to whom she had been married in July, were settled in their flat at Hampstead and Charles was at work in his legal office. Edward, as stated. was in the Sudan, being stationed at Sinkat. Geoffrey, Jean, Tony, Julian, Elfride, Ursula and David were at Aberdeen where they had planned to spend a quiet summer holiday. Tony had just finished his time at Marlborough and was going up to Christ Church as a freshman the following October. Julian had another year at Marlborough.

I was due to sail for Canada on Saturday 2 September by the *Empress of Britain*. The idea of leaving one's native country at such a time of crisis was intolerable. On Tuesday 29 August, I determined to go to London and seek advice. Before lunch I visited 'Pug' Ismay,[1] whom very fortunately I found free. He told me there was still hope war might be avoided. It was considered encouraging that Hitler had waited almost 3 days for our reply; in his latest talk with Sir Neville Henderson he had not stormed but asked questions quietly. In any case German mobilisation would not be complete till the following evening. Evacuation of children from London was starting immediately, chiefly because the Labour Party demanded it; no British Expeditionary Force was yet in France. The troops whom Ralph and Alison had seen or heard of were a few advance parties (billeting officers and so forth) and some of our planes were at Beauvais. If war broke out, one of the great difficulties would be the public demand for immediate action and there would be no fighting because it would take three weeks or so to transport the BEF to France. Poland understood clearly she could not be given military assistance by Great Britain but, as in the case of Belgium in the last war, she would be free in the end. Our military and naval mission under Admiral Sir

---

[1] Maj-Gen. George Hastings Ismay, 1st Baron (1887-1965). Sec. Cttee. of Imp. Def. 1940; Sec. of State for C.W. Relations 1951-52. CoS to Min. of Def. (Churchill) and Dep. Sec. (Mil.) to War Cabinet 1940-45; Sec. Gen. NATO 1952-57.

Reginald Ernle-Erle-Drax,[1] who had been in Moscow for some weeks during the very period the German-Russian pact was being completed, had not given the Russians any vital information; the French and ourselves were working in perfect harmony, high French staff officers having been established for several weeks in a house adjoining the office of the CID in Richmond Terrace. Italy was expected to remain neutral and it would on the whole be advantageous to us if she did as it would immensely help our control of the Mediterranean. My duty was to return to my job; everybody not directly engaged in the war should carry on his job; he hoped, if war broke out, Canada would send a division fairly soon as a gesture of Empire solidarity but it was not primarily men but munitions, aeroplanes and equipment of all kinds which were needed.

Euan Wallace,[2] Minister of Transport, lunched with me at the Travellers' and told me some of his troubles in the event of London being bombed - one of his chief problems was to provide water-tight doors to the tube tunnels, running under the Thames, the tunnels themselves being only a few feet below the bed of the river; the recent replies to Hitler had been drafted at the Foreign Office, then mulled over by the Prime Minister and Halifax,[3] after which they had been presented to the whole Cabinet for criticism and if necessary for amendments before being sent back to the Prime Minister for final confirmation. Euan was also strongly of the opinion that I should return to my men in Toronto. At the Travellers' I saw Geoffrey Dawson,[4] Robin Barrington-Ward,[5] Archie Sinclair[6]

---

[1] Adm. Hon. Sir Reginald Aylmer Ranfurly Plunkett-Ernle-Erle-Drax (1880-1967). Dir. RN Staff Coll. 1919-22; Pres. Allied Cont. Comm. 1923-24; RN. ADC to George V 1927-28 and to George VI 1939-41; RN posts incl. Dir. Manning, C-in-C Plymouth & Nore, Cdre. Ocean Convoys. 1930-45; Head of Mil. Mission to Moscow Jul-Aug 1939. KCB (1934).

[2] Rt. Hon. (David) Euan Wallace (1892-1941). MP (Con) Rugby 1922-23, Hornsey 1924-41; Con. Whip 1929-31; Pte. Sec. Bd. of Trade 1937-38; Fin. Sec. Treas. 1938-39; Min. of Transport 1939-40; Comm. for Civil Defence, London 1940-41; PC (1936).

[3] Edward Frederick Lindley Wood (1881-1959) MP (Con) Ripon 1910-25; U- Sec. of State Colonies 1921-22; Min. of Ag. & Fish. 1924-25; Viceroy of India 1925-31; Pres. Bd. of Ed. 1922-24, 1932-35; Sec. for War 1935; Ld. Privy Seal 1935-37; Ld. Pres. 1937-38; For. Sec. 1938-40; Amb. to Washington 1941-46; Cr. Baron Irwin (1925) became 3rd Viscount Halifax (1934).

[4] Geoffrey Dawson (1874-1944). Editor of *The Times* 1912-19 and 1923-41; Fellow of All Souls, Oxford.

[5] Robert Barrington-Ward (1891-1948). Barrister and journalist; Ass. Ed. of *The Observer* 1919-27 and *The Times* 1927-34; Dep. Ed. of *The Times* 1934-41; Editor 1941-48.

[6] Sir Archibald Henry Macdonald Sinclair, 4th Bt. (1890-1970). MP (Lib) Caithness & Sutherland 1922-45; Lib. Chief Whip 1930-31; Sec. of State for Scotland 1931-32, Air 1940-45; Leader of Parl. Lib. Party 1935-45; Cr. Viscount Thurso (1952).

and William Strang.[1] The latter came in to lunch after 2 o'clock, looking absolutely worn out. The failure of his mission of the last two or three months in Russia, though no fault of his own, must have been a bitter memory. He confirmed Ismay's statement that our military and naval missions had given nothing of importance away to the Russians. After lunch I saw Patrick Duff[2] on whose shoulders rests the whole responsibility for evacuating from Whitehall the Admiralty, the War Office, the RAF Headquarters, the House of Commons, the House of Lords and all government offices. Many of his plans with regard to this great trek he had explained to me in July, the main area to which they would be transferred being along the Welsh Marches. He seemed astonishingly calm, his chief regret being that he could not go back to the carefree age, don his uniform and obey orders, with no worries. He, too, begged me to go back to my young men, where I could make the best contribution.

Throughout Wednesday and Thursday it was clear that the situation was getting gradually worse and that Germany intended marching into Poland, which meant that Great Britain would implement her guarantee and thus be at war with Germany. Throughout these two days there were endless instructions over the wireless with regard to the evacuation of children, ARP precautions and many other measures to be taken in the event of the outbreak of hostilities. During these days, workmen were busy removing the valuable glass from the Cathedral and trenches were being dug with a steam-shovel in the Green court.

On Friday, at 5.45 a.m., the German army crossed the Polish frontier. At 2 p.m, that day I left Canterbury, never, I think, having felt more miserable in my life. The train was packed with reservists in uniform and with passengers returning from their holidays. Many of the trains had been taken off owing to the evacuation of children and the mobilisation of troops. The platforms at Faversham, Sittingbourne, Chatham and other places were crowded with little children, their satchels (containing food together with their few belongings) and their gas masks slung across their shoulders. They waited quietly and in orderly fashion for the

---

[1] William Strang, later 1st. Baron (1893-1978). Acting Counsellor, then Counsellor, to the USSR 1930-39; Ass. U- Sec. at F.O. 1939-43; Perm. U- Sec.1947-53.

[2] Sir (Charles) Patrick Duff (1889-1972). Pte. Sec. to Pres. Bd. of Trade 1919-23; Pte. Sec. to successive PMs (Baldwin and Macdonald) 1923-33; Perm. Sec. to Min. of Works & Public Buildings 1933-41; Dep. H. Comm. Canada 1941-44; H. Comm. for New Zealand 1945-49; Chmn. of Nat. Parks Comm. 1949-54; KCB (1932), KCVO (1937).

trains to take them to safety. On arriving in London, I went to see Jack Patteson[1] who told me that as far as he knew the *Empress of Britain* would sail as scheduled next day. I went up to Hampstead to tea with Kay. Charles came in later. While I was there a telegram came calling him up for service on a patrol boat as a river warden on the Thames. I joined Vincent Massey,[2] Alice, Lionel and Hart at Canada House about 7 p.m., Vincent having just come back from the special session of Parliament at which the Prime Minister made a statement on the international situation. In view of the blackout which was to be held that night for the first time, we persuaded Alice and the two boys to go down at once to Wentworth where they had been renting a house all summer. Lionel was planning to take a commission in the Rangers and Hart expected to join a fire-fighting squad, his new car having been made to pull an extinguisher. Vincent and I dined at the Carlton. We were the sole guests in this huge restaurant, with at least a dozen flunkies and 30 waiters to look after us. The orchestra played to us alone.

A little later Valentine Castlerosse,[3] who had landed from Canada that morning with Beaverbrook,[4] came in with two others. It was not an hilarious scene and Vincent and I went across to the Travellers' where we were joined by Ronald Storrs,[5] Kenneth Clark[6] and one or two Foreign Office men. We talked until 11 pm and then Vincent and I walked with Ronald Storrs up to Piccadilly. It was our first experience of a blackout. Pushing aside the huge black curtain which screened the great doors of the club, we came out into teeming rain and complete blackness. Busses and taxis, showing just a pin-prick of light, rushed by. So stygian was the darkness that we walked arm in arm or should have lost each

---

[1] John (Jack) Coleridge Patteson (1896-1954). European General Manager, Canadian Pacific Railway from 1936; Dir. Canadian Pacific Steamships; on loan to UK Min. of Supply 1940-44.

[2] Rt. Hon. Vincent Massey (1887-1967). Min. w/o Portfolio in Dominion Cab. and contested Durham (Lib) 1925; HM Canadian Min. to USA 1926-30; Pres. Nat. Lib Fed. of Canada 1932-35; High Comm. for Canada in UK 1935-46; Chanc. Univ. of Toronto 1947-53; Gov-Gen and C-in-C. of Canada 1952-59; Chmn. Massey Foundation; PC (1941), CH (1946).

[3] Valentine Gerald Browne, Vt. Castlerosse (1896-1952). Journalist and 'gossip' columist *Sunday Express*; 'best friend' of Beaverbrook (q.v.); 7th Earl Kenmore 1943.

[4] (William) Maxwell Aitken, 1st Baron (1879-64). Prop. of Beaverbrook Newspapers; MP (Con) Ashton-Under-Lyme 1910-16; Chanc. of Duchy of Lancaster and Min. of Info. 1918; Min. of Aircraft Prod. 1940-41; Min. of State 1941; Min. of Supply 1941-42; Ld. Privy Seal 1943-45; Cr. Baron Beaverbrook (1917).

[5] Sir Ronald Storrs (1881-1955). Colonial Administrator - numerous posts in Middle East, Cyprus and southern Africa 1917-34; Min. of Info. 1940-45; Lect. for British Council and Spec. Corr. *Sunday Times* 1942-43. Kt (1924), KCMG (1929).

[6] Sir Kenneth Clark, later Baron (1903-85). Slade Prof. of Fine Art, Oxford 1946-50, 1961-62; Chmn. of Arts Council 1953-60.

other. Parting from Ronald Storrs in Piccadilly Circus, Vincent and I walked back to Canada House, where he was sleeping that night to be on the spot in case of emergency. The next morning, after an early breakfast, I rang up Euan Wallace to say 'good-bye' and then proceeded to Waterloo. The station was packed with people but it was an entirely orderly scene. The clearest of orders were being given with a loud-speaker, "Platform so and so for children being evacuated - Platform so and so for troops proceeding to the west - Platform so and so for troops proceeding to Aldershot" - and so on. At this hour of the day hundreds of bread-winners were being deposited at this big terminus from local trains; troops were moving without confusion to their trains; women in uniform, generals and staff officers were all proceeding quietly about their business.

Curiously enough the *Empress of Britain* boat special was almost empty - most of the passengers having gone down the night before for fear of being delayed and missing the boat. Joan Pape (Lady Tweedsmuir's[1] lady-in-waiting), who had been on leave in England for a few weeks and was now returning to Canada, met me by appointment on the platform and we went down together. She was equally miserable and we made a melancholy pair. We left Southampton an hour or two late and did not reach Cherbourg until nearly 9. There we took on hundreds of passengers and a large number of cars, the loading of which from a tender always takes a long time. As we eventually steamed away, a bright moon lighting up an absolutely calm sea, we looked back on a terrific thunder storm over England.

The *Empress of Britain* can do 28 knots and for the first 36 hours she did them. One could neither read nor write in any part of the ship - the vibration was so great. At 11 a.m. on Sunday 3 September Britain and Germany were at war and at 11.15 a.m. on the ship we heard the broadcast by the Prime Minister announcing that fact. He ended with these words, "It is the evil things we shall be fighting against - brute force, bad faith, injustice, oppression and persecution. And against them I am certain that the right will prevail". At 5 p.m. that day, France was at war with Germany and at 6 p.m. we heard the broadcast from the King.

By Monday 4 September we were out of the danger zone and reduced speed to the normal 23 or 24 knots though we zig-zagged the whole way across

[1] Lady Susan Charlotte Tweedsmuir (1882-1977) w. of Sir John Buchan, 1st Baron Tweedsmuir (1875-1940). Ld. High Comm. Counc. Scotland 1933-34; Gov. Gen. Canada from 1935; Chanc. Univ. of Edinburgh from 1937; CH (1932), GCMG (1935), PC (1937), GCVO (1939). d 1940.

the Atlantic. The ship was packed and no attempt was made to prevent passengers of all classes swarming over the vessel. The broadcasts of the Sunday had been greatly appreciated and I asked the purser after breakfast on Monday at what time the next would take place. He replied that there would be no more and when I strongly objected he referred me to the staff captain who after some hesitation informed me that the *Athenia*[1] had been torpedoed on Sunday evening with considerable loss of life and as the broadcasts from England would naturally be referring to it, it was deemed inadvisable for our huge ship's company to know of the disaster and there would be no further broadcasts. He asked me not to give this information to anyone. By Tuesday, however, it was generally known, because the stewards and stewardesses had their own private wireless sets. These were later confiscated. None the less we had no further broadcasts. The voyage was uneventful though it was not pleasant having the portholes screwed down and shuttered at night. Moreover, we had to take our life-belts with us everywhere, even to breakfast.

Notes of Ralph's return from Switzerland, August 1939

Alison, Peter and I had been at the Hotel Esplanade, Locarno, for 10 days and on Wednesday, 23 August 1939 after lunch we were packing, preparing for leaving the next day in accordance with our plans for Geneva and thence to the South of France. About 4 p.m. the hotel porter knocked on our door with *The Times*, which always arrives two days late. In this we read of the Russo-German pact. Consequently we held a hurried discussion as to future plans. We consulted the hotel manager who advised us to go home. We decided not to go via the Simplon, which entailed 40 miles into Italy but return via St Gotthard. As we found, however, on the outward journey that major road reconstruction was taking place on the St Gotthard (for military purposes) we arranged to put the car on the train through the tunnel.

We subsequently left on Thursday morning at 9.30 am motoring some 50 miles through Bellinzona, up the valley to Airolo which has a station immediately before the tunnel. Here they have shunting trucks for taking cars and the whole

---

[1] Reminiscent of the sinking of the *Lusitania* during W.W.1, the *Athenia* with 1,103 passengers (among them Jewish refugees from Nazi Germany and 300 United States citizens) was torpedoed by a U-boat 200 miles off the west coast of Ireland on 3 September 1939. Out of 1,418 passengers and crew, 118 were lost, 22 of them American.

business was completed in 5 minutes. Our truck was shunted on the back of the ordinary train, which left at 11.20 am - we were through the tunnel in 15 minutes where we were shunted off the train and the car was on the road within 5 minutes of arriving at the station on the other side.

We then ran down the valley, which is most beautiful, to Lucerne, stopping for lunch at one of the most ideal spots imaginable - perfect day - and we lunched out of doors above the Lake, the water sparkling below us and the mere thought of a conflict inconceivable. We arrived at Lucerne itself at 3.30 pm and went at once to Cook's.[1] We ascertained that they had not cancelled any of their tours but were in constant touch with London and we were advised to go to Berne, where we were to consult the vice-consul or our legation. After tea, therefore, we did the 60 odd miles to Berne and stayed the night at Bellevue Palace.

The next morning I visited the vice-consul and like most of his kind he was very non-committal. However, we decided, at any rate, to make for the coast. We left Berne at 12 o'clock on Friday, 25 August and Alison and I plotted a route across France, which we thought would keep us clear of their heavy traffic. After going through Neuchatel we climbed into the Juras and lunched at a delightful little town called Fleurieur.

Almost immediately afterwards we came to the Swiss-French frontier and were surprised to see farm carts drawn across the road on the French side. Here we were scrutinised by the *agent-de-police* who combed our passports and eventually let us through. We had not proceeded more than a quarter of a mile before we came upon troops and within a further quarter of a mile the 'asparagus beds' were across the road and there was only sufficient room for one car to pass. We then proceeded through Pontarlier to Besançon, which was crowded with troops of every kind. The Maginot Line is somewhere near here but you cannot, of course, tell exactly where. We decided to continue our journey so as to get as far as we could that night and at Joinville a heavy thunderstorm appeared ahead of us, so having gone through the town we decided as it was about 8 o'clock to return for dinner, hoping the storm would give over in order that we could proceed to Rheims for the night which was another 80 odd miles.

Joinville is not much of a town and can only boast of two very indifferent hotels and we chose the most attractive and were welcomed by *madame*. There

---

[1] Thomas Cook, the travel agents.

were already other English people supping together with Dutch, Belgium and French, all with cars homeward bound. The others were all staying. After dinner we proceeded on our way but the storm came on worse than ever, and being unwilling to drive through the night owing to danger of trees strewn about the road, we again returned to Joinville where again *madame* received us with open arms and we got the last two rooms in this quaint hotel. *Madame* had never had her hotel full before, I should imagine. Everybody left early the next morning and we were off by 8.30 am going through St Dizier, Bar-le-duc, Chalons-sur-Marne to Rheims.

At every village reservists were joining the colours and in the towns it was almost pandemonium. At Chalons outside the barracks there must have been at least 200 taxis drawn up, presumably for moving the troops.

We did 84 miles in one hour and fifty minutes, which was not bad going. At Rheims I filled up with petrol. I kept the tank full throughout the run back, always filling up at 50 miles and I had no difficulty in getting petrol at all on the way back. We lunched at Laon in the restaurant opposite the station. This was crammed full with officers and hundreds of reservists were arriving by train all the time. The news was on the wireless and everybody listened to it. It did not seem too hopeful but the door was not completely closed. From Laon we went to St Quentin, Cambrai, Arras, St Pol and Montreuil. Peter had the idea of staying the night at Le Touquet. We were afraid that every town and village would be full with returning holidaymakers, like ourselves.

We arrived at Le Touquet to find nearly all the hotels shut but the Westminster booked us in. This may have been our last night on French soil for many years to come. All I can say it was a very comfortable one. I rang up the Automobile Association at Calais and after considerable delay got through and asked whether we could get the car over the next day (Sunday). Their representative was extremely helpful and immediately told us to bring the car along and he would guarantee to get it over the next day. He said be there before 12.30 p.m. Unfortunately we overslept and did not leave until 11.30 but drew into that enormous yard at Calais exactly at 12.30. The day was beautifully hot and we had to stand waiting in a queue to get our embarkation tickets for ourselves and the car for a couple of hours. We were eventually told to leave the car and take ourselves over on the normal cross-channel boat which was the *Canterbury*. We were fortunate in getting seats on deck because I have seldom seen so many people on a boat of that size before. Luckily the sea was like a millpond, and we only arrived at Dover 40 minutes late. We rang up Mother at Canterbury and she sent a car over for us and we were having dinner with her at 7.45 p.m. Burgon, Alison and I returned after dinner in the car and waited at Dover until the cargo boat arrived, which it did soon after midnight.

The chief impression one got on this somewhat hurried trip across France was the enthusiasm on the part of the French people and the numerous military activities. It was odd to see anti-aircraft guns and other guns of various calibre being put up in the centre of enormous fields, apparently miles away from any village, or town. There were hundreds of petrol wagons and long trains of lorries packed with stores of every description. Occasionally one saw tanks but it was mainly a scene of the reservists with their little handbags coming in their working clothes answering the call.

*   *   *   *

Alison to E.C.F.B., 31 August   *Felsted*

On our return to London last Monday (28 August) we found an ARP warden waiting to advise us to remove the household as soon as possible as they were evacuating all our square and district. There are only two people left in all our square and they are ARP wardens. I rang up Julian, who said he would be delighted to have us, and at 6 pm the first carload left, packed to the brim, and with two of the servants and Peter. On Tuesday I closed up the house completely - went to the auxiliary headquarters and had my kit, service gas mask and tin hat dealt out. At 5.30 Ralph returned. We had a car packed ready and left at once, getting down to Felsted at 7.30. All the servants are here, including Hignall (the butler) and Prior (the chauffeur). They fit in well with Julian's household. Nellie is the housekeeper and I am temporary head of the house. Ralph goes up to town every day.

Kay to E.C.F.B., 2 September   *London, NW2*

I had a foul day yesterday as Charles was called up and was out all night. I have not heard from him yet. It is difficult to say what else we could have done. I am afraid Germany was determined on war. I must say I do not feel any personal animosity towards the German people. I expect they are just as anxious as we.

Julian to E.C.F.B., 3 September   *Felsted*

Everyone is busy doing something. Peter has been of the greatest assistance to the ARP committee who are receiving children from Leyton and Ilford. I am organising a committee to arrange for the games and amusement of refugee children, who will soon become a confounded nuisance to their foster parents, when they get used to their surroundings. I have only had about 10 to 12 boys back so far but expect more now that war has been declared.

Ralph to E.C.F.B., 3 September   *Felsted*

There is great activity in this normally quiet Essex village. Hundreds of children have arrived, Friday, yesterday and today. Julian of course has endless things to see to. All the married masters are here and several unmarried too. Trenches are being dug, windows obscured, the sanitorium got ready for expectant mothers - a number of whom are to come here. Now as to our plans. We stay here for the present. I shall try and go to the city every day, returning here every night. I have taken a house at Staines or rather Egham, which is next door, for our office staff and shall move two-thirds of those I have left down here next week. I hope to keep a skeleton staff in the office for as long as possible as I have to keep i.. touch with our Ministry of Food. When things become more normal Alison and I will probably go back to 6 Hyde Park Square if it is there. The dugouts are finished for each house.

Julian to E.C.F.B., 4th September   *Felsted*

We had an air raid warning at 4.30 a.m. this morning and all our household got up and came down to the ground floor and stood or sat just outside the kitchen door. The warning is given here by the siren at the beet-root factory. Unfortunately the 'all clear' signal did not come through when it should - indeed it never came through at all and we eventually got tired of waiting and at 5.30 a.m. all went back to bed.

E.C.F.B. to J.B.B., 4 September   *Canterbury*

Before telling you of the events of Sunday, I must admit that after war was declared by us on Germany I had not an easy moment about your ship and German submarines, though I did earnestly try to commit your safety to God.

Then I heard the *Athenia* had been torpedoed 200 miles from the Irish Coast with 1400 passengers on board, many of them Americans. I still clung to hope and realised such a crime would make the Admiralty very careful of any other merchant ships on the high seas. It is 6.30 p.m. now (Monday) and I hope you are clear of the Irish coast. The cheap rate for evening trunk calls has been discontinued and we are asked to avoid using the telephone as much as possible.

Yesterday I went to Matins at 10.30 walking down with Miss Gray. Mrs Gardiner was also there, sitting by me. Canon MacNutt[1] began to preach and very skilfully let the congregation know war had been declared against Germany at 11 a.m. and went on preaching. Suddenly the siren went. He stopped and the Dean requested the whole congregation to move quietly and in an orderly manner to the crypt. This we did, Mrs Gardiner one side of me and Miss Gray on the other. Mr Poole also looked after me and got me a chair in the crypt. Many had their gas masks but I had not got mine (I always take it with me now). In less than half an hour the 'all clear' sounded and we all slowly left the crypt. Sir Reginald Tower's[2] niece offered to take us home in her car and we gladly accepted. We found Mollie and Norah all right. They realised it was no good coming to find me as I was safe in the Cathedral and in any case the air raid wardens would not have allowed them on the streets. The siren had only been a warning as an unidentified plane had crossed the coast.

Later, Fielding Ottley[3] looked in and said I had better register at once for a nurse, as soldiers were pouring into Canterbury wanting billets and he did not wish me to have a soldier, so I registered. We heard coals are to be rationed but you need not worry as I have all mine in for the winter. The long day ended and I was soon asleep when at 3 a.m. the siren sounded again. The maids and Miss Gray woke me up but I had hardly put on my dressing gown before the 'all clear' sounded. This morning I went to the GPO to see about air mail to Canada and also looked in at the Cathedral where glass in the windows of the north aisle has been removed.

---

[1] Rev. Canon Frederick Brodie MacNutt (1873-1949). Hon. Chapl. to Forces 1921; Archdeacon of Leicester 1920-38; Chapl. to George V from 1931; Canon Res. Canterbury 1938-45.

[2] Sir Reginald Thomas Tower (1860-1939). Diplomat - numerous postings including High Comm. League of Nations, Danzig 1919-20; KCMG (1911).

[3] Rev. Canon Fielding Hay Ottley (1877-1958). Hon. Canon of Canterbury 1927-44; Vic. of St. Luke's, Grayshott from 1944.

Julian to E.C.F.B., 6 September   *Felsted*

Just as I was about to be called this morning, the air raid warning went off
- the hooter at our beet-root factory - and we somewhat reluctantly put on
dressing gowns and came down. The sun was already bright, dispersing a ground
mist and we were thrilled to see squadron after squadron of our fighter planes
going to the attack. They disappeared from sight in the direction of the Thames
and we saw nothing of the enemy. Ralph, however, put off his departure by car to
Chelmsford until the 'all clear' went and caught a later train. We do not know if the
attack by the Hun planes was successful or not or what happened, but it was an
inspiring sight to see our own fighters going out to drive them off. I have cabled
to Miss Anderson 'Suggest postpone return till safe'. But I know she is very keen
to return and presently they will certainly convoy our ships across the Atlantic.

Geoffrey to E.C.F.B., 7 September   *Aberdeen*

With regard to the family, Tony alone at present is affected by the
Conscription Act. He is in the youngest group, which Hore-Belisha[1] has already
announced in the House of Commons is not to be called up for training until all
the other groups have. But whether this affects Public School and University boys
(between the age of 18 and 20) who, as past members of the OTC. and holders of
certificate A, are to enter, on being called up, a special detachment for men
specially qualified, on the above grounds, for being trained for commissions, I do
not know. Every university has an official recruiting committee to register the
names of such men (and others also). The Vice-Chancellor is Chairman of it.

The recruit takes three steps: (1) he enters his name on the register; (2) he
then waits till he is summoned to appear before the committee and register his
name in person; (3) he then waits till he is called up to begin his training. Tony
took the first step on the second day of the war by writing to the Oxford
University committee. He could have done so here (the Aberdeen University one,
over which Fyfe[2] presides) but preferred Oxford, naturally, as he will be with his
own friends. He is now waiting to take step number 2, i.e. to be summoned to
Oxford for the personal interview, which may come any day. He will then

---

[1] (Isaac) Leslie Hore-Belisha (1893-1957). MP (Lib then NLib) Devonport 1923-45. Fin. Sec. to
Treas. 1932-34; Min. of Transp. 1934-37; Sec. of State for War 1937-40; Min. of Nat. Ins. 1945;
Cr. Baron (1954).
[2] William Hamilton Fyfe (1878-1965). Principal and Vice-Chanc. Univ. of Aberdeen 1936-48;
Chmn. of Scottish Advisory Counc. on Ed. 1942-46; Kt. 1942.

presumably learn how long the interval is likely to be till he is called up (step number 3). If it is to be a long interval, he will go up to Oxford as a civilian and continue his studies with other undergraduates in the same case as himself. Cambridge University announced yesterday that it is providing for such, though some of the colleges have been taken over by the government. So I suppose Oxford will do the same. We can but wait till the Christ Church authorities inform us.

It is all very different from 1914. The individual is not worried by any problem of conscience. He is liable to military service from the first, if medically fit. Tony's eye-sight might disqualify him for active service. He simply has to wait for instructions, which are given according to a cut and dried plan, the government taking men, as and when it wants them. If they don't want the youngest class till after calling up all the older ones, Tony may be months before he is actually called up. Julian will return to Marlborough as usual in a fortnight's time. He will then take the same steps as Tony and may, or may not, as the case may be, be able to stay out his full time at Marlborough, which I naturally hope will be possible (as also for Monier's John). Anyway I am in no immediate anxiety about either of my two elder sons. Elfride will also return to school (avoiding London) for the coming term. I shall probably take her, however, myself as it is a long cross-country journey and there might always be air raids. The schools here continue shut till the end of this week, so both David and Ursula have gained a week's extra holiday. Both the Grammar School and St Margaret's re-open on Monday, when both will go back to school. Though all precautions - black-out lighting, sandbags around buildings, etc - have been taken in Aberdeen as elsewhere, air raids are considered unlikely here. Few people carry gas masks though the children will have to do so going to and from school. Aberdeen (the city, not the county) is a 'neutral' not a 'dangerous' area. Aberdeen (the county) is a 'receiving' i.e. safe area and is full of children from Glasgow and Clydeside.

So much then for the family. As for myself, I long ago offered my services to the government. But Fyfe, whom I had a long talk with the other day, told me that I shall certainly be required to stick to my job here, as the university will go on, and we are likely to have a lot of London University students here. Taylor (my senior lecturer) and I are both of course long past the military service age and neither medically fit for it. So we shall have to run the English Department between us. I shall probably lose my junior lecturer. So the work will be very heavy and leave little or no time for any other war work except locally as required. As for Jean, she has the house and the children to look after. The whole feel of this war is different from 1914. There is no confusion, no excitement and no news (except brief bulletins) allowed in the press. No casualty lists published, no rumours - in fact very little in the papers at all. Poland will be over-run, I suppose, in a very short time in its western portions and then, I hope, with a strategically more defensible front line will hold out indefinitely. But what exactly our plans are on the Franco-German frontier no one knows, not even our divisional commanders. On the other hand, everyone seems confident that there is a plan. I am constitutionally hopeful and I am determined not to meet anxieties before they are actually upon me. There is always a chance that I may be spared them altogether, in which case I should have caused needless self worry. A short war is not likely but it is not to be ruled out as an impossibility so I shall hope for it, a not unreasonable hope.

Julian to E.C.F.B, 11 September   *Felsted*

I reached Felsted at 2 pm and have since been going around inspecting the trenches and the black-out of windows. The latter is a terrific problem for so large a school. Miss Anderson is now on the Atlantic and should reach England next Saturday. Ralph brought back an encouraging story today. A friend of his released one of his men for service in the navy some weeks ago and this man turned up in his employer's office explaining he had one week's leave because his destroyer had strained her plates ramming an enemy submarine. This destroyer had, during the last week, brought in no less than 4 enemy submarines intact - crews and all.

There was considerable ignorance and perplexity in Canada regarding the British effort and on 12 September J.B.B. cabled Hankey[1] asking for such information as could be legitimately given concerning British diplomacy with a special reference to Poland and Italy as well as concerning military, naval and air advancement to date. Hankey's letter was a reply to this cable and in December a package of pamphlets, broadcast addresses and other literature arrived from the High Commissioner's office at Ottawa. This, perhaps, was

---

[1]   Sir Maurice Hankey, later 1st Baron (1877-1963). Sec. CID 1912-38; Sec. HMG Cab. 1916-38; Min. w/o Port. 1939-40; Chanc. Duchy of Lancaster 1940-41; Paymaster-General 1941-42.

typical of the effectiveness of the British Ministry of Information.

Lord Hankey to J.B.B., 16 September   *Treasury Chambers, Whitehall*

My name is on no account to be mentioned in connection with this letter, nor is it intended to be quoted. It is only the effort of a very much overworked man to throw off a few sentences that might stimulate your own thoughts.

You may imagine that, being plunged into the Cabinet at the outset of war, after a year of absence, with the Cabinet meeting twice a day, a vast and mixed correspondence and huge masses of papers to read, I can't find time to give you much personal help.

You seem puzzled to know what we are doing. I can tell you in a nutshell. We are doing what we have done throughout our history at the outset of our wars. Under the fairly powerful defensive shield of the Navy and Air Force we are mustering the strength of the Empire to meet an aggressor who is putting into execution a long prepared plan for which he has made preparations for using all his force from the outset. As in 1914, 1870, 1866, the Napoleonic Wars and, I suppose, pretty well all major wars in history, the aggressor has initiated it, and all he had to do was to put into execution his long prepared plans. And we, as in all our wars, have to take a longer view. Strategy involves concentrating the decisive force at the decisive point at the decisive moment. Nothing could be more foolish than to fritter away strength prematurely. Whenever we have done that in our history we have been in a mess. Naturally the aggressor, who is putting into operation his long prepared plans, has an immense advantage in publicity. That again is as it was in 1914. I should have thought it was not hard to put the position to a Canadian audience. Canada, after all, has a population of, I suppose, some ten millions. They are just as much at war as we are. The Canadians are not in a position to throw stones at us on the question of preparedness. In saying that, the last thing I would do would be to under-rate the value of Canadian co-operation. In the long run it was terrific in the last war, but this time, when the Canadian Government and people have made up their mind what to do, they have to carry their preparations out under the shield of the British Navy and Air Force and of the French Army. To that shield, unfortunately, they can make practically no contribution for a long time to come. But *bis dat qui cito dat*. The business of the Canadians is to make up their minds quickly as to what is to be their contribution to the common cause and to give a lead to their big brother, the USA, next door.

E.C.F.B. to J.B.B., 17 September   *Canterbury*

This morning I went to the Cathedral. It is terrible to see it, the whole nave piled with earth; nothing covered from the dust or dirt. Dr Mason's memorial chapel with its ebony and ivory crucifix and candles all exposed; the new choir stalls - the colours uncovered. In fact everything in a state of dirt and confusion. The nave altar has been removed and rails are placed on the steps to the choir - trucks being filled with earth, then pulled along the rails up to the choir where the earth is tipped out. All Canterbury is stirred. The roof has been camouflaged. Iron girders are to be fixed from the floor to the roof in the choir. The Dean[1] is an engineer and no doubt thinks he is saving the Cathedral but everyone thinks that bombs will do much less damage than he is doing. The people of Canterbury would like to find their cathedral a place of quiet, where they can pray. It is curious to see everyone who is out of doors and in church carrying their gas masks.

E.C.F.B. to J.B.B., 20 September   *Canterbury*

The City is now well provided with cover for anyone caught in the streets, so you need not worry. Monier is frightfully busy, as the evacuated children have meant hours of work in fitting them in. They are giving a good deal of trouble all over England. Here in Canterbury some boys took sticks and broke all the electric light bulbs in the house where they were billeted, never having seen them before. The schoolmasters who came with them seem to have no control over them out of school.

I called on my air warden, Mr Wood, to give him your message about your gas mask. You were quite right to take it and you are on no account to pay for it. The general opinion is that Canterbury is unlikely to be bombed, that is if Hitler keeps his word. Miss Gray is making hospital coats in her spare time. Each day seems to bring as much as I can manage to be attended to, though what I do seems incredibly small. There are lonely people to cheer; the daily broadcast service of prayer to take part in; necessary letters to answer, though not really many of these; a daily walk; a daily rest and then someone comes to read, and so

---

[1] Very Rev. Dr Hewlett Johnson (1874-1966). Engineer, then clergyman; Founder, prop. and Ed. of *The Interpreter* 1905-24; Dean of Manchester 1924-31 and Canterbury 1931-63; prolific campaigning writer, well-remembered as the 'Red Dean' of Canterbury.

the days go by.

Julian to E.C.F.B., 21 September   *6 Hyde Park Square, London*

London is really amazing, every house seems to have turned its area into an air raid shelter. Balloons seem to be housed on the ground, in every square and all over the place ready to be hoisted at any moment. The traffic is almost non-existent; sandbagged barricades are seen everywhere and there is a general air of officialdom with ARP helmeted wardens strutting about. Ralph's shelter in his basement is excellent and has given a sense of security to his servants, so that they seem quite happy to be back in London. I had the billeting officer for Felsted round at my house this morning and told him I was quite willing to have people billeted on me if necessary but I think he will spare me as long as he can.

Mary to J.B.B., 21 September   *Chiddingstone*

We have a house full which means a good deal of work. We've got Mr Matthew and his two daughters. They have brought a man with them who works for them in London, to help with the work here. He's a real little Cockney but seems to be settling down with our German Jews! We're having quite a lot of trouble over our evacuees. They come from Bermondsey and quite half of the children are absolutely filthy and have no clothes. So we're having to knit and sew hard and write frantic letters to the parents trying to get clothes out of them. I'm afraid a certain amount of parents will use this evacuation as a convenient way of losing their children. We've got about 150 children in this parish and are trying to organise Brownies, Cubs, Scouts and Guides for them all, not to speak of extra Sunday Schools and services. Half our mothers and babies have already gone home as there have been no air raids.

Julian to E.C.F.B., 24 September   *Felsted*

But for our trenches, which are carefully concealed, no one would know a war was on in Felsted. We start school on Tuesday with, as far as I can make out, 395 boys or only five less than our usual 400 and a few more than I expected at the end of last term. As a matter of fact I have lost about 17 or 20 boys as a direct result of the war but gained rather more, mostly from parents who do not wish their sons to be sent down to Devonshire or Cornwall where they cannot visit them. Of course I shall try to make the life of the school as normal as possible but our first rehearsal of proceeding to air raid warning stations will be on Tuesday evening, soon after all the school has got in. It would never do to have to face a serious air raid during the first night without some kind of rehearsal. Last night all the house masters were back and we had a long meeting to discuss ARP regulations.

Elfride to E.C.F.B., 24 September   *St Mary's School, Calne*

I came back to school on Tuesday. Daddy travelled down with me to London. Then I took the special train to school. They are not making a tyranny of carrying gas masks about, as I thought they would. We have to take them up to our rooms at night and they stay in our form rooms all day. We don't have to take them to church but we have to take them if we go for long walks. We have got a London boys' school here, in a building which was a fever hospital and which was going to be a new carpentry shop and kindergarten. They have the use of one of our playing-fields. A girls' school, called Westonbirt, is in Bowood Park, which is about a mile away. Having a black-out every night is an awful nuisance. I sleep with two other girls in a room and the windows are shut and the blinds and curtains drawn at dark, about two and one half hours before we come over to bed. As it is a hot-cupboard room, it is very airless when we go to bed and we don' t have the curtains drawn back till our lights are put out. School Certificate has not been put off because of the war so we have to work hard this term for it. It begins in the first week of December.

We have got cellars at school, so only a very few trenches have had to be made. We have not had any air raid practices yet, so that if there was an air raid this minute, I wouldn't know what to do. There is not much change at school because of the war, except little things like all having supper together so as to give the maids less trouble. This term there are five more new girls than usual and one of the form rooms has been made into a bedroom. We all have to knit things for evacuees. I am in the middle of a jumper. I also hope to do first-aid, though a nurse is the last thing I would be if I had to do war work. I hope the Germans don't go and bomb any of our beautiful buildings such as Canterbury Cathedral, St Paul's or Westminster Abbey. Have you got trenches or will you go to the crypt of the Cathedral if there is an air raid? I am glad you did not have to take in evacuee children. Nuns are much better.

Geoffrey to E.C.F.B., 24 September   *Aberdeen*

Elfride and I left here at 6 p.m. last Monday. There is only one third class and one first class coach of sleepers on any of the night trains now. But Elf and I had secured two berths in the former. The chief objection to travelling is the absence of all artificial light, only one dim blue electric bulb, giving less then half the illumination of a night-light for the whole compartment, so that without an electric torch no reading is possible after dark. I had not calculated on this quite unnecessary precaution so had no torch with me - an omission I rectified in London by buying one for the return journey. On arriving in London we went to Westminster Cathedral which Elf wanted to see again. It was lovely there, the space, colouring and the atmosphere of worship as the sunlight streamed down on the high altar where mass was in progress. Here was a great church being put to the main purpose for which it was built, the worship of God. To pass into it was to pass out of a world at war, into the heavenly places, an oasis of peace and beauty as uplifting and tranquillising to the spirit as it was completely satisfying to the ear and the eye. One left the place with soul and body strengthened and refreshed. What a contrast to Canterbury! I then bought an electric torch at the stores and we visited Westminster Abbey, very beautiful and all open and un-sandbagged except the portion beyond the choir. The Unknown Warrior's tomb has been converted very skilfully into a precinct shut off for private prayer and intercession and was obviously being much used for that purpose. We then strolled up Parliament Street after viewing the Thames from Westminster Bridge and passed through Downing Street (quite empty) into St James Park and then through the Horse Guards, where a balloon had just been pulled down, past the Admiralty, where I showed Elf my old haunts and the windows of Room 40,[1] to Trafalgar Square where we rested a little in St Martin's Church, just at the spot which used to be my rendezvous with Jean when we here both in London during the Great War.

Ralph to E.C.F.B., 25 September   *London*

Sir Ernest Bain[2] is in Lord Dawson[3] of Penn's Nursing Home and although

---

[1] The Admiralty's First Worls War equivalent of Bletchley Park, where the German Navy's various wireless ciphers were intercepted and de-coded.

[2] Sir (Albert) Ernest Bain (1875-1939) Insurer: controller, Ins. Dept., Min. of Food from 1917. KBE (1921).

[3] Lord Dawson of Penn, 1st. Viscount (1864-1945). Physician to George V.

he is improving he cannot, in my view, hope to be back in harness again for at least three months. Therefore I have had the whole brunt of starting an Office at the Ministry of Food on my shoulders. By the time I get home at night, all I want to do is to sit down and I go to bed very early. This also helps to save electric light. Yesterday, having filled the tank full on Friday, we went down to the South Downs and had one final day. It was really lovely. Alison, Peter and I went down to our usual place, just south of Petworth, not far from Lavington, taking lunch and tea, and we went for a good walk over the Downs and only saw five people all day, except for a game-keeper with whom we had a long talk. It did us any amount of good and we just got back before the black-out started. We have now got to reserve what petrol we have and I shall use it for business only. Prior, my chauffeur, is in the Civil Air Guard and is likely to be called up any day. Whether or not I shall licence the car next year depends on many things, taxation and how much petrol I get. In the meantime Alison will drive me and she can get a special permit from her auxiliary concern, to which she belongs, to do this. I usually spend the morning at the office and the afternoon and evening at the Ministry of Food, which is at Horseferry Road, Westminster. It is an enormous building with more than 600 or 700 rooms.

Julian to E.C.F.B, 27 September   *Felsted*

I spent last night with Ralph in London. London is really a miserable sight. The streets are empty, doorways are sandbagged, every area is an air raid shelter, and tanks of water are in every square to help extinguish fires. There are no shoppers, white painted curbs and after dark, there is a darkness that can be felt. Cars and taxis - only a few left - creep about with dimmed side-lights and no headlights. But no one is about and it might almost be a city of the dead. Ralph has more petrol being in the Ministry of Food but not enough to get very far afield. By tomorrow motor transport will have largely disappeared except for official cars.[1]

Alison to E.C.F.B., 29 September   *London*

Peter went off to Rugby by the school special at 2.15 yesterday. He and

---

[1] A reference to the war budget statement announced by the Chancellor of the Exchequer, Sir John Simon, on 27 September. Income Tax was raised from 5s. 6d. to 7s. 6d. in the £, surtax and estate duty were increased, and an excess profits tax of 60 per cent was introduced.

John went on the same carriage. They took two hours to get to Rugby. As for the linen, I will go down to Peter Robinson's and choose it for you. So many of the staff have been paid off from the big shops as there are no customers and there will be even less now after the budget. The 7/6 was entirely unexpected in the City. It was thought a shilling might be put on but never two. Everyone had a terrible shock. We shall have to gut down the household and give Hignall notice. The chauffeur goes next week and we shall take the car down to Sway where mother's chauffeur will look after it. The other servants came to us last night and said they realised what the budget meant to everyone and wanted us to know that they would like to stay with us whatever happened: if we wanted to cut down their wages they would take whatever we offered. It is a pity to upset such a good household, as we had, but everyone in London is doing the same.

October

Julian to Mother, 1 October   *Felsted*

I met Miss Anderson[1] yesterday afternoon at 4 pm. She had slept the night before at Liverpool, having been on board three weeks since sailing from Montreal. The ship, the *Duchess of Richmond*, went down first to Halifax and then waited seven days to pick up six or seven other ships and paint herself grey. These were cargo boats almost laden to the water-line with wheat, ores and all kinds of raw materials for England and all painted navy grey. The convoy set out 12 days ago with no escort and came by a most roundabout route to Liverpool only picking up two destroyers when just south of Ireland. Two of the ships were disguised as far as possible to look like naval vessels and on one occasion the flotilla came upon a suspicious little sailing ship which refused to answer their signals and which the Commander admitted afterwards was an enemy submarine disguised as a fishing boat. Apparently the submarine feared to attack, thinking the convoy was escorted by naval ships and the whole flotilla moved rapidly away from it. Each ship had naval ratings on board for signalling, and the command was in the hands of a naval commander on the *Duchess of Richmond*. The voyage was very unpleasant as there were so many restrictions. They went down almost to the

---

[1] Julian's housekeeper at Felsted.

Azores and no ship pursued a straight course. They went in curves cutting each other's wash all the time, backwards and forwards, requiring some real power of manoeuvre. There was not a single gun mounted on any one of the ships.

Ralph to J.B.B., 6 October   *London*

London is very depressing - absolute blackness at night and when there is no moon it is literally impossible to see anything. Out of 48 houses in our Square, only about three or four are occupied, all the others are empty. Practically all the shops round us have gone bust as there is no trade. Owing to Sir Ernest Bain's illness, the whole of the starting up of our office at the Ministry of Food fell on my shoulders. It takes up a good deal of my time but it is very interesting. I have one permanent man from our own staff there and I have got a secretary from the Ministry. We are working in conjunction with Sir Harry Peat[1], who is the financial director, and there are many problems. Ten of my male staff went, of course, in the first few days, but we are carrying on the office with what is left manfully. This 'war risks' insurance on saleable goods has been chaotic and has added to our labours a hundred-fold. We get no commission either which is rather aggravating. The City is just one mass of sandbags and the traffic about one-quarter normal.

It is very difficult to get into touch with one's friends. Many of them are serving, others with no business to do don't bother to come up. I lunched with Ernest Bain at the Carlton before he went into the nursing home and Euan Wallace was there, and I had a talk with him. He was lunching with Oliver Stanley[2]. My day is, office first thing in the morning and then off to the Ministry of Food from 12 o'clock to 2, office in the afternoon and then Ministry of Food from 4 o'clock till seven or more. Taking it all round, people are reasonably cheerful but nobody understands what is actually happening. I presume, of course, that the Supreme Command is carrying out the pre-arranged plan. I should imagine we had no intention of attacking on the western front whole-heartedly. The dismemberment of Poland with Russia's assistance was more rapid than was anticipated. Our business in Poland has gone west but our English staff got out with the Embassy people and are slowly drifting back. One or two came via the Baltic and had some

---

[1] Sir Harry Peat (1878-1959). Accountant. Served on numerous government committees. KCVO (1952).

[2] Rt Hon. Oliver Stanley (1896-1950). MP (Con) Westmorland, 1924-45, Bristol W, 1945-50. Parl. U-Sec. Home Office, 1931-33; Min. of Lab., 1934-25; Pres. Bd. of Ed., 1935-37; Pres Bd. of Trade, 1937-40; War Sec., 1940; Min. for Colonies, 1942-45. PC (1939).

exciting experiences. I understand Miss Anderson got back last week-end, taking three weeks to do so.

Alison to E.C.F.B., 6 October   *London*

Ralph had a letter from Roy Monier-Williams this morning and he said he and Gladys and Evelyn are picnicking in their house in London. They have been hard hit and have had to give up their car and their maids. Evelyn has apparently come down from Oxford and is trying to get a commission. Gladys is running the house. Virtually all our friends have fled and the people next door to us moved out yesterday and cleared their furniture out, so we are now the sole occupants of this square of 48 houses. It is really desolate as we never see a soul in the Square except ourselves and the ARP wardens on duty - no cars, not even cats! One seems to pass the days in a sort of odd dream or rather in a nightmare, so swiftly has the manner and tenor of one's life changed. There are bitter letters in the papers still about the 'desecration and obstruction' of Canterbury Cathedral and I think they are right. In these sad and troublous days, the beauty and calm of such a lovely place would be a help and comfort to many people. Surely they could have sandbagged the monuments.

Julian to J.B.B., 10 October   *Felsted*

Of interesting news I have but little. After the fierce and unnerving excitement of the opening days of war, things have settled down to almost the normal here in Felsted, except for about 250 East End children distributed over farms and cottages and rapidly becoming accustomed to country life. There have been many misfits and the standards of the country children in cleanliness and morals have shown up most favourably against their town cousins. The most outstanding conclusion reached by all who have come into contact with the great evacuation is the incompetence and fecklessness of the East End mothers and their inability to get obedience out of their children. However in many cases the mothers have stayed in London and their children sent down to the country have had foster mothers and are learning to be obedient and clean (gaining much from their sojourn in the country).

The next most interesting feature of war time England is the suppression of all attempts to volunteer except for ARP services. We have proceeded another step towards totalitarian methods when the individual is not allowed to offer to serve in HM's Forces. He is told to wait till he is wanted and then he will be sent for. The Englishman is no longer his own master. We had conscription it is true in the last war but not until every man who really wanted to do so had enlisted. A census has been taken of the whole population and ration cards are promised very shortly. At present there is no real shortage of food. The bacon supplies seem short as Germany is torpedoing neutral ships at sight. The most amazing feature of the present war is the silence of the press, muzzled by the Ministry of Information. We simply know nothing. We do not know how many English troops there are in France nor where they are. The censorship has been most complete. The life here at school is more humdrum than ever. All my old chaplain's keenness is re-asserting itself; I shall find it increasingly irksome to stay on here during the war, too old to be of any use at the front,

Geoffrey to J.B.B., 10 October   *Aberdeen*

Aberdeen, the University and my own domestic concerns have hardly been affected by the war at all, so far, except in respect of the nightly black-out, the complete breakdown of the school educational system (all over the country, but notoriously here) and, I need hardly say, the prospect of 7/6 income tax (with 1/- extra on the rates both here and on my Glasgow house) is appalling. But otherwise, as I say, the war has so far made little difference to us up here, even psychologically. For we are told hardly anything about it and half or more than half of that is rumour and therefore not to be believed. Our daily ration of really informing and reliable news takes about 2 minutes to read every morning and about 3 minutes to hear on the wireless every evening at 9 p.m. (which is the only time I listen to it).

The truth is this is a very queer war, though I suppose it will become normal enough once fighting begins on the western front which it may do anytime after next Thursday (the day after tomorrow) when the PM has informed the House, as I take it that he will, that he is turning down Hitler's peace offer. But no one can foresee anything. For all one knows, one may wake up tomorrow to hear that Russia has invaded Finland, or become the ally of Germany, or that Germany has gone Bolshevik, or that Hitler has been deposed or that he has made a frontal attack on the western front or invaded Belgium or Holland or Luxemburg, or that he has committed suicide or anything else you like, and one has become so inured to the strange, the unexpected, that one would accept it as quite credible and take in one's stride.

E.C.F.B to J.B.B., 11 October

Miss Babington tells me the Dean read a long statement about the Cathedral to the 'Friends' Council. Then Canon MacNutt read an equally long statement after which the Dean said he had to go. A resolution was sent to the Dean and Chapter thanking them for preserving the glass and other treasures but expressing the earnest wish that the Cathedral be restored to its proper use and offering to pay for removing the earth and cleaning the building. The Dean sent for Miss Babington and asked for the addresses of the 5,000 members of the 'Friends' but gave no inkling of what he wished to send to them. I have lately been in the Cathedral and saw King's College boys shovelling the earth up into handcarts and depositing it outside the west door. The Dean seems to have given up his idea.

Monier to E.C.F.B., 11 October   *Chiddingstone*

I heard two evacuee stories which may amuse you: a householder came to say to the Billeting Officer that she could not keep her evacuee boy any longer as his language was so bad and she was afraid for her own children. When asked to give an example she said, 'The boy is six years old and I gave him a fried egg and bacon for his breakfast, and all he said was, where's the bloody tomato!' The other story is this: A small evacuee was taken to church and behaved very badly, aged about eight: he was told that he must try to sit more still next Sunday and if he remembered the text he should have a small treat. He made a real effort and there were satisfactory signs of it and on coming out of church, when asked the text, he at once replied 'Six pieces of suet'. Such an announcement so surprised the grown-up that she forgot the real text and could not think what the boy meant; at last it came back to her that it had been 'Seek peace and ensue it'.

Monier to J.B.B., 11 October   *Chiddingstone*

The Ministry of Information has come in for a lot of criticism, partly I think owing to its unfortunate name. It can't give information when there is none. We are all well here, I will go through the family and report. Kay and Charles have been down for two week-ends. Charles is uncertain about his war job. He has been told to stand by and so lives at home with Kay and goes to his office in town, where there is one clerk, his partner and most of the office having moved to

Midhurst. Charles has also applied to the Admiralty to get on the RN Reserves. Edward is now at Port Sudan, or was when he last wrote. But men were coming back from leave and he expected to be sent back to Sinkat. He does not know if he will be sent to Torit in Equatorial Province as at one time planned. He met the new Governor, Bourdillon,[1] the other day and had a nice chat with him. Edward is very fit: his letters come through pretty regularly - air mail in nine or 10 days and ordinary mail 20-21 - air mail cost 1/3d.

Mary is very busy. She goes to Edenbridge Hospital twice a week for nursing and will have completed her 52 hours training this week. If many casualties come, Mary and Jane Meade-Waldo will have to give much more time to this. In addition running this full household takes some doing too. Rationing has not begun yet. Then she and the two Matthews girls with the Meade-Waldos,[2] and some three or four others have arranged clubs for the evacuee children on Saturdays and are running the cubs and brownies for our own children. John has made a good beginning as head of the house, as such he is in a select body consisting of the Head of the School and all heads of houses. He is service cadet officer in the OTC. He has signed on at a Reception Unit for the Reserve of officers. This means he will join up but not till he is 20, in an officers' training battalion and will not go through the ranks. Unless things are altered he will still get one year at Oxford.

It is an odd war so far and for the country districts very unlike the war of 1914-1918. You are seeing things from the Canadian centre, I from a tiny country circumference. Dick Streatfeild[3] is training at Catterick. Lots of men are special constables, ARP workers of various kinds, both men and women. But none have had anything to do, except with evacuee mothers and children. The amount of dirt brought out of the towns into the country is awful and has brought home to us what slums and casual labour really mean. Our black spot, in all this district and I understand it is true of the whole county, is the LCC teachers. With a few bright exceptions, and those religious men and women as far as I have come in contact with them, the teachers are old, lack imagination, are entirely selfish, can't keep

---

[1] Sir Bernard Bourdillon (1883-1948). Numerous postings in Africa, Mid and Far East, 1931-35; Gov. of Nigeria, 1935-39; of Sudan, 1939-44. CMG (1924), KBE (1931) GCMG (1937).

[2] The Matthew family was living in the Rectory at Chiddingstone, the Meade-Waldos were neighbours.

[3] Richard Streatfeild (1903-52). ADC to Canadian Gov. Gen, 1931-33; Ext. Eq. to George VI from 1937; Pte Sec. to Queen, 1937-46; Brig. R.A.

order, are idle and are out for themselves, only abiding by NUT hours, and prepared to take all they can get. Their conduct has made the LCC and its teaching staff stink in the nostrils of our people, of all ranks. Of course the problems faced by the LCC and the Kent Education Committee are tremendous: teachers and children long distances from school, lack of school accommodation and equipment, large numbers of children evacuated with very few teachers, small numbers of children (as here) with vastly too many teachers. We have 58 children in Chiddingstone School with six teachers and 46 at the Hoath school with four teachers i.e. one teacher to 10 children. Also many people have evacuated themselves with their own families. But the outstanding fact remains true that the teachers can't adapt themselves.

I spend hours over billeting problems. Parents are allowed to come and fetch their children home when they like and are doing so. We have lost 15 or 20 children in that way. Other parents come down Sunday after Sunday and expect the cottagers to feed them and sometimes put them up. Naturally this causes ill feeling. Again, cottagers' circumstances change and so for illness, or some other cause, the billeted children have to be removed. Practically all our children brought with them or developed verminous heads. Just think what that means to cottagers who have children excluded from school till free of infection, when they are accustomed at this time of year to be ready for hop-picking or apple-gathering all day.

John to J.B.B., 15 October   *Sheriff House, Rugby*

Rugby is at its worst - a soaking wet Sunday afternoon and I have time for a letter to let you know what life is like nowadays at school. Once I begin to think out what is different from the normal, I can think of remarkably little. Each house has its two dug-outs - barrel-roofed concrete affairs which we are only going to use in the daytime in the unlikely event of Rugby being bombed. In a night air raid we are just going to come down into a long passage, the only window of which has been sandbagged to make it splinter-proof. I sent in my name to a reception unit the other day to join a reserve of officers. We shall not be called up any earlier than if we had not joined but it will mean that we get commissions without going through the ranks. Only those of us over 18 could do it and I am sure it was worth doing, though there are obviously some advantages in starting in the ranks, as you did. I have filled in a good many forms, got a recommendation from our CO and should be called to an interview some time this week. The prospect of my getting up to Oxford next October seem very dim. Already there are 23 colleges squashed into 9 and there are several of my friends there who have got to share their rooms with one or even two more people. But if the government really stand by their assurance that we shall not get called up till we are 20, I shall be able to get a year there and I think it will be worth it as there will be nothing else to do. It will depend entirely on the number of casualties whether the age limit is lowered, I imagine.

The endless minor duties of a head of house early in the term are diminishing as the term goes on. We have started sugar and butter rationing, as the grocers find it impossible to get our large orders; rationing proper does not come in for another fortnight. The sugar is no hardship really - seven ounces a week, but the butter is rather an effort at present. On Thursday we are having our first 'tactical exercises' of the term. I am a company commander and we are being given no orders until half an hour before zero hour. I fancy a quick cavalry decision will be the order of the day.

On the Jelf side of the family, there are lots of people more of an age for service. Uncle Ralph Trench[1] is in France with the Signals and Raymond Grace[2] with The Buffs. Oliver is finishing his Territorial training and expects to go abroad almost at once. John Trench,[3] as Woolwich has been dissolved, is training in the ranks on Salisbury Plain. I was looking at the War Diaries when I was over and wondering if we could ever attempt to do the same again. The difficulty is that our ages are wrong for active service and we have mostly got that beastly job of carrying on. Also, perhaps you would feel it was an undertaking which could not be repeated. The War Diary has proved of such immense interest to our generation that I feel something on the same lines should be undertaken by us - even if of a less thorough nature. I read the lesson in chapel this morning for the first time, quite a good bit from old Jeremiah. The Public Schools Exploring Society Expedition got home about 10 days ago, after waiting a week at Halifax, Nova Scotia, taking two and a half weeks zig-zagging home across the Atlantic! It seems almost incredible.

---

[1] Brig. Ralph Chevenix-Trench (1885-1974). Act. Maj-Gen. with BEF, Royal Corps of Signals.

[2] Raymond Grace (d. 1986). Captured at Dunkirk. Later of the Royal Corps of Signals.

[3] John Trench. Ralph Chevenix-Trench's son. Killed in action, N. Africa 1943.

Geoffrey to E.C.F.B., 15 October   *Aberdeen*

Tony went off to Oxford last Thursday evening by the 6 o'clock night train to King's Cross. I hope and believe university life will be less affected by the present war than at first seemed likely. You doubtless read in Friday's and Saturday's *Times* the speech of the Vice-Chancellor and the article on war-time Oxford respectively, which supply the grounds of my hope. The authorities seem to have planned very nicely so as to enable the 19 year-olds to derive the utmost possible advantage from their year at Oxford before they are due to be called up for military service. Needless to say it is my fervent prayer that the length of the war will make it needless for Tony to be called up at all. But, at least, despite the war, he has in prospect a complete year of university life which ought to be happy and profitable. I saw him off at the station, cutting a quite important Senate meeting (the first of the session) to do so. In his compartment there was a little German Jewish boy, a refugee from Hitler's persecution, travelling south alone to join his parents in England. Otherwise, apart from the almost unlighted carriage, there was nothing outwardly to remind one of the war. Inwardly, however, I was acutely conscious that the reality of his first departure for Oxford differed much from what it would have been in peace time.

Meanwhile, things do seem to me to be going moderately well. Hitler, too, has got to pay the price and he very curiously is most unwilling and not at all ready to do so. The PM's speech has driven him into a corner. He knows that he must abdicate or fight. Either alternative appals him and he may yet try to wriggle out of his desperate situation. But he will not succeed.

I begin lecturing on Tuesday, the day after tomorrow, exactly twenty years after first coming to live in Scotland. I read the Dean's apologia for his desecration of Canterbury Cathedral in *The Times* and was not impressed by it. He does not attempt to meet the main point in the indictment brought by his critics, namely, that there was no need to turn the Cathedral into an air raid shelter at all. No church anywhere is required to supply shelter for its congregation (in case of an air raid) under its own roof. Moreover, Canterbury is a reception area. A church is a House of God, not a rabbit-hole. The latter can be supplied in the Precincts. If the 'Friends' decide to contribute one penny to the £3,000 he has spent, I shall withdraw my subscription. Let him and the Chapter find the money out of their own pockets.

Julian to E.C.F.B., 17 October   *Felsted*

Last night I had a rehearsal of an air raid for the School House just about midnight. Everybody was up, more or less dressed, with his gas mask and at his station in just over four minutes. This was not bad really as so many boys were dead asleep and had to be shaken to get them fully awake. I do not intend to have any more rehearsals now at night, as the boys are well enough coached. I may, however, have one in the middle of the afternoon in order to see how quickly they can all take cover while they are playing games. The school has really settled down to an almost normal life now. But for the precautions taken about darkening windows and a curtailed fixture list for football matches, no one would know a war was on at all. One of the boys here had an uncle on the *Royal Oak*,[1] he was the Anglican Padre and also an OF. There has been no news of him at all, so I fear he cannot be on any of the survivors' lists.

Euan Wallace to J.B.B., 20 October   *Ministry of Transport*

As soon as war broke out David[2] was asked to become press attaché in Athens and to create a new department for himself. It is a remarkable stroke of luck for him that his experiences of the last few years should have come in so very useful; I have no doubt that he is doing the job extremely well. The best criterion of how busy he is, is that I have only had one long letter and one tiny one from him since the war started. The former was chiefly to complain against the Ministry of Information under whose control our press attachés abroad originally came; but I am not at all certain whether they have not, during the drastic process of cutting down the Ministry of Information, reverted to Foreign Office control. There is clearly no object in him giving up a job where he can be of particular use to come home and try to get a commission as a 2nd Lieutenant. G. is still doing the Specialist Navigation Course which was moved from Manston to a place near Cardiff at the outbreak of war. I have seen him occasionally as they come up to London sometimes to inspect factories and such like and he comes up this week-end *en route* to Chatham. The course goes on until nearly Christmas and his great fear is that when it is over he may be retained there as an instructor. His ambition is, of course, to get back immediately to fighters and to find himself leading a

---

[1] HMS Royal Oak. Sunk by U-boat at Scapa Flow, 14 Oct. 1939 with the loss of 810 of the ship's company.
[2] David Wallace, Euan Wallace's eldest son.

squadron of Spitfires in the air. I am doubtful if he has very much chance of this, and I believe that it is even possible that he might be sent to Canada in connection with the training scheme announced recently by Kingsley Wood.[1] At any rate I do not think it wise or possible to try and exercise any influence; and I should find it difficult to know which way to pull even if I could. John[2] is at present with a crammer at Horsham and gets home to Lavington from midday Saturday until 8 am on Monday, by judicious use of his bicycle and a local train. George Lyttelton[3] offered to take him back at Eton when it became obvious that he could not go to Switzerland as arranged; but it seemed to all of us that this would be rather an anti-climax and John was not anxious to go back himself. I took him to see the Lt. Colonel commanding the Grenadiers and got him put down on their list; but nothing whatever can be done until he is 18, and by that time I am credibly informed that we shall have reached the stage where no commissions will be given except to those who have been through their militia service. It looks, therefore, as if this war will not catch John at all unless it continues for appreciably longer than our rather pessimistic three years' forecast. You can imagine what an immense relief this is to Barbie[4].

Diana and Duff Cooper[5] left here last Thursday in the *Manhattan*, we had postcards dated Sunday from them, despatched from a port in the Bay of Biscay. It is quite impossible to have any idea as to when they are likely to reach their destination. They did not mean to sail until about the middle of next month but the difficulty of getting a passage became so acute that they thought it was wise to take the first opportunity. In any case, Duff had no job here and was really very unhappy at being idle. In any circumstances we would miss them acutely; but since the war started they have been our great standby for Sunday lunch at Bognor, enabling us to get away from the hospital atmosphere, and also to have a very much better lunch than we now get at home. By the exercise of what I regard as a superhuman effort of ingenuity, Barbie and the cook have cut the feeding costs of

---

[1] Sir (Howard) Kingsley Wood (1881-1943). MP (Con) Woolwich W, 1918-43; P.M.G. 1931-35; Min. of Health 1935-38; Sec. of State for Air 1938-40; Ld. Privy Seal 1940; Chanc. of Excheq. 1940-43; Kt. (1918).
[2] John Wallace, Euan Wallace's youngest son.
[3] Hon. George Lyttelton (1883-1962). Ass. Master, Eton College.
[4] Barbie Wallace. Euan Wallace's wife, daughter of the architect Sir Edward Lutyens.
[5] Lady Diana, Vts. Norwich (1892-1986) and Alfred Duff Cooper (1885-1954). MP (Con) Oldham, 1924-29; St. George's Westminster, 1931-45; Min. for War, 1935-37; Ist Ld. Adm, 1937-38; Min. of Inf., 1940-41. Amb. in Paris, 1944-47; PC (1935), cr. Vt. Norwich (1952).

the inmates of Lavington down to 14/- a head per week; we all have the same food; and no doubt it is much better for us than the peace time diet.

Duff's lecture tour was arranged at least six months ago. He was very doubtful whether to stick to it or not but the PM was in favour of his doing so. I saw Willie Wiseman,[1] whom you will remember from New York, the other day, and he felt rather apprehensive about the tour. In his view the fact that it was arranged more than six months ago would probably not suffice to stop it being stigmatised as British propaganda, which is apparently absolute anathema to inhabitants of the USA at the present moment.

My own work here is going on as well as one could expect. In fact, I am so far pleasantly surprised that there has not been more criticism in view of the inconveniences, in both road and railway travel, with which the public have to put up. When you think that all our plans were made on the assumption that this country would be subjected from the very first day of the war to frequent and possibly devastating attacks from the air and that nothing of the sort has actually happened in six and a half weeks, you will see that we have a somewhat difficult problem of psychology and morale to contend with. There is so much that I could write to you. You must by now have seen the papers and read about the Ministry of Information muddle and the steps which have been taken to put the whole business on a more sensible footing; and I do hope and believe that you will now get a reasonable supply of news. As regards making speeches, you are certainly no worse off than we are. At the moment no public speeches of any kind are being made by supporters of the government and in spite of the obvious disadvantages of leaving the field to our opponents, I do not think it is at all advisable for any Minister to be put in the position where he may be asked so many embarrassing questions. The Turkish Treaty is a great relief, and the most satisfactory feature of the attacks on the Firth of Forth on Monday was the performance of our fighters, all belonging to the auxiliary squadrons.[2]

E.C.F.B., to J.B.B., 23 October   *Canterbury*

Mary arrived at 11.30 am today for two nights and it is such a joy. After

---

[1] Sir William George Eden Wiseman, 10th Bt (1885-1962). Adv. on US affairs to UK Del., Paris 1918-19; Chmn. Cttee. $ Exports Council.

[2] An Anglo-French-Turkish mutual defence pact was signed in Ankara on 19 October. The raid on the Firth of Forth on 16 Oct. resulted in one cruiser and one destroyer damaged and two German bombers shot down.

lunch we went to the Cathedral as John was anxious for a report as to its condition. I must first tell you that the Cathedral was re-opened for services again on Saturday (two days ago) after 100 King's Schoolboys and 50 charwomen had cleaned hard for four days. Miss Gray and I went on Sunday at 10.30. Before Dr Shirley's[1] sermon the Archbishop,[2] who was down there, stood up in his seat and said something like this, 'I am not speaking for the Dean or Chapter, but as Visitor of this Cathedral I wish to say a word of thanks to the King's School for the help they have given this last week in restoring this beautiful House of God to its use for worship. This school is one of the most ancient in the Kingdom but I doubt if the boys have ever done a greater work for Canterbury than this which they have done.' As Dr Shirley says in his letter to *The Times*, I doubt if the lower part of the Cathedral, floor, stalls, tombs, brasses, have been so clean for years. The crypt still remains blocked with boarding, etc. but the whole of the rest of the building, including all chapels, are open for use.

Leonard Burrows[3] came to see me on Sunday and his visit gave me the greatest pleasure. It made me feel young again as we talked over old Oxford days when he was up at New College and your father at St Johns. Another good bit of news is that all restrictions on gas, electricity and coal have been removed. We were puzzling how to keep warm. Now, if it gets cold I can have the stove in my bedroom lit when I go to bed. By the bye, the Dean was not in the Cathedral on Sunday morning. He may have been engaged but I wish he had been there. He might have regained his position with the city with a few generous words.

Pat Hodgson[4] to J.B.B., 29 October   *Sloane Court, London*

Here we remain quite calm waiting for something to happen, which the papers assure us is likely to come at any moment. It is an extraordinary war and as unlike the last one as you can possibly imagine. No emotionalism, no noise, just a quiet determination to see it through. There have been some bad muddles, the way hotels and schools have been commandeered amounts to a real scandal and

---

[1] Rev. Dr. John Shirley (1890-1967). Headmaster, King's School Canterbury, 1935-62; Senior Canon Residentiary of Canterbury from 1935.
[2] Most Rev. Cosmo Gordon Lang, Baron Lang of Lambeth (1864-1945). Bishop of Stepney, 1901-08; Archbishop of York, 1908-28; Archbishop of Canterbury, 1928-42.
[3] Leonard Burrows (1857-1940). Bishop of Sheffield, 1914-39.
[4] Patrick Hodgson (1884-1964). Pte. Sec. to Gov. Gen. of Canada, 1922-25; Pte. Sec. to Duke of York, 1926-33.

bureaucracy has rather lost its head. But on the other hand a great deal of valuable preparation has been effected without fuss. To what extent it will withstand enemy attacks has to be seen, but the general feeling is one of confidence. London after ten o'clock at night is like a city of the dead, nobody is in the streets and very little traffic. But the unemployment is bad and one come across tragic cases of distress among middle-aged people of the clerk type, both men and women, Their evacuation is a very serious problem. Women have taken their children away leaving their husbands behind with the inevitable result that the men seek 'companionship' from other women. Parents whose children are within reach of big towns troop out to see them during week-ends and expect to be lodged and fed by the people who are billeting their offspring! This naturally doesn't promote goodwill. And of course many children have been brought back home but no schools are opened for them, so that they run wild in the streets and forget all they have learned. The evacuation question is one that seems to me to have been handled from the start with no imagination at all by any of the authorities concerned and the social difficulties that lie ahead in consequence will be enormous.

Three Memoranda by Hart Massey[1]   *H.Q. RCAF, London*

I

It seems rather obvious, except perhaps to certain Americans, that there is a war going on in Europe unlike any other war that's ever happened and, although hopes and hunches soar high into the realms of optimism, it seems likely that this particular war is here to stay, for a while at any rate. The individual citizen. or 'little man' as portrayed by Strube,[2] can no longer be immune therefore from the responsibility for the defence of his country as he has been in the past, if over or under military age. This is why the appearance of England is like that of a beleaguered country. The streets of London are filled with the paraphernalia of war. So much so that it is inconceivable that anyone could long remain aloof from the atmosphere around him. This all pervading sense of imminent danger is just as obvious among those gaping in wonder at the four anti-aircraft guns in Hyde Park as among those enthusiastic ARP workers at Little Puddle in the Marsh - miles

---

[1] Vincent and Alice Massey's younger son; served with the RCAF.
[2] 'Strube'. A cartoonist, principally with the *Daily Express*.

away from any possible serial target. Myriads of sandbags protect the lower floors of most buildings, some smartly piled, knocked flat, and cleverly painted - others, more inefficiently stacked, bulge threateningly over the pedestrian on the sidewalk. Stuck in strips on the windows to prevent flying glass in an air-raid, can be seen mile upon mile of brown wrapping paper and cellophane. Some windows affect a rather self-conscious pattern of criss-crosses while others frankly go in for the who-the-hell-cares method of protecting the occupants of the building. Invariably, however, the efficiency and modishness of the air-raid precautions runs in a quite definite parallel with the peacetime character or aspirations of house, shop or restaurant - for obviously the condition of sand bags and brown papered windows now shows, as did the 'shop window' in peacetime, the nature of the inside.

Although it is considered unlikely that London will be bombed for some time to come, and even then it is still farther from likely that gas will be used, nevertheless everyone is advised to carry their masks and to do so religiously. Individual enterprise has an opening in the contriving of containers for these miserable little bits of rubber and tin which daily cause so much trouble; 100 are lost each day on the buses and trains of London.

This type of *ennui* and the feeling that a great deal of the precautionary measures are unnecessary, is producing an amount of impatience with the government and local authorities concerning the former's conduct of the war and the latter's old maidish observance of petty restrictions. All this is a natural outcome of plucking thousands of men and women from their daily routine of occupation and home and placing them in a completely new setting of different hours, friends, and purpose. This annoyance has no real basis and is only felt by a few, but even this will soon dissolve when things start to move.

Petrol is rationed these days and there are very few private cars on the road, but what there are all seem to have some sort of sticker on the windscreen claiming priority over every other. These are mostly authorised by local officials and are being dealt with by the government. A few examples are: LCC on ARP, Emergency Food Supplies, MYOB (mind your own business), etc.

II

Hitler's speech this morning may have ended the lull of the last few weeks and it is now possible, even probable, almost certain that we are now entering the second phase of this so far continental oratorical contest cum war. The restlessness so apparent recently is a direct effect of this lack of consistency in the daily temperature on the war fever chart. On 1 September, we were all pitchforked into what we thought at first was bound to be continued and unrelenting Hell for some time to come, although many allowed their minds to roam with confidence on the political and economic plight of Germany. Accordingly, preparations were made, but then after the sirens had been trained not to sound their voices at the sight of even a kite on the end of a string, we all relapsed into the inevitable carelessness of one who has been falsely warned several times of a lupine presence in his immediate neighbourhood, and then become slightly sceptical of the veracity of these statements henceforward. I do not wish to put the government in the place of the practical joker in this age-old story, but I do feel that circumstance should occupy this position. In a few days, weeks or months we are going to be rudely jolted from our perch of almost peacetime contentment and only then will war have begun and the full pressure of it be apparent on the ordinary men and women of England. This is not meant to be alarming.

On the ARP front, very little has happened since my last 'communiqué'. Apart from slightly fewer numbers of people carrying gas masks, activities are being carried on with just as much earnestness but, I must say, markedly abbreviated enthusiasm. It now becomes quite obvious that the defence of this country from air attack is not going to afford just part-time and amusing employment for the thousands of people engaged in it, but rather, it is going to be the permanent war-time job of the citizen with no other alternative. This is going to become increasingly plain as the war advances and more men are needed for the army. Thus does this war, like no other before it, disrupt both the individual's and the nation's routine of life.

A propos barrage balloons: There is a story of an old lady who was overheard saying, 'If those Germans think they can frighten us by sitting up there in those balloons, they are greatly mistaken.' This spirit has made the British what they are. A further indication of the bull-dog approach was apparent only the other day when the manager of a cinema, in accordance with instructions, announced on the screen the whereabouts of the nearest air-raid shelters, but then rounded off his message to the audience with this exhortation from the managerial pen: 'DON'T PANIC, REMEMBER YOU'RE BRITISH'. One gets to be pretty proud of one's passport these days! Up England! Up the Empire! Up John Bull! HAIL BLIMP!

The Ministry of Information is carrying on bravely in the face of almost overwhelming opposition and seems to be moulding itself gradually, but so far imperceptibly, into a more popular shape. Nevertheless, journalists can still be seen fuming up and down Fleet Street in droves. There is no news to speak of and there's no reason to believe there will be until the commands of army, navy and air force realise that one very necessary adjunct to a successful war is the keeping of public opinion in a contented state. This can only be accomplished by satisfying a quite natural desire for details of their army across the channel, for rumour has it that there is one there at the moment.

The Germans on the other hand, feed their own, the neutral and the enemy press with all kinds of lively propaganda illustrating her army's prowess in the field and this must, sooner or later, have an adverse effect on opinion both here and more especially in neutral countries such as America. After all, propaganda is not an evil thing in itself as so many people think. It is but the mirror of beliefs and passions, magnified and shaped, but not destroyed. In war-time it is almost as important as the army in the field. David Low [the *Evening Standard* cartoonist] has epitomised the present state of affairs in a recent cartoon in which Colonel Blimp, with the best case in the world, is portrayed with an out-of-date and puny gramophone in an equally decrepit baby carriage - competing against Goebbels,[1] with the worst case in the world, but the finest propaganda machine - overwhelming Blimp and his miserable toy, with a bombast of ingenious lies flowing from huge loud-speakers.

III

There can never be such a thing as continued military stalemate - as incident soon piles upon threat to make war the only possible outlet for the soothing of an injured national pride and the maintaining of a prestige among nations - even though there may be unwillingness on both sides. But this is not quite the situation in regard to Germany at the moment, for here, although national prestige seems to be very tender to verbal insults, Hitler seems to be anxious not to walk too precipitately into the deep end of the pool, but rather has the appearance of allowing himself to be pushed reluctantly over the edge by events. It is difficult to say what it is that has curbed the fulfilment of his former

---

[1]   Josef Goebbels (1897-1945). Chief propagandist of Nazi Party and Reichsminister for Information and Propaganda from 1933.

boasts and made him so timorous of taking the cold plunge - but it seems fairly clear that, at last, his own calculations have double-crossed him and that he has been overwhelmed by the totally unexpected - i.e. the determination of England and France to resist the final aggression in Poland. Once more David Low has discovered the essence of Hitler's predicament. In vain and with ever increasing apprehension to the trio, Hitler, Goebbels and Göring[1] search the skies for the plane which should bring Chamberlain and his notorious umbrella to appease. Now, however, the Führer seems to have recovered from the shock of miscalculation and, according to a newspaper poster just outside the window where I'm working, has already begun the war in earnest. Although it is still a matter of doubt how much the oncoming winter and attendant bad weather is going to hold up large scale military operations on the Western Front - there already seems to be great activity behind the Siegfried Line. Is Hitler going to attempt to put into practice the German theory of *Blitzkrieg*? The sporadic military and air activity of the last few days does not bear this out. Is he contemplating the success of another peace proposal? There is just enough maritime enmity to discourage this. Then what? - no one knows but there are many theories!

November

J.C. Masterman[2] to J.B.B., 1 November   *Oxford*

I can well imagine that you must chafe a bit at being away from England. I have a terrible itch myself to be doing something active and I cannot reconcile myself to sitting here teaching although reason tells me that it is my proper job. Our age is a bad one for war time, older or younger would be better. You want to know about Oxford. To my surprise the university is going on very much as in peace time. This is due to the policy of 20 rather than 19 as the usual starting age for the soldier. It means that most of the men can count on getting a full year here and a certain number a bit more. If the war goes on there will be a tendency for boys to leave school early and so ensure getting a fairly long spell at the

---

[1] Hermann Göring (1893-1946). Top Nazi and C-in-C. *Luftwaffe*. Star defendant at Nuremberg Trials.
[2] John Cecil Masterman (1891-1977). Provost of Worcester Coll. Oxford, 1946-61. Vice Chanc. Oxford Univ., 1957-58. Kt.(1959).

university. At present we have about 60% of our usual numbers - that is practically all of the freshmen and a sprinkling of the second year and a good many medical students and scientists who are in reserved classes. Unless things change it may be that the same thing will happen again next year.

As a good many of the colleges have been requisitioned for various purposes (though in many cases they are still unused) we have been crammed together a good deal: thus we have all BNC and part of Pembroke; Oriel is at Hertford; Balliol at Trinity. For games and such like we hastily put all the colleges together in pairs which seems to work well. I believe that at first the plan was to stop all debates at the Union, but this policy was changed and the weekly debate now takes place, though I understand the meetings are not reported. The first debate I think was something to do with war aims, the second on the BBC. Probably debating will go on without much fuss, certainly public opinion would not allow it to do anything foolish.

Geoffrey to E.C.F.B., 5 November   *Aberdeen*

The husband of one of Jean's old school friend came to lunch yesterday. They live at Fincastle a village in the highlands. Over 100 children from the slums of Glasgow were evacuated there but all but about thirty have returned to Glasgow. It is the same everywhere and by Christmas the vast majority of the children will have come home and the money spent in evacuating them wasted because the government planned only the first step of a revolutionary scheme and then did no more. Meanwhile ARP has caused thousands more casualties than military action. The students here were told to bring gas masks to lectures and did so for the first few days of term and then gave up the habit and now nobody does. At the senate this week it was decided they could please themselves and quite right too, we shall have no raids here or if we do no gas raids. It is clear that air raids are only against military objectives. This is proved by the German raid on the Forth last week. Warships were attacked and two were hit but the Forth bridge would have been the legitimate objective and so huge a target it could not have been missed. Moreover, the planes flew only a few feet over it and there was a train on the bridge at the time and had it been bombed this would have been blown to pieces. I am told that Lloyds are still betting 10 - 1 that the war will not continue past 1 January. What we are actually witnessing, it seems to me, is the self-stultification of war. The two most powerful armies in the world refusing to fight because each dreads the destruction of life. If I am right this war can only end in a political revolution in either Germany or the countries opposed to it. The latter is unlikely, what about the former? In my opinion the revolution when it does come will be from above and not from below. This surely is the first Great War in history which from the moment it broke out has had its course determined not by the will to fight but by the will to peace.

Lady Cripps to J.B.B., 8 November   *London*

Life is a bewildering affair just now, and, as for so many, has entirely changed things for us. We have given up everything of our own in London and are picnicking in my mother's flat. I do all the 'cooking' and have never been so glad that we are almost raw-vegetarians! Stafford[1] gave up his profession the day war started and his 'official' position is helping the solicitor to the Board of Trade. This means that he is attached to them for special work. I cannot go into this in more detail.

At 'Goodfellows'[2] we have six small boys between 11 and 13 from West Ham and a master with his wife and baby of 10 months. Evacuation has raised many problems, but we hope that with patience and understanding on both sides, some contribution may be made to the solution of some of our social problems, because already the showing up of the terrible slum conditions has opened the eyes of many who did not know such things existed. We have been lucky with our six and the difference in them physically and in other ways is surprising for the short time they have been there. John[3] is still at his job with the *Countryman* and filling in his spare time with various activities. He is pacifist and virtually a Quaker, so I do not know what fate will have in store for him presently. His small Judith is a great joy to us all. We feel very strongly that all must be done to better relations with the USSR. You will be seeing Stafford's articles in the *Tribune* which I hope is reaching you. That is his one medium for expressing his views publicly, but the freedom for this is becoming more and more curtailed, and there are tussles with the censor every week. The really hopeful sign is in the various groups who are trying to think out some new approach for the time when this

---

[1] Sir (Richard) Stafford Cripps (1889-1952). MP (Lab) Bristol E., 1931-50. Sol-Gen., 1930-31; Amb. to Moscow, 1940-42; Leader of House and Ld. Privy Seal, 1942; Min. of Aircraft Prod., 1942-45; Pres. Bd. of Trade, 1945-46; Chanc. of Excheq., 1947-50. Kt. (1930).

[2] 'Goodfellows'; the Cripps's home near Lechlade in Gloucestershir.

[3] John Cripps, Sir Stafford and Lady Isobel's son.

horror ends. Many really fine people are concentrating with all that is in them on trying to work out some plan which can be put into operation when the right moment comes.

Young Julian to E.C.F.B., 8 November   *Marlborough*

Has it ever struck you that what this country lacks is an imposing personality to which it can rally, regardless of opposing opinions and ideas in the country? I was talking about it with my form master only this morning. In the last war this country had the imposing personality, namely Lloyd George.[1] My form master said it would be interesting to forecast whether anyone of a similar type would arise in this war. I am at this moment busy on a caper for our political society here, it is to be on 'neutrality in wartime'. I shall be provocative and take the view that the uncertainty which surrounds the Neutrality Laws are due to past bad behaviour on the part of Great Britain.

Julian to J.B.B., 14 November   *Felsted*

Churchill[2] implies the longer we sit tight the better. I hear the BEF behind the Belgian frontier is getting very bored. In the last war most of the serious fighting was north of that frontier and now it is all centred in Alsace-Lorraine. I have had two uncensored propaganda letters from Germany. One containing Hitler's last public speech asking for peace, the other containing a lie about the British supplying the Poles with gas. A parent wrote to me the other day saying he was engaged at a special hush-hush factory in the Midlands and would not have even told me this had not the German wireless given a full description of the factory mentioned, its site and what it was going to produce. Espionage in England is extensive and everyone is warned against talking.

Major-General Hastings Ismay to J.B.B., 14 November   *London*

Much has gone exactly according to plan, but there has been much that is unexpected and difficult to understand. The preparations that had been made over

---

[1] David Lloyd George, (1863-1945). MP (Lib) Carnarvon Boroughs, 1890-1945. Numerous ministerial appointments from 1905; PM, 1916-22. Cr. Earl Lloyd George of Dwyfor (1945).
[2] Winston Leonard Spencer Churchill (1874-1965). MP (Con to 1904 then Lib) Oldham 1900-06, (Lib) Manchester N.W. 1906-08, (Lib) Dundee 1908-22, (Con) Epping (later Woodford) 1924-64. Numerous ministerial posts. PM, 1940-45 and 1951-55. KG (1953).

a period of years to ensure a smooth transition of the whole nation from a state of peace to a state of war worked without a single hitch. A war cabinet on the Lloyd George model of 1917-1918 was brought into being on the day war was declared, met on the same day and has continued to meet once or twice daily ever since. Within eight days of the declaration of war we had the first meeting of the Supreme War Council - somewhere in France - in accordance with plans which had been considered in every detail with our friends in advance of the war. Within a very short time all of us in this office felt that we had been a War Cabinet Secretariat instead of a Committee of Imperial Defence all our lives. At the risk of being self-complacent I quote a letter from one who has been in Whitehall for sometime and now has a glittering command (lucky Devil!), 'It has been very good to see the machine that you all prepared moving from peace to war without a tremor in its working'.

Poland was very sad but absolutely inevitable. We had made it quite clear to them and they fully appreciated that we could do nothing to relieve the pressure on them if the Bosche attacked in the east and held in the west (as we thought that he would). Their view was, 'We will get over-run but if you come in we will rise again.' They hoped to form a front somewhere well back and would have done so if the Russians had not marched. That was quite unexpected, thoroughly immoral and typical of the brutes.

We all expected intensive air attacks on this country, on the passage of the BEF and on the French mobilisation and concentration from the word 'go'. It was a great relief they did not arrive because now we are thoroughly prepared to meet it whenever it may come. Our fighting aircraft and indeed all our aircraft - both personnel and machines - have done everything that they have been called upon to do - magnificently. The navy are destroying submarines much faster than the enemy can build them and the army is in fine fettle, everybody down to and including the Colonels wear their medals of the last war and most of them are DSC or MC or both, so it really is a professional army and splendidly equipped.

To sum up we may be in for a really bad and difficult time but everyone is in great heart and I feel that every day that passes without Germany having made an effort of some kind is a day nearer ultimate victory. I don't allow myself to indulge in wishful thinking, but I can't believe that the German leaders who have let loose this devilry are not very perplexed and very unhappy at present.

I think that Mackenzie King[1] has done a marvellous bit of work in bringing in a united Canada and I regret every thought I allowed myself during the Imperial Conference of 1937 when he was not prepared to contemplate a public expression of full-blooded co-operation.

Monier to J.B.B., 16 November   *Chiddingstone*

Sometimes I feel the war will not last a second winter, such evidence as one hears about the views of those in high places is most encouraging. We are busy over endless little things. The daily round presses on one.

Edward is in Khartoum, doing a six weeks military course, mostly on the Bren gun, which ends on 14 December, when he expects to go off to Torit, in Equatoria Province, and will be about 70 miles from the Uganda border. The object of the course is to have extra officers (he has passed Cert B) able to take the place of Regulars at present seconded to the Sudan Defence Force, if they are needed in France. He keeps well on the whole, no fever or more than an occasional cold. Of course he has had a very hot spell at Port Sudan and will not have the best of weather at Torit, a hill station, where the summer is better than the rainy season. I fear he won't get home on leave next spring, for which he is due, and I admit I don't like it on his first trip - on the other hand the government do look after the health of their staff very well.

Tom Jones[2] to J.B.B., 17 November   *Harlech*

Eirene and I have been in Wales since September, first at Gregynog and then in this cottage ten minutes from Coleg Harlech. Lord Dawson prohibited my return to London until Christmas so I lent my secretary to the Cabinet Office. Theoretically the Pilgrim Trust is closed down but in fact we have just started making a few war-time grants. I leave Macmillan[3] and Lord Stamp[4] comparatively undisturbed as they are so busy and occasionally consult Lord Baldwin[5] at his

---

[1] Rt Hon (William) Mackenzie King (1874-1950). Canadian PM, 1921-30 and 1935-48. PC (1922). OM (1947).

[2] Tom Jones (1870-1955). Civil servant, administrator and author; Sec. of Pilgrim Trust, 1930-45; member of Unemployment Assistance Bd., 1934-40; confidant of Baldwin and prime mover in foundation of Council for Encouragement of Music and the Arts (CEMA).

[3] Lord Macmillan (1873-1952). Ld. of Appeal (1930). Min. of Information, 1939-40.

[4] Sir Josiah, later Lord Stamp (1880-1941). Financier. Nearly became Chancellor of the Exchequer in 1940. Killed in air-raid 1941.

[5] Stanley Baldwin (1867-1947). MP (Con) Bewdley, 1908-37; Con. leader, 1923-37; PM 1923-

home in Astley.

During the summer I arranged to transfer Coleg Harlech to the University of Liverpool for the duration for the use of their women students in their training department and about 100 are installed plus a dozen professors. All our students are of military age and most of our staff. But the course of the war is such and the calling up so slow that we are reopening on Monday in two private houses in the village and by Christmas shall have perhaps twenty men.

No one seems to have foreseen the course events were to take. I have been out of things for six months and can offer you no judgement worth reading. There does seem to be reflected in my correspondence more than the usual amount of initial thundering in Whitehall. Most of the 'planning' was irrelevant to the circumstances as they developed, and to readjust the vast machines was difficult. Probably many of the leading civil servants are dog-tired, and far too many old men have been put on committees. The Ministry of Information has been a popular joke and seems to have done most things wrong at first and then to have had a panic purge and got rid of some valuable men. The country is, I am told, quite steadfast and remarkably free from jingoism. I don't underestimate the tremendous striking power of the Germans in the short run. I quoted a conversation to Hankey the other day which I had with Lindbergh[1] after one of his visits to Göring. He said the Germans would go all out to destroy our fleet from the air by a series of relays of planes following on each other swiftly and quite heedless of casualties. I keep wondering whether all this reconnoitring around Scapa Flow and the Firth of Forth is not connected with that plan.

We are all glad to see Salter's[2] appointment. I liked Casey's[3] broadcast, quietly firm and free from bombast. Warren Fisher[4] has made two first rate speeches which were fully reported in the *Manchester Guardian*. He is a regional commissioner in north west England. Menzies[5] is much in the news. Some

---

24, 1924-29, 1935-37. Ld. Pres. 1931-35; cr. Earl Baldwin of Bewdley (1937).

[1] Colonel Charles Lindbergh (1902-74). Aviator. Famous for first solo-Atlantic flight (1927); later infamous for his pessimistic opinions on Britain's capacity to resist German air strength.

[2] James Arthur Salter (1881-1958). MP (Ind) Oxford Univ., 1937-50, and Ormskirk (Con) 1951-53. Parl. Sec. Min of Shipping, 1939-41. Chanc. of D. of Lancaster, 1945; minor ministerial office, 1951-5. Cr. Baron (1953).

[3] Richard Casey (1890-1976). Australian politician. Min. of Supply, 1939-40. Attached to British war cabinet, 1942-43; Gov. of Bengal, 1943-46. Cr. Baron (1960).

[4] Sir Norman (Fenwick) Warren Fisher (1879-1948). Chief Civil Servant; Perm. Sec. to Treasury, 1919-39; Spec. Comm. London, 1940-42.

[5] Sir Robert Menzies (1894-1978). Australian politician. Commonw. Att-Gen., 1934-39; PM

strongly resent Winston's truculence in his last broadcast - I don't. He is a useful exception to our gentlemanly rule.

SB is at Astley exiled and not well; Geoffrey Fry[1] is over, and Lady Fry is in a nursing home as usual. Patrick Duff's show has come badly out of the racket, but he would probably say that the Treasury would not give him decently paid men to commandeer hotels and colleges but only an inferior crowd of inflated sergeant majors. Eady,[2] who runs the ARP, sees the humour of it all luckily. Howorth[3] is at the Cabinet Office and obsessed with Privy Council precedents.

The drastic strain of taxation has given some of my rich friends very cold feet. At Gregynog Press it means an extra 3/- on the £ and for the first time in history they are dismissing some young members of the staff and discussing the closing of the Press. It is such a pity to have to scatter an expert staff gathered with much labour over the years.

Geoffrey to E.C.F.B., 26 November   *Aberdeen*

Nothing short of an air raid would really bring home to us that there is a war on. Moreover, one can pretend it is not there by keeping indoors after dark, not a severe self-denial (after dark) these long winter evenings. It is almost as if we ourselves were living on one planet and the war was going on on another. Such, perhaps, is bound to be the case when one has been instructed that one's normal job is one's appropriate war-work. For to do one's job properly one must think of it and not of the war.

What does the Chancellor of the Exchequer mean by telling us to indulge only in absolutely necessary expenses and to lend the money thus saved to the nation for the conduct of the war? What are necessary expenses? It is no use his employing the word unless he defines it. For instance, are Christmas presents necessary or unnecessary? Obviously we can do perfectly well without them. If that is what he means he should say so. He should quite definitely announce, 'It is

---

1939-41 and 1949-66.
[1] Sir Geoffrey Storrs Fry (1888-1960). Pte. Sec. to Baldwin, 1923-39. Cr. Bart (1929) KCB (1937).
[2] Sir (Crawfurd) Wilfrid Griffin Eady (1890-1962). Civil servant; Dep. U-Sec. HO 1938-40; Dep. Chmn. 1940-41 and Chmn. 1941-42 of Bd. of Customs & Excise; Jt. 2nd Sec. Treas. 1942-52. KBE (1939) KCB (1942) GCMG (1948)
[3] Sir Rupert Beswicke Howorth (1880-1964). Admin. Sec. Imperial Conferences 1923, 1926, 1930 and 1937; Dep. Sec. to Cab. 1930-32; Clerk of Privy Council 1938-42; Sec. of Comm. to Ld. Chanc. 1945-48. KCMG (1933) KCVO (1942).

unpatriotic to give Christmas presents. Send the money you would have spent on them to the government. Buy war certificates with it. It will of course ruin the shopkeepers. Never mind, let them be ruined.' If he does not mean this, he should say so. But in that case what does he mean by necessary? Either the word is meaningless, in which case he ought not to use it or in using it he is shirking the issue, the practical issue, and is spewing theoretically, that is to say treating human beings as if they were abstractions, mere economic units, instead of creatures of flesh and blood.

December

Monier to J.B.B., 3 December   *Chiddingstone*

A large number of our evacuees will go home for Christmas, though the government is against this. Whether they will ever return is very uncertain. Four have gone this week-end never to return I am sure. I believe these poorer people in Bermondsey and elsewhere cannot do without their children. Having very little power of thinking ahead, they cannot believe that evacuation is necessary. Some also are distinctly jealous of the foster parents; just as in our class, parents are sometimes jealous of nurses. Again others can't afford the money they are asked to pay. None of ours are paying 9/- most only 3/- but to pay out cash like that with no tangible or visible *quid pro quo* is a great trial. They could not feed their children in these days for 3/- a week but they would see the food. In some cases there is friction between father and mother about it and for the sake of peace in the home, the one with more self-sacrifice gives in. It is all very bewildering. The policy was sound and the outcry against the government would have been appalling if air raids had come and they had left the children in the cities. The children are undoubtedly happy and well and have received much affection and there's the rub for some parents as I have said. I am quite certain the commandeering of large houses and building of camps would not have solved the problem; such establishments would have needed far bigger staffs than just the usual teachers, who are quite untrained except to teach and could not have adapted themselves to catering, amusing, nursing and mothering large numbers of children. The billeting plan was the best and would have answered if the expected had happened; and for all I know may be answering now where the children are removed far from their home town, far enough for parents not to come down often.

I met an MP last week, Sir Robert Gower,[1] a former Mayor of Tunbridge Wells. He told me there was really no need to ration at all, but it was a sop to satisfy the Labour Party. As it is only butter, bacon and sugar will be rationed and that not until we have been at war over 4 months. All rationing hits, as does the urge to save, and it must be desperately difficult to maintain trade, employment and taxable incomes; while at the same time getting people to buy saving certificates and meet the rise in prices. We all wonder what the Dean of Canterbury will say about Russia and Finland.[2] I went over last week to Hever for a small committee about Christmas parties for the evacuated children. Lady Violet Astor[3] was present and is very anxious to help us in Chiddingstone. She will provide a tree and an entertainer.

E.C.F.B. to J.B.B., 12 December

Russia is having rather a surprise at the resistance from Finland and her soldiers are so poorly equipped, many with no underclothing under their thin uniforms and no proper shoes. Ralph had his first war risk insurance to arrange. A balloon exploded and came down in flames, damaging the stock of a manufacturer; so far that is all he has had in that way. Alison and her friend Vera Hope have a volunteer job at the YMCA Canteen at Victoria Station three days a week. Only ladies are employed, except the cooks who are professional. The canteen is run by the YMCA but supported by a cigarette manufacturer. The ladies meet the trains and welcome the soldiers. They work in four hour shifts. For instance, the first hour Alison and Vera push the trolley up and down the platform for the outgoing trains; the second hour they stand at the buffet in the canteen; the third hour they wait on tables and for the fourth they wash up. Only married women are employed, mostly young. They must be British-born and belong to some Christian body.

Russia in her treatment of Finland is upheld by the Dean. Ralph says he is doing the Church of England an immense amount of harm in the City. The whole

---

[1] Sir Robert Gower (1880-1953). MP (Con) Hackney C, 1924-29; Gillingham, 1929-45; Kent C. Counc. Chmn. Commons Cttee. on Evacuation, 1940-5. Kt (1919).

[2] A reference to news of Finnish resistance to invasion by the USSR. Fighting began, in what became known as the Winter War, on 2 December 1939.

[3] Lady Violet Astor (d. 1965); wife of the Hon. J.J. Astor of Hever Castle. Prop. of *The Times*.

world condemns the destruction of Finland and her loss of liberty but the Dean alone stands up for it. He goes back to his old complaint, 'It is our fault; if England had agreed to an International Conference, including Russia, this would not have happened'. The trains are lighted now, with black blinds drawn down but all lights go out automatically when the trains stop at the stations.

My heart aches for each one of my dear ones in this anxious time. It is so much easier for an old woman, though even I have to keep up my spirits with the continual wet weather, black-outs, and the sorrows of the Poles, Czechs and Finns, which are never out of one's mind. Still we are sensible and read all kinds of books, fill our minds with other subjects, help where we can and keep bright faces. *The Times* of 7 December contains an account of how one Finnish soldier will carry a searchlight on his breast to show up the Russians, and the Finns fire on them from an ambush. Of course the searchlight man gets killed but it is considered an honour to be chosen for the job. Ralph told me British soldiers cross to France daily and we have there now three army corps. Also, if you dine out now in London, no one dresses for dinner as you have to walk home in the black-out.

Euan Wallace to J.B.B., 15 December   *Ministry of Transport*

As a rule you are a much better correspondent than I am, but unless a letter of yours has been sunk in mid-Atlantic, I have for once in a way got the best of you; and talking about sinking, I hope you duly received mine of 20 October in which I tried to answer all the questions you put to me in yours of 1 October. I also hope that you have lost to some extent the appalling feeling of isolation. As I said in my last letter it is quite useless for us to try and discuss with each other current events, and what I shall be able to dictate this afternoon will, I am afraid, be rather disjointed, hopping from one subject to another.

To start with the thing in which you are probably most interested, you may like to know that the Minister of Information continues to give no satisfaction whatever to his colleagues. It would be impossible to imagine a more charming, cultivated and intelligent gentleman than Lord Macmillan, and I suppose the only conclusion that one can draw is that none of these qualities are the real *desiderata* in a job which seems to want some really tough newspaper man. I do not think

Ned Grigg[1] is at all happy as Parliamentary Secretary and if ever there is a ministerial reshuffle - and I suppose even in war that must happen sometime - I think it would be a safe bid to forecast changes in the Ministry of Information.

At the Admiralty I have been told there has been some difference of opinion and the First Lord's personal staff are known by the professionals as 'The Midnight Follies'. The destruction of the *Graf Spee*[2] has come at a very good time, for quite a number of people were beginning to be disheartened at the failure to locate the German 'pocket battleships' in view of the immense advantage which carrier-borne aircraft give the pursuing force compared to the last war. An excellent innovation, due I believe originally to the suggestion of Oliver Stanley, is a weekly meeting of Ministers not in the War Cabinet, with the Prime Minister, Foreign Secretary and the Minister for Co-ordination of Defence in rotation. At these meetings we are able to ask a lot of questions about matters which are only referred to in the Cabinet Minutes in decently veiled language; and this explicit recognition by the Prime Minister of those of us who have to carry on with Cabinet jobs without being in the Cabinet has cheered everybody up. I have had a particularly busy week with a speech at the Hornsey Town Hall last Saturday afternoon, a rather formal address to the Institute of Transport on Monday and a 15 minute broadcast on 'Transport in wartime' at 9.15 p.m. the day before yesterday.

My Hornsey meeting was in the nature of an experiment to see how far a public meeting under the title of 'National War Front' - suggested by the Ministry of Information - with speakers from all three political parties would attract an audience. The result was not particularly encouraging as only about 950 people turned up; but the Liberal, an elderly gentleman who has been associated with every peace movement for the last 45 years, made a most eloquent justification, from the League of Nations Union point of view, on our policy in determining to fight the Nazis to the finish. The Labour Party had originally responded to the Mayor's intimation that speeches must be strictly non-party in character with a refusal to participate unless they were allowed to express what was called 'the Labour point of view'. They were assured that this would be quite all right

[1] Sir Edward (Ned) Grigg (1879-1955) Pte. Sec. to Lloyd George, 1921-2. MP (Con) Oldham, 1922-5. Gov. Kenya, 1925-30; MP (Con) Altrincham, 1933-45; Parl. Sec. Min. of Info. , 1939-40; Jt. Parl. U-Sec War, 1940-2; Min. Res. in M.E. , 1944-5. Cr. Baron Altrincham (1945).
[2] The *Graf Spee*. German pocket battleship, scuttled off Montevideo after Battle of River Plate, 16 Dec. 1939.

provided it did not descend to the kind of party polemics which both the Liberal speaker and I had promised to eschew; but at the last moment they decided (as their chosen speaker was a complete dud) that more party capital could be made by refusing to come in and distributed leaflets outside the hall to the effect that the 'voice of the people will not be heard'. Like other constituencies, where the Labour party is very weak, the one in Hornsey has been captured by the communists, who kicked up a certain amount of shindy in the hall when I told them what I thought about the Russian invasion of Finland. My broadcast, which was the result of a lot of work and discussion inside the office, was made in order to try and make the most of a chance which will probably not occur again for six months at least. Rob Bernays,[1] with his journalistic experience and fundamentally different outlook from my own, is invaluable on these sort of occasions.

The Lavington Maternity Home was closed down a month ago for lack of raw material, the expectant mothers of the particular district in London allocated to us, one and all preferring to have their babies at home. We have, however, been ordered to remain at 24 hours' notice to reopen if London gets bombed, and this means of course keeping all the beds and equipment ready. But we have taken back two or three more rooms and shall be able to spend the holidays in comfort if not luxury. I had hoped to motor down there with Barbie after lunch today but have got caught for a meeting of the Cabinet Committee on the economic situation of which Simon[2] is Chairman, and Stamp the principal member. Both the railway and the road transport unions put forward schemes for very substantial wage increases 'to meet the additional cost of living'. This raises a large general question which goes far outside the Ministry of Transport and I put up a paper on it which we are going to consider this afternoon. Any attempt to allow wages to chase the cost of living is bound to fail and will result in an absolutely disastrous spiral of rising costs. Simon has already made this clear both in the House of Commons and in a speech to employers and trade unionists at a private meeting. But it will not be easy to get organised labour to take this point of view.

My other great problem is the appalling number of fatal accidents on the roads; practically the whole of the increase is due to the black-out and, at any rate

---

[1] Robert Bernays (1902-45). MP (Lib later NLib) Bristol N, 1931-45; Parl. Sec. Min. of Health, 1937-9. Parl. Sec. Min. of Transport, 1939-40. Dep. Reg. Comm. for Civil Def., 1940-2.

[2] Sir John Allesbrook Simon (1873-1954). Kt. 1910. MP (Lib) Walthamstow 1906-18, Spen Valley 1922-31 (NL) 1931-40; For. Sec. 1931-35; Home Sec. 1935-37, Chanc. of Excheq. 1937-40; Ld. Chanc. 1940-45. Cr. Viscount Simon (1940).

up to the day before yesterday, the deaths on the road had substantially exceeded the deaths on active service. As you can imagine there are plenty of people anxious to give Anderson[1] and me advice on the subject; but practically the whole of it is prejudiced and contradictory. One apparently obvious solution is to bring in a 20 or even a 15 mile an hour speed limit after dark; but since the black-out regulations forbid the illumination of the number plates on cars, it would be just as impossible to enforce them as it is at the present 30 miles an hour. Moreover, the conviction of people for negligent or dangerous driving is equally difficult for the same reason. Philip Game,[2] the Metropolitan Police Commissioner, would like to see every pedestrian made to carry a light, but that is quite out of the question, more especially as even the people who want electric torches at present have the greatest difficulty in getting them. Another contention is that drink is a major factor in these accidents; but here it is practically impossible to get any reliable statistics.

I had an enchanting letter from Diana Cooper about ten days ago. She and Duff appear to like America and they have made great friends both with President Roosevelt and Lothian.[3] But accounts which come through from various sources make it seem rather doubtful whether the actual lecture tour has been a great success or whether Duff has had audiences really worthy of his eloquence. Oliver and Maureen Stanley are the only friends of ours who keep open house in London. I go there to supper practically every Sunday night and always find the most interesting and 'topical' people.

Geoffrey to E.C.F.B., 24 December   *Aberdeen*

This afternoon, between 3.30 and 4.00 p.m., the whole sky burned with all the colours of the rainbow and as we watched this glorious spectacle, a celestial panorama of unexampled grandeur extending over the firmament from the North Sea to the Cairngorm Mountains far inland, so awe-inspiring and sublimely beautiful as to take one's breath away, we were listening at the same time to what

---

[1] Rt. Hon. Sir John Anderson (1882-1958). MP (Ind) Scottish Universities, 1938-50. Gov. of Bengal, 1932-37; Ld. Privy Seal, 1938-9; Home Sec. 1939-40; Chanc. of Excheq., 1943-5. Cr. Vt. Waverley (1952).

[2] Air Vice Marshall Sir Philip Game (1876-1961) Retd. from RAF, 1929; Gov. of New South Wales, 1930-1; Commissioner of Met. Police, 1935-45. KCMG (1935), GCVO (1937).

[3] Philip Kerr, 11 Marquis of Lothian (1882-1940). Sec. to PM, 1916-21; Sec. of Rhodes Trust, 1925-39; Chanc. of Duchy of Lancaster, 1931; Parl. U-Sec. Indian Office, 1931-2. Ambassador in Washington, 1939-40. Succ. 1930.

was no less exquisitely lovely, the seven-lesson carol service broadcast from King's College, Cambridge; so that ear and eye, nature and art joined with, and rivalled, one another in presenting us with a vision as sublime as that which inspired the author of the 99th psalm; and it did not seem difficult 'be the earth never so unquiet - to magnify the Lord our God, and fall down before his footstool, for He is holy'. We sang the psalm in church this morning, perhaps the noblest lyric ever addressed by men to the ineffable Majesty of God (though the 33rd canto of the Paradiso runs it very close): and to be simultaneously listening, as we watched the sunset, to the (really) angelic voices of King's College choir chanting carols which celebrate that same God in the person of the young child born in the stable at Bethlehem, brought home to one, as nothing else could have done, the stupendous contrast between these two conceptions of deity, for, while emphasising the contrast, it nevertheless, because the two ideas found expression in a single experience, made one realise the essential unity behind both modes of the Godhead - an experience, not often vouchsafed to one at any time and how rarely on a Christmas eve; and in itself worth a thousand times over all the arguments in support of the reality of the incarnation of all the theologians who ever lived.

1940

Hore-Belisha's resignation - Blocks of ice floating in the Thames - More Canadians arrive in Britain - 'I hate this bloody war' - The 'Red Dean' at bay - Rumours of government reconstruction - 'Halifax is still considered the only alternative PM' - 'The will to fight is fast disappearing from our people' - 'There is very widespread discontent with the government' - The Norway campaign - 'Never ... has Britannia so incontrovertibly ruled the waves' - Everything goes horribly wrong - 'Winston is too capricious to be a reliable PM' - Blitzkrieg in the West - 'The new Government are rather a scratch lot' - Felsted evacuated and J.B.B. returns to England - The aftermath of Dunkirk and the Fall of France - 'The longest three weeks in my life' -The Home Guard established - 'The entire countryside is an armed camp' - Government changes - Fear of fifth columnists - Invasion jitters - 'Can London go on?' - 'Peerless weather' - Guard duty - 'Bloody well stop or I'll shoot!' - 'How fantastic it all is' - E.C.F.B. evacuated from Canterbury - J.B.B. fixes himself up with a job - 'Our Spitfires shining in the sun' - Destruction in the East End of London - Canterbury bombed - Tony in training - The Coventry Blitz - Edward's 'paper war' - Smoke screens in the Midlands - The second Christmas of the War.

January

Vincent Massey to J.B.B., 5 January   *London*

A heavy fog hangs over the future. It is reasonable to expect that there will be renewed activity as spring approaches but where, no one can say. At the moment I suppose that events will turn to some extent on the outcome of the Finnish war. Will it involve Scandinavia? No one can say, and conjectures are rather futile. In the meantime we are relatively stronger all the time - there is no question of that.

I met both contingents of troops from Canada at the port. Both arrivals were very dramatic, the first one particularly so. Eden[1] and I saw the troopships arrive from the deck of a battleship. They came in 'line ahead' each emerging slowly from the mist over the water. As each transport passed the warships at anchor, cheers were exchanged between the blue-jackets and the troops and in one or two cases naval bands played 'O Canada'. It was a tremendously moving scene.

E.C.F.B. to J.B.B., 6 January   *Canterbury*

Julian was taken by Bishop Rose[2] last Wednesday to see the Jewish refugee camp and was simply horrified at the conditions. A certain Sir Wally Cohen[3] supplies or gets the money, and it is run entirely by Jews with an evidently inefficient Jew at the head. There are over 3,000 men there, many of a refined type such as some 40 distinguished doctors. The place is not properly heated, the food vile, the whole camp dirty, and the dirt and squalor of the hospital is indescribable. Men lie ill on pallets on the floor covered by dirty blankets. Great hunks of meat are served out to men who have stomach trouble or pneumonia and should be under a special diet.

---

[1] (Robert) Anthony Eden (1897-1977). MP (Con) Leamington, 1923-57; U-Sec. For. Office, 1931-34; Ld. Privy Seal, 1934-5 & Min. for League of Nations, 1935; For. Sec., 1935-8, 1940-45; Dom. Sec., 1939-40; Sec. for War, 1940; P.M. and Con. Leader, 1955-7. KG (1954); cr. Earl of Avon (1961).
[2] Rt. Rev. Alfred Rose (d.1971). Suffragen Bishop of Dover, 1935-56.
[3] Probably Sir Robert Waley Cohen (1877-1952). Man. Dir. Shell Transport Co., Pres. of United Synagogue. Kt. (1920).

They happened to meet Lord Reading,[1] unfortunately before they had been around the camp. Reading was at Rugby with Julian and they recognised each other. Later Julian wrote to him describing what the Bishop and he thought of the camp. (Confidential) Hore-Belisha's resignation is curious. How do you think Oliver Stanley will do who has been appointed in his place at the War Office? Sir John Reith[2] and Sir Andrew Duncan,[3] the new man on the Board of Trade, have wide business experience.

Pat Hodgson to J.B.B., 7 January   *London*

Belisha's resignation was announced yesterday. It is very unfortunate that it could not have been deferred for a week until Parliament reassembles. Then he and the Prime Minister could have made authoritative statements on the reasons. As it is, the press is full of sensational rumours that it is due to intrigues in 'high social circles!' My own belief is that he has clashed with the soldiers, while his manner and personality made him unpopular. He certainly carried out some very necessary reforms in the army, but he is a terrible self-advertiser. I know that on his visits to the front he gave a lot of trouble to those who had to conduct him round. He loved being photographed with the men, having parades in his honour and generally seeking publicity. Then he announced in the House the number of troops in France, which the General Staff wished kept strictly secret, and that did not make for concord. I thought from all I heard that his days were numbered some time ago.

Julian to E.C.F.B., 11 January   *Felsted*

I understand it is common knowledge that the objection to Hore-Belisha has not come primarily from the British generals or from the War Office, but from the French. Gamelin[4] is supposed to have said that H-B's interference with the BEF was upsetting the unity of command. If he was really to be in control of

[1] Gerald Isaacs, 2nd. Marquis of Reading (1889-1960). Barrister. Contested Blackburn (Lib), 1929; suc. (1935); Lt.Col. Pioneer Corps Training Centre, 1939-41. Col. on Staff, 1941-43.
[2] Sir John Charles Reith (1889-1971) Creator of BBC, Dir. Gen., 1926-38; Chmn. Imperial Airways, 1938-40. MP (Nat) Southampton, 1940; Min. of Info., 1940; Min. of Transport, 1940; Min. of Works, 1940-2. Kt (1927). Cr. Baron Reith (1940).
[3] Rt. Hon. Sir Andrew Rae Duncan (1884-1952). MP (Nat) City of London, 1940-50.; Dir. of Bank of England, 1929-40; Pres. Bd. of Trade, 1940 and 1941; Min of Supply, 1942-5. Kt. (1921), PC (1940).
[4] Gen. Maurice Gamelin (1872-1958). C-in-C French land forces, 1938-40.

French and British forces, he could not have a British war minister interfering with the BEF in a way in which the French war minister would not be allowed to do with the French forces. Colour is lent to this theory by the visit of Winston Churchill and the honours given to Gort[1] and Ironside[2] by the French government.

There is great speculation in economic and business circles in England as to how the Germans can possibly hold out after the coming of spring without reverting to inflation.

E.C.F.B. to J.B.B., 13 January   *Canterbury*

You were of course quite right not to mention anything about the 1st. Canadian division coming over. Every corner of Europe seems in an icy grip, snow in Italy and Romania, thermometers far below freezing point, canals even harbours in southern Europe frozen and a terrific storm in the Black Sea. The last four days German planes have been active on the east coast and in the Thames estuary. They drop bombs on fishing boats and spray them with machine gun fire.

Last week Will Hopkins came home on leave and there was a family party at Bridge, the whole family were there, Norah and Molly going over. I sent a cake and a box of crackers. Will's battalion is a good way back from the front line, naturally he was silent about the actual place. They hardly ever see a French soldier, only meet one occasionally on the road. They are warm and splendidly fed. He said he had seen more planes here in two days than in four months in France and they were 18 hours on the train reaching Boulogne at 6 a.m. and waited at the boat until 10 a.m. and then came to Dover. It was so cold the other side that if a man stood up to change his position in the train and leant against the window his uniform froze hard to the glass.

Some of the reviews of the Dean's book on Russia[3] are headed 'Gullible's Travels' or 'The Innocent Abroad'. A friend of Mrs. Gardiner was in Westminster Abbey when the Dean preached, and saw with his own eyes Sir Edmond Ironside rise from his seat in the middle of the sermon and walk deliberately out of the Abbey.

---

[1] Vt. John Gort (1886-1946). General; C-in-C of BEF, 1939-40; Gov. and C-in-C Gibraltar, 1941-2 and of Malta, 1942-4. VC (1918), GCB (1940).
[2] Gen. Sir Edmund Ironside (1880-1955). ADC to the King, 1937-40; CIGS, 1939-40; Comm. Home Force, 1940, Field Marshal, 1940. Cr. Baron (1941).
[3] Hewlett Johnson's *The Socialist Sixth of the World* (Gollancz, 1939).

Geoffrey to E.C.F.B., 14 January   *Aberdeen*

I had a good illustration at first hand two days ago of the way the government wastes time and money. Last year, in common with the rest of the staff here, I registered with the Central Council (Ministry of Labour) for war work, if required, stating the kind of work for which I was, in my own opinion, qualified by my age, past experience and special qualifications. On Friday, I received a formal communication from the Central Council (Ministry of Labour), Whitehall, asking me whether I would consent to be considered for Director of Studies to organise teaching of English Literature and Language at the British Institute at Rome, on probation for six months at a salary of £450 per annum. I was asked to reply by return - the communication was marked 'urgent' and no further information given, only a request that, if I refused I would state my reasons. I refused of course at once. The British Institute of Foreign Affairs (now at Balliol) has certain professors lent to it by Oxford University at a salary of £1,250 a year - i.e. the Govt. pays them that or would do so (tho' as a matter of fact the University contributes a thousand pounds of the salary). The job offered to me was more responsible, abroad not at home, and with no security of tenure, and yet the salary offered is only 2/3 of a professor's salary, and that altogether and apart from my special qualifications for the job concerned, which in fact are nil. For it is really a propaganda job.

It so happened that there was an article in *The Times* the same day that I received this offer, pressing the need for British propaganda in Italy to counteract the German, and giving as an example the excellent work done in this respect by the British Institute at Lisbon in Portugal. Since the war started I presume that the British Institute in Rome has acquired importance, apart altogether from its educational purposes, for the same reason. But, if so, and if they need a good man to run it, they need one with no home ties, fairly young, a modern historian with journalistic experience and a special knowledge of contemporary Italian politics and with social connections in Rome - a man in short thoroughly familiar with modern Italy, whereas I have only visited Italy for a week or two during the last thirty years, possess no special knowledge of Italian politics, cannot speak the vernacular and have never interested myself in the literature except as a pure scholar.

It will be interesting to hear Hore-Belisha's account of the reasons for his resignation, which according to the King-Hall [1]journal (which I take in) go back as far as an intrigue against him in the WO in 1938. The K-H journal is very strong on the theory that what we need to win the war, especially if it is to be over this year, is (1) the organisation of our propaganda in Germany with which it is closely connected (2) a clear statement of our war aims. The Hore-Belisha resignation was extremely badly managed in the way it was sprung on the public without warning.

Miss Gray to J.B.B., 21 January   *Canterbury*

Friday was simply terrible and you can imagine how cold when I tell you that Molly yesterday morning, going in the larder, found the two full siphons of soda water had burst, leaving glass and contents (frozen) all over the floor. Her next experience was with two eggs she broke ready to make a fish soufflé for dinner last evening. She broke the shell and the white was a clear block of ice with a yellow blob in the centre (yolk). It took quite a time in the oven to melt.. We have no excitements of German raiders but when the large Dutch ship was blown up in the Downs a short time ago, the explosion was plainly heard at Bridge. We still hear it said by unofficial people that March is the critical month and that will soon be with us and also the longer days. Great numbers of people do not use torches, partly because batteries are very difficult to buy and also do not last as they should.

Euan Wallace to J.B.B., 27 January   *Ministry of Transport*

David[2] wrote to me some time ago about his military service obligations and suggested that as he had been such an ardent advocate for going to war with Germany at the time of Munich, he felt a special obligation to fight now. I told him that I thought it was everyone's duty to do the job for which they were considered to be most fitted; and I think you would agree with me that it would be rather ridiculous for him to come home to be a rather inefficient and myopic private soldier when he appears to be doing a really important job in Greece, for which his previous education has very well fitted him. I have now written to ask whether he

---

[1] The King-Hall news-letter, founded in 1936 by the eponymous William King-Hall (1893-1966). RN retd. MP (Ind Nat) Ormskirk, 1939-44.

[2] David, Euan Wallace's eldest son who, since the beginning of the War, had been in charge of the press department at the British legation at Athens.

would like me to obtain from either Halifax or Cadogan[1] an opinion on the subject in order to reassure his conscience.

There is nothing I can tell you about the great Belisha sensation except that I am quite certain the change has been all to the good. My real regret is that Oliver Stanley should have left the Board of Trade, which is really an absolutely key position at the present time. Duncan is quite excellent but it must inevitably take some time for a complete newcomer to political life to acquire the necessary confidence in dealing with his Cabinet colleagues and with Parliament. The departure of Macmillan, charming and cultivated gentleman though he is, from the Ministry of Information was also all to the good; and I have personally every reason to be most grateful to Reith who succeeded in extracting from the Treasury enough money to run what I hope will be quite an effective press, broadcasting and cinema campaign for road safety - a thing which no Minister of Transport has so far been able to do. As soon as Reith becomes MP for Southampton some other job will clearly have to be found for Ned Grigg. One plan for a change round among the junior Ministers depended, I believe, on the resignation of George Tryon;[2] but as he did not wish to go that has fallen through.

The chief episode in my life just lately has been a debate on road accidents which took place last Tuesday. I was very glad of the chance of saying a good many things on this subject which are not possible at Question Time. I only reached the decision to put in the 20 mile an hour speed limit in built-up areas during the 'black-out' after literally weeks of thought and heart-searching. My own advisers have always been strongly in favour of it and eventually they convinced me, and I in turn succeeded in convincing practically all my colleagues who were just as reluctant in the early stages to agree with me as I had been to agree with my own officials. The great difficulty is, of course, enforcing it in conditions where registration numbers are not visible and pursuit by police cars is extremely dangerous. But I am convinced that it is only upon some definite measure of restriction on the motorist that one can hang a Press campaign directed almost

[1] Sir Alexander Cadogan (1884-1968). Ambassador in Peking, 1935-6; Dep. U-Sec. For. Office, 1936-7; Perm. U-Sec. For. Office, 1938-46. Perm. Rep. UN, 1946-50. Chmn. BBC, 1952-7. KCMG (1934), KCB (1941), PC (1946), OM (1951).
[2] George Clement Tryon (1871-1940). MP (Con) Brighton, 1910-40; Parl. Sec. Min.of Pensions, 1920-22; Min. of Pensions, 1922-4, 1924-29, 1931-35; Postm. Gen, 1935-40; Chanc. D. of Lancaster, 1940; 1st. Comm Works, 1940; cr. Baron Tryon (1940).

entirely against the pedestrian. You will see that Nancy Astor[1] raised the question of drink as she always does. It seems to me practically an insuperable problem. Even if one accepts the fact that a large number of accidents are due to this cause, pedestrians as well as motorists, no one that I know of can see any practical remedy. It would not be possible to make all motor drivers into teetotallers or to prevent the location of road houses at the places where they get the most custom. If people get killed or injured because they drink too much, it is really their own fault; but since one cannot very well say this from the Treasury bench, it seems better to ignore the question altogether and to let oneself be abused by people like Nancy.

Barbie has had several letters from Duff Cooper who seems to be blissfully happy in America speaking to packed houses and having a most enjoyable time in New York between his spells of travelling. I find Diana not nearly such a good correspondent. The best testimony to Duff's popularity is that his contract has been extended to April. I think Oliver's appointment to the WO must be regarded as a recognition of his ability. Barbie and I are going to dine with him tonight to meet Ironside. I believe the CIGS is pretty out-spoken about his late boss! Beaverbrook told Belisha he was a fool to behave so well about his personal explanation, as the Tories would never accept him as a gentleman. He had shot his way to office like a gangster and had better go on shooting. The whole thing has been a nine days wonder and I fear Hore-Belisha must have felt himself to be on a baddish wicket or he would not have gone so quietly.

Ralph to J.B.B., 30 January   *Lombard Street*

You will have gathered from the papers that we have been having remarkable weather. I do not generally comment on the weather unless it is remarkable. Ever since Christmas we have had it cold. Mother had 38 degrees of frost at Canterbury - in actual fact it was 40 degrees, 8 degrees below zero is no joke in this country. Traffic is chaotic, no trains to and from Scotland and the trains from places like Bristol last night were 10 hours late. The suburban traffic in some cases was non-existent. We had girls who could not get to the office or get home last night. The whole of our hot water system broke down last week. We had a temporary thaw but now it is frozen again. The sea is frozen also and great

---

[1] Nancy Witcher Astor (1870-1964). MP (Con) Plymouth Sutton, 1919-45; married (1906) Waldorf Astor, suc. 2nd. Vt. Astor (1919). The first woman to sit in the House of Commons.

blocks of ice are seen floating in the water. We are experiencing something which has not happened since the year I was born. However, we are exhorted to remain cheerful and courageous and our national make-up sees us through.

One interesting thing, our business in Poland is apparently being run by the Germans. Our office in Warsaw was hardly damaged at all and I gather all our records were practically intact. The Germans are utilising the majority of our Polish staff and simply running the business as if it were their own. I anticipate this will be very efficiently done and we may find at the end of the war, when Poland is restored to Poland, that our business has increased. In the meantime, of course, it is a dead loss.

February

Julian to E.C.F.B., 1-3 February   *Felsted*

Five of our maids gave notice yesterday in order to join forthwith the Land Army! They had listened in to Winston Churchill's recent appeal for one million women to come forward without delay to do jobs of value for the nation, and burning with zeal they have all decided to join up at once regardless of whether they are suitable or not. Only one of them has ever lived in the country before and apparently land girls are not wanted at present anyway. If only Winston Churchill had said that domestic service is the best form of national service.

The Polish atrocities are so terrible I can't bear to read them. Surely, surely God will not wait until the next world to punish such diabolical wickedness. But at least these cruelties make it clear that we are fighting against a horror that cannot be tolerated. The tragedy is that while we are waiting for Hitler's attack he is doing exactly what he likes behind the security of the Siegfried Line, and is transplanting populations of central Europe any way he wishes. There is a growing unrest among the younger masters who are wanting to leave the security of the reserved class in which schoolmasters have been placed and go off to serve in the army or some other branch of the services. It is natural enough for the younger men to feel like this as their own contemporaries are serving, and it is easy for them to think staying at home and teaching boys is a cushy job. I am trying to point out that the schools are national assets and it is of paramount importance to keep them at a high standard. There are one or two indications in documents coming to us as headmasters that the new regime at the War Office (Oliver

Stanley *vice* Hore-Belisha) means a restitution of the old army ideas as well as the displacement of territorial officers for regulars, and the possibility of the revival of Sandhurst and Woolwich which were abolished shortly after the war started.

E.C.F.B. to J.B.B., 10 February   *Canterbury*

In *The Times* yesterday it announced the arrival of the second expeditionary force from Canada, so I hoped your letter of 21 January would come, and it did. The main thought in my mind is the tragic fall of Lord Tweedsmuir and his critical condition.[1] You will feel it all terribly. The position of the Dean of Canterbury is most uncomfortable and his Chapter practically ignore him. Even Canon Crum[2] walked out of the Cathedral during one of his sermons. After his abbey sermon the Dean of Westminster, a wide-minded Christian man, wrote to Hewlett Johnson to say he feared he must tell him that he had abused the hospitality of the abbey pulpit. Our Dean has begun to praise Germany now and he knows that a few days ago the Gestapo in Poland shot every tenth person in one village, dragging whole families including women and children out of bed in the middle of the night, and also stopped a train and shot every fifth person in it. The Germans also bombed a light ship and shot the men escaping in boats. They say the Dean is now suffering from a martyr complex. He says all reformers must suffer. It is only 100 years after their death they are acknowledged as great men. He is one of these and lives in a fantasy made by himself. Holy Russia, and now holy Germany, are the only nations fit to govern the world. He is extraordinarily vain and loves the limelight, and yet the other side of his nature is kindly. The Lenten services in the cathedral are poorly attended. There were only twenty persons at a special service yesterday.

Sir Patrick Duff to J.B.B., 17 February   *London*

I was dining with Tom Jones the other day; he is astonishingly well and had just been staying at Cliveden for the week-end and was dilating on Nancy Astor's vitality. I think she is a remarkable woman but you would not find me at Cliveden in a hurry. She makes me feel like an invalid in a high wind. I see Euan Wallace two or three times a week at meetings. The more I see of him the more I

---

[1] Lord Tweedsmuir (John Buchan), Governor General of Canada since 1935, died on 12 Feb. 1940, aged sixty-four.
[2] Rev. John Crum (1872-1958). Canon of Canterbury, 1928-43; Canon Emeritus, 1943.

like him and the better he impresses me. He brings a good fund of robust common sense and good humour with him and, what is essential to a good minister, courage. For a young minister he has got plenty of ballast and judgement. I do not trust young ministers usually. A lot of claptrap is talked about 'young blood', but I have not seen a young minister yet who had the experience to control the destinies of people intoxicated with democracy.

I feel so sorry for you being so far away but I don't think you are further off from news than we are here. Rather the reverse probably. I hate this bloody war and being a mean black-coated civilian. I find myself being jealous of the young in quite a shameful way though I know all the time that if you shifted me out to sleep in the mud or just stand me in the reserve trench in the snow without any fighting at all, I should just crack up with pneumonia in a matter of hours. I hope you do not read the London papers which make us look as though we are squealing and grumbling all the time, which is not so. Our only trouble is that the mass of the people have not tumbled to the idea that war means sacrifices for everyone. Their leaders adopt a laudably resolute tone about prosecuting the war, but affirm that only those who can afford it, 'the rich', need pay for it. It is as pitiful a paradox as their recent attitude in shouting for war against Japan or Italy and for disarmament at the same time.

Monier to E.C.F.B., 19 February   *Chiddingstone*

We are thrilled at the exploits of the *Cossack*.[1] Here was the 'Nelson touch' for all the world to see.The navy is as great as it has ever been in our history. We got a cable from Edward yesterday saying he leaves Torit on 25 February and takes his exam in Khartoum. Then he is attached for a month to a battalion there and after that hopes for leave to England. John has had a recurrence of flu, which is bad luck in view of the coming scholarship examination.

Julian to J.B.B., 20 February   *Felsted*

We are now plunged into the most extensive epidemic that I can remember since I came here. Every Boarding House has opened dormitories as wards; matrons, masters, cooks, butlers, maids and men have all fallen ill. But we have

---

[1] On 17 Feb, the captain of the destroyer HMS *Cossack* sent a boarding party on to the German supply ship *Altmark*, even though she was sheltering within Norwegian territorial waters. Some 300 allied merchant seamen were thus freed.

struggled through and are struggling through to the best of our ability. Fortunately the epidemics are only fairly mild flu and German measles, which is apparently all over the country and is, I suppose, the secret weapon that Hitler told us that he is about to inflict upon us. The war is more mysterious than ever; we know nothing and hear nothing except of the sinking of our and neutrals' merchant ships, which seems to go on interminably. The incident of the *Altmark* provides a pleasant interlude from these melancholy naval communiqués. There is no doubt that we infringed the neutrality of Norway and cannot plead justification for it. But Germany does the same thing far more regularly; and no one in England feels anything but pleased that if the neutrality laws were to be broken, it should be done in such a cause.

There are some indications that the government intends to try and revoke what I consider one of their worst blunders, namely the closing down of the Military Colleges and Cranwell. It is now becoming apparent that a number of the best boys in the English Public Schools, who had intended to go in for Sandhurst, Woolwich or Cranwell, will now be diverted to the Navy and that the Army will lose some of the boys who might have been its best brains in post-war years. But it is impossible to find out anything for certain, though I cannot believe that Oliver Stanley would approach the Army problem in the same stubborn way that Belisha did.

I think I told you of my visit to the Jewish Refugee Camp at Richborough with Bishop Rose of Dover. The conditions that we found there were really deplorable. I first wrote to Lord Reading who is busy recruiting Jews to join the Labour Battalion, and we happened to meet him in the camp. There were 3,500 Jews there at Christmas time, and the organisation had broken down completely, apparently owing to the inefficiency of the man in charge. Reading tried to defend the situation as best he could, but I spoke of it at a meeting of the Dons and Beaks at Oxford a week later which spread information as to the camp in various directions. Riding,[1] Headmaster of Aldenham, who knows Wally Cohen, approached him to see if something could be done. Kurt Hahn[2] took up the matter vigorously and made a formal visit to the camp through his German-Jewish friends in London, and I have just heard that the Commandant has been superseded and

---

[1] George Riding (1888-1982). Headmaster, Aldenham School, 1933-49.
[2] Kurt Hahn (1886-1974). Educationalist. Exiled from Germany, 1933; Founder of Gordonstoun School. CBE (1964).

the hospital very much improved. There is no doubt that we did stir up the authorities a certain amount, but the whole affair was in the hands of a Jewish committee whose funds had become exhausted and apparently the only remedy for this deplorable state of affairs that the government could devise was to try and induce the men in the camp to join the Labour Corps. It really was odd to see in the camp a number of Tommies marching about talking German, a great many of them obviously of Jewish countenance. They have promised those who enlisted that they will not be sent to the front in case they are taken prisoner by the Germans; they would certainly be shot if they were.

Well the 2nd. Australian Expeditionary Force has reached Egypt. I do not hear very encouraging reports of the recruiting for reinforcements and I doubt if there will be much enthusiasm for coming overseas unless some very definite plan of campaign is soon disclosed. Australians are not the kind of people who will remain contented for long in camp in Egypt or even in a line like the Maginot without any fighting. They would rather be on their sheep runs or making money in their Australian cities, a very easy thing to do apparently in these times, as a wave of prosperity is sweeping Australia, owing to the certainty of good prices for wool and wheat seeing that the British Government have bought all the harvests and crops and wool clips till the end of the war. We surely must have some plan of campaign which will strike the imagination of the Australians, or there will be trouble in the AEF.

March

E.C.F.B., to J.B.B., 1 March   *Canterbury*

I fear things are bad at the Cathedral. I believe the Dean wrote a letter to the Communist party, who are encouraging sabotage in our munitions works, wishing them success in their undertakings, though I don't think he actually mentioned the word sabotage himself. The Dean insists on the Cathedral being open all night, and all the Precinct gates also. Some days ago after dark, burglars got hold of a ladder in Canon Crum's garden and entered a Burgate fur shop from the back, stealing £500 worth of furs. Miss Babington has had her office of the 'Friends' broken into and money stolen.. The Canons have now taken everything to do with the Cathedral and Precincts into their own hands, their five votes out-voting the one vote of the Dean. The postern gates and big gate are locked at 5 p.m. and the Cathedral also. All sorts of undesirable things were going on in the Precincts during the blackout, where the soldiers met their girls, and the King's School boys also. Many bicycles too were being stolen. There is not much intercourse now between the Canons and the Dean except cold courtesy. I do not think for a moment that he will resign. He considers himself champion of the communist working men.

Geoffrey to E.C.F.B., 3 March   *Aberdeen*

Last Thursday David and I spent the afternoon down at the harbour here. It was full of shipping, British and foreign, loading and unloading goods of all sorts. All our ships were armed with a gun. There was also as usual a large number of torpedo boats, mine sweepers etc. in the port, all flying the white ensign. This afternoon we were down on the beach. They have a battery of four anti-aircraft guns there and another of Lewis guns. The big beach restaurant has been handed over to, and is occupied by, the Royal Garrison Artillery. Tony has his first University exam on Wednesday next.

The Dean, or I should say, the ex-Dean now thinks the war will be over in a year. Halifax's speech at Oxford was worthy of Chatham or Burke. Tony heard it and said he spoke distinctly and evenly and the chief impression made on him was that of sincerity. Tony said the speech was an interesting contrast to that of Arthur Greenwood[1] whom he had heard the previous week and who in comparison seemed like a soap-box agitator.

Geoffrey to E.C.F.B., 5 March   *Aberdeen*

I do no special war-work, but am content to regard (as I have been officially told to do) my lecturing as war-work, and certainly my subject lends itself to enlarging and harmonising the youthful mind at a time when, above all others, that process must be regarded as of critical importance and value. The cost of living has gone up about 25% since the war began. The budget will of course seriously affect me, as it will all professional men, but it's no use worrying over it till it has come. It is, however, already possible to say that financially speaking the difference between the upper-middle and lower-middle class will be wiped out. A

---

[1] Arthur Greenwood (1880-1954). MP (Lab) Nelson and Colne, 1922-31, Wakefield, 1932-54.U-Sec. Min.of Health, 1924; Min.of Health, 1929-31; Min. w/o Portfolio, 1940-42; Ld.Privy Seal, 1945-7; Postm. Gen., 1946-7.

social revolution will be under way to which in its immensity and thorough-going character our history affords no parallel. Labour must and will enter the Government, but will (rightly, no doubt) insist on an instalment of socialism as a condition of doing so. A conscript army, which will probably be permanent, would alone suffice to alter our social fabric from top to bottom. I have complete confidence in the capacity of the nation to solve all the problems awaiting it with common sense and good humour, if only our extreme idealists can be prevented from getting control.

Julian to J.B.B., 10 March   *Felsted*

A hypocritical world pats Finland on the back but will not help her. It will be Sweden's turn next. The so-called democracies are all worrying about their own skins. All are bewitched by Germany's power and fear to be the next to be pounced on. Even we, apparently, are unwilling to strike a blow at Germany for fear of reprisals and allow our fishing fleet to be bombed and machine-gunned without any retaliation. The fighting spirit is not there and the people as a whole are getting fed up with the war and rapidly losing interest. What Europe and its terrified small countries need now is leadership. They are getting it from the Germans, and are passing one by one under their influence. The will to fight is fast disappearing from our people.

Geoffrey to E.C.F.B., 10 March   *Aberdeen*

The female medical student who were evacuated to Aberdeen from London when the war began are now returning to their own university as their mothers and fathers think there is no more fear of their being bombed in London than here. As a matter of fact a German bomber was over Aberdeen a few days ago but I missed seeing it. It flew fairly low over the coast, climbed almost perpendicularly and was pursued by our planes which brought it down and sunk it some miles out to sea.

Tony seems to have made the most of not an easy term. Certainly the Oxford undergraduate is terribly handicapped by the war. Tony had to change tutors half-way through. The House has lost all its best tutors or very nearly all. Moreover, all the older undergraduates are gone, so you do not get the stimulus of social and intellectual intercourse with men older than yourself. And entertainment is cut down to a minimum, not only between undergraduates but between dons and undergraduates. It is a poor, mutilated substitute for the genuine article.

There are times when I feel the greatest sympathy with the medieval notion of Hell, and when it would give me a savage delight to picture Hitler being made to suffer in his own person every pang, physical and mental, which has been or will be suffered by each one of his millions of victims. Surely no dignitary of the Church of England has ever been so humiliated in public as was the Dean of Canterbury in that letter to *The Times* last week by the canons. The worm has turned at last, even Crum. His letter in reply, however, makes one doubt whether the Dean himself has been in any way affected by it, unless it has confirmed him in his self-complacency and conceit. His vanity and self-righteousness would be incredible were it not vouched for by his own pen. He refers to the canons as "his" as if they were his curates. He attributes to his own efficiency and takes credit for improvements with which he has had nothing to do at all, e.g. Shirley's re-establishment of the King's School and Miss Babington's achievements as Secretary of the 'Friends'. He says nothing about his long absences abroad in China and Canada and Spain. He quotes, in support of himself and his views, the opinions of people one has never heard of in countries on the other side of the world, but neglects those of people in this country and Canterbury itself, except to imply that they admire his preaching, but for which the Cathedral would empty.

Tom Jones to J.B.B., 10 March   *Cliveden*

Everybody out of doors on this lovely afternoon except the indolent TJ who has just wakened from sleep and bethought himself of JBB away in Toronto, partly no doubt because yesterday we had here some officers to luncheon from Canada, of whom one was General Crerar.[1] I have also met England,[2] a Professor of Economics, who is in charge of Army Education and Welfare. *Inter-alia* he wants to buy up the 20,000 copies of the Penguin (or is it Pelican?) edition of SB's *On England* for distribution among the Canadian soldiers so that they may learn something of this country. Joe Kennedy[3] blew in yesterday fresh from his American holiday and talked away like one o'clock, when his mouth was not

---

[1] Maj-Gen. Henry Crerar (1885-1965). GOC Canadian HQ in London, 1939-41, and of 2nd. Canadian Div., 1941; Gen. Comm. 1st. Canadian Corps, 1942-4; Comm. 1st. Canadian Army, 1944-5. ADC to George VI, 1948-52 and to Elizabeth I, 1953. KG (1954).

[2] J.B.B.'s nominal predecessor as man in charge of education for Canadian forces in Britain.

[3] Joe Kennedy (1888-1969). American businessman and founder of political dynasty; U.S. ambassador to London, 1937-41.

stuffed with a rich iced cake. He has been put out by numerous letters from English correspondents attacking American isolationism which he found waiting his return. He reported that the atmosphere in the USA had also deteriorated because of delays over American ships at Gibraltar and our poking our noses into American mailbags. And all this at a time when Roosevelt, *sub rosa*, was stretching his powers to help us beyond their proper limits. It was up to us to keep relations sweet because presently we shall want all the money and credit America can spare - the only concrete help we are likely to get.

The Edens and King-Halls came along around tea time and the talk turned to Finland and to the probable cause of the war. An emissary from Finland has gone to Moscow. Our view is that if the terms offered are harsh the best thing would be for the Finns to put them before the world and appeal for help to go on with the fight. We could then appeal openly to Norway and Sweden to let our men and material go through. We can't send them by sea. If Finland surrenders, public opinion here will denounce once more this weak government for failing to render effective assistance.

As to the course of the war, all sorts of rumours are flying around at this moment, some perhaps inspired by the enemy. They are worth setting out: a. That Holland will be attacked on the Ides of March. That Dutch resistance will not be strenuous. b. That Germany will launch a big attack within six weeks. Hence present diplomatic activity. c. That Hitler has made up his mind that nothing will satisfy him short of a German invasion of England by his fleet and air arm in full force, either from Calais or direct to the Orkneys. This is not taken seriously. d. That he will do none of these things but will on the other hand destroy our morale by doing nothing on the Western Front, and that on the first anniversary of the War, 3 Sept. 1940, we shall be much as we are today, except for the irrepressible boredom of the troops in France. Neither side is prepared to squander the lives of hundreds of thousands of men in mass attacks. By September it will be vital to have some new binding story to cement the divisions and inspire them.

Some speculation here as to whether Reynaud will dislodge Daladier.[1] The latter is nearer to the French peasant than the former who was described as 'a clever monkey'. They have loosened the political censorship because all sorts of private news sheets were appearing. Our cabinet is always being reconstructed in

[1] He did. Daladier resigned as French premier on 20 March, Reynaud replacing him the next day. Daladier retained his post as Minister for National Defence.

clubs and corners. Halifax is still considered the only alternative PM, and his Oxford speech made a big impression. Copies will be circulated by the tens of thousands through the Ministry of Information. There are rumours that Hoare[1] may go to the Air Ministry. Malcolm MacDonald[2] went up several degrees by his speech on Palestine; the Jews say he has betrayed them by shameful double-dealing. Belisha might have stayed on if he had been given an enlarged board of Trade - 'Minister of Economics' - with a seat in the War Cabinet, but Simon opposed. Neville is said to be fit and 'to dominate the Cabinet'. Nancy Astor says that Mrs. Chamberlain is more regal than royalty and at lunch today bade Mrs. Eden beware of thinking that once you are a PM's wife you are always so - like Lucy Baldwin did, 'You may find yourself in Upper Tooting'. Eirene and I spent last week-end with Lloyd George at Churt. He takes a gloomy view of the war. He says Hankey has become an old man bothering with small points and does not possess a Cabinet mind. I had lunch with Euan Wallace recently and liked him. R.A.Butler was there too. No successor to Tweedsmuir has been found yet.

Julian to E.C.F.B., 20 March   *Felsted*

The chief and best remedy the Canons have is to preach a course of sermons in the Cathedral on the evils of an Anti-Christ state and the horrors of the OGPU, and how all Christians must beware of what fate would befall a country if it took to such desperate remedies to further economic reform. If the Dean is in his stall while such sermons are being preached, so much the better. The Canons also have a platform which they themselves can use, namely the Cathedral pulpit. But I still think their position would be immensely strengthened if they all resigned.

Euan Wallace to J.B.B., 21 March

Barbie got off to Lavington yesterday and I hope to get down there this

---

[1] Sir Samuel Hoare (1880-1959). MP (Con) Chelsea, 1910-44; Sec. for Air, 1922-4, 1924-9 and 1940; India Sec., 1931-35; For. Sec., 1935; 1st. Ld. Admiralty, 1936-7; Home Sec., 1937-9; Ld. Privy Seal, 1939-40; Amb. in Madrid, 1940-44. Suc. 2nd. Bart. (1915). Cr. Vt. Templewood (1944).
[2] Malcolm MacDonald (1901-81). Son of Ramsay: MP (Lab, NLab from 1931) Bassetlaw, 1929-35, and (NLab) Ross & Cromarty, 1936-45; U-Sec. Dominions, 1931-35; Col. Sec, 1935, 1938-40; Dom. Sec., 1935-8; Min of Health, 1940-41; High Comm. in Canada, 1941-46; Gov-Gen. Malaya, 1946-48; Comm-Gen. S.E. Asia, 1948-55; High Comm. in India, 1955-60; Gov-Gen. and High Comm. Kenya, 1963-5.

evening for at least five days. Oliver and Maureen Stanley are coming; also David Margesson[1] and Harold Balfour;[2] so we shall have a certain amount of political shop. The War Cabinet are taking a very sensible line in trying to make the eleven days' Parliamentary recess as much like a normal holiday as possible. The nine War Cabinet Ministers take duty in three squads of three; and although Oliver is one of those at short notice from Friday till Monday, he is being allowed to come to Lavington provided his car is always ready to start and he is never far away from the telephone. Although I have no doubt that our enemies would laugh at this typically British method of conducting war, I am quite certain that it is all to the good and probably more important for senior officials than for Ministers to get a few days off. Oliver is being an enormous success at the War Office, as I felt quite certain he would. Quite apart from his excellent personal relations with everybody both here and in the BEF, his speeches go on maintaining the very high quality they have always had. His introduction of the Army Estimates, at a time when there was nothing exciting to say, was a masterpiece of sympathetic understanding of the attitude of the House of Commons to the personal difficulties of our growing conscript army; and yesterday at a lunch of the National Defence Public Interest Committee he gave a simple but very striking view of our real war aims, and dropped a delicate, but very pointed and much needed, hint to the neutrals. The acceptance by Finland of the Russian peace terms was most unexpected. Ironside in particular had been maintaining that Finland was in no danger for several months; and the Prime Minister told the House the day before yesterday that the Finns did not even ask for an expeditionary force before the 1st of May.

The debate on Wednesday was another remarkable triumph for the Prime Minister. Both the House and the country had been depressed about Finland, and there was a real wave of apprehension as to the War Cabinet's conduct of the war. In two speeches - an hour in opening the debate and half an hour in winding it up - the Prime Minister managed to dispel the greater part of these anxieties and fears; although I think there still persists a substantial body of opinion in favour of a smaller War Cabinet entirely relieved from departmental responsibilities. It was of course a very considerable eye-opener to Parliament to know that an Allied

---

[1] (Henry) David Margesson (1890-1965). MP (Con) Upton, 1922-23, Rugby, 1924-42; Ass. Chief Whip, 1924-26; Whip, 1926-29; Chief Whip, 1931-40; Sec. for War, 1940-42. Cr. Vt. Margesson (1942).

[2] Harold Balfour (1897-1988). MP (Con) Thanet, 1929-45; U-Sec. Air, 1938-44; Min. Res. W. Africa, 1944-5. Cr. Baron Balfour of Inchrye (1945).

Expedition of 100,000 men was equipped, trained and ready to start for Finland; and the Prime Minister pointed out that even this limit had only been imposed by transport considerations. But you will be able to read a full account of the debate and draw your own conclusions. I think you will agree that for a man of 71, with all his multifarious other cares and responsibilities, to have not only opened the debate but sat all through it in order to wind it up is a very remarkable demonstration of vigour and determination. It may, of course, be argued that it is a pity that there was no one else to whom he felt he could entrust the second half of the task!

To get down to my own personal affairs, I have had a good deal of trouble since I last wrote you over the coal shortage. The main reason for it is the interference with coastwise shipping which the Germans have succeeded in achieving. London and the South of England get two-thirds of their coal supplies by sea in peace-time and nothing that the railways could do was able to keep pace with the deficiencies in the supplies arriving by water. The exceptional cold weather put the demand up to astronomical heights, and at one moment we were faced with a fairly serious situation. It was not possible to tell Parliament and the public the real cause of the trouble as this would only have been comforting Hitler and encouraging the Germans to intensify attacks which were obviously being successful. I had, therefore, in announcing a series of special measures to get more coal to London and the South by rail, to accept by inference a certain share of blame for the shortage - which was of course nothing whatever to do with this Department. Even now passenger facilities have had to be very much curtailed on the LNER in order allow for 'coal specials', and I am afraid this will have to go on for some months in order to build up the kind of stocks considered adequate as an insurance. Petrol rationing is naturally a source of grievance to road hauliers, and the lack of sleeping car accommodation to MPs; but on the whole I feel we have got through seven months of war with less criticism than might have been expected in a Ministry which touches people's lives at so many points. Even the higher electricity charges, made necessary by increased costs of various kinds, are sometimes laid at the door of the unfortunate Minister of Transport.

The raid on Sylt[1] was a brilliant success and it is really very fortunate that

---

[1] 19 March 1940. Bomber Command's first attack of the war against a land target - a seaplane base on the island of Sylt. Announced as a success, later reconnaissance showed no damage done to German installations.

the Germans, by bombing civilians in the Orkneys, gave us the opportunity to do it. It remains to be seen whether this is the beginning of a gradual crescendo of air activity. At the moment there has been no reply from the other side. You will be glad to hear that John got into Balliol all right and is going up there in April. I do hope you will stick to your intention of coming home this summer; and, if you do, I imagine it will be within the next couple of months. I knew you would feel Tweedsmuir's death very much. I had lunch with Eric Mackenzie[1] at the Turf today and asked him if he had heard anything as to a successor; but I gather that nothing will even be discussed until after your general election. We had a telegram from Diana and Duff Cooper when they landed in Italy; they are stopping in Paris over Easter and expect to get back here next week. I wonder very much what Duff will do now. It is a great pity if his talents cannot be harnessed to some useful work.

I wrote to Alec Cadogan about David and got a very nice letter back in ten days from Godfrey Thomas[2] (who I gather is working on Alec's personal staff) saying that their enquiries in Athens showed that David had built up a highly successful connection with Greek newspapers, editors and staffs. They added that the highly satisfactory position in Greece, where British propaganda had consistently retained the initiative, was largely due to David's efforts. I feel that in the circumstances there is every reason for him to stay where he is.

Like you I get a large number of pamphlets dealing with the post-war situation. People are certainly thinking, although most of them will have to think again. Whatever problems and difficulties we have to deal with between now and the end of the war, they will be absolutely nothing to the post-war problems in this country both politically and economically. I wish it were easier to discern a really good line of succession to the present Prime Minister.

Geoffrey to E.C.F.B., 24 March (Easter Day)   *Aberdeen*

I see the Archbishop was announced to preach in the Cathedral this morning. It can't have been pleasant in the anything but Christian atmosphere which reigns in the   Precincts. The Hebrew name Keziah (this was one of the names given by the Dean to his new-born daughter) is the Greek 'Cassia', a kind of

---

[1] Eric MacKenzie (1891-1972). Compt. to the Household of the Gov.-Gen. of Canada, 1931-39.
[2] Sir Godfrey Thomas, 10th. Bart (1889-1968). Pte. Sec. to Duke of Gloucester, 1935-7; employed by For. Office, 1939-44. KCB (1937) PC (1958).

cinnamon used as a spice and as an internal purge. May the child live to purge her father of his vanities and silliness.

As for the war, it merely for Ursula and David adds to the intense joy of being alive. We all welcome the spring, but these two children are the very embodiment of it here present in the house all the year round. Dante pictures life in heaven as perpetual spring time, and Christ said 'Of such is the Kingdom'. With children about one, above all one's own, it is not difficult to understand even in war time what He meant, and Dante too. I think our Government will soon have to imitate the French and be re-constituted.

John Wallace to J.B.B., 30 March   *Lavington*

I expect you have heard most of the news about Lavington being turned into a maternity hospital. We all enjoyed it a lot while it lasted and had lots of jokes. The voluntaries were all the sweetest of mother's friends, some of whom are still here and we have great fun with week-end parties still. Now that we have taken some of the rooms back, since there seems little prospect of the house being used as a hospital yet, it is almost pre-war.

So far the war has had very little effect on my life and indeed things seem to have changed very little and nowadays one never thinks of taking one's gas mask about. Duff and Diana have just got back to England and are spending this week-end here. They both seem to have adored their American trip. I go to Balliol in April, having just passed my college exam, and I am looking forward to it a lot. As a result I have a long holiday in the summer and there is an idea that I might go to France and help bring in the harvest. I do hope that you will get back this summer as we are all longing to see you again. David Margesson was staying here this week-end and had a terrifying experience as he shut himself in the little washing cubicle in his room at 12.00 one night. As the door works on a catch and can't be opened from the inside he was imprisoned with no air. Shouting was no good, and it took him three hours to batter his way out as the whole cubicle was walled with plate glass!

Pat Hodgson to J.B.B., 31 March   *London*

I lunched the other day with a great friend who is attached to the Supreme War Council. He told me that the French people, who are solidly anti- any patched up peace, had become discontented and restless over what they considered

Daladier's wavering policy in respect of Finland. By the time Daladier realised it and pressed for action the peace had come and he fell. At first there was anxiety on this side lest he be replaced by a weak government of a somewhat pacific nature, but that anxiety is over for the time being, although whether Reynaud can hold on remains to be seen. Nobody can suggest what more the Allies could have done for Finland in view of the attitude of Scandinavia.

The reconstruction of the French government has revived the desire for a stronger and smaller Cabinet here, which is voiced in the press repeatedly. The Contracts affair has shaken confidence in Burgin[1] while there are others like Stanhope[2] and Elliot[3] who might well be replaced. But I am informed the PM has no intention of making any changes at present though if he retains all his colleagues much longer there may be an agitation for a change of leader. The only two possible successors would appear to be Halifax (who would have to sit in the Commons) or Winston. Simon and Hoare have no following among the public. Winston is too capricious to be a reliable PM, but Halifax is respected and trusted by all parties. Chamberlain is personally unpopular with Labour largely on account of his icy manner. By the way I should have added with regard to Daladier, that it was feared his fall might involve the disappearance of Gamelin. Thank Heaven he has not gone. The morale in Britain is very good, but a working man who is a keen Trade Unionist in Chelsea informs me that he fears his class may grow weary of the war if the stalemate continues, and is very keen for some really good speakers to tour the country and rub in what we are up against.

April

Ralph to J.B.B., 8 April   *London*
There has been an enormous amount of illness this winter owing to (1) the blackout, which has prevented proper ventilation and (2) the very severe weather

---

[1] (Edward) Leslie Burgin (1887-1945). MP (Lib, and from 1931 NLib) Luton, 1929-45; Par. Sec. B. of Trade, 1932-37. Min. of Supply, 1939-40. The 'Contracts Affair' stemmed from attacks made by the opposition in Parliament about profiteering on war contracts.
[2] 7th. Earl Stanhope (1880-1967). U-Sec. for War, 1931-4; Parl. U-Sec. For. Office, 1934-6; Ist. Comm. Works, 1936-7; Pres. Bd. of Ed., 1937-8; Ist Ld. of Admiralty, 1938-9; Ld. President, 1939-40; Leader of H. of Lords, 1938-40. KG(1934), PC (1929).
[3] Rt. Hon. Walter Elliot (1888-1958). MP (Con) Lanark, 1918-23, Kelvingrove, 1924-45 and Scottish Universities, 1946-50. Fin. Sec. to Treasury, 1931-2; Min. of Agric, 1932-36; Sec. for Scotland, 1936-38; Min. of Health, 1938-40. PC (1932).

we have had. Here the war goes on very much as it has done since the beginning. The chief thing is when is it likely to become an active war? Where and how is, I agree, a problem but we cannot go on indefinitely doing nothing and spending £7,000,000 a day. A number of people think that the War is going to be over this year but personally I cannot see it. Since I dictated this the news comes of our mining the Norwegian coast and today the invasion of Denmark and Norway by Germany, so perhaps the War has really started. You will know about it all as soon as we shall.

Geoffrey to E.C.F.B., 14 April   *Aberdeen*

The news of our capture of Narvik with the annihilation of the German naval forces there, together with the further really astounding information this morning that our Navy is in the Baltic and has mined the entire German coast as far as Lithuania, has made this one of the most exciting week-ends in memory of anyone living. The old Greek proverb that 'those whom the gods would destroy they first drive mad' would seem singularly applicable to the credible folly with which Hitler has to all intents and purposes committed suicide by invading Norway without command of the sea. This last amazing feat of the navy ought to make impossible what everyone is expecting, namely, the German invasion of Sweden. The whole complexion of the war has been changed overnight. There are now only three things that Hitler can do (1) invade Holland and Belgium, who are ready for him (2) order a frontal attack on the Maginot Line, which would be suicide (3) invade Hungary or Jugo-Slavia, which would embroil him with Italy, or invade Rumania, where we have a huge army in Palestine, with our Turkish Allies, ready to come to Rumania's aid. Without iron ore from Sweden, from which it is now entirely cut off, Germany cannot long continue the war. I really think there are good grounds now for hoping that the war may be over this year. Indeed I cannot but believe that there may be already such serious division of opinion in the German High Command, or between it and the Nazi Government, that Germany herself may soon begin to crumble internally. Cut off from their base and with the German navy as good as destroyed, the German army in Norway is doomed to destruction. Scandinavia will be pro-Ally, and the wavering Balkan neutrals will be determined to side against Germany. Italy is in a very uncomfortable position and is beginning to see her chickens come home to roost. For we command the Mediterranean and could destroy her fleet as completely as we have destroyed the

German, if it dared to attack us. Poor Denmark! But, who knows? Our navy may be able to come to her assistance too before long. And what will the German people say when they discover the truth as they must before long? And how British sea-power has vindicated itself! Never in history has Britannia so incontrovertibly ruled the waves. Even far away Japan must be beginning to tremble. For Germany once beaten, what is to prevent our settling our long account with her? What an unspeakable blessing it would be if the war could be over victoriously this year and that too without any fighting on the western front!

Lord Hankey to J.B.B., 16 April

I was quite thrilled to learn from you that Mackenzie King had at last taken the plunge and decided to have a Secretary to the Cabinet. I believe Canada is the first dominion to set the example. Mark my words, they will all follow one of these days. I do not remember Heeney,[1] but if he is the right man for the job, I am sure he will never regret it. It is a good thing to start it during the war, when the whole government machine has to be tuned up to a very high state of efficiency. When peace comes it can be adapted to the slightly (though only slightly) easier circumstances. You have done good work in helping to bring about this reform.

We are up to the neck in the Scandinavian affair. It is not going too badly; the shark has got hold of the tiger's tail. It remains to be seen whether we can pull him into the sea. Anyhow, we are knocking him about quite badly. Only about half his navy is left and a good deal of that half has been frightfully hammered. We are also giving him hell on his aerodrome at Stavanger, which cannot be much fun for him.

Hume Wrong[2] to J.B.B., 21 April

The Norwegian adventure is not going too badly, although there will be many more chapters in that story before it is over. But it will not remain the chief theatre of active warfare for long. The whole continent may soon be aflame. I have the feeling that no one, including Hitler, knows what the area of warfare will

---

[1] Arnold Heeney (1902-1970). Barrister. Sec. to Canadian PM, 1938; Clerk of Privy Council and Sec. to Cabinet, 1940; Canadian Amb. to U.S., 1959-62.

[2] (Humphrey) Hume Wrong (1894-1954). Asst. Prof. History, Univ. of Toronto, 1921-7; Perm. Canadian Del. to L. of N., 1937; Special Economics Adviser, Canada House London, 1939; U-Canadian Amb. to USA, 1949-52; U-Sec. External Affairs, 1953.

be even three weeks from now.

There is very widespread discontent with the Government. I hear it from all sides and from members of all parties. For the most part, it seems to be well justified. The placing of this country on a full war basis is a task calling for imagination beyond that of which the present leaders are capable. They are, also, prisoners of their own past and cannot escape from distrust of their motives, even if it may be quite unmerited. Yet, I doubt a change is imminent. The alternative is not clear but discontent may suddenly run over and compel changes. My own chief concern is not over foreign policy or strategy but over the organisation of the home front: production, agriculture and finance. The good will and determination to win are present in the country as strongly as ever, but it is not being organised, disciplined and enlisted in the sort of totalitarian national effort which is needed if we are to catch up with Germany. I am also oppressed with the persistent social stratification of England. The 'ruling class', impossible though it is to define its limits clearly, is a very real thing and remains very complacent about its mission to rule. They are becoming more consciously on the defensive - no London revue for example is complete without some satire on the old school tie. I wish Winston were a baker's son like Daladier, and that Gort and Ironside had as humble origins as Gamelin and Georges. *La carrière* may now be more *ouverte aux talents* than a generation ago. But it's not open enough yet by a long chalk. I hope one result of this war will be to accelerate the long process of moving towards social democracy in England. I went to a dinner for Athlone[1] the other night. Very pedestrian speeches - a nice, unconceited, unimaginative elderly man, of limited capacity. But he must be agile in avoiding putting his foot into it, or he would not have stayed seven years in South Africa.

Sir Stafford Cripps to J.B.B., 24 April.

I am just back and very hectically employed in seeing people, but I must just let you know how very disappointed I was not to have the time to see you and others in Canada. John Buchan's death made me feel I didn't want to go to Ottawa - I was so fond of him and he was such a good friend to me - I shall miss him greatly. I haven't time or space to tell you all I saw and thought during 45,000 miles of travel over the last five months. It was a wonderful and exhausting

[1] 1st. Earl of Athlone (1874-1957). Chanc. of London Univ., 1932-55; Gov-Gen. S. Africa, 1923-31; Gov-Gen. Canada, 1940-46.

experience.

Geoffrey to E.C.F.B., 28 April   *Aberdeen*

Our Grandfather had sixteen children but the Government in his day hadn't yet begun the practice of taxing children out of existence by the simple process of making it pay a man to remain a bachelor, or, if married, to refrain from having children. You will have doubtless have seen the correspondence in *The Times* this week on this subject, supported by chapter and verse, which proves by simple arithmetic that the married man with, say, three children and £500 a year pays on this budget 33% more additional tax than a bachelor with the same income. And yet the Chancellor of the Exchequer, a rich man with (I believe) no children and his £600 a year MP's salary free of taxation, had the audacity to boast that he has distributed the burdens of this budget fairly and equably. What liars all politicians are! If I was to write an Inferno, I should create a nice little circle in hell for their special benefit.

Have you observed how more and more it is dawning upon people generally in this country what a fearful responsibility for landing us in this war so little prepared for it, must be borne by that lazy amateur in politics named Baldwin, who was rewarded for his gross incompetence with an earldom and the Garter, though he will probably be regarded by historians as perhaps the least fitted for his post of all the Prime Ministers on record? It is even arguable, now we see what a start he allowed Germany in re-arming, through sheer indolence, that the one achievement which still remains to his credit - his management of our ex-King's abdication - might never have been necessary had he tackled the whole thing much earlier (instead of keeping this country in ignorance of it long after it had been filling columns in the world's press) and thus have prevented it from reaching a crisis. His policy over Germany and Hitlerism was equally dilatory, though he has left it to others to get us out of that fix.

The budget is interesting for many reasons and not merely for bringing out into the open the splendid temper of the nation, so far in advance of the competence of the present rulers, among whom there is not one real leader capable of embodying in himself the fighting spirit of the people as Lloyd George did in the last war, Winston Churchill alone excepted. For we do so badly need a figurehead, a William Pitt or an Abraham Lincoln. But the budget is also interesting for its trend. I think for instance that this limitation of dividends has come to stay. If so, it is a revolution in itself of the first magnitude. We ought never to forget that the real causes of this war are economic. And it becomes more and more clear that the post-war world will be founded on an economic revolution. And, in my view, this country, as always, will once more come out on top, because it will get through its revolution by stages and not suddenly.

As for the war itself I continue to be optimistic. Norway will be the Belgium of this war. But we have command of the sea, and by the end of the year shall have command of the air as well. Japan (a sea power) has already decided, it would appear, that we must win. And the mere fact that Italy still keeps well out of it proves that she too is coming round to the same opinion. As for Norway herself, it is good for their interests to be made to realise that liberty has to be fought for. Her function has been to force all the other neutrals to realise, at last, the truth of this elementary fact. And their realisation of it is another nail in the coffin of Hitlerism. There is no neutral left now who Hitler can surprise as he did Norway.

May-June

E.C.F.B. to J.B.B., 6 May   *Canterbury*

Norway is a tragedy, and I fear bad for our prestige. I suppose we not only did not plan ahead sufficiently, nor had we yet had any experience of what it means to have concentrations of troops bombed from the air. We know very little of what our High Command has in its mind. The French army is a fine one and well-officered. Gamelin I trust, for he is a great man; so we must have some important strategy in our minds.

Julian to E.C.F.B., 15 May   *Felsted*

The early surrender of the Dutch forces is very sad. Apparently, seeing their towns and homes destroyed by aerial bombing was more than they could stand.

The very part of France we travelled through last year on our way to Switzerland is now being bombed. Do you remember the steep banks of the Meuse and our tea at Dinant? - The sunshine on the old houses, the rebuilt church, and the finger pointing to heaven on the war memorial to the 100 or so Belgian civilians massacred there by the Germans in 1914. And now the same thing is probably happening all over again in the same place.

My dear, had you not better stay at Chiddingstone until it becomes a little clearer what is going to happen? I could always have you back here if you could or would come. At least you should be with a son during these difficult weeks and not at Canterbury - until Burgon comes back.

Julian to E.C.F.B., 16 May   *Felsted*

I am sure our armies are going to do well. They may have to give way here and there, but Gamelin will fight where he wants to fight. I am told that the government are very pleased that the Dutch held out for as long as they did. At least they gave the French and British forces five or six days to get into position in Belgium before the main German forces could deploy their attack. This may prove to be of the greatest value in the ensuing days of battle.

I have the greatest faith in Gamelin; I think he means to make the Germans fight their battle where and how he wants and not as they choose. It will of course be a terrific battle, but I think we shall be able to hold them and eventually push them back into Germany.

Memorandum by J.B.B.

On Friday evening 17 May, while listening to a Beethoven concert in the Great Hall by the Hart House Quartet, I first thought of returning to England by the *Duchess of York* which was to sail the following Tuesday morning. I had a passage booked on the *Scythia* (Cunard) leaving New York on 4 June, but sailings were being cancelled or postponed without notice and I realised it was uncertain when I should get back. The news from Belgium and NE France was anxious. The English, French and Belgian armies were falling back. The German armies had broken through on the Meuse and fighting was taking place before Louvain.

By mid-day Saturday (18 May) I had decided to finish up my work by Monday evening and go. Miss Watson got me a cabin on the *Duchess of York* and the ticket arrived at mid-day. Dr Cody[1] entirely concurred with my action and I left Toronto at midnight on Monday 20 May for Montreal.

The *Duchess of York* sailed at 11 a.m. next day. The docks were heavily

---

[1] Rev. Henry Cody (1868-1951). Pres and Vice Chanc. Univ. of Toronto, 1932-45.

guarded. John Greenly,[1] who was at Charterhouse with me, was on board and we travelled together, sharing a table at meals.

After Munich Greenly had been appointed Chairman of the Prime Minister's Advisory Panel of Industrialists - a post which brought him into close touch with the three fighting services and the supply of armaments. During the months before war broke out he had full opportunity of seeing the delay and the many mistakes which the government had made in our war preparations. As regards tanks for instance, no decisions were reached as to the design of the tank best qualified to meet the new heavily-armed German tank of which the of which the government was aware. Hore-Belisha was useless. Anxious to keep himself in the limelight, he said spectacular things, sacked old generals, improved the soldiers living conditions, and increased the Territorial Army. But on the bigger issues of war policy and armaments he was utterly ineffective. Reports which Greenly's Advisory Panel presented were never mastered, even if read. On one occasion the Army Council asked for a large increase in guns and tanks. The Treasury said there were funds for either the guns or tanks but not for both. The actual effort on industry since Munich was magnificent, but far more could have been done had the government shown initiative and energy. Three weeks after war broke out Greenly was sent to Ottawa where he established the HQ of the British Supply Board with an office under Arthur Purvis[2] at New York. Every penny of the vast sums spent by Great Britain in Canada and the USA on aircraft, finished munitions, machinery, explosives, ships and chemicals pass through Greenly's office. He had with him on board a number of highly confidential papers. Two suitcases, for instance, contained the entire plans for the expenditures of Great Britain in the Dominions and the USA. These were put in the care of the Captain during the voyage - there being a special method of sinking them if any danger arose of their falling into enemy hands, and when we arrived at Liverpool I kept one suitcase in my hands and Greenly the other. We even took them into the dining car with us.

On board we had about 50 first class passengers, the Officers of 112 Sqdn. RCAF, reinforcements for 110th Sqdn., a number of army officers, including a few

---

[1] Lt.-Col. John Greenly (1885-1950). Dir. Babcock and Wilcox; Chmn. of PM's advisory panel of industrialists on rearmament, 1938-39; Cont. Gen. British Supply Board in Canada and USA, 1939-40. Kt (1941).
[2] Rt. Hon. Arthur Purvis (1890-1941). Industrialist; Chmn. British Supply Council in N. America, 1940-41. PC (1940). Killed in air-crash.

Belgians. There were about 20 civilians, among them a group of movie people who were to return to Canada shortly to make a picture of Canada's war effort centred round a spy story. The voyage was uneventful. We tied up at Quebec to take on board 200 Newfoundland fishermen who were to serve on trawlers and minesweepers in British waters. The tourist class was fairly full, and the third class packed with the men of 112 Sqdn.

The radio was kept going the whole way across and the news became more serious every day. On Thursday the Germans had reached the Cambrai-Peronne road and had captured Laon.. By Saturday the enemy were approaching the Channel ports. On Sunday came the news that 15 French Generals had been dismissed, General Weygand[1] having succeeded Gamelin as Commander-in-Chief of the Allied armies on Monday 20th.

On Monday 27 May the radio announced that the Germans had occupied Boulogne, but the Allied troops were still in Calais. It was also announced that Sir John Dill[2] had succeeded Sir Edmund Ironside as CIGS, Ironside becoming Commander-in-Chief Home Forces. The appalling seriousness of the situation was obvious to us all as we sat in the lounge of the *Duchess of York* avidly listening to the news. The Germans with their mechanised divisions had forced a gap roughly between Arras and Bapaume, and through this were pouring troops to occupy the Channel ports. It required little imagination to see that the fate of the BEF and the French and Belgian armies cut off from their base, and indeed from all means of retreat, might well be sealed. Then at breakfast time on Tuesday 28 May came the crowning blow of the capitulation of the Belgian army on the personal orders of King Leopold. Dunkirk was the only port now remaining! Neither Lord Gort nor the French commanders had been informed, and arrangements had to be made as quickly as possible to cover the left flank extending for some 30 miles to the coast till then held by the Belgian army of between 400,000 and 500,000 men.

These terrific events did not make for a cheerful voyage, which in other ways was comparatively uneventful. We had several boat drills and were warned to keep warm clothing by our bedsides ready to put on at short notice if we had to take to the boats. When 100 miles from the Irish coast regulations about carrying

---

[1] Gen. Maxime Weygand (1867-1965). Comm. of French forces in N. East; Replaced Gamelin in France, May 1940; Gov-Gen. of Algeria and Del-Gen. of Vichy in French Africa, 1941-42; Prisoner of Gestapo, 1942-45; Prisoner in France, 1945-46.

[2] Gen. Sir John Dill (1881-1944). Comdr. Ist Army Corps in France, 1939-40; CIGS, 1940-41; Head of British Joint Staff Mission in USA, 1941-44. Kt .(1937), Field Marshal (1941).

one's life belts everywhere with one were enforced. Caravenes were put out on Monday afternoon - a device for catching and severing the cable which anchored enemy mines, and allowing the mine to float free on the surface of the water. Throughout the voyage the boats hung free over the side of the ship. There was the usual complete black-out which after dark made it difficult to find one's way inside again after a stroll on deck.

By dinner time on Tuesday 28 May we were steaming up the Mersey, where the huge amount of shipping entering or leaving Liverpool was convincing proof of British command of the sea. We anchored opposite the Liver Building at 9 p.m. but no one could board and no communication whatever with the shore was permitted. Even the following morning there was considerable delay in tying up at the wharf as the *Oronsay* (Orient Line) was disembarking women and children evacuated from Gibraltar. We landed at 10.30 and found that, contrary to expectation, there was a special train. John Greenly and I travelled down together and reached Euston at 5 p.m. (Wed. 29 May).

On arrival in London I went straight to Ralph and Alison at 6 Hyde Park Square, where I learnt that Mother was at Chiddingstone with Monier having gone there on 11 May, one day after the invasion of Holland and Belgium. The question to decide was whether I should take her back to Canterbury or not. The family was doubtful, though from the first I thought she would really be better in her own home. Alison told me that the BEF was being evacuated from Dunkirk. She had talked with many soldiers who had taken part in the recent fighting. Abbeville was a smoking ruin, and Arras badly knocked about.

I went round to see Euan and Barbie Wallace. Both were very pessimistic about our being able to save more than a very small part of the BEF It was suggested that perhaps a suitable house could be found in Graffham for Mother, myself and the two maids (Norah and Molly). That evening Ralph, Alison and I talked till a late hour. Next morning I breakfasted with Vincent and Alice Massey at their flat at the Dorchester. The 1st Canadian Division is not in Flanders but is in the Midlands. It is now one of the best-trained divisions in England and with other first line troops is being kept in this country as invasion, fantastic as it may sound, is now a real possibility.. At 11 a.m. I met Edward at Victoria (he had reached England on leave from the Sudan on 29 April) and we went together to Chiddingstone where I found Mother and Miss Gray, Monier and Mary, Mr Matthew and his daughter Wendy.

The strategic railway Dover, Ashford, Tunbridge, Aldershot, Reading runs through the valley below Monier's garden. Since last Sunday trains have been passing at 1/4 hour intervals filled with the troops of the BEF. I counted three in half an hour myself; LMS rolling stock and about ten or eleven coaches to a train. On Friday I went out with Monier to the extreme end of his parish near the Sussex border. He was visiting parishioners who were lodging evacuated children, the grant for each child having been increased. The English countryside never looked more beautiful. The sound of guns was clearly audible. Troops were being transported along the country lanes. The Penshurst aerodrome was heavily guarded. The villagers had been enrolled in the Local Defence Volunteer Force. Mr Matthew and Ted went out at dusk that evening to stand on rising ground and watch for parachutists. At 11.45 their tour of duty was over. Others took their place at 3 a.m. On Friday evening (31 May) there was a rumour that enemy parachutists might be expected and many of the LDV were called out. Col. Meade-Waldo told me that 25 men were on the high ground above Stonewall, but they only had one rifle between them. Monier was arranging for the collection of scrap iron at various dumps in the parish. During these days we heard how craft of every kind from Southampton to Hull had been commandeered to bring the BEF across the Channel. The inn-keeper in the village told me that on Thursday Tonbridge was full of stretcher cases.

On Saturday 1st June I went to London and stayed the night with Ralph and Alison. That morning I found Alice Massey who showed me all over the Beaver hut in a former LCC building just inside the Mall from the Admiralty Arch. She was responsible for the admirable decorations and furnishings and general lay-out. It is administered by the YMCA, and the Canadian Red Cross has made substantial grants. It is a club for Canadian soldiers, and includes restaurant, snack bar, showers, reading rooms, lounges, information bureau and the rest. The *Blitzkrieg* has stopped all leave, so instead of being packed as it usually is, the building was comparatively empty. Alice also showed me the small Officers' Club· which Vincent and she have established at their own expense over the Cunard offices in Cockspur Street. It was becoming clear to me that as long as I was with her it would really be best for Mother to return to Canterbury where she had her own household and would be in surroundings suitable to her.

That night I dined with Vincent and Alice Massey at the Dorchester to meet the Athlones I had a talk with Athlone and also with Princess Alice. She is bright and vivacious and said they were both genuinely pleased to be going to Canada, he being particularly gratified that at 66 years of age he had another job.

On Sunday 2 June I returned to Chiddingstone. A soldier who had just returned the previous night from Dunkirk was in our carriage. He had fought the whole way back from Arras to the coast. The Germans dressed as refugees often disclosed their true identity at a suitable time. He confirmed the reports of the deliberate bombing and machine-gunning of refugees by the German airforce. That afternoon Mother, Miss Gray and I with all our luggage motored to Canterbury where we received a warm welcome from Norah and Molly. At 7 p.m. I slipped into the Cathedral to hear the Dean's sermon. He referred in the highest terms to the heroism of our troops and there was nothing in his sermon that any one could object to, which was as well as only last Sunday - the day of National Prayer - Canon Shirley had seen fit to deliver a sermon in which he had attacked the economic system of England and praised the 'idealism' of the Germans. 'We can only ask for victory if our cause is worthy of God's blessing'. The angry protests were so bitter (many soldiers had walked out during the sermon) that Shirley had written to the local paper and had also posted a statement in the SW porch, explaining he had never intended to hurt people's feelings.

Canterbury and its environment present an unforgettable scene during these memorable days. Past our house there rushes an endless stream of military traffic - huge lorries with tarpaulin-covered loads, staff cars, despatch riders, Red Cross ambulances, trucks carrying aeroplanes (folded up in bits, either damaged or new), small WD cars with officers, a train of RAF lorries, trucks with the new motor torpedo boats, military police on motor bicycles, men marching. The Dover road is barricaded beyond Bridge. Wire entanglements, strung on knife-rests and ready to throw across the road, are at the old turnpike at the top of the New Dover Road, and also on the Ashford Road, and the Sturry Road and at Harbledown, and at the top of the hill by St Edmund's School. At the turnpike there is an MG emplacement. The entire countryside is an armed camp. Trenches are being dug in good fire positions. Guns poke their noses from innocent-looking copses. In out-of-the way valleys are lorry parks. Anti-aircraft guns and search lights are legion on high ground. On Bigberry Hill there are detectors as well as guns and searchlights well sandbagged. The fields which are suitable for aeroplane landing are obstructed with posts and hurdles and farm wagons; all sign-posts are removed, even the metal plates have been taken off the milestones. The names of villages have been taken off the houses. Trenches, false and real, disfigure the fields. One's identity card (I procured mine the first morning I was in Canterbury) may be asked for several times during a quiet bicycle ride. On Monday afternoon standing on Barham Down I heard the bombardment at Dunkirk and Calais so clearly that I could detect the heavier crumps and the lighter guns. It was a superb June afternoon. In a field behind me the farmer was cutting his hay. On the Dover Road below passed an endless procession of military traffic. It was a completely fantastic scene the like of which one could hardly believe possible.

The feeling in England against the Germans is bitter. The stories of the machine-gunning of refugees, of the treacherous fifth column activities, of tanks crushing civilians trudging along the roads in flight - these and many other tales have roused a real hatred for the people as well as their leader. And now invasion is a real possibility. The enemy are at our doors. On Barham Downs it was difficult to realise that the Germans in Calais were about 34 miles from where I stood. From this house in Canterbury they are some 37 miles. The gunning goes on all day. The English people are roused at last. In England some 250,000 men have joined the LDV. In Canterbury Major H.G. James is in charge of 600 men who have joined. Each night about a hundred are on duty guarding the roads, telephone exchange, gas works, electric light plant, water works and so on. There are only 300 rifles - 250 from the King's School OTC, and 50 from St Edmund's School OTC, both of which schools are evacuated to St Austell in Cornwall. The Civil Defence Services - ARP, fire fighting, gas decontamination and the rest, all of which had somewhat languished during the tedious winter months of waiting, have sprung into activity. Each night after the nine o'clock news there is a so-called 'Postscript', generally by a Minister of the Crown. One evening recently Sir John Anderson urged every Englishman and every Englishwoman to play his or her part. Canterbury itself is a neutral area at present - that is, it does not receive evacuated children though its own children have not yet been evacuated. As far as invasion is concerned, I feel it is safer for Mother than many rural districts where parachutists might float down from the sky undetected. Here we have thousands of troops in the immediate vicinity and plans have been worked out to throw an immediate cordon round any area where the enemy might have landed.

So far enemy air activity has been more general in Yorkshire, East Anglia and Essex, though we have had two air raid warnings during this week - on Friday morning at 1.30 a.m., the sirens began their raucous wailing, one on the West

Gate, one at Nackington, one near the mental hospital - and the all clear sounded two hours later. I woke Mother but we remained quietly in bed. Then just before midnight on Friday evening there was another warning which this time only lasted for half an hour. If incendiary bombs fall we have buckets of water and buckets of sand at certain points in the house. The blackout is rigidly observed though I thought that London was not actually so completely dark as it at any rate seemed on 2 September, the night of the first black-out. About half the people one sees in the streets carry their gas masks. It is generally believed however that the Germans will not use gas. As for the invasion we are told the authorities consider Yorkshire and East Anglia as the most likely places. *The Times* of Saturday 8 June carried pictures of German parachute troops, showing how they are dressed. A troop-carrying aeroplane carries up to 30 parachutists. When dropped they immediately form into units of six or eight. They only carry revolvers as they float to earth but rifles, bombs and ammunition are dropped in separate containers. Machine guns are dropped in this way.

Euan Wallace to J.B.B., 16 May   *47 Park Street, London*

Last week's debate with a majority of only 81 for the Government was the culmination of a long series of events. Some people would describe it as the success of a carefully prepared plot. I do not think this is fair, as the real feeling of the country has for some time not been represented by the 281 Conservatives who voted for Mr.Chamberlain's Government as opposed to the 36 who voted against.

The events in Norway no doubt provided the spark, but the trail had been laid for a long time and sooner or later there would have been a determined effort not so much to oust Chamberlain as to get rid of Simon, Hoare and (I think most unfairly) Horace Wilson. The actual debate, and particularly the scenes at the end of it, were not very creditable to the House; and, as usual, members hastened to make amends by the remarkable ovation which they gave Mr. Chamberlain at the Whit Monday sitting - a demonstration which was really rather embarrassing for poor Winston.

I always thought that I should be one of those to come under the axe. In the first place they know I am not the sort of person who is likely to complain or intrigue; secondly, the Ministry of Transport inevitably attracts a certain measure of unpopularity in the public mind, as all war-time inconveniences and restrictions are so easily associated with the name of the unfortunate Minister; thirdly, the

Ministry was saddled with a considerable measure of blame for the coal shortage, which was in fact due to a combination of bad weather and lack of foresight in the Mines Department; and lastly, the raising of railway fares and charges by 10% which, as an essential part of the railway agreement, was represented by the Opposition (and, make no mistake about it, there has been an opposition) as being an arbitrary and unjustifiable action on my part. I was not, therefore, very much surprised at being told that I could not remain as Minister of Transport, but was slightly taken aback by the selection of Reith to fill the post. Winston very kindly offered me the post of First Commissioner of Works but it had, unfortunately, attached to it the condition that I should accept a peerage. By some obscure statue it is decreed that of the Lord President of the Council, Lord Privy Seal, First Commissioner and Postmaster General, one must be in the House of Lords. Attlee[1] and Greenwood were slated for the first two of these posts and we were all very anxious to keep Shakes Morrison[2] as Postmaster General. I think you will agree that I was right in refusing the offer with thanks and without hesitation. I refuse to believe that I can be of no more use in the House of Commons if not during the war, at any rate after.

You can imagine how miserable I was at being out after nine years of office; one gets used to red boxes, Foreign Office telegrams and all the other paraphernalia of government; and over the past year I have particularly enjoyed the Ministry of Transport. Barbie was even more disappointed and upset. We visualised going off to Lavington yesterday for a holiday which I did not need and which would simply have given one a lot of time to think over what else one might have done.

Imagine, therefore, my delight when at lunch yesterday Sir John Anderson asked me to become Senior Regional Commissioner for London. This is a very important job which was originally offered to Herbert Morrison[3] when the

---

[1] Clement Richard Attlee (1883-1967). MP (Lab) Limehouse, 1922-50, Wathamstow W., 1950-55. Chanc. Duchy of Lancaster, 1930-1; Postmaster-Gen. 1931; Ld. Privy Seal, 1940-2; Dominions Sec., 1942-3; Ld. Pres. , 1942-43; Dep. PM, 1942-45; PM, 1945-51; Labour Leader, 1935-55. Cr Earl Attlee (1955), KG (1956).

[2] William Shepherd Morrison (1893-1961). MP (Con) Cirencester & Tewkesbury, 1929-59; F.S.T., 1935-6; Min. of Agric., 1936-39; Chanc. Duchy of Lancaster, 1939-40; Min. of Food, 1939-40; Postmaster Gen., 1940-42; Min. of Town & Country Planning, 1942-45; Speaker, 1951-59; Gov-Gen. of Australia, 1960-61. Cr. Vt. Dunrossil (1959).

[3] Herbert Stanley Morrison (1888-1965). MP(Lab) Hackney S., 1923-31,1935-45; Lewisham E., 1945-50, Lewisham S., 1950-59; Min. of Transport, 1929-31; Min. of Supply, 1940; Home Sec.,

Regional Organisation was set up throughout the country. He refused to take it as the Labour Party would not allow him to do so. London, unlike other Regions, is to have three Commissioners, and two have been carrying on on the understanding that the Senior Commissioner-ship should be filled by someone of Cabinet status when an emergency occurred. You can see, therefore, that the post offers the prospect of a lot of work and of still keeping in touch with the government. I believe that the Senior Regional Commissioner for London will act as the *alter ego* to the Minister of Home Security in times of crisis.

I hope it is not being 'catty' to say that the new Government are rather a scratch lot and Winston must have had an extremely difficult job in deciding who to put in and who to leave out. Very clearly there is a considerable element of 'spoils' for the victors in it; in some cases past services are rewarded, in others outstanding efficiency recognised - as in the case of people like Rab Butler - by retention in their posts. Nobody quite knows how Beaverbrook is going to organise the production of aircraft and I should have thought myself that this would have been a more suitable job for Reith, who at least was an engineer for many years. The main thing is, however, that for the present there will be no opposition in the House of Commons and, even in a country which is fighting for democracy, that is a considerable advantage in the prosecution of the war in its most critical moment. I think, however, there is very little doubt that a section of the Labour Party will refuse to accept it as their duty to be loyal to a government in which they have two of their leaders in the War Cabinet and, perhaps regrettably, there will be a section of the Conservative Party which will find it very difficult not to show their preference for the last regime as compared to this one.

Duff has just been broadcasting. He is going to do it at least weekly and perhaps oftener. I believe he will make a great name as Minister of Information.

Tom Jones to J.B.B., 19th May   *Cliveden*

I am prompted to scribble a line to you as at this time one is actively thinking of friends near and far. It is a time for which we have no precedent in experience. We have within a week suddenly begun to apprehend that the unparalleled beauty of this little island may soon be defaced, deformed, destroyed.

There has never been such an unbroken spell of springtime loveliness and I

1940-45; Ld. Pres., 1945-51; For. Sec., 1951; Leader of LCC, 1934-40; cr. Baron Morrison (1959).

think what haunts many of us is that the ripe perfection of the English inheritance will be horribly gashed and stabbed into ugliness and into ruin. We are the enemy, not France, that Hitler desires should be made to eat dirt, because it is we more than France who lie athwart his imperial appetite. The issue lies today in the balance. The number of his divisions, the power of his machines, the ubiquity of his planes in the air are marshalled with such an accurately calculating genius that resistance to their tremendous shock seems bound to fail. Courage the Allies have in reckless profusion. One hears incredible tales of the individual heroism of the youth of the Empire, but the enemy directs an overpowering mass of metal. Our unpreparedness in the air is now openly confessed and were we not at war one would wish Ministers impeached and lynched. Scape-goats are sought - some Treasury clerk is blamed for refusing credits; or Lord Weir[1] for playing about with many types of planes; or Baldwin, blind and deaf to what Germany was up to; or latterly Kingley Wood for manipulating figures to deceive his Cabinet colleagues and the public. It is useless today. We can only turn beseeching eyes to Canada and the States and pray that planes by the score and the hundred may reach these shores in time.

After eight months of relative complacency NC has been removed from the top and Winston takes his place - in which there is gain and loss. Several of the feebler Ministers have at last been removed, including your friend at the Ministry of Transport, Euan Wallace. But Kingsley Wood at the Treasury inspires no confidence; he would have been better as Leader of the House. Woolton[2] and Duncan are well spoken of. Hudson[3] and Cross[4] were doing well and are now moved about and will have to learn new jobs from overworked civil servants. Horace Wilson[5] vanished into the recesses of the Treasury overnight, very unfairly

[1] Rt. Hon. Lord Weir (1877-1959) Industrialist; Adviser to Air Ministry, 1938-39; Dir. Gen. of Explosives, Min. of Supply, 1939; Chmn. Tank Board, 1942. PC and cr. Vt. (1938).
[2] Lord Woolton (1883-1964). Company Director; Min. of Food, 1940-43; Member of War Cabinet, 1943-45; Min. of Reconstruction, 1943-45; Ld. Pres. 1945 and 1951-52; Chanc. of Duchy of Lancaster, 1952-55; cr. Baron (1939), PC (1940), Vt. (1953) and Earl (1956).
[3] Rt. Hon. Robert Spear Hudson (1886-1957). MP (Con) Whitehaven, 1924-29 and Southport, 1931-52; Parl. Sec. Min. of Labour, 1931-35; Min. of Pensions, 1935-36; Sec. Dept. of Overseas Trade, 1937-40; Min. of Shipping, 1940; Min. of Agric., 1940-45. PC (1938), CH (1944) and cr. Vt. (1952).
[4] Rt. Hon. Colin Cross (1896-1968). MP (Con) Rossendale, 1931-45; Govt. Whip, 1935-37; Parl. Sec. Bd. of Trade, 1938-9; Min. of Econ. Warfare, 1939-40; Min. of Shipping, 1940-41; H. Comm. Australia, 1941-5. PC (1940). Cr. Bart (1941).
[5] Sir Horace Wilson (1882-1972). Civil Servant; Chief Industrial Adviser; seconded to Treasury for service with the PM, 1935-40. Used by Chamberlain as confidant and envoy. Kt. (1933).

blamed for much, though he had gathered power into his hands too obviously. His successor not fixed - Morton[1] of Economic Warfare mentioned; also P.J.Grigg.[2] Lindemann[3] and Brendan Bracken[4] are duly installed at the PM's elbow. Dill is praised at the War Office - an exception to the universal denigration.

Geoffrey to E.C.F.B., 19 May   *Aberdeen*

The news is tantalisingly brief, and one can but exist from day to day. I should doubt myself whether Hitler has really, as we are insisted to believe, staked quite his all on this battle. He surely still has some cards up his sleeve, e.g. some arrangement with Mussolini (or possibly Russia) to come to his aid at some pre-decided moment, when he delivers a similarly heavy attack (to the one now in progress) against Switzerland, Italy attacking from the south, with the object of turning the other end of the Maginot Line; or alternatively, an onslaught on Rumania, with the aid of Hungary. All that seems certain is that he is pressed for time and cannot face a second winter of war, so that if we can hold him in France, and in any other country, for the next three months, we shall have beaten him. Meanwhile, in the background, the British Navy is there, and whether he over-runs France or not will continue to strangle him.

The French ought not, I think, to have been taken so much by surprise, and I expect there was treachery at work. For they must have known of the vast concentration of troops at that section of the line facing the Ardennes. But after the first shock they seem to be pulling themselves together, and are getting accustomed to the German tank and aeroplane tactics. After all they are the most seasoned army in the world, and are fighting for the very existence of France and have many very able generals.

The situation most resembles 1918 and if so, that is of good augury for us. In open warfare victory and defeat are quickly interchangeable. And even the German Airforce cannot, one would think, stand losing aeroplanes at the rate of a thousand a week, i.e. of 50,000 a year, or even more. The RAF is wonderful, and

---

[1] Desmond Morton (1891-1971) Princ. Asst. Sec. Min. of Econ Warfare, 1939-40; Personal Asst. to Churchill, 1940-46. Kt. (1945).

[2] Sir Percy James Grigg (1890-1964) Civil Servant; Per. U-Sec. for War, 1939-42; Sec. of State for War, 1942-45. Kt. (1936), PC (1942).

[3] Prof. Frederick Lindemann (d. 1957). Personal Asst. to Churchill, 1940; Postmaster Gen., 1942-45 and 1951-53. Cr. Baron Cherwell (1941), Vt. (1956).

[4] Brendan Bracken (1901-58) MP (Con) Paddington N, 1929-45, Bournemouth, 1945-50 and Christchurch, 1950-51; P.P.S. to P.M, 1940-41; Min. of Info., 1941-45. Cr. Vt (1952).

I am glad to see that many German planes fall to anti-aircraft fire. That justifies one in believing that if, and when, they attack this country they will lose a high proportion of their numbers through action from the ground.

Norah Hopkins to Mother, 21 May   *Canterbury*

I will get the windows done for your return. Everything seems to be going on much the same here; children have left Canterbury and from the villages around. The soldiers are having to guard all bridges and railway tunnels. Just for the short journey from Chartham on my bicycle I had to stop and show my identity card six times.

Extracts from Kay's letters to Monier   *Weymouth*

24 May. On Sunday (the Day of Prayer) we went to Matins at St John's Church and had a very nice service, only marred by the most appalling sermon. It was given by the Vicar, aged well over 70 I should think, and lasted about 35 minutes. It was far too long. The tone of it felt exactly like the Salvation Army, the hell fire touch. This was really a great pity as the Church was packed with people, most of whom didn't go regularly but went because of the King's appeal. There must have been 600 or more people there and they were quite obviously bored.

3 June. We have had a tremendous week-end, 10,000 French soldiers billeted on the town, most of whom knew no English! We have 21 officers staying in this hotel, most awfully nice, and we have great conversations about the evacuation. They are simply marvellous, taking great care of their men, and so charming to talk to. I have done a lot of interpreting both for Officers and men, and on Thursday spent three hours at the Services Club serving meals etc. Very few people here seem to know French and they broadcast an appeal for interpreters. It is nice to be able to do something to help. Charles finished his first course on Saturday and passed second out of 15 in the exam, which I think is very good. He is doing cable testing this week (also hush-hush please!). We still have no idea how long he will be here and think of getting a tiny flat as this hotel is so horribly expensive.

7 June. I've done a lot more interpreting this week, taking six French officers out shopping on Tuesday. Poor things, they had lost everything, so we had to buy shirts, underclothes, socks etc. They laughed a lot, and we had great fun over it. Yesterday I spent the morning in the Services Club, and served a lot of French Tommies. I am most impressed by their bearing, and their reception here has been wonderful. People have given them clothes, free hair cuts, repaired their boots etc. They are pathetically grateful. Most of them went yesterday, but the Chief Liaison Officer is still here in the hotel, a most charming cultured man, speaking perfect English.

Kay to E.C.F.B., 7 June   *Weymouth*

The papers, as usual, grossly over-rated the heroism stuff. Many of our men were shot on the beaches by Guards Officers stationed at the water's edge, because they tried to get into the boats too quickly. The French say the young English officers were brave but utterly foolhardy and inexperienced, which I suppose is inevitable.

Both French and English loathe the Belgians. They apparently were frightfully treacherous. Some people think half the Belgian army were Nazis, certainly a large proportion were not loyal to the Government. They dressed up in every conceivable clothing and sniped our men from the roofs of houses as they went along. Dunkirk is certainly no use to the Germans. Everything is blown up, and the town razed to the ground. I talked yesterday with a Sergeant of the Royal Artillery who, with 15 other men, held a bridgehead for 14 hours against three German tanks, thus giving the engineers time to get there to blow up the bridge. He was extremely diffident about it, but it must have been awfully brave, as they only had one small house for shelter and one anti-tank gun.

Notes by E.C.F.B, 9 June   *Chiddingstone*

I heard today that Mrs Gardiner's nephew Randolph has landed in England from Dunkirk.

His Mother writes - 'He looked awfully well though I thought a bit strained, and no wonder after all he has been through. The terrific rear-guard action took them back and back until they were told to abandon their guns and make for the coast. Then the long wait in big queues on the battered pier at Dunkirk. He said if it had not been for the thick pall of smoke from the burning oil tanks which blew over their heads they could hardly have escaped the bombing. It must have been an inferno. He came over in a troop ship; later, when the last piers were destroyed, men were grouped in big circles on the beach and many, as you know, waded and swam out. He had many narrow escapes. They slept by day in a hole dug underneath their gun-carriage. He said it was so tragic moving through Belgium, all the houses empty, things left just as they were. The men slept in any one they liked and fed on all the good farm stock which ran wild. He said it was awful to see all the wagons and piles of good munitions abandoned. He says there were so many fifth columnists even amongst them. One day a 'British' soldier asked one of the men what Brigade they were, '29th' promptly replied a sergeant (they were not, but their tanks were marked 29). 'Who are you?' 'I am from the Hopkinson Military Mission, can you guide me to your HQ?' The sergeant winked to a man in the background who fired over the man's head and he put up his hands at once, and was marched off under guard where he was disposed of.'

Notes by J.B.B., on visit to London, 11-13 June.

Winston Churchill keeps difficult hours. He goes to bed for three hours every afternoon and then works till all hours of the night. When First Lord of the Admiralty, his staff found this very difficult as they had their duties during the day and yet had to be with him till 1 or 2 a.m. The PM is a terrific talker and spends much time in the control room. Horace Wilson has returned to his duties at the Treasury and has no further influence. Labour made his dismissal a condition of their joining the government. Wilson was not very tactful. Cabinet ministers did not relish receiving a note from him requiring their presence at No.10. The three men closest to the PM are Brendan Bracken, Morton and Lindemann. Bracken is now PPS to the PM, and has just been made a Privy Councillor. He has stuck to Winston throughout his ups and downs of fortune and they are devoted to each other. Morton was in the Department of Overseas Trade and then in charge of Economic Intelligence; he is a close personal friend of the PM's. Lindemann is a don at Christ Church - for long an expert in air problems and has been the chief adviser to Winston for many years past on our unpreparedness. Winston dislikes Hoare. Eden and Duff Cooper he felt he should take back owing to their resistance to Chamberlain's policy. Eden has to prove himself. Few think he will make a great Secretary of War.

Stanley Baldwin is at Astley unwell, presumably crippled by arthritis, and feeling deeply the criticism of his regime. Patrick Duff and many feel this criticism is unjustified. Had he proposed in 1936 rearming on a scale equal to what we now know Germany was, his government would have fallen. The moderate rearmament plan then initiated was all the British public would tolerate. Had the government gone out there would have been a Labour Government which would have cut down even the mild rearmament then planned. It is forgotten how great a part the League of Nations and international understanding played in the by-elections of those days. Chamberlain is more to blame. He was warned on at least two occasions about our inferiority in the air - but perhaps Simon and the Treasury will come in for the most criticism when the inevitable clean-up takes place after the war. Chamberlain's refusal to cultivate good relations with Labour, and still less to take them into his government, was a tragedy.

The foundation of the LDV was badly managed by Eden. He announced it on the wireless without having thought out, still less established, the machinery to deal with those who wished to enrol. The response was instantaneous and enormous. Tens of thousands of men applied during the first few days. They were required to give their names to the police, who then examined their credentials to ensure they were not fifth columnists. If found satisfactory the applicants then filled up the enrolment form which was signed by the Company Commander. In London alone some 80,000 men presented themselves. The police were not ready for such an invasion and there was much delay. In small towns and country districts the police were not in any case competent to deal with possible undesirables. When many thousands had been accepted there were no proper HQ staffs, no rifles, no uniforms and no funds. Dugout generals and colonels were put in charge. In London General Pereira[1] is OC of the LDV. HQs were established in the Imperial Institute. There was no staff to help him - no clear instructions - no administrative help of any kind - not even any furniture or stationery. Pat Hodgson offered his services to Pereira and was accepted. Files, postage stamps, boxes for confidential papers he supplied out of his own money. Even now (12 June) there are only 2,000 rifles for the entire London Area. Many of the factories and terminal stations are providing their own guards. A few days ago Ironside (GOC Home Forces) met representatives of the LDV at the Cannon Street Hotel and assured them there would soon be rifles for everybody. Pat Hodgson fears he said this merely to encourage them. His remarks do not agree with Philip Game's, who takes the view that all men who serve in the inner London area should have truncheons and help the police, rather than be armed with rifles. Pat thinks that

---

[1] Maj. Gen. Sir Cecil Pereira (1869-1942). GOC Territorial Army (1923); Comm. London Home Guard, 1940-41.

quite a number of fifth columnists will find their way into the LDV They can copy the arm-bands even if they are not accepted by the police which many probably will be, as careful enquiry is impossible.

Opinions differ about Ironside's ability. Gort is admittedly able (he was Commandant of the Staff College at one time) and he has come out of the retreat to the Channel ports with flying colours. It was only by a small Cabinet majority that Gort got command in the field and Ironside became CIGS. The vote nearly reversed these two positions.

The activities of the fifth column are prodigious. The Queen of Holland's own Chamberlain was sympathetic with the Germans. In England, Ramsay,[1] the MP, was detained because conclusive evidence was discovered that he was closely in touch with a spy who had been employed for years in the cipher department of the American Embassy, having presumably conveyed to the Germans full reports on all important messages between Great Britain and America for some time. During the last few weeks there has even been grave suspicion about the integrity of the staff in the cipher department of the British Foreign Office and recently the whole staff of clerks and also the King's messengers have been changed.

Hore-Belisha's behaviour had become intolerable. Both Gamelin and Gort disliked him. He talked against Gort to Gamelin. He loved self-advertisement, showed no breeding - when staying at GHQ he insisted on a special car being sent to fetch a barber to shave him. On another occasion in Paris, when Gamelin and Georges[2] came to see him by appointment at 10 a.m., he received them in his pyjamas. *Truth* had already published two articles about his activities as a company promoter in London before the war, and had a third ready. It was the knowledge that this third article might be published which had much to do with his willingness to accept dismissal quietly.

The King is doing magnificent work. Sir John Weir[3] reports that HM is in excellent health. One criticism I heard was that up till the National Government under Winston he did not see enough of Labour members. Each Monday the Queen and he give a small private dinner. There are present besides themselves one equerry, one Lady-in-Waiting and eight men guests. Labour representatives

---

[1] Capt. Archibald Ramsay (d. 1955). MP (Con) Peebles, 1931-45; Detained in Brixton Prison under Reg. 18b, 1940-44.

[2] Gen. Joseph Georges (1875-1951). Cmdr. of French armies in the NE sector, 1939-40. Joined CFLN in Algeria in 1943.

[3] Sir John Weir (1879-1971). Physician-in-Ordinary to George VI and Elizabeth II.

are included in these dinners but not enough of them. Alec Hardinge[1] is not a particularly imaginative No.1 on the secretarial staff.

Unity Mitford[2] always told Hitler that if war between Germany and England came she would blow her brains out. And this she attempted to do in Munich. Hitler, who was really fond of the girl, was very concerned but took no action except to provide a special train to the frontier. The bullet still remains in her head and surgeons cannot extract it. She is not normal.

The Horse Guards and the surroundings of the Admiralty and War Office - Whitehall in general - present an appearance of an armed camp; wire entanglements, MG posts and barricades ready to be thrown into position, are at strategic points. An officer visited Sloane Court the other day and inspected Pat Hodgson's flat which is at the corner commanding four roads near Chelsea Barracks and Chelsea Hospital in order to see what field of fire was possible from the windows.

The iron rails are fast disappearing from the Parks. With the German armies almost in Paris, Londoners looked strained and anxious and there were not many light-hearted people in the streets. And yet Vincent Massey said that in the last two days there seemed a spirit of greater confidence in official circles than two weeks ago. If it is so, I cannot imagine why.

Gamelin was described by a high French official as resembling a medical man who is good at diagnosis. He told the government that the Germans might break through on the Belgian-French frontier. But he is not a good surgeon. He was quite incapable of doing anything about it. He was surrounded by useless generals, contemporaries of his at his Military College, and was unwilling to get rid of them. Depending on the power of defence he was lulled into a false sense of security, enjoyed his special train and all the fruits of being Generalissimo, without being prepared to shoulder the responsibilities and especially the unpleasant responsibilities.

Kenneth de Courcy,[3] of the Imperial Policy Group, informs me that there is a considerable body of opinion in England in favour of making a 'Treaty of

[1] Rt. Hon. Alexander Henry Hardinge (1894-1960). Pte. Sec. to Edward VIII and to George VI, 1936-43; PC (1936), GCB (1943); Succ. Baron Hardinge of Penshurst (1943).
[2] Unity Mitford (1914-48). Fourth daughter of Baron Redesdale; an admirer of Hitler and the Nazis.
[3] Kenneth de Courcy (b.1909). Journalist; publisher of numerous semi-official foreign affairs digests.

Amiens', *reculer pour mieux sauter*. England's fortunes were low in 1802 but within 14 years she had conquered Napoleon. If Hitler refused to accept reasonable terms suggested by the USA, then the USA would come into the war. It is possible that France may give in and a new French Government formed which will be hostile to Great Britain and, under someone like Laval,[1] friendly to Germany. Is it in actual fact possible to continue if France is out? Hitler has threatened to annihilate the English. If his aeroplanes lay flat huge parts of England including our aircraft and munitions factories, can we go on? And what about the general starvation of Europe which is possible anyhow owing to the failure of the crops? The protagonists of the 'Treaty of Amiens' maintain that if Hitler's army is once demobilised he will never be able to mobilise it again.

Personally I think the whole proposal is fantastic but it shows the way some minds are working and should be recorded.

Notes by Tony, 19 June. Trinity Term at Oxford

During the summer term at Oxford, which is now over, there has been an increasing feeling among the undergraduates - at any rate most of those I know - that life at the University was just a farce when men no more than a year older, and sometimes even our contemporaries, were fighting in Flanders or Normandy. 'I was at Oxford during the war'; that is hardly the answer one would like to give to questioners afterwards. Something however was done to give us national service. Those of us who were members of the OTC, by signing our names on a list, became Local Defence Volunteers.

The first time we went out, a platoon from two colleges were on from 8 till 12 midnight, another from 12 till 4, and again another from 4 till 8 a.m. A dozen of us, mostly from Christ Church, were on from 12 till 4 a.m on 24 May. We were provided with army overalls and carried our gas masks. There were only enough rifles for one between three. We all carried batons; these were wooden, and apparently weapons of offence used by bullers. I doubt they would have been much use as one man hit a tree with his baton and the latter promptly broke! Our task was to patrol the labs - particularly the Clarendon Laboratory - and protect them from fifth columnists. We were of course frightfully keen, but nothing happened. The hour of dawn towards the end of our four hours, was enlivened for

---

[1] Pierre Laval (1883-1945). French PM and For. Minister, 1935-6. Strong advocate of peace with Germany; Numerous offices under Vichy régime; Executed 1945.

me by conversations with two bobbies who were doing the rounds. We deplored the state of the war and thought that the Froggies had let us down. The previous evening the news had come through of the Germans reaching Boulogne.

Notes by Teresa Brown (formerly Teresa Brodie), 20 June

My cousin (a Lieutenant in the RAOC) having been in northern France since January, was with the 1st. Recovery Section to go into Belgium when Hitler invaded that country. They were met by a tightly packed line of refugees on foot and on all manner of vehicles, and he cannot forget the horror of seeing Nazi bombers descending to tree-top height to machine-gun these helpless men, women and children.

They proceeded into Belgium as far as Louvain and soon after began to retreat. Passing through Brussels (not very greatly damaged) they had a slight gas attack scare, when the sewers were blown up and a great cloud of black vapour enveloped them. As they retreated they had to forage for food and my cousin became an expert pig slaughterer and chicken killer at the farms and chateaux on the way.

When the news of Leopold's capitulation came it was not wholly a surprise as there were many whispers and rumours. But the following morning Jerry appeared in large numbers on the opposite bank of the river where they had paused, and they hastened on, having had no sleep or rest for five nights. Then came the order 'destroy all vehicles', and that nearly broke Geoff's heart. Their travelling workshops cost £6,000 each to equip and they had two of these in the most perfect order, besides all the other vehicles and his own private Morris. They ditched the large lorries, broke up all the mechanisms and fired them. His last job was to pile all his private belongings and papers into his small car, pour petrol over the lot and set fire to it. He estimates they destroyed about £75,000 worth of perfect mechanical equipment.

At Dunkirk the men were ordered to break their rifles and throw them into the sea. They were ordered to embark with their men at once. When the men had been taken on board there was no room for the officers, so he and his Captain remained behind to help the other officers - they were few. They were on the beach for 36 hours, wet through, during which time remnants of the Belgian army panicked along the beach and swamped the boats, so that our men were forced to fire on them. The whole time they were bombed and machine-gunned and constantly had to run and scatter about the beach. He got off at last, swimming for the boat fully equipped, and reached Dover in his birthday suit at 5 a.m. on Thursday 30th May. Only three officers and 80 men returned out of his unit of 400. They left Dunkirk a complete ruin.

Notes by J.B.B., 22 June

Colonel Howe of the Buffs, the OC of the Infantry Training Centre at the Barracks, and CO of all troops in Canterbury, dined with us last night, a serious man and a bachelor. He was a prisoner of war in Germany from May 1915 to November 1918. He has built up the vast training centre at Canterbury. There are usually about 1,200 young militia men there, 300 or 400 coming in and an equal number going out after about four months intensive training, when they are drafted either to various new battalions of the Buffs now being formed, or to other regiments. When the *Blitzkrieg* started on 10th May all training stopped and his young men were put to guard road blocks and other strategic points in Kent. But now that the LDV has taken over most of this work his lads can have their nights in bed and carry on with their training as usual by day.

Col. Howe said that the 5th. Buffs, which was the second Territorial Battalion (the 4th. Buffs being the original Territorials) was not well officered when the war broke out. For the first three months of the war they were guarding various points in Kent. Then the senior officers were changed and the battalion was sent to France at the end of November, to train in a back area. They were in the neighbourhood of Arras when the Germans reached them, and were without proper equipment as it was never contemplated they would be in action. They fell back towards Boulogne and suffered heavy casualties. Some got back from Dunkirk but hundreds of these young, untrained boys were killed or taken prisoner.

One cannot help asking why, in view of the immense increase of young soldiers, the government did not use the services of the hundreds of ex-regular officers (aged 40-55) who have experience of the last war to officer the new battalions. It is true that such officers are not familiar with all the new forms of mechanised warfare, but they could have picked this up fairly quickly, and they would have at least provided that stiffening of discipline and judgement which young officers cannot be expected to possess. Take for instance 'Puggy' Howes[1] who only left the army two or three years ago - an admirable soldier, efficient, calm in a tight place and used to command. In September 1939 he put his name down for service of any kind and said he was prepared to drop his present rank of Brigadier and become a Colonel, or Major, or Captain if necessary. He was placed in the Colonels' Pool, and in April was appointed to take charge of records at Canterbury. A foolish waste of admirable material.

Notes by J.B.B., 24 June

Today the armistice terms imposed by Germany on France are published in full in the morning papers. The armistice was signed at Compiègne at 5.50 p.m. on Saturday 22 June, and the French delegates immediately left for Rome to conclude an armistice with Italy. Yesterday on the 9 a.m. news a statement by the PM was read, branding the terms as so humiliating that it was incredible France could have accepted them. All day yesterday we speculated as to what the precise terms were, and the future of the French fleet and air force seemed to be mostly on people's lips, and then on the 9 p.m. news we heard. But it is only today the twenty four points as published in the press can be clearly studied.

There can be no question that to win the war Germany must decisively defeat Great Britain, and to defeat Great Britain it clearly necessary for Germany to invade and to occupy this country. There is much speculation at the moment as to whether Hitler will attempt an invasion within the next few weeks, or whether he must first reorganise his army, navy and air force, and restore his depleted supplies of petrol and oil - in other words will he leave us alone for two or three months, packed tight in our little island, while he goes for Romania and then when all is ready strike his final blow on England in September? Bombing, no doubt, will greatly increase whatever happens. That we must expect. But will actual invasion be deferred? Hitler has announced his intention of making peace in London by 15th August, and so far he has kept to schedule. And every week he postpones attacking this island our power to resist increases. All our estimates of his lack of petrol and other essential stores seem to have been wrong, so perhaps he possesses everything necessary to strike at once. Certainly there has been no serious bombing of railways and ports, administrative centres such as Whitehall,

---

[1] Brigadier Sidney Howes (d. 1961). Comm. 6th. Cavalry Brigade, TA, 1934-38.

factories, or aerodromes so far. On Tuesday and Wednesday last, about 100 German planes bombed this country - on the Tuesday the area attacked was from Yorkshire to Kent and there were civilian casualties in Cambridgeshire, and on the Wednesday bombs were dropped on the North East Coast, Yorkshire and as far west as South Wales. It seems as if the Germans wish to demonstrate at this stage that no area in England is safe. It is only recently that children have been evacuated from east and south-east coast towns to Cornwall, Devon and Wales. We had air raid alarms both nights here; bombs fell on Sheppey on this second occasion and the windows of this house rattled and the house shook five separate times.

It is known that the enemy have assembled 800 to 1,000 motor boats at Boulogne and the Channel ports, also a large number of flat-bottomed boats each holding eight twenty-ton tanks and 200 men and drawing only four and a half feet of water. A night with poor visibility and a calm sea would be necessary and any attempts at landing would probably be made at the same time under cover of a devastating bombing attack. The Navy cannot guarantee being able to stop the enemy landing at every point from Scotland down the East Coast of England and along the South Coast to Wales. There is also the possibility of an attempt on Ireland. We in the Local Defence Volunteers have been told that we may have to assist the local troops in dealing with the enemy landing small groups of tanks at different points, and in that event must do our best to fight a delaying action: our main forces would not move until it was certain where the real attack was being made. There are a number of naval guns on lorries in this corner of Kent ready to go to the threatened point, but it is obvious these must not go rushing off after a few stray tanks when the principal attack is being exploited elsewhere. Roads and bridges are mined all over this part of Kent and I presume on the East Coast too. The sea front at Whitstable is stiff with gun emplacements. The shores all round Kent are covered with barbed wire five feet high. Strong points constructed of concrete guard strategic positions where the coastal road to Thanet leaves the Faversham-London road.

During past years parties of Hitler Jugend boys have been entertained in East Kent. They have been shown the Cathedral and have toured the country. Many of them carried cameras. It is quite possible that parachute troops may actually be these boys.

There has been a general rounding up of fascists in England and

Canterbury has provided her quota. The fascist HQ was in St Margaret's Street. A bus driver, Smith-Elvy, was one of the leaders, also a pub-keeper in Union Street; these are now arrested and detained. The LDV lads say there are a few men with fascist leanings around still - notably a milkman who wears a dirk with the swastika on its hilt (no doubt nonsense, but typical of what is being said).

Notes by J.B.B. Guard Duty East of Canterbury, 25 June

Let me attempt an account of my experiences on the road block last night. I left this house at 8.15 p.m. and reported for duty in the Mint Yard (i.e. the main quadrangle of the King's School) at 8.30. By this time the Mint Yard is the scene of the greatest activity. Men who have been drilling since 7 p.m. are just being dismissed. Those detailed for the various guards are arriving.

Besides the road blocks the LDV is responsible for finding guards for important points in Canterbury itself, such as the Post Office, Telephone Exchange, Water Works, Power Plant, and one or two observation posts such as the Dane John. The Southern Railway guards several bridges with its own men though these are on the strength of the LDV, and the Post Office also finds some of its own guard. The LDV, with a strength of some 700 or 800 men, is divided into three 'platoons' each consisting of 200 to 250 men under a Commander and a second in command, also an officer. Each 'platoon' is divided into three sections, each section being under a Section Leader and a second in command, both of whom are officers. I belong to Section 2 in A Platoon, Mr Maple the book-binder being my Section Leader and Mr Akroyd second in command. Mr Dawton, of Amos & Dawton (the house agents), is my Platoon Commander. My sergeant is Sgt. Roberts, 'born with a rifle in his hands' as he said to me, a first class instructor, a veteran of the Great War, with the Military Medal.

On arriving in the Mint Yard I find Roberts already getting his guard together. I report. We are 10 in all, Sgt. Roberts, Cpl. Osborne, also an old soldier of the last war, and eight men. Of the eight, four of us are old soldiers, the other four young fellows. We fall in and then file into the Quartermaster's store to draw our rifles, ammunition, blankets, waterproof sheets, hurricane lamps and tin helmets. Thus equipped we fall in again and are then ordered to board one of two or three lorries standing in the Mint Yard. We climb in and a few minutes later are joined by the men of two other guards. With much laughter and swearing we are packed tight, some 30 men, sitting on the floor or perched precariously on the side, our rifles between our legs. About 9.20 we reach our road block which is at a road junction some two miles east and a little north of Canterbury. We pile out of the lorry with all our equipment and inspect the post. There are two wooden barriers covered with barbed wire (knife rests) under the hedge ready to be thrown across the road in the event of an emergency. Additional rolls of barbed wire (concertinas) stand ready against a tree to strengthen the barriers if necessary. At the top of the bank which borders the road on one side are two sandbagged emplacements offering shelter and a reasonably good field of fire for men with rifles or MGs. At the right of the road near the advanced barrier is a sandbagged rifle pit level with the road. Ten yards down the road in front of the barrier the road is mined. The bridge on the side road just north of the road junction is also mined. An army bell tent stands in a field a few yards from the road junction. First relief is posted at 9.30 p.m., and the rest of us, it being a perfect summer evening, stand round and talk. The Sergeant, who is terribly keen, puts us through some rifle drill and tells the younger members of the guard about the care of their rifles under active service conditions. About 11.30 we go into the tent and doss down. At 11.45 the orderly officer comes round, a further divertissement. And then the talk goes on though the Corporal and one or two others doze off.

I was just munching some chocolate and biscuits when, at 12.30 the siren, or rather a number of sirens from different points of the compass, shatter the evening calm. 'Turn out the guard,' shouts the Sergeant, and we all pile out of the tent. I shake the Corporal who, with a heart felt, 'Hell,' struggles to his feet. We fall in outside. 'Load and run up to the advance post and take these two young fellows with you,' says the Sergeant to me. I ram a clip into my magazine and run about 40 yards up the road and drop into the trench. Behind I can hear the barriers being placed across the two roads near their junction. One of my lads who was quite thrilled over the whole business whispered, 'There's a man coming down the road on a bicycle,' and true enough there was. So I yelled, 'Halt,' but he did not stop. I then yelled, 'Bloody well stop or I'll shoot,' whereupon he dismounted and I told him to come on. 'Only ARP,' he said, to which I replied, 'I don't care, who or what you are but you'd better stop when you're challenged.' We examined his identity card (which obviously is almost entirely useless as identification) and had a good look at him, and then shouted back to the Sergeant and the others at the barrier, 'Man coming through OK'.

After the warning sirens have ceased there is a short interval of complete calm. Then the whole countryside springs into life. Searchlights pierce the sky. The ARP posts become active and one hears shrill whistles. The bugles in the barracks at Canterbury two miles away sound the alarm for every man to get up and dress. Motor cyclists begin dashing up the roads as well as military cars. Everywhere one can hear challenging on the roads. Our planes go roaring overhead. Soon there is the sound of firing to the north and east - the Thames Estuary presumably and perhaps Margate - flashes of gunfire - a few tracer bullets. Great fingers of light stab the starlit sky - a yellow June moon stares down unconcerned. About 2 a.m. a military patrol comes by - a regular convoy consisting of officers in the leading car, then two small trucks with wireless apparatus and men with ear phones on - then a large lorry, then motor cyclists; only the first car and the rear motor cyclist have dim lights. These patrols cover the whole of East Kent every night, continually on the move.

By now things were calming down, though there was no 'all clear' signal. I sit in my post talking with the two youngsters. The Sergeant joins us and also the Corporal and we talk about the old war days and the trenches - and then about Canada - and finally about professional soccer. It grows quite cold as the dawn approaches, and we shiver. We can't smoke. At last it begins to get light. Still no 'all clear'. The dawn discloses us (as it always does) looking tired and dishevelled. By 3.30 a.m. it is full daylight. We are still on our posts. The 'all clear' goes. It is not worth turning in. The Sergeant, seeing we are cold, says, 'What about a little rifle drill?' We agree. And so, from 3.30 to 4 a.m. on a road east of Canterbury in the Year of Grace 1940 you might have seen a Sergeant and eight weary, rather bleary-eyed men going through rifle drill. At 4 a.m. we tidy up the tent, unload and inspect rifles, and shortly afterwards, in the early morning sunshine, march back to the Mint Yard, hand in our equipment, and I slip into No.16 New Dover Road just before 5 a.m.

Julian to E.C.F.B., 26 May   *Felsted*

Yesterday was a busy day for me. I managed to persuade S.A.Courtauld[1] and two other Governors to come to Felsted to discuss our possible evacuation. It proved very difficult to come to any decision, but eventually they accepted my suggestions - (1) to try and get into touch with the Home Office for advice, (2) to

---

[1] Samuel Augustine Courtauld (1865-1953). Director of Courtaulds; Chmn. of Governors, Felsted.

allow any parents who wished to take away their boys now.

Later I got on the 'phone to the regional office of the Home Office at Cambridge and they advised us to stay here, but said it would be a good thing if we had an alternative place to go to. If a real attack on England started then it might be necessary for the government to refuse to allow us to move as any place with dug-outs would be preferable to wandering along roads open to gun fire!

I then decided to open up negotiations at once by 'phone, and arranged to take Hill Court and to be allowed as much accommodation in Goodrich Court (Ross-on-Wye) as was possible. I sent two large lorries down to Goodrich this morning filled with mattresses, blankets, camp outfits and stores of food..

My darling, you see how things are - wobbly. If we go the school would be instantly taken over by the military or the government, and we should see it no more till the war was over. To have even the possibility of Goodrich and Hill Court as places to go to would give us the chance of some continuity in our school life.

If I take the school, or part of it to Ross, I shall try and get a cottage on the estate, and if you would like it I should love to have you too, although I expect you feel as safe at Chiddingstone as anywhere. The truth of the matter is there is no place in the British Isles that can be considered safe now.

Between 27 and 30 May, Julian, after consultation with his Governors, decided that the school must be moved from Felsted. He gave the boys ten days holiday. They went to their homes on 30 May with orders to reassemble in Herefordshire on 10 June.

Julian's notes on talk with Brigadier Stuart King.   *Felsted*

Brigadier J.Stuart King,[1] Deputy Engineer in Chief at GHQ, arrived in Felsted on Thursday, 30 May, having been sent down by the WO to deal with home defence against enemy attacks on the Eastern Counties. He is an old boy of Felsted and has two sons in the school. He had got out of Dunkirk the previous Sunday night - the last night the port was able to be used for evacuation of troops. Two days previously Gort had been told to diminish his staff by half, as their brains were badly needed. If the whole GHQ were to be captured or killed the loss

---

[1] Brigadier (later Lt-Gen.) Charles Stuart King (1890-1967). Engineer-in-Chief, War Office, 1941-44; Special Mission to India and SEAC, 1944; Commdt. RE, 1946-56. KBE (1945).

would be very serious. There was little bombing in Dunkirk the night he got away; there would have been much loss of life if the Germans had sent over more planes as the port was chock-a-block with troops, embarking on many kinds of vessel. There was a double line of English ambulances for two miles to the harbour, and a line of French ambulances alongside, and the rest of the road occupied by troops. A thick pall of smoke hung over the town which may have helped to keep the Germans away.

King said that originally the hope was to get about 50,000 of the BEF away, but it looked very doubtful if more than this number would ever be evacuated. Events proved him to be wrong over this, but evacuation was continued from the beaches when the port could no longer be used. He spoke warmly of the bravery and endurance of the English troops, it was well up to the best standard of the old BEF of 1914-18. Man for man we were infinitely superior to the Germans and he felt sure the Germans knew it.

Bombing was more terrifying than dangerous, especially the new kind of whistling bomb which made a shrieking noise as it came down. Anywhere 300 or 400 yards off roads and railways there was little danger from bombing as the enemy seemed always better able to strike at a road or railway in the hope of hitting transport. GHQ had escaped molestation from enemy bombing by always announcing where they were moving and then going half a mile or a mile down a side road to a farm or house, so they had been able to get some sleep on their trek northward.

King spoke of the capitulation of the Belgium army and that 48 hours before the King had given in, the Belgian army had 'chucked up the sponge', and Gort knew his left wing was undefended. King was therefore surprised to read in the press that the King of the Belgians' move was supposed to have been the first indication of the Belgian failure. GHQ had known two days before that no help was to be expected any more from the Belgians.

King himself had been responsible for seeing that every bridge and culvert in Belgium on the line of the BEF retreat had been prepared for demolition. He said that GHQ were satisfied that the reports that every one of those bridges had been blown up by our retreating troops were accurate. He had also been responsible for preparing the block ships for the harbours of Boulogne and Calais. These ships were prepared as far back as last October by the Admiralty. They had been completely filled with reinforced concrete mixed up with iron and old scrap and as far as GHQ knew both the harbours of Boulogne and Calais had been successfully blocked before the Germans captured them. It was estimated by the Admiralty that many months would elapse before the Germans would be able to clear away these obstructions.

King spoke of the magnificent training and capacity of the better German troops and said that their equipment was wonderful. The close co-operation between the German tanks and their air fire was astonishing; they never stopped to mop up a stray point which was still resisting but pressed on, flowing round enemy obstructions like the sea round sand castles, leaving to troops coming behind the job of clearing up.

Notes by J.B.B., 3 and 11 June   *Canterbury*

On Tuesday 4 June Julian arrived from Felsted at Canterbury. It was his only chance of seeing Mother and me before he settled in Herefordshire for the remainder of the summer. He had been at Goodrich for two or three nights inspecting the accommodation available at the three large houses, Goodrich Court, Hill Court, and Pencraig for the Senior School, and Canon ffrome near Ledbury for the Junior School, and had then returned to Felsted for a few nights from where he came to Canterbury.

He and I motored to Dover about 6 p.m. that evening, up past the Castle to St Margaret's Bay and so to the Dover Patrol Monument. A pall of thick black smoke drifted along the French horizon from Dunkirk and Calais entirely obscuring the coast. Immediately below the cliffs where the Monument stands, two hospital ships rode at anchor about a mile from the shore. Off Dover harbour was the strangest assortment of ships which had been and still were bringing over the BEF The evacuation was officially finished that night. There were pleasure steamers and life boats, and trawlers, and tugs, and row boats, and motor launches, and fishing smacks.

Between Canterbury and Dover there were road blocks at the Gate Inn, beyond Bridge where the road to Kingston forks right, and at Kearsney. There were also MG emplacements and trenches at various points. The fields were obstructed to prevent planes landing. On the road from Dover to Deal there was a huge in-and-out sandbagged barrier, so constructed that an East Kent bus almost got stuck in it.

Julian left after lunch on Wednesday 5 June to return to Felsted for one night and then go down to Herefordshire for the remainder of the school term.

He wrote to me on 11 June saying he was much disturbed to find that the military authorities might take over Goodrich Court as a convalescent home for officers some time in August and would I see Patrick Duff (Permanent Secretary of the Office of Works) about it. It so happened that I was meeting with Patrick Duff that Wednesday, and he was aghast at hearing that Julian had moved 420 boys into the Wye Valley area without the Office of Works knowing anything about it. If the government were evacuated from London this area (Worcester, Gloucester, Hereford) would become one of the most congested districts in England, and incidentally if the Germans knew (as they certainly would) that the government had migrated to this part of England it would immediately become extremely unhealthy. Patrick could not have been more charming about it, but said he simply could not promise that Felsted would not be turned out if he had to move the government. Every house, every cottage, every bed in these three counties was earmarked. He could not understand how Julian had managed to move there without his knowing, but it was obviously the result of a slip up between the War Office and the Office of Works, and as this was not Julian's fault he would do his best not to disturb him. Naturally I emphasised the fact that if a great public school like Felsted had to make two moves it would, quite apart from the expense, practically break up the school. I wrote two letters to Julian, one to show to his Governors, the other telling him the extreme delicacy of the situation.

Geoffrey to E.C.F.B., 23 June   *Aberdeen*

I think the Archbishop of Canterbury is 'finished', and ought to resign and let William Temple[1] take his place. This is not a time for old men, or men belonging to a past world, to be ruling in the Church or state. His utterances cut no ice and are obviously those of a disillusioned and brain-weary mind. William's on the other hand are as vigorous and as relevant to present needs as ever.

P.S. Bevin[2] is the man it seems to me. Why had the Labour party never made use of him before? If Churchill died or dropped out, I'd make him PM.

---

[1] Most Rev. and Rt. Hon. William Temple (1881-1944). Bishop of Manchester, 1921-29; Archbishop of York, 1929-42; Archbishop of Canterbury, 1942-44. PC (1929).
[2] Rt. Hon. Ernest Bevin (1881-1951). MP (Lab) Wandsworth C., 1940-50, Woolwich E., 1950-51; Gen. Sec. TGWU, 1921-40; Min. of Labour and Nat. Service, 1940-45; For. Sec., 1945-51. PC (1940).

Pat Hodgson to J.B.B., 26 June.   *5, Sloane Court, S.W.3*

Many thanks for your letter. Your LDV life is strenuous but it must be interesting meeting all those men: You have probably heard that it has been decided by the powers that be that the whole force shall be run by the Territorial County Association. It is a wise decision, but as far as I personally am concerned involves the end of my job I fancy. In the meantime we work longish hours and yesterday received a lot more rifles for issue to factories, etc. Still no uniforms to speak of and the supply of armlets has given out, causing much dissatisfaction.

I had no idea that the duties of the LDV were to be so militant. How can you fight any action with such limited equipment And how many men of your men have ever fired a rifle? I do hope Pownall,[1] Ironside's No. 2, will get a move on quickly. My own feeling is that if there is to be any attempt at invasion it will come very soon. Hitler has promised his people peace in August and a 'Peace Rally' in September at Nuremberg. He must beat us first and cannot afford to delay. I expect to hear of his seizing the Southern Irish ports any day.

If we don't get the French Fleet the outlook is dangerous The blockade and the position in the Mediterranean will be gravely disturbed as we relied on France for the latter. Moreover Japan is being troublesome. We have no ships to speak of in the Pacific as she well knows; but if we don't stand up to her we shall alienate Russia and the USA. That is the Foreign Office view. It is all becoming more and more chaotic and difficult.

Geoffrey to E.C.F.B., 30 June   *Aberdeen*

The whole of this evacuation scheme (sending children to USA, Canada, etc.) seems to me quite wrong and simply a sign of panic. At any rate as far as our children are concerned nothing would induce me to exile them from parents, home and country thousands of miles away to be with perfect strangers (and in a damp hot tropical region like St Louis!) when, however serious the air raids may be, the worst of them are likely to be over in twelve months for reasons stated by the Secretary of State for War, and even as it is, and taking them at their worst, the casualties they would cause among children are not likely to be anything like so numerous as those due to motor car accidents in times of profound peace.

---

[1] Maj-Gen. Sir Henry Pownall (1887-1966). Dir. of Military Operations, 1938-9; Chief of Staff, BEF, 1939-40; Insp-Gen. Home Guard, 1940. Lt-Gen. (1942); C-in-C, Persia and Iraq, 1943; Chief of Staff, SE Asia, 1943-44. KBE (1940), KCB (1945).

Of course, if I did by any chance want to evacuate the children across the Atlantic, I'd send them to Canada rather than the USA, and preferably to Toronto. But a woman friend of ours here, who wants to go at once to Canada to a friend who has offered to put her up for the duration, can't get a berth by love or money, nor, she is told, will any be available on any ship till the end of July at the earliest.

The war, in my opinion, has now reached the stage when we possess the offensive and, what is more, are making use of it: i.e. the offensive in the air, in which we have already won complete moral ascendancy over the Germans, and shall soon add to it numerical superiority also: in other words, we have, or shortly shall have, a command of the air as complete and effectively in operation as our command of the sea. On land too, in the only region in which fighting is now going on, we likewise possess (and are using) the offensive, i.e. in Africa, against Italy. The simple fact is that when we are in actual contact with the enemy on sea, air or land, we possess the offensive, are making full use of it, and are beating the enemy. Every day that passes our strength is increasing relative to his, in ships, aeroplanes, manpower and munitions. It it is possible for him to invade this country without command of the sea, and without command of the air, by parity of reasoning it must be much more possible for us, who possess complete command of the former and shall soon possess complete command of the latter, to invade France at any point on her enormous coast line which we decide to be most suitable for the purpose, when he will have - I mean Germany will have - the further disadvantage of having to fight in a country whose inhabitants will use every opportunity of assisting us and ham-stringing our enemies.

I am quite happy about the future. I think we are doing admirably and our tails are up and morale is as firm as a rock. And as for the invasion of England, apart from a few isolated landings here and there - which would do us good - I shan't believe in it till I see it.

Notes by J.B.B., 30 June

I was on guard duty all last night at the Gate Inn road block at the junction of the Old and New Dover roads. There is an MG post there - also another sand-bagged firing position on the roof of a low-lying wing of the inn, as well as a trench badly sited in the orchard to the south of the road. The barrier consists of two huge concrete pipes turned on end and filled with concrete. There are also deep holes in the road (now covered with wooden lids) into which huge steel beams would be placed end-wise when the need arises

I got back to No. 16 at 5 a.m. and went to bed for two hours or so. At 9 a.m. I was on parade at the Mint Yard for the GOC.'s inspection. We waited about, being stood at attention and then at ease in turn, army fashion, for three quarters of an hour, and then marched to the Dane John, when we formed up. As there are only about 50 rifles, a special platoon of men with rifles had been formed. I was in this special platoon, and we gave some extra time to drill last week. Lt. General A.L. Forster DSO[1] arrived at 10.35 - tall and distinguished-looking. We presented arms very creditably I thought. Then the General, with James and the platoon commander concerned, passed slowly down the ranks. I was in the rear rank and James very wrongly told the General I was 'the son of the late Canon Bickersteth'. The General said to me, 'Was your Father Vicar of Lewisham?' 'Yes, Sir.' 'Well, I met him and your Mother in Ceylon many years ago. Do you live in Canterbury?' 'No, Sir, in Canada.' 'Will you join up with the Canadians over here?' 'No, Sir, not allowed to, Sir, can only join them in Canada, Sir.' 'What was your regiment? 'The Royal Dragoons, Sir.' Altogether much too long and embarrassing a conversation - I standing stiffly at attention like a stuffed monkey, eyes front and I hope not moving a muscle of my body. When the inspection was over we broke ranks and sat on the grass and the General talked to us. He congratulated us on our turn-out and drill and spoke of our duties - guarding road blocks until taken over by the regulars, dealing with parachutists, stray tanks, etc; promised uniforms very shortly and also rifles from the USA. We then marched past and back to the Precincts. As we passed along under the old city walls our rifles at the sling and whistling old war songs I wondered whether in all their long history those fortifications had looked down on a stranger scene.

Three weeks with the 44th (Home Counties) Division by Eric Duncannon;[2] written at J.B.B.'s request

In the afternoon of 10 May, the siren sounded over the modern red brick

---

[1] Lt.-Gen. Alfred Forster, RM (d. 1963). Asst. Dir. Naval Intellignece, 1943-46; Comm. RM, Chatham, 1936-39; ADC to King, 1939; Member of Church Council, 1940-41.

[2] Eric Duncannon (1913-93). Succ. Father as 10th. Earl Bessborough (1956); keen actor; contested Islington W (Con), 1935; L. of Nations High Commission for Refugees, 1936-39; ADC to Comm. Canadian Corps, 1940; First Sec. British Embassy, Paris, 1944-47; Jt. Parl. U-Sec. Education, 1964; Member of European Parliament, 1972-7.

building of the town hall of Estaires, five miles from the Belgian frontier. For three weeks the Division had been occupying a defensive position on the Belgian frontier, well consolidated by a series of blockhouses designed to receive anti-tank guns firing along the anti-tank ditch partially completed. However when the sirens sounded on this occasion the flag had fallen and these comparatively well developed defences were abandoned. The Germans had invaded Holland and Belgium and the 1st and 2nd British Corps were ordered to advance on to the river Dyle around Louvain and in front of Brussels, and the 44th Division in the 3rd Corps into a reserve position on the River Escaut with a front including Syngem, Oudenarde, and Kerdove. These advances were made in accordance with a plan which had been made some months previously.

On this hot afternoon only a few German bombers were sent over Estaires before the Divisional operation order had been issued to units. One bomber was brought down by a Bren gun from an RASC unit, which though well behind the lines thus drew the first blood in the Division. The advance of the mechanised columns of the Division, amounting to at least 2,500 vehicles in all, was timed to start that afternoon. The 150 vehicles attached to Divisional Headquarters were fitted into the march tables, so that the head of the column might pass the starting point at about midnight.

The first assembly area in Belgium was at Wervicq where we were extravagantly welcomed by the Belgians. Not for long, however, were we to indulge in their fine flattery. The following afternoon we proceeded to take up our position on the Escault where we had four apparently peaceful days, uninterrupted save for the drone of high flying German reconnaissance planes whose thorough work was only later appreciated. Meanwhile the 1st and 2nd British Corps were fighting desperately on the river Dyle in defence of Louvain and Brussels. But they were soon to withdraw from this line. The French 7th army under General Giraud[1] had failed to join them on the left, and the bridges over the Meuse along the Belgo-German frontier had not been blown due to the successful efforts of fifth columnists who had cut fuses. In consequence the Belgian Army was retreating from Namur in front of German armoured columns which they did not dare engage.

---

[1] Gen. Henri Giraud (1879-1949). Comm. Fr. 7th. and later 9th. Armies (1940). Captured and escaped in 1942 to become civil and military chief in Algeria. Favoured by the US as Free French leader preferable to de Gaulle.

While the BEF made its way across Belgium, probably in accordance with German designs, and in company with two French divisions, extracted by General Gamelin from the Ardennes, the German High Command launched the full force of its attack with eight or nine armoured divisions of tanks through the Ardennes, now only lightly held by the French, towards Sedan. The German penetration was effected with such speed that the gap created was never again closed. They swept up through Douai, GHQ at Arras, Amiens, and St Omer with no substantial opposition. The battle of the 'bulge' was fought, lost, and the 1st and 2nd British Corps were ordered to withdraw from the River Dyle to a line extending roughly from the right of the 44th Division on the Escaut in a south westerly direction. The 44th were, so to speak, the northern pivot on the new line. The Belgian Army withdrew from Namur to our south, swung up behind us northwards, and were supposed to take up a position on our left on the Escaut.

It may be of historical interest to note here that any reference to the Belgian HQ tended to provoke discreetly disparaging remarks from the Corps Staff Officers as to King Leopold's ability as Commander-in-Chief. Though the latter had, it appeared, a well-trained team of staff officers, I gathered that they were frequently not consulted and that no one could prevent the amateur strategist from taking independent and somewhat impulsive decisions. Perhaps also his chief of staff obeyed the King's orders almost too readily. In the light of Leopold's subsequent defection it seems likely that this was the case. Even if the King gave no order to the effect, his Chief of Staff should have informed British GHQ in good time of the intention to capitulate. Such an action might have made the difference between the loss or salvation of 350,000 lives in the Allied cause. Indeed, it seemed to me at the time that it was only the Germans' omission to occupy territory already ceded to them that enabled the armies of the north to withdraw unopposed to Dunkirk. In fact the withdrawal of the 44th Division was covered by the French Cavalry Corps.

Despite the absence of tanks and dive bombers the effectiveness of the German attack on us south of Oudenarde cannot be gainsaid, although our troops were made to withstand it for four days. Its effectiveness was due in the first place to their accurate artillery fire, continuously assisted by spotting planes unopposed by our fighters, which were all being employed elsewhere (probably further south in an effort to stem the main German air and tank attack through Sedan). The German artillery was consequently able to register fire on nearly all the cross-roads, Brigade headquarters and battery positions in our divisional area. Retaliation by counter battery fire was impossible owing to our having no artillery observation planes whatever and no high ground on which posts could be established. Secondly, the Germans crossed the river at one point south of Petegem with extraordinary rapidity. All the bridges had been blown up by our engineers, but unfortunately the water level was reported to have fallen two or three feet in as many days and the Germans had scarcely to use the rubber boats which they had brought up to the bank. Many of them displayed great gallantry in stripping their clothes and wading across the river with their weapons held above their heads. A number undoubtedly filtered into Oudenarde where in some cases they put on civilian clothes, Belgian, French or British uniforms and advanced towards our lines either in the guise of friendly refugees or as comrades in arms. As soon as they were able to entice our men to raise their heads from their section posts they would fall flat on their stomachs and use their Tommy guns with disastrous effect on our troops who were hardly expecting such deception.

After two days of fighting the Germans were able to get their artillery across the river and from then on it seemed doubtful whether we would be able to hold the position. Our old Divisional HQ at Reseghem and Brigade HQ were heavily shelled. Our right front was turned and the enemy infiltrated along our right divisional boundary and on the third day launched a heavy attack against our neighbour on the right, the 4th British Division. On the fourth day the shelling became more persistent and accurate until we were finally ordered by the 3rd Corps to withdraw to a position facing south with a front inclusive of Courtrai and Menin. We had not occupied that position for more than 18 hours before fairly. reliable reports intimated that the spearhead of the German attack in this sector was directed against and had nearly reached our left flank at Courtrai. Having been fighting hard for some five days and on the move for more than ten, the Division was ordered to retire to a rest area at Quesnoy near Lille.

Both on the withdrawal from the River Escaut and from the Courtrai-Menin front, our lines were supposed to have been taken over by the Belgians, but it is very doubtful whether they fought any rearguard actions whatever. They were always hard on our heels and followed us closely in their two withdrawals. We were to hand over the Courtrai-Menin front at 2 a.m. the following morning but at midnight 3rd Corps HQ telephoned to say that GHQ might want us to do another job, and that we would not be able to settle down at Quesnoy. In the meantime however we were to complete as far as possible our move to the rest area and we would be informed of our ultimate destination when we reached Quesnoy the following morning.

By this time definite orders regarding 'the other job' had been received. We were to take up a line facing west between Hazebrouck and Merville evidently in the hope of checking the scythe movement of German armoured divisions. By this time our troops had had no sleep for about seven days and vain protests were made at this effort to throw us into a line again at such short notice. In fact owing to the difficulties in assembling the units disregarding stragglers altogether, our move towards the new front, to which previously our backs had been turned, was delayed by about ten hours. Moreover disturbing reports, which subsequently proved inaccurate, to the effect that St Venant and Merville were already occupied by the Germans and that Cassel was beleaguered, made it necessary for the Division, without consulting Corps HQ, to revise the line which it was originally intended we should take up. We occupied Strazeele and the Forest of Nieppe and were able to advance westwards some distance beyond these areas. Three or four days fighting followed during which we were able to deal successfully with minor German tank penetrations. Finally however we had to withdraw to the Strazeele - Neufberquin/Estaires road simultaneously with the collapse of the British 2nd Division on our left. In fact, the General commanding this division informed us that night with complete *sang froid* that he was out of touch with the French on his left facing south and that owing to heavy German attacks his division had in effect ceased to exist. By then news had reached us of the Belgian capitulation and the Allied governments' intention to withdraw all the northern armies within the perimeter of Dunkirk. This news was not confirmed by 3rd corps HQ with whom we were temporarily out of touch. Nevertheless, the Commander of the 2nd Division decided to order his troops back to Dunkirk. This example was followed by the brigadier commanding our left brigade group, which had not received many casualties, without reference (as far as I could make out at the time) to Division HQ. Despite this complete opening of our left flank our General decided to hold out as long as possible with our other two now considerably depleted brigade groups. Indeed, assuming that we had been cut off from Dunkirk, the only course open was to fight to the last man. Consequently the whole of the division, less the left brigade group, held on until it was virtually surrounded. A promise of support from the two French light mechanised divisions with tanks did not come up to expectations and finally, after jettisoning the greater part of our transports, equipment and those guns which had not been abandoned on the Escaut, we made our way by night, the majority of us on foot, to the Mont-des-Cats where it was intended we should fight another desperate rearguard action during the day and continue our journey to Dunkirk the following night.

Meanwhile, definite orders had come through from Corps, tardily it is true, to the effect that we should withdraw at once to an assembly area within the Dunkirk perimeter. In view however of the Belgian capitulation several hours previously, and news of the German advancing eastwards through Steenwoorde and Godewaersvelde, the reasonable assumption that we had been cut off developed into an apparent certainty. Our General therefore nobly decided to hold the 'garrison' until relief came. But relief was unlikely, as we guessed that every other division in the BEF had already arrived, or was about to arrive, within the Dunkirk perimeter. Few of us wished to stay on the Mont-des-Cats, though the romantic nature of the General's decision to hold out in the monastery was fully appreciated. However I think most of us hoped against all reasonable hope that a way was still left open to Dunkirk and felt that we should take it while we could. But there were of course no good grounds for such optimism.

The earnest desire to withdraw to Dunkirk was even more strongly accentuated when the following morning we were subjected to very heavy shell fire and dive bombing. Nearly two-thirds of the Division were closely packed on the hill around the monastery. Advance parties had arrived on the Mont-des-Cats the previous afternoon. The main body marched there at night arriving at about 4 a.m. Five hours were spent in preparing the defensive position by which time the German shells and bombs began to burst around us with such devastating effect that at 10.45 a.m., after a lengthy conference with brigadiers, brigade majors and COs, the General was persuaded to withdraw the Division from the position under heavy fire from the German artillery and trench mortars. The remainder of our transport and reserve provisions were abandoned and we set out on foot by devious routes in a north-easterly direction towards Poperinghe.

During the first part of the journey we were seriously harassed by trench mortar fire which caused a certain number of casualties, in addition to the men we had already lost by remaining on the Mont-des-Cats. By some miracle, however, our advance north-east back into Belgium was unopposed and after an hour's halt outside Poperinghe where we were twice machine-gunned and dive bombed from the air, we trudged our way north west towards Bergues.

In the course of this march we saw for the first time the full fury of the destruction wrought by the men of the BEF on their transport, arms and equipment. For thirty miles around Dunkirk the roads were choked with abandoned vehicles and guns making the roads impassable for those who still remained to come. On all sides were blazing lorries and the dead horses of French artillery and supply columns. In some cases this transport had been abandoned deliberately, in others voluntarily after heavy machine-gunning by enemy bombers. Such havoc can never before have been seen on any battlefield, such waste of stores and equipment never before contemplated. The best army in the world was abandoning the finest equipment ever made to the encircling armies of the Bosche. Moreover that night as some of our men reached the beaches and lay down exhausted in the sand, the process of exploding all the petrol dumps around Dunkirk was begun. In this historic withdrawal it can be said that the whole of the BEF was virtually disarmed. All that remained to be done was to evacuate the men from the twelve mile stretch of beach between Dunkirk and La Panne.

When we reached the beaches many thousands of men, particularly those towards the eastern end around Bray Dunes, had been on the beaches at least two or three days with very little food, for which we searched in vain. It took us three days to evacuate the majority of our men under heavier shell fire than dive bombing, and it is doubtful whether evacuation could have been delayed longer. We were at the mercy of our own fleet and merchant navy which strove under the most difficult conditions to embark in somewhat irregular fashion the 350,000 men comprising the Allied armies in the north. The final accomplishment of this feat might have been accelerated had the organisation of the embarkation been controlled by the high command. As it was the men of each division were directed to a very approximate area on the beach and had to wait the arrival of ships opposite that area. In many cases however the areas chosen on the beach did not coincide with the most convenient points of embarkation, due in some cases to tide and the contours of the beaches, and in others to the presence of wrecks in the vicinity. Ships opposite one division area might therefore wait for a day or two before embarkation could be effected in any large numbers, whereas more recent arrivals at other points along the beach where embarkation was less difficult were able to board their ships almost immediately. As a result many men were able to embark at once on arrival, whereas others had to lie on the beach or queue up in the water for up to five days without food, during which time embarkation was proceeding continuously and fairly rapidly from the jetty at Dunkirk. This of course was not made generally known and the risk of an uncontrolled movement towards Dunkirk avoided. The jetty, which was already under fire, provided a tempting target for machine-gunning and bombing from the air. At least a hundred experienced staff officers under central control with motor-cycles were needed to organise the embarkation. In fact I believe barely half a dozen were sent out from Wellington Barracks.

Much might be written of the organisation on the beach. Not, however, knowing exactly what the situation was it is difficult to make any useful comments on it, nor suggestions as to what further efforts to control embarkation might have been made. Owing to the need for information, and the feeling on our part of the beach that the situation there might not be appreciated by the authorities, I was lent a small Morris and proceeded towards Dunkirk in the hope of either finding our own General or other staff officers of higher formations. On the way I was asked to give a lift to a French Captain to show him that most of the French were at the Dunkirk end of the beach and that they were not supposed to stay around Bray Dunes. I took the French Captain and one of his subalterns in the car. The former told me that he had the address of *Amiral Nord* and he wanted to report there. I said I would try and get him there and make enquiries for myself as to who was responsible for our embarkation and where their headquarters were.

We went to the end of the beach, but found it was impossible to get the car off it on to the road to Dunkirk. So we returned to Malo-les-Bains, where the French Captain and I left the car in charge of the French subaltern. We borrowed a side-car motorcycle from a French Corps HQ in Malo and proceeded to Dunkirk. On the main cross-roads with the monument on the eastern outskirts of Dunkirk, our motorcycle 'conked out' just when the German artillery was registering on the cross-roads. Shells were bursting all around us and one just above us knocked the French Captain and the driver off the cycle and wounded them mortally. The motorcycle itself was flattened out, but in some miraculous way I was only slightly hit by a ricochet off the road. More shells burst nearby and in a minute there were twelve men lying around me badly wounded. They were all French soldiers. I managed to find two unwounded French soldiers who helped me to load up the casualties into an abandoned 30 cwt lorry which fortunately still functioned and I was soon joined by a French marine who knew the neighbourhood, and together we eventually found the casualty clearing station. Having unloaded the French wounded, I went round to the British side of the hospital which was just about to be evacuated, managed to obtain a tin hat and finally transport to take me back to Malo and the car on the beach. On the way we called in at the sub-area HQ where an officer on the staff suggested I should embark that night (Thursday 30 May). His men were all going to board a hospital ship. A liaison officer from 3rd Corps informed me that my General had already embarked the night before. Despite this I felt I had to return to our divisional area on the beach. When I returned to the point on the beach opposite Malo where the car had been left I found the French subaltern was still guarding it. I told him of the probable death of his Captain and he decided not to return towards Bray Dunes but to remain with some other Frenchmen he had met who had just reached Malo. On return to our division area I found our report centre had been shelled, and that it had moved down to a coastguard station. Embarkation from that point was proceeding at a very slow pace and all that night (Thursday 30 May) only four lifeboats loads got off.

Now I had ascertained from several sources near Dunkirk that embarkation at that end from the Mole, and the beaches near the jetty, was proceeding rapidly and in the latter place and saw for myself the men being marched in only very shallow water towards the lifeboats and being rowed out to waiting ships in much calmer water than we experienced the following day. I therefore reported all this to the Divisional Commander and advised him to move west, but he said that while I was away it had been suggested the division should embark at Bray Dunes. The following afternoon most of our men were marched thither, though I remained behind to collect some unattached stragglers belonging to various units. I embarked these men on to a destroyer and we arrived at Dover that night. We entrained at once and reached a reception camp at Warminster early in the morning of Saturday 1 June, exactly three weeks after we had moved up into Belgium. They were the longest three weeks in my life, and the red brick towers of the Town Hall at Estaires seemed to belong to the remote past.

Dictated at Stansted, 4 June.

July

Notes by J.B.B., 3 July

Mother and I went to the bank about her securities and also about the possible moving of her current account in the event of Canterbury being evacuated. We also took away Mother's despatch case containing her jewels, as these she would wish to take with her if she were ordered to leave Canterbury. Monier told me on the telephone yesterday that if Canterbury was evacuated nobody would be allowed to use the roads, but a special train or trains will be provided and the evacuees would go to the place the train took them to, and would have to stay there. Mother and I however have not changed our decision that she should remain here unless ordered to move.

I was at the barracks again this afternoon on the LMG. (i.e. Bren). As I was bicycling back again the sirens sounded, and nearly everybody in the streets ran for cover. Traffic seemed to stop and the streets became empty. Air raid wardens and their assistants proceeded to their posts and the fire engines started off on their patrolling of their allotted areas in the town. I was interested in seeing this procedure, and bicycled about for a quarter of an hour watching precisely what happened. Being in uniform nobody stopped me.

Bombs were dropped at Bekesbourne (an attempt to hit the aerodrome). Two civilians working near were killed and several wounded. Norah, who was at home at Bridge, saw the plane which cruised about in and out of the clouds quite low. Other bombs were dropped near Lyminge, and this morning bombs were dropped at Wye.

4 July

Personally I am doubtful about the wisdom of this migration of children to Canada. Quite apart from the impression of panic it will surely make on Canadians and Americans, it separates children from their parents, involves a risky voyage, and prevents the children from taking part in the crisis which awaits the country. Spencer Leeson's[1] letter in *The Times* is essentially sound. Such schemes as there are really apply to the children of well-to-do parents. It is good stock to send to Canada - no doubt about that - and from the point of view of Empire solidarity

---

[1] Rt. Rev. Spencer Leeson (1892-1956). Headmaster of Winchester, 1935-46; Canon of Chichester Cathedral, 1940-9; Bishop of Peterborough, 1949-56.

may have far-reaching results. But after the first few weeks of rapture I can see many recriminations arising - the children expecting English conditions and not finding them, and their parents not understanding that Canada is a 'foreign' country; their hosts becoming tired of their small guests, many of whom will not fit into their new homes. Moreover the numbers are a mere drop in the bucket.

I lunched at the Travellers' with Tommy Lascelles.[1] The streets round Whitehall at lunch time are an astonishing sight. There are high naval and military officers in uniform proceeding to their clubs. Belgian and French troops are conspicuous at every corner. I also noticed a number of French sailors. English soldiers in khaki jostle Canadian airmen, while civilians seem as numerous as ever.

Tommy Lascelles who, besides being No.3 Secretary to the King, works at the War Office in the afternoons, says that many of the fifth column stories prove to be mares' nests. He told me of the case where an officer in the 48th. Highlanders (1st. Can: Division) had detected a man skulking about in some heath-land in Surrey and had arrested him. The man said he had been dropped by parachute about two hours previously and had given the names of several fifth columnists who formed a cell in that part of the country. He spoke with a foreign accent. Ironside thought the matter of such importance that he personally went down to investigate it and found that the man was lying from start to finish and was in actual fact an English soldier who was a deserter from the North of England for whom the authorities had been searching for several weeks.

Tommy Lascelles is not sending his children to Canada, though he has many friends who would be glad to take them. He says that with the King and Queen announcing their intention of keeping their two daughters in England he could hardly do otherwise himself, though in any case he questions the advisability of the whole idea of this huge emigration. It may be good for the Empire, but there is an element of defeatism in it - something a bit panicky and 'yellow'.

Geoffrey to E.C.F.B, 7 July   *Aberdeen*

Saturday's issue of *The Times* made good reading. Our destruction of the French fleet at Oran out-Hitlers Hitler at his most spectacular.[2] It was not only

---

[1] Sir Alan Lascelles (1887-1981). Asst. Pte. Sec. to George V, 1935, and to George VI, 1936-43; Pte. Sec. to George VI and Elizabeth II, 1943-53; Keeper of the Royal Archives, 1952-3. KCVO (1939), PC (1943).
[2] On 3 July 1940, in Operation 'Catapult', British warships attacked and sank French naval vessels in their North African bases of Oran and Mers-el-Kebir.

magnificent, but it was war, and of the most effective kind, for it has staggered the world; and in its moral effect alone has already compensated us for the débâcle of France. Its material effect will probably be of no less critical value and may well prove the turning point in the war, so that historians will from it date Hitler's eventual downfall.

Trevelyan[1] in an old-mannish, rather plaintive article in today's *Sunday Times* deprecates the attempt to compare the present war with the Napoleonic. No doubt there are profound differences, and naturally so; for history never exactly repeats itself. But principles don't change, nor, despite modern scientific inventions (the aeroplane, etc.), does geography. We controlled the seas then as we do now, and it was our control of the Mediterranean that counted most. It was from there working northwards that we beat Napoleon. Spain was his Achilles' heel, and Italy may well be Hitler's. We ought surely, now, to give France her quietus in Syria as we have done in Oran, and then destroy the Italian Fleet as we have the French (which was sunk in a French harbour and under the protection of French land guns). The Italian Empire would then collapse, and Italy would not take long to follow suit. If at the same time or thereabouts we were to destroy a German expeditionary force sent against these islands, we should start the winter with complete victory in our grasp.

Is it not also obvious that the entry of the USA into the war is now only a question of time (she is as good as in it on our side already)? The moral effect of that, especially if it came before Christmas, would be enormous.

Moreover I don' t think the new French government are going to find it easy to govern France. The French nation are, in the end, the clearest-sighted in the world, and cannot for long be fooled. The FO and our Secret Service ought surely to possess many means of assisting their enlightenment, especially with so many able and loyal French men with brains in this country. And with Russia - it is Stafford Cripps's big chance - such a very uncertain quantity, the Axis can't be happy about the Balkans.

Lord Baldwin to J.B.B., 7 July   *Astley Hall, Stourport on Severn*

Your letter from Toronto was one of the kindest and most welcome that I have ever had and I now send you my belated but grateful thanks. I put off

---

[1] G[eorge] M[acaulay] Trevelyan, OM (1876-1962). Regius Prof. of Modern History, Cambridge, 1927-40; Master of Trinity Coll. Cambridge, 1940-51.

replying because I thought you might very likely be in England before my letter reached Canada.

I wish we were near enough for you to run over here, but that cannot be. I am all right but disgracefully lame which prevents my getting about. Until the end of April I had paid short visits to London regularly and had long talks with all my friends, but now I couldn't ask them to come and see me, and indeed they couldn't if they would want to. Hence I know little of what is going on and I have much time for thought, and doing little odd things for the folk round about as one did in the days of one's youth. I have a feeling that we are in the supreme testing time for our people - throughout the world - and the first part of our trial is the stripping from us by treachery and faintheartedness of all external worldly support, so that we stand alone; and in the eternal scheme of things we have been chosen, if we cast ourselves on God, as His instrument for the regeneration of Europe and through Europe of the world. May we rise to it!

Kay to E.C.F.B., 9 July   *Savoy House, Sandown, I.O.W.*

We came here yesterday from Weymouth as Charles is to be stationed near here. I don't know if I'll be allowed to stay, probably not, but we don't know our plans yet.

We didn't really see very much of the Portland raid last Thursday. Charles was on his way there and just got in, and spent the rest of the morning in a dug-out. He was shaken by blast, but unhurt. I saw the bombs dropping before retiring to the cellar, and when it was over walked up the hill and looked down into the harbour. The auxiliary cruiser they hit was a very important anti-aircraft ship, specially built for the defence of Portland. The Huns knew just what they wanted and came down to 200 ft. above the ship to dive bomb her.

At least 50 men were killed by the first salvo which burst in the engine room. They got off the survivors, most badly wounded, and she then became a total wreck, burning furiously for five hours before sinking. It was a terrible thing and ought never to have happened. I'm afraid she never got the air raid warning. Two other small ships were sunk and 11 civilians killed on shore. There was no damage done in Weymouth.

We had air raid alarms three or four times every day there, so this place seems calm by comparison. On Sunday there was another raid on Portland, and we felt the blast before taking refuge in the cellar.

This place is completely deserted, the beach banned and the whole town dead and covered with pill boxes and barbed wire. I should not have succeeded in getting here alone, but being with Charles I was allowed in. I do wish Jerry would be quick and launch his attack. It's awful waiting and not knowing what is coming.

Dick Stancliffe to J.B.B., 9 July   *Great Smeaton, Nothallerton*

Like you I am one of those who has found something of a semi-military nature to do, and have just been authorized to buy my own uniform and revolver. I'm sure I shall carry both with my well known *esprit de corps* and trepidation in case I am 'had up' by the Police or LDV.

I am Deputy Commandant (*anglice* bottle-washer) of the Northern Area Observer Corps. I deal in anything, and as far as I can make out I'm like Euclid's definition, but I cannot remember which one it was! It's an entrancing business and if you would like to join me as official historian and unofficial Intelligence Officer, it will keep you busy seven days in the week until this party is over. I can't tell you what I am doing in a letter, as I've signed so many documents that I only dare have a bath in the dark.

My most interesting game is to visit the most secret places in England without a pass and without previous warning; most fascinating. I also deal in latrines, income tax, enemy raids, insurance, ammunition and underclothes. I can stay up all night, motor all night (and get put into the guard room by the LDV) or go to sleep all night (as our siren is out of action, fifth column they say!). And I've still got to work all day with interesting correspondence to answer from Berwick to Flint and Carlisle to Grimsby. I'm awfully sorry to have to agree that I am feeling quite guilty. You know it is rather fun.

Julian to E.C.F.B., 10 July   *Goodrich Court*

The school cricket eleven is to go to Shrewsbury all being well on Saturday, and if I can get enough petrol I shall try and take the day off and go too by car, though it is over 60 miles from here. It all seems rather strange and futile carrying on with games while such momentous things are happening so short a distance away, but boys must be occupied and they cannot always be thinking about the war.

I am so glad Burgon finds satisfaction of soul in his war service. I thoroughly understand this and hanker after it myself. I find the old routine of this school life not very easy. The complexity of the problems appertaining to our new surroundings, and the difficulties that obviously lie ahead in keeping the school together in the future, occupy much of my time, but all the same underneath is the feeling of dissatisfaction with all one's efforts. I must of course get something of a holiday, that is if Hitler does not strike this summer. If he strikes no one will be allowed much freedom of movement as far as I can see, and of course if it is at all possible I shall come to Canterbury. We break up on 6 August, and hope to do a Shakespeare play in the grounds here after the school and higher certificate exams are over, with our Morris dance club doing country dances. But who knows what another three weeks will bring forth.

Accommodation for all the staff is our great difficulty. I am naturally very tired, but not too tired, only one does not rally to fatigue quite as quickly at 55 as I did at 35!! I have been offered free accommodation and even financial help by a newspaper proprietor at Windsor, Ontario in Canada, for ten boys - and their sisters - from Felsted, but I am doubtful if I shall have any boys willing to go, and indeed I am not encouraging them. I agree with Burgon, this departure of what can only be a small proportion of English children to Canada is a bad advertisement for our solidity and may even be engineered by the Germans!! If some are to go, why not all? and what process of selection can ever be fair?

Notes by J.B.B., 11 July

Last night I was on guard duty at the Gate Inn road block. I was actually on guard from 12.45 a.m. to 2.30 a.m. On three occasions Boche planes were over the coast and the three main groups of searchlights presented a perfectly superb sight - (1) the Sheppey, Thames Estuary, Sheerness, Gillingham, Rochester and Chatham group, (2) the Whitstable, Herne Bay, Margate, Ramsgate group, and (3) the Dover, Shorncliffe, Folkestone, Hythe group. When, as was the case last night, all these lights were in action at once, it made the night (which was particularly dark) as light as if there was a full moon.

At 11.45 p.m. last night we were in our tent but awake. Sgt. Roberts put his head in and said to me, 'John, load your rifle and come quick.' I jumped out of my blanket, rammed a clip of cartridges into my magazine and joined him outside. 'There's a car just drawn up down the road I don't like the look of,' he whispered. We advanced on the car, the Sgt. a small man, muscular, athletic and full of pep, with his rifle at the ready. 'Steady there,' came a voice from the car. 'Steady be damned,' said the Sgt. 'Who the hell are you?' 'Police,' came from the car, a large black limousine. ' Police eh?' said the Sgt, 'let's have a look at you,' and he shoved his head through the window. 'All right, all right, here you are - that's my pass, and here's my tin hat and uniform,' and he turned on a torch to show his credentials. 'Well, what do you want?' said Roberts, mollified but still suspicious. 'Well, there's lights been reported in the orchard up on the hill here, and the Chief Constable sent us up to have a look.' 'John,' said the Sgt., 'go into the orchard and have a look round, cock your rifle and put the safety catch at safe.' I went into the orchard and for a few minutes patrolled round inside. It was pitch black and had there been anyone there it would have been impossible to see them. I returned and suggested to the Sgt. that if the orchard, which was a large one, was really to be combed from end to end he would have to turn the guard out. The pub keeper came out, hearing the voices, and said, 'I'm sure they come from occasional cars moving on the back road from Patrixbourne towards Canterbury.' The Sgt. decided it was not worth calling the guard out, and I was ordered to unload and go back to the tent, which I did and smoked a cigarette before the hour for me to turn out on guard arrived.

There are many alarms of parachutists landing. Yesterday afternoon the police rushed up to the high ground near Nackington to deal with reported parachutists, but it was a false alarm and probably arose from the white puffs of our AA guns being taken for parachutes.

All this week the tides have been right for invasion. On Monday night the enemy were definitely expected to make a landing and we were all warned to be ready for an emergency. My Sergeant Instructor at the barracks took a platoon of men to Herne Bay and manned a trench all night. Along the Dover Road passed many lorries full of soldiers proceeding to various coastal points; this was between 7 and 8 p.m. There was a general feeling of expectancy all this week.

We removed all our motoring maps to-day from their usual shelf in the hall to a trunk in the box room. The government has urged everybody not to leave maps about in their houses where they might be of use to the enemy.

Geoffrey to E.C.F.B., 14 July   *Aberdeen*

We had a fine sermon from the Bishop of Aberdeen this morning on the necessity of cheerfulness in war time. The pessimist is the worst kind of traitor. Our fighting forces (of whom he sees a good deal in the Orkneys) are full of confidence and in the highest spirits: the civilian population must follow their example. As a matter of fact I do not think that the bulk of the nation requires any exhortations under this head. It entertains not the slightest doubt of victory, was never in its history so united and ready for every kind of sacrifice to achieve victory, and is not in the least down-hearted by the defection of France, but on the contrary is, if anything, rather relieved to be fighting on its own, and no longer in danger of being let down by its allies.

But while I take this to be the fact, one would never guess it from the behaviour of our so-called Ministry of Information and the numerous other public bodies and private individuals who take it upon themselves to exhort and admonish us, day in and day out both on and off the wireless. The truth is that as a people we have a natural distaste for, or even hatred of, propaganda. I neither listen to nor read it myself, its sole effect upon me (if I happen to do so by mistake) being to incite me to indulge in the exact opposite of what the propagandists recommend or command. The only speakers on the wireless I have liked so far are those who treat propaganda, I mean propaganda for home consumption, humorously, like J.B.Priestley.[1] As for sentimentalists like Duff Cooper, they should be shot. From the very first the Ministry of Information (i.e. of propaganda - why not call a spade a spade?) has been mismanaged and still is, by the government, and in my opinion it has done, and still is doing, much more harm than good. Its methods of procedure stimulate the very nervousness they intended to counteract. An hour of P.G. Wodehouse,[2] such as we got on the wireless last night, is worth all the propagandists in the world as a stimulus in war-time and as a preserver of mental and emotional sanity.

When the air raid bulletins mention a Scottish NE town, it does not necessarily mean us. But, as a matter of fact, in Friday's 9 p.m. wireless news and in the next morning's papers, it did. A lone raider came in from the North Sea about 12.45 p.m. and dropped some half-a-dozen bombs on houses between Aberdeen and Old Aberdeen and on a ship-yard near the harbour, killed 25 persons and wounded others (I don't know how many) and then was shot down by three Spitfires on the (though not yet completed) ice-rink just on this side of the

---

[1] John Baynton Priestley (1894-1984). Well-known author and broadcaster. OM (1977).
[2] Pelham Grenville Wodehouse (1881-1975). Author and broadcaster; the 'finest writer of modern English' who, interned in Germany in 1940, notoriously made five broadcasts to America. KBE (1975)

Bridge of Dee in Anderson's Drive, about half a mile below our house, the plane being burnt out and all its occupants killed. For this raid there was no warning given. If there had been, there might have been much less loss of life.

I was sitting in my study when I heard distant gunfire. It might of course have been practice (just AA artillery) only, but, as I wished to take no risks, I ran up to the nursery to see if the children were in. They were; so I told them to come downstairs at once to our air raid rendezvous - the passage just outside our bedroom. (The servants go to their bedroom in the basement.) The gunfire got near and louder, and after about four or five minutes very close - indeed all round us - and very loud. The children weren't a bit frightened, for we spoke in our ordinary tone of voice, and treated the whole business as all quite ordinary, and consequently they did the same. I felt sorely tempted to run upstairs to the nursery and see what I could see from its window which commands a magnificent view of the whole Dee valley to the harbour and the sea. But conscience forbade (for it is really very silly to risk standing at a window in the very middle of a raid with high explosive shells plastering the sky overhead). So I stayed where I was with Jean and the children. If I had gone upstairs and looked out I should have seen the whole fight, which must have been, and indeed was, most thrilling, and been able to watch the German plane throughout the whole course of its long slanting fall to earth. As it was we simply heard the gunfire come to an abrupt conclusion with a rat-tat-tat of machine gun fire which (though we didn't know it) was that of the German plane's machine guns which went off by themselves, as it burnt itself out, half in, half out of the empty ice-rink building, which it ignited after striking it and bursting into flames. We then went downstairs and had our lunch at 1 p.m. as usual, the whole thing not taking more than about ten minutes. We assumed that the raider had been driven off, and in a few minutes we had dismissed the whole matter from our minds.

After lunch I took the two children for a bicycle ride through the Countesswell woods across the Dee at Cults, and home by the Banchory road. It was then, and not till then, that we discovered what had actually occurred in the raid. The ice-rink building, which has just been completed, but has not yet been fitted up inside, stands to the left of Anderson's Drive about 150 yards up it from the bridge. After crossing the bridge, which is an LDV station, and also a military guard post (there are always regulars there), a special Constable stopped us and others and said we could proceed no further, or at any rate no further than 50 yards up the Drive. 'Why', I said, 'has a bomb dropped?' 'No, an aeroplane,' he replied. 'Ours?' I asked. 'No, a German one,' he answered, and then he gave me further particulars. So we took a small detour - you can imagine how excited the children were - and by a side road got to a point level with the fallen aeroplane (tilted, burnt out, up against the ice-rink building) and separated from the Drive by a narrow field. We crossed this field and so got to the edge of Anderson's Drive and within some 30 or 40 yards of the scene of the crash. There was an armed guard keeping away the spectators (of whom there were hundreds), but one could see exactly what had happened. A row of small houses on the opposite side of the Drive to the ice-rink had had a narrow escape, as the aeroplane in falling had just missed them by inches, and hit the ice-rink wall sideways and just below the roof, against which we saw the blackened remains leaning.

A young LD Volunteer on a bicycle told me, then, about the loss of life in Aberdeen. A lot of the lives lost were in small houses, and some (in the shipyard) due, I believe, not to a bomb, but to an explosion in a boiler caused by fragments of one of our own shells. A large number of windows were broken in Old Aberdeen, including one in King's College Library (which happened to be a stained glass one that nobody likes).

We returned to tea, the children of course quite thrilled at such an unexpected close call to their ride. 'I've never seen a wrecked German aeroplane before,' observed Ursula, as we climbed the steps from our garden to the drawing-room, 'but then, you see, this is the first time I have been in a war'.

Dick Stancliffe to J.B.B., 15 July   *Thorpe House, Sowerby, Yorks*

My most interesting work is in the study of the people in the same show. The unemployed carpenter, for instance, who turned up at a lonely spot overlooking the North Sea when war was declared. He brought his carpet-bag with him full of tools and nothing else. When asked his business he tersely said 'A've coom.' 'What for?''For't War', was the laconic answer. He built the post, he pinched a tent, he's still there. What he doesn't know about the job is not worth knowing, and he even recruited his own father. You could write a book about him alone.

Notes by E.C.F.B., 16 July

Last night, just as Burgon was going on night duty, the Dean called to bring me a donation for the LDV. The Dean met Maisky[1] the Russian Minister at a lunch last week. He (Maisky) was anxious to know if we were really serious in our determination to prosecute the war, asking if our defences are good. He has a great opinion of Churchill (as has the Russian Government), and two and a half years ago told the Dean that he was the man to lead the British nation in a war. If we can hold out for two months, said the same oracle, in September Russia might come in on our side. She has no military alliance with Germany and fears her as a powerful neighbour. To-day Sir Stafford Cripps had an audience with Stalin.

18 July

The *Daily Telegraph* to-day reveals that the King, a day or two ago, paid a visit at midnight to some big munitions work. His car was immediately stopped by the Home Guard (LDV) with a peremptory, 'Halt, who goes there?' The chauffeur replied, 'His Majesty the King.' Not satisfied with the chauffeur's word the guard peered into the car, recognised the King, and with the word 'Pass' allowed the car to go on.

During the long air raid last Saturday from 3 to 9 p.m., the Archbishop was taking a Confirmation in the South East of his Diocese. All the bus services stop during a raid, and only some of the candidates had arrived when the service commenced. He had just finished when eleven more turned up; he took a second service for them, and then when that was finished he cheerfully started a third service for two more belated candidates from a distance, whose bus had not been able to bring them.

Notes by J.B.B., 18 July

The Bishop of Dover tells me that with the voluntary evacuation of the coastal towns, i.e. Hythe, Sandgate, Folkestone, Dover, Deal, Sandwich, Ramsgate, Broadstairs, Margate and Westgate, the Archbishop proposes to close some of the churches at the end of July. This is not to be done piecemeal, because it might give the impression the clergy were deserting their job, but according to a set plan which will be announced. The clergy thus set free will be sent to parishes which happen to be vacant through the death of the incumbent or because he has left to take up a chaplaincy. The financial situation of the churches is serious. In a

---

[1] Ivan Maisky (1884-1975). Soviet Ambassador to Britain, 1932-43.

Church at Margate which is usually packed, the Bishop, when he took the services there last Sunday (14 July), had 15 at the Holy Communion, 20 at Matins, and 40 at Evensong. The quota for the Diocese for general church needs is usually £13,000: this year it will hardly be £6,000. The disappearance of the people means no money for the vergers, the lighting, insurance and other necessary church expenses.

A few days ago a small bomb fell in the Vicarage garden at Buckland (Dover), broke all the windows and also blew out the east window of the Church (which was a particularly ugly one) but caused no loss of life.

In a typically English way there is great divergence in the regulations about evacuation in the various towns. So far there has been voluntary evacuation only. The next stage would be compulsory evacuation of all civilians except the essential persons - doctors, nurses, clergy, ARP and the rest (this would be ordered by the Ministry of Home Defence). The last stage would be total evacuation; this would be ordered by the military authorities. The divergence arises with respect to the second stage. The Vicar of Margate, who has a woman housekeeper, was told he could not keep her when compulsory evacuation was ordered; but the Vicar of Ramsgate was told he certainly could keep his housekeeper. Those to be evacuated would be ordered to report at the railway station at stated times when special trains would take them to their destination, and they would go to whatever place the train took them and nowhere else. There is no question of Canterbury being evacuated even as regards the second stage, let alone the third.

Notes by J.B.B., on visit to London, Friday 19 July

I lunched with Euan Wallace at Buck's. As Chief Commissioner for the London Civil Defence he is having a busy time. If the government was forced to leave Whitehall, Euan would be in supreme control of London. He told me that 'G', his second boy who has been for months with the Coastal Command in Cornwall, was recently brought to HQ at Northwood near Harrow and is now flying round Scotland visiting all aerodromes and teaching the personnel some new details about navigation, in which he is one of the chief experts in the RAF. His marriage to Elizabeth will probably not take place for some months as, though the divorce has gone through, it is not made absolute and now that Gerry Koch de Gooreynd is officially missing it is not likely to.

Euan told me that 'Bulgy' (Andrew Thorne)[1] is in command of the Corps in this part of England. 'Bulgy' Thorne had a division in the Flanders fighting and did very well. He's a brother of Nancy Dalrymple, Hew's wife.[2]

Euan and Barbie Wallace have recently each purchased a motor van which takes food and drink and magazines round to the troops in their area. John, my godson, is driving one of these vans. They each cost £275 and are administered by the YMCA.

At 2.15 I attended a meeting of the Council of the Friends of Canterbury Cathedral at Lambeth Palace. The Archbishop welcomed us all personally and made a short speech. It was the speech of an old and tired man. Among those present was Canon Jenkins,[3] whose general appearance was appallingly untidy. He told me that J.C. Masterman had recently got a job in Intelligence, and was in uniform and stationed at Colchester. Pakenham[4] was in hospital at Oxford, having been shot in the leg by a colleague in the LDV - a young fellow who knew nothing about a rifle. John Lowe,[5] the Dean, is doing excellently. There are 67 entries for next October. The University chest shows a deficit of £15,000 for the present year, and will probably show a deficit of £30,000 for the next year, in which case the Colleges will, as in the last war, have to come to the rescue.

I had tea and an hour's talk with 'Pug' (now Major-General Hastings Ismay, secretary of the Committee of Imperial Defence and a sort of informal chief of the PM's staff). Ismay goes everywhere with the PM and spends many week-ends with him at Chequers. He was going off there directly after tea. He said that the PM was much impressed with the coastal defences in Kent after his visit here ten days or so ago. Earlier this week Ismay accompanied the PM on a visit to Portsmouth and Weymouth. Churchill was delighted with the enthusiastic reception he received from the tens of thousands of tradesmen employed by the

---

[1] Maj-Gen. Andre Thorne (1885-1970). Comm. 48th. Div., BEF, 1939-40; Lt-Gen., 1940 and comm. XII Corps (Kent), 1940-1; GOC Scottish Command, 1941-45. KCB (1942).

[2] Hon. Sir Hew Dalrymple (1857-1945). MP (Con) Wigtownshire, 1915-18. KCVO (1932).

[3] Rev. Claude Jenkins (1877-1959). Chaplain to Archbishop of Canterbury, 1911; Canon of Canterbury, 1929-34; sub-dean, Christchurch, 1943-57.

[4] Frank Aungier Pakenham (1905 -). Politics Lecturer at Oxford, 1932-45; Pers. Asst. to Sir William Beveridge, 1941-44; Parl. U-Sec. War Office, 1946-7; Chanc. D. of Lancaster, 1947-8; Min. for Civil Aviation, 1948-51; Ist. Lord Admiralty, 1951; Ld. Privy Seal, 1964-5 and 1966-8; Sec. of State for Colonies, 1965-6; Leader of H. of Lords, 1964-8. PC (1948); cr. Lord Pakenham (1945) and succ. to Earl of Longford (1951).

[5] Rev. John Lowe (1899-1960). Canadian; Dean of Christ Church, Oxford, 1939-59; V-Chanc. Oxford University, 1948-51.

Admiralty in the dockyards. These men are notoriously difficult in peace time, strong Trade Unionists, veering much to the Left, and though in Admiralty employ, are not under naval discipline but are civilians. They cheered the PM and told him to 'go to it'. Churchill, on this occasion, also visited a number of the French ships which we had forcibly taken over two weeks ago. Some 200 ships of varying size, all belonging to the French Fleet, had been taken over by us. In some cases the officers and men had elected to stay and fight side-by-side with us, but the majority expressed the desire to return to France and they had accordingly been sent back. In this latter case the French ships would be operated where necessary by British crews: in the former case English sailors would supplement the French crews. The PM addressed the French officers and men in the most execrable French and they were delighted!

Ismay said that Lindemann (of Christ Church) was constantly with the PM but did not seem to do much, and people wondered why Churchill saw so much of him; but Churchill likes him personally, as he does Morton and Brendan Bracken, and is very loyal to his friends. Ismay finds the PM difficult to get to know well, but likes him immensely. There is almost something feminine in his nature, and he likes those who are sympathetic to him around. Ismay, whether at Chequers or at No.10, is always prepared to stay up talking till 2 a.m. or 3 a.m., the hour the PM likes to go to bed.

I reminded Ismay that in July 1939 and again a few days before the war broke out, he had emphasised to me the very cordial and intimate character of the relations of the British and French Governments, and that at the CID he had had three or four high French Staff officers working in Richmond Terrace in close co-operation with the British General staff. Had he personally been surprised at the way the French had chucked in their hand? He replied that until the war started he had no idea of the rotten state of the French government, but that even after the first Supreme War Council held at the end of the first week of the war he had remarked to his wife on his return to England that he did not feel 'the French were taking the war seriously'.

He told me that it had been agreed by the French and English General Staffs, that directly Holland and Belgium were invaded, the British and French armies were to attack the Ruhr. But the French had refused to co-operate when the moment came, being deadly afraid of retaliation. He also told me that it had been arranged that our bombers should bomb the triangle in Northern Italy (the great industrial area - Fiat works, etc. - round Turin) immediately Italy came into the war. At this moment Ismay was with the PM, at Orleans where Churchill had gone to try and put heart into the French. During the conference, Ismay was called to the telephone by Barratt,[1] OC our Bomber Command, who told him that our planes were all bombed up and ready to go but the French, under whose command they technically were, refused to allow them to leave the ground. What should he do? Ismay called Reynaud, Weygand and Churchill out of the Conference and Weygand, after some discussion said, 'Tell my people who are on the spot that the English planes are to start at once.' Ismay so informed Barratt who had held the telephone line. About twenty minutes later Barratt rang up again to say the execution of the plan was now quite impossible, as the French had driven lorries on to the aerodrome and left them stranded there in such a way that not one of our machines could leave the ground.

Reynaud is by no means the intrepid fighter we had supposed. He is shouting at one moment, 'I will fight on the Somme, I will fight in Paris, I will fight behind Paris, I will fight every step of the way to the Mediterranean, I will fight in Africa,' and at the next moment weakly giving way to political intrigues, as for instance, when having brought de Gaulle,[2] the great expert in Tank warfare, from the front to take over an administration post at the Ministry of War, he was prevailed upon to send him back to the front line again to carry on as a General. Reynaud's mistress is a strong pro-fascist. Churchill while actually with the French on his two visits during those critical days, almost succeeded in making them continue the struggle, but directly he had departed defeatism again ruled.

I asked Ismay what his personal opinion was about the invasion of this country by the Germans. He replied that he considered invasion was most unlikely. He pointed out that, when planning to land troops in England, the Germans had counted on the main British army being engaged on the Continent, and that they would therefore be opposed by five or six second line British divisions. The situation was now very different, with thirty divisions in this country, of which eight were battle-tried: moreover the element of surprise through troop-carrying

---

[1] Air Chief Marshal, Sir Arthur Barratt (1891-1966). AOC-in-C., British Air Force in France, 1940; AOC-in-C., Army Co-operation Command, 1940-3; AOC-in-C, Technical Training Command, 1943-5. KCB (1940).

[2] Gen. Charles de Gaulle (1890-1970). Comm. Fr. 4th. Armoured Div., 1940; U-Sec. Nat. Defence, 1940; Chief of Free French, then Pres. of FNCL, 1943; Pres. of Fr. Prov. Government, 1944-6; Pres. of Fr. Government, 1958-9; Pres. of Fr. Republic, 1959-68.

planes, parachutists, and fifth columnists was exploded, and we had had many weeks to prepare our defence: our aerodromes were now admirably protected and our coastal defences were extremely strong. Ismay further stated that our regular troops were now admirably equipped and when I expressed surprise, said that four hundred 75's had come from the USA. These, though not new, were perfectly good guns, identical with the French 75, and had proved very effective in dealing with tanks: further, we had plenty of heavy guns, the Admiralty having been found, rather characteristically, to have a number up their sleeve. Material to equip a new BEF was not yet available, but in two months it would be, and there was no question that in 1941 we must once again break out of this country.

Ismay said Stafford Cripps was doing an admirable job in Russia, and that his conversation with. Stalin on 1 July had been 'very satisfactory'. Hankey, as Chancellor of the Duchy of Lancaster, had done some very useful special reports, e.g. (1) on German oil supply, (2) on plans to destroy bridges, essential factories, and oil dumps, and blocking the harbours in the event of Belgium and Holland being overrun. When the débâcle ensued, the plans drawn up in this report were efficiently carried out as far as Belgium was concerned, and had this work not been done by our men it would not have been done at all.

21 July

This morning Mother and I went to Matins at 10.30 in the Cathedral. It was a sad experience. We entered the Precincts by one of the postern gates which are open all day. Shirley's house was shut up and the garden untidy. McNutt's house was also empty and the blinds were drawn; his wife is away and he sleeps in his dug-out and feeds with the Crums. It was a glorious summer morning. We saw two persons, and two only, in the Precincts; one was sitting on a seat and the other met us near the Dark Entry. Meister Omers stood silent and deserted. The Choir School was shut. The Precincts were unkempt. The sand bags blocking the Crypt windows were dirty, mis-shapen and falling to bits. There were of course no bells. We entered the Cathedral. It seemed dark, many of the windows being blocked. It smelled musty from the damp earth in the ambulatory. The congregation numbered about 80. They sat in the block of seats east of the Choir. They were shabbily dressed. There were 10 soldiers in the chairs below the High Altar. The head Verger and the Bedesmen stood about with little to do. The organ was not played till just before the choir entered. The atmosphere was one of complete gloom. The procession entered from the entrance by Chichele's tomb. The cross bearer came first, followed by Poole[1] who is very leftist and out of sympathy with the war; and Canon Crum bringing up the rear. No other Canon was present, nor was the Dean. The service began - the temporary organist sitting at the manual of the metallic-sounding Hammond organ placed in the middle of the aisle. The Psalm was 44. The service was dead. The only bright spot was the sermon preached by Crum on the heroism of our airmen - a sacrifice of self - a sacrament which we must not take as paid to ourselves but to God. The experience of Matins in the Cathedral during the war was disillusioning and melancholy. Afterwards Mother and I walked in the unkempt garden of Meister Omers, and then returned through the deserted Precincts. The Dean is unaware how ineffective the Cathedral and its services are - a great opportunity lost.

Geoffrey to E.C.F.B., 21 July   *Aberdeen*

We have had more raids this last week, but no bombs dropped. On Friday evening, I think it was - or it may have been Thursday - just after dinner we saw the repeated flash of shells bursting in the sky, with sound of distant gunfire from a raid on a convoy southward (over the sea) off Stonehaven. The Germans were driven off and no ships were hit, but according to what Tony heard from our neighbours (who know all the airmen at Dyce - our local aerodrome) three of our Spitfires were lost. We have been having heavy thunder, rain, low clouds and, generally, bad weather for air raids, during the last two days. Altogether we have had so far eleven raids in three weeks, about one every two days on average. One cannot but suppose that once Hitler has realised the contempt with which his absurd peace gesture to this country has been received, he will launch his much advertised air-attack *en masse* on this country; in which case, I suppose, we must expect continuous waves of bombers day and night over us for days and perhaps several weeks on end. But the prospect is quite calmly envisaged up here, and everyone is determined to see it through.

Notes by E.C.F.B., 21 July

Teresa Brown, who is at Kingston-on-Thames with her husband employed in the Leyland works, writes:- 'I heard from Bill last week, he is near the New

[1] Rev. Joseph Poole (1909-89). Minor Canon and Sacrist of Canterbury, 1936; Precentor of Canterbury, 1937-47; Canon Emeritus of Coventry, 1977.

Forest and forms what they call a flying patrol. They (three men and himself in a small car) patrol the forest at night and specially during air raids, on the look out for spies showing lights etc. He had the satisfaction of catching one red handed with a wireless transmitting set, and says he was very roughly handled and is now well disposed of!'

Notes on Dr Lucas by E.C.F.B., 22 July

Dr Lucas has just been in to see me. His hospital in France was at La Baule near St Nazaire on the Bay of Biscay. On Sunday 16 June he had 1,500 wounded soldiers in it, and received information that the French were cracking, and he must get the wounded away. There were two ambulance trains in the station and a hospital ship at St Nazaire eight miles away. He and the staff set to work and filled the first train with 700 patients and sent it off. It took from 11 a.m. till nearly 10 p.m. He and the staff then got some food at a restaurant and he tumbled into bed. At 4 a.m. on 17 June a staff officer entered his bedroom very anxious, saying the Germans were getting near and he must get the remaining wounded (700) into the other train that was waiting, by 10 a.m., and must get them through, if possible, to Quiberon where a transport would be waiting. The first train had got through to St Nazaire, and the wounded were on the hospital ship there safely, but the Boches were now so near that the next train must go no further. I forgot to say that after loading the first train on the Sunday he himself had gone by an ambulance the eight miles to St Nazaire and seen all the wounded on board personally as he had several anxious cases. He only got back to La Baule about 10 p.m. that night.

At the staff officer's order Dr Lucas sprang from bed and set to work with his staff and orderlies. There were no ambulances and they were to get them on the train by 10 a.m., as well as all the mobile hospital equipment. The men had to be carried on stretchers. There was an engine on the train, and by 10.45 all were aboard. They were told not to stop at St Nazaire as the French were disaffected already, but to pass through to Redon and so to Quiberon. The Germans were not really so near as reported. The wireless said they must hurry on every soldier, wounded or not, and all English would be made prisoners. This was a German broadcast lie. However, at St Nazaire the engine driver said he could go no further, took off the engine and left them. Dr Lucas and one of his colleagues found the station master who said there were no longer any engines available.

They said, nonsense, they had seen plenty of engines with steam-up in a siding or shed, and lifting the station master out of his chair forced him to come along with them. As they passed the train Dr Lucas said to a wounded soldier, a gunner, 'Let me have your pop-gun (a revolver) as we are going to have trouble with this fellow.' They got to the engine shed and all the drivers seeing them coming ran away. They pursued one and seized him, Dr Lucas keeping his revolver at the man's ribs, and forced him to bring out his engine and attach it to the train. Dr Lucas stood on the step, revolver in hand, till the train got to Quiberon. Once clear of St Nazaire, the French driver gave less trouble, but Dr Lucas never left him till he had his train load at Quiberon station about 6 p.m.

There were thousands of English soldiers there waiting for transport, and Dr Lucas said the whole thing was very humiliating. A worried transport officer said the transport was not there yet and they had better get some food. They scouted round and got some for their patients and then for themselves. The transport officer had nine wireless or telephone messages telling him to hurry up, and they decided to get the wounded out of the train and along the one and a half miles to the quay. They had no transport but stretchers and the task seemed almost impossible. Dr Lucas was in command and he went down the train telling all who could walk that they must do so, or they would have to be left behind. They pulled themselves together and, though many were stretcher cases, they walked the one and a half miles with the help of orderlies or nurses, the doctors and other medical staff carrying the worst cases on stretchers. At Quiberon quay, the transport was seen one mile out. They secured barges and rowing boats, the RAMC manning the latter, and backwards and forwards they went from the shore to the *Dorsetshire* till all were on board. Some of the men were so badly wounded they ought not to have been moved at all.

It took 48 hours to get to Portsmouth and they slept as never in their lives before. At Portsmouth they could not land, the harbour was full of transports loaded with soldiers brought back from France. Nor could Dr Lucas send any message to his wife till they got to Southampton on Thursday 19 July. After landing their wounded and seeing them off to various hospitals, he wired to his wife, and then he and others were sent straight to Leeds where he has been since. He had applied for a home hospital, but hearing he was probably being sent out to the Middle East he had got 48 hours leave and had been to the War Office, saying he was too old for this, and hoped for England. He and his wife and two sons were off this afternoon for a good evening in London. Sam, his eldest son, a gunner, had a wonderful escape from Dunkirk.

Dr Lucas said for some time they felt the French were giving in, principally from corruption among themselves.

Tony to E.C.F.B., 27 July   *Aberdeen*

I stayed one evening after finishing work at 5.30 and had a few sets of tennis with Fiona and the two land girls (Sylvia and Diana Haig). About half way through one game just as I had served, we heard two or three successive bangs in the sky almost directly overhead. It was cloudy so we could see nothing. We looked at each other in wild surmise, except for Sylvia who had succeeded in getting half way to the summer house in the twinkling of an eye. We came to the conclusion it was an aeroplane back firing or playing high jinks and calmly went on with our game. Planes, you see, are continually over Grandhome which is only half a mile or so from the aerodrome here. Actually it wasn't a plane at all but bursts of AA fire from the guns at the aerodrome. Pieces of shrapnel had fallen within only 50 yards of where we were playing (quite small pieces). I had dinner that evening with the Patons and then biked home in the gloaming. Sitting in the drawing room before we went to bed I saw two or three flashes in the air to the south as it might be out to sea and we heard gunfire. Then there was a deep rumble - more felt than heard - a distant bomb. Apparently a large convoy had been passing up the coast, and this accounted for the firing we heard and the presence of Nazi planes over Aberdeen during the day. Convoys are fairly frequent going up the coast and account for several raids. A few days ago on my way back from work at a point where I can see right over Aberdeen and the North Sea, I stopped to watch a huge convoy steaming slowly north. We have had 12 raids on Aberdeen in the last month (i.e. since the collapse of France). This is not counting the one I was telling you about which disturbed our tennis. Two of the 12 had no warning and in most of the remaining 10 no bombs here dropped. One of those which was unheralded by Wailing Willie (Father must have told you about - the occasion when a German plane was brought down not so very far from this house), I was sitting in the library at Grandhome and we heard bombs being dropped (in Old Aberdeen as a matter of fact) about four miles away, but they were loud enough. The windows rattled and the set of valuable plates (which they've now taken down) shook in their brackets. That lone raider did more damage and loss of life in one town (Aberdeen) at one time than any other so far anywhere else in the Kingdom.

Yet Aberdeen is not classed as an evacuation area for school children. Of course if there had been a warning the loss of life would have been much less. I have slept through two air raids at night so far without being woken by the sirens, though there is one just up the road. It shows how hard exercise in the fields brings sound sleep. Britain really is an armed camp, absolutely seething with troops and gun emplacements and tank-traps and barricades. In fact to go to the beach here is enough to make one feel one is living in a fortress. The large granite concrete blocks, put at a few yards from each other along the coast, remind one of the walls of a medieval castle greatly enlarged.

How by the way is Private Bickersteth of the Home Guard getting on? Please give him my love. I shall soon equal him as Private Bickersteth, or perhaps he is now a Corporal. Anyway I hear he is now familiar with the Bren gun. He will of course know what the body-locking pin is, but I bet he doesn't know what (and where on the gun) is the barrel-nut-retainer-plunger! What I am interested about is the Tommy gun, and am wondering whether it is replacing the rifle as the personal weapon of privates like him and me. As Uncle Burgon is the only member of the family so far on active service I hope he is being careful to put some account of his own work and doings in the War Diary.

Julian to E.C.F.B., 29 July   *Goodrich Court*

The difficulties here increase rather than decrease and I begin to wonder if we shall be able to live out the winter here. If only one knew the attack on England was not coming off, I should move heaven and earth to get the WO to move the soldiers out of Felsted and go back.

I foresee nothing but dwindling numbers in our entries in a county which does not know us. I have now 100 boys either leaving this term, or who have already left, and I fear we shall be under the 300 mark next term, instead of 400. One gets such shocks still. Only yesterday a subaltern of the 2nd. Middlesex Regiment, now at Cheltenham, said they had plenty of officers, far too many, but no men! Yet the government boasts of having registered over four million men! What nonsense! If the word was 'enlisted' I should sit up and take notice. I know of quite a number of men, registered over six to nine months ago and not yet called up - forgotten perhaps , or the machinery broken down!

We see searchlights every night in the far distance from here, but nothing else to remind us of war!

Notes by E.C.F.B., 29 July

Burgon and I want to go out, but wait for the 'All Clear', which comes at 11.30. We sally down to Lloyds Bank, where I sit while he goes on to the General Post Office to send a cable to Canada. He returns to pick me up, but as he enters the Bank door at 12.40, an air raid warning sounds again. We begin to speak to a clerk, when suddenly a shrill whistle sounds and bells ring. 'Excuse me,' said the clerk, 'I must go to our cellars,' and in the twinkling of an eye the Bank is empty! The porter, a member of the Home Guard with Burgon, said to him, 'What are you to do?' 'Walk quietly home for lunch,' said Burgon. Shocked, the porter said, 'But what about your mother, surely she had better come down with me to the underground shelter, it is very comfortable.' I thanked him but said I was going home with my son. The streets were rapidly emptying, some taking shelter, others walking quietly home if their homes were near. Shopkeepers were all putting up their shutters, and locking their shop doors, and some issuing out to their war work, such as ARP or ambulance work. We walked on, looking in at the tobacconist's first. We saw or heard nothing, and seldom do in these air raids, but the danger of a German bomber, under cover of a cloud, dropping a bomb and then diving down to machine gun anyone they see is always present. So far this has not happened in Canterbury. We stopped again at Twyman's to speak to Mr Harris of the Home Guard, and ask why his shop door was open during a raid. He replied, 'We have decided to go on with business. It is impossible to keep shutting up two or three times a day.' As he spoke (12.50) the 'All Clear' went, and we reached home soon after to a peaceful lunch.

We heard from Mary this morning that she has formed a women's fire fighting squad at Chiddingstone, as men are few and are doing ARP or Home Guard work. Her Austrian cook, Siddie, has joined, and they have two manual pumps and a stirrup pump. They are, I believe, the first women's squad, at any rate in that part of the country.

Notes by J.B.B., 30 July

Eric Haldenby who commands the 48th. Highlanders of Canada, was in Canterbury yesterday and spent the evening with us, much to the joy of four corporals from the cadet course who were dining here. Eric gave us a full account of their amazing few days in France in mid June. The 1st Canadian Division, with the 51st. and 52nd. British Divisions, was to form a defensive flank to protect Brittany and particularly Brest. The Division reached Plymouth from Aldershot on 14 June. They landed at Brest, where nobody seemed to expect them, the following morning and spent the day in the woods above the town with HQs in the moated fort. That evening (15 June) they entrained, and their orders were to go to Sablé about 70 miles east, and a little south of Rennes, and about 110 miles SW of Paris. The stations were full of refugees - Rennes had been bombed. The French populace gave them an enthusiastic welcome as the train meandered slowly through the countryside. At Laval (40 miles east of Rennes) the French expressed great surprise that the Canadians had been ordered to go as far as Sablé. They reached there at dawn on 16 June and pulled up in the yards, which were full of British stores. At first they could find not a single person to advise them, but finally an English RTO, called Oates, appeared who informed the Brigadier and Eric that the Germans were known to be only 40 miles distant the previous night. A scheme by which these two regiments could be disposed in defensive positions round Sablé, if emergency arose, was worked out, but the men did not leave the train in view of the uncertainty of the general situation. While they were there a German reconnaissance plane flew slowly overhead several times. They had no rations other than stores they had purchased in Brest. Oates said everybody had left Sablé and strongly advised them to go back.

Having satisfied themselves with Oates's credentials, they thought it best to go back at any rate to Laval. Their French engine driver refused to take them back saying *Guerre finie*. Argument failed to budge him. Finally the *Chef de Gare* was unearthed, but he said he could not give the engine driver any instructions. Eric then sent for Sergt.-Major Laurie of the 48th. who by profession was a CPR. engine driver. They held a revolver to the back of their French engine driver and forced him to get up steam with the help of Laurie. The return to Laval was all up hill and very slow, the engine finding it difficult to haul such a heavy train. There were frequent stops while sufficient steam was again got up. They worked out a careful scheme for engaging the enemy if they were attacked, and it was decided that a position should be taken up on the south side of the railway track. The men had their rifles and 50 rounds each, and they had some Bren guns. Holes were knocked in the roof of the railway carriages, so that the Bren guns could deal with hostile aircraft. At Rennes they thought they would go to St Nazaire to embark, but finally were ordered to make their way to St Malo though nobody seemed certain that they would not find the railway cut. They reached St Malo and found a ship already more than half full. But both Battalions managed to get on it, and they eventually arrived at Southampton on 18 June after surely one of the strangest expeditions on record. They discovered afterwards that German motor bicycle patrols had actually crossed the railway track between Rennes and Laval, while they were at Sablé. The men call this episode 'The Brest Bust'.

The 1st. Canadian Division was also nearly involved in the defence of Dunkirk about 23 May. General McNaughton,[1] with his GSOI, took a car across the Channel and did a quick reconnaissance on 21 May. The idea was that the Canadians should hold a defensive position on the high ground round Cassel, and thus defend Dunkirk. But the Germans were in Boulogne on 23 May, and the two regiments of the 1st. Brigade chosen to go - they were actually on ship in Dover harbour and had cast off - were ordered to return.

Eric says that the Canadians are naturally a bit fed up after these fruitless expeditions. They have now been in England for seven months and have not fired a shot. They are trained stale. There is nothing more they can be taught about their arms. At the moment, in their new area they are digging hard, but simply long for a chance of having a go at the Boches. In addition to two and three inch mortars, Bren guns and anti-tank rifles, they now have Tommy guns. Eric also explained the newly-formed reconnaissance squadrons - motor cycles with side cars carrying a Bren. This takes a leaf out of the German book.

Notes by J.B.B. on a visit to Sarre, 30 July

I bicycled over to Sarre this afternoon to see Nicholas Ignatieff[2] who is a subaltern with the 1st. Canadian Engineer Battalion RCT. The high ground between Sturry and Upstreet has one road block near the miners' houses, much wire and trenches and a number of strong points, the latter cleverly concealed, one in a hay stack, another in a slag heap. The fields are all blocked with concrete posts and other obstructions. On the Wantsum Flats at the bridge just short of

[1] Lt-Gen Andrew McNaughton, DSO (1887-1966). Comm 1st. Can. Div, 1939-40;GOC 1st Can. Corps, 1940-42; GOC-in-C, 1st. Can. Army, 1942-3; retd. as Gen., 1944; Can. Min. of Nat. Defense, 1944-45. PC (Can.), 1944. Son killed in action (RCAF), 1942.
[2] Nicholas Ignatieff (d. 1947). J.B.B.'s successor as Warden of Hart House.

Sarre, is a road block permanently manned by troops. Ignatieff showed me the defensive system of the village of Sarre, which is based on the idea that enemy motor cyclist patrols and light armoured cars should be allowed to pass by and then engaged from behind. He first took me into a cottage on the right of the road which bears left handed towards St Nicholas-at-Wade. It is a veritable fort inside. Just beyond it on the top of the rise is a windmill (made ready for demolition) and at the foot of it a farm with the usual out-buildings, sheds, pig sties and the rest. A somewhat tumble-down-looking black-boarded cart shed strikes the eye as nothing particular. Inside it are three feet of concrete with loopholes commanding the country towards St Nicholas. One line of pig sties is a veritable strong point to hold a section of infantry and MGs. Beyond the farm is a brick house standing on the road to Ramsgate at the top of the rise and commanding the entire countryside towards Ash. A few feet away one would say it was an ordinary bungalow. It shows no signs whatever of its sinister transformation inside. Enter the door and you will find all the floors and partition walls removed, and the interior divided into several concrete compartments with three feet brick walls - the loopholes about a foot back from the windows so that they cannot possibly be detected. To fire one simply breaks the glass or opens the windows. The modern pub where the buses stop is rapidly being converted into a miniature Gibraltar. The famous Crown Inn (15th. Century) visited by so many celebrities, is fortunately not to be touched and Ignatieff and I had a cup of tea there. But Baxter's lovely 16th. century house down the lane to the north is ruined; one end of it is de-gutted and Bren guns from behind concrete defences will fire through the old leaded windows. The heavenly garden lies derelict. These Canadian sappers are a fine body of men, drawn from all over Canada. I spoke to men from Quebec, Alberta, and Nova Scotia, and loved the free and easy attitude. They were under canvas, cleverly concealed under the trees where the road forks to Ramsgate. HQ is in the cricket pavilion. The men's cook is a nigger who went all through the Spanish Civil War on the government side. Ignatieff says they do not expect to be at Sarre much longer, and will then move possibly to Surrey, where they will proceed to make another lovely English village a death trap to the invaders.

Notes by J.B.B. on a visit to Romney Marsh, 31 July

A glorious midsummer day with blue sky, high fleecy clouds and a brilliant sun. The Kent countryside quite exquisitely lovely. The Bishop of Dover who is visiting clergy in the Marshes has asked me to accompany him. He has his ARP arm band, and we both have our respirators and steel helmets. We motor along that entrancing valley to Ashford - road blocks at Milton Bridge, Chartham, Chilham, Godmersham, Wye cross-roads and Kennington. Most of these had sand-bagged MG posts and trenches connected with them. Through Ashford to Ham. At the top of the hill above Ham village, a strong road block. The marsh looked its attractive self; cattle and sheep grazing as usual - farmers putting up posts and other obstructions in the fields - little or no civilian traffic. The canal at Ham fortified at suitable points - a column of light tanks proceeding along the road near Brensett. At Lydd, our furthest point, the Bishop lunches with the curate, and I eat my sandwiches on the top of the church tower with a private of the Somerset Light Infantry who had not heard me ascending the tower and as I emerged on the leads seized his rifle and was suspicious till I succeeded in satisfying him I was not a fifth columnist.

The lighthouse at Dungeness about 6000 to 7000 yards distant looked further. It was misty. Rye was not visible. The shore is well fortified. Private Smith, with whom I shared my lunch, resented one thing only and that was lack of sleep. Regular daily duties and constant patrolling at night; and now of course the 'stand to'. There is a curfew; no one is allowed out later than half an hour after sunset. Round the Rectory is a huge park of lorries, wireless trucks, and transport of all description, all hidden under the trees. The old Rector (aged 86) does not relish it. There is a searchlight in the field opposite. Four heavy tanks on flat cars, with their crews in coaches behind, pulled into Lydd station as we passed.

We went on to New Romney which is extremely heavily defended. It struck me far more so than any other place we saw all day. There were batteries of heavies and field guns - houses and inns cleverly and effectively organised as strong points, tremendous blocks, trenches, MG emplacements and the rest. The sea wall along to Dymchurch was topped with thick coils of wire and sailors were in charge at several points. Well-constructed pill boxes and guns (so camouflaged it was impossible to make out what they were) were to be seen facing at fairly frequent intervals along or near the sea wall. At Dymchurch a good many of the shops were closed. The famous miniature railway looked derelict. The name 'Dymchurch' had been painted out on the board at the doll-sized station. There were no civilians about at all, the whole place had a completely deserted air; but contrary to what I expected, that glorious expanse of sand was completely devoid of wire; except for one or two strong points children could have taken possession of it as long as they kept away from a long line of posts which stretched out into the sea (it was low tide) and which we understand is connected with a net or some underwater contrivance to which mines are attached. At some points on the south coast barbed wire stretches far out to sea, some of it disclosed at low water and a horrible obstruction just below the surface at high tide.

As we entered Hythe we saw from the lack of traffic and the ARP officials at every corner that an air raid was in progress. We put on our tin hats, the Bishop looking most imposing in his. Out of 9,000 people only 3,000 are left. Norris, the Vicar, and his wife gave us a warm welcome and provided tea. The noise of a severe air battle over our heads was very noticeable, but the machines were too high or the upper air too misty to detect what was happening. But there was the weird screech of planes diving, or zooming up, and the rattle of MG fire. Norris said the shore is covered with wire. The public lavatory on the sea front is a strong point and OP, and I could see figures on it. The canal bridge was mined and powerful barriers block the bridges. A steam-roller formed the chief obstacle across the avenued way from the town to the sea front, which as children we had so often traversed with Nanny. In Hythe itself there are solid concrete road blocks near the terminus of the light railway. Norris said the police check-up every single house in the town on Sundays to see that no unauthorised people have appeared.

There is considerable resentment over the way in which some of the more aged poor who have been evacuated have been treated. They have virtually been placed in what amount to old-fashioned work-houses; have to wear the uniform of the establishment, and are under discipline. This seems to be chiefly in Wales which anyway is a generation behind England in her social services. The air raid was still in progress when we left Hythe and throughout our run back to Canterbury along Stone Street. The only occasion when we were asked to show our identity cards was at a particularly strong road block at the Ashford-Hythe and Lympne-Westenhanger cross-roads. We stopped at the usual point above Horton Priory to look at the famous view of the Weald spread at our feet in the soft evening sunlight. The air scrap went on high above our heads. The 'all clear' sounded about 7 p.m. long after we had returned to Canterbury.

Archdeacon Sopwith[1] has a young friend in the New Forest called Jane.

---

[1] Ven. Thomas Karl Sopwith (1873-1945). Archdeacon of Maidstone, 1934-9; Canon and Archdeacon of Canterbury, 1939-42; Archdeacon Emeritus, 1942-5.

Jane has a riding mistress and the riding mistress entered a bus in the New Forest a few days ago and found herself sitting next to a none-too-clean gipsy woman. The gipsy noticed her embarrassment and said, 'I notice you don't much like sitting next to me, but I can do a thing you can't. I can at least pay my fare, and you can't.' The riding mistress replied she had plenty or money with which to pay her fare, but when the conductor came round she searched for her purse in vain. The gypsy said, 'It is no good your looking for your purse as I saw you leave it behind on the mantelpiece in your house.' And the riding mistress recollected that such was in actual fact the case. The conductor who had been an amused witness of this scene said to the gypsy, 'Well, Mother, you seem to know a lot about what is happening; perhaps you can tell us when the war is going to end'. 'I can,' said the gypsy woman without a moment's hesitation. 'It will be over by February, but Hitler will have gone a long time before that month.'

I was on guard tonight (31 July - 1 August) at the Broad Oak road block. We all had to stand to from 3.30 till 4.45 a.m. Apparently the tides are right; there is a great massing of troops in northern France and an invasion is definitely expected in the next ten days.

The small shopkeepers of the towns in this part of Kent have been ordered, in the case of an invasion, to destroy all their canned stores to prevent them falling into the hands of the Germans. Betteshanger School house is the centre of the air raid signals as far as raids are concerned.

Experiences of Frank Lionel Montagu Rundall, 1939-1940

On August 26th. 1939 I was called out on partial deployment. I was stationed in Hyde Park, with an Anti-Aircraft Battery, composed mostly of London Bankers, I myself being in the ICI Technical Dept, dealing with ARP organisation. On 15 October my regiment went overseas, and came under the orders of the Advanced Air Striking Force. Our Headquarters were at Rheims, and the various Batteries lay within a radius of 20 miles, defending light bomber aerodromes. My Battery (the 158th. Battery of the 53rd. HAA Regt. RA) was at Berry-au-Bac, on the Aisne. We were attached to the 76th. wing of the BEF which comprised 12 and the 142 Squadrons. I was in command of a Battery of four three-inch guns, and was responsible for the defence of 12 Squadron. This Squadron was the one which blew up the bridge over the Meuse at Maastricht. A friend of mine, Don Garland, won the VC for this job. Out of the six planes

(Fairey Battles) which volunteered for the job, one only returned. After three weeks fighting there was only one pilot out of the original set left in the Squadron.

In May, during the invasion of Belgium, I was engaged in building a new gun site, and we were not yet ready for action when a formation of German bombers came over and dropped the first bombs we had seen at close quarters. During the next five days a German mechanised column broke through the French line at Sedan, and a battalion of enemy tanks penetrated into our area. We were not organised for defence against ground troops, as we had only thirty rifles among a hundred men; the aerodrome had been repeatedly bombed, day and night, and the evening before we retired, 50 Parachutists were seen to land in the neighbouring woods, and our telephone lines were cut. At midnight we received an order to move as quickly as possible, taking with us only our instruments, and such personal kit as we could carry, but leaving our guns behind us, as there was no transport available for them. We retreated through Rheims, and across the Marne and Aube, without incident. When we reached the Troyes area we found that our Regiment had lost over half its guns. Here the Brigade reformed, (the 12th. AA Brigade). The 53rd. Regiment, less my Battery, the 158th., was sent down to the base to re-equip. My Battery was attached to the 73rd. HAA Regiment, defending the aerodromes round Troyes. We could not bear to lose our guns, so the next night a party of us went back across the Aisne to try and save them. We split up into three parties; my party consisted of myself and 10 men, with a couple of towing lorries. The French, who were at that time holding the line of the Aisne, said that there were no French on the opposite bank, only German mechanised units. The Lieutenant in command of the Bridge at Berry-au-Bac, however, thought that it might be reasonably safe for us to have a try at reaching our guns on the opposite bank. My own party worked hard all night, and we returned across the Aisne with both our guns, to the rendezvous arranged, before dawn. Party number two also turned up, but the third party was never seen again.

We then returned to the Troyes area with our guns and all our clothing which had previously been left behind, and a lot of stores, but we had lost two officers, and half a dozen men. We were at Troyes for about a fortnight, and during this time I was involved in an accident. We had had no sleep for three nights, and were ordered to attend a conference of officers that lasted from 8 p.m. till after midnight, at which time we climbed into a car, and all fell instantly asleep, including the driver, so that we must have run into a French lorry, which smashed our car to smithereens. The French found that we were all unconscious, and bleeding, so they dragged our bodies to the side of the road, and after taking our cap badges as souvenirs drove on without having attempted any first aid. However they reported our plight to the first British they passed, who came out and salvaged us. They said afterwards that we had all looked too awful for words, lying unconscious in great pools of blood. I was the least hurt, as I had been in the back of the car wedged in between some others, but I had a great gash across my forehead, and another under my chin, and was unconscious for twenty-four hours. We were all taken to Number Nine General Hospital, at Grand Luce, near Le Mans, where we had to stay for a week. We were informed when we were convalescent, that we were all to be sent home, but I persuaded the medical commandant after some difficulty, to let me stay in France and rejoin my unit. I pointed out that I was a 'walking case' with no broken limbs. He said I was a young fool, but gave in. I returned to the Battery just as they were about to retreat to the Vendôme area. This retreat was far better organised than the last one, but the RAF, whose vehicles kept no sort of convoy discipline and careered along at any speed they thought fit, and very much hampered the Army columns, which maintained the ordered speed of 15 m.p.h.

My Battery had now only half its number of guns; this meant that two of our four sections had no guns, and so we were sent into rest billets. We were billeted at a lovely old mill, beside a charming river, where we fished and bathed and thoroughly enjoyed ourselves. I can tell you the water looked good to us, as we had not had a bath since we left Rheims. This mill was owned by an old miser, who looked like a gorilla. He had made such a lot of money out of the mill, that he did not bother to work it any more, and lived alone, very penuriously in one room of the house where we officers were billeted. He was evidently slightly mad, and we all agreed that the formidable-looking woman, whose portrait hung in our mess room, must have been responsible. (A pity he didn't enjoy his money while he had it. I expect the Germans have found it all right by now). During this week of rest, I was able to visit Château d'Un, Vendôme, and Blois. It was at a pub in Blois that I heard from a refugee that the Italians had come into the war. I knew that would put our Navy's tails up! The French at this time seemed very disheartened, and the crowds of refugees that thronged the roads were more than half composed of French soldiers, numbers of whom sat around in cafes, drinking and smoking and gossiping, never seeming to think of fighting at all. Some evinced the greatest faith in the Maginot Line, but never seemed to think that it was up to them to do anything at all to help matters. Most of them though just shrugged their shoulders, and hardly seemed to care about anything. The further we went, the more French soldiers we saw, sitting around and drinking. I forgot to say, that while we were at Rheims, I captained a football team against a regiment of Chars Legers - Light Tanks - at a place called Stenay on the Luxembourg frontier. I was thus able to take a look around, and found it mainly interesting for the fact that there was no sort of Frontier defence at all.

From Vendôme we retired to Ancenis, on the Loire. Here we had been ordered to report to the Gendarmerie, where a British officer, alleged to have been sent on ahead, would show us our billets. After a whole day's driving, from four o'clock in the morning, we arrived, dead beat, only to find that no British officer had yet arrived, and that nobody knew anything about us or were ready to afford billets. So we slept under the trees that night, and hung about all next day, wondering what was going to happen, and waiting for further orders. At last an officer arrived, and said that the French were offering no organised resistance against the oncoming Germans, and he advised us to get to the nearest port as quickly as possible. We therefore went on to Nantes, about thirty miles. Here things seemed much better, for though the town was packed with British troops, there seemed to be some sort of organisation. My whole regiment collected in a large château and its grounds, outside the town. During the night, half 158 Battery was sent south of the river, to St Brevin, to cover embarkation from St Nazaire.

At breakfast the next morning the Adjutant asked me to take some petrol to them. I had no idea how far away it was, and hopped on to a lorry, just as I was, without any kit, and of course leaving all my valuables, such as field-glasses, family photographs and snapshots, plus my Grandfather's gold watch nearly a hundred years old (its date was 1860) with the rest of my kit and accoutrements. I did not even pause to take a tin hat, or a gas mask. The battery's position proved to be about forty miles away, on the south bank of the river's mouth. When I at last reached it, I was immediately told that all British troops in Nantes were embarking that night, and that I could not possibly go back and collect my kit. So I stayed where I was, but the next morning I got up at 4 a.m. and found a small boat to ferry me across the river, as I meant to have a dash at rescuing my kit. I arrived at St Nazaire without any form of transport but there were several deserted cars lying around, ownerless, so I got into the biggest I could find, (which incidentally had a wireless in it, which was great luck), and drove back to where all our British vehicles had been carefully and tidily parked in a large field, ready to be fetched if possible. French soldiers and civilians were busily looting everything they could lay hands on, snatching and grabbing, and trampling things down in the mud. It was absolutely hopeless to try and find one's own belongings. I returned to the battery, however, with half a dozen rifles, and a Bren gun, and hundreds of rounds of ammunition, which I had contrived to pack into the car.

During the general embarkation, which we were covering, German bombers appeared, and dropped bombs, which however did no damage. At 4 p.m. we were informed that the embarkation had been completed, and that as it was impossible for us, covering troops, to reach St Nazaire in time, we were to make a very hasty retreat to La Rochelle. Half an hour after we left, three Heinkels appeared at St Nazaire harbour, and sank the *Lancastria*, which had aboard, among many others, about 120 men of our Battery. 6,000 men were on that boat, and about 2,000 were saved. We had been told to arrive at La Rochelle that evening at 9 p.m., but this was later extended to midnight, when the French closed the port. There were only two British colliers in the harbour, and we all crammed on to these, being obliged to leave all our guns, stores, and lorries etc., on the quay. This time the French were all lined up on the quay, waiting almost to snatch things out of our hands as we went wearily on board. They seemed to grudge us everything we were able to take away with us. They were like jackals. When our lorries drove up, the French jumped madly on, even as we were alighting, and snatched and tore at everything they could. We had a struggle to get any of our own things before they were seized from us. While we were waiting for the French to raise the boom, to let us out of the harbour, German planes appeared, and dropped magnetic mines just outside. This, we were told, happened every night. Luckily our collier was fitted with an anti-magnetic mine device, so we passed over the minefields unhurt. We were four days on board without any life-belts, before any escort appeared, but we had bully beef and biscuits to eat, though nothing but buckets of sea-water to wash in. Finally we docked at Newport, Monmouthshire, terribly dirty, but thankful to be in England once more. We were tremendously impressed at the different standard of living over here, to that in France, in fact the different standard of everything. We felt this is certainly a land to fight and die for, or better still to live for.

August

Notes by J.B.B. on a visit to London, 2 August

I heard that the GOC of the Canadian Division, Andy McNaughton, had a high reputation in military circles in England, and would probably go far. At present he has a Corps (7th) consisting of the 1st Canadian Division and a British mechanised Division. Whether he will now take over the 2nd Canadian Division, the arrival of which is announced in to-day's evening papers, I don't know. McNaughton impresses the army pundits here with his knowledge of gunnery. Recently at a conference some new artillery calculations were presented. McNaughton looked at them for a few moments and then announced they were inaccurate, which indeed they proved to be, though British gunnery experts had been working on them for some weeks.

Euan Wallace, with whom I had a long talk on the telephone, told me that Duff Cooper had had a pretty hot time in the House last night, being bitterly attacked for the house-to-house enquiries which representatives of the Ministry of Information had been making, in order to ascertain the trend of public opinion. This was said to smack of Gestapo methods. Actually this procedure had been arranged by Duff's predecessor. Euan said Duff had made an admirable speech and he admired his courage in coming right back at the press who now have their knife into him. He also says that Eden agrees too much with the military heads. What one wants is a Secretary of State for War who has his own ideas and will often over-rule the Generals.

I lunched at the United Services' Club with Hankey, who told me about the means taken to demolish all material which might be of use to the Germans in Belgium and even in France - such things as the burning of petrol and oil stocks; the removal of gold from the banks; the destruction of railway centres and factories, and of stores of all kinds; and the blocking of harbours. As early as last September he had begun working on this problem, though it was difficult work as Belgium refused to discuss the matter for fear of breaking her neutrality. All arrangements about the gold, for instance, had to be made privately by the Governor of the Bank of England approaching his opposite number in Belgium and various private banking interests. Hankey had his demolition squads (mostly naval men) and the destroyers to take them across the Channel, all waiting at

Dover directly the Blitzkrieg began. The officer in charge of the detachment for Le Havre, Rouen and Brest reported to the French GOC at Rouen, who thanked him but said all arrangements for demolition had already been made by his engineers. A French Colonel was deputed to take the naval officer round. At one oil tank they found a French soldier who, when asked what the plans were for destroying the tank, said he would put a match to it and *mourir pour la patrie*. The destruction of tanks of this kind is a highly expert and delicate job. Hankey's squads eventually carried out the demolition themselves and destroyed 1,500,000 gallons of petrol in Le Havre alone. The French fortunately did destroy the valuable oil refineries at Dunkirk. The Germans got no oil or petrol in Northern France or in Tours, Orleans or Bordeaux. But Marseilles with large oil and petrol stores and material of all kinds fell untouched into their hands.

Hankey said that the British military High Command did not realise how rotten the state of the French army was, though Hoare and he had serious doubts after their visit to the Maginot Line in January last. Some of the forts were not very efficient (in one of the largest the lift was out of order). Hankey thought the whole Maginot Line was very under-gunned. Gamelin was specious and always had a good answer for every problem. They met General Corap,[1] whose army later broke at Sedan. They were not impressed with him. His equipment was not up to date: practically all his transport was horse-drawn. Hankey had two days previously had General de Gaulle and Spears[2] to lunch, and found de Gaulle slow of speech and very deliberate. Pétain,[3] de Gaulle said, was a very vain man. He disliked having had no prominent military post in the war and had seized the opportunity of becoming Head of State. That very morning the lunch took place de Gaulle had received information of the low morale of the German troops, especially in Brittany, where according to his agents they were sullen and thoroughly fed up and anxious to return to Germany. The French colonies are wavering as to their allegiance to France or England, the older generation tending towards France, the younger towards fighting on with England.

---

[1] General André Corap (1878-1953). Cmdr. of French Ninth Army, which broke before the German onslaught around Sedan in May 1940.
[2] Maj-Gen. Sir Edward Spears (1886-1974). MP(NLib) Loughborough, 1922-4, and (Con) Carlisle, 1931-45; PM's personal rep. with Free French, 1940-45.
[3] Philippe Pétain (1856-1951). Marshal of France, 1918; Fr. Amb. to Spain, 1939-40; Chief of the French State, 1940-44. In detention after war till death.

Hankey is himself engaged on various special jobs: at the moment he is particularly occupied with a device for dealing with hostile tanks. He said the military mind was singularly unresponsive to new ideas, and then when a new device was demonstrated expected it to accomplish results it was unreasonable to expect. He has been twice in East Kent recently - at Ramsgate, and then at Hythe.

With regard to invasion Hankey thought the air attack on Dover two days ago was significant as showing the enemy really wished to wipe out our destroyers - but he said there was no sign of ships in the Channel ports, of a type which could be used for landing - e.g. as at Gallipoli: there were plenty of barges, but these were for show. *The Times* to-day reports that the German press seems to be preparing the people for there being no immediate direct invasion on England, but pointing out that England will be brought to her knees by separate blows - the blockade - air attack - a war of attrition. The Italian fleet was skulking in Taranto, we could bomb it when the nights get longer.

I had a talk with Tom Jones at the Pilgrim Trust office. He has resigned from the UAB (Unemployment Assistance Board) and will give up the Pilgrim Trust after the war. He is 70 years old shortly. He told me of the Guerilla Warfare School at Osterley Park, financed by Edward Hulton,[1] owner of *Picture Post*, and run by Tom Wintringham[2] who was in the Spanish Civil War and wrote recently on how to stop tanks. The Osterley Park course lasts two days and teaches all the dodges of guerilla warfare. TJ's cottage at 'Snick' is occupied by gunner officers. 'Snick' is apparently not being fortified as is Sarre.

Geoffrey Dawson told Vincent Massey that the Germans had recently dropped seven bombs in an isolated part of the Yorkshire Moors, apparently for no other reason than to get home more easily.

I came down on the 7.15 from Victoria with a number of soldiers and sailors. One soldier, a Welsh Fusilier, returning from leave, told me a policeman at Swansea had actually shown him a German bomb filled with sawdust. It was marked Skoda.

There is much uncertainty about this bell ringing in case of a German landing. (1) Are the vergers or bell ringers chosen, and do they know their job?

---

[1] Edward Hulton (1906-88). Magazine publisher; founder and prop. of *Picture Post*, 1937-58. Kt (1957).
[2] Thomas Henry Wintringham (1898-1949). Author and adventurer; helped found Osterley Park Training School for Home Guard, 1940.

(2) Should the Churches remain open, and should one bell or a peal be rung and for how long? (3) How to guard against fifth columnists ringing the bells?

Sir Philip Gibbs[1] to J.B.B., 3 August   *Shamley Green, Guildford*

I was in France all through the dreary winter and then until a week before the Germans entered Paris. But I escaped the ordeal of Dunkirk and most other adventure as I was cut off from the BEF at the most interesting time, alas, through no fault of my own. Now I have 'chucked' all work as a war correspondent owing to the conditions of censorship which make it futile and humiliating.

A week ago today my family, that is to say my son Anthony and his wife and two small children, departed for the USA. I shall suffer from acute anxiety until I hear of their arrival which I shall not do for another two weeks as they are in a slow-going cargo-boat.

Notes by J.B.B., 4 August

Tuzo Wilson (Ottawa) and Neelands (Toronto), both Lieutenants in the Tunnelling Company, came in for a drink tonight. They are mining the roads by means of diamond drilling, a far more speedy and efficient method than the old one of digging a trench and putting in the explosive and filling it up again. The mining industry in Canada has taken a great deal of interest in these methods and has provided the machinery and the funds.

Three days ago two of Wilson's men got very drunk in Canterbury. When military policemen tried to run them in they knocked down at least five men, broke the handcuffs and were with difficulty eventually overpowered. They were huge men - a fine type - and apparently got tight on doped wine. Mrs Gardiner says she knows this is the case, and this pub ought to have its licence taken away. All Canterbury was talking of the superhuman strength of these Canadian soldiers. They are miners by trade.

This morning (Sunday) I paraded at the Mint Yard at 9.15 and 50 NCO's (I was one of the few privates) went in lorries to the London Fusiliers' HQ at Harbledown, and then marched to a large quarry on Bigberry Hill, where the anti-tank company of the Fusiliers gave us a demonstration of various tank-fighting methods. The first was the Molotov bomb. I threw several at a dummy tank. They

---

[1] Sir Philip Gibbs (1877-1962). Prolific author, war correspondent. Kt (1919).

are ordinary beer bottles filled with two parts petrol, one part paraffin, and one part creosote-tar. Only the first has to be lit with a fuse - the next catches fire from the first - the flare up of flame is terrific and the heat intense. They envelop the tank and the occupants frizzle to death. Various types of mines were exploded, some for blowing up a road, others which will explode when the tank passes over them. It was a perfect summer morning. As we marched through the shady lanes the countryside, with harvest and rapidly-ripening fruit, looked entrancing.

Geoffrey to E.C.F.B., 4 August   *Aberdeen*

Tony has received his notice to join up (on the date arranged last October) at Warwick on the 15th of this month, so that we have only another ten days of his company. Two days before receiving this notice the Oxford OTC officially notified him that if he had not already received it - which he hadn't - the WO had now issued a regulation that all men like himself who had passed even a part of Certificate B (as he has) were to go straight into officers' training units. Nevertheless, when two days later, he received his call-up notice it was a notice to join an ordinary (service) unit, and not an officers' training unit. One can only suppose that the new regulation had not yet reached the local military authority that called him up.

Nevertheless I hope that, in the circumstances, he will be soon transferred to an officers' training unit: even though it is, of course, hoping against hope to expect that the WO should act, at any time, with efficiency or reason. Utter chaos reigns there at present, I understand, and always will, unless they alter, root and branch, the entire system upon which the WO has from its origin been organised, the product of which is the mind of the professional soldier, i.e. a mind that is no mind in the ordinary sense of that term. It is sad to reflect that the army has learnt nothing at all from the last war and is still being run on the principle that the professional soldier, merely because he is a professional, must never rank below the non-professional, though the cirumstances may have conclusively demonstrated that the latter, in this case or in that, posess vigour, brains and initiative, and the former none. It is a tragic fact that professionalism in the army is such that (a) it cannot itself produce a genius, but on the contrary nips it in the bud, (b) is so hide-bound that it cannot detect military genius outside its own ranks, and even if it could, would never allow it to rise to the top. For to do so would, in its view, be equivalent to admitting its own inefficiency. Our political system succeeds, or has succeeded hitherto, because it discourages professionalism. William Pitt was PM at 24. So, too, in the commercial world, brains can rise to the top at once, whatever the age of its possessor. Oliver Cromwell, one of our few military geniuses, was a civilian till after he was 40, and when he became a soldier never lost a battle (the same is true of Julius Cæsar). You will see that in our present army, as was the case in the last war, age (i.e. youth) and civilian status, will prove as complete a handicap to military advancement as they always have in the eyes of the professional. Nothing short of a political revolution could break the spine of military professionalism, whose unbreakable law is 'rank goes by seniority, and seniority by length of service in the regular army.'

In short I do not think that our War Office is competent to deal with an army composed of men who are 90% civilians by profession. For it will automatically place them and keep them all, and throughout the war, under the command of the 10% who are professional soldiers, since it will provide no means by which the civilian (now become a soldier) whom circumstances may prove to possess military genius, may be raised to the highest command. I doubt whether it is even capable of discovering such individuals, who yet must exist in an army of four million men. Such individuals won't be used because they won't be discovered, but even if they were discovered they wouldn't be used. Our army system, which is a vicious circle, renders it impossible. For it is professionalised through and through; (as the navy and, still more, the RAF are not) possibly because the army operates on land, and they on the sea and in the air respectively. Water and air would seem to have that advantage over the grosser element earth. They foster, and do not kill, the spirit and the initiative of the individual, as earth does: and they also love youth and the fire of youth. At any rate, and for whatever reason, the navy and the air force are controlled by brains that seem ten times as much alive as those of the army command: fertile of new ideas, new methods, and new men. Nor are they disinclined by nature to take advantage of the civilian. The navy saved the army at Dunkirk by calling in the aid of civilians, i.e. non-naval vessels of every description manned by non-naval men - a device which saved a desperate situation and converted it into a triumph. Such an idea would not even have occurred to the army, or if it had, would have been turned down because not mentioned in the professional text-books.

Ralph to E.C.F.B., 5 August   *Lombard Street*

We had a glorious weekend at Langton Green. Peter played cricket for the village side on Saturday afternoon and you could not have wished for a more typical English scene. It is a lovely old fashioned green with the cricket pitch in the middle. It was a glorious afternoon and war seemed miles away, except, of course, there were loads of lorries and trucks beetling along all the time. Langton Green won handsomely. Peter got some hard hitting in before he was bowled. He had the satisfaction of getting the fellow out who bowled him - a very good catch.

Notes by J.B.B., 7 August

The papers are full of German statements about the coming attack on England and there are constant references to secret and mysterious weapons. For instance (*The Times* 7 Aug) foreign correspondents were informed that one of the secret weapons to be employed against England was that used only once before, and that was in the capture of the key fortress of Eban Emael near Liège. At the time there was much talk of a new type of gas which rendered the Belgian garrison powerless for some hours - producing a sort of lethargy, semi-unconciousness which made it impossible to use the limbs, but was innocuous except for that,

To-day there are quotations from the 'Schwarze Korps', the official organ of the SS, to the effect that 'the time of waiting is over, we are coming.' Or again, General Sander, of the German Air Force broadcasting says, 'The German Air Force stands ready in a wide crescent from Trondheim to Brest. In the centre of this crescent lies the main objective, a comparatively small island, England. The attacks of the German Air Force will be directed against important military objectives, against the centre of English industry and against harbours and docks'.

Ralph Alderson to J.B.B., 8 August   *Bemerton Rectory, Salisbury*

I have been doing various jobs starting with billeting officer for this place - and then I did a six weeks period twice in the local Food Office, as we had 45,000 ration cards to write out, and a great deal of filing and sorting - a very tedious and tiresome job. However it was all done here by voluntary work and did not cost the country a penny. Now I am in the Home Guard which is quite amusing. I did guard all night at the Water Works about three and a half miles off on the Plain, but now only do 5 a.m. to 8 a.m. about twice a week, which is a great improvement. I have an alarm clock and so far have not overslept myself! I hear tonight that the military are shortly going to take it over.

We had a Field Day last Sunday and I impersonated a German parachutist, and with three others had to get to a certain farm which was supposed to be an aerodrome, and strange to relate, we did it. We were the only three of the enemy who got in, all the others were taken prisoner - I hid in a wood and crawled along the edge of cornfields, and crept through beds of nettles, and was in the objective long before the 'cease fire'. It was really a most amusing day's work.

Eric Duncannon turned up here on 1 June straight from Dunkirk after going through thrilling experiences and finally wading into the sea and being picked up by a destroyer, which took him to Dover, where he got a train which deposited him at Warminster about 18 miles from here. I was the nearest friend he could think of, so he got a car and came here, and we fed him and bathed him, and I fitted him up with pyjamas etc. He got home to Stansted the next day, and has by now rejoined his regiment. I don't know where he is at the moment.

Notes by J.B.B., 10 August

Last night I was sitting in the Garden room about 11.30 p.m. There was the sound of AA fire and German planes overhead and then four bombs dropped, I would judge about five or six miles away. This is so usual that I took little notice, but when another bomb fell rather nearer I went upstairs and looked out of my bedroom window. I then saw at least 10 parachute flares floating serenely in the sky at about 2,000 feet, in the direction of Sturry and Sarre. They were of great brilliance and even at a distance which I judged to be at least six miles, they illuminated our garden. The countryside below them must have been as clear as day.

I got Mother out of bed for a few moments to survey the skies. It was a very lovely scene, with the parachute flares shining like enormously brilliant roman candles, and scores of searchlights searching the skies in their attempt to pick up the German planes, which were droning overhead. The Boches remained in the neighourhood for some time, as there was the explosion of a very heavy bomb about 12.15 a.m., which shook this house and rattled the windows,

Sergeant Berk says that there have been many rockets and other light signals in this neighbourhood lately, and the Field Security and civilian police are doing their best to track these down. So far though their efforts have been without much success. Moving about among the civilian population and among the troops in pubs and elsewhere, Berk says he finds that morale is excellent. It is not considered there are many fifth columnists, but those that exist are evidently very efficient.

'The Artist at work in South East Kent' by Marjorie Linnell, 10 August

At any of the crossroads and other strategic points on the high roads between Canterbury and the coast are now to be seen miniature buildings which make one wonder if one has jumped back into one's childhood and is realizing the child's dream of an ideal 'castle in the air'. But these fascinating small buildings are built with deadly intent, and are the pill-boxes from which our soldiers will shoot 'if the invader comes'.

To describe a few outstanding ones:- just outside Deal stands Sholden Church, commanding three important roads. Now, in front of the main building there is a perfect imitation, small and square, but built in the same stone, with lancet windows, and the appearance of stained glass; in fact the whole pill-box was hardly distinguishable from the Church in the background. Another such was in course of construction outside Upper Deal Church (St Leonard's); this was being built of old mellowed red brick, to tone with the brick Church centuries old. Outside the village pub at Mongham a pill box appears to be part of the main whitewashed brick building

At the corner of a wood on the Canterbury side of The Half Way House, on the way to Dover, before knowing it, one is right on one of these shooting boxes. It is most cleverly painted with leaves and boughs, and literally fades into its background. But the real gem is about 500 yards nearer Canterbury, by Broome Park. It is built in the form of an old toll house, whitewashed brick, with little casement windows, draped with dimity and lace curtains; a rose tree climbing up its walls; a tub of evergreen by the steps leading up to its tiny front door; and the guttering round the eaves standing out in the most realistic way. All this is painted on the flat walls, and is a piece of real artistry, as in fact, they all are.

One can imagine Sergeant Artist, Corporal Architect, and Private Stonemason finding a sense of deep satisfaction in having accomplished such imaginative works of art, and at the same time providing defensive points in the countryside which they have not defaced.

Notes by J.B.B., 11 August

I was on guard at the Gate Inn road block last night and got home about 5.45 a.m. - was up by 8.30 a.m. and at 9.30 paraded at the Mint Yard for Church Parade. About 500 men on parade, all in uniform. Behind The Buffs band we marched by Broad Street and the High Street and Mercery Lane to the Cathedral, where the service took place in the Choir. General Forster read the first Lesson, and the Dean the second, speaking first of the work of the Home Guard, whom he welcomed to the Cathedral. He said that when Major James asked whether the School buildings in the Mint Yard might be used for the HQ of this force he (the Dean) had gladly given his consent as such an organisation was his ideal type of army, being a real people's army.

Geoffrey to E.C.F.B., 11 August   *Aberdeen*

Yesterday afternoon Jean, Tony, Julian and I went to tea with the Bishop of Aberdeen and his wife by invitation. The Bishop is 72, was going to have retired, but the war, which he is enjoying immensely, has done much to rejuvenate him. He loves flying up to the Orkneys and Shetland (part of his diocese) and visiting the military, and of course naval forces there, and hopes soon to get leave to fly to Iceland. As to what he sees and gets to know, he is of course sworn to secrecy. When he flies, he does so from Aberdeen, over the Moray Firth, then overland to a rendezvous where the aeroplane has to report itself, and fly round till told to go on, which it must do absolutely accurately to the second i.e. where it is expected to be at a given point, there it must be exactly, or else it would be at once shot down. The Orkneys and Shetlands and north of Scotland are thick with troops, guns and fortifications and ships; and the fleet, he says, is in fine fettle and supremely confident, longing to fight the invaders by land, sea or air if they would only come. Even the highest naval officers are not allowed into the ship-yards: all that is known or rumoured is that the new battleships are so heavily armoured that the heaviest bomb falling on deck would be about as effective as a squib, and they are said to be torpedo proof.

Tony has to be at his OCTU at Warwick at 6 p.m. on Thursday next. He has not discovered yet if he can get there by that hour from here starting the same day. If he can't he will travel south on Wednesday night. We shall miss him. He views the prospect with perfect equanimity. I do hope he will find some congenial spirits among the men he is to be with, and some intelligence in his officers. He can drill a company, knows his Bren gun, is quite a good shot, etc. It seems absurd that he must go right back to the beginning, and be wasting his time and the taxpayers' money. But what else can you expect in the British army ?

As soon as one has a son actually in the army one can't help wishing our military authorities had more brains than history has shown them to possess. In my opinion retreats, however conducted, should not be rewarded with decorations. Decorate the victorious General only - that should be the rule. *Finis coronat opus*; time enough to decorate our Generals when they've beaten the enemy. I dislike the way in which at the present moment the country is being cajoled into regarding our retreats in Africa (necessary as they may be) as if they were victorious, whereas they are merely a tribute to our military inferiority - only temporary perhaps, but still unquestionably, inferiority to the enemy locally.

Notes by J.B.B., 12 August

This afternoon I rode to Marley to see Mr and Mrs Sharp, parents of Harold Sharp (Barrie, Ontario, and now in England with the 1st Canadian Division). Mr Sharp is in the Kingston Home Guard and goes on duty at the Kingston waterworks, where I was on guard last Monday, August 5th. Canterbury Home Guard is no longer to help Kingston who will alone be responsible - two men patrolling this pumping station at intervals during the night. This hardly seems adequate protection considering the extreme importance of the place. It supplies water to Dover Castle, to the Admiralty at Dover pier and to most of the aerodromes in the district. The two engines pump 100,000 gallons of water an hour, and hardly lower the head of water in doing so.

I returned via the lanes, running through Mount's orchards. The digging of huge trenches, tank traps, on each side of the railway line wherever the actual track is level with the land on either side, is going on apace. The railway line itself is mined and there are numerous barriers and some pill-boxes sited to fire down the line. On the bridges there are concrete blocks to hold steel beams as barriers to motor cyclists.

If the Germans attack from North and South and join forces, thus cutting off East Kent which would become their bridge head, then this defensive system along the railway might serve to isolate one section, where the German attack had succeeded from another section, where it had failed - in other words it might isolate certain areas where the enemy had been able to exploit his primary success from other areas where he had been help up.

At 5.30 p.m. today the fourth air raid alarm sounded. Hardly had the sirens ceased their wailing when a series of terrific explosions shook this house to its foundations. I thought the windows would be shattered. We heard later that 217 bombs (many of them small ones) fell round the aerodrome at Bekesbourne and in and near Patrixbourne. This was direct from the Bishop of Dover, who went to see the Rector of Bekesbourne. The number of holes were officially counted by the RAF. The house at the corner where one turns down to the village of Patrixbourne just beyond the Bifrons Lodge gates was hit. Trees in neighbouring orchards were uprooted. The sanatorium near Bekesbourne Hill was badly damaged, and workmen engaged on making concrete road blocks and trenches were killed. A number of airmen and soldiers were wounded or killed near the aerodrome. Two bombs fell on the golf links about one mile from this house. A German bomber was brought down on the marshes near Stodmarsh village. One of our Spitfires came down on the railway line near Bekesbourne station, and traffic was limited to one line till the tracks were cleared. An enormous one-ton bomb fell plumb in the middle of the pylons on the top of Dunkirk Hill, and many fell in Boughton, west of Dunkirk, causing a number of civilian casualties. The bus station (near the Duke of Cumberland pub) at Whitstable and the adjoining houses were badly damaged. The runways at Hawkinge aerodrome were damaged. The aerodrome at Lympne was hit.

J.B.B., 13 August

At 7.30 a.m. today, heavy air fighting over Canterbury. Three Messerschmitts came down in the sea off Whitstable, and one of our Spitfires came down on the jetty.

A lad from Deal, who was in Canterbury to join up, informed me that yesterday morning (12 August) some mysterious shells fired apparently from some vessel at sea (though none was seen), landed in and around the barracks at Deal, where it took off the leg of one of the marines. This happened just after an air raid when the 'All Clear' had gone some minutes. One or two of the shells were duds, and had been actually seen by the lad, who told me about the episode. They are being examined by experts. The theory is that they may have been fired by E-Boats, but none were actually seen from the shore.

This evening my section of the Home Guard paraded at the quarry behind the Broad Oak road block and practised throwing Molotov bombs, and the new phosphorus bomb, at a dummy tank, which we constructed from bits of sheet iron and blocks of wood. The phosphorus bomb needs no fuse. It explodes as soon as the bottle breaks and the liquid comes in contact with the air. It therefore needs very careful handling.

Kay to E.C.F.B., 13 August   *North Cottage, Yaverland, I.O.W.*

I know you'll be wanting to hear about the big attack yesterday. First let me tell you that we are safe, though it was pretty nasty while it lasted. Charles was on watch at the time (12.00 noon) of the first big attack, and counted 50 bombers coming over him,

Two bombs fell right over the station but missed all the buildings and fell over the cliff into the sea; that was the nearest they got. I was shopping in Sandown and took refuge in the grocers! I waited downstairs for a time, and then went up to a window facing away from the sea and which had no glass in it.

From there I could see the big attack on Portsmouth; masses of planes going along in formation and then suddenly throwing up their tails and dive-bombing among the balloons, almost certain death. They got the station, where an empty train was standing, which caught fire and blazed furiously, and the whole station was soon gutted. Also the brewery went up in flames, and minor damage was done in the dock-yard, really very little though, for the number of bombs dropped, though the worst thing was two bombs falling on an air raid shelter, killing all the forty people inside it.

I saw one Hun come down in flames on Ventnor Down, after circling over Sandown three times with smoke pouring from it. The whole sky at one time seemed to be filled with planes, wheeling and turning in all directions. One of our fighters came down on Sandown Golf Links, the pilot unfortunately being killed. But Charles saw another make a crash landing on Bembridge aerodrome, and calmly get out and light a cigarette before walking away! It was certainly the most impressive raid we've had, though every day now two or three planes come down either on the island or in the sea.

The 'All Clear' finally went at 1 p.m. and I biked home furiously, however just getting in before the second wave came over at 1.15; this lasted till 2.15, after which Charles at last got down from Culver, very hungry, having had no lunch.

I'm sure the Huns don't drop bombs here on purpose, when Portsmouth and Southampton are so close, but of course they do throw them out sometimes if they're being chased.

Mary to J.B.B., 14 August   *Chiddingstone*

Today the village has been seething with Canadians from Vancouver. They must have been doing some large scale manoeuvres; wherever one went they were hidden behind hedges and lying about in fields. Daddy talked to some of them when he went to teach at the Hoath, and they all were frightfully keen to get at the Germans and hoped things were really beginning at last.

Janie Streatfeild came to lunch to-day. She's home for a couple of nights to make arrangements for Dick's sister's wedding, which is due to take place in September. She was her usual charming self. She told us Dick is very busy and doesn't even get Sundays off. He's not getting quite such a good type of man to train now. Catterick has got about a hundred thousand troops and they're all praying the Germans will try invasion! We told her of Colonel Harry Streatfeild's theory that German airmen make forced landings and so on; they fight furiously for a time and then quite suddenly entirely collapse and often break down and cry.

The other night when Mr Matthew was on Home Guard he saw rather queer lights over in the Tunbridge Wells direction, and many people have seen similar lights. Edenbridge has gone all spy-conscious as two spies were caught there last week.

Our river defences seem to be progressing fairly fast at last. We've got funny little brick and concrete pill boxes all along the river at intervals of about 200 yards. I suppose so that it is possible to see from one to the other, they are lopping off branches of trees and even felling whole trees, and the river looks awfully untidy. They are also digging it out in some places and making the banks very steep. The bridges have got concrete barriers and all the ones which had stone parapets at the sides have been taken down and flimsy wooden railings put up in their place. We are told this is called the second line of defence but no doubt it's really about the twentieth. The men working on the pill boxes get paid exhorbitant wages, and all the tree-felling has been done by New Zealanders.

Tomorrow I go for my fire-fighting practice in the village. Visitors to the village think us quite mad as we rush about in tin hats and top boots running out lengths of hose and pumping madly. We have been doing a lot of knot-tying and the other day I was let down out of one of our upstairs windows in a chair knot - really most comfortable. We are getting much more efficient now, and I think could cope with a fire if we caught it in time.

Today hundreds of Canadians ended up their route march in the grounds of Stonewall. They swarmed into the house and sat about behind bushes in the garden changing maids every five minutes! The evacuees had the time of their lives and none of them went to school this afternoon.

Notes by J.B.B., 15 August

I have been reading a Penguin book just published. It is called *Science and War*, and is written anonymously by a group of 25 eminent scientists. It is a terrible indictment of government inactivity, short-sightedness and lack of imagination. The chapter on tanks, for instance, shows how the War Office was warned after the close of the Spanish War as to the best method of dealing with tanks, but did nothing. Another section on camouflage proves how completely opposed to the basic ideas of disruption, counter shading, coincident pattern, and deflection the present system of camouflaging our buildings and lorries is. Artists and not biologists have been consulted. Other chapters on nutrition, agriculture and factory administration tell the same story.

Notes by J.B.B., 16 August

Air raids over England are now terrific, but let it be said at once that the loss of life and damage done are small in proportion to the German losses. Yesterday (Thursday 15 August) the biggest air invasion of this war up to date took place. The actual periods of air raid alarms as they affected Canterbury were as follows :-

9.55 a.m. till   10.45
11.25.   "   12.35
2.45   "   5.45
6.35   "   8.00 p.m.

As far as this corner of England was concerned the German bombers came over in waves from 25 to 50 at a time. It was a peerless day with clear skies. But they flew so high they were invisible. The afternoon attack extended to Croydon, where the aerodrome was damaged. London had an air raid alarm. Short's aircraft factory at Rochester was hit and a there were a number of casualties at Detling aerodrome. Of the bombs dropped on the northern Kent coast, 21 were duds. These mostly dropped near Herne (on the way to Herne Bay). We brought down 169 German planes yesterday - 34 of our machines are missing, but 17 of the pilots are safe.

Last night I was on guard again at the Gate Inn road block with our gang. We were told to keep a sharp look-out because about 200 soldiers (in brown overalls and forage caps) were masquerading as parachute troops and attempting to get through our road blocks anywhere in this part of Kent. I was on from 11.30 to 1.30 with Fred Newman and Eric Miles. We vacated the actual road block which is in a cutting and took up positions of vantage near, but we heard and saw nothing.

This morning at about 11.50 a.m. I started with Mother into the town, intending to do some shopping. We began by entering the Precincts by the postern gate from Burgate. The siren sounded. We went to Canon Crum's house to enquire about Jim (who is progressing) and as we walked across to the Cathedral heavy bursts of machine gun fire were heard directly overhead, but the planes were high enough to be unobservable. We took shelter in the SW porch of the Cathedral. The fighting became more intense, and the Air Wardens blew their whistles and everybody was ordered to take cover. There were only a handful of people around the Christ Church gateway and on the benches, and they ran to the SW porch. There we waited for nearly half an hour while the fight overhead waxed furious. One of our machines came streaking down across the sky and disappeared behind Mrs Cotton's house. It was some miles distant. The shrill screech of planes diving to the attack and loud bursts of fire were heard as our fighters engaged the enemy. As far as we could see there was no one moving in Mercery Lane, nor in the High Street. Towards 1 p.m. the noise of fighting died away and Mother and I, although the 'All Clear' had not gone and in actual fact did not go till 2.20 p.m., walked home through streets which were still more or less deserted.

This afternoon I bicycled out to see the Dornier lying straddled on the fields on the left of the road just before it descends into Stodmarsh village. Sentries of the 9th London Fusiliers were guarding it, and the lad I talked to, in civilian life an accountant in London, had been there when the machine came down and its four occupants were taken prisoner. He said the pilot, who was wounded, made a very skilful landing. The other three were unhurt. They surrendered without trouble. One of the Germans was quite a boy. The contents of his despatch case were his shaving kit, six bars of Nestlé's milk chocolate, and eight bottles of hair oil.

I then went on to see the Spitfire which had fallen in the orchard of a farm just north of Wickhambreaux. This was probably the machine we saw falling this morning from the Precincts. The pilot who was wounded had baled out successfully. The Spitfire lay among the apple trees and the RAF were engaged in removing the instruments and equipment before an attempt was made to cart the whole machine away.

Monier to E.C.F.B., 17 August   *Chiddingstone*

The day before yesterday came a raid, a real one. We are all quite all right, one fatal casualty in the village, one pony had to be killed, and several sheep - a good many houses damaged, including ours, but no direct hits except on one barn. All the house damage done was due to blast.

No one quite knows how many planes there were, and it is clear our fighters were after them: most people feel the bombs were jettisoned to try to escape. Some 50 bombs at least were dropped, all high explosive of various sizes, none very big and some quite small.

The planes came over in a straight line from Westerham, Toys Hill, Bough Beach, Chiddingstone, the Hoath and then on south to the sea. Westerham had one man killed in the open and some damage. Then, when they got to my parish, they went right down its length from north to south. Eight to ten bombs at Bough Beech, one man cut by glass, and his little shop knocked about. The Mill, two bombs at least. The farmer and his wife and children were out. The barn was destroyed here and the house knocked about. The cottage where Mother and I walked to was not touched, and the woman in it unhurt; but her husband, who was outside about his work, was hit by a splinter and killed instantly. Two big bombs fell between the road and the Castle in which many panes of glass were broken, but so oddly. Many smaller and one big bomb fell by two cottages near the cross roads, and hurt the cottager, but the two families insisted on sleeping there last night. The village Church and our house had many windows blown out on the north and west sides but again most oddly, and tiles were brought out. One woman at the Castle was slightly cut by glass. Then the planes went over Stonewall and a cluster of cottages beyond called Finch Green. The children at

Stonewall were outside, but the Colonel got them in in time. Mary dashed upstairs and fetched a child from bed. Much glass was broken and the house rocked. But no one was hurt. A bomb in one field full of cattle and sheep touched none, but some sheep were killed on the way to the Hoath. I and the Cresswells went to our cellar, which felt quite safe, and was.

In the Church, the three unstained windows facing north were blown out, the stained glass window between them was not touched, The main east window was untouched, and yet another facing east was damaged. Some three or four feet of plaster came down over the choir.

In the Rectory the scullery window went, Sue's room over it had no glass broken, but some of the ceiling came down. A lot of tiles came down in the walls, and in two or three places in the roof facing west and south, and the bombs were north and west. Panes were unbroken and yet the woodwork round the windows fell in - pictures on the wall came down outside my room, and all the books in John's room fell out of the shelves. When I crept up the damage seemed slight.

Geoffrey to E.C.F.B., 18 August   *Aberdeen*

We have good news of Tony from Warwick just after his arrival, saying he had met *en route* an Old Marlburian, one of his exact contemporaries and an old friend, who was joining up at the same depot as himself, and the second from Warwick saying that he and this OM had lunched together on Thursday (before reporting at Warwick in the evening), and then gone to see the Wilsons, parents of another OM, who live at Leamington, who gave them a most cordial welcome and offered them hospitality at any time, e.g. baths, meals etc. Mrs Wilson is a sister of John's housemaster, Johnson, at Rugby, who was killed last week in an air raid, presumably at Rugby, while on duty as a special constable. I am afraid John will feel his death very much, having just been head of his house. Tony added that he is in barracks at Warwick and that there are numerous other Oxford and Cambridge men among the same lot of recruits and more than one Old Marlburian. They had been drawing kit on Friday and didn't get down to things, he believed, till Monday.

Colonel Streatfeild believes, as some others do, that the war can be won, militarily speaking, in the air without any serious resumption of hostilities on land. He means of course that in a few months' time we shall be in a position to destroy Germany from the air - in fact, do to Germany what she is at present attempting, but so far without success, to do to us. Moreover, it is worthy of remark that our successes so far have all been accomplished without resort to any of our new types of aeroplane, whether fighters or bombers, which are known to be superior both in speed, range of action and manoeverability to our Spitfires and Hurricanes. They are, presumably, being kept in reserve for our own air offensive when it begins in earnest, after it is certain that the German air offensive on this country has failed (as it will fail) and invasion as a practical possibility has been ruled out.

I think myself there is a good deal to be said for the view that we shall win this war by our sea and air power, and not by our sea and land power. Never in our history have we ever had any success with our expeditionary forces. Our victory in the end has been the result of effective use of our fleet. Our expeditionary land forces have always been defeated, compelled to retreat or been at any rate ineffective until after the blockade has so weakened the enemy that they (our military forces) could administer the *coup de grace*. What is new in this war is that besides what we have always won our wars by, namely command of the sea, we shall shortly also possess command of the air. And the difference is this, our command of the sea is bound, by itself alone, to bring victory in the end, but it involves a long war. To shorten the war naval power must be supplemented by land power, which we have never possessed, because we have always had to create our armies after the war had begun; and this takes a long time, during which we have had to face one military defeat after another, until our armies were ready, so that we never win any battle but the last one and wouldn't even win that unless, as mentioned above, the enemy by that time had been rendered weak by the naval blockade. But air power supplies us with the extra (military) weapon - extra, I mean, to our fleet - which, owing to our military weakness, we have in our previous wars lacked.

We possess in our air force, or shall very shortly as soon as we have won command of the air, a substitute for the army, which can be employed in destroying from the air the enemy's military forces, not only or chiefly by actually defeating them, but by destroying their material means of supply at the source (i.e. in the factory) and in accelerating the effect of the blockade by destroying their food supplies in Germany (which the fleet cannot do) also at the source, not to mention the effect of all this on the morale of the German nation. So do not be greatly exercised by what happens to such relatively small military forces as we still have abroad in the Near East and Africa; but we should during the coming winter concentrate all our energies (i.e. our aeroplanes) in bombarding Germany and Italy from the air, every day and every night.

If we can avoid invasion for the ensuing six weeks, I think it reasonable to hope, granted that we employ our air force in an incessant offensive on Germany and Italy during the coming winter, that we shall have both well beaten by next spring. In which case it is probable that there will be a revolution in both these countries and in France, and our armies would have to be employed not in defeating the enemy, but in reducing the already defeated enemy's countries to order - we in Germany and Italy, General de Gaulle and his troops in France.

Minna Crombie[1] told me a good story of an old lady concerning fifth columnist activities. It was in London and the old lady was rung up one evening by a strange but cultivated voice telling her that her son wished her to pack up and leave London at once. He (the speaker) gave his name, but she didn't know it, but he claimed to be her son's friend. She very cleverly asked him, 'which son, my elder or younger?', she actually having only one son. He replied, 'Your elder son.' 'Oh,' she replied, 'but I must meet you and hear more details before I can consent to take such a drastic step.' So they arranged to meet at Victoria station next morning, she in a white mackintosh so that he might recognize her. She then rang up the police and arranged that a detective should be there, and should intervene if, but only if, she took off her mackintosh. She did not, I think, go herself, but sent a maid in the mackintosh, who was at once accosted by a gentlemanly stranger. After a moment or two's conversation, on the excuse of heat, she removed her mack; the detective instantly came up and arrested the man, who turned out to be a leading fifth columnist, and was of course at once interned.

As for the diary tell Burgon we up here see, hear and know nothing about the war, and I am well aware that my own opinions about it are worth absolutely nothing at all. Nor for that matter are anyone else's. You had something to put in the diary in the last war beyond opinions, rumours, etc, because you had sons at the front, and I was in a government office. But there is now no front, and if there was, none of us would be at it, nor, as yet any of our sons, so what is there to record except worthless opinions, not certainly worthy of recording and rumours equally worthless? I simply treat my weekly letter to you as a weekly

---

[1] Mrs Minna Crombie (d. 1951). Widow of John Crombie, and a cousin of E.C.F.B; lived for most of the war with her daughter (Mrs Fenella Paton) at Grandhome, near Aberdeen.

conversation, which from the nature of the case can refer to nothing so interesting as to merit permanent record.

The following contribution was sent by Minna Crombie, concerning the experiences of Frank and Violet Younghusband in West Africa, 18 August

Frank was Liaison Officer to the French Naval Staff at Dakar. From the time of the French débâcle, neither cables nor mails were accepted for Dakar. His Mother wrote to the Admiralty and was told that anxiety was felt for him and his staff, as the French authorities refused information and refused to allow him to leave. Their position was against international law, for Frank was an officer on active service, and had diplomatic status. The Admiralty had asked for leave to send a cruiser to take them off. Permission was refused. They then said a cruiser would be sent to the three mile limit if the authorities would send them out to the cruiser. This was refused. After Oran, fearing that the *Richelieu* might be attacked, Frank, Violet, the staff, and another Englishwoman and some children were put into a collier and anchored across the mouth of the harbour, where they would have been in the line of shell or torpedo. A French Lieutenant Commander was in command and much perturbed. He said to Violet, 'I am signalling to the Captain of the *Richelieu* that ladies and children are on board, he cannot know this'. The reply to his signal was, 'English women and children must take the consequences of Oran.'

Frank says it was wonderful seamanship by which Onslow avoided the collier and damaged the *Richelieu*.[1] When he withdrew, they were landed. Frank and the staff under close arrest were lodged in the common gaol under a guard of black soldiers. Frank should have had a guard of white naval ratings. Violet, the other woman and the children were taken to the women's prison.

The Governor-General, Admiral, and GOC, all of whom had been very friendly dining them, and dining with them, refused to see Frank and Violet. They refused to allow the Consul to see them. Violet was not allowed to see Frank, or to write to him, and the Governor-General sent her a message to say Frank was going to be shot.

---

[1] Capt. R.F.J. Onslow, commander of a force of British warships which attacked the French battleship *Richelieu* in Dakar harbour on 8 July 1940. *Richelieu* was sufficiently damaged to need a year's repair work.

Violet was two nights in gaol and then returned to her hotel with a sentry at her door. She says they had all lost their heads, and orders and counter-orders succeeded each other. She is a very determined person, so she sent a message to the Admiral to say she must see him, as well as the Consul, and would go out taking her sentry with her. This she did. At the Consulate she found a machine-gun in the gateway and a line of armed police to prevent ingress or egress. She then went to the Governor-General and demanded a pass to see Frank as well as his release. He told her to see the Admiral. She had only five francs and the Bank had orders not to cash her cheques or to change English notes. She asked the Governor-General to get her some money. He refused. thereupon she said, 'Your Excellency, my credit and my husband's is good, so I will run bills for what I require and shall send them to your Excellency to be paid.' She was not allowed to use Frank's car, but a negro taxi driver put his taxi at her disposal and refused payment, while her sentry occasionally stood her cups of coffee. She then went to the Admiral, and was told he was out. The sentry, a French sergeant, said, 'Probably in, come round to the back door.' At the back door they were told he was in, and Violet walked through the kitchen and took a chair in the drawing room. Presently a secretary came in and repeated that the Admiral was out. Violet said, 'I will wait for him.' The secretary returned in a few minutes and said, 'The Admiral would be busy till late at night!'. It being then about noon. Violet said, 'I will wait for him - this chair is very comfortable.' Shortly after the Admiral came in and wept on her shoulder, saying he was in an awful position. 'Not so bad as ours,' said Violet. 'You must free my husband, and give me a pass to go to him at once.' He wept again, and said Frank would not be shot, and they would be allowed to leave soon.

Finally they were motored over 200 miles of desert into Gambia, thence by sea to Freetown, Sierra Leone, and then a Dominion Liner was held up for them and they were put on board without landing. They say it took them 24 hours of constant baths to get clean. Violet was allowed to bring away her luggage, but all Frank's belongings were confiscated - uniform, sword, medals etc. He only had what he stood up in. A charitable man on board, about his build, fitted him out with some clothes, and would not let him pay for them. They were made much of on board - were given a cabin and a sitting room, bathroom, and a private bit of deck, fed on luxuries - caviare and *foie gras* amongst them. At the end of the voyage, Frank was told there was no bill, as the company was proud to have him.

They arrived at Frank's Mother's house about 8 p.m., calling out to her, 'We have been in jug.' You should have seen the driver's face.

Notes by J.B.B., 18 August

This has been quite an eventful day. I put on uniform and after an early breakfast, paraded at the Mint Yard with some 50 men from 'A' Company. We proceeded in lorries to the hill above Fordwich where the 9th London Fusiliers took us in hand, and we were shown various methods of dealing with enemy tanks. The first was a well-arranged ambush in a road running through a cutting - explosives attached to a board which is pulled across the road by a cord just before any tank arrives, followed by bombs hurled by men from concealed positions. We were then shown how to make home-made bombs, mine roads, use the Tommy gun and Bren gun (from the hip), attach a cylinder full of saxonite to a Mills bomb, and other stunts. An air raid warning from 11.15 to 12.15 made it inadvisable to carry out one or two demonstrations with smoke and flame.

We got back to Canterbury about 12.30, and the second air raid warning went at 12.45. By the time I was bicycling back to No. 16 there was a merry scrap going on overhead. Machine guns and pom-poms and screeching of planes diving to the attack and the zoom as they shot upwards again. Many of the machines were visible above the market place where I stopped for a few minutes with the ARP wardens to watch the scrap. A little later one of the German bombers was brought down and I saw the thick black smoke as it came down towards St Edmund's School. This machine fell in the new building estate near Kent College on the top of the hill. It did no damage, coming down in two back gardens. The crew of four were killed, their bodies being burnt beyond recognition. During lunch, at which Dr Munro Kerr[1] was our guest, the gunnery continued, but by 2 p.m. it had all calmed down, though the all clear did not go till 4 p.m.

J.B.B's notes on the first bombing, 18 August

Mother and I had tea in the garden. It was a superb summer afternoon. At 5 p.m. the siren sounded again. I telephoned to Mrs. Gardiner, who was coming to read to Mother, to stay at home until we saw what sort of a raid it was. About 5.15 we saw a very remarkable sight. Fifty German bombers, flying in perfect

---

[1] Munro Kerr (1868-1960). Prominent Obstetrician and Gynæcologist.

formation, passed overhead at about 3,000 feet. They looked like a flight of great black vultures. There was something sinister and awe-inspiring about them as, guarded by their fighters, which wheeled all around them like mosquitoes, they moved steadily forward towards their goal. After they had passed there was silence, and then suddenly fighting began almost above our heads. Apparently one or two of the bombers detached themselves from the formation; the idea of this maneoeuvre being to attract the Spitfires away from the main body. Mother had suggested we go indoors and we had not been in the house more than a few minutes when bombs began falling in the park into which our garden juts. Norah was looking out of the window halfway up the stairs and pulled it down quickly as she heard the bombs descend. She saw one of them. It was Mother who actually heard the first whistler and remarked on it. Curiously enough the explosions were not very great, and the house did not rock or the windows rattle. A few minutes later I went to the bottom of the garden (with my tin hat on!) and could see some mysterious looking hillocks thrown up at various places in the park, which immediatly suggested delayed action bombs. The fighting was still going on overhead, so I decided to wait. As soon as this had passed over I went into the park and several ARP wardens and police appeared from the other end. One bomb had fallen about 50 yards from the house formerly occupied by the Russells, leaving a fairly large crater. Another had fallen at the end of the park about 50 yards from our garden wall, leaving a hole about six feet deep from which a lot of moist chalk was scattered all over the grass for 100 yards or more. There were four mounds which looked as if a gigantic mole had been at work.

Molly was at her home at Bridge during the attack, and saw the 50 German bombers come over. Then all of a sudden our fighters appeared out of the sun and swooping in a circle round the enemy tried to intercept them. Molly and her family heard one shell splash into the lake in the park near their house. One bullet made a gash all down the leg of a cow. Another cow had a bullet through the loose flesh hanging on its neck. Neither was permanently hurt.

Ralph to E.C.F.B., 20 August   *Lombard Street*

We have had German planes over our house continually, and in the two raids on Sunday afternoon a number of battles were fought over the house. Five bombs were dropped about half a mile away, and Peter has picked up a lot of cartridge cases in the fields of the farm where he works. He has also been given a bit of bomb which fell on Sunday - a nasty-looking object. The farmer gives him and all his men previous instructions as to what to do if there are any Huns about. They all have to lie in the hedges or under a haystack. He enjoys his farm work intensely. The hay-fever passed off after 48 hours although he was quite sneezy whilst it lasted and he could not play cricket on Saturday afternoon.

Mary to J.B.B., 20 August   *Chiddingstone*

Here is an extract from Kay's letter of 17 August which we received this morning:

'We have raids all the time now, in fact the warning is on practically all day some days. Yesterday we had a terrific one, at 12.30 mid-day. I was at home at the time but Charles was on watch. The bombers came in waves attacking Portsmouth. One balloon caught fire and came down blazing and I saw two machines destroyed, one exploded in the air and fell to pieces, and one fell over and over sideways into the sea. It is very difficult to believe one is actually seeing these really terrible things, or that the planes have living people inside them. One is inclined to regard it all quite impersonally.

I do not feel afraid at present, not during an ordinary raid, though I was very frightened for a few moments on Wednesday when a German bomber, hedge-hopping out at sea, nearly hit this cottage. It just escaped the roof by inches and fell into the bay about half a mile out. It really was very frightening, and I could see the pilot's white face looking out of the cabin, obviously wondering when he was going to crash. Everybody came dashing out of their houses when he'd gone over to see what they thought would be a blazing and wrecked cottage. But they were most kind and gave me a cup of tea which was welcome. It was just a nasty moment, but it is extremely unlikely it will happen again, so I don't really worry.'

Daddy has told you about the raid of 15 August from his end. I promised I would write about my doings. I'd gone to Stonewall to help Jane look after the six evacuees. We had had our tea and were waiting for the children's tea bell to ring, when suddenly we heard Colonel Meade-Waldo shout at the children (in a parade ground sort of voice) who were playing in some hay quite a long way from the house. We were wondering why, when we suddenly heard bombs. The children were really rather slow, and weren't all in by the time we'd rushed downstairs, and then I remembered that one of the children was in bed at the top of the house. She'd had a slight temperature for a day or two. I've seldom run up stairs so quickly - three flights. The child was lying with her face in her pillow, pretty petrified, poor kid; I picked her up and said we'd go and join the others. By this time bombs were falling pretty fast and the noise was deafening. I ran downstairs in fits and starts, trying to time my descent past windows when there wasn't an explosion. Just before we got to a blacked-out skylight it lifted right up and there was a terrific flash, and then in no time we were in the basement. The children were really awfully good, only one small girl getting a bit tearful. It was over very quickly and we gave the children their tea, with them all talking excitedly. In the middle of the raid Donald, aged five, shook his fist and said, 'I'll smash old Hitler's face in when I see him.' All the children recovered very quickly, though they're a bit jumpy over noises now. When the 'All Clear' went we walked around the house altogether to survey the damage and to show the children that everything looked much as before. One large French window had blown in and a good many other window panes had gone.

I then biked home, meeting little groups of people all the way comparing the damage done to their houses with that done to their neighbours'; there's great competition. I looked in here to find Sue Matthew and the Creswells clearing up the debris, and then went on on my bike to find Daddy. Everybody was very calm and already hunting for souvenirs round the craters. So far 47 craters have been found, and one probably fell in the Castle lake; also the flash that I saw was a bomb exploding in the air over the house at Stonewall. The Colonel said he thought one had done so, and people rushed over from Penshurst and other places thinking to find the house in ruins as they had watched it explode. Also the garden is littered with bits of bomb but there's no crater. Edmund has found a tracer bullet which he has polished, and everyone is awfully jealous.

Rather ironically there was a public lecture planned for the evening of the raid on 'How to protect your houses and belongings from bombs.' Perhaps if we'd had it the night before, we might have done better. Needless to say we didn't have the lecture.

All Saturday people were taken up with cleaning their houses. The filth was indescribable. In this house besides the broken glass and fallen plaster, all the boards opened up puffed up the dust of centuries I should think.

Not content with bombing Chiddingstone (they couldn't have bombed Daddy's parish much more successfully if they'd tried) we then had a pretty hot aerial battle directly overhead at Sunday lunch-time. A British pilot baled out and landed unhurt at the Causeway, and his plane crashed yards deep into a field in Bough Beech. Another plane narrowly missed the church tower. We didn't see this as we had departed to the cellar till the machine-gunning stopped. When we emerged the sky was full of smoke coming from the Ide Hill direction, where we afterwards heard a Dornier had been shot down.

Our local worry at the moment is what will happen if there are raids while people are in the hop-gardens. There might be anything from 100 to 160 people with no means of shelter. Three bombs in Friday's raid fell in hop-gardens. Quite a lot of people are a bit doubtful about having a bin; and I honestly believe if we have another raid before hopping starts, the farmers won't get the people to come out unless they provide adequate shelter, which would be very difficult.

Lt. Nicholas Ignatieff to J.B.B., 20 August   *Barrosa House, Aldershot*

Somehow or other Canterbury has stamped this war for me as a crusade - the sort of crusade that it must become if we are to prevail in the end. It is not enough of a crusade yet - that is our tragedy and our mistake. There is still too much of the ordinary war about it yet, where people are ordered and paid to work and fight - if we are to really win, we must go into it in the sort of spirit you are showing. It is no use defining in intellectual terms our 'war aims' or 'peace aims'; through the frightful experience of war, we must be crusading for, actually building, a new world now.

When I actually work with my men with pick and shovel or with wheelbarrow or axe, I feel a new bond spring up between us - 'We', not simply 'You', are rolling up our sleeves and not shirking. 'We' are digging-in and begin to build a new world now on new foundations, which are fundamentally old and not based on any fantastic theory or political promise.

The enemy is crusading - we must crusade better. It is that, and not military success, that can save us - for what I can see coming is this: Russia will wait until the moment that Germany's air force is depleted and she is so involved that a lightning thrust with her tremendous air strength will shatter Germany in a matter of days. Stalin will do this, not to help us, but to steal victory from our grasp and impose his own in Europe, Asia and Africa. That is the frightful test ahead of us, and then we will have a new challenge and a new fifth column and our only hope is to have a clear definition of our own aims and of our way of life. The words 'Democracy' and 'Parliament' are not enough - we must have travelled some distance along the path of a 'new life'; a life that holds real promise and inspiration to our broad masses, our army, our youth. It is us - the better endowed - that must take the lead and show the example - it is not yet being done sufficiently - there is yet not sufficient hope and promise for the broad masses of England, let alone the world, in our victory. The masses are still apathetic because there is no wide spread inspiration. What is 'freedom' if it is not going to be any better than the pre-war years? We failed miserably in peace, and in order to triumph in war we must triumph on the civil front - we must cease simply ordering and paying men to work and fight, and we must inspire them to follow us into a world that will be beautiful for them as well as for us.

I would like to see the army work, work at everything - harvesting, building, transport - everything but sitting around. The worst possible thing that can happen is if we sit around and train lethargically all winter - it will kill morale and spirit - I am sure of that. If we put these vast millions of men to work - in defence, or building a better Britain now - this island will not only be an inpregnable fortress by next spring, but it will be a transformed Britain, and a Britain well on the way to peaceful revolution. That is far more important now than an attempt at military adventures overseas - for we have to cope with both the Fascist and the Bolshevik crusade - the latter becoming the far more formidable as the war progresses.

Notes by J.J.B. concerning air raid on Canterbury, 21 August

Julian and I bicycled to Whitstable, leaving Canterbury about 2.30 p.m. There had evidently been an air raid alarm shortly afterwards, as on reaching the top of the hill above Whitstable about 3 p.m. an ARP man told us the 'All Clear' had just gone. We inspected the sea front with its concrete posts and stakes running out into the sea, and saw the houses knocked down near the bus terminus. Most of the shops are boarded up and the houses on the sea front empty. There was hardly anyone about. We returned through Blean Woods and down Tyler Hill. At the Home Guard HQ, I learnt that bombs had fallen in Canterbury, but it was not known where. At the crossroads at the market I saw Fred Newman who told me a bomb had fallen in Cossington Road, and another in Ersham Road. We bicycled round to Oaten Hill and found it littered with debris; and demolition squads, ambulances and fire engines at the narrow end of Cossington Road. The lower end of the Old Dover Road was also covered with debris. We hurried round to Ersham Road and found that a huge bomb had fallen just behind the Telephone Building, about 100 yards from the Cossington road one; the crater was enormous. The bomb must have been at least 500 lbs. Dust was floating across this part of Canterbury like a thick mist. We then returned to No. 16 where we found Mother full of her experiences, which she evidently went through with flying colours.

Tony to J.B.B., 22 August   *Budbrooke Barracks, Warwick*

We came up to the barracks here at about 4 p.m. in the afternoon, rather wisely I think. We were directed first to the race course just outside Warwick where A and B companies are billeted. From there we were directed across the Common to Budbrooke barracks. Here we saw the CSM of our company, X coy, which with Y coy, is billeted in the barracks. We at once met two other men, one Oxford the other Cambridge, and we went round collecting: pay book, three blankets, mug, fork, spoon, knife. Then we had some tea. I was very glad to find myself in barracks with a decent bunk to sleep in. I met two other OM's which makes four in all in our barrack room, besides numerous other Oxford and Cambridge men. The next day we spent mostly in drawing kit, including uniform and didn't have much else to do. Saturday was also rather an idle day, though we learnt how to turn to the right and to the left and how to march - despite the fact that the majority of us already have Certificate A! However I can see the reason for it. We have all got to learn to work together and to learn discipline - army discipline. And the best way to do this is to get us moving together in three ranks. The Warwickshires are obviously very keen on the drill and turn out. I hope they prove as good on the weapon training and tactics side. On Sunday we had nothing to do all day really - no parades for our platoon. But there is always cleaning to do. One seems to spend half one's time cleaning boots and cleaning equipment in the army. Battle dress itself has no brass to clean, but there are two buttons and the regimental badge on the cap, and our web equipment - belt and so on - has plenty of brass on it and has to be groomed fairly regularly. We haven't been issued with rifles yet, but when we are, that will be another thing to keep clean.

And now for a typical day. Reveille goes at 6.30 a.m., the time we must get up, though if you still have a lot of cleaning to do it is advisable to get up earlier. Breakfast is at 7.15, parade at 8.15, which means we must be ready outside our block by 8 o'clock, properly dressed and equipped. It is a company parade, but usually we are inspected just by our platoon commanders. On Saturday, however, we have a march past and band playing. After parade we have several periods. These are about an hour long, and we have breaks of five or ten minutes in between, and a break of nearly half an hour in the middle of the morning. We have four periods in the morning and two in the afternoon. One of those in the morning is always PT, which is very energetic. We do some of it outside and some in the gym. Otherwise so far all we have done is marching and drilling and a little weapon training with the Ross rifle, which is what we use. It is a Canadian make and practically the same as the short Lee Enfield, though I don't like it so much. Lunch is at 1.15 and a good meal. In fact I think the food is good, but there is not much of it. We have our tea at 4.30, after the two periods and it is really the last meal of the day. There is supper of soup and bread at 7.15 every other night, which however doesn't amount to much, and is rather a scramble. We are allowed out after 5.30 nearly every day, though we may not go further afield than Warwick and Leamington. We have to be in again by 10 o'clock, and lights out is 10.15. On Saturday and Sunday we are allowed out of barracks from 12.30 to 11.30, which is pretty good. Up till yesterday I was out every day in Warwick and Leamington, and with some of the other chaps have established myself in one of the hotels there, so that I can use it for writing letters and so on.

Our platoon is 25 strong. We are all recruits. There are about thirty of us in this room. At least twenty are university men, of which about ten are also public school. Thus Marlborough, Rugby, Malvern, Radley, and Bedford among others are represented. Of the universities, of course, Oxford and Cambridge predominate. We have Christ Church, Trinity, Exeter, Queen's, Teddy Hall, and several others represented from Oxford, and from Cambridge Pemmy, Magdalene and Trinity Hall. One is always meeting university men too from other units stationed in the barracks or on the race course. The remainder of our lot vary from the lesser universities and grammar schools via the clerk type and workers, down to a barrel shaper from Birmingham. As a squad of recruits we are pretty good, because of course most of us have done the stuff before. In our room there are two room orderlies - very good fellows - who are regulars of some standing. Then we have Corporal Woodward who is 2nd. in command to Sergeant Jones, our platoon commander and instructor. He is a grand man and a good instructor, very keen on the team spirit, viz: that we should have pride in our platoon and company and make them the best in the training centre. Our Company

Commander is Major Keeble[1] and looks and is like all majors - short and a trifle tubby, with a fattish face and moustache. He interviewed us all a few days ago singly. I gathered from him that in a month we see the CO and then the Area Commander, who is responsible for transferring one to an OCTU. The Major said we should probably be here for about twelve weeks. There are two subalterns to our company, 2nd. Lt. Lucas and Winstanley. The former has been through the ranks and is an OCTU like us, but he was in a Guards regiment and so very keen on neatness and spit and polish, and for that reason is disliked by the men.

I am far better off than one or two other chaps I know and I think I am lucky to be with the Royal Warwickshire Regiment. I went and saw another Old Marlburian friend (Eric Yarrow) at Elgin the day before I left home. He is in a Royal Engineers' training battalion and in a hut camp. Previously they were in a church hall where conditions were pretty foul. He hasn't the company of any other public school men, and says that if it were not that he knew a family in Elgin he'd never have stood it. At the end of this month he will be going to an OCTU after three months in the ranks.

Notes by J.B.B., 24 August

Mother, Julian and I motored over to Broomlands, Langton Green, two miles west of Tunbridge Wells, to lunch with Ralph, Alison and Peter in the house they had taken for two months. A peerless day. Never have I seen the Weald look more entrancing. The harvest was being carried - the deep midsummer green of the trees and meadows, the ancient timbered cottages of Kent, the country people moving quietly about their business - all made a picture of peace and solidity. But we had left Canterbury as the sirens sounded their third warning that morning, and as we stopped on the side of the road near Pluckley for a cup of tea, enemy planes were overhead. When we returned in the evening it was a curious experience to feel relieved in seeing the Cathedral standing there untouched, and also our house.

Walking up to see Sergeant Roberts at about 11 p.m., I realised how stygian is the blackness of Canterbury at night. The flashes of the big guns bombarding the French coast lit up the sky to the east.

The bombing of Ramsgate this afternoon was particularly severe. The gas works were hit. A bomb was also dropped at Barham. Indeed there are few

---

[1] Probably Major Robert Keeble (1911-88). Terr. Comm. 1939. DSO, MC. Later Dir. Portland Cement Company Ltd.

localities where German bombers are not now seen and bombs may be, and are being, dropped promiscuously all over the country - with remarkably little damage.

I fear that some, at any rate, of the Canadian troops are pretty wild. A certain unit quartered in Gatton Park, belonging to Jeremiah Colman[1] (where as boys in St David's, Reigate days we used to be turned loose in the strawberry beds) killed a swan and ate it, and worse still removed all the vegetables from the kitchen garden.

J.B.B., 25 August

Sergeant Major 'Bill' Crean, No 35 Section Field Security Corps, stationed at Eastwell Park (HQ 1st. London Division) dined here tonight. He tells me that there is still much trouble in this part of Kent about signalling by lights to enemy planes - though except for this the fifth column problem seems fairly solved. Of 280 aliens who were in the Ashford area only 30 remain at large, and they are mostly American.

I was on guard tonight at the Gate Inn road block. At about 10 p.m. Barber, formerly Dr Lucas' chauffeur, who lives in the cottage adjoining the inn, called me up to the attic at the top of his house from where there is a wide prospect towards Nackington and Lower Hardres in order to show me two flickering signal lights. These had disappeared however by the time I got to the top of the building, and though I waited for half an hour they did not reappear again till later in the evening. I have little doubt these lights are genuine and are not the headlights of a car. The Canterbury police have asked me to look out for signalling of this kind, which is constantly being reported. I tried to get a line on the position and Sergeant Roberts entered it on his guard report.

The Germans are known to be practising embarking and disembarking troops on the Brittany coast. But perhaps all this is a blind, though if an invasion is to come it will be before the equinox of September 21st.

John Cripps to J.B.B., 25 August   *Lechlade*

My Mother and my two youngest sisters have left within the last week or two for Moscow by a long and tedious route across Canada to Japan and then

---

[1] Sir Jeremiah Colman (1859-1942). Chmn. J. and J. Colman Ltd.; High Sheriff of Surrey; Pres. Surrey CCC, 1916-23; Vice-Pres. of Boy Scouts Assoc. and YMCA.

through Manchuria to Moscow across Siberia. A journey of seven weeks' almost constant travelling. We had a cable today to say that they were safe in Montreal.

My Mother has been quite overwhelmed these last few weeks with my father's work (he no longer has a secretary) and things of her own, as well as with arranging to move from Goodfellows to a smaller house that is being got ready over in the Stroud district at Oakridge (just by the Rothensteins). Leaving 'Goodfellows' has meant a great deal to her naturally after more than 20 years, but the new house sounds more suitable in present conditions and is in a district to which both my parents are very attached.

Only my eldest sister is left here now and the rest of the family will be in Moscow for the winter at any rate. I believe things go very slowly there and are not at all easy, but we get no real news, although more letters are getting through now. On the whole life out there sounds dull, and it will be a great thing for my father to have some of the family with him to keep house and help with what entertaining has to be done.

How much I admire you for what you have been doing! It makes me feel so insufficient, but my wife and I are Quakers (we have only joined the Society of Friends lately, although we have been what they call 'attenders' for a long time), and I have refused as a conscientious objector to take part in activities connected with the war. I have not yet been before a tribunal, although I registered in May. You might like to see my statement, with which you will, I am sure, wholly disagree!

I find it difficult not to do as others do (a public school education leaves its mark!) and it does not involve just one decision, but a host of them. And the matter is never really decided in my mind, not in the sense that I feel hesitant about my general attitude (however great one feels the responsibility for non-cooperation to be), but we cannot and do not want to live by ourselves apart from the community, although this in itself must involve compromise at some point, and it is the point at which compromise should cease that is so hard to determine. And the temptation is great to try to rationalise in explaining to others what one feels, rightly or wrongly, to be a right decision, dictated not by reason but by that thing called conscience, which means something quite real to some of us and almost nothing to others.

I am continually tempted to 'join in' but so far have not done so. I am still with *The Countryman* and there is no one there to take my place, although we have tried to find someone for several months. The trouble is that the Editor is 74 and has so much to worry him at present that he has not the energy left to train new people in what is a very individual business. If he were younger it would be easier.

All my future plans depend upon the tribunal. In the meantime Ursula and I are planning to let our house here (I suppose you don't know of anyone who would like to take it unfurnished for the duration?) and to move over to 'Goodfellows', which has been lent to us, as they could not sell it. We are putting what resources we have into the venture and intend to live there ourselves with our two children in the three rooms that were the nursery wing. We are going to have 25 children from the poorer parts of Bristol with a nursery school staff provided by the Corporation, and we hope to run the gardens - with some adjoining land - as a market garden, where refugees and conscientious objectors can get a proper training in addition to doing useful work. I shall probably work two days or three days at Idbury and the rest of the week in the garden. It may not work as we hope, but it seemed worth trying and the best we could do within our beliefs to make a contribution to the life of the community.

Here everything still seems unbelievably peaceful with no more than the very occasional and distant thud of bombs.

Ralph to E.C.F.B, 26 August   *'Broomlands', Tunbridge Wells*
Alison was told the following story by a YMCA worker at the canteen in Victoria Station where she (Alison) works. This worker, a very meek and mild woman of about 55, was attached to a YMCA canteen in France. When the Blitzkrieg started she found herself isolated and determined to make a go for the coast. She was not a good walker but she started to 'leg it' and fell in with a wounded British Tommy, whose arm had been damaged by a bullet. They both walked together and after the first day the British Tommy was inclined to give up, but this good lady was determined she would, at least, save the life of one British soldier. She told him if he did not carry on she would knock him on the head with his tin helmet. To continue the story, she got clothes for him at a peasant's house and, to use her own words, 'I actually stole food, a thing I have never done before in my life'.

They walked by night and hid by day and they were told to go to Dunkirk by a friendly peasant, as they understood British troops were being evacuated from there. They eventually arrived at Dunkirk in the early hours of the morning but found all the ships had gone; they had arrived a day too late. They hid in the sand-dunes all that day and then found a farm where the occupants were friendly, who told them where they could get a rowing boat. They set off that night in the rowing boat and started to row to England. They had no idea of the direction and in actual fact were heading for Norway, but fortunately for them they were picked by a destroyer and safely landed in this country. The YMCA lady, therefore, had her wish; she saved the life of a British soldier to fight another day.

Notes by Julian, 15-16 August

On Friday August 15th I decided to pay a visit to a camp on Salisbury Plain where some of the Australians of the 2nd AIF are encamped. I had just enough petrol in my car to make this journey by road - 95 to 100 miles each way. I set off at 2 p.m., with William McKie,[1] organist at Magdalen College, Oxford, who had been staying for a few days with Mrs Trafford at Goodrich Court. We went through Gloucester up via the Air Balloon public house on to the Cotswolds. We stopped at Cirencester and had a look at the beautiful 15th. century church. It was market day and the streets were crowded. Then we went on to Fairford but did not go into the church as all the glass had been taken out, but we got some tea at the Bull Inn, and then on to Lechlade where I dropped William, who was to get a train into Oxford later, and on via Raillmore and Swindon to the Plain. I had great difficulty in finding the Australian camp; there are of course no sign posts and to ask a passer by or a local inhabitant the whereabouts of such and such a camp produced always a negative result, but I had Lobscombe Corner as the name of a crossroads to make for, and eventually at 6.45 p.m. I reached a point where a passer-by said he knew there was an Australian camp down the road two miles further - to my delight. I found the Brigade I was seeking at this spot, the 12, 9 and 10 battalions of the 2nd. AIF. The tents, all camouflaged, were scattered in a most higgledy-piggledy way, with no attempt at lines - to avoid offering a good target to the German airmen. The whole Brigade had only just got out of their slit trenches at the end of an air raid, when a neighbouring aerodrome had been attacked. Only 800 to 1000 yards from the officers' mess marquee were some enormous craters made the day before by German bombers. Only one man had

---

[1] William McKie (1901-84). An Australian; Organist and Master of Choristers at Westminster Abbey, 1941-63. Kt (1953).

been hit by a machine-gun bullet as it passed through his seat 'in and out, in and out' - a neat affair - in the last war it would have entitled him, I suppose to four wound stripes!

This unit came over to England some five or six weeks ago in six or seven of the largest British liners of the British merchant service, including the *Queen Mary*, *The Empress of Britain* and the *Aquitania*. The troops on board constituted the remainder of the 1st. Australian Division, the majority of which had already landed at Suez and had proceeded to Palestine, but when this second contingent reached the neighbourhood of Colombo, sudden orders were given to turn about and proceed via the Cape. This order was given, apparently because Italy had come into the war and the French front was cracking. The flotilla waited five days at Cape Town. The troops were allowed ashore and were 'pretty lively', as one of the AIF officers said to me - I imagine the Cape Town authorities were thankful to see the men go. There were a number of desertions - or rather missing the boat. These men were rounded up and sent on, on tramps, even without escorts and most of them landing in England proceeded on their own initiative to London to look for their units. When the convoy reached the Bay of Biscay, the final scenes of the French débâcle were being enacted and the Australians expected to be flung in to the French fighting, ill-equipped though they were, with only rifles and some Brens. However they went on and all landed at Liverpool and were sent straight down to Salisbury Plain, where they are encamped on the old site of the Canadian Camp in 1914-18.

I had much interesting talk with the CO of the 2/10 Battalion, who was a sergeant in the same unit in the last war. He said his unit was now fully equipped with all the accessories and additions which a modern infantry battalion has to have, in Bren guns and carriers, anti-tank rifles, heavy trench mortars, motor cycle detachments, wireless sections, etc. and 'his boys', as he put it, 'are ready for anything.' They expect perhaps to be taken to Egypt and there to join up with the other Australians. He hinted that we had still one or two surprises up our sleeve for the enemy, though he did not specify what the nature of these might be. He considered the fighting spirit of the present Australians was quite as good as that of the old AIF, but feared long inactivity in England. 'Anyway,' he said, 'the War Office will not be able to leave us here in tents on Salisbury Plain during the winter months.' His crack brigade was on one hour's notice, i.e. it had to be ready to move day or night in any direction with only one hour's delay for getting off the mark. I noticed all the officers had their equipment ready to hand all the time. Next day I went straight back to Goodrich, and left there for Swansea that afternoon.

Swansea had had 53 air raid warnings on 54 nights and had suffered some damage, though none was apparent to the ordinary visitor. The air raid sirens moaned out their mournful sound just after I had got into bed. I went into the next room and found a boy named Walter Cobbold whom I had brought to Swansea to see off to South America, and we descended to rather a grim air raid shelter under the hotel. I soon got weary of this and the sight of a number of old women, deshabillées, sitting aimlessly round, and went back to bed, though shortly after the AA batteries got busy making a terrific noise. I told the boy to stay down which he did till 2.30 a.m. I slept throughout the raid which lasted most of the night. Bombs were dropped a mile from the hotel and some people, I heard next morning, were killed,

I said good-bye to the boy at 11 a.m. and friends took him on to the ship, and then I spent the whole day travelling to Canterbury. As I crossed in my taxi from Paddington to Charing Cross, the air raid warnings were going, but my taxi man kept on. I did not get to Canterbury West till 9.30 p.m., the train on the main line never travelling more than 15 m.p.h. The line had been bombed shortly before we passed Paddock Wood. I arrived to find that six more bombs had fallen in Russell's Park, just behind 16 New Dover Road during that afternoon. Mother appeared, and was unperturbed!

John Lowe, Dean of Christ Church to J.B.B., 26 August.   *Oxford*

We have had a very peaceful time here on the whole. So far there have been no bombs in Oxford or the immediate neighbourhood. My only experience was on Friday when we were taking the two boys for a picnic in the country and ran into a raid; a bomb crashed a couple of fields away from us, perhaps 350 yards. No district seems to be quite immune from the stray raider but I fancy we are as well off here as anywhere. What next term will be like, I do not know. There have not been many withdrawals yet but it is too soon to make an estimate. My rough guess is that short of invasion or complete chaos, we shall have a little over 100 men, compared with 150 last term. Of the dons Masterman, Ryle,[1]

---

[1]   Gilbert Ryle (1900-76). Commissioned in Welsh Guards, 1940. Prof. of Metaphysical Philosophy, Oxford, 1945-68.

Foster, Dillwyn and Gray are in the army. Colin Dillwyn is missing. He got pretty far into Flanders with his battalion of the OBLI, and very few of them came back. He may possibly be a prisoner. Lindemann, Harrod,[1] Grant Bailey, Collie and Page are doing special jobs. The censors now are Russell and Bob Mortimer,[2] and the latter is doing very well at it. He never had enough responsibility before. I suppose it is no use asking you to come and see us and get all the news at close quarters. It would be very nice if you could snatch a day or so; I can always put you up. If you are staying on, you must come some time.

Notes by J.B.B., 26 August

Since the bombing attacks of last week the streets empty much more quickly than they used to do when there is an air raid alarm. Today I made three attempts to send a cable to the Controller of Hart House and succeeded the third time. At 11.45 Mother and I did not go out as the siren sounded just then. At 2.45 I had gone out to do a few odd jobs in the town and the sirens went at 3.05 p.m. The Post Office, the Municipal buildings in the Dane John, the Beaney Institute and (if before 2 p.m.) the banks all immediately close their doors; the trades people put up their shutters (if their plate glass is not already protected by wire netting); many of the shops are closed to business; the people go indoors, and if away from home make quickly for shelter; the ARP wardens, donning their helmets, bicycle quickly to their posts; the Control Room behind the Municipal Buildings is manned; police in a car motor quickly down the High Street exhorting everybody through loud speakers to take shelter and not stand at their doors or move about in the streets, and the whole place becomes strangely silent. Within three or four minutes one generally hears the deep sinister hum of large German formations passing overhead, generally out of sight above the clouds, or if in clear weather very high. Then our fighters are heard and generally a fight or series of fights with machine-guns and pom-pom fire bursts out above our heads.

Volunteers for raiding parties to raid the French coast are being called for. The rougher type of soldier from the poorer parts of Glasgow and Liverpool are

---

[1] Roy Harrod (1900-78). Lecturer in Economics; served in PM's office, 1940-42 and thereafter in an advisory capacity. Kt (1959).
[2] Robert Cecil Mortimer (1902-76). Lecturer Christ Church, Oxford, 1929-44; Junior Censor, 1940-44; Canon of Christ Church, Oxford, 1944-49; Bishop of Exeter, 1949-73.

being accepted. It would be better to take detachments of Canadian and Australian troops, who are fine scrappers and intelligent.

28 August

I was in London yesterday and spent part of the afternoon with Euan Wallace, the London Regional Commissioner, at the HQ London Civil Defence Region, which is in the Geological Museum in Exhibition Road, Kensington. One has to pass many guards to reach Euan. He introduced me to Harold Scott,[1] the Chief Administrative Officer, who has been lent by the Ministry of Home Security to the London CD Region HQ. He used to be one of HM Prison Commissioners. Euan then showed me the 'holy of holies', i.e. the control room, buried in the ground with 30 feet of concrete above it. This room and many others adjoining it, such as the telephone exchange, sleeping quarters, offices for the Regional Commissioner and his assistants, and so forth, cannot be hit by even the heaviest bomb. The air conditioning system is not yet quite finished, so these large subterranean quarters were stuffy. The previous evening there had been an air raid alarm for six hours, and during this period Euan and his staff had been down below sitting up all night. They have not yet worked out a technique for dealing with such a situation; obviously if everybody is to remain up during an air raid in the night they cannot do their work next day.

The walls of the control room are covered with maps, one is a huge map of London and its suburbs. Areas 1, 2, 3, 4 and 5 comprise inner London. Area 1 is Westminster, Kensington, Chelsea and the City. Area 6, to the north, is so large it is divided into sub-sections A, B, C and D. Another map is of England with little hooks stuck into all the large towns and each district named by a series of letters. A ticker tape system, connected with Fighter Command HQ, ticks out reports unceasingly. Every minute is recorded night and day, and if there is a raid the code letters of this district are ticked out with YY (yellow) or RR (red) or at night PP (purple). While Euan and I were standing in front of this map the girl who operates the ticker machine came to the map and hung a yellow disc on the hook sticking out of the blob which represents Canterbury. It was 3.35 p.m., so we knew that the yellow, or 'stand-ready', warning had been given in this part of Kent.

---

[1] Harold Richard Scott (1887-1969). Civil Servant; Dep. Sec. Min. of Home Security, 1940-2; seconded as Chief Admin. Officer, London CD region, 1939-41; Sec. Min. of Home Security, 1942-3; Comm. Met. Police, 1945-53. KBE (1942), KCB (1944).

The red, I found later that night, had been given about 4.10 p.m. In one of the other rooms representatives of all the great London departments sit during a raid, e.g. War Office, Air Force, Police, Gas, Water, Electricity and so on. These are senior men qualified to give instructions immediately the area bombed is known. Directly a bomb falls the ARP officials or Police who get to the scene first, immediately telephone the local ARP control centre, and the local centre telephones London HQ control room.

Euan told me they were having a lot of trouble with people reporting delayed action bombs, which in reality were bits of concrete or other debris. Sappers have to go out and investigate all these cases, and much valuable time was wasted.

Vincent Massey gave the amusing account of difficulties he experienced in keeping an appointment with Edward Halifax during an air raid alarm two afternoons ago. He found locked doors everywhere, most of the FO staff in their cellar shelters, and on finally being allowed into the FO building was warned against crossing one of the inner courtyards. He finally reached the Foreign Secretary's usual room and found him there quietly working away with all the windows open.

Lionel Massey gave me a most interesting account of his light tanks and armoured cars. His battalion is part of the 2nd. Armoured Division and is in Cambridgeshire. The armoured cars are something very new and exciting. They take the greatest care to camouflage themselves, but the other day when the PM inspected them between 200 and 300 motor vehicles of various kinds were drawn up in the open fields - what a chance for a few German bombers on patrol. Lionel said they are having, as we are, much trouble with signalling with lights in Cambridgeshire.

A problem in this part of Kent at the present moment is the number of East-End Londoners who are picking the hops. These people are often dressed in bright colours and are dispersed over big areas, thus being a wonderful target for German bombers. Moreover there is the difficulty about their food. They were clearly told to get their ration books counter-signed and special permits issued at their food office in London before they started but most of them, according to Mr Tassall, Town Clerk of Faversham, have failed to do so. He is issuing them with an emergency ration card, good for one week.

Young Tassall, who has recently joined the RAF and is stationed at Detling as an AA gunner, was fortunately on 48 hours leave when the Germans did so much damage to the huts, canteen and tents at that aerodrome. Most of the officers and men had their kit destroyed, but Tassall found his kit bag blown to about 300 yards from his tent, but otherwise intact.

The death of Lord North, Lord Guilford's heir, was announced in the press two days ago. He was blown up by a land-mine in a prohibited area on his own estate at Waldershare. In actual fact he was playing golf and lost a ball. He went to look for it in an area which he knew was dangerous. His sister was also killed, and his wife very badly wounded.

This afternoon (28 August) I was out on the hills round Nackington, when the sirens went. I had been examining the ground to see if I could find likely vantage points for the signal lamps which we often see at night from the Gate Inn road post. I was squatting in an open field on high ground. Within five minutes German bombers, coming from the Dover direction, passed overhead at about 1,000 feet. The formations were of different sizes - three, six, or eight, - and operated separately. Spitfires were soon on the scene, and many individual fights took place in and out of the clouds. After a burst of machine-gun fire I saw the complete wing of a German plane fall to the ground; it fluttered and turned like a falling leaf. A few minutes later I caught sight of a Dornier chased by a Spitfire. The Dornier came out of a cloud and dived low. The Spitfire emerged from the same cloud further on at the higher level and thus missed the Dornier, which made off towards Dover. Clouds of smoke rose from the Ramsgate and Margate direction where bombs were falling.

After I had got home we saw a German baling out. His parachute shone white in the sunlight and he, a tiny figure, swung at the end of it. I watched him for five minutes over towards Sturry, but a west wind carried him towards Stodmarsh and he disappeared from view.

29 August

Of the many German pilots who have baled out or been shot down during the last two or three weeks in this part of Kent, some have been truculent and tried to show fight, others have only been too thankful to be out of it for the duration. A German pilot officer who came down near Wingham appeared pugnacious but the farmer in whose field he descended took off his coat and showed he meant business, whereupon the boche thought discretion the better part of valour. The airmen are being taken up to London as prisoners most days by the morning train from Canterbury East station.

J.C.Masterman (senior history don at Christ Church) went through a course in Intelligence at Swanage and is now at Colchester as an Intelligience Officer. He confirms that Dundas,[1] Pakenham and one other were shot by a colleague in the Home Guard (a cook in the House kitchens) and are still in hospital. Gilbert Ryle (a Greats don at Christ Church) writes from Sandown Park where he is a subaltern in the Welsh Guards in their training battalion. Eric Gray and Ayer[2] (two of the House dons) are cadets at Sandhurst and join the Welsh Guards before long. Ryle says he has been given his weapon training by a former pupil of his at the House.

31 August

Yesterday afternoon I was on the hill above Harbledown when the siren went at 3 p.m. German planes went over towards Maidstone. Two formations, one of Hurricanes, the other of Spitfires went over my head to engage them but too far off for me to see what happened. As I was returning by St Edmund's School, the Germans came over in a huge formation. Standing with one or two others at the top of the hill I counted about 100 - they were Dorniers with Messerschmitts flying in formation with them. They were in groups of 30. At about 10,000 feet they were clearly visible - shining in the sun, and with my field glasses one could see the outline of the machines quite easily. Others in Canterbury counted 180. In all there were probably 300 in the wave. About one hour later, fighting began over and in the vicinity of Canterbury. I saw three come down probably out of control; a parachute was seen slowly floating to earth above Barham and Bridge.

At 8.15 I paraded at the Mint Yard and we were up at the Gate Inn by 9 p.m. and the first guard was posted. From 9.30 to 10.30 p.m. there was the greatest activity. Every searchlight in East Kent was probing the skies for German machines - they were operating alone or in pairs; other larger groups could be heard in the distance. At about 10 p.m. bombs were dropped on Broad Oak hill,

---

[1] Robert Dundas (1884-1960). Emeritus Student of Christ Church, Oxford (1910-1957).

[2] A.J. 'Freddie' Ayer (1910-85). Lecturer in Philosophy, Christ Church Oxford, 1932-35; Commissioned in Welsh Guards, 1940; Dean of Christ Church, 1945-46; Wykeham Professor of Logic, 1959-78. Kt (1970).

setting fire to two cottages and some ricks, and causing a terrific blaze visible for miles round. Towards Faversham and possibly Eastchurch or Sheppey there was heavy AA fire, the flashes of the shells bursting in the sky being incessant. There was sound of heavy bombing - more AA shells towards Chatham; then flashes towards Dover; then sound of firing and bombing towards Ramsgate. We seemed to stand in the centre of a circle, on the circumference of which there was the most intense action. It was a superb star-lit night. Some 70 or 80 searchlights making patterns across the sky, the bursting shells, the flares from the Dover direction, the steady thud of bombs, the motor buses rushing past completely unlit inside, the Bridge fire engine dashing by about 10.15 p.m., the glare of the Broad Oak fire all made a weird and fantastic scene. Things quieted down before midnight, and Fred Newman and I had a comparatively uneventful guard except for late travellers walking doggedly along to their destinations: first came a soldier returning to Broome Park from leave in Newcastle; next came a civilian who had left Stoke that day at 2 p.m. and was now making for Barham; and third came another soldier returning to Bridge after spending his leave at Portsmouth. Newcastle had had its worst bombing the previous night. The man from Stoke told us about Lewis's department store at Birmingham being set on fire and factories damaged in the suburbs, and the lad from Portsmouth said that the town had suffered, but not the dockyards. All agreed that the damage done was not really very serious in comparison with the German losses.

We no longer stand to at 3.30. It is still dark then, but we continue the regular guard duty till 5 a.m., at which hour we return to the Mint Yard. The run down on our bicycles to the Precincts at this time of the morning was a very lovely experience. Dawn was breaking over the coast towards Ramsgate and Margate. A crescent moon hung over the gradually lightening sky. The stars in the west were still bright. A fresh clean wind had sprung up. All was absolutely peaceful and quite lovely as we ran into the town, which in the half light looked like a stage set with its mediaeval houses and deserted streets into which figures straight from the Middle Ages might be expected to step. The first show of dawn lit up the Angel Tower and then, in turn, the western towers and the rest of the huge building which brooded over the still-sleeping town caught in the light of the new day.

I was in bed by 6 a.m., and two hours later was woken by the siren, and a few moments later heard sounds of savage fighting in the sky overhead. German bombers could be heard crossing overhead in their usual long procession, but only a few were visible in the blue misty sky. Desultory fighting continued. At 10.40 I had just left the house to walk up the road about 100 yards to Sgt. Roberts's cottage. There were not more than four people in sight. Suddenly bombs began falling very close. Those four people and myself made for cover. I ran back to No.16 and found Mother and Miss Hewitt and Molly and Norah in the hall - the spot we sit in if bombs are near. A few minutes later things quieted down and Roberts and I went to the Mint Yard to draw rifles, blankets etc for the Osterley course. At 11.40 the 'All Clear' went and the town, deserted till then, sprang into instant life. Crowds were set on doing their week-end shopping. People waited three or four deep in the banks which were forced to remain open after mid-day; the counters in the shops were besieged by women, queues stretching out of several butchers' and grocers' shops. Hundreds of people coming out of work were bicycling home while the going was good; motor traffic jammed the High Street; everybody smiling and good humoured and telling each other where the bombs had fallen, namely in Grey Friars Gardens, the moat in front of the city wall near the old railroad locomotive at the corner, and on the tennis courts just opposite. The Grey Friars one smashed the greenhouses of Mr Smith one of whose employees is our gardener, and also broke windows in Mrs Gardiner's house and in the Post Office and Methodist Chapel. But there was no loss of life. At 12.40 the sirens went again and the streets once more emptied with much of the shopping uncompleted. The 'All Clear' went at 2.10 p.m.

A quiet afternoon, but at 5.45 the sirens again. The dull roar of hundreds more of the enemy machines overhead. Our Spitfires shining in the sun thousands of feet above us, and continuous fighting with machine-gunnery and screeching dives and bombing in the distance - what a life!!

September

Mary to J.B.B, 4 September   *Chiddingstone*

When we started hopping last Thursday the people were definitely getting jittery and, directly there was a warning of German planes around, everybody departed to ditches round the field. This was most delaying to the picking, but people are getting much calmer now and go on picking while aerial battles go on overhead. We have seen a lot of planes shot down during the last week and several parachutists coming down to earth. Today Daddy was in the hop garden at lunch time and John, Nicholas and I were here when we heard firing etc. We looked out with care and saw a man floating down quite near. One could see his arms and legs waving about. Actually he was further away than it appeared and Colonel Meade-Waldo found him beyond Stonewall. There were two men came down - both German. One fell at Penshurst and was dead, and the one the Colonel found died shortly afterwards.

Twice last week I went to Stonewall to sleep with Donald aged 5 - Jane's evacuee, who has broken his arm. He turns on to it in the night and moans and groans and wakes up so one doesn't get much of a night. He fell off a tree and dislocated it as well, so he's had a lot of pain poor child.

Hopping makes one awfully sleepy and I'm feeling overcome now. I did 7 - 9 a.m. and 2 - 6 p.m. today.

Notes by J.B.B., 5 September

On Sunday afternoon, 1 September, Sgt. Roberts, Maple and I motored in Roberts's car from Canterbury to Osterley which lies just north of the Great West Road, nine miles from Hyde Park Corner. We expected to sleep in camp but found the accommodation was in a small villa in Bassett Gardens, devoid of all furniture except palliasses. Here we dossed down with our blankets and then spent the evening at the Osterley Park Road House. At 1 a.m. three bombs were dropped about 1000 yards from us. We stirred in our blankets, cursed and turned over to sleep again.

The whole of Monday from 9 a.m. to 6 p.m. was taken up with lectures and demonstrations on the training ground in the park. There were 270 men, all Home Guard, on the course. They came from as far north as Edinburgh and from Gloucestershire and Wales, and indeed from every part of the British Isles. The programme is given below. The weather was peerless. When work was over we went to Harrow where, after much trouble, we found Bob Henley (Bomb Disposal Section). Ted Emptage of Maidstone HQ came with us, and he and I had a meal at the King's Head on 'the Hill'.

On Tuesday (3 September) the course continued, ending with a lecture from Tom Wintringham from 5 to 6 p.m. Edward Hulton, of *Picture Post*, finances the course and Wintringham, who was in the International Brigade during the Spanish War, is head of the Training School. A similar school has just been started by Hubert Gough[1] at Hurlingham, and the government is shortly establishing another at Liverpool. There will eventually be four or five in Great Britain. After the end of September Osterley will stop courses for the rank and file and give a week's course for instructors. I slept at the Royal Empire Society that night. On Wednesday (4th September) I saw Major G.Lester in Room 055 at the War Office about a possible job. It is MI6 - very hush-hush, dealing with our agents abroad - job certainly available if I want it. Lunch at Travellers with Pat Hodgson, Mike Pearson and John Lowe (Dean of Christ Church). At 3 p.m. saw Lt. General Sir John Brown[2] at the War Office. Sir Horace Wilson had written to Sir James Grigg (Permanent Under-Secretary of State for War) about me, and Grigg had forwarded his letter to Brown, who is in charge of all questions touching the welfare of the British Army. The problem of keeping such a huge body of men (one and a half million) happy during the coming winter is one which is exercising the time and thought of the War Office greatly at the present moment. Brown, who is an interesting person, 'h'-less, self-educated, and somewhat proud of it, outlined to me some of the plans in this connection - entertainment pure and simple (local talent where possible), games, BBC broadcasts, education. Welfare officers who already exist all over the country will be used. As regards education, Brown said that R.S.Wood,[3] Principal Assistant Secretary of the Board of Education, and F.D.Bendall,[4] a senior inspector of the Board of Education, were working hard on a comprehensive scheme. He took me in to see these two officials. Neither Brown nor they were quite clear how the 1st. and 2nd. Canadian Divisions fitted into the picture, but Brown said he hoped I would write to McNaughton, GOC 7th. Corps (which includes the 1st. Canadian Division). Wood gave me an idea of the general plan to provide facilities in education for the troops this winter. For the great mass of men there would be lectures, rather of the popular type - the rise of National Socialism, French History, Middle Eastern politics, simple poetry and so forth. For the second (large) group who wished for more serious study, e.g. a language, a science, there

[1] General Sir Hubert Gough (1870-1963). Cmdr. of British 5th. Army in France, 1916-18; retd. 1922; Colonel and Zone Commander Home Guard, 1940-2.
[2] Lt. Gen. Sir John Brown (1880-1958). Dep. Dir. of Territorial Army, 1937-9; Dep. Adj. Gen., War Office, 1940-1. KCB (1934).
[3] Robert Stanford Wood (1886-1963). Civil Servant at Bd. of Ed. since 1911; Dep. Sec. of Technical Branch, 1940-46; Vice-Chanc. University of Southampton, 1952. KBE (1941).
[4] Col. Francis Bendall (1882-1953). Director of Army Education at War Office, 1940-42.

would be lectures of the WEA type. For the third and smaller group (though of course very large too in actual figures), whose educational careers had been interrupted by the war, arrangements would be made with the universities to provide courses e.g. in economics, engineering, languages and so forth, either by sending the men to the universities if billeted near a university town, or by travelling lecturers. As regards Canada, Mr England had already worked out a very comprehensive scheme and was just returning from a visit to Canada. Wood also hoped I would get into touch with McNaughton, and hinted that if there was no opening with the Canadian forces there might be work with the British troops in this regard.

About 9.30 a.m. on Wednesday 4 September, ten bombs were dropped, probably almost simultaneously, by a German plane on the western section of Canterbury. The first demolished some houses adjoining the up platform of the West Station. The second destroyed Hammerton's bicycle shop (at the corner where the Station Road joins St Dunstan's Road) and a sweet shop next door. The third damaged a shop near the Falstaff Inn. The fourth hit some houses looking on the Stour. The fifth, part of the ruined City Wall in the Tower Gardens. The sixth fell on the shelter near the Methodist Chapel, and other bombs fell on houses as far as Beer Cart Lane. It is almost unbelievable that nobody was killed. In some cases people crawled out of the ruins unhurt. One end of the shelter was blown in and a woman sheltering in it had her pelvis broken. Only four people in all were wounded, three women and one man. Willie Blore's ARP dugout was immediately next to the houses knocked down by the first bomb, but he was just inside the entrance to the dugout and unhurt.

Ted Emptage, a member of the Maidstone Home Guard who lives near Detling and holds a position of some local importance in the GPO, being responsible for keeping all communications in this part of Kent in good working order, told me that when the aerodrome at Detling was so badly bombed some weeks ago and between fifty and sixty officers and men were killed, only three bombing machines were destroyed. The machines are distributed over the surrounding country under trees and various kinds of cover. Asphalt paths enable the planes to reach the main runways. A travelling workshop goes round to each machine enabling all running repairs to be carried out *in situ*. Holes made by enemy bombs on the 'drome are dealt with by a huge steam shovel which lifts five tons of soil at one go, deposits it in the holes and then proceeds to lumber over it pressing the soil in. In this way the 'drome, however badly bombed, is quickly restored to use. The first raid on Berlin started from Detling; every night the bombers start off somewhere. They rise in pairs and continue circling round the aerodrome till all the machines are up and then they go off together on a signal from their leader, gaining height all the way so that when they pass over Canterbury and the coast they are too high to be seen or even heard. They have had much trouble about light signals by fifth columnists. All roads passing Detling aerodrome are now barred to civilian traffic. A Home Guard the other day procured a rifle rest and when he saw a light he sighted his rifle on it and in the morning they went to the precise spot the rifle pointed to. They found it was a window in a house and that the woman concerned was careless, not a spy. Hornchurch, Northolt and Heston are also the starting points for any raids on Germany.

6 September

Julian and I motored to Ramsgate this morning with Bishop Rose. The stories that Ramsgate is laid low are untrue. Passing through the main streets one notices little damage except for one or two demolished houses and many broken windows. But certain streets have been badly hit. In Farnsworth, the Vicar took us to one of these - two rows of working-class houses, the people still engaged in salvaging what they could. The caves are astonishing. A foreseeing Town Council managed to impress the government with the need for deep air shelters and finally procured a grant. The work began about the time of the Munich agreement and hundreds of tons of chalk were brought up a shaft at the bottom of Ellington Road, and carted away. The result is a vast shelter consisting of long corridors cut in the chalk, nearly three miles long under the central part of the town. These corridors or galleries, which are electrically lighted and possess their own generating station, are equipped with seating, first-aid posts and lavatories and are reached by 23 entrances with wide concrete steps; they are 80 feet below ground. They provide accommodation for 60,000 people, and as soon as the siren goes the population of Ramsgate go there.

The Rector of St Martin's (Day) is in the habit of standing at the open door of his Rectory in Lower Bridge Street during an air raid and inviting people in to take shelter. The other day he saw an old lady coming along the street as the enemy planes were droning overhead and said couryeously, 'Madam, would you care to come inside here for a little to take cover,' to which the old lady made the somewhat cross and unexpected reply, 'Don't be ridiculous, young man, trust in the One Above!'

The Home Guard has been warned that certain persons are posing as Home Guard Officers. The other day (not in Canterbury) a man in civilian clothes, stating he was an officer in the Home Guard, visited a local HQ and was given much information about road blocks and location of posts.

Last week four men in a rowing boat landed near Lydd. Three of them were immediately captured. They said they were Dutch refugees and wished to get to the USA. They were well supplied with English money and possessed a portable sending set and a code book. The fourth man apparently got away. Subsequently another boat which was empty was found on the beach, and probably there had been also four men in this. We were informed about this just before going on guard on Wednesday last (4th September), and told to stop anyone who looked suspicious.

8 September

The next two weeks (8th - 21st September) are supposed to be extremely suitable for invasion and the greatest vigilance is being exercised. Many of the men in the Home Guard simply cannot remain on duty after 5 a.m. as they must be at work at 6 o'clock. But those whose duties will allow them to do so are asked to volunteer to continue on guard for at least another hour. Last night the Home Guard had a lecture on gas from the Brigade Gas Officer. He predicted the use of gas by the enemy in connection with the invasion. Cloud gas can be brought in ships and there is always an on-shore wind for a little time. The Boche can also spray gas from planes and can drop gas bombs and even fire gas shells across the channel. Recent intelligence leads to the belief that he will not so much use the killing gasses such as chlorine, arsene, phosgene or chloro-picrine, or even the blister gases, but the so called nose gases, DM, DA and DC. These gases do not kill, they do not permanently injure, but they lower fighting ability, making the throat constricted and giving a feeling of a bad attack of flu, and the deepest depression and lethargy and unwillingness to exert oneself. You don't know you have been affected until you begin to feel the effects, often an hour afterwards. The only way to resist it is to summon all the will-power one possesses and fight on. When discovered one should put one's gas mask on. It will shorten the length of time the DM has effect.

This morning Mother, Julian and I went to 10.30 Matins at the Cathedral, it being the special Day of Prayer. Halfway through Canon McNutt's sermon the siren went and we all proceeded to the eastern crypt which was packed, a fair number of soldiers being present.

Last night London had by far its worst air raid of the war - big fires raged in the docks area and in East London - fires in the City and considerable damage all over South and South-East London. The raids lasted from 4.30 to 6.30 and then again from 8.30 onwards till dawn: 400 are estimated killed, and another 400 wounded,

9 September

Julian left by the 9.36 for London and two days at Felsted before returning to Goodrich. London was heavily bombed again last night and trains, telephones and all Post Office services are dislocated. No papers have come today at all, but the wireless tells us the immense damage which has been done to London. Julian was very uncertain when he would reach London.

I was going on guard that night so was in uniform and as soon as the Boche planes had gone off (one was brought down by a Spitfire near St Stephen's: the Spitfire did a victory roll round the Angel Tower of the Cathedral) I went down to the Precincts. I bicycled past Browning's yard in St George's about 150 yards from our house where three men were killed, into the Mint Yard and so to the Green Court. The east end of the lovely Cellarer's House was fearfully damaged, the roof, top and second floors having subsided on to the ground floor. Since the Hardcastles left, the house has been divided into two - the east end being occupied by two King's School masters, the west end by Alec Sargent[1] with whom Canon Bradfield[2] was living. Alec's lovely white-panelled drawing-room is heaped up with rubble and his furniture was sticking out from under it. His old Mother had just left the room and with the servants was below. They were unhurt. The Norman walls stood up magnificently. The two masters were away, the school

---

[1] Rev. Canon Alexander Sargent (1895-1989) Archdeacon of Maidstone, 1939-42; Archdeacon of Canterbury, 1942-68; Canon Emeritus, 1974.
[2] Rt. Rev. Harold William Bradfield (1898-1960). Hon. Canon of Canterbury, 1938-46; Bishop of Bath and Wells, 1946-60; Pres. Somerset CCC, 1954.

being in Cornwall and they were not home in Canterbury in spite of it being holiday time. Another bomb fell just at the foot of Lady Bertram's house blowing in part of her dining room and throwing bricks of the dividing wall between her and Miss Mary Mills's house in a huge heap which blocked the shelter under her garage. I found everyone unhurt and both Mary and Dorothy Mills very calm and cheery.

At 8.15 I went on guard at the Gate Inn road block. Invasion is once again expected. The Buffs were also on duty all night at this road block. There is a state of emergency. We drew rifles and ammunition to keep in our houses. The AA barrage both at Dover and on the island of Sheppey was tremendous on several occasions during the night. The weather was cold, dry and clear and the bursting shells made a noisy and magnificent display. The sky above Dover was also constantly lit up with the flashes of our heavy guns shelling the French coast.

10 September

At 2.15 p.m. I went to Wright's the saddler to see about a leather sling for my Lee Enfield rifle, and he asked me whether I had seen the public announcement advising evacuation of certain sections of the population. I hadn't, and we crossed the road to read a placard on a board in the High Street near the Arcade. This printed statement signed by Auckland Geddes,[1] Regional Commissioner, said that if invasion took place every inch of ground would be contested but there would be much troop activity and it would unquestionably be of assistance from the military point of view if aged and infirm persons, children and all whose business did not require their presence in Canterbury left the town as soon as possible. Those who could do were asked to leave quickly and avoid coastal areas. Trains would leave Canterbury West station the following day, beginning at 11 a.m. Members of the Home Guard, clergy, doctors, ARP officials, and others engaged in essential services were instructed to stay.

I immediately realised this meant that Mother should leave, and within three minutes was in Skam's yard arranging for a car the following day. Mother hated the idea of going but agreed with me that it was clearly the right thing to do, as the authorities had made it clear it would assist the national effort.

---

[1] Auckland Campbell Geddes (1879-1954). MP (U) Basingstoke, 1917-20. Numerous govt. posts during that time; Ambassador to USA, 1920-4; Regional Commissioner for SE and NW regions, 1939-42. Cr Baron (1942).

Much had to be arranged. First a wire to Julian at Felsted. Mother, with characteristic efficiency, had all her packing done in a short time; for weeks she has had a suitcase filled with personal papers ready for such an emergency as this. I saw Ian White-Thomson[1] and then the Archbishop himself, who said I might certainly come and stay at the Old Palace for two weeks or so. That will probably be long enough, because if *der Tag* has not come by then, I should certainly have found more permanent work which will take me from Canterbury.

Julian to E.C.F.B., 10 September   *Goodrich Court*

I must record my experiences of yesterday as some of them will be interesting for the War Diary.

The 9.36 train was about 15 minutes late, no papers were at the stations and we made quite good pace until we got to Rochester, but here our train was deflected on to the Maidstone line and meandered in a very leisurely way along the Medway until we reached Maidstone, then still more slowly to Tonbridge, and so on to London Bridge which we did not reach until 1.10 p.m. I bought some chocolate at Maidstone and shared it with an RAF Sergeant who occupied my otherwise empty carriage, and with whom I shared a taxi at London Bridge station. As our route lay through the Bermondsey area, several large fires could be seen blazing, or rather smoking away towards the docks area - London Bridge itself was not in use, police turned us further east to cross at the Tower Bridge. I could see a great fire burning at the north end of the Bridge - perhaps a large warehouse or block of office buildings. When we got near Liverpool Street station our taxi man put us down as a cordon had been drawn all round the approaches and police were on guard. It was explained to me on enquiry that three unexploded bombs were in the vicinity, and until they had been dealt with by demolition squads, the station on that side was railed off.

I said good-bye to my RAF Sergeant, and went into the hotel and got some late lunch. After this I decided to try to get to the East End to call on Canon Steele, our Felsted school missioner. I left my luggage with the hall porter and sallied out to try and find means of transport. I could have taken a taxi but thought I should see far more if I went on a bus if one could be found. The Metropolitan railway was closed and there were no trains running to the East End, so I asked

---

[1] Very Rev. Ian Hugh White-Thomson (b. 1904). Chaplain to Archbishop of Canterbury, 1939-47; Vicar of Folkestone, 1947-54; Chaplain to George VI, 1947-52, and to the Queen, 1952-63.

about buses and was told if I walked to Aldgate I might find a bus going east. This I did and hopped on a No. 40 and from the top managed to get a very good view of a great deal of the damage done, as it went from Aldgate to Shoreditch past the London Hospital, through Stepney and Whitechapel and on to the docks area. Everywhere were signs of the big attack by air made on the two previous nights. Several fires still burning with firemen playing water from hoses on to ruins; glass everywhere in the streets, but always swept up into heaps - consequently many broken windows. Here there were signs of direct hits on office buildings, or a crater in the road, but the damage done was far worse as we got more into the slum area. Nearly every pane of glass seemed to have been broken in the front of the London Hospital facing the Mile End Road. The bus could not keep a straight route: it took side streets and quite often had to retrace its way, being held up by a rope across the road, with a large shell hole just beyond it. Every now and then we came across a whole three or four houses collapsed in the street. In the meaner streets the houses which had been destroyed looked so feeble of structure that it did not seem surprising they had collapsed at the slightest blow. At the doors of hundreds of houses stood little knots of people discussing the situation. In Whitechapel and Stepney whole streets seemed to be occupied by Jews.

After a time my bus decided it could go no further and the passengers were all bundled out. I then managed to get a trolley bus which was going in the Plaistow and Victoria Docks direction. This took me considerably out of my way and I discovered this a bit late, so that I had to retrace my steps - this time I jumped up into the cab of a lorry coming back westwards from the docks, and then took a lift from a baker's cart going in the right direction. At last I found myself in the neighbourhood of the School Mission and, walking through one or two familiar streets, reached the vicarage where I found Canon Steele who gave me a warm welcome.

The Mission people had had a bad time on the previous two nights and had had little sleep. Steele took me round the parish and showed me a good deal of the damage that had been done there and whole houses that had been destroyed. In one spot, only 150 yards from the mission, an enormous bomb had fallen, destroying the fronts of about 20 houses, any one of which looked as it it would fall down at any moment.

The headquarters of a balloon barrage were behind the Vicarage, and these have been smashed to smithereens by an enormous bomb. Fortunately all the occupants were engaged on their balloon and there were no casualties. Actually only one person has been killed in the parish and 20 wounded, but they have had a bombardment every night since; I fear that there will have been an increase in this number. No sooner had Steele and I sat down in his sitting room for a cup of tea, when an air raid warning went. I, accustomed to our habits at Canterbury, refused to take any notice of it and we went on quietly with our tea. After a quarter of an hour I said I must get back to Liverpool Street somehow, and he very kindly walked with me to the entrance to the Victoria Docks gate, where there were trolley buses picking up workmen from the Docks. I entered one of these with a crowd of stevedores, but it only took us about half a mile and then turned north-east, so we got down and about ten of the stevedores and I clambered on top of a lorry going west. It was interesting to see how every street had been emptied since the air raid warning started, only ARP wardens were standing about on duty. From the top of our lorry we had a magnificent view of a fight going on, and AA guns firing on the raiders. The lorry drove at great speed and once more through Bethnel Green and Stepney to within about a quarter of a mile or so of Liverpool Street.

I picked up my luggage and went to get a train. There were quite a number of people waiting about, but in a few moments the 'all clear' went and the whole station was crowded with City workers who had been released from their shelters and were seizing the chance of beginning the journey to their homes. Fortunately a train to Chelmsford was announced, and I managed to get a place in it. On reaching Chelmsford I found that my wire had obviously not reached Chappel, and I had to take a taxi out to Felsted, which cost me 15/-.

Notes by J.B.B., 11 September

Mother, Miss Hewlett and Norah left at 8 a.m. in one of Skam's cars (driven by Parker) for Herefordshire. It was horrific seeing them go off. But I am sure it was the right thing to do to carry out the desire of the authorities in a crisis such as this.

All day there have been many lorries with troops passing along the New Dover Road. Military police control the traffic at various cross-roads which are not usually controlled at all. All morning I carried out various duties, such as notifying the Telephone Co., the police, and various friends that No.16 will be shut indefinitely. All afternoon Maple, Sgt. Roberts and I reconnoitred the Gate

Inn road block and the country to the south of it which our emergency squad of 38 men is responsible for defending. There are many rumours as to why the evacuation has been ordered. Invasion is genuinely expected as the PM's broadcast at 6 p.m. made clear. But perhaps even more the reason is that many AA guns are being placed round Canterbury, and a heavy barrage will be put up when the hordes of Boche planes pour over the town on their way up to London. This will probably bring retaliation. There is also the question of feeding the civilians and of accommodation for troops. The prospect of invasion is (to me) fantastic. I do not believe it will be tried. But the military authorities have ordered cancellation of leave and a general 'stand to'. At the barracks the troops practically sleep with their clothes on. The date of invasion has been set for 13 September, or failing that any day up till 21st. The *Daily Telegraph* this morning reports that in Berlin the offensive is spoken of as planned for around 11 November.

After tea I migrated to the Old Palace. All my kit was packed into a taxi, and I bicycled down with my rifle slung over my back and my ammunition in my pocket. Alec Sargent, Canon Bradfield and I dined together. Rose, the Bishop of Dover, came in afterwards. That very morning his garden boy had gone to the marrow bed in the kitchen garden to get a marrow for the cook. He espied a huge unexploded bomb lying among the marrows and rushed off to tell his friend the kitchen maid. Together they viewed the bomb. 'Lawks,' said the kitchen maid, and ran off to tell the cook. And they all came to tell the Bishop, who in turn viewed the bomb from afar with considerable respect. The police came and notified the bomb disposal section and a sergeant arrived and taking one look at it said, 'Oh! that's an easy one.' He went up to it, smacked it in a friendly way, and took the detonator out, and with the help of one of his men hurled it into a lorry and took it away. A small typewritten note stating where it was made and giving its number and other particulars was removed and given to the Bishop to keep.

Bradfield, who went to Dover this afternoon, came in for considerable shelling. The immediate surroundings of the harbour are getting rather messed about by German guns, and the large apartment block on the sea front was damaged by water after its large water tank on the roof was destroyed. Stories that shells have fallen on the top of Lidden Hill, near the Half-Way House, and even at Barham Cross, are without foundation, though unquestionably Canterbury could be shelled if the Boches so desired.

I drew 10/6 in pay from the Home Guard this evening.

Ralph to J.B.B., 11 September   *London*

We have, of course, been having it pretty grim up here. The damage, of course, is considerable, but as the communiqué states, set against the whole of London and the country at large it is a drop in the bucket. They have simply plastered the City. The Docks too have had terrible fires and St Katherine's Dock apparently got it this morning, as I see volumes of black smoke rising in the sky.

We saw, or rather Peter saw, a good number of the planes coming over on Saturday evening and realised there must be a big raid on London. It took me four hours to get up on Monday morning and about the same time going back at night. In fact I bring some clothes up with me in case I have to stay in London. The only stations working are Blackfriars and Holborn but they got Cannon Street working the same day. St Mary Abchurch and the pub opposite and this end of London Bridge have received a hit. All the buildings round about there are badly damaged. On Monday night they got Cheapside and Queen Victoria Street - a building in Budge Row has been demolished, but fortunately they missed Bow Church. They got the Bank of England - one plumb on the top- which went down three floors and came to rest on the sixth floor, and one in the road between the Bank and the Royal Exchange - 70 yards from this office. Fortunately we had our windows treated a fortnight ago and we are one of the few firms with no broken windows. Glass damage in the City is tremendous. Funnily enough even in the small streets you come across windows completely out. Heaven alone knows why.

The East End, of course, has got a packet and it is dreadful to see the poor people dragging what few belongings they can carry coming through the City either on foot or in lorries. However, the people are generally cheerful and it has created a feeling of enormous anger, which is not going to help make peace at the end of the war. The people are determined to stick it until the end. The general opinion is they would like to do in the entire German country. That is the worst of war. Nobody will be happy until all the big German cities have been razed to the ground and as many women and children killed as possible.

Notes by J.B.B., 12 September

Skam's chauffeur brought me a note from Mother telling me they had reached Goodrich about 4:30 and had received a warm welcome. Julian is expected to-day.

At 10 a.m. I went to see Miss Babington at the West Station. A queue four deep of adults and children carrying suitcases and bundles stretched right down the station road. One train full of children had already left, and as I arrived another train bearing about 500 adults and children steamed out of the station amid much waving and cheery farewells and a few tears. It is hoped to get one train away every hour. The YMCA were providing tea and sandwiches; many of the travellers had not had breakfast. It is not quite clear whether the children will receive the weekly subsistence allowance as the evacuation is apparently voluntary. Fielding Ottley said the parents were singularly feckless and helpless and this was perhaps typical of Kent where the people do not possess the sturdy independence of the Yorkshireman or the Londoner. I understand it is hoped that at least 15,000 people will leave Canterbury, i.e. about half the population. So far about 3,000 have gone.

Many of my pals in the Home Guard have evacuated their wives and children. Already the town seems emptier. I spent the afternoon reconnoitring the country round our post once again. The orchards and enclosed character of this country might make it difficult for tanks, but certainly restrict the field of fire for the defenders.

Canadian host reactions to British evacuees.

Maude Grant to J.B.B., 20 August   *Otter Lake, Ontario*

The position of the well-to-do women without any money is hard, as people here will put up children, but they do not want mothers so much - especially the rather grand, smart, bridge-playing, undomesticated women who hoped to get into rich homes. It is all difficult and will continue to be. So many of the women were so splendid that one hates to be critical of others.

Mrs. David Dunlop to J.B.B., 11 August   *Toronto*

You are quite right about the war guests from England not all fitting into the life in Canada. I hear some are very discontented, even those in good homes. One woman demanded from her hostess a car and chauffeur, as she had to leave her Rolls Royce behind!

Monier to E.C.F.B., 12 September   *Chiddingstone*

I had hardly posted my letter yesterday when our biggest and longest battle started, and stretched from Edenbridge to Tonbridge. We were having tea at home when a German bomber went lowish over the hop garden with two British fighters on its tail. He never got back to Germany.

We are quite as safe here as in Surrey, our evacuated children are still with us. The weather, of course, is too marvellous for words. We have not had any rain for 18 days I think, and then it was only a sprinkling.

Notes by J.B.B., 14 September

The date foretold for the invasion was 13 September. That has now passed. The Dean said this morning that 15 September was now supposed to be the *Tag*, and all danger would be over in about another week. Why this should be, I cannot see. The long winter nights, often providing fog and a calm sea, would seem extremely suitable. Certainly there is still a state of emergency, and the regular troops man their posts from dusk till dawn as well as the Home Guard. Last night Bradfield, returning from Broadstairs, was stopped nine times on the road by troops in full kit and asked to show his identity card.

Last night with German planes droning overhead and the searchlights making superb pyramids and cones in the sky, and a full moon flooding the Cathedral, the nightwatchman cried-out, '11.45, fine night and all's well,' itself perhaps an epitome of the spirit of England.

Up till last night about 4,600 people, including children, have left Canterbury since Wednesday morning. We hear that the first lot are temporarily housed under canvas and in halls in Reading.

I spent a good part of this morning learning the mechanism of the Browning automatic rifle, which is American and takes .300 ammunition, not .303. Sgt. Stringer (the antique furniture dealer) has been doing a course at Ashford and is now to instruct members of the Home Guard.

J.B.B., 15 September

During our guard last night there was a heavier and closer AA barrage than ever before. The shells from guns on Dunkirk Hill, where the Boches were attacking the pylons, seemed to be bursting almost over Canterbury.

All this morning we spent at our road block. The entire emergency squad of some 40 men were there and we worked out the disposal of these men, working with four sections of 10. Some of the heaviest air fighting I have ever seen broke out overhead. At one point a Messerschmitt 110 appeared out of the clouds immediately above us, about 1,000 feet up; a little smoke was coming out of it. Right behind came a Spitfire overhauling the German rapidly. A short sharp crack of fire, and the German machine burst into flames and fell like a bit of lead. The pilot baled out and was seen a few moments later swaying gently at the end of his parachute. We saw as many as four parachutes in the air.

As we went to the Gate Inn for a drink about 12.30 a Lieutenant in the RNVR rode up on a motor bike and joined us. He commands an MTB and said that the stories which have been so current during the last few days about an attempt by the enemy to invade this country, having been already stopped by the navy, are entirely groundless. Yesterday there was a report all over Canterbury that at least 50 barges had started across the channel for the Dymchurch area and had been entirely wiped out by the navy, and the sea was thick with the bodies of German soldiers.

This MTB Lieutenant thought invasion was most unlikely even if the RAF had not caused havoc among the barges and small freight boats collected, especially at Calais and Boulogne, apparently for the purpose of landing troops in England. He also said the tides were now wrong again and would not be high again till the neap tides came. Winter invasion would be very difficult - in spite of the long nights, the sea and wind were seldom helpful and the barges required an absolutely calm sea.

I went to Evensong at 6.30 tonight in the Cathedral. An air raid warning had just gone 'all clear', another might begin at any moment. All day long such terrific fighting in the air had taken place over Canterbury, wave after wave of invading German planes being broken up over the city. As we assembled in that vast building which for centuries has witnessed so many historic scenes in the life of the nation, all was for the moment quiet. Except for the choir, the Cathedral was shrouded in darkness. The High Altar, illuminated by special lighting from the pillars on either side, stood out against the black background of St Thomas's Chapel and the blocked east windows. The cross dominated the scene. We were a small company - perhaps 150 in all. The only clergy were the Archbishop and Ian White-Thomson (his Chaplain), and the Dean, who read the service from his stall.

The Archbishop read the lessons from his throne. The Dean took the intercessions from the pulpit and called us to pray. He then preached on the elemental human instincts of pugnacity, curiosity and acquisitiveness, and how these instincts could be abused or transformed into something good - something new. The final hymn was 'Through the night of doubt and sorrow', and the Archbishop blessed us in most moving words, and we dispersed through the vast unlit nave. Within half an hour the sirens sounded again. German machines were overhead, and bombs were dropped on the outskirts of the town.

J.B.B., to E.C.F.B., 16 September   *Canterbury*

This morning a big bomber was brought down at Walmer, the crew of which was Italian. A yellow-nosed German machine, meaning it belongs to a squadron of crack fighters, fell in Hartley Churchyard, near Sittingbourne, this morning, missing the church by inches.

The fight yesterday (Sunday) morning and afternoon over Canterbury was perhaps the most intense that has taken place here since the war began. The wireless mentioned Canterbury and Maidstone by name, stating that the main attacks on London had been broken up over those two places. The Archbishop was most amusing, 'I saw nothing,' he said, 'nobody ever shows me anything. Why am I never allowed to see these exciting things'. A bomber which came down near Sturry was found to contain 25 rifles, 25 helmets, flares, parachutes large and small, and thousands of rounds of ammunition. There is no doubt of the truth of this; Cussans, our CO, had it officially. Exactly what it portends is difficult to say. Were they to be dropped for fifth column men or are the German pilots under the impression German troops are already in England?

The Dean tells me that up to to-day about 7,000 persons have left Canterbury. The authorities hope many more will do so, and new placards all over the town urge all who can leave to leave quickly. Frankly, it is difficult to see the reason for this half voluntary, half compulsory order, and many are in great doubt as to their duty. Most of those who have gone are in the Reading and Newbury neighbourhood.

Notes by J.B.B., 15 and 18 September

A terrific gale developed last night. The skies cleared by mid-day but the gale continued. This change in the weather, together with the terrific attacks by our RAF on barge and ship concentrations in the Channel ports, has certainly deferred Hitler's plans for invasion, though the PM, in addressing the House tonight, stated that there was every reason to think he would make the attempt.

I was out on guard last night. It deluged from 10.30 p.m. to 4.30 a.m. and we all got soaked. The tent proved watertight, but even so the rain came in through the flaps, and as each relief came in everything and everybody got very damp. It was not a pleasant night. The AA guns are much closer to Canterbury than formerly.

ARP officials have been informed this morning that the enemy have dropped cylinders (about two feet long) from planes. These may be magnetic mines and they should be reported at once. No one with steel helmets or any such equipment should go near them.

Euan Wallace to J.B.B., 16 September

Six successive nights sleeping in our War Room did rather get me down and I went off to Lavington for two nights and a day, getting back early this morning. Luckily it was quiet here and at Lavington on Saturday - but yesterday (Sunday) was not so good. We had a bomb just the other side of Graffham, and London had a pretty good doing, though fortunately not in Stepney, Poplar and the Docks. A lot of damage has been done, of which roads and railways are the most awkward, and gas and cold storage the most potentially serious if it goes on. But London is not 'out', or anywhere near it. I have forbidden Barbie to sleep in London, so she is at Ascot tomorrow night with Helen Fitzgerald, after dropping Peter and Bill at Eton. John went off to Oxford to-day for his fortnight's military course. I think he will enlist in a Young Soldiers' Battalion.

To-day's technique (owing to cloud cover) of keeping London under red alert most of the day is going to be awkward if it continues. We shall have to try and re-organise our lives entirely. Yesterday's aerial victory was an epic.

Having cabled to his father at Chiddingstone, on 18 September, that his ship had reached Mombassa after a voyage of 33 days, Edward added:

'We only saw one ship out of harbour since we left convoy off Ireland. As soon as we saw it we dashed off in the opposite direction, wirelessing the Admiralty that we had sighted an armed enemy raider. Flashes appeared from the bridge of the ship, which turned out to be a British merchant cruiser, curtly telling us to cancel our message'.

Lt. Col. R. Heyworth to J.B.B., 19 September   *Palestine*

Here we keep jogging along. We all feel rather *embusqués* and I put up a letter recently asking for the future policy, and saying we liked our horses, but if it meant being used always on internal security duties, all ranks would welcome mechanization. We could be used as a Machine Gun battalion, or Recce. unit on motor bikes after very little extra training.

The last two months we have spent in the most comfortable quarters in Palestine. But now we move next week to a much hotter and more unpleasant part. I had a cable today saying our charming friend Wintle (the Royals officer who was court-martialled but acquitted) was now coming back to us after his escapades. He is a wizard how he gets away with it. As you know he was sent to the Tower for threatening his superior officer. Curiously enough, the superior officer in question, Air Vice-Marshal Boyd,[1] was last week flying out to Egypt to take up an appointment there; unaccountably his aeroplane flew over Sicily; it was either attacked by the Italians, or had engine touble and was forced to descend. He and several other officers were taken prisoner. Two days ago I was speaking to a Flight Lieut. about this incident and he remarked, 'A good thing too, he is no loss,' which shows the fault was not all on Wintle's side.

Notes by J.B.B., 21 September

Today I went to Dover with the Bishop of Dover, in his car. Our object was to inspect the area of the town which had suffered most damage last Wednesday week from bombs and shells. The Bishop had to decide whether St James's Church, in which parish this area lies, should be shut or not. While Rose had lunch with one of the Churchwardens and the Rector, I ate my sandwiches at the sea front! I found a section not barred to the public and sat on a seat with the eastern gap of the harbour to my left and the western gap used by the cross Channel service almost straight in front of me. The western gap is closed by a boom, and also by the old freight ship, the *Sepoy*, which was badly damaged by a bomb while lying in harbour and was then towed to the gap and sunk there. The

---

[1] Air Vice-Marshal Owen Boyd (1889-1944). AOC Balloon Command, 1938; Captured, 1940. CB (1939).

eastern gap is used by ships leaving and entering the harbour and has a net against submarines. The harbour was deserted except for a number of mine-sweepers and a few small naval craft. Coils of barbed wire were two feet in front of me and stretched along the entire front to the water's edge. A kiosk to my left announced that 'Ice cream is sold here', but it is 13 months or more since it was; next to it was a camouflaged pill box. The asphalted sea wall was covered with shingle and other debris deposited there by two bombs which fell on the shore a week ago. Above were eight or ten barrage balloons. The houses facing the sea were empty: many had been damaged and there was hardly a sound pane of glass among them. Of traffic along the sea front there was none: indeed there was little movement of any kind: from the channel Dover must have looked completely dead. A few soldiers passed; then three lorries carrying cement lumbered by followed a few moments later by two more carrying sailors: that was all.

Re-joining the Bishop, we proceeded to go round the area, going first to the caves. These are old smugglers' caves in the cliff under the Castle. They were used occasionally during the last war but are in constant demand now. Dover Town Council did not show the foresight of Ramsgate, where the caves were specially dug and well ventilated and lighted. The Dover ones stink, and of lighting there is little except an occasional bulb. About 50 people were in them when we went round. Some of them practically live there - there was a collection of rickety furniture, beds and deck chairs and old boxes. Men, women and children sat and lay about the place. Lavatory accommodation was of the most primitive character.

We then walked along the sea front and turned inland by the Grand Hotel. Whole blocks of buildings are here demolished or merely skeletons of the houses stand. The Bishop and I went into one small house up a very unsafe stairway, and under the guidance of the City Surveyor looked out from the back on a scene of utter desolation. The space between the backs of two rows of houses was a mass of rubble and beams, and old furniture and doors and window frames - it was the remains of some dozen working men's houses - on one door, lying flat on a heap of debris, lay a black cat peacefully asleep. In front of St James's Church Schools was an enormous crater in the road, and the boys' school had completely disappeared except for one gable and chimney; the girls' school was so badly damaged as to be useless; on a heap of rubble near the ruins a Union Jack had been placed.

The normal population of Dover is 40,000, and about 50 per cent have left. But those who are left do not slink about as if they were waiting for the next shells or bombs to fall, but proceed quietly about their business. St Barnabas Church, which we passed on our way to St James's, received two direct hits from shells and is damaged beyond repair. This town, 21 miles from the Germans in Calais and four minutes from the Germans in flying time, is certainly in the front line.

Alan Don,[1] the Archbishop's senior Chaplain, came down from London to-night and gave us a more detailed account of the bombing of Lambeth. He himself lives in a flat in Westminster, just across the river. He heard this late lone bomber and it was apparently his last bomb for the night, which fell on Lambeth. Don heard the explosion and, fearing for the Palace, he walked out on to Lambeth Bridge. But there stood the Palace apparently intact, and he went back to bed. Only at 10 a.m., when he went there, did he learn of the tragedy. The bomb, which must have been a large one, fell behind Ian White-Thomson's bedroom and Miss Fuller's bedroom (the typist), and going through the big drawing room, exploded there. It destroyed this room and the adjoining small drawing rooms and the debris fell through into the pantry and a room where the balloon men were sleeping - fortunately under a table. They burrowed their way out.

To-night we had a talk about the future of the Palace. Should it be built up after the war? The house is thoroughly badly planned and the Archbishop thought that as it is now virtually cut in two, the end which contains his rooms and the Chaplain's and secretaries' quarters, with bed rooms above, might be converted into a suitable residence for the Archbishop of Canterbury. He said, 'No successor of mine would, in any case, have been able to continue to live in Lambeth as it was before this tragedy.' If the part destroyed is restored, it might be made into some Church office. But Church House, just completed, has removed the necessity for more offices.. The whole section of Lambeth, part of which is now destroyed, dates from 1832. It had a veneer of stone over the brick. It is Victorian architecture and building at its worst.

Alan Don says that what the authorities are really anxious about is the possible flooding of Millbank and the area round the Tate Gallery, if the enemy

---

[1] Rev. Alan Don (1885-1966). Chaplain and Sec. to Archbishop of Canterbury, 1931-41; Canon of Westminster, 1941-46; Dean of Westminster, 1946-59; Chaplain to the Queen, 1959-66. KCVO (1959).

secured a direct hit on the wall between the road and the Thames, where the level
of the river is above that of the land.

Notes by J.B.B., 22 September

At lunch the Archbishop, Alan Don and I discussed the prospects of the
war. Can London go on like this? Every night at about 6.30 millions of Londoners
have some food and then, if they are not at home, go home so that they are at the
place where they will be sleeping before dark. About 8.30 p.m. the people of
London descend to dug-outs or shelters of some kind (mostly cellars below their
houses) and sleep there as best they can until the 'All Clear' goes about 5.30 a.m.
They then go upstairs and go to bed for about two hours, then bath and have
breakfast and go to work. Can this curious life continue all winter? And especially
when it gets dark by 4.30 p.m.?

We three discussed the outlook. The Archbishop thought it very grim. I
mentioned that before long Hitler would stake everything on one gigantic gamble,
sending thousands of planes over on the night before the *Tag*, and destroy the
Admiralty, the War Office, the RAF Headquarters, and other nerve centres; he
would attack every railway terminus, every essential bridge and all the chief
aerodromes. Just before dawn he would land thousands of troops from aeroplanes
and would also attempt several landings from the sea, having detailed hundreds of
planes to deal with our fleet. The Archbishop does not agree. He thinks Hitler will
confine his activities to bombing on an ever-increasing scale but will not try actual
invasion.

J.B.B. to E.C.F.B., 23 September

At the moment we have the curious spectacle of some million and a half
troops billeted throughout Britain and many of them in comparative safety,
watching about six million civilians being bombed in London and able to do
nothing about it.

I showed 60 New Zealanders over the Cathedral this morning. Such
magnificent men, drawn from both islands. They were thrilled at seeing the
ceremony at 11 a.m. in The Buffs Chapel. The air raid sirens sounded and
screeching and zooming developed overhead. What thoughts it conjured up. These
troops from a young Dominion standing in front of Chichele's tomb, who in the

same Cathedral had conducted the triumphal service for the victory at Agincourt - and a fierce air battle going on overhead.

This afternoon about 3 p.m. Lt. General McNaughton, and Eric Duncannon came to the Old Palace by appointment. McNaughton and I had a long talk. He asked me to make a survey of the educational requirements of the Canadian troops - namely the 1st. Canadian Division, the troops in the Depots at Aldershot and Borden, and many isolated groups. The 2nd. Canadian Division would not be included as it is busy training. He suggested that I spend two days in London at Canadian military HQ with Major Humphreys,[1] who has the result of a questionnaire which the troops answered some weeks ago, and that I should then go to Corps HQ for a week or ten days and visit all units and find out what they need. After this he thinks that Vincent Massey, Mike Pearson and Hume Wrong might discuss with him (McNaughton) and me the whole situation. Whatever is planned he thinks should begin not later than 1st. November. As there are some 45,000 troops concerned, it is obviously a superhuman task, but I said I would come and do my best. The job is a civilian one. Whether it involves staying on to administer the system when it has been drawn up is not certain. Anyhow I have leave of absence from Hart House till Christmas. The Canadians are situated over a huge area of Surrey, and the first thing I must do is to get in touch with them. Corps HQ is at a village called Headley, SW of Leatherhead (absolutely confidential). If you writer to the Travellers' I will leave word where they are to forward letters. You must not, of course, put Headley. The addrress is really HQ 7th. Corps, Home Forces.

Later the Archbishop and I strolled round the Precincts and went into the garden of Meister Omers. It was one of those superb golden September afternoons, and the old house with its red Virginia creeper and 13th. century stonework was bathed in sunlight. Never has it looked more attractive. But it was locked and empty, and the garden was unkempt and overgrown.

Geoffrey to E.C.F.B., 25 September   *Aberdeen*

So profound was the Victorian peace and so firm men's faith in its permanency, that you would have refused to believe this vision of the future even had it been granted you. And yet the little girl and the old lady were and are you.

---

[1] Maj., later Maj-Gen. George Humphreys (1899-1991). GSO2, Public Relations, War Office, 1938-9; Asst. Dir. Public Relations, 1939-40; field postings thereafter. CBE (1948).

Though years have enfeebled your frame, I venture to think that could Lewis Carroll have seen you the other day, passing through Oxford on your way from Canterbury to Herefordshire, he would have failed to detect the smallest change in your essential self. He would have recognized with delight, but without surprise, the same lively, adventurous, eager and capable spirit, determined, as always, to present a gay and indomitable front to the slings and arrows of fortune, however outrageous, and never losing her presence of mind.

Your memory must be just about as long as the modern German Empire. The changes that have taken place during the four score years of your life are more numerous and far more staggering than any that occurred in the whole course of the 10,000 years of preceding history. In your childhood, for instance, the coach, as a means of public transport, was not quite yet obsolete. In the 1860s, travel by train was comparatively new. No such revolutionary changes are likely to occur during the next eighty years, and if they do I doubt if they would be desirable.

I think it certain that Austria will be given an independent government again after the war, perhaps as part of a confederation of Danubian states. I, for one, hope that the submarine and bombing and fighter aeroplane will, as weapons of war be, if not abolished, internationalised. The USA and the British Empire will be so powerful in alliance - which is what they are as good as already - that they may compel both Russia and Japan to consent to this proposal. Russia is going to be the chief difficulty. The British Empire and the USA. could destroy Japan by economic means alone at any time they chose if she proved refractory.

Notes by J.B.B., 25 September

A farmer who owns extensive orchards at Wickhambreaux told me today that several Dorniers had been brought down on his property. The pilot of one of them was somewhat truculent to begin with, but he calmed down after a little and talked interestingly. He said the people were not short of food in Germany and that their rations in the Luftwaffe were very good. Hitler was not responsible for the promiscuous bombing: it was the order of the group round him. As for the shooting of our pilots when baling out, this had been done by some Germans entirely on their own responsibility. Most German pilots would not do such a thing. This particular German pilot was well dressed and smart. He had on him a photograph of a very pretty girl and two tickets for the Berlin opera on the very night of the day he was captured. He said he was very disappointed at not being able to take his girl there.

About 200 people of those who left Canterbury two weeks ago have now returned.

J.B.B. to E.C.F.B., 26 September   *Travellers' Club, Pall Mall*
I left Canterbury early this morning. Molly was splendid about everything and looked after me and fed me and was so sensible. We went very slow, and the journey to London took about three and a half hours. Traffic diversion makes many traffic complications and we crawled down Queen Victoria Street. *The Times* office was completely out of commission, but no damage to any one I understand. It was 2 a.m. the night before last - much damage in this district.

After establishing myself here I went round to see Major Humphreys in charge of Auxiliary Services whom McNaughton asked me to see. He suggested lunch at 1 p.m. and then I went off to see Vincent. He was delighted to hear of McNaughton's request to me, and I am going off to dinner with him and Alice as soon as I have finished this. I also saw Mike Pearson and Hume Wrong - they and Vincent all knew of the probability of the offer to me, I think Hume may be free to help.

At lunch with Humphreys at the Guards' Club, I met Harry Crookshank[1] (Financial Secretary to the Treasury) and we all three talked. From 2.30 to 4.30 I buried myself in files of memorandum and official reports. At 4.30 I went over to see Major-General Montague[2] who is in charge of Canadian Military HQ.

Mary to J.B.B., 26 September   *Chiddingstone*
We had a cable from Ted yesterday evening, sent off from Torit the day before. It said, 'Excellent journey. Good luck immediately at Torit. Well content. Letters 18 August received. You all did well in exciting raid.' We puzzled over 'good luck immediately at Torit' for ages, and then someone remembered that we had made up a code for telegrams. 'Good luck' was to mean 'joining Equats'; this

[1] Rt. Hon. Harry Crookshank (1893-1961). MP (Con) Gainsborouugh, 1924-56; Parl. U-S Home Office, 1934-5; Sec. for Mines, 1935-9; FST, 1939-43, PMG, 1943-5; Min. of Health, 1951-2; Leader of House of Commons, 1951-55; Ld. Privy Seal, 1952-5. Cr. Vt. (1956), PC (1939), CH (1955).
[2] Maj-, later Lt-Gen. Percival Montague, DSO, MC (1882-1966). CoS Canadian Mil. HQ, London, 1940-42

means the Equatorial Battalion of the Sudan Defence Force, composed entirely of southern Sudanese troops. The headquarters have always been at Torit. Whether Ted will do any of his own job or simply become a soldier, we don't know. We shall hear in time.

Friday. Today has been one of the most exciting days we've had from the point of view of aerial battles. We had been hop-picking all day and had dress circle seats from the garden. There were two big battles this morning, but the really exciting one was this afternoon. I've never seen such a barrage as the AA put up, which turned the formation of German bombers making for London. Then the fighters were at them and the machine-gunning was terrific. Then the hop garden went mad as a German bomber in flames appeared coming quite low. For one awful moment we thought it was going to crash into the Church, but it swerved and actually fell about a quarter of a mile away. It must have got rid of any HEs it had, as there were no explosions, only clouds of black smoke. Two men baled out, but one parachute didn't work and the other was dead. I suppose there must have been others in the machine. When I came home for tea, I biked down to the scene of the action. The debris was still blazing in some places with a very bright flame, rather as if there had been incendiaries in the plane. You weren't allowed into the field which was a mass of soldiers and police, but you could see very well over the hedge, and I picked up (like an awful souvenir hunter) a bit of plane lying in the road. It's simply amazing how quickly a crowd gathers, even in a remote country district. By the time I got there, there were cars parked up the road and at least 50 people gazing over the hedge. The village is very excited to have had a crashed German bomber so near. We have become known as 'the Dornier bus route'.

The man on duty at the Home Guard post thought he heard an unexploded bomb drop near a group of cottages just north of this house. So Daddy and Mr Matthew have set out, complete with tin hats, to see if it is so, and whether the people ought to be evacuated. John went off to Osterley yesterday evening to start the course today. He's gone off with another man from this parish called Belahonbek. I say it's unfair for two men with names like Belahonbek and Bickersteth to go together!

Saturday. Daddy and Mr Matthew got home after searching unsuccessfully for the unexploded bomb and having walked miles. They tried to report the incident, but couldn't get through on the phone. Just after midnight there was a terrific explosion, and we all leapt up and met on the landing. Daddy dressed and went up to the village and along to the Home Guard post. Everyone seemed to think the bomb had fallen in the park, and it certainly had sounded in that direction. So he undressed and we got back to bed. There were a few more bangs that night, and Daddy was just setting out to the hop garden at 7 a.m., when Colonel Meade-Waldo arrived saying the bombs had been at Thresher's Field, about a mile in the opposite direction to where we had thought. He had been there since 4 a.m., and had nearly got blown up by the bomb going off about 10 yards from him. Luckily it was in very soft sandy soil and he was quite unhurt.

Notes by E.C.F.B., 29 September   *Goodrich Court*

Keynes's[1] wireless talk on the financing of the war and the relative cheapness of restoring the material damage being done to London, was most cheering, just as the Dakar fiasco[2] was most depressing. I think there is bound to be a revolution in France before they recover. I cannot see why Frenchmen should not now fight against Frenchmen, if the process helps us to beat the Germans.

The rottenness of post-war France must have been known to our Foreign Office, and their failure to take it into account makes it impossible to acquit them of the grossest incompetence. Baldwin and his advisers have a fearful responsibility in this matter. Our government must have entered on the present war knowing quite well that France would be a broken reed, and yet they let the British people remain in entire ignorance of the fact.

J.B.B. to E.C.F.B., 28 September

This is the most fantastic life. Last night I walked in pitch blackness to the Dorchester where I found a merry party. Vincent, Alice, a lad called Lewis - who has just got the DFC. - another Canadian officer with a Russian wife, Hart and Alison Grant. We dined and drank Lewis's health in champagne. About 8.45 p.m. the bombardment began - the nearest battery seemed to be in the park just opposite. The noise made talking quite difficult at first but one gets used to it. The

---

[1] John Maynard Keynes (1883-1946). Fellow and Bursar of King's College Cambridge; Editor of *Ecomonics Journal*, 1911-44. Wrote numerous influential books and 'invented most of modern economics'. Cr. Baron (1942).
[2] 'Operation Menace', 23-24 September 1940, in which a large force of British warships tried without success to persuade the garrison of Dakar to declare for de Gaulle and the Free French.

Strathconas[1] dropped in, she (a Loder - I was at St David's with her father) just down from Scotland - a western island - many German bodies always being washed up and the water so covered with oil, bathing is difficult. Above us German machines droning about continuously and 3.7" and 4.5" guns firing every minute or so. I left about 11.30. I had my tin-hat. Not many people about. I walked down Piccadilly and turned into St. James's Street. A German machine quite low, much bursting of shells overhead, but no shrapnel dropping. Suddenly when I was two thirds of the way down the street and St James's Palace was just looming through the darkness, a curious swishing noise and there fell a shower of incendiary bombs all round me, one just at my feet, literally, on the pavement. It spluttered and let off a sort of firework in a most amusing way - another fell by the Carlton Club - others, I counted about a dozen, fell on the houses. I ran across the street to where the bomb near the Carlton Club was burning right up against the wall. The street had seemed empty - there must have been many invisible watchers - as, no sooner had the incendiary bombs fallen and their funny spluttering flames lit up the street from end to end, then men began to appear, whistles blew, and fire engines could be heard approaching. A man rushed out with a pail of sand to throw on the Carlton Club bomb. I helped him stamp it out. Flames were now appearing on the roof of one house, other small fires were starting. Actually I heard this morning that Burg's - a wine merchant- was burnt out. I did not wait much longer but walked back down Pall Mall, the great club frontage illuminated every few seconds by the flash of guns. I went up to my room and undressed. As I stepped into bed three whines and three terrific detonations about half a mile off or less, I judged - Green Park I thought was likely. Curtains and blinds floated gently out into the middle of the room and then returned to their normal position. I turned the lights off, drew back the curtains and blinds and opened the window wide. That odd acrid smell of explosives drifted in. I got into bed and went to sleep in spite of the gun fire. The bombs I heard fell near the India Office I discovered this morning. A curious evening you must admit.

I met Bendall (Director of Army Education) this morning. Not a very imaginative or inspiring person. But for over an hour I picked his brains. A whistle blew announcing heavy bombardment over this area of London. All office staff

---

[1] Donald Strathcona and Mount Royal (1891-1959). MP (Con) N. Cumberland, 1922-26; Parl U-S for War, 1934-9; war service, 1939-45. Lady Strathcona was the daughter of Lord Wakehurst.

filed past our door to shelters. But we decided to stay where we were - and indeed at Canterbury you have sat in your corner unconcerned in many similar situations. Had lunch with Ralph and Hume Wrong at the Travellers'. Hume stayed on after Ralph had gone to talk of the work I am trying to do for the Canadians. He could, I think, be set free from Canada House and would be prepared to help which would be an admirable idea. All afternoon I worked hard in Humphrey's office on files, trying to get this very complicated situation clearer in my mind.

I think I could work out a plan for educational machinery. But the fact remains that the Canadian Legion officials who know the Canadian end, who have devised a scheme by which Canadian universities agree on common educational requirements, and who have been labouring on this problem for months, have returned to Canada disgruntled. Moreover, they have sent a cable stating that they were entrusted with the educational work for Canadian troops, that they have a complete scheme, and that directly suitable arrangements have been made for the status of their officials, they are prepared to come over and run the educational work for the Canadian troops. This holds a pistol at McNaughton's head, and he is not the man to submit to it. But you see what a difficult position it places me in.

To-night I dined with Euan Wallace at the Turf. He, poor man, has my trouble, gastritis, and I don't wonder, considering the strain under which he lives.[1] But as usual he is cheerful and amusing. Today he took the King and Queen to some strafed areas. The King was in great form. Euan says that the casualties as given in the press are as correct as they can possibly be made. The ARP people find much money and jewellery in the debris and are, Euan believes, extremely honest in handing it in. One ARP man found £60 in £1 notes and handed it in to the Town Clerk. Euan also gave me facts to make one optimistic about our ability before long to defeat this night bombing.

October

John to J.B.B., 2 October   *Chiddingstone*

I got back from Osterley on Saturday night. I was extremely glad that I went, and I was lucky to get in at all, as the school in its present form has come to an end. The course, I expect, was much the same as when you were there. The commandant opened the two-day series of lectures by stressing the fact that they

---

[1] This was the early stage of the cancer from which Wallace died in February 1941.

would not be teaching us how to carry on a gentlemanly war. The Germans do not play cricket, and we must temporarily give it up; for instance, they used dum-dum bullets - we must have no compunction about using them too.

The whole lot of us (about 190 men of every age) lined up for the bomb-throwing practice - after the demonstration by two Spaniards. That was the most energetic half-hour of the whole course. Did they make you run 10 yards, monkey-run 10 yards, crawl another 10, and then fling your bombs? It was great fun; and I am getting some bombs made by one of the men here, so that the Home Guard can practice it.

The scouting person was excellent, I thought. I expect you had him. What he said made me wish we had done more of that kind of stuff in the Corps at school. Was 'Yank', the Canadian who has fought in two Mexican revolutions, and done a bit of gun-running among other things, lecturing on quick ways of doing-in Germans, when you were there? He was most entertaining, and gave us lots of information - mostly for use in guerilla warfare. I liked Slater's lecture on street-fighting. He described the capture of Belcite in Spain, which he had organized three years ago. He's rather Bohemian, didn't you think?, but a very able lecturer.

The attack through smoke, which you described to me at Canterbury, was a great success. An old general, who was in the Argylls, acted as umpire - sitting in the pill box - but he got hit by a sawdust bomb, and the fighting spirit made him forget he was meant to be umpiring, and he started slinging bombs back at the attackers.

There were men of every sort and description taking the course: in my digs there were two businessmen from Leicester, and two more from Manchester. I talked to a captain in the gunners (he and a sergeant were the only regulars attending the course). There was a retired general, GPO Home Guardsmen, factory workers and an office boy. There was, of course, a very large proportion of old soldiers.

J.B.B. to E.C.F.B., 2 October   *H.Q. 7th. Corps*

I have had many talks with General McNaughton, whose abilities I have come more and more to admire. The Canadian troops are making a tremendous contribution to the conduct of this war. There is no part of the army where more constructive thinking, more practical experiment, or more definite realisation of the technical issues at stake are in evidence than in the 7th. Corps, and especially in the Canadian part of that Corps. Staying here has given me the welcome opportunity of long informal talks with the head staff officers, which has been valuable.

Yesterday I went to see the holding units in Hampshire. A car and a driver were put at my disposal, and I went by myself. Then I went to Aldershot to see the GOC 2nd. Canadian Division and one or two others. I am shortly off to spend two days with the 1st. Canadian Division, where I hope to see various units in the field. Humphreys is coming down on Sunday afternoon to talk over a number of matters before the final draft of my report is decided on. My task is a colossal one, and I can but make a number of general observations. I am pretty clear on one thing, and that is that I myself do not intend to run the educational work for the Canadians during this winter. And I am also pretty clear that they ought to get back representatives of the Canadian Legion to do so - or at least to be associated with the man who is asked to run the show. I should be finished by Monday or Tuesday, and what happens then I don't quite know. I am getting very good at living from day to day - a procedure which under normal conditions is so difficult for me.

Notes by E.C.F.B., 2 October

I had this morning rather a vivid picture of conditions in the East End from Mary Hardcastle.[1] She has been working in a Dockyard Settlement, and came in for part of the terrible raids. The Settlement itself is untouched, but all around the buildings were demolished and people were brought in for shelter and first-aid. The inferno with the dock fires, she said, was unforgettable. Though she had to step through roads of broken glass to visit people, she was glad to have had the experience, tragic though it was, and to have personal knowledge of the people's wonderful spirit. Some of the homeless women and children from the East End have been sent down to empty hop-pickers' huts near Canterbury, where people have been collecting clothes and fitting them out. Such quiet uncomplaining people, most of them, never speaking of what they have been through, and so grateful for any help. When asked what they wanted most, they nearly always said, 'Underclothes, so I can wash what I have on.'

---

[1]   Possibly Mary Hardcastle (1901-64). Vice-Princ. Charlotte Mason College, Ambleside; Member of Church Assembly (C of E), 1950-2.

J.B.B. to E.C.F.B., 5 October   *H.Q. 7th. Corps*

You all seem to take it for granted that I have got a fixed job here. Such is by no means the case, nor am I at all certain that I want one. I might stay on for a few weeks until qualified educationalists arrive from Canada who, I am convinced, must come from the Canadian Legion. It is, I hope, possible that my report may result in the creation of some machinery capable of operating a simple educational system for the men. But I am certain I am not the man to run it. It looks to me as though three experts should be cabled for from Canada. The whole business bristles with difficulties, and the main problem is that it has to be done quickly, and at best can only last for four or possibly five months.

The bombing round here is continuous, but nothing nearer than a mile or two. One minor casualty the other day was a fellow's eyebrow cut with a bit of a bomb! Every night we are treated to a superb display of the AA barrage - guns of all calibre and searchlights by the dozen - in fact the outer defences of London I suppose.

Tony to J.B.B., 8 October   *Budbrooke Barracks, Warwick*

I cannot say I have noticed much boredom among the troops here. But then at Budbrooke we are all still training, which means we are all doing something new and interesting. But I notice that very few of these men are capable of amusing themselves. They must have entertainment provided or else all the week's pay has gone by Monday on drinks and smokes. Since the middle of last month some enterprising people have started a canteen. It is in a church hall and contains a billiard table, piano (which has been vigorously tapped all evening), and the usual supply of old magazines, besides, of course, food.

We are lucky here in having Leamington close at hand, which has a number of cinemas and even more highbrow entertainment, such as orchestras at the Pump Room. But men stationed on Salisbury Plain or in the Yorkshire moors, miles from anywhere, must have a pretty boring time. Most of the lads who come here for training are from Birmingham and Coventry. All the rest of our Company (excluding ourselves) left a week or so ago as their training was completed. All have gone further from home than they have probably ever been before; and that is one of the most trying obstacles to keeping the men cheerful, especially when they know their homes are being bombed. We have a man in our platoon from London. He is a typical cockney, a thorough rogue, but a likeable person. He is 24, with a wife and two kids. He has had to take French leave (technically deserted) to go and see his wife who has been ill and who, of course, has been in all these raids on south London. I don't blame him, since official leave was not granted. The family tie is far stronger than the patriotic tie in such cases. He thinks it worth having 14 days jankers (i.e. defaulting) just to see his wife and children for a day or two. I do not know how this can be avoided when a man is not actually on active service and who has nothing else to occupy his mind.

As you may have heard I volunteered for India at the end of August, and have heard nothing since. But as far as those who volunteered from this place are concerned, I think India must be off because the course starts at Bangalore on 1 December. I wish they would tell us definitely that we are not going.

Our platoon continues to be a happy family. Indeed I have been very happy here. The great thing about being a private is that there is no responsibility. I take care not to worry over-much about the future (which has been my policy since this wretched war began), and so life is pleasant. What has really helped me is being with a fairly large number of Oxford and Cambridge men - all of them decent chaps. Although we have been eight weeks together, we have never really got on each others' nerves. The rest are a fairly decent lot. Only about four of them are really rather objectionable - and I don't say this because I am an Oxford man and they are not, for this is quite the opinion of the men of their own standing. The rest are as good as any Varsity man. There is that Londoner I was telling you about. I can get on with him all right. We are lucky too to have among us an old soldier who has seen seven years' service in India and Egypt. He is Irish and his name is Paddy. He knows all the tricks of the trade and is typically the old soldier.

Soon, however, I see I shall want more and more to leave this place. They have only taught me (or will have taught me) two new things that I hadn't known before - the grenade and the 2" mortar. Thus much of my time, if not all, has been wasted. What I have learnt are: the conditions under which the private soldier lives, the sort of man he is (and that is not much different from you and me), and what men and NCOs expect an officer to be like in his attitude to, and dealings with, his men.

Geoffrey to E.C.F.B., 13 October   *Aberdeen*

I begin my term with one short on the staff of the English Department, as my assistant lecturer has been called up. He only came last year and has joined a searchlight detachment in the army, down at Taunton. I believe the six Divinity professors have only one student this session between the lot of them. No Divinity student need join the army, but (much to their credit, for they are still laymen) they have insisted on doing so.

I think all fear of invasion is now past. Apart from the increasingly unfavourable weather, that naval attack on Cherbourg must have administered the *coup de grace* to the German preparations. I do not, by the way, see any special difficulty in getting the Germans out of the countries they have occupied once we have secured - as we inevitably shall - complete mastery over their air-force. Given that condition there is nothing to prevent us, since we have command of the sea, in forcing the Baltic and, by landing an expeditionary force in North Germany, turning their flank and attacking them in the rear. We could also land troops at any time in France if we want to. I think we shall begin to move much more quickly once the USA presidential election is over.

Mrs Gardiner to E.C.F. B., 13 October   *St Peter's St., Canterbury*

Today has been very sad for Canterbury. In another raid, and without a warning, bombs fell on Burgate, demolishing three shops. Alas! our dear, nice Mrs Carver was killed, and her cousin, Miss Staniforth, is in hospital. Mr Williams, the furrier, was also killed as well as an apprentice of the Chapter, a boy named Taylor.

In the Precincts, the Crum's house had ceilings down and windows smashed. Other houses were damaged. Some windows were broken in the Cathedral, and many in the High Street and Broad Street.

Burgate is indeed a sad sight. So many of the buildings have suffered grave damage. But I daresay it will rise up again in much of its old beauty! One does wonder what all this incessant bombing is going to lead to. I see Rome says it is intended to make English people rise up against their leaders. I wish our bombing of Germany would have the same effect!

I am afraid this is rather a melancholy letter, but I feel sure you will want to hear. Anyway, I trust Goodrich is as calm and peaceful as ever.

J.B.B to E.C.F.B., 17 October   *H.Q. 7th. Corps*

A few evenings ago Eric Duncannon and I went over to the McNaughtons for a glass of sherry before dinner. Eric is always in and out, but it was the first time I had been there, and Mrs McNaughton gave me the warmest of welcomes. I told her I had met the General on the stairs at HQ only half and hour before and had told him I was talking as a civilian and wished to inform him that he was doing far too much and would break down. Mrs McNaughton said my words had evidently had some affect as he had rung up only a few minutes before I arrived and said he was coming home and going to bed. When he arrived he greeted me with all the great charm he posseses and said, 'Well, you see I am carrying out your orders.'

As I came back from my billet where I went to have a bath and change into a dark suit, a bomb came hurtling down about 300 years to the west of the lane along which I was walking. I did not throw myself down on the ground as the high shrieking noise it made was loud enough to tell me it was not so close as to be really dangerous. It was a gorgeous moonlit night. The barrage towards London was terrific - just like looking at a real strafe three or four miles back from the front line in the last war. I love the walk between the HQ and my billet. It lies along a lane with over-arching trees, and is on high ground so that I can look towards London. Every night when I go back to change at 7.30, and again when I go back to bed at 11, I am given the most marvellous display of searchlights and shells bursting like great fireworks in the heavens. The flash of guns all along the horizon, the flares dropped by the enemy and the drone of their planes above, the sharp crack of the AA guns, and the deeper note of the heavier guns are a continuous chorus. What an amazing life it is. And unless they drop quite close, like to-night, one thinks little of it.

Geoffrey to E.C.F.B., 19 October   *Aberdeen*

London is exciting the admiration of the world for the spirit in which it is reacting to the most cruel, and senseless, bombardment that any great city has ever had to submit to in history. The government at last seems to be tackling the question of proper shelters with the organised effort that the situation so pressingly demands. In another month or two matters, one hopes, will be so arranged as to reduce the loss of life to a minimum, however great the severity of the raids.

But alas for our beloved Canterbury, and for Burgate, one of the most adorable streets. Only a year ago I remember you taking me into Miss Carver's bookshop there, and our pleasant talk with Miss Carver herself, such a charming woman. Her death, and the ruin of her flourishing business, is tragic beyond words. And but for your recent and timely removal to the safety of Goodrich you might, for all one knows, have been in that shop at the very moment it was bombed.

I see in *The Times* today (Friday) that the Dean has stated - and I should say he was right - that the Germans were deliberately aiming at the Cathedral. Perhaps this is why they missed it! One can but hope and pray it may continue to escape.

As the Germans have occupied Rumania and will shortly occupy Bulgaria, one can but hope that our General Staff will not commit the inexcusable error of allowing Greece to become a second Norway or Dakar. For this time they have been well-warned beforehand. We need the 'Nelson touch' in the Mediterranean just now, and I hope we will get it. So long as the axis powers do not pocket Greece, I think Germany will rue the day when she bogged herself down in the Balkans, which have always in the end defeated their would-be conquerors. In fact Hitler's diversion thither is but another proof that the initiative is really passing into our hands. But it remains true that our military High Command has still to prove that it is equal to the responsibilities laid upon it. We do so badly need a really signal victory in Egypt or the Near East. It would at one stroke change the face of the war. For it seems clearer and clearer that the war is going to be won in the Near East, and not in Europe.

Monier to E.C.F.B., 19 October   *Chiddingstone*

The Church House was hit about a week ago, and the new Great Hall damaged, and I am told people were killed in the restaurant on the top floor at dinner. The bombing was so bad that Mr Matthew had to get out and return from Peckham Rye station, and took three-and-a-half hours each way.

Our RE Company at Bough Beech has orders to move. I had Church Parade last Sunday. We had the Major (in command) and the Captain to dinner last Wednesday, such nice Territorial officers. Now the London Scottish are getting the Castle ready to move in next week. I met a charming Major today who tells me they have their own Presbyterian Chaplain, and I have offered the Church for their services.

Angela Woolley[1] to E.C.F.B., 24 October   *Cheltenham*

My brother Roy and his wife Gladys have had a marvellous escape, but a very sad loss. They were staying with Gordon at Epsom for a few nights when a high explosive bomb got a direct hit on their lovely house at Phillimore Place and utterly destroyed it. A neighbour rang them up at Epsom, and they went straight up to town to find it was only too true.

The miracle is that they were not there. Their son, Evelyn, had just joined his training unit, and the only person in the house was the poor old caretaker, who is buried beneath the pile of rubble and debris. They don't think they will even find her body.

Our first thought is Thank God. He has surely been wonderful to have given them the intuition to spend those few nights out of London, the first they have had since the raids began. Roy telegraphed me, 'We have lost everything. Gladys and I have a few clothes left and that is all...' They have indeed been through it, having first the unexploded AA shell right through their house, and then this.

With their characteristic courage they will face up to it well. As Roy has said, 'Thank God the family is safe. Things don't matter so much in these days.'

We have got Paul at home with a broken leg - a simple fracture of the shin-bone. He is in plaster now and hobbling about. In fact he will probably go to watch the match between Felsted and Cheltenham on Saturday, and will soon go back to school as he can hobble about there. He did it playing football.

J.B.B. to E.C.F.B., 27 October   *H.Q. 7th. Corps*

General McNaughton was very kind to me in what he said about the value of my report. He was in favour of cabling to Ottawa to approve of Dr Chatwin's appointment as Director of Educational Services to be stationed in HQ in London, and he said he wished me to take over the supervision of the general arrangements in the Corps and to be down here with him. Chatwin had already been suggested by the Canadian Legion, and I have always been in favour of a Legion appointment for the post. An answer finally came which was entirely satisfactory in that it did not seek to dictate terms to the General.

It was decided to ask the Canadian Legion (through Crerar, the Chief of Staff in Canada) to send over not only Chatwin, but also five civilian educational

---

[1] Née Angela Monier Williams, J.B.B.'s niece.

advisers, one each for HQ 7th. Corps, each of the Canadian divisions, HQ Canadian base units, and the convalescent depot at Brixham in Devon. The Director and each adviser are to bring with them a good clerk, and are to be provided with cars and drivers. This was precisely what I had advised in my report, so I was very pleased. The cable also stated that the GOC intended to appoint unit education officers in each battalion to be responsible for the general educational interests of his unit to his CO, and to begin making preparations by discovering what their men wanted, what accommodation there was in their unit areas, what instructors the unit itself could supply, and what more serious study through correspondence courses and classes was desired. This again was precisely what I had suggested and I can honestly say that the restoration of cordial relations between the Legion and the military authorities over here has been achieved.

It was clear to me that my work was finished, and I so remarked to the General. He said, 'On the contrary, if you are free to stay I want you to stay.' I replied, 'I am free to stay till Christmas, and possibly the whole winter if I am really needed, but I don't see in what capacity I am to remain, considering you have done practically everything I suggested in my report.' To this McNaughton answered, 'I would like you to stay for the time being.' So there the matter rests, and nothing more can happen before we get a reply to the enormous cable (above mentioned) which was despatched last night.

The general impression here is that things in Germany (not materially but psychologically) are considerably worse than we know. I don't mean that German morale is likely to crack or any such 'wishful thinking' as that. But that the troubles facing Hitler are very great and his anxieties far more serious than we imagine. I hope it is so.

Mrs Mann to E.C.F.B., 28 October   *Canterbury*

Here we lead a queer life. The last three attacks were very bad. When Burgate was so badly hit, we just lay on the floor while the bombs came down, and the noise was awful. During the last raid when the Deanery was hit, I was lunching with my brother at the Fountain - the room was full and everyone (officers included) threw themselves on the floor. It is really very funny when one recovers from the fright. It has made people much more nervous, and they go to the shelters quickly when the siren goes. The Crypt is used a great deal and quite a few people sleep there. They have mattresses or camp beds and say they sleep comfortably. It is warmed now, and cups of tea are provided at a small charge. The uppper part of the Cathedral is very cold and also damp, owing to so many windows being broken. I think they are having most of the services in the East Crypt. People are happier there when there is a warning on.

November

Notes by E.C.F.B., 1 November

Deaconess Waller came to see me a few days ago. Her work lies in Southwark which is much devastated. St Peter's Church is destroyed, and in one shelter nine Air Wardens were found absolutely uninjured, but killed by blast, one man lying dead with his hands in his pockets. On her way to early service, the Deaconess meets the people coming home from the shelters where they have been all night. They carry their bedding and say cheerfully they have passed a good night, and are going home for a wash; occasionally they find the home not there but a heap of ruins.

Geoffrey to E.C.F.B., 3 November   *Aberdeen*

Jean and I went to see that really first-rate naval film called 'Convoy'. Jean had already seen it with the children and they were so enthusiastic about it that I determined I must go too, so Jean came with me as she was quite pleased to see it a second time and we made sure they would be safe with neighbours in case there was a raid.

About half-way through the film and at the most exciting point - just when an English cruiser was about to engage a German pocket battleship - the film was switched off and the manager came on the stage to announce the sirens had just gone; that people who wanted to could go, but that the performance would continue for those who cared to stay. Knowing the children were all right, we of course stayed, as did most of the audience, and we sat watching the most realistic representation of a sea battle I have ever seen. German bombers were zooming overhead - over our heads, I mean: which, had one stopped to think about it, greatly added to the excitement.

We emerged from the cinema about 7.30 into pouring rain and pitch darkness. No traffic, as all the trams had stopped in their tracks the moment the alarm was sounded. We could hear the German plane or planes loud overhead, but couldn't see them as there was low cloud. Fortunately for us they suddenly switched on the searchlights, which served as an excellent illumination to the streets. So we walked the mile home through the pouring rain.

Monier to E.C.F.B., 5 November   *Chiddingstone*

I am delighted that Burgon has been so successful in his report, and gets on well with General McNaughton. I mentioned McNaughton to Dick Streatfeild yesterday, and he said at once what a charming and talented man he was. It certainly looks now as if Burgon will stay on in England, at any rate until next summer.

Our troops arrived today and are settling in. They will, I am sure, need the Village Hall for a canteen, which means the schoolchildren cannot use it. But they are now so reduced in numbers that this will not matter. Including evacuees, Miss Thorne has only 45 children in all.

Mary to J.B.B., 5 November   *Chiddingstone*

We've got some very smart officers here. The London Scottish arrived yesterday, and one can't move outside the gate without hearing bagpipes or seeing a soldier. They seem to be very nice men. By getting to know the Chaplain first, we managed to stop them taking the Village Hall as billets, and they are going to have a canteen there every day, not to speak of evening entertainments. Most of the men seem genuine Scots and some have lovely accents.

Before the London Scottish arrived we had got to know the RE officers fairly well. One of them told us some good stories about how they were stranded for six days on an island just off Brittany, a very short way from German occupied territory; there were fifteen of them and they fed on carrots and potatoes before being taken off by a French smuggler's boat. He also told us how difficult it is to get men to Ireland on leave. You have to fill in forms galore and find out all the particulars about the man and who he's going to, and so on. One day one of their men said he wished to go to Ireland, so he started away on getting permission. It took some days, and just before the permission came through, the soldier came in and said, 'Is it a bother sending me to Ireland, sir?' 'Well it is rather,' replied the officer. 'Very well then, I'll go to Gravesend instead.' Gravesend was about six miles from where they were stationed.

We've had a very noisy time with bombs, although nothing has actually fallen very close. During this last fortnight I've got to know what a bomb sounds like coming down, and I've got jolly good at diving under the dining room table or my bed. I believe I'm about right in saying that we have had 400 bombs in this parish alone.

I saw a Spitfire and a Hurricane on the aerodrome at the Causeway the other day, and was amazed to see how very small they looked. I can't think how one sees them at all when they're flying high. A Messerschmitt was brought down on the aerodrome on Sunday.

Alison to E.C.F.B., 6 November   *Groombridge*

On Thursday I went up to Town by the early train with Ralph to see about the house, change the books, and do odd bits of shopping. Our poor house is a pitiful sight with all the windows gone, and pools of rain water on all the floors. A lot of bricks and soot have come down into every room; it's the concussion. It is sad to see our home like this, but we are amazingly lucky to have got all our furniture safely out - and ourselves. Several of our friends have lost their houses and all their things.

Jean to E.C.F.B., 7 November   *Aberdeen*

Eden has reversed Hore-Belisha's policy with regard to university OTC's. The latter disregarded them, but Eden says that a man who has certificates A and B and has served three terms in a senior OTC is considered to have done the same as a man in an ITC, and can go straight to an Officers' Cadet Training Unit. Tony doesn't wish Julian to waste time in an ITC as he is doing, and he certainly mustn't join one of those 'young soldier' or Home Defence Battalions, which just contain the scum of the earth.

J.B.B. to E.C.F.B., 10 November   *H.Q. 7th. Corps*

I think General McNaughton looks at the entire educational business as he would any other purely military problem. Orders are given and carried out. That is however not the case with regard to a question of this kind. I hope to get a good talk with him tomorrow morning, and am preparing a few points which I think he should emphasise in his remarks to those attending the conference tomorrow. He has so many tremendous problems on hand, that he really has not the time to give to the educational one, and yet we are in actual fact trying to start an immense programme of education affecting thousands of men. And at present I am alone. It is quite fanastic. But I am remaining calm and have not lost my sense of humour.

On Wednesday, Commander Woodruff[1] dined, addressed a meeting and slept here. He is the man who gave the famous broadcast about the Coronation review of the fleet in 1937, when he was rather tight. 'The fleet is lit up and I am lit up ...!' He spoke admirably on the work of the navy to officers and men.

Geoffrey to E.C.F.B., 10 November   *Aberdeen*

The Poles have a section of the coast here, for the guarding of which they are responsible. We have let off one of our Divinity professors (who has no Theology students this year owing to the war) to do social and educational work among them.

Neville Chamberlain's death has come rather suddenly, but it is not really to be wondered at when you consider his age, and all that he has gone through since he became PM, and the terrible blow which the failure of his foreign policy must have inflicted upon him. I think, and always shall, that he was right about Munich, but wrong not to have voluntarily resigned when the war broke out, or even earlier at the time when Hitler invaded Czechoslovakia. The real culprit was of course his lazy predecessor, Stanley Baldwin, and his predecessor, the vain and egregious Ramsay MacDonald. These two men will have to answer a terrible charge at the bar of history, of neglecting, not willingly of course, but through culpable incompetence the best interests of their country.

J.B.B. to E.C.F.B., 17 November   *H.Q. 7th. Corps*

Chatwin arrived from Canada today. He is a funny little man, thoroughly competent, I would say, to run a huge and complicated system of classes and correspondence courses based on text-books and card-indexes. I am just thankful he has come to take all this detailed office work over

His HQ will be at Guildford, and I spent several hours there with him on Thursday helping him find suitable quarters with the Surrey area billeting officer present. We finally discovered a vast billiard saloon containing nine or ten billiard tables, not now in use owing to lack of business. Directly he saw it his face lighted

---

[1] Probably Douglas Woodruff (1897-1978). Press Officer, Empire Marketing Bd., 1931-33; on staff of BBC, 1934-36; Ed. of *The Tablet*, 1936-67.

up. He said, 'This is the place. I will partition off one corner for my own office and leave all the rest one large room, so that I can keep everything under my control.' I think he saw the look of surprise on my face, and explained that in keeping an office of this kind it saved time and labour in keeping his clerks together and was much more efficient.

There was very bitter feeling among the Legion heads in Ottawa at my being called in, as indeed I foresaw there would be. The military heads over here were much criticized for sending Robert England back to Canada and taking me on as an independent adviser. But when the long cable arrived from General McNaughton, the Legion Council was delighted and did at last realise (Chatwin informs me) that I had been responsible for effecting a rapprochement.

Notes by E.C.F.B., 18 November   *Goodrich Court*

A week ago, on the night of 11 November our bombers attacked part of the Italian fleet lying in Taranto harbour. They sank a battleship of their newest type and two cruisers. They also sank and damaged several auxiliary vessels, thus proving to the Greeks that we can give them effective help in the gallant stand they are making. During the week they have effected many losses on the Italians, defeating their crack Alpine troops , taking large numbers of prisoners, tanks and ammunition.

All this is good news, but bad is to come. On the night of 15 November the city of Coventry was brutally bombed by the Germans. The old city, consisting of many Elizabethan and Georgian houses, was practically wiped out. The magnificent 14th. century Cathedral was destroyed. Nothing was left but the ancient tower surmounted by its beautiful spire. The King spent five hours walking about the stricken city the next day, hearing with great sorrow of the casualties, 200 or more having been killed. Hardly a day passes but we hear of the King and Queen visiting bombed areas. They talk to homeless people in the shelters and wherever they go, by their words of sympathy and understanding, encourage all whom they meet.

Mary to E.C.F.B., 14 November   *Chiddingstrone*

I had such fun last night. Wendy and I went as canteen staff to an ENSA concert for the troops in the Village Hall here. We sold cigarettes and chocolates in the interval, but otherwise watched the show which was extremely good and very funny. After it we went round to the officers' mess and imbibed sandwiches and drinks. They are a very nice crowd.

Mrs Gardiner to E.C.F.B., 14 November   *Canterbury*

The Cathedral is more than ever deplorable. Did you hear they had altered the statutes to allow Canon Ottley to take a residence,[1] no canon being available? Of course we love having his beautiful sermons and reverent readings, it is a great treat. On Sunday week, he and Mr Poole were the only clergy present at Matins. Last Sunday, only he and the Dean, who read Morning Prayer. Canon Crum has 'gone away till Christmas'; Canon McNutt is ill, and some say will not return; Canon Shirley is in Cornwall with the King's School. I can't think how the Cathedral will live it all down. But, of course, there must be a resurrection and reconstruction after the war.

Peter to his parents, 16 November   *Sheriff House, Rugby*

I expect you have all heard about the Coventry show, well we had a ringside seat until one or two loud bangs sent us into the passages. Coventry is a total wreck! For three-quarters of a square mile in the middle of the town there is nothing except tons and tons of rubble and ruins.

The carnage is unbelievable. The Rugby hospital is full, ambulances and buses have been bringing the wounded in hour after hour. I myself have seen the people swathed in bandages being lifted into the hospital while some of the walking-wounded limp in after them. All Thursday night death rained on Coventry from the sky. It had to be seen to be believed, and even then you thought you were having a nightmare. I never got to sleep until 1 o'clock and I was looked upon as lucky because I managed to get to sleep at all.

The nearest thing we had was a land mine that came down near Bilton Grange. The whole house trembled on its foundations, and the roof spotter was knocked on his back by the blast. All the road and rail communications are cut with Coventry. Nobody is allowed within ten miles of the city, and only people who are fleeing are allowed out. And by gosh, there are hundreds and thousands of people leaving the town. It is terrible to see these poor bombed creatures trudging along the road to no one knows where. People are pushing prams piled high with clothes and getting lifts off lorries. Still, I don't want you to get the idea

---

[1] This was unusual in that Canon Ottley was not one of the Cathedral's residentiary canons.

that we are in danger here because we are not - yet. So don't get panicky because I will let you know when we get bombed.

On Thursday I saw a balloon come down in flames and also a Jerry. He was blazing like a comet and when he struck the ground he went up with a devil of a bang. There was also a colossal flash, which went up red and changed colour - an incredible sight.

Tony to J.B.B., 17 November   *O.R.T.U., Warwick*

The big news of the week of course is the raid on Coventry on Thursday night. I woke up on Thursday morning to hear someone cursing away trying to get a black-out up, so that the lights might be put on. It took him about five minutes to adjust the wretched thing when someone else calmly announced that the blasted lights weren't working anyway. We learnt later that a barrage balloon had broken loose and its cable was responsible for fouling the electric wires somewhere, and depriving us of electricity.

That morning we spent in Grove Park doing some rather futile tactical exercises. It was a very clear sunny day and we saw afar off over Coventry some aerial activity. The planes were thousands of feet up and we could only see them occasionally glittering in the sun. They may have only been British planes, but I think in view of what happened that night they were Jerries reconnoitring.

I did not go into Warwick on Thursday evening as I was attached to the anti-parachute platoon. It does not involve much except being prepared to be called out at a moment's notice during the night. The disadvantage is that members of the AP platoon are not of course allowed to leave barracks while on duty.

Bombing began, I suppose, about 7.30. I went over to the NARP about 8, and there was plenty of AA fire then, besides explosions over Coventry. It was a gorgeous night, perfectly clear with a full moon. When I returned across the square at about 8.30, hell had obviously been let loose. Chaps were crowding out of the barrack rooms watching the display. There were flares slowly descending; terrific flashes and explosions, and what looked like a direct hit, because huge flames shot up at once and then died down quickly to a red glow. There were one or two searchlights on around our part, but at this period the bombing was on Coventry. We could even see tracer bullets firing up at the sky. The bombing went on and on, and sometimes came nearer, making the barrack room windows rattle away in their frames. Our electric light had not been restored, so we had to make do with candle-light.

Just before 11 o'clock the AP platoon was called out. Our job was simple. We merely had to comb the Common (which lies behind Warwick and the barracks) for parachutists. We were told that parachutists were reported as having landed there, but I believe it was merely a precautionary measure. At any rate it was genuine, and I did have two rounds of live ammunition in my pocket. I ought to have had five, but there were not enough to go round, so I and another chap shared a clip. All we did was to walk across the Common and back again, and of course there was not a German to be seen. Over Coventry there was a thick pall of smoke, which glowed red from the simply enormous fires started there. Sodom and Gomorrah were not in it. I heard for the first time those whistling bombs, and shrapnel thudding down. Half a dozen balloons over Coventry went up in flames and slowly descended, bright lights trailing white smoke behind them.

Next day we were told we were going to help move furniture from damaged property, and we were taken by lorry to Lillington, a northern suburb of Leamington. Here untold damage had been done by a land mine. These land mines are dropped by parachute and make the loudest explosions and cause the worst damage, as the blast drives outwards (not upwards like a bomb). The mine had landed at the corner of two roads of small, jerry-built, semi-detached houses; for 700 yards down one road and 200 down the other, all the windows were broken and the frames skewed. Slates were off the roof, the ceilings of the top floors were in holes, and in more than one case the walls were giving way. I helped to move furniture from one house most of the afternoon. Strips of paper did not seem to have prevented glass splintering. It was all over the place, and the damage done to the house rendered it quite uninhabitable. The owner was a nice fellow, with a wife and small son; a typical 'small man' I suppose. We helped to move all his furniture into a lorry and two army trucks which some Czechs had brought up. The Czech army was everywhere doing valiant work.

The man's wife looked very tired and upset, yet she and her husband both carried on just as if they were in the normal process of shifting house. The poor little boy was looking very wistful and rather lost amidst the general wreckage of his house. Sgt. Jones was extraordinarily tactful and very nice to them, and saw that we moved the stuff with the greatest of care. Then several of us went over in the lorries and helped the man unload his furniture. We went about eight miles to

Bishop Islington, which is south of Leamington, and unloaded the furniture in the stable courtyard of a house where the man had relations. It was a dull, grey day. Then the Czechs, with whom we fraternized in French, drove us back at breakneck speed.

On Saturday I went into Leamington for lunch. The damage to the central part of town is not that great. It gives an example of the freakish way bombs behave. One bomb had dropped in front of the statue of Queen Victoria and moved its granite base some two inches, and so it still stands looking as ugly as ever. Not one of the Town Hall windows were so much as cracked, yet the whole way up the other side of the parade, plate-glass windows in the large shops were smashed. A bomb had completely demolished Liptons, and half of Boots. Even so a sign saying 'Business as Usual' was up in that half that was still standing. The casualties are remarkably few.

On Saturday evening we met some Polish airmen in the canteen at Warwick. They had been evacuated from Coventry. Some of their chaps, thinking the land mines descending were parachutists, had rushed to capture them and were blown up. We also chatted with some RASC chaps, who had been sent from London to help. They said they had not seen anything in London to compare with Coventry. Until today the wretched town has been without gas and electricity. The chap I was talking to said there wasn't a single house that hadn't been damaged. 'Three sweet lads,' as he put it, 'came on a land mine that had landed without exploding, and tried to pull off the parachute as a souvenir; of course the thing blew up and destroyed them and the street with it.' The RASC chap finished saying, 'We are still looking for the bits.'

John to E.C.F.B., 21 November   *Chiddingstone*

Ten days ago I spent a week at Cambridge by invitation of two medical friends of mine in Caius. I stayed in the guest room there, and had a first view of the other University.

On Sunday morning I went to Holy Trinity for Matins and the church was packed ten minutes before the service began. Max Warren,[1] the vicar, is very

---

[1] Rev. Dr. Max Warren (1904-77). Author and Vicar of Holy Trinity Church, Cambridge, 1936-42; Gen. Sec. Church Missionary Soc., 1942-63; Canon of Westminster, 1963-73.

popular with the undergraduates and the town. It was a very moving service. A Mr Lunt,[1] Chaplain of Downing College, preached a good sermon.

That visit to Cambridge also finally convinced me that my decision in July was the right one. There might not have been a war on at all up there, except for a lot of RAF cadets in many of the colleges; even some of my friends who are reading medicine or engineering (both of which schools will ultimately make them be of use to the war effort) said that they found their existence to be very shallow at times. From this three days at Cambridge I now know quite definitely that I should have been wrong to pursue a luxury education for another year, when a war is being fought in which everything that I hold most precious is at stake. I count myself lucky to have had ten years of first-rate education; and one day I hope very much that I shall be able to follow my relations to a peace-time Oxford.

I have written to the Kent War Agricultural Committee, and have hopes of getting to a forestry camp. I am vastly happy here, but I feel I could be doing a lot more to help; and forestry work would be a healthy way of doing so.

J.B.B. to E.C.F.B., 24 November   *H.Q. 7th. Corps*

The Canadian Legion has sent a cable asking for my services, so I presume the General will now definitely suggest to me that I should stay on. But he has been so busy the last few days I have had hardly two minutes with him. But I seem to be getting more and more dug in. For instance, I have been posted in Part II Orders (Julian will explain that) as attached to the 7th. Corps, which means that I can apply for billeting expenses and ration allowances. Also, yesterday a batman driver and a two-seater car for my exclusive use turned up. The man's name is Sanders, and he comes from Toronto, but has been living in England for four years before the war. He joined up with the British army in January 1940, was in France and came through the Dunkirk affair. He transferred to his native Canadians three months ago. He seems a nice fellow, and it will be very useful having him and the car - though I wish it had been a sedan - as the two-seaters are somewhat draughty and cold. Still, I am lucky to get a car. They are difficult to come by and I shall be the envy of many staff officers who would give their eyes to have a car of their own, however small. Sanders will look after me, but in actual fact he will have a fairly soft job. I expect he may have to help in the mess at times.

---

[1] Rt. Rev. Francis Lunt (1900-82). Chaplain Downing Coll., Cambridge, 1934-43; Rector of St Aldate, Oxford, 1943-51; Dean of Bristol, 1951-7; Bishop Suffragen of Stepney, 1957-8.

Elfride to E.C.F.B., 24 November   *St Mary's School, Calne*

We had four air raids last week; one on Tuesday morning, one that evening at supper time, and one on Wednesday evening which lasted till early on Thursday. We all had to go to our shelters for these raids. In the house I am in, there are only 14 of us, and one half sleep on the ground floor, so they went back to bed leaving almost a camp bed each for the rest of us. And as we got up at least an hour later the next morning, I don't feel any the worse.

We have had three lectures since I last wrote to you. We had one on birds, one was on the eighteenth century, and the third on the radio dealing with the recent developments. The lecturer said that she thought the Prime Minister had the best broadcasting voice of anyone she had heard, because he is so sincere. She also told us how the BBC combats enemy propaganda. I like a lecture on something modern like broadcasting. I know so little about it.

I have been reading a very good book called *Reaching For The Stars*,[1] I have forgotten the author's name. It describes her experiences in Germany from 1934-38. I had got into the habit of thinking of all Germans as cruel, wicked people, who machine-gun defenceless women and children. But this book reminded me that there are many more nice Germans than not.

Ralph to E.C.F.B., 25 November   *Lombard Street*

Peter wrote a most excellent letter last week, although it took three days to come. Mercifully no bombs were dropped near Rugby. He seems very well, and I am delighted to say that he has passed Certificate 'A'. He went in for it, I believe, the first opportunity he could, feeling that he might have a chance of passing, and apparently he has done so with flying colours.

The description he wrote of the Coventry raid was very good, and it certainly must have been a most appalling experience. The Rugby hospital, and even the sanatorium, are full of casualties, and they talk of taking over the new House as a hospital.

This Paper War. *Edward Bickersteth, 26 November*   *Torit, Sudan*

I get down to the office about 9 o'clock. I have already been there for an hour and a half before breakfast; but that does not really count because I am left

---

[1] Presumably Nora Waln's *Reaching For The Stars* (Cresset, 1939).

pretty well alone, so I get through a lot of work. Generally I have an attractive cypherine sitting opposite me to cope with the never-ending flow of telegrams, but today she is away looking after a sick husband in the Political Service. Furthermore it is mail day in, so I expect a black morning. I get it.

A cypher-wire is waiting on my desk. After ten minutes labour, I learn the interesting fact that Mohd Bakheit Ali, recently transferred to the North, has gone without his last Pay Certificate, and therefore can receive no pay for December as no one knows how much is due to him. I scribble a note to the Staff Officer, who ought to have remembered to send it with the man, and then Faud Effendi brings the mail in. He is our chief clerk and a very good one too. He is an Egyptian by birth and openly pines for the delights of Cairo and Alexandria, but he works very hard all the same. He always makes me sign for every confidential paper that I take over from him; and when I give him a secret letter for the post, I always get a solemn little receipt for it.

The mail today consists of 12 envelopes, eight from HQ in Khartoum, three from the outside Companies, and one from the Governor of Equatoria. That's not bad: last week we had 21. I open them carefully, preserving the envelopes for future service, glance through them all to see that there is nothing urgent and write them in the 'In' book. Before I have time to open the cabinet and search for the files, the CO pokes his nose round the door and calls me in. 'About those ammunition returns,' he begins. When I get back to my table five minutes later, the pile of files in my in-tray is rising rapidly. The clerks have been getting busy on the non-secret mail. I look at one or two in a hopeless sort of way, when suddenly there is a smell like a French train. I know without looking up that the Staff Officer is approaching. This very faithful native officer, who has a good old Arab name, but, judging by his face, is of slave descent, has an unfortunate habit of using cheap scent in enormous quantities. Almost invariably I smell him before I either see him or hear him. He has a little problem about Ration Strengths. He knows much more about this intimate subject than I do, but I listen courteously, and at the end make the only obvious decision, which is what he wanted me to do: he could easily have made it himself, but it is all part of the game that I should do it. He departs satisfied, and I metaphorically open the windows of the railway carriage.

Next comes the officer commanding the MT Company to talk about the petrol return. He makes this one up, but I put it into cypher and send it off.

Consequently almost my only contribution to a 10 minutes' conversation is that at all costs the return must be short. Having arranged a game of squash for the afternoon, he pushes off. As he gets to the door, he stiffens to attention and salutes. He is some ten years my senior, but we always salute each other in our own offices.

Another wire comes in and I settle down to it. This announces that one of our outside companies has broken the signalling arm of their heliograph; this is serious, for we use the helio. a lot. So I send for the signalling officer (native) and indent for a new one from Khartoum at leisure. He brings another indent for me to sign. This demands 'Gun Vickers Tripod Gear Raising Pin One'! Having no idea that such a thing exists, I sign glibly.

Then comes another wire, this one 'Immediate'. At whatever hour of day or night an 'Immediate' telegram arrives, I have to do it at once. So I get out the code book and struggle with it. Just as I get to the point where you simply must not stop or you lose your place, my Sergeant-Major comes in. He advances to the front of my desk, left-turns with a slap of bare feet on stone floor, does a quivering salute, and announces in the bastard Arabic, which we call Mongallese and which does duty for a *lingua franca* all over the southern Sudan, that that woman is waiting to see me. After a lot of patient excavation, I discover that she is the wife of a soldier who is up on the frontier who has directed that she be paid £1 out of his stored-up pay, which I keep in a sort of bank. She is dressed up to the nines - i.e. has a skirt of bright red cloth wrapped round her middle. Her baby is on her back, slung in a goatskin with half a gourd over his head to protect him from the sun. He doesn't think much of my office and cries, she soothing him by jogging her shoulders. I get out the bank book and the money box , make the relevant entry and give her £1. The Sergeant-Major salutes himself out of the office, shepherding the woman with him and I start my 'Immediate' wire again from the beginning. When it comes out it proves to be an interesting intelligence report from the Eastern Frontier, so I write it in the book and take it straight to the CO. He says, 'Pass it on to Khartoum.' So I go back and put it all back into cypher and despatch it all to the powers that be.

I look at my watch and discover that it is 11.30. So I open a drawer and furtively produce a bit of cake and sit back for my five minute 'stand-easy'. As soon as I have got my mouth full, the CO comes in. This happens without fail every single morning, and embarrasses me frightfully. However, I stick manfully to this excellent Political Service habit; I find I am fresher than most when 2 o'clock draws near. In fact everybody except our office packs up soon after 1!

The CO has brought in a Secret letter for me to type, so I send for the machine and tap painstakingly away. When I have done about eight lines, I discover that the CO has written in minute writing at the bottom of his draft 'Copy to HQ.' This means that I ought to have had another carbon in, so I start again.

The noon bugle goes, and the strokes of the hour are beaten out on the rusty bit of old iron that does duty as a station clock. The squads of the depot Company march briskly past my window on to their parade ground, with the sergeants yelling themselves hoarse, and the men making a soft pad-pad with their bare feet on the sandy soil. The commander of the depot Company comes in for a cigarette, and I hear the latest exploits of his gentle savages who, ten weeks ago, were tilling the soil in nakedness and peace, and had never dreamed of becoming soldiers. But that was before the big recruitment drive.

I get back to my work cheered by the fact that Faud Effendi has just brought in the private mail. I stuff three or four letters into my pocket, to be read at leisure after I have had my lunch. The pile in my in-tray is now two feet high, so I decide to tackle that. Some letters I merely sign as having seen. Some are very interesting, but others were obviously designed for British troops and I wonder why they ever bothered sending a copy down to us. A couple of wires always come in at 1.30, making it impossible for me to get back to lunch punctually at 2, and certain that I shall have to return here in the afternoon. But at last the CO comes in and says, 'Home.' I lock the safes and another morning is over.

December

Julian to E.C.F.B., 1 December   *Goodrich*

I met Mr and Mrs Wimperis[1] on Sunday, and had an interesting talk with him on the war. His job is to give the final verdict on all the aeronautical inventions for the RAF. He has a staff of 30 who sift the vast number of inventions that are sent in, both by amateurs and professionals, and he deals with the final selection.

---

[1] Harry Wimperis (1876-1960). Dir. of Scientific Research Air Ministry, 1925-37; member of Aeronautical Research Cttee. CB (1935).

He told me that the famous American bombing sight has never been tried properly in war; undoubtedly it is extraordinarily accurate if the plane is travelling as it would in peace time; but as the chief method of fighting flak by a modern aeroplane is to upset the sound-ranging system of the anti-aircraft gun by constantly changing speed, height and direction, another kind of bombing sight which is independent of the simple conditions of ordinary flight is probably much better.

He told me that they were trying now to discover means of detonating all the bombs in a night-flying bomber while it is still in the air; but nothing satisfactory has yet been discovered.

Five years ago he had a great argument with Trenchard[1] as to the amount of effort that should be put into defence and offence in the RAF. He pleaded that the ratio should be fifty-fifty, but as it was defence was left far behind; which now seems to be a great pity.

A few days ago I met the parent of one of the boys who works in an aeroplane factory. He told me about our wonderful new fighters which will shortly be in the air. Their names are *Typhoon* and *Tornado*. Their speed is 450 m.p.h., and they are more heavily protected with their powers of firing and flying higher greatly improved.

Young Julian to his parents, 7 December   *Marlborough*

We had our match with Clifton last week. We left Marlborough at 9.45. On arrival in Bristol it seemed to us that the populace was in one of two minds; one half had taken to its heels, and the other was waiting around poking its head out of windows as though eager to miss nothing. Evidently an air raid alarm was in progress, a theory reinforced by the fact that everyone who had a tin hat was wearing it. It was about noon and we saw three planes some way off, circling like hawks. I hoped hard that they were Jerries, but I don't think they could have been. Later we had another half-hour air raid alarm which, like the rest of Bristol, we ignored as it was only half-an-hour before the start of our game.

The start gave us a moral superiority we never lost, so we won, 16-9. They only crossed our line once. Our return to Marlborough was jubilant. At Calne, just before 6 o'clock, we stopped for half an hour and the master said he

---

[1] Lord Trenchard (1873-1956). Marshal of the RAF; Chief of Air Staff, 1918-29; Comm. Met. Police, 1931-5.

didn't object to us having a little drink if he wasn't there. And anyway, beer is of course permitted when allowed out with parents and so on. So we had a pint all round and came on back to Marlborough.

John Owen and I had Jennings (a master) to tea on Thursday. We got on to the war, and we agreed the USA has done next to nothing for us yet, and is behaving disgracefully. In the war there are four things to be considered; what the USA will do, how effective is the blockade, the state of German production and of German oil supplies. If all four are for in our favour we shall beat Germany before next winter. It never really struck me before that Hitler first missed the bus at Munich; when he should have had us on toast. For that reason it was a stroke of brilliance on Chamberlain's part.

Geoffrey to E.C.F.B., 8 December   *Aberdeen*

The Fyfes asked us to tea to meet William Temple who came to give the annual Myrtle Lecture. The war, he says, has made his work to an extent less heavy. He hardly ever, if indeed at all, goes up to London now as, owing to air-raids, it is no longer used as a general rendezvous. No church meetings are held there, and he has given up going to the House of Lords. As far as his province is concerned, he says, bomb damge has been slight so far.

As for France, which surrendered to Germany at the cost of her honour in order to save Paris, he thinks that she will not have saved it by her shame. For the Germans, in his opinion, are very likely to destroy Paris in mere revenge, if military pressure compels them to leave, as one hopes and expects it will.

He would like the public schools after the war to re-form themselves on the model of Christ's Hospital, and charge no fees except to those who could afford them, accepting of course state-aid on that condition. He thinks this would solve their financial problem while preserving all that is of value in the public school system. When I asked him if he thought, say, Eton would accept such a proposal, he admitted that Eton probably would not and should be allowed to preserve (for some time yet at any rate) what has always been her rather exceptional position. But he thought that Winchester would be ready to fall in with the others, and certainly Harrow (already hard-hit by the war). The public schools would thus revert to the position originally intended by their founders, a position which Christ's Hospital still maintains, i.e. that of schools intended for poor scholars, with the addition of such richer ones as were ready to pay for the kind of education boarding schools afforded, and which only they can supply.

Temple sketched as desirable after the war a form of government for this country in its main features socialistic. The state should control the banks, dividends for capitalists should be limited, and capital itself, though not abolished, should be allowed to dwindle till in three generations it has entirely dispppeared from e.g. the possession of the descendants of the individual whose industry and abilities had originally accumulated it. Death duties, of course, are already effecting something like this. His main point was that it was useless to try and create off-hand an ideal Christian state. The right method was to take the already Christian features of our present civilization and slowly strengthen, develop and build up on them, gradually eliminating the unchristian elements.

Ralph to Julian, 10 December   *Lombard Street*

London had a nasty night on Sunday, the planes came over us, I have never heard so many nor so low. A good deal of damage was done, but it won't win the war. Poor All Hallows Barking has been very badly knocked about. I saw it yesterday, the whole of the East window and Altar has disappeared. The Port of London Authority building also got it badly. We had an incendiary bomb on the roof of this building, but it was soon put out and did no damage.

The news of our attack in North Africa is certainly cheering, and we seem to be giving the Top Wop something to think about. If we can only knock the wops out of the war quickly it should shorten it by years, otherwise the general view here is that it will go on for some three or four years at least.

Tony to his parents, 12 December   *Warwick*

In B Company we are supposed to be on a special course of advanced training in tactics. All the OCTU candidates who have passed the board are in one platoon. By the by, the board which interviewed me was composed of three soldiers, one of whom was a full colonel (probably an acting brigadier) who knew Uncle Burgon in the last war. One of the other colonels was an Old Marlburian.

However, yesterday we were told the course was suspended for a few days as B Company has been given a job of work to do in Coventry. What we have to do is to light and look after, during the hours of darkness, these oil burners which set up smoke screens round vulnerable targets such as aerodromes and factories.

The screens are only put up during the period of the full moon, and they are useless in a high wind. The smoke which the generators emit is very like the filthy factory smoke which I knew well enough in Glasgow. The idea of course is to intensify the atmosphere so as to combat the night bomber. Apparently it was suggested by the Prime Minister himself, adapting the idea from the smoke screens warships set up to protect themselves in battle.

We were taken on to this aerodrome and were dropped in batches of six or seven along the road. Each man had about 15 of the generators to look after. They are in pairs, about 10 yards apart along various roads surrounding the aerodrome and works district. We reached the spot about 9 o'clock and soon created a beautiful fog. It got you in the eyes and throat. An air raid was on, so we had to be very careful lighting the things, and also careful to see that the chimneys didn't catch fire, which they were very liable to do, especially if they had not been properly cleaned. Actually, though lighting them had looked a simple enough matter when we had the demonstration, in fact the brutes were very averse to it, and often went out as soon as you turned your back on them. What with the filthiness of the fog and the extreme cold, I did not exactly enjoy myself.

I don't think Jerry dropped any bombs, but the barrage was terrific. Little pieces of shrapnel were falling like rain all around me. I badly wanted a tin hat. I can't think why we have not been issued with them yet. As I was bending over helping the chap on the beat next to mine to light one of the burners which had gone out, a small piece struck me sharply on the shoulder; I thought at first the other fellow had hit me. I also saw something quite remarkable - an AA shell in the air; it was going away from me and upwards straight at the moon, so was clearly visible against the background.

Eventually at about 1.30 the order came to put burners out. This was a job in itself which took a little time. Our night out finished with one of the most frightful bus journeys I have ever had. We all piled in with our equipment, so the bus was abnormally crowded, and it was beastly cold. The roads were slippery, a ground mist had come up and the blackout was severe. We were not back in our new camp till 4.30, though luckily we were allowed to sleep in till 10 a.m. when the orderly sergeant came and dragged us out. This business makes one frightfully dirty - filthy with soot and petrol and oil, and when the water supply is behaving badly, as it is at the moment in the camp, it is difficult to get clean.

Geoffrey to E.C.F.B., 15 December   *Aberdeen*

The war news is almost unbelievingly encouraging. At last the British army has given evidence of its efficiency - evidence far to seek till now - namely a major victory in the field against numerically superior forces, won by first-class staff work and with full use of all the latest tactical devices in support of a strategic plan, which Napoleon himself couldn't have improved upon. It's the beginning of the end of the Italians, and will oblige the Germans to think furiously, since by next spring we shall be in a position to do unto them what we have just done unto the Italians. They (the Germans) are already far more nervous of being invaded somewhere on their 200 mile coast-line, than we are of being invaded by them. In fact we should like them to try. They are making no military progress by their bombing of houses and civilians: and as to the submarine campaign, if we can hold it for another month or two, we shall then have the Mediterranean fleet available for reinforcement in the Atlantic. I am beginning to think that Julian may miss this war altogether, as he certainly will if it is over before the midsummer of 1942.

Mary to J.B.B., 16 December   *Chiddingstone*

I have been doing a good deal of work at the canteen started for the men in the village hall here. It's most amusing work and I love it. Being the London Scottish there are of course a great many gents in the ranks, but now the battalion is getting the ordinary army intake, and there are some men from the slums of Glasgow. Whatever they are and wherever they come from, I've never had a rude word said to me, they're always perfectly charming. A few have got very Scotch accents, and I've more than once been done when they come and ask for things through the hatch! I'm very good on the prices of cigarettes and have at last learnt that a 'double Woods' means ten Woodbine. We sell copious cups of tea which they imbibe five minutes before their tea, and are back for another cup five minutes later. The NAAFI has now come to the Castle, but the men all hate it and hardly patronise it at all. When they first came the Colonel told us we weren't to open in the morning as he thought the men were sitting around too much. But the men were so furious he had to say he would open for an hour. Now most of the men know me by sight, but to begin with it was a fearful business getting past the sentries into any of the big houses.

The troops have been having some very good concerts in the village hall, which I get into as 'canteen staff'. Last night, the London Irish gave a first-class show. They even managed to tap dance on our very rickety stage. Unfortunately there's some silly rivalry between them and the London Scottish, who didn't turn up to watch the Irish show. The week before we had a not very good but very sporting show from some office workers in Tunbridge Wells who have got up their own company. There was a not very good conjurer and two mediocre singers. But the men enjoyed it thoroughly and were very enthusiastic.

Monier to E.C.F.B., 26 December   *Chiddingstone*

The second war Christmas has passed, absolutely quietly here - and on the whole was a really happy day. I had a nice number of Communicants, though less than last year, at the four services - 10 at the 7.30 in the Rectory dining room, which with Mary's and John's help we made very like a church, and clearly this hour was appreciated. After lunch, to which we had a London Scottish private who knows Canon Crum's family, we all listened to the Empire broadcast and the King - all good we thought. Then we had a walk to get warm. Mary had provided a Christmas cake, having saved up a little icing sugar. Dinner was roast goose from Mr Hale's farm, excellent, and plum pudding made last July, when the ingredients could be got, and Mr Matthew produced a bottle of Champagne. Freda had sent a box of Turkish Delight and we had ginger. So it was hardly a war dinner! None of us slept badly after it either.

Evelin Jackson (née Faithfull) to E.C.F.B, 28 December

It was Christmas Eve and I had taken the precaution of securing an Emergency Ration Card before I left home, and came to spend Christmas in Gloucester. I went into the first shop to get my meat ration. I waited my turn very patiently, but it was useless. No meat to be had. A tall man in the rear, very dirty, was hailed with joy by the butcher who had refused me, 'What can I do for you Sir? A nice leg of mutton?' He answered grandly, 'Yes, that will do.' One more effort I thought. 'Couldn't I have a few pork chops?' There they were, most temptingly, on the counter in front of me. 'Well,' he said grudgingly, 'I could give you one.' I had visions of returning to the family with but one large pork chop and wondered how far it would go among the three of us. I begged for two thin ones and came away in triumph.

Next I visited a grocer for lard, butter, bacon and tea. The waiting seemed endless for the shop was packed, and I was despairing when I found the flighty young girl serving seemed to know all the customers except me. When my moment came and the Emergency Card was sighted, all her smile went. 'No bacon, no lard, and I doubt about butter or marge!' I was granted two ounces of tea, and that was the result of my long wait. A fat woman and a small boy, who came much later than me, were served at once - the Emergency Card condemned me. When I asked for meat for the dog the answer was, 'Not for you or for me.'

Ralph to E.C.F.B., 29 December   *Groombridge*

I feel definitely more confident myself, and although we have an arduous furrow to plough with many unpleasant surprises in store, we have surely turned the corner. If only old Pétain would really tell Hitler where he gets off and start the fight again. I fear it is too much to hope for. But the Greek victories, coupled with our own magnificent show in North Africa, fill one with courage. A devil of a raid is going on now over London. It started at 6.15 p.m. and a number of German planes are still going over us. We twice have just walked out along our private road to have a look at our London barrage. It is a magnificent sight. I fear there are some large fires, as the sky (we are 35 miles from the centre of London) was a horrid red colour. Although we are so far away, the barrage shakes windows and doors in this house.

I only had Christmas Day off. We went to the 9 o'clock Holy Communion and had a walk after lunch, and had dinner at night. Alison, Peter and I solemnly dressed. It is lovely having Peter home and he really is an admirable companion. He is just my height, pretty broad and definitely stronger than I am. So I have to be careful!

1940 has certainly been a year. It will, I expect, prove to be the last year we shall have lived in London. Twenty one years is a longish time to live in one city. It was November 1919 that we first came to town. Our house there looks too awful now, the majority of our front windows broken, holes in our roof and two ceilings nearly down! also bricks down all the chimneys. I have had to do essential repairs to keep the weather out, having claimed £28 for damages. I do not see our son being able to afford to live in it again, and although I have just under fifteen years of lease left - if it is still there at the end of the war - I may be lucky to let it.

We have had good health too this year, which has been very fortunate. In fact we have a great deal to be thankful for.

1941

'The destruction of the City of London is just deplorable' - Colonel Bingham and the 'Old School tie' - John joins The Buffs - Table talk with Bevin and Eden - Cliveden in wartime - Renewed invasion fears - Ralph and the Home Guard - 'The war news really is extremely cheering' - The Oxford Bermondsey Club and a visit to the shelters - Tales of Commando raids - Mary's war - Contacts with CEMA - Tony joins his regiment - The 'Red Dean' and the Socialist Sixth of the World - The great London Blitz - 'I think this war is going to be a long one' - 'The gloom in the mess is at times considerable' - Grim news from the Mediterranean - The sinking of the Bismarck; 'a tragic but also triumphant few days' - The Germans invade Russia - 'Certainly a country to give everything for' - Training; 'but for what?' - The 'Red Dean' triumphant - Talk of a Second Front - 'One's whole world turned topsy-turvy' - The Tots and Quots Club - War prospects - Montgomery; 'a pugnacious little man' - Operation Crusader - Days of Infamy - Tony sails for India.

January

Geoffrey to E.C.F.B., 1 January   *Aberdeen*

I must send you a line to tell you what a happy beginning of the New Year Tony's visit has been for us all. His train up here was actually six hours late yesterday, a large slice out of his brief leave. But at 3.30 he arrived and we had a great family reunion. Ursula and David performed their play - the third in their repertoire - for him, and then after supper a long cosy evening in front of the fire. Such a long way to come for so short a time, but it was worth it.

We saw Tony off at 5 p.m. the next day. He is now going straight to an OCTU, where he will be really learning things, and living an interesting though of course a very strenuous life, not wasting his time, as he has been at Warwick at his ORTU for the last four-and-a-half months.

The OCTU course lasts three months; it used to be six but is now telescoped into half that period. So if all goes well he ought to pass out and get his commission by the end of March or beginning of April. He then gets a fortnight's leave: supposed to be used for fitting himself up with uniform, etc. This, if it comes off, would be extraordinarily lucky for us, as the first fortnight of April would coincide with that portion of the Easter holidays when we would all be at home.

Ralph to E.C.F.B., 3 January   *Lombard Street*

Our office is intact, and in fact to all intents and purposes undamaged. We believe one or two windows were broken on the upper floor, but not ours. We were extremely fortunate, but we have always had efficient fire watchers every night since war began. The destruction of course in the City of London is deplorable. Whole streets are simply destroyed. They will all have to be pulled down and rebuilt. Everything was very chaotic on Monday. Poor London Bridge station is just a shell, completely burnt out; the platforms however are all right.

Tony to E.C.F.B., 4 January   *168 OCTU, Droitwich*

I am lucky to be in a company billeted in a huge hotel which stands in its own grounds about a mile the Birmingham side of Droitwich. We only arrived on Friday, but as far as I can make out we have come to a good OCTU, although it will be hard work as the course is pretty intensive. Our Company Commander is

Major Haslam of the Somersets. In civilian life he was a schoolmaster. A most amusing man in a dog way. I am in No. 5 platoon and the Commanding Officer of the OCTU is Lt.-Colonel Bingham,[1] DSO, of the Royal Fusiliers. We have not met him yet.

J.B.B., to E.C.F.B., 5 January

On Thursday afternoon I motored up to London to discuss a number of problems. I tried to see Ralph but just missed him. The damage even in that immediate neighbourhood is bad enough, though not as widespread as around Newgate and Mark Lane. All Hallows Barking has gone. Trinity House has also been destroyed, and the same bastion of the Tower was again damaged. Lombard Street was piled up with rubble. The people were pouring out of their offices just when I was there in order to reach home before the blackout - quiet, a little grim, but good-humoured as they queued-up for the long line of special buses. Hoses were still being used for smouldering buildings, while great boards covered holes in Queen Victoria Street over which traffic bumped at a crawling pace.

I dined with Vincent and Alice Massey at the Dorchester. Vincent said it was not certain about Gerald Campbell[2] joining Halifax at Washington, but I hope he does. Campbell is British High Commissioner at Ottawa. He knows the USA intimately and is popular there. Did you realise that Neville Butler,[3] Counsellor at our Embassy, was also a Christian Scientist?

Howe,[4] who is Minister of Supply in Canada, was dined and slept here at Corps HQ on Friday. I know him well and was glad to get to talk to him. He lost everything in the torpedoing of his ship except what he stood-up in.[5] He has bought several reach-me-down suits, and the one he was wearing looked like that kind of ready-made clothing. All his essential papers had been duplicated, and they were immediately flown over in a bomber, so one of the worst inconveniences was

---

[1] Lt.-Col. Ralph Bingham (1885-1977). Bt. Comm. Royal Fusiliers, 1934-7; CVO (1953).
[2] Sir Gerald Campbell (1879-1964). High Comm. in Canada, 1938-41; Minister in Washington, 1941 and 1942-45; Dir-Gen. of British Info. Services, New York, 1941-42.
[3] Neville Montagu Butler (1893-73). Joined FO 1920; Counsellor at Washington Embassy, 1940; Minister, 1940-1; Asst. U-S of State, FO, 1944-7; Amb. to Brazil, 1947-51; Amb. to Holland, 1952-4. KCVO (1947). The Christian Science reference is, presumably, connected with Halifax's predecessor as Ambassador, Lord Lothian. He too was a Christian Scientist.
[4] Clarence Howe ((1886-1960). Canadian Min. of Transport, 1935; Min. of Supply, 1940; Min. of Reconstruction, 1946; Min. of Trade and Commerce, 1948-57. PC (1946).
[5] The ship, the *Western Prince* (10,000 tons), was sunk on 14 December 1940. At least one of the Canadian government mission's members was drowned.

avoided. They were six hours in an open boat and were only saved because the skipper of a small freighter which had passed them in the night turned back in answer to the SOS. Such action is strictly against orders, as obviously such rescuing vessels may be carrying vital freight and be torpedoed themselves in picking up the shipwrecked people. Howe told me that when he recounted to Alexander[1] (First Lord) what the skipper had done, Alexander said he really ought not to have done it, with which Howe did not agree.

The fall of Bardia is marvellous. The Canadians, I think, rather wish they had been in it and feel the Australians will be very much above themselves.

Notes by John Bickersteth, 10 January

On Monday of this week I got back from work soon after 5 o'clock to find that my calling-up papers had come. I am to report to the ITC, The Buffs depot, Canterbury, before 1600 hrs. on 16 January. This is extremely good news, both because I have been waiting for my papers since October, and also because I can think of nowhere I would rather go than Canterbury. I want eventually to get my commission in The Buffs, and this should help me do so.

I discovered from Father that my posting was not pure chance. As usual the Bickersteth family had got to the top. Father had asked Uncle Ralph (otherwise Brigadier R. Chenevix-Trench, CB, OBE, MC) if he would write to General Scarlett,[2] the Colonel of The Buffs, and ask him if he could help me to get a commission in the regiment when the time came for me to leave my OCTU. Scarlett obviously interpreted the letter differently. Father heard from Uncle Ralph the same day, who explained what had happened and said he hoped he had done right. We have assured him that he has.

I went to work on Tuesday for the last time. And I thus completed four weeks of forestry, in which I have learnt a great deal and kept extremely fit. I have done a bit of everything - felling, measuring-up and sawing off props, stacking them and loading them on to lorries for delivery by train to various collieries. I have also used the stripping spade and draw-shave in the process of stripping the bark off trees which are destined for the GPO as telegraph poles.

---

[1] Albert Victor Alexander (1885-1965). MP (Lab) Hillsborough, 1922-31 and 1935-50; First Lord of the Admiralty, 1929-31, 40-44 and 45-66; Min. of Defence, 1947-50; Chanc. of D. of Lancaster, 1950-51. Cr. Earl Hillsborough (1963).

[2] Maj-Gen. Gerald Scarlett, MC (1885-1957). Dir. of Mobilization, 1940; Dep. Adj-Gen., 1940; Col. The Buffs, 1940-45.

And the actual work has been varied and interesting; and I have enjoyed too the talks with the men round the fireside at lunch and dinner time (picnicking, as it really is, would be jolly cold in a snowstorm if it were not for the roaring wood fire). I have picked up dozens of things that interest me - country ways and words, anecdotes about Chiddingtsone 70 or so years ago. The early morning ride to the wood - though it has been bitterly cold sometimes - was a good experience; the countryside looking very wintry, trees stark against the snow. Then there is the ride home in the evening with a red sun sinking behind Stock Wood, and a 'goodnight' to the labourers leading home their horses in the dusk. Very romantic it may all sound; but work on the land is not romantic. It is a bitter, never-ending struggle against the forces of nature, ever chary of giving up her bountiful store. Townspeople who come out on trips to the country at hay-making may think it looks an easy life, even an idyllic one. But always the winter haunts the farmworker. The layman does not know what it is like going to work on a bitter January morning - hands blue with cold; or spreading manure in the pouring rain, one's feet clogged with clay. I do not know what it is like either. But four weeks on the land has shown me to some extent what it must mean.

The average farmer now is working harder than ever. He knows he can make a valuable, even an essential, contribution to the war effort. Whatever he produces is the result of unremitting toil, day in day out, the whole year round. But he could grow more if he had more men to help him. If the government were to take 10,000 skilled men off the farms in the spring and put them in the army, they are not doing their best to put farming on its footing. If farming in this infinitely fertile country of ours is set on its feet again as a result of this war, then Hitler will certainly have done England a thoroughly good service.

J.B.B. to E.C.F.B., 12 January   *H.Q. Canadian Forces*

Before the dinner for Howe I had a good talk with David Margesson (the new Secretary of State for War), whom I had not seen for several months. I told him a little of what was going forward down here, and he said he would like to come down one evening and have a good talk with General McNaughton, whom he does not know. He asked me to tell the General this.

At the dinner I sat between Bevin and Oliver Lyttelton[1] (President of the Board of Trade). Beyond Bevin was Eden, and Bevin, he and I had a good deal of three-cornered talk during the meal. Bevin is very proud of his training schools for munition workers. He was most interesting too on the necessity of breaking up what he calls the 'groove' system, whereby a man makes the same tool or the same bit of a tool all his life. 'What's the good,' he said, 'of talking about raising the school-leaving age when we do all we can by our economic system to atrophy a young man's brain directly he starts work?' Eden chipped-in and said, 'I have a boy at Eton - 16 years old and mad to get into the Air Force. But there's no technical training at Eton. What shall I do with him? Surely the public schools are finished in their present form; in a mechanised age like this, when boys' minds turn towards the machine, they cannot provide any help.' I took up the point from the obvious angle that boys needed something beyond technical training if they were to live full lives. Eden agreed but said there was no reason why a boy should not get both. At this point I told Eden I hoped they would send Gerald Campbell to Washington to assist Halifax. He agreed it would be a good combination, but nothing had yet been settled.

Bevin, by the way, said he would like to come down here and speak. I must arrange it. He is proud of his success in building up the dockers' union. The dockers and the more extreme elements in the Labour Party feel he has deserted the ship in accepting £3,000 or £4,000 a year, or whatever is the salary of the Minister of Labour. But he made it clear, as he told me the history of his life, that he means to go back to Labour as soon as the war is over. I also had a talk with Cranborne[2] (the one and only 'Bobbety') whom I had not seen since he was at the Dominions Office. He knew I was with McNaughton and asked how things were going.

On Friday I was at Reading University, making final arrangements about the visit of 30 men there next Wednesday, and the three succeeding Wednesdays, for lectures and practical work in agriculture. I came back via Farnham and had

---

[1] Oliver Lyttelton (1893-1972). Controller of Non-Ferrous Metals, 1939-40; MP (Con) Aldershot, 1940-54; Pres. of Bd. of Trade, 1941-2 and 1945; Min. of State, 1941-42; Min. of Production and member of War Cabinet, 1942-45. Cr. Vt. Chandos (1954).
[2] Robert Arthur James Gascoyne-Cecil - Lord Cranborne - (1893-1972). MP (Con) S. Dorset, 1929-41; Parl. U-S. F.O., 1935-38; PMG, 1940: Sec. of State for Dominion Affairs, 1940-42 and 1943-45: Sec. of State for Colonies, 1942-43 and 1951-52; Sec. of State for Commonwealth Affairs, 1951-57. Succ. as 5th. Marquis of Salisbury (1947).

lunch with John and Mrs. Macmillan[1] at Farnham Castle. It was a superb day and I have never seen the place looking more lovely. The other half of the castle is used for a military school and I visited it - flourishing my pass, as it is very hush-hush. The Macmillans' son, Peter, is at Hong Kong and is also G.3 on the China command.

Kay to E.C.F.B., 15 January   *Yaverland, I.O,W.*

We had a dreadful night last Friday with the 'blitz' on Portsmouth, and have been quite cut off since. Everything has to come via Southampton, which takes twice as long. Our AA fire was excellent, and several planes were brought down, but the damage they've done is really terrible. Both stations, the Town Hall, the two main shopping centres and several piers are completely destroyed. The dockyard miraculously escaped, which is lucky for us as there are always a lot of ships being repaired there.

Ralph to E.C.F.B., 16 January   *Lombard Street*

We have had an awful lot of snow, of course. It started on the evening of New Year's Day and did not disappear until last Saturday. Now we have got a whole lot more. It is very cold.

We have one of the largest holes outside our office I have ever seen or want to see again. It was caused on Saturday night. As you know the booking office of the Bank station was constructed some years ago under the very extensive roadway. It is a huge place with shops, etc. The bomb came at an angle and, apparently, went down the escalator, and the damage it caused is colossal. The blast could not get away and therefore came up again, and the entire roadway has collapsed. To give some idea, the hole is just over 300ft. from lip to lip. in one direction, and about 250ft. in the other. We have a grandstand view from this office as we look right into it. The casualties, I am sorry to say, were heavy, over 300. They even extracted four people alive on Tuesday afternoon. They have hundreds of Pioneer Corps and Royal Engineers, with four or five 40ft. cranes. It is all steel and concrete to take the weight of the traffic and it looks as though a giant has been playing marbles with it. None of the buildings was touched.

---

[1] Rt. Rev. John Victor Macmillan (1877-1956). Archdeacon of Maidstone, 1921-34; Suffragen Bishop of Dover, 1927-34; Bishop of Guildford, 1934-49. OBE (1919).

The damage in the City following the fire has got to be seen to be believed. It is aggravating to realise now that if everybody had had firewatchers, there would have been practically no damage at all. We in this building have had firemen and firewatchers since the war was begun; they are on duty every night. We have had incendiaries on the roof but they have been dealt with at once.

Tony to E.C.F.B, 16 January   *168 O.C.T.U., Droitwitch*

Major Fielden[1] of the 10th. Hussars is 2nd. in command of 168. I have not come across him yet but am interested to hear that uncle Burgon knows him. As for our CO, Lt-Col. Bingham, he wrote a letter published in yesterday's *Times*, which you may have seen, and which supports the 'Old School Tie'. Today's gutter press have of course seized on it with relish and headlined it to death. But I think what he says is in the main true. Bingham is a remarkable man. He doesn't know what fear is. They say he used to spend his leaves in the last war with a rifle in no-man's -land.

Willie Blore (Canterbury Cathedral Librarian) to E.C.F.B., 17 January

In Canterbury the sirens are going continually. Sometimes we have as many as 10 in a day; and the total score since the beginning of the war is now 631. Sometimes I have to get up and go out three times during the course of the night; this is a bit trying in the bitterly cold weather we are having, but I don't mind that as much as the pitch blackness which makes me run my nose into a wall, or trip up and fall in a muddy puddle. Anyhow, it does not seem to have any evil effects on me, and I have now so well trained myself that I wake up directly the siren goes and spring out of bed and get dressed and out in a very few minutes. I am generally on duty on alternate nights; and during the day I usually go whenever the siren sounds as well as being on duty from 4.00 to 8 p.m.

I cannot do anything in the Library as there is no heating at all. The temperature is now below 40 there, and it seldom gets much above that.

This afternoon I was crossing Mercery Lane walking behind a stationary military lorry opposite the chemist's. Just as I was passing, it suddenly moved backwards and knocked me over. Before I could get up it had just about run me

---

[1] Edward Fielden (1886-1972). Retired as Major, 10th. Hussars (1921): MFH, South Salop Hounds, 1925-9 and North Cotswold Hounds, 1929-32; re-employed as 2nd. in command 168 OCTU, 1939-42; Lt.Col. Home Guard, 1942.

over. However, I let out a fearful scream which the driver fortunately heard so that he stopped his lorry an inch or two from my body. I had great difficulty in persuading the crowd that at once gathered that I was quite unhurt, and had only given out the piercing scream to call the driver's attention and stop him from crushing me to death.

It is 10 p.m. now and if the siren goes I shall have to turn out at once. I am afraid this is rather rambling scrawl. But I have to do everything in a hurry, as I never know how long I have before the bally siren goes again.

Notes by E.C.F.B., 19 January   *Goodrich*

Heavy snow continued to fall yesterday, no cars could be used and Julian had to plough his way on foot four or five times between this house, Goodrich Court and the church. The snow was deep and the roads slippery. Julian in the evening was quite exhausted.

No buses could run on the roads, so no boys could come from Hill Court, which disorganised all the work, especially as five masters were away for the same cause. A case of mumps occurred today, followed by others of measles. No car could take them along the icy roads to the sanatorium. The case of mumps slept in Julian's study, a small dormitory being kept for the other sick boys.

J.B.B. to E.C.F.B., 19 January   *H.Q. Canadian Corps*

The University of Toronto has extended my leave of absence until June, which of course means the autumn. At lunch when I saw the General, he said, 'Well, you can be with us for a while now!' whereupon all the brigadiers pulled my leg and said with groans it was a terrible prospect. In actual fact it is highly unlikely I shall be here much beyond Easter. Already military schemes and exercises and training of all sorts are beginning to make inroads on educational programmes. For instance, the course I had with much trouble worked out for four successive Wednesdays for a number of keen farmer-soldiers at Reading University, is already down to three owing to a three-day route march for the entire Division, and possibly another Wednesday may be ruled out too.

But the first day - last Wednesday - was a great success. As far as the weather was concerned it could hardly have begun worse. When Sanders called me at 5.30 a.m. I looked out and saw it was a thick fog. When we set off at 6.00 a.m., the blackness and the fog made me wonder if we would meet the lorries, and even if we did whether we could get them to Reading. It took us nearly 40 minutes to crawl down the road to our rendezvous. Two sections were marching smartly up the road as we arrived, but there was no sign of any lorries which had 15 miles to come. At 7.05 a.m. one lorry turned up full of French Canadians. The Sergeant was terribly difficult to understand, but I gathered he thought some sections had gone to the wrong place. I waited till 7.15., then gave the order to leave without the Carlton and York party. We nosed along but by the time we had passed Guildford the grey light of dawn made travelling easier and the fog had lifted. We reached Reading at 9.23, being due at 9.30 a.m.

Coffee and buns were provided for the men, who were cold, and then we went to the lecture room in the agricultural building. Here the Vice-Chancellor, Sir Franklin Sibly,[1] welcomed the party and I made a short speech. There was a first-rate lecture on changes in British agriculture between 1870-1949, with notes and figures written out and a copy for everyone. I had arranged for a young lecturer from the French department to be present, and about every five minutes the lecturer stopped while his French-speaking colleague interpreted the main points of the argument. At 11.00 a.m. the Carlton and York lads turned up, just in time for the second lecture, which was on climate, soil and population as determining factors in British agriculture.

At 12.15 we all had lunch in the University buttery. We had brought our meat ration as obviously the University could not manage that, but everything else they supplied and the men had a first-class meal. Then we clambered into cars and lorries and went off up the Basingstoke road to a large, successful private farm. The men asked innumerable questions, and again our 'French interpreter' was there. Back to the University by 3.15 for tea and buns and by 3.45 we were on our way back. It was snowing and cold, but we made good time and had returned to billets by 5.30. I need hardly say that we shall pay for everything we had, including proper remuneration for the lecturers. We had cause to be grateful, and I hope we showed it.

I have rearranged next week's second visit somewhat, and we are leaving later. This leading a convoy in the dark in fog, or on slippery roads, is too nerve-

---

[1] Sir (Thomas) Franklin Sibly (1883-1948). Prof. of Geology, Cardiff, 1913-18; V-Chanc. Univ. of Wales, 1925-6; V-Chanc. Univ. of Reading, 1929-46; Chm. Geological Survey Bd., 1930-43. Kt (1938).

wracking. It would have been awful to have lost the party. Thank goodness I didn't.

I had lunch with Hankey in his icy house one day last week. How these English people exist I don't know. It is just straight silly. Nobody wants overheated 'American' houses, but the sheer discomfort of living in a refrigerator is not a sign of hardness but stupidity. Hankey thought it disgraceful giving Gilbert Murray[1] the OM after all his 'misleading work' with the League of Nations Union. I don't agree in the least. He thinks Bob Cecil[2] is as bad.

On Tuesday I had a jolly day at No. 5 Canadian General Hospital at Taplow - in the grounds of Cliveden. I had a long talk with the RC padre who is keen about the educational work among the hospital staff and patients. There is no chapel, largely because Nancy Astor is a Christian Scientist and has made difficulties. The men would like it, and also a good many of the officers on the staff.

I sat next to Nancy at lunch and we talked hard, or rather she did. The conversation ranged from Russia, which she thought wonderful in conception but pathetic in execution, to Roman Catholicism, about which she is well-known to have an obsession, considering Rome as a menace second only to National Socialism. She mistrusts the RC padre at the hospital, but I told her she was wrong and also that there ought to be a chapel for the use of all denominations. I did not find her as hostile to this as I had been led to expect. She was not unreasonable either about the drink question, though she said Christmas and New Year celebrations at the hospital left much to be desired. She wanted an order against treating in drinks - and in this I think she is right.

Before lunch I talked to Trenchard, the Marshal of the RAF. I had met him several times before and he is very able. But his difficulty, I always think, is in expressing himself. Tom Jones came in, as did Sir Walter Monckton[3] and Waldorf

---

[1] (George) Gilbert (Aime) Murray (1866-1957). Australian born Regius Professor of Greek, Oxford University, 1908-36. Chm. LNU, 1923-38. OM (1941).

[2] Rt. Hon. Edgar Algenon Robert Cecil (1864-1958). MP (Con) C. Marylebone, 1906-10, and Hitchin, 1911-23; Min. of Blockade, 1916-18; Ld. Privy Seal, 1923-24; Chanc. of Duchy of Lancaster, 1924-27; Pres. of LNU, 1923-45. Cr. Vt. Cecil of Chelwood (1923). Nobel Prize Winner (1937).

[3] Sir Walter Monckton (1891-1965). Barrister turned politician. Dir. Gen. of Press Censorship Bureau, 1939-40; Dir.-Gen. Min. of Information, 1940-1; Dir. of Propaganda in Cairo, 1941-2; Solicitor-Gen., 1945; MP (Con) W. Bristol, 1951-57; Min. of Labour, 1951-55; Min. of Defence, 1955-56; PMG, 1956-7. KCVO (1937), PC (1951). Cr. Vt. (1957).

Astor.[1] We all five talked politics until lunch. Trenchard and TJ were singing the praises of D'Arcy Cooper,[2] Chairman of Lever Brothers, who they thought should be in the Cabinet. I fear I have never heard of him before. Monckton and I had a short talk. He is a great friend of Stafford Cripps, and promises to send me some of his letters to read. I gather that Stafford is very disillusioned about Russia and sees how it is impossible to change human nature in a generation. Maisky is quite frank in stating that Russia would have liked friendship with England but all her advances were repelled, and so Germany, who cultivated her assiduously for years, was finally accepted. Now Russia is not in a position to say no to Germany (as anyone who sees the maps as I do occasionally, showing the dispositions of German divisions along the Russian frontier, will agree).

Later in the afternoon TJ and I walked over to see Joyce Grenfell.[3] Do you remember her at Gregynog with Bob Brand?[4] Joyce is now playing in 'Farjeon's Diversion' at Wyndham's Theatre, and very successfully too, I gathered. She does sketches rather *à la* Ruth Draper.[5] With her were Tony Thesiger and his wife.[6] He is stationed in Bristol with his AA battery, and they have had a pretty grim time.

Mrs Constable Curtis to E.C.F.B., 21 January   *Goodrich*

The reason that Hitler has not bombed Oxford is that he intends it to be his capital, with Christ Church as his Reichstag. He will live at Blenheim as it will annoy Churchill.

John to E.C.F.B., 25 January   *ITC, The Buffs, Canterbury*

I am in an unusually small platoon with a few men who have only been here three or four weeks; a Sgt. Dighton is our instructor, and from what I have seen of him this first week he lives up to his reputation of being the best instructor there is in the depot. We have four three-quarter hour periods every morning,

---

[1] Vt. Waldorf Astor (1879-1952). MP (Con) Plymouth, 1910-19; Chm. Royal Inst. of International Affairs, 1935-49; Ld. Mayor of Plymouth, 1939-44.
[2] Sir Francis D'Arcy Cooper (1882-1941). Chm. of Lever Brothers and Unilever Ltd. Member of Industrial Export Council, BOT. Cr. Bart. (1941).
[3] Joyce Grenfell (1910-79). Actress, broadcaster and writer. OBE (1946).
[4] Robert Henry Brand (1878-1951). Head of British Food Mission, Washington, 1941-4; Chm. British Supply Council in N. America, 1942 and 1945-6. A Director of Lloyds Bank.
[5] Ruth Draper (1884-1956). American-born character actress and 'monologue' artiste. CBE (1951).
[6] Anthony and Virginia Thesiger. She was described by Joyce Grenfell as 'my oldest and dearest friend.'

when we do foot drill, rifle drill, Bren gun instruction, and so on. In theory we have two more periods after lunch, but on three afternoons this week we have been free.

Our Company Commander is a Major Argles - most awfully nice; and I have also had an interview with Colonel Howe, who told me to work hard, which I certainly intend doing. Our barracks are very comfortable, with hot water all day at the end of the passage. We have sheets of a sort with our army blankets, which I was not expecting.

I went to a late celebration in the Crypt last Sunday, and tomorrow I shall go to the Garrison Church. How I wish the services could be held in the Choir again.

J.B.B. to E.C.F.B., 26 January   *H.Q. Canadian Corps*

Bingham's dismissal from the OCTU was inevitable but David Margesson told Barbie Wallace the other day that Bingham had written his letter anonymously, sending of course his name to *The Times* with it. But *The Times* refused to publish the letter unless it was signed, and Bingham then gave his consent. All the officers and men in the OCTU sent Bingham a kind of round robin asking if they could do anything to help and expressing confidence in him.

I dined with Mrs Ronnie Greville[1] last night at Polesden Lacy. There was only a small party including the Dutch ambassador and his wife, both quite charming, Lady Austen Chamberlain[2] and Sir George Clerk.[3] I talked with her for a while about the British Council, but the most interesting conversation was with Clerk. He thought we were being very foolish about the way we intern British Fascists. In many cases, though the young fellow before the tribunal might have been secretary of the Fascists in the locality, say Bermondsey, the entire group in that district only amounted to a handful of people. Clerk's view is that it would have been better to have left fellows like this at large, though under observation. As it is, he is detained and put into an internees' camp with scores of other Fascists. There he gets the idea of belonging to a big movement.

---

[1] Hon. Mrs Ronnie (Margaret) Greville (d. 1942). Society hostess; described by Harold Nicolson as 'silly and selfish'. Bequeathed her jewels to the Queen Mother.
[2] Lady Ivy Chamberlain (d. 1941). Widow of Sir Austen Chamberlain.
[3] Rt. Hon. Sir George Clerk (1874-1951). Amb. to Turkey, 1926-33; to Brussels, 1933-34; to Paris, 1934-37. KCMG (1917), PC (1926).

Mrs Ronnie Greville has not been at all well and disappeared shortly after dinner. She seems to meet everybody and two days ago had a long talk with Mr Hopkins,[1] Roosevelt's nominee, whom she liked very much. Hopkins is apparently completely in sympathy with us and is lost in admiration of the Navy.

Notes by E.C.F.B, 29 January

London has had no night-bombing for nine days; what does this portend? Hardly any daylight bombing either. Some say it is the bad weather which is also hindering our offensive; some say it is the effect of German reorganisation, so many of their planes being sent to the Mediterranean; others that the German pilots are getting leave while the planes are being overhauled for the invasion of England.

One interesting fact is that there is to be no Grand National, or any substitute race, run this year. The first time for 104 years.

February

Miss Barrow to E.C.F.B, 1 February   *Canterbury*

When my sister came home from hospital, in a wonderful way she started to get better. Then the order came out to evacuate Canterbury as far as possible. I went to the Police and they said it was my duty to stop as I was in food. So my sister came to live in the home over the cafe, so as to always be together. When the sun was out we walked in the Precincts before I got busy, and often met and talked with Mr White-Thomson who was a great friend of hers. She got better and better. She had her meals in the cafe with her friends, and all the old customers welcomed her back.

Then the first raid came, one day when my sister and I were underground in the shelter we had made. The kitchen and cake room were damaged, and the small dining-room at the back with the glass roof was made unusable. We shut for a day and a half, all staff and myself clearing up breakages and making the place ready to open again, which we did, screening the dining-room off, which it took six men a fortnight to patch up. Half an hour after they had taken their tools away, another raid came, and did all the damage over again. We had spent about £72 on

---

[1] Harry L Hopkins (1890-1946). U.S. Sec. of Commerce, 1938-40; Special Adviser and Asst. to Pres. Roosevelt, 1940-55.

teak shutters, wire netting and supports, etc. to make the place as safe as possible, and although the street was badly damaged and nine people killed, no one in our premises had a scratch. I was lifted from the cake room and put on a mat in the big dining-room, but only sprained my ankle which soon got better.

The gas and electric were both cut off in this raid and the street was shut for rescue work, so this time the cafe was out of action for four days. During that time we tried as best we could to get tea and meals for the rescue men. By this time we had made our underground premises into a dining-room for 35 people, and a service pantry where six staff could work in safety. Here we had bought and installed new gas equipment. In five days another raid came, the worst of all, and after clearing up after this one we received letters and messages from most of our customers to say they were afraid to come as our premises seemed to be doomed. We talked things over with our solicitor, who advised us to rent the undamaged part of the premises as a warehouse, store our equipment, and re-open when things had settled down. We spent a fortnight packing all our stuff. I said I thought the time was given to me to get her quite better, and then we would rise again together after the war.

A month longer we had her with us. She was patient, gentle and thoughtful for others until the end. She had a beautiful service and many lovely flowers. Now I am going to gather up the threads and start again. I have been doing the cake business here as it is a way of earning money and yet be near her. I shall continue, all being well, for a time and decide later if I shall re-start without her.

J.B.B. to E.C.F.B., 2 February   *H.Q. Canadian Corps*

I spent two days in East Kent last week. There is an atmosphere of tenseness in that area. It is so close to the enemy one feels in the front line in a way one is not conscious of further inland. The people live under a strain. The night before I arrived, shells had dropped for the third successive evening at Bridge and Barham. Fired as they were from the French coast, the range must have been somewhere about 30 miles.

The constant references in the press to plans for invasion are disquieting. Knox's[1] recent statement in Washington that Hitler will strike in the next 60, or at most 90, days is not calculated to allay forebodings, though frankly there seems

[1] Franklin Knox (1874-1944). Prop. *Chicago Daily News*; Republican, but appointed by Roosevelt as Navy Secretary (1940).

little in intelligence reports to suggest an attack is immediately likely. That the Germans must strike within the next few months is obvious. But this may as likely take the form of more intense air and submarine activity as invasion by troop-carrying planes and surface ships. Preparations are being made throughout East Kent for a blitz from the air.

The face of Canterbury is scarred. In Burgate, where the charming old bookshop stood, there is now a gaping hole full of rubble. Among the pile of bricks and masonry were books and torn leaves and broken bookshelves. The Precincts are a sad sight. They were completely deserted. When I drove in under Christ Church gateway on Thursday afternoon, there was not a person about and nothing moving and not a sound. Inside the vast building was even colder than outside and it was completely empty. The tombs were covered with sand bags and corrugated iron; gaunt, hideous but no doubt effective. On the wall of the St Augustine Chapel were the names of all the Archbishops for 1450 years, and I read them through and speculated whether any of them had seen stranger times than these. I made my way down into the crypt. It smelt musty and airless. People sleep there every night, including two town councillors. I stood there for several minutes. There was not a single sound of any kind. It was indeed a strange experience. I came up and walked to the far end of the Cathedral and stood in Becket's Crown behind the pedestal where in normal times sits the stone chair on which every Archbishop for 700 years has been enthroned. Before me stretched this vast building, gloomy, cold, yet utterly majestic and as yet (and pray heaven always) untouched by German bombs as regards its structure.

Next morning I went out towards Ramsgate and visited a unit. On my return I had a long talk with Cousins who, on the whole, was less unimaginative than I had expected about the work I am trying to do. He said they would welcome me back into the Home Guard in case of emergency. I said I would get back if humanly possible. In the afternoon I had tea with my former Sergeant, now RSM Roberts, and a great swell. The Canterbury battalion seems to have progressed. Slackers have been weeded out and several officers have changed. The drill is smarter and the men, all of whom have battle serge and greatcoats, must do their job or get out. RSM Roberts promised, as we sat at tea, there was a place for me when I get back.

With John, who turned up at 6 o'clock looking extremely well and smart in the uniform of a private soldier which fitted him, I walked down pitch-black streets to visit Mrs Gardiner. I saw Canon Gardiner[1] for a few minutes. He looked frail and wizened, and was lying in what looked like an Elizabethan four-poster, canopied bed. This odd-looking piece of furniture was constructed of rough timber and is supposed to protect him from a collapsing ceiling. He said, 'I am 83, and I have been in bed for nearly four years, but I can read and I can sleep, and have nothing to complain of.' At 8.45 John and I presented ourselves at the Old Palace and found the Archbishop alone. We three dined together. He asked John all about his present life and wanted to know about Monier and Mary, and he questioned me about my work. But he is old - very old - and seemed strangely out of touch with the great stream of military life which flows past his door. As always he was kind and interested in his guests, but I do wish that a man like William Temple might be called on to deal with the problems the Church has to face.

I have not mentioned how many people asked about you, but everybody did. When you do go back you will certainly be welcome. But at the moment I am convinced that you are best where you are.

Molly Hopkins to E.C.F.B, 8 February   *Bridge*

I expect Norah told you about our night of fireworks last Wednesday. I heard there were 200 fire bombs dropped on and around Canterbury, wonderful they did no damage. The whole place for miles around was ablaze with lights and flares. We have had no more shells lately. They were rather frightening at first, but we did get used to them. I saw Mr John and a chum yesterday. He does seem to like the army life doesn't he?

We often see our bombers and fighters going over to France and coming back. Rather a wonderful sight.

Notes by E.C.F.B., 12 February

On Sunday last, 9 February, Burgon's great friend Capt. Euan Wallace died, and today Burgon went to his funeral at Lavington. David Margesson also attended, and Burgon tells me that Barbie Wallace, though clearly distraught, maintained herself with quiet dignity throughout the day. She asked Burgon to keep her son David's last letter from Athens to his father. He was buried in the old

---

[1] The Rev. Thory Gage Gardiner (1857-1941). Ordained 1880; Chaplain to Archbishop of Canterbury, 1903-28; Residentiary Canon of Canterbury, 1917-37.

Churchyard close to the House. Bishop Samuel Wilberforce and Cardinal Manning's wife lie there.

Geoffrey to E.C.F.B., 16 February   *Aberdeen*

With any luck Edward's period of active service is likely to be co-terminous with Italy's complete collapse in all her African possessions, a blessed consummation of his forthcoming marriage [to Jane Meade Waldo].

No one can say, of course, what will be the state of the war by mid-summer. All one can be certain of is that much of great importance will have happened by then. The attempt at invasion will by then be either a thing of the past, or else never likely to occur. Japan, too, will then be either definitely in the war (and consequently the USA too) or will be as definitely out of it. If she does come in, I think she won't last long. She could not stand more than six months' blockade conducted against her by American and British fleets more than twice the size of her own, and she, too, with ships and aeroplanes inferior in quality, and herself exhausted by four years of a still continuing war with China.

How one wonders whether Wavell[1] is trying to, or will, occupy Tripolitania, and then transfer his army to the Balkans to meet the German threat against Greece, or whether he is already doing this!

They raised over two million pounds here in War Weapons Week.

Ralph to E.C.F.B., 18 February   *Lombard Street*

As you know, I am now in the Home Guard and have all my accoutrements. Our particular Company is being somewhat reorganised, and we have a very pleasant Commander. I am on duty every sixth night, and we have a parade every Sunday. I have made arrangements for Peter to do his Home Guard in the holidays with my platoon, so in all probability Father and Son will go off to war together. He, of course, is a Lance Corporal, also a drill instructor; I, of course, am only a Private. Peter very much hopes that the invasion will take place in the holidays, and will go on for a very long time.

The war news really is extremely cheering, and although I fully anticipate we may be in for a difficult time during the next six months, I am quite convinced

---

[1] General Archibald Wavell (1883-1950). C-in-C Middle East, 1939-41; C-in-C India, 1941-43; Supreme Commander, SW Pacific, 1942; Field Marshal (1943); Viceroy and Gov.-Gen. of India, 1943-47. PC (1943). Cr. Earl Wavell (1947).

we shall win this war, probably a little quicker than some people think. I know Burgon feels it will be over this year. That I think is too premature.

Visit to the shelters in the railway arches of Bermondsey with George Grant.

J.B.B. to E.C.F.B., 19 and 23 February   *H.Q. Canadian Corps*

I had long wanted to visit George Grant and see for myself the work he was doing. Last weekend I went to Bermondsey and had a fascinating time. Somewhere about 1910 I visited Alec Paterson[1] at what was then the Oxford and Bermondsey Mission. Now, according to the new idea whereby one avoids the word 'Mission' and the implication of patronising the poor, it is called the Oxford and Bermondsey Club.

George and I met in the West End and had tea. We then took a bus over Westminster Bridge, and walked from the Elephant and Castle along drab streets on a damp, cold afternoon. There were signs of destruction almost at once - here a church laid open to the sky, there two or three houses in a row gone, further on a pub at the corner, a gaunt skeleton with rubble piled high inside. I had my tin hat and respirator and my shaving kit - no other gear of any kind. I dumped my shaving kit at the OBC and we went first to a pub where we had a drink. 'Hullo, Georgie dear,' from a woman sitting at the bar drinking her Guinness. 'Well, Mrs Brown, and how are the children? This is my Uncle,' and we shake hands and chat. A drink is bought for Mrs Brown and we talk with the bar-tender who had a pub of his own till a week ago when it was destroyed.

We then go to the Abbey Factories shelter where later we are to sleep. It is a large cellar-like room below the factory, and it has recently been fitted with bunks. Access by a steep ladder, a rope to help the aged in descending. 'Mrs Burke, here's my Uncle, 'says George to a sprightly little woman of 73. 'Glad to see you,' says Mrs Burke, 'that's my husband there but he is very bad with wind tonight - gets him all queer inside, and no wonder either. You see a bomb came right through the house next to ours, did quite a lot of damage to our house too, but the furniture is mostly all right and we are paying rent still.' There is considerable criticism of landlords; if a house is destroyed, obviously the tenant

---

[1]   Alexander Paterson, MC (1884-1947). Sometime elementary schoolteacher, Bermondsey; Princ. Officer, Min. of Labour, 1919-22; HM Comr. of Prisons and Dir. of Convict Prisons, 1922-47. Kt (1947).

ceases to pay rent. But if it is only damaged and the furniture is still there, the rent must be paid, though sometimes it is lowered. George says that in many such cases the house is not really habitable. The people, if possible, hang on to their few bits of furniture and would do anything to avoid moving themselves and their furniture, and then the landlord demands rent. 'We are a real family party here,' says Mrs Burke. 'On Christmas Eve we 'ad tea, games and dancing, and d'yer know I dressed up as a pirate.'

In the next shelter, Millers, we walked through great rooms piled high with cloth and flannel. Then, descending to a lower storey - vaulted roof like a crypt - we met a group of people preparing for bed. There were no bunks but beds of various kinds, some with sheets, most not. At the far end we met 'Gran' who, George whispered, was 'one of the real characters of Bermondsey,' and I was introduced as 'my Uncle'. George told me that she had lost everything when her house was bombed, but what roused her to a white heat of fury was the fact that she had lost 30/-. She was found sitting on the curb cursing Hitler, almost knocked silly by blast, and swearing she must return to find her money.

Stumbling out into the pitch-black streets, the evening had cleared and the stars looked down on acres of untenanted houses as everyone had gone to the shelters. Until recently the long immunity of several weeks had made people bold and they slept at home, but the night before I was there, eight people had been killed at a pub about 400 yards from the OBC. The night before that there had also been casualties, and these two episodes had brought the people crowding back to their shelters. We turned left towards London Bridge station. You remember how the railway runs on a viaduct from Canon Street to New Cross? Hundreds of the viaduct's arches have been made into shelters - not that they would be much use against a direct hit, but then few shelters would be - but they do afford some protection. And the most famous of these arch shelters are Stayners and 61 Arch. Imagine huge, vaulted chambers - not only long but broad, because here above us the railway opens out to run past the platforms of London Bridge station. These chambers seemed to open one into the other. Off the main thoroughfare, so to speak, were many smaller rooms and passages. These were catacombs on a vast scale, and on each side were beds contiguous. We passed Mr and Mrs Jones sitting up in bed, with six little heads of the six little Joneses all popping up in the most intriguing manner on either side of their parents. George knew scores of people and we stopped often to speak to his friends.

There was a soldier on leave standing there in uniform looking down on his wife and two daughters. Beyond was an elder brother nursing his small sister, who only now was beginning to recover from the shock of being bombed. I talked to an old couple sitting completely immobile on their bed. They seemed dazed and quite impervious to their surroundings. Then six young boys, all aged about twelve, and three of them most obviously Jews, rushed up. "ere, what about them boxing gloves, Mister?' they say to George, and to me, "ere Mister, come and see our bed,' so I go with them and sit on their bed and we talk amidst the noise and bustle - two old men on my left quietly playing draughts, babies crying, and two uniformed nurses (very clean and smart-looking) making their way slowly through the crowd. It is a scene of confusion and yet of order, of bustle and yet calmness, of gaiety amidst sadness.

A shelter marshal is in charge. 'How is a place like this controlled?' I say to George, 'Can anyone get in? Surely with the entrance so dark anyone could slip in.' George replied, 'Public opinion controls its use. It's full as you see. If any stranger came in and tried to take somebody's bed, it would be known at once. If you weren't with me, someone would have asked you by now what you were doing. These places develop a type of *esprit de corps*, a sort of family feeling. In an uncanny way everybody knows everybody else, at least by face.'

These people, or most of them, have been in Stayners or 61 Arch since the first big blitz began. At first they lay on the floor. It was muddy and became indescribably filthy. Gradually a floor and low wooden beds were provided. Blankets are available if necessary from the LCC. They are fumigated once a month. At first there were no proper sanitary arrangements. This is now all improved. Adequate lavatories, medical services and general control have all been provided. On the whole the people are clean and, as George says, 'We have little or no trouble about morals. Indeed, they are almost puritanical - a very definite code which frowns-on promiscuity. People don't see much wrong in a lad living with a girl, but if a baby is coming it must be marriage or complete ostracism.'

George has had some truly horrific experiences as, for instance, when an underground billiard room used as a shelter was hit and a fire started. The place was a shambles - scores were killed, either by HE or blast (a person killed by blast shows little sign of being hit - in this case one or two men playing billiards at the time stood propped up against the table , cue in hand but dead). Others caught fire and George had to play a hose on them to extinguish the flames. He takes all these experiences calmly, and I am bound to say showed few signs of strain. But I begged him to arrange to get quite away out of the area for a weekend once a month.

He tells me there are only four things which would cause trouble in Bermondsey among the people. (1) If, when their house had been destroyed by enemy action, they were forcibly removed from the area. They wish to stay where they are, in some other house even though that is likely to be hit before long. (2) If their children are compulsorily evacuated. Many parents are sensible enough to send their children away where they can get schooling; there are no schools open in Bermondsey. But many do not wish to be parted from their children, as is the case of the lads in 61 Arch who talked to us. They are running wild. (3) If there is a shortage of tea. They seem to drink tea on every occasion, and (4) if there is a shortage of beer. The pubs are crowded, and the people enjoy themselves, especially on a Saturday night.

Later that evening we went to a pub called 'The Raven and the Sun'. It was so full we could hardly force our way in. George introduced me to a whole crowd of his cronies. They were all drinking beer, and I stood drinks all round and had a gin and lime myself. The atmosphere was hot and when one had passed the blackout curtains, one found oneself in a brilliantly-lit room, with everyone packed like sardines talking at the top of their voices. There was singularly little hostility expressed towards the Germans. They seemed to take everything as it came. Shortage of beer would be a catastrophe, and I am sure lead to demands for a negotiated peace within a week.

George told me that there is not much talk about a new order or better economic conditions after the war, but what he does hear talked about is education. They have got hold of the idea that education is what counts. Better living conditions, more money, shorter hours - all these are useless unless they have education. Only then can they compete with the upper classes and make their own way. Give them education and all else will follow. As for the extremes of Fascism and Communism, George says there does not appear to be much. The Fascists pay 10/- to a working man to walk in one of their party processions, and 15/- if one works the gramophone on a lorry. The Communists pay only 3/- for marching.

George and I sat talking till nearly 1a.m. Then we crossed the road and entered the Abbey factories. The room already described was full of bunks, like a

Western Canadian bunk-house. There were sleeping human beings in all of them, except the two reserved for George and me near the door. We slipped off our boots and jackets and then got in under the blankets - supplied by the LCC. In the bunk above me was Mrs Lovat, in the bunk next to me on the same level was another woman, we were head to head. 'We all sleep in tomorrow,' whispered George, 'being Sunday and that means we get up about 7.30 and not 6 a.m.' I fell asleep almost at once, but woke several times during the night ; one or two people were restless and were sitting up or moving silently round the room. At 6.45 Mrs Lovat awoke, and there was some creaking in the bunk two feet above me. She slipped dexterously to the floor and went out, only to reappear a quarter of an hour later with a jug of tea and some mugs. She saw I was awake and tip-toed across with a mug of hot tea. "ere,' she said, "ave some tea.' I thanked her warmly and took it and felt in my trouser pocket for a penny. 'What yer doin'? No penny for guests.' I remonstrated but she would not take it. 'You 'ave another 'alf 'our at least, so lie down again.' I did so, and she tucked the rather dirty eiderdown round my neck, gave me a friendly pat and went off.

At 8 a.m. George and I went over to the OBC. I shaved and then we had breakfast. Several people were there who were homeless and using the place as a rest centre. One was a lad of 14 who was starting work the next morning at Peak Frean's biscuit factory: too young to start, and perhaps a blind alley job, I don't know. But anyhow, too young. Why should he not have better education? And of course the economic factor does come into the picture. If the parents did not need the money he would earn, he probably would get two years more schooling.

Later: My dear, I had got this far last night and then today after lunch (20 Feb) came a letter from George telling me that Stayner Street shelter (or Stayners as it is usually called) was 'smashed to ribbons' last night (i.e. Monday 17 Feb) The casualties were enormous - 300 mentioned in the papers, but certainly far more than that. 'After this morning, nothing worse can happen to Bermondsey,' adds George. This was the shelter where we spent so much time two nights before the catastrophe. It was there where we met the six lads who wanted the boxing gloves, the soldier and his wife and twins and the others. It is too appalling - 'this slaughter' - as George describes it quietly and without melodramatics. They must all be dead or maimed. George writes, 'Can you not get something done to get the government to provide proper shelters and forbid the use of the arches? After all, they are under the railway which is a military objective.' If only Euan Wallace was alive - as Chief Regional Commissioner for London, I could perhaps have done something.

On that very evening we had the Duke of Gloucester to dine and also Howard Kerr,[1] his equerry, and we had a jolly evening. I talked with them both, but how trivial it all seems when one thinks of the tragedy in those narrow squalid streets. Of course I wrote to George at once. The thought of those people done to death *en masse* is a continuous nightmare - a horrible background to all one does and thinks.

Geoffrey to E.C.F.B., 23 February   *Aberdeen*

We are now getting on an average one raid a day. The German planes come over, I suppose, from Norway, sometimes in a blizzard of snow; they seem to be quite indifferent to bad weather. Nineteen people were killed in the raid of the week before last, but as far as I know, none since. Nor have the bombers done any material damage either. Why they should have started their attacks on us again I can't think, unless it is in some way connected with the threat of invasion.

I can but hope that by mid-summer the situation will be clearer. The Germans can't delay doing something on a big scale soon. And we evidently have something big up our sleeve too, either with reference to meeting or forestalling the German blow. Why otherwise is Eden out in Egypt? And why are we turning over, as we evidently are, so large a proportion of our Merchant Service to military purposes with the consequence that the whole country is being warned to turn vegetarian this summer? What is Wavell doing in Libya, or perhaps in Greece? He is our greatest soldier since Wellington - perhaps even since Marlborough, and how he must be longing to practice his art on the Germans. He is said to be the one general they really fear.

March

Mrs Gardiner to E.C.F.B, 2 March   *Canterbury*

We have had a most successful War Weapons Week, with a really excellent exhibition of English and German weapons, model aeroplanes, posters

---

[1] Lt. Colonel Howard Kerr (1894-1977). Equerry to Duke of Gloucester, 1924-46; Comptroller, 1946-50. KCVO (1948).

drawn and invented by Canterbury school boys, etc. One interesting feature was the full equipment of a German escape boat for airmen brought down in the Channel (one broke loose and was captured off Dover). The equipment was complete, even down to sets of games (Halma, Backgammon, etc.) for the airmen to pass the time till picked up! The entrance fee was 6d, and I believe they made a lot of money. The City aimed at a quarter of a million, and I heard last night that the amount was well on to half a million.

Geoffrey to E.C.F.B., 2 March   *Aberdeen*

Perhaps the worst of the winter is over, as I am sure the war is - not, of course, the worst for the individual, but for the nation. We have now Hitler where we want him. He is playing to our tune, not we to his. Every day that passes he declines and we mount upwards. We are now in the position to call his bluff.

The Germans have so far thriven on bluff, as Mussolini did till he met someone who was at once prepared and eager to fight him. Then he collapsed instantly like a pack of cards or a punctured balloon. German victories up to date have all been won not owing to superior skill, but to either (1) lack of preparedness or (2) lack of the real will to fight them on the part of their foes. We have, of all their enemies alone hitherto, possessed the latter qualification for beating them and, even without the former, it has enabled us to beat them in defensive warfare. Now we have got the weapons to wage offensive war. I shall be therefore much surprised if the German armies, when they meet ours, do not collapse before them exactly as the Italians have done and for the same reasons. Materially our weapons will prove superior in quality to the German (and will be now no less numerous than theirs). In addition, our soldiers want to fight, and the German soldiers, like the Italians, at heart do not. They are sick of the war and want to go back to their homes. A Balkan war will eat up Hitler's armies, his aeroplanes, his tanks and his petrol. Even if, at terrible cost, he reached the Mediterranean, the sea would be no good to him since we command it.

There is a good deal of sheer bluff, I think, in the German boast about what their submarines are going to do. They do not possess a quarter of the number they say they have. They may, and probably will, temporarily have a measure of success at sea. However, not only are we well-prepared, but as soon as the USA Lend and Lease bill is passed, President Roosevelt will put at our disposal the 150 ships, and more, interned in American ports which would more than make up for any extra loss we incurred through the intensified submarine campaign.

Notes by E.C.F.B., 7 March

A Squadron Leader (an Old Boy) came to visit Felsted School at their quarters in Goodrich. Julian has written the following account of his conversation, told privately and not for publication, on 7 March.

'An OF Squadron Leader lunched here today. He is in charge of a station which deals with the Parachute Corps. The government asked his group a short time ago to organise a stunt against the enemy, and as a preliminary canter they decided to try out an evening attack on Boulogne. They chose 12 of the toughest guys among the Parachute Corps, and dropped them in Boulogne where they attacked a number of cafes in which were numerous German officers. Each was armed to the teeth with Tommy-guns, knives, knuckle-dusters and stones in socks. Secret information told of the cafes most frequented by German officers, and within half an hour the parachutists had killed about 200 of them. Then they made their way to a selected point near where a British submarine took them all off. The only casualty being one of them who left with them lying flat because he had to be knocked out by one of his own party to prevent him bringing back as a prisoner a barmaid from one of the cafes.

This was a preliminary to the attack on southern Italy. Six large troop-carrying planes flew from Mildenhall across France to Malta, where they were held up for three days because while there a bombing raid was made on the aerodrome by the Germans and one or two planes were injured. After the attack and the necessary repairs, they set out and dropped 36 parachutists at a spot about 40 miles inland from Naples with orders to destroy as much of the railway line and bridges as they could, especially as these were lines of communication for taking munitions and reinforcements down to Albania. Nineteen of them were taken prisoner, and it is hoped the remaining 17 have been taken off successfully. One of their jobs was to destroy two bridges which were thought to be made of concrete, but subsequent photographs showed both bridges intact, so apparently they had not sufficient explosives to complete this part of their job. But all reports say they did a great deal of damage elsewhere and threw the Italian authorities into great confusion.'

J.B.B. to E.C.F.B., 9 March   *H.Q. Canadian Forces*

I have seen Malcolm MacDonald three times this past week. First at a luncheon which Vincent Massey gave and where Geoffrey Dawson rushed up to know how I was getting on. I sat next to Donald Strathcona, who used to be Under Secretary of State for War, and is now working with General Willans.[1] I went to see him at the War Office not long ago on this welfare work. Then I saw Willingdon,[2] who looked extremely well and said the press had greatly exaggerated his illness and consequent return from South America. I had a good talk with Tommy Lascelles.

The second time I saw MacDonald was on Tuesday, when he and Vincent came here, and on Friday, at Vincent's particular request, I lunched at the Canadian Club at the Savoy. There was a great turnout and the PM was coming until the last moment. R.B. Bennett[3] was there. He must find it riling to see Vincent so much in the saddle. I found myself sitting opposite the Lord Chancellor, the Greek Ambassador (M. Simopoulos) and Kingsley Wood. Simon began talking about modern Greek to the Ambassador, and told me that often while on the woolsack he often rendered stanzas of English verse in Greek iambics.

On Tuesday afternoon I went to Ford Manor near East Grinstead to have tea and dinner with Guy Simonds,[4] who is Commandant of our Junior Staff College there. The House belonged to the Spender Clays[5] and the garden includes one of the finest collections of shrubs, heather, water plants and kindred things in England. Between tea and dinner Guy and I sat in two chairs rather like the King and Queen, with 30 young Canadian budding staff officers on either side of us. Before us was a huge sand table, and we listened to syndicates (teams of six) explain the incompetence of Gatacre at Stromberg, and the competent handling of Tel-el-Kebir by Wolseley.

---

[1]   Maj-Gen. Harry Willans, DSO, MC (1892-1943). Dir. Gen. Welfare and Education, War Office, 1940-42.

[2]   Rt. Hon Lord Willingdon (1886-1941). MP (Lib) Hastings, 1900-06, and Bodmin, 1906-10; Gov. Gen. of Canada, 1926-31; Viceroy and Gov. Gen. of India, 1931- 36; Lord Warden of Cinque Ports and Ambassador at large from 1936. Cr. Marquis (1936).

[3]   Richard Bedford Bennett (1870-1947). Canadian PM, 1930-5. Cr. Vt. (1941).

[4]   Guy Grenville Simonds (1903-74). Brig. GS Canadian Corps, 1941-42; Brig. GS 1st. Canadian Army, 1943; Div. Commander, 1943-44; Lt-Gen. and Corps Commander, 1944; CGS, Canadian Army, 1951-55. DSO (1943).

[5]   Rt. Hon. Lt-Col. Herbert Spender Clay (1875-1937). MP (Con) Tonbridge, 1910-37. PC (1929).

Geoffrey to E.C.F.B., 10 March   *Aberdeen*

The air raid sirens have this moment (3.50 p.m.) sounded. It is a glorious afternoon, hardly a cloud in the sky. So if raiders appear, which is on the whole unlikely, they will be easy to spot and will get a warm reception. No one here takes much notice of the alarms now. We had two yesterday, morning and afternoon respectively, and for weeks now have had one a day, if not rather more, on an average. But outside my study window the pavements of Queen's Road are full of young people strolling along, and nurses and perambulators, as if there were no such thing as hostile aeroplanes in existence. There goes the all clear siren five minutes after the alarm! What, I ask you, is the good of taking any notice of either? or of allowing them to have even a nuisance value?

Ralph to E.C.F.B., 10 March

I was on duty on Thursday night in the Home Guard, and in spite of very adverse conditions I had a very amusing time. There was an awful gale of rain and wind but fortunately I was on the first patrol from nine to midnight, consequently I was able to get a bit of sleep from midnight to 5 a.m., and when I got home about 5.30 of course went to sleep again. They are an awfully good crowd in my section, and we have most interesting talks.

The office was again untouched in the blitz the last two nights, nothing nearer than 200 yards away. The restaurant which caught a direct hit on Saturday night was the Café de Paris. I knew the Manager, and have often been there in peacetime. He was killed and I fear the casualties were heavy.

Mary to E.C.F.B., 15 March   *Chiddingstone*

I shall remember my twenty-third birthday as the one in which I entertained seven Bermondsey children to tea, ages varying from 3 - 12. Miss Thorne, the school mistress, had made me a cake, we had managed to save up enough fat for some buns, and I discovered that the Inn had some chocolate biscuits, so one wouldn't really have thought there was a war on. Jane brought all her 'evacs' to tea and I enjoyed it as much as they eventually did. We sang and danced and Daddy read aloud a Beatrix Potter book. When they left they asked when the Rector's birthday was so they could come to another party at the Rectory.

Every day seems to be crammed full with things to do. After I've fed the chickens and do household chores I aim to get to Stonewall by about 10.30. Jane Meade-Waldo and I always work till 12.30 and then go out for a walk. If we don't it means Jane gets no exercise, though of course I have plenty with the bike ride both ways. We lunch at about 1.10 - the Colonel likes to hear the news - and we are at it again at 1.45 till 4.15. Now that it's light after tea I nearly always go out again on my bike visiting parents of my Cubs or Brownies; taking wool for somebody to knit into socks for the Balloon Barrage crew adopted by the Brownies; collecting money for the village contribution to the Prisoners of War Parcels Fund, or having a rehearsal with the women with whom I am getting up a play. Nothing seems to be ready but I live in hope.

It is rather difficult to explain what fills our time at the office. You see we are doing two separate jobs. One is acting as secretaries to Lady Violet Astor[1] for the Kent Prisoners of War Parcels Fund, and the other is organising the National Flag Day for Kent which is on 5 June. We have been especially busy lately, as we have had to make up a circular letter, which has been cyclostyled, to be sent out to all British Red Cross and St John Ambulance officials. This has meant a lot of envelope-addressing, and we've written 180 personal letters to last year's organisers hoping they will help us again. At the same time as all this, we are getting permission from all the big towns and the Chief Constable to hold the flag day. So far Chatham has refused, but we are hoping our persuasive letter will take effect.

As I expect you have read in the papers, the prisoners' 'adoption' scheme has been stopped. As it was this personal touch which was so popular, we have to write long, careful letters explaining why contributions to a general fund will lead to much fairer distribution, and there will be no risk of a personally-addressed parcel missing the man when he is moved around, which apparently used to happen quite frequently. We get about £700 a month, and I think it may go up more.

Really our household with one maid and two land girls is working very well, though of course when we have visitors it makes extra work for Daddy and me. We spent an hour choosing hymns for the Day of Prayer on 23 March, and it's jolly difficult choosing hymns for such a mixed crowd. The padre of the Royal

---

[1] Lady Violet Astor (d. 1965). Wife of J.J. Astor, MP (Con) Dover, 1922-45 and Prop. of *The Times*, 1922-66. Cr. Lord Astor of Hever, 1958.

Sussex is coming to preach, and the soldiers billeted in the Castle, the Home Guard and local fire-watchers will be there for Matins. As I write there's a burr of 'Jerry' planes and occasional bumps, but nothing very close. We have been much quieter lately.

J.B.B. to E.C.F.B., 16 March   *H.Q. Canadian Forces*

Our little conference on Tuesday went well. The Corps Commander, Major-General Montague, Brigadier Page,[1] Major Humphreys, Brigadier Turner,[2] Chatwin and I were present. The General started off by saying that my memorandum deliberately dealt with mistakes and failures and the lessons to be learnt from them, and that I was preparing a further report for the end of April recording what had been achieved. We then proceeded to discuss my memorandum point by point, deciding that correspondence courses should go on indefinitely and 'directed reading', but that classes, unless they were being well-attended or had only recently been started should, as a general policy, close down at Easter. We then approved of a cable being sent to Canada saying that 12 civilians would be needed for staffing the educational policy. All my other recommendations were also approved. All this was most satisfactory, and I suppose one can feel one has had a good deal to do with the general policy which will govern the development of this effort for the next 18 months or so, that is unless Hitler upsets it all.

On Wednesday evening Colonel Donovan,[3] one of President Roosevelt's personal representatives who had visited all the crowned heads, prime ministers and governments of the Balkans during the past two months, dined in 'A' mess. I gather it is considered the Greeks may put up a pretty good show before their country is over-run by the Germans.

I forgot to mention that General Paget,[4] the father of Tony's friend young Julian Paget, lunched here on Tuesday and also dined on Wednesday. His son went to Caterham ITC and is now at an OCTU at Sandhurst. Paget had as his

---

[1] Brig. Lionel Page (1884-1944). Commanded Canadian Base Units in England, 1940-41: Maj-Gen. Comm. 4th. Canadian Division, 1941.
[2] Brig. Guy Turner (1889-1963). Dep. Adjutant and QMG, 1st. Canadian Division, 1941; Maj.-Gen. and Dep. Adjutant and QMG to First Canadian Army, 1942-45.
[3] Col. William 'Wild Bill' Donovan (1883-1959). Visited Europe as adviser to Pres. Roosevelt on many occasions, 1939-41.
[4] Gen. Bernard Paget, DSO, MC (1887-1961). C-in-C S.E. Command, 1941: C-in-C Home Forces, 1941-43; C-in-C- 21st. Army Group, 1943; C-in-C Middle East, 19444-6. KCB (1942).

ADC, at least I think he is an ADC, J.R.M. Butler.[1] He was an Intelligence Officer at GHQ in France and got away at Dunkirk all right.

On Friday we went to see a group of gunners training on Salisbury Plain. On the way out we stopped at Stonehenge for five minutes, while on the way back we made a longer stop at Salisbury. The Cathedral stood there unharmed, shining in the sun with that most lovely of all Closes with broad and spacious lawns all around it. I shall never forget the superb spectacle of that glorious spire, 404 feet high, brilliantly lit by the western sun, so that all the details of the carving stood out, soaring into the sky. We stood in the Cloisters, a scene of complete peace, and then after tea had a glorious run back. What an amazing sight England is these days - with its enormous camps of all kinds being erected by vast numbers of workmen. One wonders what will happen to all these very permanent-looking buildings after the war.

Did you see that Barbie Wallace may be adopted as Conservative candidate for Hornsey in Euan's place? Apparently it is not settled.[2]

Ralph to E.C.F.B., 18 March   *Lombard Street*

I have had quite an active time with the Home Guard lately. We had some good night operations on Friday night, as we manned our defence lines some four miles from the village. We were taken there in lorries and then did it all in the dark, at least it was not so dark as there was a good moon. Some regulars had a big do on so the roads were pretty crowded.

On Sunday afternoon we had a Company parade at Ashurst Park. We marched for two and a half miles there, then did some drill taken by a regular Sgt. Major, finished up with some bayonet fighting, and then marched back again. I skipped about like a young ram. Last night I didn't, as it was my night for duty and nothing exciting happened. We stopped a few people on the roads and put the fear of God into one young man. At a quarter to five we were woken up as a whole lot of cows had got out and were parading through the village. At five o' clock this morning I was driving cows, all very fresh, back to their farm. It is wonderful what the Home Guard tackle. I believe we could even assist at an *accouchement*.

---

[1] James Butler (1889-1975). Historian; Fellow of Trinity College Cambridge since 1913; MP (Ind) Cambridge Univ., 1922-23; historian of the Official Military Histories of War, 1939-45.
[2] It was not. Capt. Gammans was the Conservative candidate for the 28 May by-election which he won. He held the seat until his death in 1957.

Thomas Jones to E.C.F.B., 19 March   *Harlech*

Burgon seemed to me well and cheerful with his mind full of projects for the benefit of the Canadians. I have told Sybil Eaton, the chief promoter of CEMA (Council for the Encouragement of Music and the Arts), to get in touch with him so that she might take some concert parties to the troops. That was on Sunday. I little thought that on Friday she and I would again be together in Bristol Cathedral, saying good-bye to Sir Walford Davies.[1] We were both fast friends of his over many years and since CEMA began we had been greatly helped by his infectious enthusiasm and his passionate desire to give the multitude opportunities of hearing the best music and the best musicians. His dying thoughts were busy with this, and his last message sent to me on Monday was to say he would not be able to help me 'for a month' owing to his illness. Early on Tuesday morning he died.

J.B.B. to E.C.F.B., 23 March   *H.Q. Canadian Forces*

As you know I was in London all Wednesday and spent most of my time seeing people with regard to the development of music and art here. I am convinced that among the Canadians there is a demand for good music, good exhibitions of pictures and so forth. The War Artists' Exhibition now going the rounds in England, chiefly in industrial towns, was recently on view at Colchester and was visited by more Canadian soldiers than by any other troops. I slipped into the National Gallery for half an hour to see the War Artists' show there, and first rate it was. The Colchester show was partly drawn from this.

CEMA - Tom Jones's scheme and backed by the Pilgrim Trust and the Treasury - is responsible for most of the musical activity, and the art exhibitions are also being backed by this organisation. So I went to see the British Institute of Adult Education about getting them to come and visit the Canadians. I am meeting Sybil Eaton, the violinist, in Leatherhead tomorrow, and have asked Chatwin to come too.

On Friday evening Mr Bevin, Minister of Labour and National Service, arrived about 6.45 p.m., and I met him at the door, being responsible for asking him here. After dinner he spoke for over an hour and then answered questions.

---

[1] Sir (Henry) Walford Davies (1869-1941). Composer, conductor and educationalist; Master of the King's Music, 1937-41. KCVO (1937).

For the first 20 minutes of his speech he maintained that Labour had always been more alive to the dangers of Fascism and Communism than the government of the day, but he did not deal with Labour's attitude to rearmament.

Then he described what the Ministry was doing. Speaking of the so-called unemployables he told us that 154,000 of such people (many unemployed for five years or more) had been drafted into industry, and employers had been told they must keep them for eight months. With some pride Bevin told us that only 5% had proved impossible to employ. He said too that in 1914 about 12% of the women in the country were gainfully employed, whereas in 1940 at least 45% were. Just before he finished speaking I whispered to the General that he really must not call on me every time to say a few words, as he always said a word of thanks himself. All he did was to grin and say he intended on calling on me to speak and if I did not I should be court martialled. And he did call on me, and it gave me a good opening to explain to Mr Bevin, much to his and everybody else's amusement, that I stood there only because I did not want to be shot next morning.

Geoffrey to E.C.F.B., 30 March   *Aberdeen*

Tony has heard that he has been posted to none of the regiments he had put his name down for (The Buffs were his first choice) but to the South Staffords which neither he nor any of us know anything about. Their depot is at Lichfield and it is there that he has to report himself next Friday. It is annoying not to be able to join the regiment he asked for, but few can nowadays, as so long as he is posted to a battalion with a good CO and congenial fellow officers it doesn't really matter which the regiment is, for like all English regiments it is sure to have a fine record and tradition. The only connection of our family with Staffordshire, so far as I know, is that a Bickersteth was once Dean of Lichfield, and it was dear old Ninny's[1] home county. Tony looked very smart in his trench uniform and officer's great coat, and is lucky in having been issued with full service kit, e.g. sleeping bag, camp chair, etc., which at many OCTUs they are not.

Whoever was responsible for the Yugoslavian *coup d'état* must have been planning carefully for some months beforehand or it would not have come about so smoothly. Anyway, a blow has been struck for our cause which may well be decisive. Hitler's plans are completely upset, and not only has he lost his chance of

---

[1] 'Ninny' - Miss Peters - had been nanny to Geoffrey and his brothers.

conquering Greece, but also of bringing Japan in on his side. Last week was about our best week in the war so far, and may well have curtailed its length by months. I doubt if Italy can stick it out much longer, and Germany's subject countries are causing her more and more trouble. Norway is now under martial law while Holland is on the verge of revolt. Germany's army and air force are spread out, and she seems already to have yielded us control of the air over Northern France. Over the whole field of the war everything is most promising.[1]

Ralph to E.C.F.B., 31 March   *Lombard Street*

The happenings of the last week surely bring out the efficacy of the National Day of Prayer yesterday week. No one, not even a confirmed agnostic, can surely say that the Hand of Providence has been withheld from our cause bearing in mind what has occurred. The interesting point is that so many unlikely people in the City who did not really bother their heads with prayer or religion, seem to have at last tumbled to the idea that there might be something in it.

April

Hewlett Johnson to J.B.B., 2 April   *Canterbury*

I passed on to RSM Roberts what you said about returning in case of Blitz. I feel however that there will be no Blitz, at any rate in the near future: what has happened in the Balkans confirms this view. How good all this is.

I see the Home Guard regularly. The Major is as wheezy and as assiduous as ever. The canteen is a great boon and a social asset of incalculable value: men get to know one another. I have learned much there. The improvement in the men's bearing is most marked: they are workmanlike and their equipment appears to be first-rate. The preponderance of young men is a healthy feature. The congregations are very good and I get the most interesting talks with men and officers. There is considerable - and to me most interesting - ferment amongst them.

---

[1] The official war communiqué for the week reported British successes in East Africa, Greek successes against the Italians in Albania, and the replacement of a pro-German government in Yugoslavia with an all-party pro-British coalition.

My Russian book is having a remarkable career.[1] If I had arranged for royalties - which deliberately I did not - I should be rich: it has become a world's best seller - seven editions, despite no advertisement in England, and editions of 100,000 each quickly following one another in the USA. I was told that two of the largest presses in America are working incessantly to meet the demand. I have had to cable permission for translation into the Finnish, Greek, Hebrew and possibly Spanish languages. The epilogue, as to the political future of Russia, written seven months ago, is fully justified by events.

Ralph to E.C.F.B., 7 April   *Lombard Street*

Peter and I went on duty together on Friday night, and had an amusing time. We held up some drunks. Yesterday morning we had a longish do with some regular troops having a demonstration of the new 3" mortar. Very interesting but bitterly cold.

We had a small party for Peter's birthday last Saturday, and were very fortunate in the weather. We had eight children to tea and had a treasure hunt in the garden, and then their respective parents and a few grown ups, including some of the regular officers billeted in Groombridge, came in for a drink. I think we can look upon it as our Swan Song before the budget, as I feel quite certain that after the budget we shall have to cut down everything to the very minimum, and quite rightly so.

Notes by E.C.F.B., 9 April

Yesterday, as we had hoped, we took Massawa, the Red Sea port. This means we, and the Americans, will be able to send supplies round the Cape this way for our troops fighting in Egypt. This important victory is however clouded by the announcement that the Yugoslav army is no longer able to fight as a unit. They had very little time for preparation and were overwhelmed by the German hordes of mechanised troops. This exposed the flank of the Greek army, so the Germans pushed through and today took Salonika and totally destroyed the Yugoslav capital, Belgrade. King Peter and his government have however escaped to Egypt.

---

[1] Presumably *The Socialist Sixth of the World* (Gollancz, 1939), which ran into 22 editions and was translated into 24 languages.

Kay to E.C.F.B., 11 April   *Yaverland, I.O.W.*

We're now having very bad nights, but I hope it's only while there is a moon, and that things will quiet down again in a week or so. Poor Portsmouth has had several more bad raids, and is the scene of terrible destruction. Really there is not much more to destroy round the harbour. Any more bombs would be sheer waste.

The war seems to be going pretty badly but I've given up worrying about it now. It seems to me that it will last at least another 18 months, possibly longer. But the end is so distant one cannot foresee what conditions will be like.

Geoffrey to E.C.F.B., 13 April   *Aberdeen*

It is difficult to follow the Balkan war so far. But beyond the joining up of the Italians and the Germans, whose initial successes were to be expected, no decisive victories seem to have been won yet. It was unfortunate our losing those generals in Libya,[1] but no one is indispensable and our army there knows all the strings far better than the Germans. The bombing of Kiel was grand, and the Germans must know it to be the merest foretaste of what is to come. I believe that once our authority in the air is completely established, our victory will be assured and not long delayed.

Tony to E.C.F.B., 15 April   *I.T.C, Whittington Barracks, Lichfield*

I am not sorry now to be in the South Staffords. Here at the ITC I am in a good mess. It is comfortable enough and the food is good (excellent, considering the general food situation). I am leading a remarkably idle life - a subaltern in an ITC has really nothing to do. In fact except for the Adjutant and Company Commander the officers can hardly be said to be hard worked. The only real job I have had is Orderly Officer, and my turn for that duty unluckily fell on Easter Sunday. However, I found time to go to Matins at the Garrison Church. Present were the CO, the Adjutant and his wife, and one other officer beside myself. There was also an NCO and two privates. Since joining the army I have found continual cause to be ashamed of the C of E.

---

[1] These were, according to the official communiqué, Lieut.-Gen. Sir Richard O'Connor, Lieut.-Gen. Neame and Maj.-Gen. Gambier-Parry. These, along with some 2,000 troops taken prisoner during the withdrawal from El Agheila, were adjudged ' a remarkably small number'.

Perhaps one advantage of this mess is its cheapness. On average last month the cost of mess bills was 1/3d a day. The reason for this is, of course, the large numbers (there are over 50 actually feeding here) and neither the food, service, nor bills can be so cheap in Battalion or Company messes. Of the other officers I cannot say much at present. They are a pleasant crowd, but nothing very exciting.

I only hope that if an invasion is attempted this summer I am somewhere on the coast where the Germans attempt a landing.

Notes by E.C.F.B., 18 April

On the night of 16 -17 April there was a terrible raid on London. The destruction caused exceeding that of all other previous raids on London put together. Buildings totally or partially destroyed were Guy's Hospital, Chelsea Hospital for Pensioners, Christies, Selfridges and Maples. The following letters describe some of the damage:-

Miss Hewett to E.C.F.B., 17 April   *Richmond, Yorkshire*

I heard a sad thing yesterday. One nurse at the Newcastle Nursing Home has just come from the Middlesex Hospital in London where she was in charge of a maternity ward. The babies - 20 of them - were in a ward in their cots. They got a direct hit and none of them lived.

Monier to E.C.F.B., 17 April   *Chiddingstone*

I should not have liked to have been away from here last night. The German planes droned overhead from 9 p.m. till 4 a.m., quite continuously. There were no bombs near here, but I fear London had a bad time. Our windows shook all night from gunfire. I went out once in a tin hat. The sky was bright with flares and the glow to the north illuminated the whole countryside.

Ralph to E.C.F.B., 17 April   *Lombard Street*

It took me nearly four hours to come to the City this morning. The office is intact. It certainly was a pretty bad raid, but it is difficult to see the extent of the damage done despite the fact that I had to walk from St James's Park station to the City.

This is one of the times when we have to keep our peckers up, and however long it takes we must be determined to do Hitler and all his works in.

Personally I think the war is going to be a long one, I am afraid another two or three years. .

J.B.B. to E.C.F.B., 20 April   *H.Q. Canadian Corps*

I received a warm welcome on my return from Oxford today. Eric Duncannon (who had himself just returned from leave) told me about the raids on London. The damage round Piccadilly, Jermyn Street and Pall Mall is appalling. Many of the big houses looking on the Green Park below the Ritz are gutted. The middle part of Jermyn Street is flattened, as is the Burlington Arcade. Houses are hit in St James's Square, and the Royal Automobile Club is damaged. Scores of windows are broken in Pall Mall (including the Travellers') and the back of Fortnum and Mason is destroyed. There is also much damage in the Strand.

When one hears of such destruction in London and elsewhere, one wonders can it go on indefinitely, in view of our damage to Germany which is equally severe though spread over a wider area. Well, we can but wait and see.

Oxford is packed. The foreign element is considerable in addition to evacuees. There are many Czechs and Hungarians, and until recently there was a bevy of French admirals at the Randolph. There are many Jews to be seen, and a wide selection of foreign languages can be heard in the High. Shopping is a long and tedious business, and the permanent residents find standing in queues to get their provisions an irritating experience. Hotels are doing a roaring trade and one cannot get a room unless one books it a week or two before. Julian and I stayed at the Mitre where they did us well - a single room and three meals a day at a guinea each - very reasonable.

Ladders giving access to roofs, water, sand and other fire-fighting appliances are in evidence in every college. In most college gateways there is a special board to which is affixed a card giving times of the blackout. In some cases walls and arches are shored up against the blast. Colleges are still occupied for war purposes. For example, the Security Police HQ is at Oriel, there are WAAFs at Magdalen and St. John's is occupied by the Ministry of Food and goes by the name of 'Fish and Chips'.

On the night of the great London Blitz (16 April) I walked up the High to the Mitre about 11 p.m. The sky was criss-crossed with a dozen searchlights, and numerous Bren gun carriers hurtled by us in the blackout. I nearly ran into the great tank of water on the pavement in front of Queen's. Looking down the High past Magdalen I saw the sky lit up with the flashes of guns - a curious experience in Oxford.

Geoffrey to E.C.F.B., 20 April   *Aberdeen*

I begin tutoring again on Tuesday, and have a very busy term before me, more work than usual owing to my being a lecturer short. To go on with one's ordinary avocations up here where, despite constant air raid alerts, we are still really only on the extreme fringe of the war, seems like fiddling while London is (literally) burning. But the students must be taught and (this term) examined, however difficult it be - and it is very difficult - to keep one's mind off the war.

I think this summer will be like that of 1918, or more so. If by the end of July we have won or as good as won (as we shall have) the battle of the Atlantic, and hold up the Germans in Libya, thereby keeping the new route from the USA to Egypt and Turkey open, the crisis of the war will be over in our favour. I still trust the Turks. Russia is the uncertain quantity, for she is as unscrupulous as Germany and might yet join forces with her. That, I think, explains why Turkey has not yet come in on our side. She is suspicious of Russia and must wait until she sees which side Russia takes. Japan too would be ill-advised to trust her much. What, I think, would decide Russia finally to oppose Germany would be the USA's coming in on our side (which she will certainly do before the summer is out).

J.B.B. to E.C.F.B., 23 April   *H.Q. Canadian Corps*

The news about Yugoslavia and Greece is not very bright - but frankly I believe the more countries Hitler adds to his repertoire the more trouble he is storing up. I also think that the present experiences of these Balkan countries will show them the need for a common life which in the end may make for unity. I expect Turkey will go the same way as the rest. But somehow I am not unduly perturbed.

I have had some pretty busy days as, in addition to everything else, the library van has been in our area. This is our own Canadian van well-stocked with novels and books of various recreational kinds. It is making a round of the units and leaves 100 or more books in each battalion and 50 or so in small units. These form a little library and in about six weeks the van goes round again and changes the books.

I rang Barbie Wallace two nights ago. She was staying at the Dorchester. The poor woman has had endless misfortunes. The curtains and carpets from Lavington, which were being altered and cut-down to fit the smaller dimensions of Beechwood, were in Maples on the night of the Blitz and were entirely destroyed - representing a loss of £1,500 - and they were only to be at Maples that one night before being sent to the factory to be altered. Bad luck, isn't it? But Barbie was very calm and unruffled about it.

Geoffrey to E.C.F.B., 27 April   *Aberdeen*

With regard to invasion you have to remember that the extreme north of Scotland, which is flat and full of aerodromes, is that part of these islands where, if anywhere, it may be attempted with most likelihood of success. The whole of Scotland north of Inverness and the Caledonian Canal is for that reason an area closed to the public, and anyone living in it may pass out or back into it only with a passport. An old Glasgow student of mine who lives in Dingwall (just north of Inverness) came to see me yesterday on business, and told me that eleven German spies (probably landed from submarines) have been caught there in the last few weeks alone. He spotted one of them himself.

I heard yesterday that poor Professor Dixon[1] and his wife and daughter have been bombed-out of their London home. All his books are gone. It is hard lines on a man of 75 who had retired and was living on his pension. He possessed some beautiful pictures, furniture and a valuable library, none of which could be replaced even could he afford to do so. I heard too that Beresford,[2] of the University Grants Committee, whose literary work you may know, was killed by a bomb last year.

J.B.B. to E.C.F.B., 27 April   *H.Q. Canadin Corps*

I spent Thursday in London. The damage of the 16 April Blitz is very marked. In Tottenham Court Road and that part of London there is extensive damage. The Victoria League Hostel in Malet Street is knocked-out. This was full of soldiers at the time, including Canadians. The wounded ones were brought to

---

[1] Prof. William Macneile Dixon (1866-1946). Hon. Fellow of Trinity College Dublin, and Professor of English at Glasgow Univ., 1904-1935.
[2] John Beresford (1888-1940). Sec. of University Grants Cttee.; on Standing Commission on Museums and Galleries. CBE (1938).

the Beaver Club where Alice and Vincent Massey, who spent the night in the basement of the Dorchester, went at 5 a.m. when the all clear went, and helped to organise their treatment. The destruction I describe I saw personally. Ralph tells me that the City is in much the same state. So there it is, and yet people say the war will go on for years. I don't see it myself, because we are doing just as bad damage to them though on a more spread-out area.

I spent all morning talking to W.E.Williams[1] about possible art exhibitions. There is one called 'Living in Cities' of which there is a private view on 1 May which I hope to go to and arrange for them to get it to Aldershot later in the month.

It would be idle to suggest that the work here is not without its various difficulties. With the Australians doing such heroic things, you can imagine how terribly hard it is for the Canadians. The gloom in the mess at times is considerable, though we seldom talk about it. However, two nights ago we did, and everyone speculated what people were saying about the Canadians living comfortably in England. I am told that the local inhabitants rag the men about it sometimes - probably quite good-humouredly, but nonetheless it is hard for everybody. And the prospect for me personally of living on here for months and months in an environment which is kindly but unresponsive is not exhilarating. But then again, it would be worse to return to a truncated Hart House in Toronto. So it seems the better of two evils to be staying here, doesn't it?

Notes by E.C.F.B., 29 April

Our troops captured Dessie in Abyssinia this week, the last stronghold of the Italians, finding large stores of food, guns and ammunition. Many prisoners were taken.

On Sunday 27 April the Germans entered Athens and proudly raised the swastika on the Acropolis, setting up a Quisling government. They also completed their infamous destruction of Belgrade by looting the town. The Australian government announces that the evacuation of our forces from Greece has commenced and is being carried out satisfactorily. We sorely needed Winston Churchill's stirring words that same Sunday evening.

---

[1]   William Emrys Williams (1893-1977). Sec. British Inst. of Adult Education, 1934-40; Dir. Army Bureau of Current Affairs, 1941-45; a Director of Penguin Books, 1935-65. Kt (1955).

J.B.B. to E.C.F.B., 29 April   *H.Q. Canadian Forces*

I am just back from a day at Bordon where I think I can say the concert was in every way a great success. There was a varied programme organised by Sybil Eaton, and in the middle I made a little speech and talked about CEMA and the whole idea of holding such concerts. At the end the Brigadier expressed our thanks to the artists and said he had come afraid he would not understand one word of the programme, but he had in actual fact enjoyed every moment of it. It was quite evident the men did too. To get 400 soldiers together with hardly a cough and all obviously interested and appreciative was a great satisfaction - and I am bound to say a relief, as I had no idea what would happen.

I hope other concerts may come out of this - and I am to meet Jacques[1] who runs CEMA music in London before long. One cannot of course suggest that the programme was the highest kind of good music, but it was good and brilliantly performed. Everybody seemed very pleased, and Brigadier Page thanked me in his little speech at the end.

Memorandum by J.B.B., 30 April

The following quip was made about military intelligence - 'Never in the field of human conflict has so little been known by so many about so much'.

'Pug' Ismay, who has been present at every meeting of the Supreme Council, either with Chamberlain or Churchill, from the beginning of the war until the break up of France, gave me an account of the meeting at Bordeaux[2] when Churchill met the French politicians and soldiers during the fateful days of June. Reynaud had said to Churchill , 'Do you realise that when we lay down our arms the entire might of the German forces will be turned upon you?' Churchill stuck out his jaw and remarked, 'That contingency has occurred to me.' Reynaud said, 'What will you do?' Churchill, looking up at the ceiling remarked casually, 'Frankly, I have not given the matter much thought, but if the Boches attempt to cross the Channel I think I am safe in saying we shall drown as many as possible, and as for any who succeed in landing on our shores we shall knock them on the head.' Churchill also told Reynaud that whatever happens we shall go on for ever.

[1] (Thomas) Reginald Jacques (1894-1969). Dir. of Music, CEMA, 1940-45. Founder-member of Arts Council. CBE (1954).
[2] Probably a mistake as there were Churchill-Reynaud conferences at Briare and Tours but there is no record of meeting in Bordeaux.

Ismay is Chief of Staff to the Prime Minister in his capacity as Minister of Defence. The general idea of the Ministry of Defence is that it co-ordinates the functions of the Navy, Army and Air Force. But when 'Pug' recently discussed the exact duties of the Minister with the PM, Churchill observed, 'I think it would be best if we don't try to define my functions too precisely'.

Admiral Darlan[1] is an intensely ambitious man who wishes the Germans to win, in which case he thinks he is certain to play an important part in the public life of France, whereas if the British win he is obviously finished. He would willingly swing the French fleet which remains over to the Germans, but the officers and men of the fleet are not prepared to go that far. However, if we sink more of their navy they could fall in behind Darlan. It is for that reason we are careful about intercepting French convoys. We could hold them up and if necessary destroy the convoys, but we cannot at present run the risk of having the French fleet in the Mediterranean actively engaged against us. After all, 50% of the Italian fleet, even after the battle of Matapan, is extant. The Littorio class battleship damaged some months ago at Taranto is probably now in action again. Battleships are often very rapidly reconditioned. The *Barham*, which was badly damaged by shore batteries at Dakar, is now at sea again. There is the further point that there is a considerable body of American opinion which is very sensitive about food ships for the French civilian population and, again, we do not wish to antagonise the Americans.

At the present time Sir John Anderson is universally regarded as the only possible alternative successor to Churchill as Prime Minister.

I had a long talk with Patrick Duff who shortly leaves to become Deputy High Commissioner at Ottawa. The idea is that Malcolm MacDonald will travel extensively through the Dominion making speeches, while Patrick holds the fort at the office in Earnscliffe (the High Commissioner's official residence). Sheila MacDonald is going out with Patrick.

---

[1] Admiral François Darlan (1881-1942). Appointed Minister of the Navy, June 1940; named by Pétain as his successor. Surprised in Algiers by the Allied landing in November 1942, he changed sides only to be conveniently assassinated the next month.

May

Geoffrey to E.C.F.B., 4 May   *Aberdeen*

I bicycled up to Grandhome yesterday afternoon and had tea with Minna
Crombie out of doors in her revolving summer house. It was quite warm enough
to make this most enjoyable. The grounds were looking lovely and the long grass
for a wide area around was thick with wild daffodils. The pleasure of living in such
a beautiful place has, however - or so I think - been considerably diminished by the
almost incessant noise of the aeroplanes flying low over the tree tops from the
neighbouring aerodrome. It often makes conversation inaudible, and goes on by
night as well as by day. The aerodrome has never been bombed as, apparently, it is
very difficult to discover from the air.

Minna, who as you know is rather deaf, is not bothered by the sound of
the aeroplanes, and never hears the siren at all. Her London house, which costs
her £600 a year to keep going, though inhabited only by a caretaker, has had its
windows smashed, but has so far escaped other material damage. She has not been
there since the war began, and all her things, many of great value, are still in it.
She says that the looting of damaged house property has become a serious evil.
What is not destroyed by bombs is almost certain to be stolen. The ruins are now
so extensive that it is quite beyond the power of the police - much occupied with
more pressing duties - to guard them properly. It is this that she fears for her own
house if it should be only partially destroyed. Yet she cannot make up her mind to
remove its contents or even the valuable parts of them, as this could only be done
under personal supervision, which would involve her going up to Town for the
purpose, and this she does not want to do. So she is trusting to luck. Miss Sorley,
who reaches the age of 90 this week, continues - very wrongly I think - to defy the
Hun by remaining in residence in Onslow Square, only a few doors away from
Minna's house there.

Notes by E.C.F.B., 8 May

Our garrison in Tobruk are gallantly resisting every attack of the enemy
who find our occupation of that place a great thorn in their side. Our troops
counter-attack and take many prisoners, both German and Italian. Julian is
particularly interested in this battle as the Australian brigade fighting there is

commanded by a Brigadier called Morshead,[1] who was a master under him in St Peter's Adelaide, and also fought in the 1914-18 war. Last summer Julian met him when he went to visit the Australian troops on Salisbury Plain. He thought then what keen soldiers the Australians were.

Margaret Hopkins to E.C.F.B., 8 May   *Bridge*

Our gun at Bishopsbourne is called the Boche Buster (only we are not supposed to mention it). They have been firing it lately. It goes off with a loud bang, but they warn us when it is going off and tell us to open our windows. We feel quite safe with it to guard us.

Notes on the Liverpool Blitz sent to Miss Anderson by a relative, 9 May

We have had seven nights of bombing, as well as the bombing by day. It seems as if it will never cease. The noise of bombs and gunfire has been terrific and we all feel a bit worn out, for we have had no sleep. Sunday night our turn came, and the bomb dropped right in the middle of the lawn, blowing the back kitchen, coal shed, and wash-house, etc. sky-high. All the back part of the house is so badly cracked with the blast that it is no longer safe.

Liverpool is in a dreadful mess, and Bootle is worse. Blocks of shops and houses are down; it's just awful to see it all. There's no Lewis's and no Lord Street, and dozens of churches are destroyed. Whole streets are but piles of rubble. We are wondering when it will all end. The casualty list I am afraid is very high, but the people have been marvellous, to say nothing of the Home Guard and ARP wardens, who were at the house five minutes after we were hit, and who helped to put out the fires in the next-door house occupied by an old lady.

We were all sheltering under the stairs at the time the bomb dropped, and when it was all over and we looked at each other we were as black as sweeps. We had to laugh; so we had a wash, and a good cup of tea, and then felt more fit to tackle things again.

Ralph to Julian, 12 May   *Lombard Street*

Poor old London had a dickens of a do on Saturday night, by far and away the worst yet. The damage is colossal, it is no good beating about the bush.

---

[1] Brig., later Lieut.-Gen, Leslie Morshead, DSO (1889-1959). Comm. 9th. Australian Div., 1941; GOC New Guinea, 1944.

Fortunately this office only had about seven windows broken, but our fire-watchers are first class. One incendiary went down the lift shaft and burned the lift, but it was put out in no time, and another on the roof was dealt with just as promptly. Other concerns are not as efficient as ours, and often fire-watchers are non-existent. Consequently there is a complete burn-out with whole streets on both sides gone.

Our house in Hyde Park Square survived; it was surrounded by high explosives, leaving nine huge craters, but received no damage. Several houses in the Square, and all Clarendon Place and the house next door but one to us, have all gone.

Notes by E.C.F.B., 13 May

The Germans carried out the most serious raid on London that has yet taken place on 10 - 11 May, lasting from sunset to sunrise. The debating chamber and the lobby of the House of Commons were totally destroyed. The debris in the chamber was 50 ft. high, burying everything under it including the Speaker's chair. The House of Lords did not suffer much, but the lantern in the centre part of Westminster Abbey collapsed leaving a large hole. Incendiaries fell all over the roof, but the band of fire-watchers extinguished them quickly, others rushed into the nave and put out flaming beams as they fell. The main fabric is unhurt. Much damage was done to the historic roof of Westminster Hall, however. The Deanery, a perfect specimen of a Medieval house, was laid flat; as were the houses of most of the Canons in Dean's Yard. Canon Barry[1] had to preach at Reading on Sunday morning. He kept his engagement although he had been up all night helping to save the Abbey, and went in the only clothes he had left to him, an old flannel suit which he was wearing at the time.

It has been announced this morning that on the same night, Saturday 10 May, Rudolf Hess,[2] Hitler's former secretary and whom he had named as his successor after Göring, had escaped from Germany by himself in an aeroplane and had landed in Scotland at night, descending by parachute. This is mysterious, as Hitler had given out that he was missing and was suffering from hallucinations.

[1] Rt. Rev. [Frank] Russell Barry (1890-1976). Fellow of Balliol Coll. Oxford, 1928-33; Canon of Westminster and Rector of St. John's Smith Square, 1933-41; Bishop of Southwell, 1941-53.
[2] Rudolf Hess (1894-1987). One of the earliest Nazis; his flight in a new Me 110 to Scotland and his wish to meet the Duke of Hamilton has led to the persistence of as many conspiratorial theories as has the manner of his - eventual - death in Spandau prison.

Does this mean that Hitler wishes our government to believe that Hess is mad and not to credit any revelations that he may make? Or has he been sent by Hitler with peace overtures?

Memorandum by Julian on the visit of Wing Commander Barlow to Felsted School, 13 May   *Goodrich*

In addressing the boys, Wing Commander Barlow stressed the urgent need for more personnel in the RAF. He spoke of the objective before the country of securing at least 200,000 officers trained for air crew work by December of this year.

Later, he explained to me how well ahead of Germany we already were in the number of officers now training and in the number of machines being produced. But, he says, we must have two-and-a-half times as many of both as Germany if we are to gain the definite superiority. The Empire was producing an ever-increasing number of pilots, and this was most helpful. The training of observers overseas was not, however, proving so successful as had been expected, as visibility in the Dominions is so much better than that which is almost invariable in this country, so that observers trained for instance in Canada have to learn their job again when they get over to Northern Europe.

The Germans have made a brilliant advance in their aeroplane engines. Four or five years ago the British engineers said that in their opinion the best type of aeroplane engine could not be produced to function really satisfactorily without a high grade petrol. The Germans, knowing that in wartime they would be cut off from these supplies, experimented on producing engines which could depend only on a low-grade petrol, and have had the ingenuity to produce an engine which for its horse power has a better performance in climbing and in work at high altitudes than British machines. The Germans, he added, are brilliant in their use of 'ersatz' material for all kinds of purposes when they cannot get the real stuff.

Monier to E.C.F.B., 14 May   *Chiddingstone*

I feel we must not set too much store on this flight of Rudolf Hess from Germany. It must take him some time to stabilise his ideas - and he has clearly fled for his life. The attack on the Abbey and Houses of Parliament are, to me, a more significant sign of Hitler's madness and that things are not going well for him.

J.B.B. to E.C.F.B., 14 May   *H.Q. Canadian Corps*

Vincent and Alice Massey have word through private channels that their son Lionel is wounded in the leg. They think he is in a general hospital in Athens which was left there entire when the British troops were evacuated. But they don't know anything for certain, and it is very trying not hearing anything official nor being likely to for weeks. Naturally they are anxious to know whether his wounds are serious or not.

Today we had a small conference at which the Corps Commander presided. We had a number of problems to discuss - pensions for civilian workers in the army in the field, music and art, personnel and the weekly cabled report to Canada. Under 'personnel' my own position was discussed - or rather McNaughton merely announced that in a letter Dr Cody had stated the governors of the University of Toronto were prepared to extend my leave for as long as he (the GOC) wished for my services, and that he (the GOC) wished me to stay on. So that, I suppose, is settled, and I think it is for the best.

Geoffrey to E.C.F.B., 18 May   *Aberdeen*

In Rudolf Hess we now have under lock and key in this country one of the foulest criminals of the innermost Nazi gang, and I hope we shall treat him accordingly, and not as if he were a film star. His mere presence here must worry Hitler terribly, for there is none living to whom the latter has so freely unbosomed his own black heart. We have men in this country who can be trusted to make the utmost possible use of him. And he certainly ought to be, or ought to be made to be, of the utmost possible use. Nor need we have any scruples as to the methods by which we bring pressure to bear on him to compel him, willy-nilly, to serve our cause. Personally, I would put him under the guard of the Poles, Jewish Poles for preference, and give them *carte blanche* in their treatment of him, on the one proviso that they do not actually torture him to death. We could return him to Germany after the war, or what remains of him, like an orange out of which the last drop of juice has been squeezed.

His flight must serve to spur Hitler to even greater haste. During the coming weeks we must expect the full fury of the German offensive. If, for the next three or four months we can hold him - for we do not need to beat him - then I think there is a good chance of Germany collapsing by internal disintegration before the winter is well under way. For in Hess's flight I see the first overt symptom of the maggot gnawing away at the core of the apple. Even if Russia joins in with Germany, it won't help Germany much in the longer term. America will deal with Japan. As for France, I doubt whether French armies could be trusted to fight us in North Africa or the Near East, whatever their generals might wish, though it would be awkward to have Bizerta in German hands. But I hope and believe we have check-mated the Germans in Syria. This summer will stretch us to the utmost, especially in the Mediterranean, for I believe the worst of the battle of the Atlantic is over, serious as the strain there still is.

I am very busy now with exams, and shall be until the end of June.

J.B.B. to E.C.F.B., 18 May   *H.Q. Canadian Forces*

On Friday Mr J.G. Winant,[1] the American ambassador, came to lunch, with him was General Lee,[2] the military attaché. I sat near them for the meal and he told us how the unions in America were behind Britain in this struggle if for no other reason than the way Hitler has treated the Trade Unions in Germany. He also said that the Hess episode had caused more excitement in the USA than any other single event since the war began. He himself thinks Hess is perfectly sane and is completely disillusioned with National Socialism. I suggested that whether Hess did or did not give us valuable information, it would be most undesirable for the Prime Minister to make any statement about it, and he agreed.

General Lee is the most English-looking American I have ever seen. He is the typical English colonel, with a large moustache, goes dressed in rough tweeds, and is full of fun. He seemed to assume as a matter of course that the Americans would come in before long. At tea, General McNaughton asked me to talk with Lee about our educational work here because the same kind of programme would be very useful 'when they come over'. This event, he seems to assume, will happen as a matter of course.

On Thursday a very different person came to lunch, namely Lord Melchett.[3] He looks the typical Jew - fat and sleek and unattractive. I sat next to Colonel Blacker[4] who lives at Coates Castle near Lavington. He is one of those

---

[1] John Gilbert Winant (1889-1947). US Ambassador in London, 1941-43.
[2] Probably Brig-Gen. John C H Lee (1897-1958). Became Eisenhower's logistics chief (1942).
[3] Henry Mond, 2nd. Baron Melchett (1898-1949). MP (Lib) Isle of Ely, 1923-24, and (Con) Toxteth, 1929-30; Dep Chmn. ICI, 1940-47.
[4] (Latham Valentine) Stewart Blacker (1887-1964). Soldier, inventor and explorer. Author of *First Over Everest* (1933).

Englishmen who has served in the army, regular and irregular, all over the world. He also flew over Everest with Hamilton - or Clydesdale as he then was - and is now an expert on gun equipment. I have seen his 'Bombard' in operation at the Home Guard technical school near here.[1]

John to E.C.F.B., 20 May   *Chiddingstone*

I expect you know already that I got my commission in The Buffs. Needless to say I am tremendously pleased. I go back to Canterbury on Friday, but for how long depends entirely on vacancies in the various battalions - of which there are eleven. Last Friday I met Father at Humphreys and Crook in the Haymarket where I had my uniform made, and sallied forth an hour later as a very newly-hatched second lieutenant. I went straight on to Rugby where I spent a very happy twenty- four hours. There were numerous air raid alarms while I was there, but none of these came to anything.

Notes by E.C.F.B., 21 May   *Goodrich*

On Sunday and Monday nights, 18 and 19 May, the RAF observed great concentration of German aeroplanes and air transports on aerodromes in the south of Greece in obvious preparation for the invasion of Crete, and bombed them heavily. At 4 a.m. on Tuesday, the air-borne invasion began. The Germans landed 4,500 soldiers by means of air transports and gliders, accompanied by aeroplanes carrying guns and ammunition. The men wore battle-dress, some British, some New Zealand and some Greek, but as Mr Churchill comically announced in the House, they were speedily accounted for. Later on Tuesday, and today, 3,000 more troops were landed by air, protected by dive bombers, the fighting increasing in intensity. Unfortunately, there being no aerodromes in the country, we could not keep any of our airforce on the island.

J.B.B. to E.C.F.B., 21 May   *H.Q. Canadian Forces*

I have heard from my old platoon commander at Canterbury that the Home Guard were 'at home' to the public last Monday week (their first

---

[1] Wing Co. Douglas Douglas Hamilton (1903-73). Styled Lord Clydesdale, MP (Con) E. Renfrewshire, 1930-40; 14th. Duke of Hamilton and 11th. Duke of Brandon (1940). PC (1940). J.B.B. was probably unaware at this time that Hess, claiming to have met Clydesdale during the 1936 Olympics in Berlin, made his flight to Scotland to see him in May 1941.

anniversary) and gave demonstrations. They marched through the streets on Tuesday - 350 strong - and looked very smart, I hear, ending up with a service on the Green. They have any amount of equipment now, MG's, Tommy guns, light automatic rifles, and find there is not enough time to practise.

Yes, the General Thorne who has got the Scottish Command is 'Bulgie', Nancy Dalrymple's brother. It's nice for her to have him so much nearer than Kent. Montgomery,[1] who goes to Tunbridge Wells succeeding Thorne, is a great fire-eater. He makes all his staff officers go for long runs - and if it knocks the older ones out says, 'Better to find that you're too old now than in the middle of a battle!'

Notes by E.C.F.B., 24,26 and 29 May

One has the feeling that this invasion of Crete is a rehearsal of the tactics Germany wishes to employ in an invasion of England. At the same time the securing of the island of Crete is a matter of great importance to Hitler in the eastern Mediterranean and the prevention of which is of still more importance to us. Our anti-aircraft guns brought down 16 air transports, and though serious at present, the situation seems well in hand.

All yesterday (25 May) the Germans were flooding Crete with more air-borne soldiers. It is hoped they may still be held by our troops, but it became necessary for the King of the Hellenes regretfully to leave Crete - as his house was threatened. He spent the previous night in the hills accompanied by his Prime Minister and staff, then got away on a waiting ship. There seems to be no respite in the struggle for Crete, but our long-range fighters and bombers are assisting, and our guns have brought down 250 aircraft.

Our fleet was engaged with the enemy in the North Atlantic yesterday. We have damaged the *Bismarck*, a battleship. The enemy, however, has sunk the *Hood* with all on board (42,000 tons) by an aerial torpedo.[2] Our fleet is still in pursuit of the enemy. There is so much that is grim and anxious about our present situation in the war.

---

[1] Bernard Law Montgomery, 1st. Vt. Montgomery of Alamein (1887-1976). Maj-Gen., 1938, Lt-Gen., 1942, Field- Marshal, 1944; GOC 12 Corps, 1941, Comdr. SE Command, 1942; Comdr. 8th. Army, 1942-44 and 21st. Army Group, 1944-45; Dep. Allied Supreme Comdr. Europe, 1950-58. KG (1946). Cr. Vt. (1946).
[2] Actually the *Hood* was sunk by the *Bismarck* on 24 May, and by gunfire not 'aerial torpedo'. There were three survivors from the ship's company of some 1,300 men.

On Tuesday 27 May, at 11 o'clock, the news came that we had sunk the *Bismarck*, after a pursuit of over 1,700 miles, in which units of our fleet, aeroplanes and seaplanes were all engaged. So the sinking of the *Hood* has been avenged.

Monier to E.C.F.B., 27 May   *Chiddingstone*

Last night we received a cable from Edward. He is being posted to Wau, a place about 200 miles west and north of Juba. I fear it is not a very healthy spot as it is on a river and I do not think so high as Torit. I think it is in the middle of the Dinka country. He has had malaria again, I am sorry to say. Of course he needs home or cool climate leave. But that cannot be got. Still he has had every attention when ill, and I gather this has not been a bad bout.

Whatever the issue in Crete, I believe we shall win. I am sure this attack has and will cost the enemy so heavily that an attack on England must be postponed.

J.B.B. to E.C.F.B., 28 May   *H.Q. Canadian Forces*

Last weekend I went up to London and met George Grant again at the Travellers', now operating after months of inactivity. The place has been damaged but is in many respects just the same, except for the library being filled with tables and a few maids supplementing the men servants of whom those left seem so old as hardly to be able to get about at all.

George and I walked in St. James's Park and sat on the grass and talked. Then we had a somewhat meagre tea at the Travellers'. I had to order more for him. Then we taxied across Waterloo Bridge and got out the other side and walked. Much sign of Blitz immediately. The Old Vic, for instance, shattered - whole streets with almost every house gutted. In many places the roads were impassable and we climbed over rubble and helped women with perambulators and babies, all laughing at the strange predicament. There has been some looting, George tells me. Recently, 17 of the Southwark ARP officials were arrested. Professional thieves employ children of 14 and 15 to steal for them. A few days ago a man caught looting was left unconscious in George's section as a result of the way he was handled by the infuriated people. The area round the Elephant and Castle is a terrible mess. That the Elephant should go means almost more to Bermondsey than Westminster Abbey.

Everyone was most welcoming. Mr Hobson of the 'Raven and the Sun' was doing a more roaring trade than ever because so many pubs are out of action. And leaving the slummy houses to enter the brightly lit pub with its noise and laughter and fun, clinking of glasses and gay shining faces, one could understand what pub life means to these people.

George and I then made a tour of the shelters. First Miller's, which I had seen last time. We all sat down for a chat and old Mr Burke was lying on his bunk the other side of the gangway, no longer, I am glad to say, 'troubled with the wind,' but just going to sleep. Then from the other end of the shelter the curate of St George's Bermondsey read prayers. These consisted of the Lord's Prayer, 'Lighten Our Darkness' and the Blessing. Then the curate announced that the next day there would be a memorial service for Mr Henley, the much respected late Mayor, who had been killed the previous Saturday while walking from one shelter to another. Mrs Henley has been nobly carrying on with War Weapons Week.

We then visited George's post and found the lads on duty - some playing cards, some chatting round the electric stove - ridiculously cold still for late May. We had a long talk about Canada and about fire-fighting. The real trouble with the new incendiaries is that they jump - as often as six times - and five or six feet each time, and then blast. It is curious how that word, blast, which one hardly heard 18 months ago, figures so much in everyday life now. The effect on people seems to show itself in what look exactly like bruises which emerge sometimes hours, but sometimes a day or two after exposure.

Finally we returned to Abbey Factory shelter, and I occupied the same bunk as I had last time. Mrs Lovatt, who I should have said fed us with sausage and chips earlier in the evening, was there. Talking with George, he told me that among the youth of Bermondsey there is tremendous admiration for Hitler as the wielder of successful power - ruthless power, which gets results. There is no love for National Socialism, nor any desire to see it in England, but just respect and admiration for power - for the big leader - the king of thugs. What a chance for the right kind of leader. I took off my jacket and boots, and slipped into the blanket. The pillow was very dirty. Next morning we got up at 7.30.

On Friday night Noël Coward[1] came down to dine with us in 'A' Mess. He gladly accepted Eric Duncannon's invitation to sing, and certainly provided the

---

[1] Noël Pierce Coward (1899-1973). Actor, playwright, composer, lyricist, producer and author. Kt (1970).

most amusing evening. After dinner he went off for half an hour and entertained about 200 men in the YMCA hut at Leatherhead, and returned to our mess by 9.45 where some 50 officers had by then gathered. He sat down at the piano and sang old favourites and new songs off and on for two hours. In some ways Noël Coward is a genius, a sort of portent of the age combining jazz, modernity, realism, humour, wistfulness and seriousness; almost a philosophy of life. He does not really play the piano well. He does not possess really a good voice. But he put his stuff across because he has that indefinable thing, personality.

The sinking of *HMS Hood* and then the sinking of the *Bismarck* has made for a tragic but also triumphant few days. Crete, I should say, cannot hold out much longer. Tides and rough weather have been against us. What an amazing war it is.

June

Notes by E.C.F.B., 1 June, Whit Sunday

Received bad news today, as it is announced our troops have been withdrawn from Crete during the last few days. By today our Navy have evacuated 15,000 men with great difficulty under hourly bombing and machine gunning.[1] Our troops could have contended with the parachute and sea-borne troops, had not the enemy had complete command of the air. On the other hand we have signed an armistice with Iraq, have entered Baghdad and settled the revolution, though it seems a poor exchange for our loss of Crete.

Winston Churchill, in return for a broadcast from the Canadian Prime Minister, broadcast today. It troubled us to hear his voice, which sounded so weary and worn out.

Geoffrey to E.C.F.B., 1 June   *Aberdeen*

Tony is now in Gt. Yarmouth. He says he quite likes the place, and his job is to command a mortar platoon. Fairly shortly the regiment, he thinks, will be taking part in grand-scale manoeuvres under war conditions, and these may continue for two months.

---

[1] In addition to heavy naval losses, some 12,000 British and Commonwealth troops were left behind in Crete.

The war situation seems to me to be taking on a far more promising aspect, and the Crete affair (though it has itself gone against us and was, or is, a remarkable feat of arms on the part of the Germans) in my opinion makes the attempted invasion of these islands, even of Ireland, much less likely. Our stubborn and protracted resistance in Crete has upset their timetable completely. We have definitely check-mated them in Iraq and are now, I fancy, in a position to do so whenever we choose in Syria. In Libya, too, we shall soon be much more favourably situated.

Nor is that all. Dissension in German headquarters is certainly developing. The internal revolution which brought about the collapse of Germany in the last war will repeat itself. German submarine officers (and men) may refuse to sail as too many of their craft are being sunk. The Navy, and possibly the army too, hate the Gestapo, which in any case is functioning with greater and greater difficulty over the vast region over which they have to operate. Moreover, the Gestapo itself is honeycombed with traitors and self-seekers. Hess did not escape to this country for nothing.

I have always said, and I hold to it, that Germany's collapse will come like a thief in the night - her Day of Judgment. And it will be Hell for Germany, not because we shall slaughter her then, but because they will turn and rend themselves - a seething mass, a disillusioned hate-consumed rabble, each man's hand against his neighbour, maddened, half-starved, desperate. But whatever the suffering of the Germans it won't amount to a tithe of what they have brought on Europe by their simply monstrous iniquity. Hitler will be murdered or, to escape that fate, will commit suicide.

I see the Kaiser is dying.[1] I don't think Hitler will long survive him. Hell has long been crying out for them both.

p.s. from Jean

Our neighbour Mrs Crump was shopping the other day in a small grocer's shop where she was not a usual customer, and she happened to be wearing her very oldest coat and hat. When she had finished her purchases the man leaned over the counter and whispered confidentially, 'Would you like an onion? We have got some and keep them to give to the poor.' Moral, go shopping in your oldest clothes!

---

[1] Wilhelm II, ex-Kaiser of Germany and King of Prussia died on 4 June 1941 at Doorn, Holland, where he had lived in exile after his abdication in November 1918.

Mrs Gardiner to E.C.F.B., 1 June   *Canterbury*

I have a new job, a Polish officer who comes two or three evenings a week to learn English. I was asked to take him on, Mr Mieczystar Powlowski (such names!) which I was very glad to do. He was a teacher of Slav languages in the University of Cracow before the war, and had written numerous books. He is a nice little man of about 45, and has left a wife and twelve-year old son in Cracow. But after two years' complete silence he does not know if they are living or dead - poor thing. His zest to learn English is immense, and he gets on rapidly as far as reading it goes, but he is a poor performer at speaking. Of course, his own tongue is so utterly different from ours. He knows a little German, and so do I, and 'speaks Latin', so we manage to get on somehow. The Poles are all at Barton Court, not too comfortable I fancy. We all find our pupils like to prolong the lessons as long as possible, and fill in one or two evenings away from their billet.

John to E.C.F.B., 3 June   *Abbots Barton Hotel, Canterbury*

Uncle Burgon gave me a grand weekend. Molly was her incomparable self, and I thought the relationship between officers and men in the Canadian forces was clearly illustrated by Uncle Burgon and Sanders, his driver.

'Could you call me at half past seven in the morning?' asked Uncle Burgon on Friday night as we were going out. 'Well,' says Sanders, heaving himself slowly out of his chair, 'I think I can do that, but why not have a little lie-in as it's Sunday?' A tiny thing, you'll say, but that little incident would never occur in the British army. The Canadians talk to each other as equals, and probably consider themselves such. Partly owing to that that they are an untidy, and apparently ill-disciplined lot; but again owing to that easy comradeship, they are among the finest fighters in the world, and it is a thousand pities that they have been cooped up in Surrey for 18 months, getting, very naturally, more and more fed up.

Uncle Burgon took me with him to Dover where, at the Police station and the Castle, we visited the ARP control rooms. At the Castle observation post, which is manned night and day of course, they can see the flashes of the German guns, and are able to give a 70 second warning between the flash of the gun and the landing of the shell. In this way the men in the control room have to sit there waiting for the crump of the shell for what must be a very long minute!

We then walked down the High Street, which was seething with people, and is comparatively undamaged by shell and bomb. The sea front is, however, fairly knocked about, and of course was comparatively deserted. The big hotels are pitted with splinters, and not a building has glass in its windows - just grey sheeting nailed to the frames. Out in the harbour lie barges to which some of the barrage balloons are moored. The sea was looking innocently blue and friendly, and it was fantastic to think of the Germans barely 20 miles away. Perhaps Dover should have been denuded of everyone who was not absolutely bound to be there; but as Bishop Rose was saying to me last night, there is something tremendously inspiring about the friendliness arising from common danger which unites the small community, as it does in perhaps no other town in quite the same way.

We are of course extremely comfortable billeted in this hotel. 'George' Howe has decided that the 30 or so subalterns in the depot ought to take their share in fire-watching duties; so once in 10 days each of us is nabbed for fire patrol. All five of us who are down here got our turn last night, and including the rounds on patrol and the walks to and from the hotel (we come back for lunch every day) I think I've walked over 10 miles since midnight; so we get our modicum of exercise, which should keep us fit for the constant training and marches we shall get when posted to a battalion. At the moment all the battalions are full, and I may be here some weeks yet.

J.B.B. to E.C.F.B., 4 June   *H.Q. Canadian Forces*

John will have given you an account of our trip to Dover, so I won't - except to say that we saw the most up-to-date fire engine I have ever dreamt of.

We got back to Canterbury for tea and then I went straight down to see the Dean, having arranged with him that morning to call in at 5.15. He was just the same, and there is something I like about him in spite of his vanity and muddle-headedness and obvious gullibleness. His book, of which he gave me a copy, is having a phenomenal success, he tells me, in the USA, where it sells for 50 cents - a paper-bound affair. The English edition is stiff binding. He regretted that he had not been allowed to go to America at Easter-time to address a large conference of all the leftish societies. Walter Monckton of the Ministry of Information, he says, wished him to go on the grounds that it was of value to send a leftist who was entirely in favour of fighting Germany to the finish, but he was over-ruled. He certainly does want to fight Germany, but friendship with Russia is an equally important plank in his platform. He says that peace is her one desire, but that if Germany attempts to attack Russia and invade the Ukraine, Russia will give a magnificent account of herself, having more first-line aeroplanes than any other nation. He adds that if only we would make really friendly advances to Russia she would respond, whereas we do exactly the opposite; our present growing collaboration with the USA being seen as based on the assumption that we draw away from Russia.

The People's Convention, which has in a sense taken over the Left Book Club and the leftist organisations in the country, has been badly hit by the suppression a few months ago of its official organ, the *Daily Worker*.[1] It has, to my mind, a somewhat naïve programme, but apparently the movement has many adherents, all of whom regard Bevin and official Labour as Yes-men who have sold their souls to business interests. It began with Pritt's[2] big meeting in January 1941, and it caused a big break with Gollancz[3] and the Left Book Club, which the Dean says is now a spent force. Pollitt[4] is a keen supporter, though apparently Maxton[5] does not belong to it.

The Dean tells me he was recently asked to address 120 medical students in London who were graduating. He spoke about Russia, compulsory medical insurance and other plans in the People's Convention programme, and received the keenest attention and enthusiastic applause. Everywhere he goes he is tremendously impressed with the profound desire for radical change which he finds in soldiers and civilians alike.

After breakfast and Matins next day, I proceeded to the Mint Yard where some 200 of the Home Guard paraded for inspection by the GOC 44th. Division, General Mason McFarlane.[6] He spoke to every man on parade - an unheard of thing - and it took so long that I had to leave for my talk with the Archbishop at

[1] Using his powers under Defence Regulation 2D, Herbert Morrison, the Home Secretary and Minister of Home Security, suppressed publication of the *Daily Worker* on 21 January 1941. The ban lasted over the next 18 months.
[2] Denis Nowell Pritt (1887-1972). QC (1929): MP (Lab, later Ind. Lab) N. Hammersmith, 1935-50.
[3] Victor Gollancz (1893-1967). Left-wing publicist and publisher. Kt (1965).
[4] Harry Pollitt (1890-1960). Secretary CPGB, 1929-56; Chm. CPGB, 1956-58.
[5] James Maxton (1885-1946). MP Glasgow Bridgeton, 1922-46 (Lab to 1931, then ILP); Chm., ILP, 1926-31, 31-39.
[6] Maj-Gen. (Frank) Noel Mason-Macfarlane, DSO, MC (1889-1953). DMI with BEF in France, 1939-40; Head of British Mil. Mission to Moscow, 1941-42; Gov. and C-in-C, Gibraltar, 1942-44. MP (Lab) N. Paddington, 1945-46. Lieut-Gen. and KCB (1942).

the Old Palace before the end. He was extremely well, I thought, and in the circumstances cheerful. For as you probably know he was at Lambeth on the night of 10 May when the worst damage of all was done to the Palace. He himself stood there to see the Chapel burning, the Library badly damaged, and the Lollards' Tower hit. He observed to me, 'I was not conscious of any physical discomfort or any particular fear, only a feeling of complete helplessness. No fire engines were in when we telephoned, they were all out at other fires.' He said that the sight of the Deanery at Westminster was heart-rending.

I cannot say Cosmo looked any older, but by some he was described as a man who has been overwhelmed by the Flood, as indeed is the Church over which he presides. There were many ominous cracks in the fabric of the Church before the deluge came, and it has not been able to stand. What will happen to the old Church of England, I wonder? Personally, I hope that William Temple will be called to the helm before long. But some say it will be Williams of Durham.[1] I think Temple is the only hope.

Geoffrey to E.C.F.B., 8 June   *Aberdeen*

I see in today's paper that old Charterhouse has been completely destroyed by fire in one of the air attacks on London, all of it except the Gate House and Chapel. It makes me furious. It was one of the most beautiful groups of old Tudor buildings in the country. I should like to see Hitler (and his gang) live to a great old age, and have crammed into every second of it the maximum amount of physical and mental pain which the utmost ingenuity of man could invent in the way of the most exquisite torture. And if I could have the pleasure of seeing him suffer, I should kick him on the head, as Dante did to a particularly black-hearted villain whom he encountered in the lowest pit of Hell, excusing himself for the insult on the grounds that 'it was courtesy to be rude to such a devil as he'. We have at least got the dastardly Hess under lock and key. Let us keep him there till he dies. Evil always destroys itself, and modern Germany is evil. There is no reason that I can see why she should prove an exception to this universal moral law.

---

[1] Rt. Rev. Alwyn Terrell Petre Williams (1888-1968). Fellow of All Souls Oxford, 1911-18; Headmaster of Winchester College, 1924-34; Dean of Christ Church Oxford, 1934-39; Bishop of Durham, 1939-52; Bishop of Winchester, 1952-61.

Mary to E.C.F.B., 9 June   *Chiddingstone*

It was a great pity it was so wet for our Flag Day and I think it will affect the final total. All the same, Lady Violet, Jane and I had a very successful tour, if rather a damp one! Jane and I had mapped-out the route and told the people the approximate times, and we kept to the schedule well. It was an awful strain being polite to people all day, but it was interesting meeting the people with whom we have corresponded so much, which makes it so much easier to write letters now. The organisers varied from Mayors and Mayoresses to plain Mrs X living in a tiny villa in Snodland, but they were all dead keen to beat last year's total. The results we have so far received have all got more than last October, and a few even more than last June.

At Chatham we were ushered into the room where the Mayor and Mayoress and lots of helpers were busily counting money. After much shaking of hands the Mayor took us up to the Parlour where, in asides to Jane and me, he tried to find out if Lady Violet would like some sherry. We both swore she never drank it, knowing that if we embarked on drinks we should get hopelessly late for our next call!

Lady Violet is so charming with everyone one meets, though she is constantly being muddled-up with her sister-in-law, Lady Astor, which I don't think pleases her much.

J.B.B. to E.C.F.B., 11 June   *H.Q. Canadian Corps*

All day I have been out on exercise (what in the old days we would have called manoeuvres) with the Hamilton Light Infantry. The weather was fine, and I thoroughly enjoyed a good day in the open. Everybody was extremely kind in their welcome and willingness to give information and explanation. I was amazed (and I think Julian would have been too, as an old soldier) at the immense amount of mechanical transport one battalion possesses, and what a clutter it all makes. Under actual war conditions, of course, it would go off the road. But even so it is terrific, and I cannot help feeling that in dealing with invasion in this country, where operations would almost certainly be in a closed-in, restricted area, much of this MT would be a liability rather than an asset. Except for Bren carriers and MG's on lorries (which do make them mobile) most of what was done this morning could have been better and more quickly done *à pied.*

On Tuesday we had a farewell dinner for Dempsey,[1] who left today to take over command of the 46th. Division. It was just 'A' Mess, with one or two others, and we drank the health of our guest of honour, the Corps Commander merely getting to his feet and asking us to do so. But about 10 p.m. the Corps Commander suddenly called on me to say something! So I did my best without any argument and they said it was all right. I am very fond of Dempsey and shall miss him.

Notes by J.B.B., Waterloo Exercise, 14-16 June

The general idea of this exercise was that the enemy had landed parachutists and airborne troops on the South Downs from Amberley to Firle, many of whom had infiltrated down from the Weald. More troops were engaged than in any other exercise to date. The enemy consisted of an infantry division from 4 Corps, a brigade of Guards, an armoured division and other units. The duty of the British forces was to drive the enemy back into the sea. They consisted of the Canadian Corps (i.e. 1 and 2 Divisions and Corps troops) and an infantry division, with a brigade of 'I' tanks.

The exercise began at 08.30 on Saturday 14 June. Corps HQ expected to move at some time during the exercise, but not at once. I had the General's permission to do a little fifth column work, and decided to push off at about 15.00hrs. and try and reach Findon Manor which was the HQ of the staff directing the exercise. I was in my little Austin car - a military car bearing the Corps sign, and Clark was driving as Sanders was on leave.

We kept to side roads as far as possible, once or twice passing near to enemy posts, but no one tried to stop us. On the main road between Arundel and Worthing the civilian police were stopping all civilian cars and turning them aside from the manoeuvre area, but my little military car was always waved on without question. Getting near the village I waited for a promising civilian to question, and an old lady coming down the road informed me where Findon Manor was and added there were troops there. I then boldly entered the village. The Control Staff were in the Manor House; other officers were in the village hall opposite. On

---

[1]   Maj-Gen. Miles Dempsey, MC (1896-1969). Comm. 13 Infantry Bde., 1940; BGS 1st. Canadian Div., 1941-42: as Lieut-Gen. Comm. 13 Corps, 1943-44 and 2 Army 1944-5; Comm. 14 Army, S.E. Asia, 1945. Chm. Racecourse Betting Control Board, 1947-51. KCB (1944), General (1946).

alighting from my car I was immediately surrounded by a number of military police who wished to know my business. They seemed surprised I had got through with a Canadian car, but an enormously fat red-faced sergeant said, 'Excuse me, have you a padre brother in Herefordshire?' so my *bona fides* as a spectator were confirmed.

Next day I sallied forth going NE via Petworth to Billingshurst. Troops were everywhere, all our 2 Div. it seemed. At Billingshurst there was a real mess-up. Some of our troops, some of the Guards (enemy), some were bare-headed (the sign they had been taken prisoner), with umpires appearing from different directions. No one seemed to know what was going on, which was very typical of any large-scale operations. A number of the enemy I talked to said they intended to try and attack Headley Court (Corps HQ) that night. I said I knew Corps HQ had moved, so there would not be much to capture.

The whole exercise has been full of surprises. When shown the maps a few days before, I had visualised an attack on the Downs with both sides maintaining a fairly definite line. Nothing was more inaccurate. For the parachute troops were brought up in buses from the XII Corps area and dumped surreptitiously, and mostly at night, two days before the exercise began. This placing of the parachutists was perhaps the only feature of the exercise which was not true to the real conditions of war. If they had been dropped from planes, some at least would have been seen by the Home Guard. As it was, they were not seen at all, enjoyed plenty of time to make their plans, and had an immense initial advantage. Almost before the Canadians had started, the enemy had infiltrated behind them. Half a recce battalion was taken prisoner on Saturday morning, a whole Field Ambulance was captured, and our men found themselves facing in every direction.

There were many amusing incidents. When the 2 Cdn. Div. arrived at Horsham, where they were supposed to find billets, they found the Guards (the enemy) already in possession of the town. There was a real scrap and tempers were lost. The civilian police at Horsham rang the directing staff at Findon Manor and said, 'We don't like your war, please remove it altogether.' At Cranleigh, the civilians were such a nuisance standing around and asking questions that the officer in command ordered the Rector to ring a curfew. The Rector said this was illegal unless the Germans had landed. The officer said he would take full responsibility, so the bell was rung after which all civilians had to remain indoors, much to their annoyance.

I came across a Guards officer in the 'P' section who was on the Canadian side, and he said he knew where Corps HQ was. So I followed him, and about dusk we reached Rusper. The village was the scene of the greatest activity, Corps transport of every description - lorries, cars, station-wagons, motor-bikes - was pouring in, and everybody was trying to discover where they were to go. I approached a military policeman on point duty. 'Where is 'G' office, please, Corporal?', to which he said he didn't know, while eyeing me suspiciously. A station-wagon was drawn up further down the street. I poked my head in and said to the young officer, 'Is this General McNaughton's Canadian Corps?', but got no further. I heard the words, 'Arrest that man,' and two enormous corporals seized me by the arms, swung me round none too lightly, and brought me face-to-face with a young security officer who, fortunately, I did not know. 'Steady,' I said, 'I do actually belong to this Corps myself.' 'You do like hell,' was the answer, and I was marched off to the Chief Security Officer up the road. I produced all my passes, but it was no good. I was told they could all have been forged. 'Who can identify you?' I said I thought one of the brigadiers would, so with some difficulty we found 'A' mess. Corporal Steward, who gave me a cheery hello as we entered, nearly gave the game away. The first brigadier we came across was Hertzberg;[1] with him was one of the ADC's. I saw that 'Hertz' had twigged the situation and by the naughty twinkle in his eye intended to have some fun at my expense. Standing a prisoner before him , I asked very correctly if he would identify me. 'Hertz' looked me up and down with a blank expression on his face and said, 'Who the bloody hell are you?' and 'Never seen you before.' And did the two corporals give me a dirty look?. But of course we could not keep it up for long, and eventually the security corporals saw I was known and I walked back with them to the Security Officer, and commended them and him on their efficiency.

It was a good exercise in that our lads learnt many lessons, chief of which was that the enemy in modern mobile warfare are in front and behind and on the flanks. In fact, as we discovered rather quickly, there are no flanks at all.

Julian to E.C.F.B., 19 June   *Goodrich Court*

All went well in London yesterday, and the meeting with various bishops passed off successfully. I had a few words with the Bishop of Liverpool who told

---

[1] Brigadier Charles Hertzberg, MC (1886-1944). Chief Engineer Canadian Corps, 1941-42; Maj-Gen. and Chief Engineer 1st. Canadian Army, 1942-43.

me with confidence that when it is thought necessary to make an appeal, there would be immense contributions from all over the world to rebuild the burnt-out churches of England; at the same time he is quite certain that a number of churches in Liverpool, if he has anything to do with it, will never be rebuilt, as they will not be worth rebuilding and did not serve any useful purpose even before they were destroyed.

Burgon picked me up and went to the Dorchester where, after five minutes with Barbie Wallace, we were warmly welcomed by Vincent and Alice Massey. We had a most interesting dinner. I sat next to a Mr Michael Powell,[1] who has just finished producing a film called *The 49th Parallel*, which he thinks ought to be a great success. During dinner, Vincent produced a long handsome-looking cigarette box, which was placed on the table at his side. When he opened the lid (he must have timed it very well) we heard Big Ben striking 9 p.m. and heard the news. Apparently there are only two or three of these yet in England; they are an American invention.

J.B.B. to E.C.F.B., 19 June   *H.Q. Canadian Corps*

Yesterday Julian and I dined with Vincent Massey. He had seen Stafford Cripps that afternoon. Stafford returned from Moscow a week ago to report to the War Cabinet. He is of the opinion that the Germans will attack the Russians. Hitler could get all he wants, e.g. oil, grain and other war material from Stalin by negotiation, but that is not his main purpose, which is to eliminate the Russian army which is a constant menace to his eastern frontier. This must be done at once in view of the growing strength of the British Empire and the USA.

Barbie Wallace told me that Duff Cooper had informed her that the reason Hess had made his amazing flight to Scotland was to try and persuade Great Britain to come to an immediate understanding with Germany. Otherwise, Russia would be the only gainer, as the Empire and Germany bled each other to death. Hess came without Hitler's knowledge, and because he was, and always has been, actuated by a profound hatred of Bolshevism.

---

[1]   Michael Latham Powell (1905-90). Film Director. *49th Parallel* (1941), starring Eric Portman, Laurence Olivier, Leslie Howard and Raymond Massey. Remembered as 'one of the better wartime propaganda films', Emeric Pressberger's script won an Oscar.

Notes given to J.B.B. by E.C.F.B. at Chiddingstone on 22 June. She had moved there from Goodrich on 18 June.

The exciting news of today is that the Germans have invaded Russia. It has been known for some time that the Germans had been massing troops along the whole Russian frontier from the White Sea to the Black Sea.

Tonight we listened to a thrilling speech from the Prime Minister, announcing the government's decision to assist Russia in every possible way in their fight against Germany. That we should do this will bring great content to the Dean of Canterbury and satisfy his wildest dreams. This may postpone Hitler's invasion of England as, no doubt, his aim is to finish off Russia first.

The reception of Churchill's speech has proved most satisfactory, approval of help to Russia having come from the USA and all parts of the Empire. The proviso usually added is that although help must be given at once to fight Germany, this does not carry with it approval of Russia's internal government.

Geoffrey to E.C.F.B., 22 June   *Aberdeen*

Well, here's a pretty kettle of fish, a complication of an already sufficiently complicated situation. It pleases me immensely to contemplate the two great satanic causes of the modern world, namely National Socialism and Bolshevism, furiously engaged in destroying one another. Nor do I see how it can be argued that it is not to our immediate and ultimate advantage to have our principal enemy compelled to undertake that war on a double front which he had planned so far to avoid. Doubtless the German armies will run over western Russia, but they cannot conquer the Russian Empire; nor if there is a Russian revolution will the resultant chaos help Germany to hold down and make profitable to herself so vast an extent of territory inhabited by populations who all hate her and whom already she has the greatest difficulty in controlling. Moreover, what is to prevent the Russians retreating into their boundless hinterland and destroying as they go all the wealth Hitler is fighting them to secure? And will not he, in the end, bog himself in Russia as Napoleon did, and as the Japanese have done in China?

Russia, of course, may put up a better show than is generally expected. She has vast quantities of tanks and aeroplanes, as many as the Germans (though of inferior quality and unlikely to be deployed with any military skill), but on so enormously wide a front and under the fluid conditions of modern mechanised war, it would be strange if she utterly failed to do Germany any serious damage with them. How she fights must, it seems to me, largely depend on Stalin's ability to command the loyalty of the Russian people and draw out the full consequences of the traditional Slav hatred for the Germans, which goes much deeper than the bitter opposition between Communism and Hitlerism. Will Stalin, unlike the average autocrat, discover an able general? Events alone will determine.

Julian to E.C.F.B., 22 June   *Goodrich*

Yesterday I spent a quiet jolly afternoon visiting some gardening squads, watching cricket and lying on the river bank while crowds of happy and naked boys disported themselves in the shallows of the fast-flowing Wye. Then I went along and saw the steel-wired swing bridge which the Scouts are flinging across the river just below Goodrich Court. It is more than half finished, and they have done a fine bit of work in carrying out a rather difficult job.

I have no room to comment on the Germano-Russian outbreak of war. Will Russia resist? I suppose so. Is she our ally? I suppose not. But the thought of the two anti-God totalitarian states disposing of each other is not altogether unpleasing.

Margaret Hopkins to E.C.F.B., 23 June   *Bridge, Nr. Canterbury*

Did you see in the paper that a Jerry was brought down on the line near Bekesbourne? It was so low, and one of ours was after it machine-gunning for all it was worth. The pilot baled out, but he was too low; he broke his ankles and his plane burst into flame on landing, which put the railway out of action for a while. There is nothing left of it but a few bits of metal. But we don't get half as many Jerries as we did last summer. They seem to be getting them before they get as far as here now.

Tony to E.C.F.B., 30 June   *Gt. Yarmouth*

I have had quite an interesting first three months as a commissioned officer, but much of it has been dull, for when you are neither in training nor in action the routine becomes rather deadly and everybody gets fed up or, as they say 'browned-off'. How the army in this country longs for an invasion and a bit of action.

I had a week in Liverpool doing fire-watching on those vast warehouses. That was before the first week in May when Liverpool had its blitz - eight nights in succession. About a week after that I went for a ten-day course to Warrington - a dirty, dismal manufacturing town if ever there was one, even Glasgow would compare favourably with it. It was while I was on this course that I received the papers posting me to the 14th. South Staffs at Yarmouth. I think I am lucky to have come here, as it is a fairly large town within easy reach of Norwich and Cambridge.

Our job here is to guard the coast to the last man and the last round. We are a static force - in the front line really, if you look at war with a 1914-18 mentality. Our CO is a regular soldier and came back with the 2nd. Battalion from India just before the war started. My Company Commander is a very tall thin major, who inevitably gets nicknamed 'Lanky'. The Signals Officer is a Scotsman from Edinburgh, who no more intended to get into this regiment than I did, while the MTO is one of the few Midlanders in the mess. The padre is a Channel Islander from Jersey, and a Methodist. He is good company, and I play tennis with him occasionally.

My own platoon is made up, for the most part, of men much older than myself who are married. This is one objection I have against being in the 14th. Battalion. I would much rather be in command of men nearer my own age. The married men, who are approaching middle age, and who have been called-up for service from decent jobs in the Midlands, now find themselves away from their families on the bleak North Sea coast endlessly waiting for an invader who never comes, and who anyway when he does come will do so by parachute far behind our lines. These men are decent enough, but they do not take easily to the army and are therefore easily discontented and ready to go absent. However, I am getting to know them better. I will say for them all that, although they grumble, they get the job done.

I am most interested to hear that John is to go abroad, and shall be even more interested to hear if he really does sail soon. The army idea of 'soon' never seems to be less than three months later. Several officers, more or less my contemporaries at Lichfield, were warned for embarkation at the beginning of May. They got their kit and their leave, and they have said their good-byes. But I don't believe they have gone yet. I do envy John going, though for myself I am rather keen to be in this country if an invasion comes.

July

Julian to E.C.F.B., 1 July   *Goodrich*

Just a few words to tell you how much I am thinking of you today. My thoughts are naturally full of our dear Morris.[1] To me his loving personality is as vivid and uncomplaining as if it were not a quarter of a century ago that the dear boy was with us on this earth. I can see him now as if it were yesterday, calm and serene in doing his duty regardless of the cost to himself. Well, he lives on anyway. I am not one who considers that our brave dead in the Great War have given their lives in vain.

Notes by J.B.B., 3-5 July

Yesterday Brigadier Inglis[2] of the New Zealand forces dined with us and afterwards spoke to a number of officers about the fighting in Crete. He said the preliminary bombing of the area in which the Germans intended to land their air-borne troops and parachutists was simply terrific. Directly after the troop-carrying planes arrived, the gliders and parachutists were dropped all over the island. Apparently there is no place except woods and towns where the Germans are not prepared to drop parachutists. It is a great mistake to think they only go for aerodromes or flat surfaces. We had no air support whatever. During the entire Greek fighting, only one lot of English planes came over - eight Blenheims. They dropped their bombs and disappeared. Also, we had no guns to speak of. There were three six-inch guns guarding the beaches, about 20 Bofors and some light calibre guns, but no 25 pounders. The Germans didn't bring any light armoured vehicles by air, but they brought fairly heavy mortars. As regards the parachutists, the leader had a white parachute, the men had ones of green, while the equipment had reddish-brown parachutes. It is said the Germans had controlled fire within ten minutes of landing. They are very good with their automatic weapons, and their tactics are always the same. First they get together, organise and almost at once try to work round the flank which they do with great rapidity if not watched.

---

[1] Morris Bickersteth, the brother who was killed on the first day of the Battle of the Somme, 1 July 1916.
[2] Brig. Lindsay Inglis (1894-1966). Comd. 4 NZ Brigade (Egypt, Crete and Syria) 1940-42; Comd. 2 NZ Div. for periods, 1942-43. Retired as Maj-General.

Inglis said that individually they have little initiative, and if they saw our fellows really going for them with the bayonet, they fled.

The Germans, apparently, fought clean and respected the Red Cross on field ambulances. The only casualty clearing station they made untenable was so situated that it commanded an admirable field of fire they hoped to (but never actually did) use.

On Friday 4 July I dined with Mrs Ronnie Greville at Polesden Lacey with Leo Amery[1] and his wife. Amery said General Auchinleck,[2] who has just succeeded Wavell as C.-in-C. Middle East, is a soldier of outstanding ability. He is an Indian Army officer, understands the country and its peoples and enjoys their confidence.

As far as India was concerned, Amery said Congress was rather like the Fascists - strong because wonderfully organised. Most of the provincial governments that have recently resigned did not want to do so, but were forced to by Congress. The Moslems, who are about a quarter of the population, are not so well educated as the Hindus, but are much more virile, and provide about nine tenths of the Indian Army. Amery thinks the final constitution for India will not be a reproduction of the British, but will incorporate some of the best points of the American, Swiss and Scandinavian models.

On Saturday 5 July I was at Lavington with Barbie Wallace. David Margesson was the only other guest. He told me that the PM and others all realised that Wavell's despatches were those of a thoroughly tired man, and that it was essential he should have a rest. Margesson and I had a long talk about Willans's idea of a newsletter or pamphlet for the British troops next autumn. I said we certainly would want to come in on it, and I said that Emrys Williams had a first-rate mind. As regards Russia, Mason-Macfarlane, who heads our military mission to Moscow, was received in a friendly way but got no information at all at first, but is now fully in touch with General Staff plans.

Margesson said that everybody was wondering whether we could attack Germany, or German-occupied territory, now that the enemy has its back turned. The idea seems attractive, but how could we do this? Shipping for transporting a

---

[1]   Leopold Charles Amery (1873-1955). MP (Con) Sparkbrook, 1911-45; Ist Lord of Admiralty, 1922-24; Colonial Sec., 1924-29 (and Dominions, 1925-29); India Sec., 1940-45.
[2]   General Claude Auchinleck, DSO (1884-1981). C-in-C India, 1941 and 1943-47; C-in-C Middle East, 1941-42. GCB (1945), Field-Marshal (1946). Kt (1946).

large number of troops across the Channel, even for a raid, was an insoluble problem. We were not yet supreme in the air, and our armoured divisions were not numerous enough to undertake big-scale operations on the continent. Our troops could not be maintained overseas, there would be casualties, and eventually our men would have to be taken off. Then everyone would cry out, 'Yet another evacuation'. Margesson was optimistic about the possibility of the Russians at least holding up the Germans for three months or so, though I gathered Dill was not.

John to his father (Monier), 14 July   *I.T.C. The Buffs, Canterbury*

Yesterday four of us officers went by car to Maidstone for Major Peter Fleming's[1] lecture. It was in the Corn Exchange, which was absolutely packed with most of the front row full of 'brass hats'.

Major Fleming was not a brilliant lecturer, but he spoke quite interestingly on the air aspect of the Greek campaign in which he took part, and certainly gave us something to think over. When asked by one of the 'brass hats' during question time at the end whether he had anything to say on the subject of blowing up bridges, he paused for a second, and replied, 'No Sir, except never leave it to your allies!'

I had a glorious run back. Kent was looking indescribably beautiful with the wheat beginning to ripen. Certainly a country to give everything for. I saw the sea away to the left just before coming into Chilham. And as for the view of the Cathedral from the hill and in the light of the setting sun at about 9.50, it just took my breath away.

Geoffrey to E.C.F.B., 20 July   *Aberdeen*

I am in better hopes than ever about the war. I believe the Russians, though retreating, have the situation well in hand and know very well what they are about. They possess ample reserves. Our shipping losses are down, and the RAF is working devastation on Nazi shipping centres. Italy is in a bad way, and Japan is not much better. I am filled with confidence.

---

[1] (Robert) Peter Fleming (1907-71). Travel writer and author. Pre-war special correspndent for *The Times;* married to the actress Celia Johnson, and elder brother of Ian Fleming, creator of James Bond.

Notes by E.C.F.B, 22 July

Today changes in the Cabinet have been announced, among which are Mr R. A. Butler to be President of the Board of Education, Mr Churchill's Parliamentary Secretary, Brendan Bracken,[1] to be Minister of Information, and Lord Hankey to be Postmaster General. The latter's successor as Chancellor of the Duchy of Lancaster is Mr Duff Cooper, who is being sent to the Far East on a special mission to report on the general situation there. It is a matter of great satisfaction that Ramsbotham[2] has been removed from the Board of Education. Butler is the right man for the post. He is a governor of Felsted and feels strongly about the necessity for Religious Education, the lack of which has been shown by the evacuated children, who are practically pagans.

J.B.B. to E.C.F.B., 23 July   *H.Q. Canadian Forces*

Yesterday I went up to London. First I visited CEMA to see about some more music for several units, and then met Coulter[3] at Canada House. He has been selected to go round the munitions factories and talk about the Canadian war effort. He and I went to the Ministry of Information to see officials of the Public Meetings Branch and we discussed finance and general arrangements there. I had a talk with George Ignatieff[4] and Vincent about 6 p.m., then dined alone and early at the Travellers' for Sanders to drive me down to Bermondsey at 7.30, where George Grant had organised a concert in the Oxford Bermondsey Club.

A stage was rigged-up in the large room, and there were chairs and benches to accommodate about 100 people. The audience were the parents and friends of the boys acting. I went behind to see the boys being made up as I always do in Hart House productions, and then Sanders and I sat in the back row and

---

[1] Brendan Rendall Bracken (1901-58). MP (Con) N. Paddington, 1929-45, Bournemouth, 1945-50, and E. Bournemouth, 1950-51; PPS to Churchill, 1940-41; Min. of Information, 1941-45; Ist. Lord of Admiralty, 1945; Chm. *Financial News*, 1926-45, and of *Financial Times*, 1945-58. Cr. Vt. (1952).

[2] Herwald Ramsbotham (1887-1971). MP (Con) Lancaster, 1929-41; Min. of Pensions, 1936-39; Ist Comm. of Works, 1939-40; Pres. Bd. of Ed., 1940-41; Chm Unemployment Assistance Bd., 1941-48. Gov-Gen. of Ceylon, 1949-54. Cr. Baron Soulbury (1941), and Vt. (1954).

[3] Robert Coulter (1914-87). Schoolmaster commissioned in the war; later made a career in broadcasting, becoming controller of BBC Scotland.

[4] George Ignatieff (1913-89). Canadian Civil Servant and diplomatist; 3rd. Sec. London, 1940-44; in Ottawa, 1944-5; Adv. to Canadian Delegn. UN, 1946-47; Councillor Canadian Embassy Washington, 1948-53; Amb. to Yugoslavia, 1956-58; Asst. U-Sec. of State for External Affairs, 1960-62; Amb. to NATO, 1962-65, and to UN, 1965-68.

watched the show, which was a typical Bermondsey production. The boys sang blues and jazz songs, there were boys playing accordions and boys playing mouth organs, interspersed with 20-minute plays and several skits. The war was only mentioned twice; once at the start about evacuating to the Abbey Factories shelter if a raid began, and once in the interval when we were told how the air-raids had so disrupted club activities during the winter that now they were trying to cram several months' work into a few weeks. Many of the people there had been blitzed out of hearth and home, but it was never mentioned. Everyone seemed intent on forgetting the war.

I managed to get a talk with George Grant about his future. He is now thinking of joining the Merchant Marine - a sort of subtle distinction between active offensive warfare as would come his way in the Navy, and defensive action which is presumably the only fighting a freight ship would do. I told him I was not impressed, and advised him strongly to stay where he is because there can be no doubt there will be a recurrence of air-attacks in September. He said he would take no action till he had talked the matter over with me again. It is very difficult to know quite what is best.

Kay to her father (Monier), 25 July   *Yaverland, I.O.W.*

As you probably heard on the wireless, we had a German bomber down near here yesterday. It landed quite close to here after running out of petrol and the crew of four gave themselves up after having, however, unfortunately enough time to blow up the plane. Charles was called at once to the fort, and at very short notice had to do the preliminary examination, and remove all their belongings and papers.

He was up there practically all day and got a lot of useful information for the officer who came over to interrogate them. This I shan't put in a letter, however, but it will wait till we come home. They were all armed, but behaved quite well when captured.

It was a nasty moment till we saw where they were going to land. They swooped three times low over this cottage, and finally came down in a cornfield about a quarter of a mile away, rather wrecking the corn! The whole neighbourhood is frightfully thrilled, and there is a constant procession to view the remains.

Mrs Gardiner to E.C.F.B., 27 July   *Canterbury*

The military here, so far as I can judge, seem very divided in their ideas about likely happenings. Some say if invasion comes, it is most unlikely to be on this part of the coast. They have, however, fortified us strongly; masses of barbed wire and iron pipes have appeared all among the polyanthus roses and summer bedding in the West Gate garden. My Pole (my pupil) is always very encouraging and assures me there will be revolution in Germany and the war will be over by Christmas! It is very interesting to hear Polish views of Russia.

The Dean is, of course, in great feather. There is an immense pile of his 'important book on Russia, ninth edition, millions sold' in Goulden's window; while the local press tells us he has a pressing invitation from many parts of the USA to go on a lecture tour, but has put himself in the hands of the government! I think they should make it a condition of his going that he resigns his Deanery!

Notes by E.C.F.B, 28 July   *Chiddingstone*

John telephoned tonight that he had just been posted to the 11th. Battalion of The Buffs stationed at St Margaret's Bay. He is much pleased as he hears that the CO is greatly liked and the officers are a nice set. We are glad he is still in Kent and can get home easily.

Tony is attending a course at Thetford in Norfolk, and spent his twenty-first birthday there. His brother, Julian, has been accepted for the KRRC and has finished his time at Oxford, which alas was only two terms. All his belongings, and Tony's from Christ Church, have now been sent home. Tony had one year there, but both boys have passed their necessary examinations, which we hope entitles them to a war degree.

J.B.B. to E.C.F.B., 30 July   *H.Q. Canadian Forces*

My visit to the Tank Brigade on Salisbury Plain last week was a great success. The Brigade Commander, Worthington[1] (or Worthy as he is known by his friends) has long been known to me. I did what I could to help him in February 1940 when he was commanding the armoured units at Camp Borden (60 miles from Toronto) and was meeting with little assistance in his fight to get tanks. Actually, I did for him what I have never done for anybody else, and that was to

---

[1] Brig., later Maj-Gen. Frederick Worthington (1889-1967). Comm. Canadian Tank Brigade, 1940; GOC Armd. Div. 1942; Pacific Comd., 1945.

write personally to Mackenzie King, and I think it did help. With the invasion of Flanders, all changed and everybody was out to get Worthy all he wanted. The Armoured Division is being formed, and should be over here before very long.

Worthy is a splendid little man, 48 but looks older because of his grey hair, and has always been crazy about tanks. There is not much he doesn't know about heavy 'I' tanks or the lighter cruiser variety. He has already got a good many heavy tanks, the latest model is called the 'Churchill', and the one from the latest is called the 'Matilda'. You saw in the press the PM sitting in one of the new monsters called after him. I had a ride in one. It was a very interesting experience. Of its peculiar features I will not write, but it is certainly calculated to put fear into the hearts of those who meet it.

I had particularly wanted to be at Chatham House (Royal Institute of International Affairs) tomorrow to hear George Ignatieff speak about Russia, but the Tank Brigade job on Salisbury Plain prevents it. But George did send me his paper to read, which is very interesting. He is quite certain that Russia will be prepared to play her full part in post-war reconstruction. The real trouble, from what I can hear, is that the Foreign Office and War Office are still profoundly suspicious of, and even hostile to, what they consider is a system of government essentially incompatible with British ideas. Indeed it is true. As George Ignatieff points out, the Russian spirit must be freed, so as to present an opportunity for the genuinely sound and democratic characteristics of the Russian people to show themselves.

August

J.B.B. to E.C.F.B., 3 August   *H.Q. Canadian Forces*

All Thursday I was on Salisbury Plain and had a very interesting day. I lunched in Salisbury with Colonel White,[1] chief education officer for Southern Command, and W.E. Williams, who is to run this new War Office bulletin called 'Current Affairs' for the troops. Williams is one of the outstanding younger men in the field of popular education. I know him well and am much impressed with his ability. He is to have three deputy directors, and it is hoped that the first issue will come out in early October. The whole plan is in a preliminary stage , and we had a

---

[1] Col. Archibald White, VC, MC (1891-1971). Served with Army Education Corps, 1920-47.

long discussion about the functions of what is to be called ABCA. I shall do my best to ensure that any facilities which may be made available to English troops shall be available also for the Canadian Corps.

You will have seen the account of the arrival of the 3rd. Canadian Division. Basil Price[1] who commands is a delightful person. He was in command of a Brigade here all last winter and I know him well. The number of Canadian troops in this country is now very large, and is to be further increased by the Armoured Division in a few weeks' time.

Notes by E.C.F.B., 3 August

The seventh week of the Russian-German war has begun and the Germans are making a third desperate push in three directions in their endeavour to reach Leningrad, Moscow and Kiev, meeting strong and determined opposition.

Today, walking from Chiddingstone Rectory towards the Castle, eight huge RAMC lorries passed us and turned into a big field. There were big trees on the other side of the field, but to reach them the lorries passed down the sides close to the fence. We were told that this was to prevent their tracks being noticed by aeroplanes, such tracks being visible from the air for a week afterwards. Once under the trees the lorries were camouflaged, first by big nets and then by heavy boughs. When Monier went to shut the church at 10.00 p.m. he found about twenty lorry drivers inside. He showed them all over, and they were full of interest. One of the men said, 'There is one good thing about this war, we are all seeing a good deal of England'.

Notes by J.B.B., 5 and 7 August

I attended a meeting at the War Office with Major-General Willans and W.E. Williams (receiving his memorandum on ABCA). Then I met Ivison Macadam,[2] secretary of the Royal Institute of International Affairs, at Chatham House. Shortly after the outbreak of war, he was lent to the Ministry of Information and was only released from this post a short time ago. He was in charge of talks, propaganda talks, all over the country. He was very caustic about

---

[1] Maj-Gen. (Charles) Basil Price, DSO (1889-1975). GOC 3rd. Canadian Div., 1941; seconded to Canadian Red Cross, 1942; demobilized, 1945.
[2] Ivison Macadam (1894-1974). Sec. and Dir-Gen. RIIA, 1929-55; Principal Asst. Sec. Min. of Information, 1939-41; Ed. Annual Register of World Events, 1947-73. KCVO (1974).

the management and policy of the Ministry of Information. Duff Cooper, though extremely able, was unsuitable for the job of Minister and was lazy. Many of the appointments, such for instance as Mr. Pick,[1] were grotesque. There was no continuity of policy, little imagination in the planning, and among the staff a feeling of insecurity. He hoped the new Minister, Brendan Bracken, would do well. He is by profession a journalist, and is therefore keen to give out as much news as possible.

Later I met Lady George (Ti) Cholmondeley[2] to discuss steps which might be taken to bring some outside interest into the lives of young officers at Canadian base units. In each of these there are perhaps 40 or 50 young officers waiting to join their units, here today and gone tomorrow, away on courses or just arrived from Canada. They know very few people, are stuck away in camps in the country in a narrow environment, are bored by the inaction, and are stewing in their own juice. The idea is to arrange for some interesting visitors, such as Sir Joseph Addison,[3] Hilary Saunders[4] (author of 'The Battle of Britain), and the like, to go down to these camps, dine and spend the evening in the mess talking informally to the young officers about general topics and world affairs. I am to see General Price Montague in London, and also Brigadier Phelan,[5] Commander Base Units, about this idea.

On Thursday I was in uniform all day. I spent the morning on the ranges near Bisley going through my Bren gun firing tests. I did not do too badly. One has 40 seconds to get off two magazines (each containing 15 rounds for this particular practice), and I got 22 well grouped on the target at 200 yards out of 30. Later, I spent two hours with a company of Engineers learning from a Sergt.-Major specialist all the most dastardly ways of doing a German in, some of it a form of ju-jitsu, but mostly clever trick ways of disposing of an enemy in single-combat.

---

[1] Frank Pick (1878-1941). Vice-Pres. London Passenger Transport Board, 1933-40; left Min.of Information, Dec. 1940 'somewhat embittered'.
[2] Lady Sybil Cholmondeley, wife of 5th. Marquis of Cholmondeley and sister of Rt. Hon. Philip Sassoon; Supt. Women's Royal Naval Service, 1939-45. CBE (1946).
[3] Sir Joseph Addison (1879-1953). Diplomatist; numerous central European postings. KCMG (1933), retd. (1936).
[4] Hilary Aiden St John Saunders, MC (1898-1951). Writer; author of many official publications of the war; librarian to House of Commons, 1945-50. CBE (1951).
[5] Brig., later Maj-Gen., Frederick Phelan, DSO, MC (1885-1970). Adjutant-Gen. Ottawa, 1940; Dep. Adjutant-Gen. London, 1940-41; Comm. Canadian Reinforcement Units, Aldershot, 1941-43; Dir-Gen. Reserve Army, Canada, 1943-45.

John to his father (Monier), 8 August 11th. Battn, The Buffs, St Margaret's Bay

Our 'binge' started at 1.30 a.m. on Thursday morning when we got the 'stand to'. I had only taken over 18 Pl. that morning, but as it happened the 'roughing it' together, which the exercise entailed, has enabled us to get to know each other much better than any formal introduction would have done.

The 'stand to' was only a practice, and the Battalion did not move off until 4.45, when we set off for Sandwich to smash imaginary air-borne landings. We had a first-class scrap with the 'enemy' which everyone enjoyed tremendously! We stayed near Betteshanger most of the day, then we marched off by moonlight, the food only arriving at 12 o'clock, and we dossed down under the trees on our ground-sheets as we were.

However, it was only half an hour after our suppers - hot broth and tea, very good - when we were woken, and there followed two and a half hours of forced marching in a driving rain. We covered the nine miles to Barham by 4 o'clock; our job was to protect the southern flank of the force attacking Canterbury which was presumed to have fallen to the enemy. It was sad to reflect, as I passed down Barham hill as the clock struck four, that the last time I was there Mary was Marjory's bridesmaid in a peace-time wedding on a midsummer's day. We were pretty tired, and the platoon slept for an hour at the side of the road after I had posted guards.

About 10 o'clock we went a further mile or so to Kingston, where we were surprised to find the cooks had got us a hot breakfast waiting - tea and bread and marge and sausages. So we were new men when we set off down the Elham Valley to Elham itself where a 'pocket' of parachutists and air-borne troops had to be cleared up. It was only six miles, but the day was hot and MT kept passing and re-passing us. You have no idea of the quantity of trucks, cars, bikes and mobile artillery when a brigade is on the move. We attacked a hill behind Elham and there was a colossal barrage (imaginary) pounding the top of it. It was rather disconcerting to find that the enemy had deserted it after all that!

By then I gather there was a pretty fair muddle, as generally arises when these big exercises get far advanced. All the same, by 7.30 that evening we were established in the Elham ex-servicemen's club. The officers slept in the billiard room. Plumley and I got an excellent egg-bacon-bean dish in a local cafe, we couldn't wait for 'lunch' which arrived at 8.15.

I know the supply sounds appalling, but it must be tremendously difficult, and a big scheme like this is partly to test the supply services. In the case of food, as you can see, they were found wanting. Petrol supply, almost as important, was I believe, excellent. All the same, the Battalion had to march the 16 miles back to St Margaret's the next day.

Of course, after a long spell of coast defence we are not in very good training, with the result that with the heat and the distances marched, many feet gave out. But, as one of my section commanders said to me last night, 'Now we've done it, it's good to look back on.' For a well-trained battalion the 48 miles in two days, which I believe it totted up to, is nothing to write home about, but for us who have been static for so long it was not a bad effort.

Tony to J.B.B., 10 August   *Thetford*

Churchill tells the army in this country to be on its toes for invasion around the beginning of September, but he doesn't say who is going to do the invading. Why should we not invade them? Even if we only established a bridge-head strongly held, we should have a job to occupy us for the winter, and a big start for next spring which is the date I put for the end of the war.

I know from personal experience the general shortages of weapons and so on in the army, but can see too how rapidly they are now being made up. I am in charge of the 3rd. Mortar Platoon in the Battalion, and when I arrived in May there were two mortars, in many respects incomplete. But by the end of June I had four, and I am expecting the remaining two shortly which will bring me up to full establishment. It is however interesting to note that the new mortars are not such good pieces of workmanship as the old ones. Several of my men used to work in iron and steel factories in and around Birmingham, and they are quite scornful of the 'mass production' way these new mortars are put together, and of the quality of the metal. They are right too. A mortar barrel should not get heated, however many bombs are fired through it. My old ones don't heat up, but the new ones do after firing only a dozen practice bombs.

In about a week we are going back to Yarmouth. In Thetford we are at least doing proper training, which I really prefer to sitting on the coast. The officers are billeted all over the town. I am in furnished billets in a house belonging to an oldish lady. I sleep in a big double bed that is comfortable enough, though I sometimes think I prefer army blankets and a camp bed. It seems silly to be on intensive training and yet sleeping between sheets at night. Eating in one place, sleeping in another, and working in a third is awkward.

Geoffrey to E.C.F.B, 10 August   *Aberdeen*

I had a very happy birthday yesterday despite bad weather which made it impossible to be much out of doors. Jean, however, managed a surprise in the way of food in the shape of a leg of venison (unrationed) for lunch. Any extra meat nowadays is an event. For myself I confess I hate a vegetarian diet, and whatever food experts, who are mostly cranks, may assert, history proves that our climate demands that we should be, what in fact we are, a nation of meat-eaters. I get sick of nothing but vegetables and fish - much too much soft starchy food.

The food situation in the country is appalling. The War Office is, as always, the chief culprit. Most things that go wrong are due, in the ultimate analysis, to the inordinate greed of the WO for manpower, which it can neither arm nor use. Moreover, for months it wasted the food, especially the meat, it demanded for the army - wasted it on a colossal scale. We are short of coal. Why? Because the WO has impressed 60,000 miners for the army, and refuses to release them. It should never have been allowed to have them. We are short of agricultural labour and of factory workers for the same reason. No one knows what the army does with its men. It keeps its generals abroad so short of men that they cannot win battles owing to inferiority of numbers. If the excuse is that it cannot equip the men owing to shortage of weapons and tanks, etc., why call up the men till they can be equipped? In this, as in all our wars, the inefficiency and stupidity of the WO has been proved to be a more formidable enemy than the enemy itself.

I am not surprised Hewlett Johnson is triumphant over Russia. He has the right to be. For the press, the government and people generally have boxed the compass with regard to Russia, and are saying about her just about what he was saying months ago. The Church, on the other hand, has only made the feeblest effort to explain why we are now right to discriminate between Communism and Nazism, though there is nothing to choose between them as enemies of Christianity, and both are equally stained with the blackest crimes. It is doubtless very embarrassing for the Church, but only because it will insist on moving out of its proper orbit by preaching crusades against pagan governments when its proper function is to convert the individual sinner to Christ.

Notes by E.C.F.B, 11 August

A propos Geoffrey's remarks about the Dean, Mrs Sopwith, wife of the Archdeacon of Canterbury, writes, 'I think the Dean is very happy now. He has started a new way of arranging his hair, over his ears! He came to see me the other day and I was much struck with his *coiffure.*'

Random notes by J.B.B., mid-August

American officers who visit Corps HQ from time to time tell me that on the whole Lindbergh's ardent isolationism has helped the Allied cause. English women in the USA - mothers of evacuated children - are rather unkindly called the Free English. This refers to their inability to produce funds to pay for their keep. I also hear that over there the British are called a nation of 'Wop-keepers'.

Quentin Reynolds,[1] the American who has recently become famous for his BBC broadcasts which advocate America's entry into the war, was furious the other day, because the last paragraph of one of his broadcasts was cut out by the BBC officials who are responsible to the censors that nothing undesirable is said over the air. This particular paragraph was a terrific indictment of Hitler and German methods. When Reynolds went to Broadcasting House to ask whether Great Britain was at war with Germany or not, he was met by a long-haired, be-spectacled official who said, 'Oh yes, Mr. Reynolds, we are at war with Germany and a reasonable hate is permissible, but such expressions as you use are not desirable. The English do not hate like that, especially on a Sunday evening.'

Jean Norton[2] who has a cottage on Beaverbrook's estate (just near our Corps HQ) told me that Hess, who came over really believing he could persuade us to take common action with Hitler against Russia, was deeply hurt when he was not given a few gallons of petrol to take him back to Germany. There has been no break between Hitler and Hess, though Hess flew to England without the Führer's knowledge. It is believed that one of the reasons why Darlan is so bitter against England is that when we bombed the French ships at Oran after the Fall of France, his son was on one of the ships and was killed.

---

[1] Quentin Reynolds (1902-65). Writer and broadcaster; Assoc. ed. *Collier's Weekly*, 1933-45; author of *London Diary* (1940), *Don't Think it Hasn't Been Fun* (1941), etc.
[2] Jean Norton (d. 1945). For 20 years '... Beaverbrook's most intimate woman friend.'.

Notes by J.B.B., 13 August

Yesterday Mother, Julian and I had tea with Guy and Helen Pawson[1]. She is busily engaged in managing and developing 'British Restaurants' in Kent. With the help of the government only recently obtained, the WVS has been establishing restaurants in the country areas. The initiative came from private quarters - local women, but questions in Parliament forced the government to assist by making initial grants, the restaurants being expected to make their own way once established. Three forms of service are provided: the mid-day dinner for villagers or, in small towns, for factory workers, ARP workers and the like, eaten on the premises - 8d per head; if you bring your own bowl and jug to take the meal away with you - 6d per head; meals from the mobile canteens which go round the villages and serve the agricultural workers in the fields are also to be had at 6d per head.

Geoffrey to E.C.F.B., 17 August   *Aberdeen*

Churchill and Roosevelt's manifesto[2] is good propaganda and well-timed for taking the wind out of peace proposals shortly expected from Hitler. What is said supplies what the people of the USA, and many in this country, have for a long time been demanding; a succinct statement of the ideals for which we are fighting. This is all very well, but it still remains true that what we, and now Russia, want more than anything else from the USA, is not talk about the future that will succeed the war, but belligerent action here and now. American inaction is exasperating. I sometimes wish Japan would invade Thailand or Siberia, as I believe such action would drive the American people to declare war.

Julian to E.C.F.B., 21 August   *Felsted*

Brigadier W.P. Buckley[3] has been and I have agreed to let him take my house in Felsted from 25 September. It will be let furnished, but I shall retain my bedroom and study and a big room upstairs for my stuff, though I expect I shall

---

[1] Albert Guy Pawson (1888-1986). Oxford Cricket Blue; joined Sudan Political Service, 1911; Gov. Upper Nile Province, 1931-34; Sec. International Rubber Regulation Cttee., 1934-42; Colonial Office, 1942-4. CMG (1934). Helen Pawson died in 1980.

[2] The so-called Atlantic Charter; an eight-point declaration of human rights and war aims drawn up by Churchill and Roosevelt on the *Prince of Wales* off Newfoundland, and made public on 14 August 1941.

[3] Brig. William Buckley, DSO (1887-1968). Asst. Adj-Gen. Aldershot Command, 1937-39; Comm. Eastern Area, 1939-41; retired 1942.

have to let him have the bathroom for his own use. I liked him, although he was perhaps a little pompous. There are two daughters and a grandmother. I see my home being a rendezvous for subalterns! I have not yet fixed the rent. He suggested three and a half guineas, I smiled and said I thought that hardly enough. I am not however leaving him any plate, cutlery, crockery, blankets, sheets or dining-room curtains, so he will have to bring in a good deal. I suppose the 'let' is a good idea, but I shall be sorry to hand over my house. In many ways however it will be a good thing to have the furniture used and the moths kept at bay. I hope his daughters are not the modern fast type with painted nails and leaving cigarettes burning all over the place!

J.B.B. to E.C.F.B., 24 August   *H.Q. Canadian Corps*

On Wednesday afternoon I first visited the Empire Talks Department at Broadcasting House, where MacAlpine[1] liked my draft broadcast but asked me to insert in it a personal anecdote about some soldier if I could. He also wanted to know whether the Americans were interested, as the broadcast was for Canada and the USA. I replied that the American ambassador had recently talked to me about army education and was certainly interested in it. On him suggesting I should include a reference to this, we agreed I should ask the Corps Commander's permission first. There is no hurry as they have enough speakers in the series for the next two or three weeks. But I am to make a recording some time in September.

At 5 p.m. I drove up to 'Buck House' where the policeman, after inspecting my pass, asked me to drive in (much to Sanders's satisfaction) to the Privy Purse Door. I was then conducted along some narrow winding corridors to Tommy Lascelles's room. He gave me a warm welcome, and tea was brought in. I gave him copies of Nick Ignatieff's broadcast scripts, stating that General McNaughton and I thought them excellent. Tommy willingly undertook to telephone Ogilvie[2] and say he knew all about Nick. He also asked me about the Canadians in this country, and whether I had written anything. When I said I had been discussing a broadcast that morning at the BBC, he asked for a copy and, I gathered, intended

---

[1]   John MacAlpine (d.1956). Minister Presbyterian Church in Canada, 1927; contested Maidstone (Lab), Gen. Election, 1935; joined BBC, 1937 in publicity dept.; Controller of Overseas Services, 1952-55.
[2]   Frederick Wolff Ogilvie (1893-1949). Dir-Gen. BBC, 1938-42; Principal Jesus College, Oxford, 1944-9. Kt (1942).

to show it and Nick's scripts to the King. I fear mine is terribly dull compared to Nick's.

We then walked in the garden and inspected the damage from the most recent raid. The mess must have considerable, although it is now cleared up. Tommy said the King and Queen were standing together at a window looking into the central courtyard. The King saw the aeroplane and the Queen saw the bomb drop. They have filled up the holes and covered them with asphalt again, but you can see where they fell.

Next day (Thursday) I was in London again for a War Office meeting with Williams about ABCA. The prospectus, with a foreword by General Dill, explaining the whole plan, is now being sent to all officers in the British army all over the world. The first issue of 'Current Affairs' is to be on 27 September, and thereafter they will appear regularly week-by-week. The War Office wishes to know whether ABCA publications are to be sent to all officers in the Canadian army overseas. McNaughton is to hold a conference early in September to settle our policy.

Yesterday it poured. It deluged all day, which was a pity as it was Sports Day for the whole Canadian army at Aldershot. I was bidden to the lunch given for Mackenzie King. It was the biggest collection of 'brasshats' I have ever seen. There must have been 25 brigadiers and 20 colonels, and of course the Corps Commander and divisional generals were there. We all had drinks first and while King gave me a very cordial greeting, the only thing he really had time to say before passing on to the next person was, 'Please tell me how is your mother?' This is typical of King's courtesy and makes him so different from R.B. Bennett, who possesses no polish of this kind. After lunch we all went to the sports, but it poured so much I did not remain long. When King inspected the Guard drawn up on the sports ground for him, there were quite a number of boos. King is not a popular figure. Many consider him an opportunist, but I think they are wrong and in 100 years hence he will be considered a great Prime Minister who kept Canada united, and under whose regime the Dominion developed into a truly self-governing nation, yet maintaining her connection with the Empire.

John to Mary, 26 August   *11th. Battn. Buffs, Dover*

On Monday we did a 26 mile route march, starting at 9 and getting back at 6. It rained as far as Dover, then going along the inland Folkestone road for six miles or so, we ran into a thick sea mist. We came back up Castle Hill, which was a terrible sweat, and through the Duke of York's school back to home. We sang a good deal of the way, and I started 'John Brown's Body', sung leaving one word off each time, until at the end you just sing, 'Umph ... Umph ... Umph ..., and his soul, etc.' I was surprised nobody knew that way of singing what is otherwise a very dull song. It was rather a success.

Last night we were out on 'night ops.' until 2.30. At first there was a lot of enemy activity and we all saw a German plane caught in the searchlights - the first time for me for some time - and emitting sparks and flame after being hit by our AA. I think it got away, although we couldn't be sure as there was also see a lot of flak and tracer (just like fireworks) over Calais. Our night scheme was pretty hectic - patrols and so on; and there was quite a free fight at the end with C Company, during which my stick was broken and the chinstrap of my tin hat torn off!

I went to Matins with one Roger Keane at Eythorne on Sunday. What a service. The rector had the loudest singing voice I have met yet, at least ten choirmen strong. As a result all the choirboys shouted too, and the din was ear-splitting. He read the prayers at a great pace - interpolated, 'Don't forget the Amens,' to the choirboys in the middle of the prayer for the Royal Family, and preached an amusing sermon on Bartholomew. Really an amazing hour. I don't think I can face it again.

Random notes by J.B.B., late August

Beaverbrook was actually seated on the plane that crashed killing Purvis.[1] He was on the plane, with all his luggage, when an official came up and said, "There is another plane over there, Sir, which is a bit slower but much warmer. Would you prefer it to this one which is fast but cold?" Beaverbrook immediately said, 'Anything for warmth with my asthma,' and changed from the ill-fated plane, thus saving his life.

Halifax has been a failure as ambassador in the USA. Though he has tried hard and the Americans respect him, he can't put it across. Trying to eat a hot dog, and trying so much to be popular, instead of just being a good democratic mixer,

---

[1] The death of Purvis, then chairman of the British Supply Council in North America, on 14 August 1941, is a matter of record. That Beaverbrook should have been on the same aircraft is not mentioned by his biographers.

as Philip Lothian always was, does no good. They understood Lothian, who either really enjoyed a hot dog and showed he did, or did not like a hot dog and said so. Halifax is not likely to return. Who is to be his successor, nobody can think. Archie Sinclair (Secretary of State for Air) is mentioned.

Notes by J.B.B., 30 August

I had an hour's talk with the Dean before lunch today. It is only natural that he should feel immense satisfaction that we are at last ranged on the same side as Russia, whose ardent supporter he has been for so many years. He points out that at last England is discovering what he has always maintained; which is that Russia is strong. Such strength is based on two things; that there is a moral basis behind her productive machinery and industry, not merely a private profit motive, and that she stands behind Science - she has a belief in truth.

The Dean sees a good deal of Maisky, the Russian ambassador, who is very bitter about the paucity of British support. So far we have only sent Russia 200 fighter planes and six American bombers. The Dean marvels at the shortsightedness of this country not going all-out to help Russia to the utmost. I said, 'What about the Anglo-American mission we were sending to Moscow?' He replied, 'Why the delay? Every day is important.' I am bound to add that General McNaughton agrees with him, and pours scorn on Canadian and English soldiers who say 'Let the Germans and Russians kill each other off.' Even a Polish general I met the other day has been saying, 'This war is going to lead to a new more sane and liberal Russia than the ultra-revolutionary one'

The Dean is constantly addressing huge meetings. 'I ration myself,' he said, 'to one or two meetings a week.' Invitations are pouring in from all over the country, and attendances are never less than 3,000 people. The audiences, says the Dean, are always enthusiastic, but there is still much suspicion of Russia in this country. He cannot broadcast, and White Russian influence is strong at Broadcasting House. There is never a single word in the press about these big meetings he is addressing. 'Would not Russia have fought against us as willingly as against Germany?', I asked. He said, 'No, the Russians loathe Nazi Germany, whereas we, the British, are half-way between friend and foe.' He continued, 'We have no theory of racial superiority , though it must be admitted we do not always behave as if this were the case - in India, for example, or the West Indies - where in spite of the good things we have done, our motive is based primarily on private gain.' He said that in his speeches the biggest round of applause invariably greets his description of the Russian parliament, where each member is equipped with earphones and can listen to any speech, though delivered in a foreign tongue, in his own language because it is instantaneously translated. 'Why cannot we have Hindu and West Indians in one parliament,' he said, 'making their case heard and understood in the language of each of their hearers?' 'This', he maintained, 'is true internationalism'.

Julian to J.B.B., 31 August   *Felsted*

I have much enjoyed my comparatively quiet time in my own house, especially the last few days during which it has become restored to its usual appearance and comfort. Now only my house, soon to be let by me to Brigadier Buckley, and the old School House which is chock-a-bloc with masters' furniture, and the chapel are not requisitioned. I only hope when the war is over that we shall be quickly able to turn the occupants out.

On Sunday, immediately after Holy Communion at which, I am glad to say, I saw the Brigadier, I motored over to Stansted Hall to lunch with R.A. Butler. There he was *en famille*, and after lunch Sam Courtauld,[1] Rab and I had over an hour and a half on the education problems of this country. Rab told me he had been determined not to give himself away when he replied to the important delegation of Church leaders last week. He felt it would be fatal to estrange any powerful group if he were to appear on the scene straight away with a firm policy. He hopes, however, to introduce a very comprehensive Education Bill during war time, say by Christmas 1942, which rather looked as if he felt the war might go on some time after that.

He would not go into details as to measures he is considering, but felt it would be quite impossible to raise the school-leaving age to 16. There are over 1,000 schools either destroyed or badly damaged, and there will be a great paucity of teachers for many years after the war. He hoped rather to legislate for post-school education, night classes, or part-time teaching out of employers' time. He would not commit himself about the public schools, but we discussed the many difficulties of bringing the boarding schools into the public system of education; not only the introduction of state-aided scholars, but also of some state training

---

[1] Samuel Courtauld (1876-1947). Chm. of Courtaulds Ltd., 1921-46. Butler's father-in-law.

for teachers. He did not seem to think the Preparatory Schools could easily be included, but, as one would expect, he was most discreet. He was more keen on asking me questions than in stating his policy, so I came away, as I am sure he intended me to, with no very clear idea that he has as yet any settled policy.

He spoke of the difficulty of finding any good spokesman in the Lords for a progressive education policy, and said he had toyed with the idea of getting put there himself. It was not impossible, he pointed out, to run the Board of Education from the Upper House, as of course Halifax had done so for a time, but I doubt if Rab really meant this, as the chief battle must be fought out in the Commons. He depreciated the attitude taken by many Churchmen, and even by the Archbishop himself, by which they seek to thrust the un-Christianity of the modern age on to the schools, leaving out the failure of the Churches to influence the parents to demand better from the schools for their children. But he told of one amusing incident, when a deputation of distinguished Churchmen visited him ten days ago. He managed to cover the Archbishop in momentary confusion by whispering to him at the end of proceedings, 'Will you close with prayer?' The deputation, all Churchmen or prominent non-conformists, were unprepared for this and rose somewhat awkwardly to their feet, while Cosmo sought round in his mind for an adequate prayer to meet the occasion.

I think Menzies made a blunder in resigning the premiership.[1] He had so good a press in England, he wanted to get back here, and I fancy public opinion in Australia is against having its best troops in the Middle East while Japan threatens to attack. So he wanted to get back to put this before our War Cabinet, but I also suspect he has designs on the premiership as Winston's successor, though this would mean of course his resigning from the Australian Parliament and finding an English seat. This last idea may be grotesque. I think Menzies is most patriotic, but it is hard for politicians not to look out for their own advantage; and he is very ambitious.

---

[1] Having spent a good part of the year in Britain, Menzies resigned the premiership of Australia on 28 August 1941, having tried and failed to form an all-party government.

September

Notes by J.B.B., 7 September

I was at Lavington today with Barbie Wallace, and David Margesson was there. His reply to Maisky's criticism of the paucity of English assistance was (i) his figures were not correct, we have sent many more planes than that, and (ii) that had not Russia come into an agreement with Germany in 1939 there would have been no war. I replied that the Dean of Canterbury would probably retort that Russia would have made a defensive alliance with Great Britain had the government really been in earnest. To this Margesson countered by saying, 'How could our government come to an understanding with Stalin when he demanded as a pre-requisite of any agreement that Russia should have a free hand to march into Finland and the Baltic states?'

Notes by E.C.F.B., 10 September   *Chiddingstone*

On Monday last, 8 September, Burgon recorded a broadcast to Canada at the BBC studio, which was placed on the air at 1.30 a.m. Also, a son, Robert Erskine, was born to Kay in the Isle of Wight, where she is with her husband Charles Beveridge. In two weeks' time I am to move back to Goodrich to be with Julian once the school term has begun.

Notes by J.B.B., 14 September

David Wallace, who was with the Legation at Athens in charge of the press propaganda and got away to Crete and then to Cairo, arrived in England in mid-August. Prue (his wife) and the baby left Athens a week before he did. David told me they all had the greatest admiration for the Greek character. They appreciated everything we had done and tried to do, and realised that more was impossible. The people in Athens, for instance, received the New Zealand troops retreating through the city to embark with as much enthusiasm as they had shown upon their arrival.

The British Embassy at Washington is 200 strong and badly needs co-ordination. Halifax, who contrary to expectation returns to the USA, takes with him Angus McDonnell[1] who has lived in the States a long time and understands the Americans. He will be able to interpret Halifax in Washington and New York, and see that he offers the right people a drink, which the Ambassador frequently forgets to do. There should be somebody to reorganise the embassy staff and really take in hand our attempt to present the British case in America. There is now doubt whether Sir Gerald Campbell, who is in charge of the propaganda work, is really the man for the job. There is talk of giving him an ambassadorship somewhere. Vernon Bartlett,[2] who Campbell had chosen to follow him directly to the USA, was deflected to Russia where he now is. There have been many plans and attempts to put across a really sound British propaganda case from coast to coast, but nothing has happened. We are as badly served as we were two years ago when the war broke out. India is perhaps the most fruitful source of misunderstanding. There are millions of Americans who believe India is a down-trodden country, used merely as a revenue-producing subject race. The American universities are especially unenlightened on this subject.

Sam Hoare, our Ambassador in Madrid, badly wants to succeed Linlithgow[3] as Viceroy of India. Hoare is admittedly doing a first-class job in Spain, and it is evident that the Spanish government has some doubts about the ultimate success of the Axis. Amery is not against Hoare's appointment, but the last word lies with the PM.

One night early this month I was awakened by an aeroplane flying very low over my billet which, a moment or so later, crashed about 50 yards away in a clearing in a wood and burst into flames. As I rapidly put on trousers and a coat, I saw through the window two figures suspended from their parachutes floating down over the golf links on which our garden abuts. The parachutes were pink in the light of the burning plane. Not being certain whether they were British or German, I loaded my revolver and slipped it in my pocket. On rushing out I found Doucet, a young staff officer billeted in the next house, already helping the pilot-parachutist out of a tree. He immediately asked where the three other members of

---

[1] Col. Hon. Angus McDonnell (1881-1966). MP (Con) Dartford, 1924-9. Attaché to British Embassy, Washington, 1941-45. A 'Falstaffian character' who, as Halifax's nephew by marriage, was appointed to 'de-ice Edward'.
[2] (Charles) Vernon (Oldfield) Bartlett (1894-1983). Journalist and broadcaster; MP (Ind. Prog.) Bridgwater, 1938-50; temporarily British wartime press attaché in Moscow.
[3] Victor Alexander Hope, 2nd. Marquis of Linlithgow, KG, PC (1887-1952). Viceroy and Gov-Gen. of India, 1936-43.

his crew were. I said I had seen two baling out, but not the fourth. The pilot told me they had been bombing Frankfurt. Their petrol tank had been hit and all their instruments knocked out, and that he and his crew had known they would not be able to reach their base, which was Waddington in Lincolnshire. I went off to look for the rest of the crew. The two other parachutists I had seen soon turned up none the worse for wear, but the fourth man was discovered dead in the plane, and we could not get at him. The three survivors were taken into the next billet for some food and drink, while Doucet phoned the police at Leatherhead and got through to Waddington to report the accident. The pilot said he had seen the beacon on Headley Heath, but having no instrument or wireless, could not tell where he was. He had circled round trying to find a place to land, and realising he must crash in a minute or so, shouted to the crew that it was every man for himself. The fourth man had been seen trying to bale out, but apparently had not been quick enough. When, next evening on the wireless news, we heard that 'Six of our aircraft are missing', we knew where one was.

Geoffrey to E.C.F.B., 15 September   *Aberdeen*

What seems to me certain is that Russian ideas, as the result of the magnificent resistance put up against Nazism by Russia, will acquire great prestige after the war. The European centre of gravity may well shift from Paris, not to Berlin, but to Moscow, just as that of the British Empire may well shift to from London to Ottawa, which is in closer touch with New York. And after the war, financially at any rate, New York not London will be the world centre; and New York not Paris will be our most important embassy.

I have no knowledge of the workings of the Japanese political system, but it looks as if the Emperor has bestirred himself to take - as I suppose he has the right to do - a personal hand in politics, with the object of trying (if there is still time) to drag his country back from the brink of the precipice over which it is in mortal peril of plunging. In other words, nothing short of the Emperor's personal support can now avail to put the Japanese foreign office in a position of ascendancy over the military clique which apparently rules the country, and thus save it from war with the USA.

I registered this afternoon for fire-watching, and now await the event with interest, for I am already an ARP fire-watcher for eight private houses. Julian joined the King's Royal Rifle Corps OCTU at Perham Down, Andover last

Thursday. I confess I hope that we shall not send any troops to Russia. The latter is fighting well, and will beat Hitler as they did Napoleon. What we ought to do is to try and bomb Berlin every night for a month.

J.B.B. to E.C.F.B., 21 September   *H.Q. Canadian Forces*

My busy week began on Monday when I was chiefly occupied with proof-reading and correcting the pamphlet called 'Educational Opportunities Available to Canadian Forces Overseas', which I have drawn up to provide unit education officers and others with full information about our programme. When it is all set out on paper it does not make a bad showing, especially if you remember that when I came here almost exactly a year ago I was completely alone.

On Tuesday evening, Sir Paul Dukes[1] dined here and afterwards spoke to a captive audience in the Sergeants' mess on 'Russia'. He was one of our chief agents there for several years after the last war, and speaks the language perfectly having lived among them as a Russian. He thinks they will not give in , because it is their own soil which is being invaded. This is comforting in view of the news from the Russian front these days. He pointed out, however, that it is a grave mistake to think that the winter will necessarily make military operations more difficult for the Germans. Frozen country is good for tanks - and as for the attack on Leningrad, the entire stretch of water around Krondstadt freezes over, and tanks can, and no doubt will, attack over the ice.

On Wednesday afternoon I was at Cliveden, dealing with a number of problems which had arisen at No. 5 Canadian General Hospital, and for the whole of Thursday I was in London. I went to see Ralph first, and then met Tom Jones at the Athenæum where we lunched. We talked a good deal about the '1941' Club, who meet at the house of Edward Hulton of *Picture Post* every week. There, Priestley, Joad,[2] Julian Huxley,[3] Kingsley Martin[4], and other intellectual radicals of varying degrees and little experience of day-to-day administrative problems, meet. TJ also told me that Keith Feiling[5] is writing Neville Chamberlain's life. We

---

[1] Sir Paul Dukes (1889-1969). Travel writer; war service as lecturer and broadcaster for Min. of Information, Royal Inst. of Int. Affairs and Council for Adult Education in HM Forces.
[2] Cyril Edwin Mitchinson Joad (1891-1953). Philosophy lecturer, 1930-46; broadcaster.
[3] Julian Huxley (1887-1975). Biologist and writer; like Joad an original member of the BBC's 'Brains Trust' panel. Dir-Gen. UNESCO, 1946-48. Kt (1958).
[4] (Basil) Kingsley Martin (1897-1969). Editor of *New Statesman*, 1930-60.
[5] Keith Feiling (1884-1977). Tutor of Christ Church, Oxford, 1911-46; Chichele Prof. of Modern History, 1946-50. Kt (1958). His *Life of Neville Chamberlain* came out in 1946.

discussed who could write Stanley Baldwin's, who personally I feel will be vindicated by history. I am one of those - perhaps there are not many - who believe he is being most unfairly criticised at the present time 'for getting us into this mess,' as his detractors say.

On Friday I set off with Chatwin for Chichester where we had talks with Education Officers and regional committee secretaries. In Southampton we went down to the docks near the South Western Hotel, where the big Cunarders, the *Queen Mary* and the rest, and the White Star liners used to berth. There was nothing; just one ship in the whole port basin. The new docks, from where I have so often sailed on the *Empress of Britain*, were very badly damaged. We returned along the coast and came back through Portsmouth. What is remarkable is to see the fine old Mother Church of Portsmouth, where Nelson and Hawke and St Vincent all worshipped, standing erect and (except for some damage to the roof) untouched by the bombs that have laid waste several acres all round, so that all one sees of the houses, many of them famous, which stood there six months ago, are burnt-out shells, twisted iron girders and heaps of rubble. It is difficult for you to realise what grievous harm Portsmouth has suffered.

Geoffrey to E.C.F.B., 27 September   *Aberdeen*
I am interested to hear that Julian has taken an ex-lawyer, a German-Jew, on to his staff, as Miss Holland, Ursula's headmistress, has done the same. The man in question was not a judge but a well-to-do solicitor with a large and lucrative practice in Halle. He and his wife escaped from Germany penniless, in the last aeroplane which was allowed to bring Jewish refugees. They managed to bring their four grown-up sons with them, or thought they had until immediately after starting they discovered that their eldest, a businessman, had been prevented from leaving by the Gestapo. The three remaining sons were interned in this country, one (a student) being sent to the Isle of Man, another to Canada, and the third to Australia! The two former have been released and are back in Scotland, but the third is still in Australia. The old couple are now installed here in a small two-roomed flat. This is paid for, and they are supplied with a modest sum for their livelihood, by a rich Glasgow Jew, who acts as guarantor of their harmlessness. They heard, not long ago, that their eldest son had died in a German concentration camp.

We went, all of us, yesterday to see the film, simply first-rate, entitled '24 Hours in Soviet Russia', a marvellous picture, most beautiful, eloquent and convincing of the 'goodness' of the life, habits, achievements and disposition of that vast nation created since the last war by Lenin and Stalin, at the cost of murdering millions of their political opponents. It seemed to me like an unreal dream to see vast crowds of my fellow-countrymen cheering to the echo the image of 'dear old Uncle Joe' Stalin on a tank, and the Russian ambassador as he stood speaking underneath, wonder of wonders, the Union Jack side by side with the Red Flag - the so lately abominated ensign of the 'oppressor of poor little Finland'. One's whole world seemed turned topsy-turvy. What, thought I to myself, shall I be cheering next?

Elfride is now a fully matriculated student of this University. She devotes all her mornings now to reading Latin and Greek, and on two afternoons a week is temporarily helping at a local ARP centre. I have been spending much time on Shakespeare, re-writing, or rather re-thinking, lectures for next term. There is noboby like Shakespeare (except Dante) for clearing up one's mind on present affairs. Julian writes very happily from Perham Down. He seems to take to the army like a duck to water.

J.B.B. to E.C.F.B., 27 September   *H.Q. Canadian Corps*

I came on the staff of this Corps exactly one year ago today. It is incredible that I have been here this long, but it has been an interesting year and I do not regret it. I have made some friendships, notably with the Corps Commander, and these I am sure will endure.

I spent Friday evening with the General and Mrs McNaughton. After dinner we heard the news and Colonel Drew's[1] broadcast in which he made a great plea for the intense training of a highly specialised powerful fighting force in Canada. Drew pointed out that Canada is infinitely better suited for training mechanised troops than this country. The General's face as he listened was an interesting study. I asked him at the end what he thought. He said, 'Well, it is largely a re-hash of what I told Drew here a few weeks ago, but perhaps it would have been better to have asked me before publishing it to the world. Moreover,

[1] Lt-Col. Hon. George Drew (1894-1973). Barrister and politician in Ontario; Leader of Canadian Conservatives, 1949-56; High Commissioner for Canada in UK, 1957-64.

the fact that George Drew has suggested such a plan is hardly likely to commend it to the government in Ottawa.'

On Wednesday I went to London. First I was at London University for the meeting of the British Association of Adult Education, then I had a talk with W.E. Williams and two Cameron Highland Officers at the War Office about ABCA. At 6 p.m. I went to a reception at the Savoy given by the Bessboroughs for the Free French, and at 7.45 I went to the Café Royal to attend a dinner given by the Tots and Quots Club - a group of scientists who meet monthly to dine and talk. The members of the club are all outstanding scientists and I was very frightened when it became clear to me that I would have to speak, and the only people I knew besides Winant, the American ambassador, were Julian Huxley and Roy Harrod. I was introduced to Zuckerman,[1] the anatomist, who seemed a fascinating man. The talk centred first round the need to organise science for social reconstruction, as has been so brilliantly shown in the Tennessee Valley plan. It was agreed that the ownership, use and control of land all needs to be revolutionised. It was also agreed that employment, and security in that employment, were the two things people would demand after this war. When it came to my turn near the end of the evening, I tried to say this: that we had heard all evening about the benefits, the material benefits, science can confer - housing, beautiful cities, a juster economic system, shorter hours, health, nutrition, and so forth, but what good are these unless the people are educated to enjoy them and use them properly. And education, precisely because it touches human values, is not answerable to the exact sciences. Ethics and the formation of character, the humanities - are all part of education, and on these science can and should speak with reserve. I am sure what I said was immature and inadequate, but like all truly learned people they were kind in their comments.

Tony to his parents, 29 September   *Gt. Yarmouth*

It is amazing how quickly one slips back into the rut. Not much has happened really to alter the usual and rather deadly routine. But as I now feel part of the battalion, and have a niche in it, life is quite comfortable even if dreadfully unexciting.

---

[1]   Solly Zuckerman (1904-1993). South African-born zoologist and broadcaster; scientific adviser to numerous govt. deptartments during and after the war. Kt. (1956), OM (1968) and cr. Baron (1971).

I had meant to tell you something about my first platoon huddle over ABCA last week, but as time and paper were short, had to save it for this week. The CO always calls informal and spontaneous discussions on everyday subjects 'huddles', and so they were. That though was before ABCA inflicted its pamphlets upon us. This amazing body issues a lurid red pamphlet called 'War' every second week, and every other week a slightly less lurid but equally cheap and nasty pamphlet which, on the outside, looks like a cheap propaganda leaflet. I daren't produce it in front of the men while I am talking on the subject it deals with, because the immediate reaction would be, 'He's had this propaganda shoved down his throat, and now he's trying to shove it down ours,' and they will not play.

You know how the average Englishman hates propaganda, and the first issue of 'War' was rather a disappointing and inadequate subject. It dealt with the war in Libya of a year ago. The men weren't really interested in this, though an interesting discussion did develop on whether it is worth our while to drive the Germans out of Libya. My platoon is interested enough in current affairs, but they must be 'current' not a year old. I have just been looking at the first issue of 'Current Affairs', the other fortnightly issued by ABCA. Its main subject is America and her attitude, written I gather by an expert. The introduction gives some fairly sensible hints on how to give a lecture.[1]

October

Notes by E.C.F.B., 4 October   *Goodrich*

Two days ago Julian gave an 'At Home' to his masters and their wives and also the household staff. There was good music, the viola being played by the new German refugee master, who had been a leading judge in Hamburg and is a man of culture. Because of some Jewish blood, he and his wife were exiled from Germany with only 10/- in their pockets. He told us that he is brilliantly happy at Goodrich, and he seemed astonished at the courtesy of the boys and the friendly way they came to talk to him out of school. Julian has given them a little home by themselves in one of the Hill Court Lodges, and is so glad of the opportunity of helping people who have suffered so much.

---

[1] Probably Tony did not know at this stage that his Uncle Burgon - for whom he had a high regard - was in large part responsible for the ABCA enterprise.

It has just been announced that a long stretch of railing surrounding the Ambassadors' Court at Buckingham Palace has been removed with the King's approval. It is said that the material will be sufficient for one tank.

J.B.B. to E.C.F.B., 5 October   *H.Q. Canadian Forces*

Last Monday I was driven down to Brixham beyond Torquay for Operation 'Bumper', one of the biggest exercises ever to take place in this country, and now that it is over it can be mentioned. About 12 divisions were involved.

We stopped at Salisbury, where the Cathedral was like a peerless silver jewel set against a blue field - a cloudless sky, and again at Sherborne for a quarter of an hour to see the Abbey. By the time we reached Crewkerne it was raining, just as it had been in August 1926 when Julian and I drove along that high ridge to Chard. But that soon cleared up, and we slipped down the Exeter by-pass and chose the coastal road through Powderham, Dawlish and Teignmouth to Torquay. We were not charged any toll on the Teignmouth bridge, being a military car, and the run was superb. On the high ground north of Torquay the views back towards Exmouth were extraordinarily like those of the real Riviera. We reached Brixham just as it was getting dark.

Our object was to visit No. 1 Canadian Convalescent Depot, a convalescent home for soldiers and non-commissioned officers. The entire depot is housed in beach huts, and the sleeping quarters are all 'chalets' joined one to the other. Each 'chalet' is about as large as a good size bathing-machine, enough room for a narrow bed and a table and chair and that is all. I had a long talk with Wright, the CO, about ways and means of occupying the spare time of his patients. It is almost incredible but no attempt at occupational therapy has been made. We knew that there was an admirable training centre of this kind in Exeter, but Wright has been so occupied in restoring an effective administration that he has had no time to give to this method of ensuring discipline through useful employment. Later, when I talked with naval officers and found them more than ready to give lectures to the men about diesel engines or the construction of motor launches, I wondered why neither the CO nor the padre had had the idea of asking before. Travelling on to Dartington I was able to see Hans Oppenheim,[1] who left Germany in 1933, and persuade him to organise some music for our Brixham depot. I also learned from

---

[1] Hans Oppenheim (1892-1965). German-born composer and conductor; Dir. of Dartington Hall Music Group, 1937-45.

Dorothy Elmhirst's[1] secretary that as Dartington was the distributing centre for documentary films in the south west, some could be shown at Brixham. Both these suggestions I have since passed on to the CO and padre there.

Everybody is now back from 'Bumper', which apparently was a very good exercise, and I gather the Canadian Corps did well. The 1st. Canadian Division, or rather the West Nova Scotia Regiment, took the GOC of the 54th. Division prisoner!

Mrs. Gardiner to E.C.F.B., 19 October   *Canterbury*

I have, much to my satisfaction, got a new Pole to learn English with me. He is an older man than my last, a Captain Stanislaw Lodzinski, and very much a gentleman! He has worked on his English without a teacher for six months, and reads and writes astonishingly well. He admires the Cathedral enormously and is busily translating Mr Warner's guidebook into Polish. Such industry. He too, like Dr Pawlowski, has a wife and daughter in Poland, but knows nothing of their fate. The Poles are so brave and good. But one feels underneath they are so heartbroken, not only about their dear ones, but about their country and its sufferings.

The Russian position does haunt one, but I can't help believing they will pull through. Captain Lodzinski tells me the Polish airmen who are coming over here from the prison camps in Russia were so starved they are nearly all ill, and will have to be cared for and fed for some time before they are efficient. I fear that the Russians - brave as they are - have been awfully cruel to Poland. If only they can make a fresh start.

You will have heard of the bad raid on Whitstable on 11 October. A sea mine fell behind the Bear and Key Inn and, they say, 500 houses were damaged. I believe five people were killed and about 30 hurt, but the figures vary; one thing is certain, that the casualties were extraordinarily light in the circumstances.

Geoffrey to E.C.F.B., 21 October   *Aberdeen*

The important news is that Tony volunteered for India again. There were four others besides himself, and they all have been interviewed and accepted. Unless there is a further interview at the India Office, Tony says he will

---

[1] Dorothy Whitney Elmhirst (1897-1968). American-born philanthropist who, with her husband, bought Dartington Hall in 1925 and founded the Dartington Trust.

presumably hear no more about his posting until he gets his embarkation leave and is sent off. Wavell, it seems, wants 700 officers from this country for the Indian Army and for British troops. Tony thinks he is forming big armies in India to man what will be our Eastern front up to the Caucusus, and to deal with any trouble in the Far East if Japan really does try and march on Malaya and Burma. I had rather have Tony under Wavell's supreme command than anyone else. And abroad he will at least be seeing life and enlarging his experience - not stagnating.

Teresa Brown to E.C.F.B., 27 October   *Whitstable*

We are all quite safe after the raid. That Saturday night Daddy happened to be fire-watching and had just come to call me to look at some especially beautiful stars. We stood at the gate as the Hun plane swooped overhead, he must have been unloading his beastly burden, as two parachutes each carrying gigantic magnetic mines floated down. One landed harmlessly in the tide just off the beach, and I saw it next day after the Navy had rendered it harmless. It was like a black pillar box in shape, about ten feet long. The other landed at the junction of two streets just behind the High Street, and has done incredible damage for a great distance around. We feel very thankful it was early on a Saturday night with most of the population indoors at home, or at the cinema. Otherwise the death toll would have been very heavy.

Our life continues in its even way, and sometimes one longs to do something more vital to help the anguish of the multitude enslaved by Germany. On Saturday I registered for National Service. Sometimes I almost wish I wasn't married so that I could be up and away on real war work. I know you will say that is very wrong of me.

We are hoping for a visit from Bill soon. He recently went to Ireland and wrote us a very long denunciation of the Irish, both North and South, especially from the security point of view. It is no secret that all the army exercises in Northern Ireland are observed by Nazi staff officers who go over the border from their legation in Dublin and view what is being done. The German Consul in Dublin even had the cheek to go to Belfast to inspect air-raid damage. The Nazis go over the frontier in plain clothes, and unless we happen to be lucky enough to catch one, there is nothing to stop them wondering about, seeing what they want to see and reporting what they find out. The Irish, of course, think they are being good neutrals.

J.B.B. to E.C.F.B., 28 October   *H.Q. Canadian Corps*

Last month, we hear on good authority, some 50,000 French veterans sent their decorations of the last war back to Pétain as a protest against his collaborationist policy. This is as good a sign as any that the spirit of resistance in France is growing, and it does seem unfortunate we cannot seize the opportunity to make a diversion. But I feel we cannot express any opinion on this matter without knowledge. Certainly it is not the opinion of any regular soldier of experience that an invasion of Holland or France (a bridgehead for instance in Brittany) would result in anything else but disaster. How could we advance into France with the troops that we would have available? To occupy even a limited area merely involves the almost insuperable problem of maintaining them there. The Germans could easily detach 20 or 30 divisions to hold such a British force *in situ*. Even if we could advance, where would we advance to? To Paris? And if we did, we would immediately have to set up long lines of communication and expose vulnerable flanks. Moreover, there is the difficulty of shipping and the fact that we have not established air supremacy as yet.

On the other hand I think we must be careful not to become what the soldiers call 'Maginot-minded'. It is all a very difficult problem.

Notes by E.C.F.B., 31 October

Today the American destroyer *Reuben James* was torpedoed and sunk with considerable loss of life off Iceland. This event should strengthen the majority in the Senate's voting next week on the amendments to the Neutrality Act.

General de Gaulle has issued a call to Free French people to observe today at 4 p.m. a five minute silence and cessation from work in honour of the hostages recently shot in France. No details of observance in France were given in the press, but there was a sympathetic response in England and in other countries. In the harbour at Alexandria, even the Vichy ships flew their flags at half-mast.

November

J.B.B. to E.C.F.B., 2 November   *H.Q. Canadian Corps*

On Tuesday I was in Colchester visiting our AA Group HQ, having lunch with a number of officers, and spending the afternoon with the padre who has been supervising the educational work among the AA detachments in the two large barracks they occupy. This padre is one of the few I have come across who is almost entirely useless - from our point of view he is no use at all. He has been given a nice little house as an educational centre, but it is the centre of nothing. He tells me the men are too busy training and are all congregated in large barrack rooms which makes individual work impossible. I asked to inspect the North East Essex Technical College, which we did that evening, and we found it a hive of activity, but there were no Canadian soldiers there at all. Then there are a number of detachments out in the field manning isolated AA posts. One of these is some 30 miles from where the padre lives, but in all the time he has been with the unit he has never been near the post. Dear me! I only wish Julian were here. He would have the whole place buzzing in a week.

I had a letter from Tommy Lascelles the other day saying he had shown our pamphlet 'Educational Opportunities for Canadian Forces Overseas' to the King. I will send it to you after I have shown it to the General.

Notes by E.C.F.B., 2 November

All over England there is great difficulty in obtaining servants. All women over the age of 18 have to register, and are usually sent to join the forces or do other important work. Householders, therefore, in many cases have to do their own work. Geoffrey and Jean, for instance, are now servant-less. Another cause is the general restlessness among all the girls.

Mary to E.C.F.B., 7 November   *Chiddingstone*

I have been meaning to write to you ever since Kay's baby, Robert, was christened, but each night something seems to have turned up which had to be done, or I have been sick of letter-writing and too lazy to settle down to it. Jane and I are very busy because we have been asked to organise a Flag Day for Russia in Kent, in response to Mrs. Churchill's request to support the Aid to Russia Fund. This is to be held in December, and we have been writing for permission to hold the day in the main towns, and today we sent off 154 letters.

Besides the relations at Robert's christening there were a lot of village children and some grown-ups too. Last Sunday at the children's service, Daddy asked what we had done the Sunday before, and one small boy upped and said, 'We were christening your baby,Rector'!

Geoffrey to E.C.F.B., 9 November   *Aberdeen*

Snow fell again this week and it is still lying. It is bitterly cold. But just think of our airmen over Berlin on Friday night, enduring 60 degrees of frost but still doing their job; and of those facing and fighting through the terrible Russian winter. So one is ashamed to grumble. All the same it is cold, and I felt it particularly so last Thursday when I spent my first night (to recur every tenth day from now onwards) fire-watching up at King's. I was in control of a party of eleven students, eight men and three women, whom I divided into four sections of three each. Beds are supplied for the party in two rooms and, luckily, there was no siren that night. Personally I got very little sleep as one man had a graveyard cough and several snored loudly, but I shall try and manage better next time.

Tomorrow afternoon Dr. Benes,[1] the head of the Czechoslovakian government, is being given an honorary degree and will make a speech after it. He should be very interesting as he is a great statesman, and likely to be one of the big men in Europe after the war. Jean and Elfride and I will be there to hear him.

J.B.B. to E.C.F.B., 10 November   *H.Q. Canadian Corps*

I was in London all day yesterday, first to fix up a series of CEMA concerts for units in the coastal towns, then I went by appointment to see Arthur Greenwood, minister without portfolio in the Cabinet. We had a half-hour's talk about the plans of his ministry as regards reconstruction. He is not in favour of a Ministry of Reconstruction as in the last war, but thinks each department should shoulder its own responsibility in this regard. He outlined a number of committees which had been set up, but frankly admitted the whole thing was in a very early stage. He told me I could come to him whenever I liked and also introduced me to Sir George Chrystal,[2] the permanent under-secretary, who was equally cordial and said he would keep me in touch with what happened. All this I want for the work I am doing in connection with Canadian demobilisation plans.

There followed lunch at the Dorchester with Vincent Massey as host. I was talking to a group of visiting Canadian MPs, when up came, of all people,

---

[1] Eduard Benes (1884-1948). For. Min. of Czechoslovakia, 1918-35; President, 1935-38; recognized by Britain as President of Czech govt. in exile in June 1940; restored to office in May 1945, he resigned in June 1948.

[2] Sir George Chrystal (1880-1944). Attached to Min. of Reconstruction, 1917; Sec. of Min. of Pensions, 1919-35; Perm-Sec. Min. of Health, 1935-40. KCB (1922).

Reith,[1] who said to me in the most affable way, 'Hullo. How are you?' I thought he must have mistaken me for someone else, so said, 'My name is Bickersteth.' He replied, 'I knew that.' I said, 'Well we haven't talked since our rather acrid conversation across the Atlantic, and then our exchange of cables.' 'No,' he said, 'that's right. Why didn't you come to the BBC?' 'For the reasons I gave at the time. I was very happy at Hart House, and the staff at Broadcasting House was changing with such rapidity that I felt I must demand security of tenure and also independence. Also, I was far from sure if I could get on with you.' He said, 'Well, now I have seen you, I think I should have got on with you alright.' 'Perhaps it might have been easier for me than I thought,' was my reply, 'but Dawnay,[2] who came instead of me, died after two years of it.' 'Not as a result of the BBC,' Reith said, 'he was a sick man when he came to us. I wish you had come, I'm sure we would have got on.'

It was quite a burying of the hatchet. We sat three feet from each other at lunch, and he leaned across asking after you and telling me to keep in touch. After lunch I had a talk with Eden and Cranborne. They and Winant had been down to review some troops near Winchester and had seen David Wallace who, Eden said, was enjoying life immensely.

J.B.B.'s notes of his interview with Lt-Gen. Hastings Ismay, 10 November

'Pug' Ismay went to Moscow with the Beaverbrook-Harriman mission. He was the only person in uniform and was present on the chance of any strategical matters coming up for discussion. They did not; but as he was the only General there, Stalin expressed a desire to have a talk with him. In Stalin's room in the Kremlin, with an interpreter in attendance, the atmosphere was oriental in its serenity, lack of emotion and long silences. After a silent opening, Stalin in a slow measured tone said through the interpreter, 'Has the General anything he wishes to say to me?' 'Pug' said yes he had, and began to give reasons why it is impossible for us to form another front in the West or to create anything in the way of a diversion. In the middle of this Stalin suddenly stopped him to say he knew all there was to be said and that the Soviet Union was well satisfied with what Britain

---

[1] Baron John Reith (1889-1971). Manager of BBC, 1922; Dir-Gen., 1927-38; Chm. Imperial Airways, 1938-9, and of BOAC., 1939-40; MP (Nat) Southampton, 1940, Min. of Information, 1940; Min. of Transport, 1940; 1st. Minister of Works, 1940-42. Kt (1927). Cr. Baron (1940).

[2] Col. Alan Dawnay (1880-1938). GS, War Office, 1930-33; Controller Programmes Division BBC, 1933-35; OC Irish Guards, 1935-36; Instructor Imperial Staff Coll., 1936-37.

and America were doing. There was a further long silence, which Stalin showed no sign of breaking. Then 'Pug' said to the interpreter, 'Has Marshal Stalin anything he would like to say to me?' Stalin's response was that we must have conscription in Britain, and when 'Pug' began to explain that we had had conscription for several years, Stalin, getting as excited as he ever did, said, 'No, no, I don't mean that. I mean you must have conscription after the war. You must always have conscription. You English rely on your fleet. It is a great fleet. But things have changed and you must have a large standing army as well. There will always be Pétains in France, and you must not rely on the French army ever again. I suppose you would like to know why I signed an agreement with Germany at the end of August 1939. I will tell you. I have good information about the countries of the world, and all the information I had about France led me to think she was rotten through and through, and all the information I had about England led me to believe she was unarmed and completely unprepared. What therefore was I to do?' 'Pug' said that he made no attempt to answer that one!

The Russian military authorities were extremely secretive. They were of course ready enough to say what guns, tanks, aeroplanes and munitions they needed (that was the reason for the conference); but if 'Pug' asked a Russian general how many guns they had in an infantry division or how many tanks in an armoured division, he received no definite information. Mason-MacFarlane has seen nothing. Neither he nor any foreigner has been allowed to wander around and pick up what information they can. I asked 'Pug' why we had not sent 50 or 100 carefully selected officers - experts in tanks, gunnery, wireless, etc. - to see the difficulties of campaigning on a large scale, and his answer was that the Russians would not allow it. This seems very silly, though it is natural they should be suspicious of a people who have always shown a lack of sympathy for the Soviet social experiment. The first question Stalin asked Beaverbrook was about Moore-Brabazon's[1] unfortunate remark in Liverpool when at a private luncheon (no press present) he said he hoped the Russians would kill as many Germans as possible, and the Germans would kill as many Russians as possible. Trade Unionists were present at the lunch and gave him away. 'Pug' said that he had no reason to think that the Russian Department at the War Office was still fundamentally hostile to

---

[1] Rt. Hon. John Theodore Cuthbert Moore-Brabazon, (1889-1964). Aviator and self-publicist; MP (Con) Chatham, 1918-29, Wallasey, 1931-42; Min. of Transport, 1940-41; Min. of Aircraft Production, 1941-42. PC (1940). Cr. Baron (1942).

the Russians (I had heard a different story), and he denied that our politicians in general were hostile either. The Prime Minister (with whom he spends hours day and night) is absolutely sincere in his hope that Russia will beat Germany hands-down, unsympathetic towards Communism though he still is.

We are giving Russia as much help in equipment and raw materials as we possibly can. This inevitably reduces the equipment of our own troops in this country and, I suppose, makes the chance of a break-out next summer even more unlikely. But it is better for our tanks and aeroplanes to be used where they are desperately needed that to lie idle in this country. 'Pug's' personal opinion is that there are two main possibilities:- the Russians will not give in and the fighting will gradually get bogged down (unless the threat in the Caucasus, which is serious, develops further) so that early next spring the German army will quietly put Hitler aside and mount some form of negotiated peace. The second possibility is that Hitler, knowing that the army is thinking of some such plan, may make the terrific gamble of trying to invade us. 'Pug' thinks the second alternative is much the more unlikely. He points out that the question of invasion will settle itself. Either the Germans will have superiority in the air by day, in which case they will quietly blow this island to bits, or they will not have air superiority by day, and then invasion is impossible anyway. He believes that the Germans, having turned East, will never be able to turn to the West, and that the war will be fought out to an end in the Middle East.

Mary to E.C.F.B., 11 November   *Chiddingstone*

We thought you would like to know that Kay has just rung up from the Isle of Wight to say that Charles is ordered off on a five-week course on Friday, and will not return to the island. They don't know where he will go, it might be Iceland, but there are other English stations. Either Daddy or I will go to Yaverland on Friday for the night and help Kay pack and bring her and Robert back here on Saturday, at any rate for the present. They will try and get a proper mover such as Pickfords as they have got a great deal of stuff after living there for over a year. Kay was of course upset, but they have been expecting something like this to happen for some time, and Charles may still go to a place where she can join him.

Jane will have told you of her cable from Ted - that he won't be getting leave in 1942, so in order to get married the best plan is for her to travel to stay with her aunt in Kenya and then they can get married there. Such permits are difficult to obtain in wartime. But we shall help in every way we can. Really, everything is happening at once.

I have not forgotten Uncle Morris this Armistice Day, and our poppies are above his photograph.

Ralph to E.C.F.B., 14 November   *Lombard Street*

Peter is extraordinarily happy at school and, in spite of the war, is enjoying himself enormously. He has just got his Proficiency Badge in the Home Guard for shooting. To get this one he had to obtain an 8" group on the big range at 100 yards; he distinguished himself by getting a 4" group. This new call-up business will, I fear, make it quite certain that Peter will have to leave Rugby at the end of next summer term, if not earlier. In fact I may be in the bally thing myself before I am very much older.[1]

John to his father (Monier), 16 November

On Friday afternoon I was told that I was to defend one Pte. Thomas in a Field Court Martial at Dover Castle the next morning. Very short notice, but I got down to it straight away and spent a couple of hours with the prisoner in the guard-room, finding out what he had to say. I had never met him before, though he was with this Company. As he was palpably guilty (of desertion) and wanted to plead guilty, I had merely to make a speech in plea of mitigation.

We managed to get a lot of good points into the plea - bad varicose veins were, rather obscurely, the cause of the trouble - and I based my argument on the theme of, 'This man has never been given a fair chance, his case has never been sympathetically dealt with, leniency of sentence would show that the Army is prepared to admit its mistakes in not giving the accused a square deal according to his individual merits.' I wrote it all out in draft form - two and a half pages of foolscap, which I did not think would be excessive. As the accused pleaded guilty there was no prosecution speech, merely a summary of evidence read out. I said my stuff. It did not go as well as I had hoped, I felt I read it too much, and when I sat down and the President asked me to write out the main headings and give them

---

[1] At the beginning of December 1941 new regulations extending conscription were announced, with the minimum age for call-up being reduced from 19 to 18½, and the maximum increased from 41 to 51.

to him, I felt utterly depressed! However, when I returned, after the court had been closed, he said, 'That was a very good speech, were you a barrister or solicitor?' My depression vanished at once to be replaced by a swollen head, which I have been trying to knock out of myself by thanking my lucky stars that I had only a guilty case to deal with.

But I was extremely glad to have had this experience. It was interesting, and I now know that I could do it again without getting the wind up. I do not suppose I shall ever learn whether the speech had any effect on the severity of the sentence, as the court is of course sworn to secrecy. But I intend to see Thomas again before he goes off. I am afraid he is rather a bad lot, and will find himself doing about 18 months or so.

J.B.B. to E.C.F.B., 16 November   *H.Q. Canadian Corps*

This must be a very short letter as I am off in a few minutes to our new quarters (confidentially they are in Paddockhurst in Sussex). I had tea with the Corps Commander yesterday in his bedroom. He is recovering well from his illness and getting on splendidly. He does not look in the least ill, and says he feels well. I think he will be back towards the end of January.

I am sending Sanders to spend the afternoon and evening with his wife in Sutton, as in future this will be more difficult to do, and shall do the move in party with General Pearkes[1] and Guy Simonds. It is bound to be chaotic for a few days but we shall soon settle down.

General Montgomery, with whom our Corps will shortly be closely in touch, is considered a great martinet and a pugnacious little man.

Notes by E.C.F.B., 18 November

It was announced four days ago that the aircraft carrier *Ark Royal* has been torpedoed in the Mediterranean, so she is really sunk after two years of fine service, including a share in sinking the *Bismarck*. All but one of the 1,600 officers and men were saved, owing to the magnificent seamanship displayed by one of our destroyers which managed to get alongside the heavily listing ship, and to the marvellous discipline shown by the crew as, one by one, they slipped down ropes on to the deck of the destroyer. A few officers and men were left on board while

---

[1] Maj-Gen. Hon. George Pearkes, VC, DSO (1888-1964). GOC Ist. Can. Div., 1940; GOC-in-C. Pacific Command Canada, 1942-44; Minister of Nat. Defence, 1957-60.

attempts were made to tow her into Gibraltar, as well as to try to close the big hole in her side. But within 25 miles of Gibraltar she sank.[1]

Monier to E.C.F.B., 20 November   *Chiddingstone*

Today John ceases to be in the infantry as his whole Battalion is being turned into a Regiment of Artillery and will be armed with light mobile AA guns to accompany armoured divisions and give them protection from aircraft. He leaves for Yeovil on 27 November, and after two months there, goes on to Watchet, just under the Quantocks. The training altogether will last about four months, and then they will probably go overseas.

Jane and Mary have been asked by Mrs Churchill to 10 Downing Street on 3 December over the Russian Flag Day - rather a thrill. So the offensive in Libya has begun. May it be a success.

Geoffrey to E.C.F.B., 23 November   *Aberdeen*

Tony had no sooner reached Netheravon last Sunday than he was informed that the WO had postponed the course he had come to attend till the middle of December. So he simply returned to Yarmouth the next day.

Our weather continues to be vile; almost incessant rain and gales for the last four weeks, and barely a glimpse of the sun. Our siren alerts continue, and yesterday a bomb was dropped on the beach, but there were no casualties and only trifling damage.

We seem to have begun well in Libya and to have an excellent chance of destroying the whole German army there.[2] Moreover, I do not think the whole plan of our operations has yet been revealed. We may well be planning an encirclement movement on a vast scale. In that case, should it succeed, it would not be long before we would capture Tripolitania, thus inducing the whole of French North Africa, which is strongly anti-Vichy, to join us. We should then command the Mediterranean, and Italy would be at our mercy.

The Russians also, despite the German claim to have captured Rostov, seem strangely confident. The German communication lines get longer the further

---

[1] The *Ark Royal* sank on 14 November 1941. It was acknowledged at the Court of Inquiry that the loss stemmed from faults in the ship's design.

[2] A reference to the opening days of a series of engagements known as 'Operation Crusader', in which Axis forces were obliged to withdraw from Cyrenaica.

they advance. So Napoleon's fate may still await the invaders even during the present winter. Roosevelt's settling of the miners' strike in America showed the patience of a statesman of great ability. In short, things are looking hopeful all round.

J.B.B. to E.C.F.B., 23 November   *H.Q. Canadian Corps*

We have been here a week now and have shaken down, but I do not think anybody likes our new HQ as much as they did Headley. We are stuck away in wooded country, very lovely in itself, but inconvenient as regards accommodation and badly served by towns. Local towns are, to the private soldier, the saving grace of any locality, and we are five miles from a town of any size, too far for the soldier to walk in the dark nights, so when he gets in at 5 or 6 p.m. of an evening, he has nowhere to go. We work in a large country mansion - a rambling grotesque place, and 40 officers also sleep and mess in it. Another 40 or 50 sleep and mess in another country house four miles away, and special transport arrangements take them backwards and forwards for meals.

Yesterday there was a lunch here for the new Army Commander, Lt-General Montgomery. It was attended by the divisional generals, brigade commanders, and a few full colonels. I was the only civilian there. We each in turn had a chat with Montgomery, and I found, as I expected, he is the son of the late secretary of the Society for the Propagation of the Gospel. He is a man of about my age, small and spare, gray-haired, and has the reputation of being a bit of a fire-eater. For instance, he makes all members of his staff over 40 walk or run five miles a day. He was pleasant enough to me and asked about my work. At lunch itself I sat next to his ADC, a perfectly charming lad who had only finished his OCTU a few months ago, having been at Charterhouse till 1938, and then one year at St Johns. After lunch, as we stood around talking, the BGS of the Army, Brigadier Sinclair,[1] came up to me and said, 'You are Bickersteth aren't you? I said, 'Yes, and I believe you are son-in-law to Archdeacon and Mrs Sopwith.' He smiled and said he was. So it is a small world, and I find I have a link with the Army Commander, his BGS and his ADC, all of which is useful from the point of view of the work.

---

[1] Brig. John Sinclair, OBE (1897-1977). Dep-Dir. Mil. Operations, 1941; BGS SE Command, 1941; Dep. CGS Home Forces, 1942; Maj-Gen. 1943; Dir. of Mil. Intelligence, 1944-45. KCMG (1953).

Monier to E.C.F.B., 28 November   *Chiddingstone*

It is now 9.30 p.m. and Kay and Robert should have started on their way from Euston to Glasgow, *en route* for Dunoon, which they should reach just before mid-day tomorrow. Late on Monday night Charles phoned from Dunoon to say he had found lodgings, and would Kay and the baby come up. Kay was overjoyed. I saw them off at Edenbridge at 2.30 this afternoon.

Charles will notice a change in Robert even in the fortnight he has been away. He now smiles a lot and chuckles deliciously. Charles has no instructions yet as to when and where he may go. But I am sure he and Kay are right to be together now, in case he is sent overseas.

Notes by E.C.F.B., 30 November

After a pause to refit and repair tanks, another severe tank battle has been going on in Libya for the last day or two, with losses on both sides. The South Africans made a fine stand at Sidi Rezegh, suffering very heavy casualties. The battle at present seems to be in our favour. The Germans seem hemmed in but are fighting with great determination to escape to the west.

German pressure on Moscow increases without much progress, but Timoshenko[1] has re-formed his army and re-taken Rostov.

The situation in the Far East is beginning to look serious; a strong force of Japanese ships being seen off mandated islands. Roosevelt has returned unexpectedly to Washington and we have sent troops to Rangoon.

Mary to E.C.F.B., 30 November   *Chiddingstone*

We ought not to be taking Wednesday off to go to London really, but it will be fun, and I'll write and tell you about our visit to 10 Downing Street after the event. Jane and I are looking forward to it.

Michael Harker (the Old Felstedian RE here) was in Church this morning. Shows Uncle Julian's teaching! There is one quite regular communicant among the privates, and we asked him to breakfast this morning as by coming he misses his at the Castle. His home is in Leeds, so he and Daddy had much in common. There was no Church parade, but we had the CO from the Castle who is such a

---

[1] Semion Timoshenko (1895-1970). Marshal of the USSR and C-in-C of several army groups; vice-commissar of defence, 1941-5.

dear, and one other officer, two or three men and one singing in the choir. This last is going to play the organ next Sunday as he was an organist and choirmaster before the war.

We had a very boring girl to lunch who is working in the Land Army near here, and is the daughter of the late Vicar of Edenbridge. But tonight we may have a couple of sergeants in after supper to smoke a pipe and chat and listen to the wireless. So each day fills up with something.

J.B.B. to E.C.F.B., 30 November   *H.Q. Canadian Corps*

I was in London on Tuesday and had a long talk with Harold Scott, the director of the Borstal Association, which now has very little to do as most of the boys, when they come out of a Borstal institution, go straight into the army. The Association generally finds jobs for about 1,000 boys a year. This past year, 700 of these entered the fighting services. Not all of them turn out well, and they get into trouble and go back to a civilian prison or to a place of military detention. In other words, as Scott pointed out, his work really lies within the services, keeping touch with soldiers, sailors and airmen in trouble. And there is some prospect that before long he may be so employed. He told me of a most interesting experiment at Pontefract where a kind of military Borstal for the Northern Command has been set up. It was started with the co-operation of Sir Ronald Adam,[1] at that time GOC Northern Command, who I had always heard was a man of imagination. He is at the War Office now.

I did a little shopping, which I hate, and found I could not do much both because the shops had not got what I wanted, and when they had, I had forgotten to bring my margarine coupons. Vincent Massey and I lunched alone in his flat at the Dorchester. He told me that his son Lionel is still a prisoner in Athens, and that George Grant, of the Oxford and Bermondsey Club, has signed on for the Mercantile Marine. He was supposed to have reported on a certain date, but did not do so and nobody knows where he is. It is not for a moment suggested that he is shirking his job, rather that he has sailed on another ship without telling anybody where or how. He is an extraordinary youth.

---

[1] Lieut-Gen. Sir Ronald Forbes Adam, DSO (1885-1982). Dep. CIGS, 1938-39; Comm. 3rd. Army Corps, 1939-40; GOC Northern Cmmd., 1940-41; Adj-Gen. to the Forces, 1941-46; General, 1942; Dir-Gen. of British Council, 1946-51.

December

Monier to E.C.F.B., 4 December   *Chiddingstone*

Charles, Kay and Robert are here again. Kay managed the journey so well last Friday night (28 November) and Charles met her at Dunoon. On Monday he was told he was to go overseas, probably to the Far East, and was to have a fortnight's leave starting on Tuesday. So they came down on Tuesday night (2 December) - two hours late due to fog - and after breakfasting and doing a little preliminary shopping at Gieves for tropical kit, they got here for lunch. I gave up going to London and was here to greet them.

Charles is of course torn between duty and love of wife and child. Robert is none the worse for his two long journeys, and has begun to be quite happy lying in his cradle and talking to a toy animal.

Mary and Jane enjoyed their trip to 10 Downing Street very much and came back so enthused.

Tony to E.C.F.B., 5 December   *Aberdeen*

This morning I had a letter from the Adjutant of my Battalion, saying that I shall be going to India on or about 25 December (secret) and can consider this as my embarkation leave. It has been extended two days but I shall spend them in London as I want to get some kit, and I think I shall be going down to Chiddingstone just for the day on Wednesday. I also want to see Uncle Ralph in London to ask him about insuring my luggage on the voyage and the like. On Thursday I return to Yarmouth and await more precise instructions as to where I have to report and when. I only hope that I do sail round about Christmas. So often one hears of sailings postponed, and officers and men saying goodbyes 'for the last time' about six times over before eventually leaving.

We had the Bishop of Chichester[1] to tea last Wednesday. I hadn't met him since he was Dean of Canterbury in 1927 or 28! Of course, we had to argue with him about the war and religion, and in my usual way I began to tell him that the Church should try and keep clear of politics. However he didn't think so.

---

[1] Rt. Rev. George Bell (1883-1958). Ordained 1907; Resident Chaplain to Archbishop of Canterbury, 1914-24; Dean of Canterbury, 1924-29; Bishop of Chichester, 1929-58. Prolific writer on ecumenicalism; his 'courageous condemnation of the indiscriminate Allied bombing of German cities undoudtedly contributed to the disregard of his strong claims to succeed William Temple as Archbishop of Canterbury in 1944.'

Notes by E.C.F.B., 7 December

Today, while Japan was still negotiating with the USA, negotiations which they said were actuated by their sincere desire for peace in the Pacific, suddenly and without warning Japanese planes bombed the Hawaiian islands. Roosevelt, in announcing this fact in a speech to Congress, said that 7 December would always be remembered as a day of infamy, because of Japanese treachery in attacking a nation with whom they were at peace, without first declaring war. In Honolulu there were about 1,500 killed and 1,500 wounded. They also bombed the Philippines, Hong Kong and Singapore, and landed troops in North Malaya. After doing all this, Japan made a formal declaration of war against America and Britain, a perfect imitation of Nazi methods.

J.B.B. to E.C.F.B., 7 December　　　　　　　　　*H.Q. Canadian Corps*

Owing to the present pressures I had to put off an engagement last night and turn-down Mrs Ronnie Greville's invitation to Polesdon Lacy. I rang her to explain the situation and she was very nice about it, though it was very short notice to be told two weekend guests were calling off. But war conditions cannot be altered. She said the King and Queen had had lunch with her at the Dorchester alone this week, and were very interesting, and she wanted to tell me about it. I spent all afternoon seeing NCOs and men of various kinds who wanted help, and this was far more worthwhile than talking to Mrs Ronnie Greville!

On Friday I dropped in at Leatherhead on my way back from No. 5 Hospital at Taplow to have lunch with General McNaughton. His lung is now absolutely clear, and all he has to do is rest for some weeks and then he can come back. But he will find this a difficult period, as his restless active mind will get hopelessly bored, and he will become depressed. I believe the doctors will realise that too long a rest is defeating its purpose, and he may come back about the second or third week in January. In the meantime there is the question of Lieut-General Crerar to consider. As you saw in the papers, he has been appointed GOC 2nd. Canadian Division, taking a step down to Maj-General to do it. He is senior to Pearkes, and if he arrives from Canada before McNaughton recovers fully I do not see how he can avoid taking command of the Corps temporarily. He is an extraordinarily nice man.[1]

Notes by E.C.F.B., 10 December

There is bad news for us today; before Question Time the Prime Minister told the House that *Prince of Wales* and *Repulse* had been sunk off Singapore. The former was our newest battleship of 35,000 tons. The second was a battlecruiser like *Hood*, of some 32,000 tons and over 10 years old. Later we heard that more than 2,000 crewmen had been saved from the combined ships' complements of 3,000 men, though Admiral Sir Tom Phillips[2] and the Captain of the *Prince of Wales* were lost.

John to E.C.F.B., 10 December   *8th. Light A.A. Regt. (The Buffs) Yeovil*

The Japs have certainly achieved a great measure of tactical surprise, and by attacking in so many places at once have had initial success. The sinking of so many fine ships, both ours and American, can be nothing but a very serious blow. But I hope and trust we shall recover from it; the difficulty will be in finding a place where we can really hit back. The only amusement I've got out of the whole business so far is the reports of air-raid alarms in New York; the war must have come as such a shock to the vast majority of Americans. Incidentally, I see no reason why the Lease Lend programme should be seriously curtailed. It is not as though the Americans have got busy on production at all up to now.

There, you may say, is your grandson laying down the law about something of which he knows very little. But I find it rather fun doing this in letters. It reminds me of the occasion when I wrote to Ted a few days before Germany attacked Russia, saying firmly I thought Hitler would never attempt it. He got the letter nearly two and a half months after the attack started, of course!

On 11 December 1941 Italy and Germany declared war on the United States. On the same day, President Roosevelt asked Congress to recognise a state of war with those countries.

---

[1] Such 'Canadian musical chairs' did not please Montgomery whose relations with Crerar and McNaughton 'suffered for the rest of the war'. See N. Hamilton, *Monty: the Making of a General, 1887-1942* (Hamlyn, 1982) pp. 500-1.
[2] Acting Admiral Sir Tom Phillips (1888-1941). Vice-Chief of Naval Staff, 1939-41; C-in-C, Eastern Fleet, 1941.

Notes by E.C.F.B., 14 December

The Russians announced yesterday great successes in pursuing the Germans along the whole front. They have recaptured over 400 towns and villages, and have secured huge booty of every kind.

This morning at dawn, the Japanese launched their heavy attack from the mainland on Hong Kong, after sending an insolent ultimatum to Maj-General Norton[1] calling upon him to surrender. This was promptly refused. The Royal Australian Navy is giving efficient help, while the Australian government is sending troops and airmen direct to Singapore.

Tomorrow Charles Beveridge will have to say goodbye to his wife and son, leaving Chiddingstone for his place of assembly, Dunoon, prior to embarkation.

In the USA, Lindbergh, the former airman and pro-Nazi who has abused England day in and day out, has requested to rejoin the Air Force and will go 'anywhere necessary'. He has even given up his Nazi decorations. Is he, I wonder, a fifth columnist?

J.B.B. to E.C.F.B., 14 December   *H.Q. Canadian Corps*

There are two Canadian battalions in Hong Kong, so they are seeing some fighting before us. The Home Guard seems to be tightening up a good deal, and in the New Year I must go and see Cussans in Canterbury. I hope they will allow me to stay on.

I left here on Thursday and spent the night with Brigadier Jim Stewart[2] at Borden. He commands all gunner reinforcements. Next morning, at Stewart's request, I addressed his CO's and senior instructors. I was not prepared for this, and it was a strain, but I spoke not about any detailed educational programme but from a comprehensive point of view. I then went round and saw our civilian educational adviser, a decent enough fellow but (as Jim Stewart pointed out) nothing more than a country school teacher. That, of course, is our trouble. We

---

[1] Maj-Gen. Edward Norton, MC DSO (1884-1954). Member of Everest expeditions, 1922 and 1924; Comm. Madras District, 1938-40; Acting Gov. of Hong Kong and temp. Lieut-Gen., 1941; retired 1942.

[2] Brig. James Crossley Stewart, DSO (1891-1972). CCRA 1st. Canadian Corps, 1941; served in Italy and NW Europe; rtd. from Army, 1947; Manager Indust. Assoc. of British Columbia, 1947-60.

are 13, including Chatwin, and except for a couple of them there is not one I would have on my staff at Hart House. We have really got to the stage where we ought to have some of the ablest brains in Canada on our staff. As it is, we peg along and give the Army what they want - i.e. a modicum of educational opportunity, but not too much - certainly not enough to interfere with military duties.

Ralph to E.C.F.B., 18 December   *Lombard Street*

I do not like to think what it will be like if we lose any more men under this new call-up. They are now talking of opening Lloyds all day on Saturday, which would mean we would have to work all day. The pressure of work is terrific; however, 'sufficient unto the day'.

Peter is full of the course which he will attend for a week in early January just outside Tonbridge. I know all about the place as one of our officer instructors, an excellent chap, took us there with the Home Guard last Sunday. It is supposed to be one of the best schools in England, so he should have an interesting time even if it will be very hard work. His recruits platoon has just won some kind of competition, apparently for the whole school, so he must have taught them pretty well. There are no two ways about it, Peter has the makings of a fine soldier.

The Far East situation is serious - no wonder Australia is angry. We are prize muddlers. Our lack of first-class staff officers is a tragedy.

Notes by E.C.F.B., 20 December

Burgon has eight days Christmas leave and has been allowed to bring his car as far as Cheltenham tomorrow, where Julian will meet him. Arrangements are being made for Burgon's driver to stay in a hostel overnight in Cheltenham, as he and the car have to be back at Corps HQ the following day.

News from the Far East is not good. We evacuated our garrison from Penang yesterday, and all European civilians. Unfortunately this gives the Japanese a port on the Indian Ocean, enabling them to harass our ships on the way to Singapore. The Japanese announce that they took Hong Kong yesterday. This is not confirmed, but seems probable, as all communications to the British government have ceased. If true, our garrison has only held out for five days.[1]

---

[1] The Hong Kong Garrison surrendered to the Japanese on Christmas Day, 25 December 1941.

Today Hitler has taken over command of the German army and dismissed von Brauchitsch,[1] making him the scapegoat for failing to take Moscow.

Notes by E.C.F.B., 26 December

On Christmas Day Kay had a letter from Charles, written from a ship, but whether before or after she had sailed she does not know.

Monier had no one at home except Kay, Mary and the baby, but entertained the CO from the Castle and another officer to dinner.

Geoffrey and Jean had the happiness of all their five children with them. Tony, who was at his assembly place at Leeds, was unexpectedly given leave as long as he was back on 27 December. It is not known what date he actually sails for India. As he has previously been in Norfolk, he provided a Norfolk turkey.

Burgon was at Goodrich with Julian and me. Miss Mathews provided an excellent turkey and plum pudding, and an old bottle of port was produced.

Julian to E.C.F.B., 29 December *Felsted*

I discovered this morning that the WO have definitely said that my house is not to be requisitioned unless I desire it. The Signals mess wanted to rent it as it stood, furniture and all, but this I have refused point blank as my furniture is not suitable for a mess. I have also refused to come to any decision for the moment on them renting my house with the furniture stored on two rooms. Fortunately the Major responsible for billeting is rather on the school's side against the Corps of Signals.

J.B.B. to E.C.F.B., 31 December

We listened in the 'A' mess last night to Churchill's speech in the House of Commons in Ottawa. It was interesting to hear it in the presence of the acting Corps Commander (Gen. Crerar) and his staff. The PM's strictures on the Vichy government were, of course, aimed at those considerable sections of the French Canadian population who, if not now, at any rate a year ago, were strongly pro-Pétain. The sentences in French at the end, though delivered with an execrable accent, would give almost childish pleasure to the Province of Quebec.

---

[1] Field Marshal Walter von Brauchitsch (1881-1948). C-in-C of German Army, 1938-41. Credited with saving Paris contrary to Hitler's order to destroy the city in 1944.

Jock Houstoun-Boswall[1] told Julian and me an amusing story the other night. He said that when the Australians left Colchester it was decided to give the local police chief a gift as a token of their esteem. It was agreed that a boomerang would make an appropriate present, and accordingly a boomerang - beautifully polished and in every way a particularly fine specimen - was presented to the police chief at a special function. A few days afterwards the Commander of the Australian troops received a note from the curator of the local museum saying that a boomerang was missing from the collection and did he know anything about it!

---

[1] Probably Sir (Thomas) Randolph Houstoun-Boswall, 5th. Bart. (1882-1953). A landowner who was a member of the Travellers' Club.

1942

Charles posted overseas - A variety of views on Russia - The shape of the post-war world - Elfride's war - 'In Malaya the situation is very serious' - Confused fighting in Libya - 'The war does not seem to be going well for us' - John returns to Rugby - 'Churchill will have to continue as PM' - 'Stafford [Cripps] will be all right ... he is unquestionably a future PM' - Beaverbrook's departure from the government - 'The so-called 'governing classes' seem to have lost confidence in themselves' - 'The Far Eastern situation still seems to go from bad to worse. But I still think we shall hold Australia' - Burgon's offer from the WO - The enthronement ceremony in Canterbury.

January

Julian to E.C.F.B., 2 January   *Felsted*

It is quite clear that I shall have to spend at least ten days here. There are a large number of questions to be settled concerning the Signals Corps taking over the remainder of our un-requisitioned buildings, as well as the task of moving all the furniture, except in my study and bedroom, from its present position. So I reluctantly wired to Geoff telling him I could not attempt Scotland.

On Tuesday and Wednesday I was in London attending the Headmasters' Conference at County Hall. Winant, the American Ambassador, gave us a delightful talk. He started in a very halting fashion, but in a few minutes he had quite won our attention and approval. We were free by 1 p.m. on Wednesday, and I lunched at the Royal Empire Society. At about 3 p.m. I was walking along the Strand doing some shopping, when who should I pass but Burgon, striding along so fast I do not think he saw me! I joined him later at the Travellers', from where we took a bus to the Dorchester to dine with the Masseys.

Most of yesterday was spent moving furniture. The Signals Corps mess is anxious to hire from me as much as they can, but it is very unwise to let furniture to a mess - for no one person will accept responsibility for it, and a mess in wartime is so easily dispersed and cannot be got at to meet damages. So I fear I shall leave them very little.

J.B.B. to E.C.F.B., 4 January   *H.Q. Canadian Forces*

Julian and I dined with Vincent and Alice Massey on Wednesday night. Leonard Brockington,[1] a lawyer by profession and a former personal adviser to MacKenzie King, was there. He was in admirable form and is a good conversationalist and *raconteur*. The others there were Sir Leonard and Lady Woolley,[2] and we had much interesting talk about the failure of the British government to stop criticism in the Dominions of its conduct of the war. We discussed Crete, which is held up as an example of outright failure, but which in

[1] Leonard Brockington (1888-1966). Welsh-born Canadian barrister; special war-time assistant to Canadian PM, 1939-42; adviser to MOI Empire Division, 1942.
[2] Sir Leonard Woolley (1880-1960) Museum Keeper and Archæologist; Major GSPR Directorate, 1939-43; Lt-Col., 1943-46. Kt (1935).

fact gave us time to stabilise the position in the Middle East. We are not good at explaining our case.

At 11.45 Vincent, Julian and I went in a taxi through the dark streets to Piccadilly and along the Strand to St Paul's Churchyard. There were, perhaps, 2,000 people there - the rowdy ones dancing and singing below the portico of the west front, where there was a blacked-out Christmas Tree. After the clock had struck midnight, we joined hands and sang 'Auld Lang Syne', but the whole affair was a pale reflection of the peacetime crowds and excitement. Through a gap to the north, one's eye wandered freely over the great arid waste of destruction around Paternoster Row - the result of the Blitz of 29 December 1940.

Next night, back at HQ, I dined with the officers of Corps signals There were 35 of them present, and the smartness of the turn-out was reminiscent of peacetime guest nights. The Colonel and I discussed the set-up of present wartime signals. How tremendously technical is every department of the army now.

Mary to E.C.F.B., 5 January   *Chiddingstone*

The excitement for us was certainly our visit to Downing Street. We had to show our invitation cards to two policemen at the entrance to the street, but were then swept in to No. 10 down a longish red-carpeted passage, the walls covered with signed team photographs of cabinet ministers. At the top of the staircase we were announced, and Mrs Churchill shook hands with everyone. I suppose there were about 120 people there. Mrs Churchill spoke quite charmingly first, and was followed by Sir Charles Wilson,[1] who had been on the Moscow mission with Lord Beaverbrook, and was very interesting about the tremendous need for various medical supplies. Lord Iliffe[2] spoke about the actual organisation of the Flag Day, and we felt rather honoured to be told this was the first reception held at Downing Street for over two years - in fact since the war began. Mrs Churchill ended the meeting reading out a message from Madame Maisky, then said in her charming voice, 'This isn't really a meeting but a tea party, so let's all go

---

[1] Sir Charles McMoran Wilson, MC - Lord Moran - (1882-1977). Dean, St Mary's Hospital Med. School, 1920-45; Pres. Royal College of Physicians, 1941-50. Kt (1938), Cr. Baron (1943). Because Churchill's doctor from 1940, Lord Moran should, perhaps, have kept quiet about his patient. Hence the publication of his memoirs in 1966, *The Struggle for Survival*, caused considerable controversy.
[2] Lord Edward Mauger Iliffe (1877-1960). MP (Con) Tamworth, 1923-29; Company Director and Newspaper Proprietor; Chm. of Red Cross and St John Fund, 1939-45. Kt. (1922). Cr. Baron (1933).

next door!' Whereupon we all surged in for a truly pre-war-like tea to which Jane and I did full justice.

Sarah Churchill was there in WAAF uniform, and Randolph's wife as a VAD. We had hoped to see Winston, but he did not appear. Although it was horrid and foggy outside, it was very cosy inside No. 10. Quite a lot of window panes have gone, and the gaps have been boarded up.

Tony to J.B.B., 5 January   *Golden Lion Hotel, Leeds*

I expect the poor old Canadian Corps would not be sorry to be on the high seas bound for Europe or the East. However, the PM insists on holding up the bogey of invasion, so I suppose General McNaughton will have to be attacked before he attacks. I think the boredom of coastal defence really drove me to volunteer for India, so I do not blame them for being browned off.

I have been in this town scarcely more than a week waiting to embark. Of course I have made my pilgrimage to what was the Vicarage, Leeds, in Grandfather's day. Of Leeds itself I have little to say. It is like Glasgow, a dirty industrial town and in winter none too bright. What the country round about is like, I have not had the opportunity of discovering. The war goes well in the Near East and badly in the Far East. I expect therefore to find myself in the latter area of operations.

Peter Macmillan, son of the Bishop of Guildford, had been in Hong Kong at the time of the Japanese invasion. This extract from his mother to E.C.F.B. expresses the family's anxious relief at his escape.

Mrs Macmillan to E.C.F.B., 10 January   *Farnham*

Yes indeed, you are very right. Our Peter is free, safe and unharmed. It is almost too glorious to believe now that it has happened, though directly I heard that a party had escaped I felt sure that Peter would be one of them if he were alive to do it. Nothing can alter the joy and relief at his escape, but, grievous to say, we have no news for him of his wife and little boy.

J.B.B. to E.C.F.B., 15 January   *H.Q. Canadian Corps*

On Thursday Sir Ronald Adam came to lunch. He is now Adjutant-General, and commanded 3rd. Corps up to Dunkirk. He is an extremely able and imaginative man, a great friend of 'Pug' Ismay, and genuinely keen on the educational experiments in the army. When General Crerar introduced me to him he said charmingly, 'I have heard all about the educational work here, and do so hope that you will come and have a talk about it with me in London sometime.' I certainly shall do as, like McNaughton, he was obviously full of ideas and vitally interested in the whole project. Before becoming Adjutant-General he had the Northern Command for a bit, and during his tenure of that office he did an enormous amount to encourage education among the troops he commanded.

He was also very interesting about the war, especially Russia, saying that the Russians had been far more forthcoming during Eden's visit than they had been at the time of the Beaverbrook-Harriman mission. Their 47-ton tanks, heavily armed and with terrific armour-plating, have proved too much for the Germans, but there are only a few of them. Stalin asked Nye[1] (the Deputy CIGS) whether the English generals got drunk, adding, 'Mine do, and I think they are rather better generals when they are drunk than when they are sober!'

From various sources in London I gathered there are two very different opinions about the Eastern front. There is still much fear and suspicion about Russia, and there are those at the War Office who minimise Russian achievements in the field, maintaining that the German casualties are far fewer than the Russians claim; that the German withdrawals are far more orderly than our daily press would suggest, and that the morale of the German army and of civilians is by no means undermined. This, for instance, is the opinion of some of the soldiers who went with Eden to Moscow. Other English military experts are convinced the Germans are defeated in Russia, and will never recover sufficiently to be really dangerous again. Those who are so convinced, and who think we should go all the way with Russia, fear that unless more cordial relations are built up with Stalin, he is quite likely to make a separate peace with Germany as soon as Russian soil is clear of the last Hun. They also think that Russia will then form a tremendous Slav 'bloc' in Eastern Europe with Russia as the dominating partner. They maintain that this bloc system is the only possible outcome of this war if future wars are to be avoided. That is, an Anglo-Saxon bloc (British Empire and USA), the Russian bloc, and a Far Eastern bloc of China and, grotesque as it now seems, Japan with

---

[1] Lt-Gen. Archibald Nye (1895-1967). Enlisted in the ranks, 1914; Dir. of Staff Duties, 1940; Vice CIGS, 1941-46; Gov. of Madras, 1946-48; High Commissioner for UK in India, 1948-52, and Canada, 1952-56. KBE (1944).

her. During the Eden visit, Stalin did his best to get him to agree on the occupation of the Baltic states as a permanent part of the peace treaties. It was the old trouble of the summer of 1939 again. Eden, quite properly, said he had no power to make such commitments.

I am now just off to see my opposite number at HQ 12 Corps, and then to lunch with Ralph, Alison and Peter. Incidentally, I have to pay Ralph £1, the extent of my indebtedness for a bet I took with him more than a year ago, that the war would be over before Christmas 1941. I must be more careful in future, though I still do not think this war will last as long as the last.

Elfride to E.C.F.B., 18 January   *Aberdeen*

The West Report Centre, where I go once a week for my 'war work', has taken to paying its receptionists. Apparently in Aberdeen alone, where there are only three centres, it will cost the government £62,000 a year. The silly thing is that it's quite unnecessary, for all we telephonists volunteered to do the work for no pay. The amount wasted on all the report centres all over the country must be simply terrific. Why should income tax be so high when the government can afford to throw so much money away?

The amount of trouble the whole business causes is amazing, for we have to be paid at the end of our time on duty. There are four shifts every day, and the poor officer in charge has to pull out his (or her) money bags four times a day, and dole out 9d all round. Then he has to write our names, addresses and several other things on a special sheet of paper which we have to sign. And even then it isn't over, because there are refreshments in the form of tea and biscuits for every shift, and he has to ask us exactly how much we've eaten and charge us for that. Then of course they've got to work out the accounts and make them balance. So now I get 9d. a week, which usually comes down to 6d because 3d is taken off for refreshments. What I find most amusing, however, is that I earned my first money without doing anything to earn it! For there was no alert, so I did nothing but sit in a nice warm lounge and read Jane Austen.

Notes by E.C.F.B., 19 January

In Malaya the situation is very serious. The Japanese are pushing slowly and systematically towards Singapore, from which they are only 65 miles distant.

They have also made a deep penetration into Burma and secured most of the tin mines.

In North Africa the Halfaya garrison has surrendered, 5,000 prisoners being taken, among them being two Italian generals and one German. Though the position was strongly fortified, we only lost 60 killed, 100 wounded, and gained large stores of guns and ammunition. I learn from Burgon however that Rommel, though he has lost many tanks, still possesses hundreds of the combination anti-aircraft and anti-tank guns. These have held up our advance very materially.

There is still no cable from Tony who sailed for India on 6 January. It is difficult not to be uneasy, as Axis U-boats are very active on the East coast of America.

Edward has written from Wau saying that the Governor of his Province has told him there is no objection to his marrying this year, although he has not been four years in the service. Jane is naturally anxious to get a permit to go out to Cape Town if possible, and be married. Edward would try to get leave to meet her there. Monier and Jane went to the Blue Star Line office this week, and were told by an official that such a permit was almost impossible; practically all the berths were under government control. I think Jane still hopes that private pressure might be brought to bear on the Foreign Office.

J.B.B. to E.C.F.B., 25 January   *H.Q. Canadian Corps*

So the Archbishop has resigned.[1] To me personally he has always been the soul of kindness, and I knew him very well. Some months ago he spoke to me quite openly of resignation, and clearly considered William Temple was the only possible choice as successor. I hope he does succeed, as I think he is well fitted to cope with the colossal problems of the post-war world.

On Wednesday I attended the third day of the so called 'Study Week'. This brought all the senior officers, down to and including Lt-Colonels, of the Canadian Army together. There were about 300 of them, and they sat in tiers round a large rectangular space, where, on the floor, there was a large 'sand table' - more precisely material bulging into hills and valleys with some kind of packing underneath it. Each day the 'sand table' represented a different bit of country -

---

[1] Dr Cosmo Lang, the Archbishop of Canterbury, announced his intention to resign at the Convocation of Canterbury at Westminster on 21 January 1942. He was only the second Primate to do so since St Augustine's founding of the See in the ninth century

sometimes real, sometimes fictitious - with each formation taking it in turn to attack or defend, or handle the co-operation of tanks and infantry.

It was a curious experience, though I am now fairly used to being the only civilian among so many officers. But everyone was very kind. Looking around at these 300 officers, the military talent of the Dominion of Canada, they would have looked very much like any other crowd of human beings, had they been in civilian clothes. But they are an able and enthusiastic group, and certainly they are patient. There is an immense amount of practical defensive work to be done, and I think it can quite honestly be said that the fact we are here in England makes invasion less likely. All the problems discussed had a bearing on air-borne and sea-borne invasion. Montgomery and Crerar sat in armchairs at one end of the hall, and Montgomery summed up each day.

MacKenzie King's decision to refer the matter of conscription to a plebiscite is shrewd and, though criticised here, can, I think, be defended. There are many who hold that he has not the courage to face a general election, to which can be answered (a) that he received an overwhelming mandate from the people of Canada less than two years ago, and (b) that the situation has not materially changed since then except on the one point.

You will have seen in *The Times* of yesterday the charming tribute paid to my great friend Reggie Heyworth,[1] CO of the Royals, who was recently killed in Libya. He and I went through many battles together in the last war, and, you will remember, we last saw him at Shorncliffe in 1938.

Geoffrey to E.C.F.B., 25 January   *Aberdeen*

I can't say I am looking forward to my fire-watching tonight. As I look out of my study window, I can hardly see across the street through the thick columns of whirling snow driven in from the North Sea by a south-easterly gale. It is the third successive blizzard we have had to endure in the last ten days, and yet, as the Red Queen would say, quite summer-like compared to that we read of in Russia, where, notwithstanding, the Russians still manage not only to fight but to drive their enemies before them. I can't imagine how they do it.

We had a letter from Tony on Tuesday, which must have been delayed at least ten days in the post. We presume it was written on board ship just prior to

---

[1] Lt-Col. R.F. Heyworth (d. 1942). Mil. Sec. to C-in-C India, 1932-35; OC Royal Dragoons, 1938-42.

sailing. He told us the vessel was crammed with troops, both officers and men, and that he was sharing a cabin with another officer deep in the bowels of the ship. This was so ill-ventilated that he wondered how it would be tolerable when they reached the tropics. Let's hope he will then be allowed to sleep on deck.

Australia seems to be losing its nerve about Japan, which is, after all, even if it captures New Guinea, not really so near her vitals as the Germans were near ours after Dunkirk. Moreover, I imagine that Japan is not much longer going to have it all her own way. In other words, it would seem that help is being sent and is already near. Japan seems to me to be fighting like a gambler, and spreading herself too much, unless of course she succeeds in capturing Singapore.

Mary to E.C.F.B., 26 January   *Chiddingstone*
Isn't it a coincidence that John should be sent to Rugby for part of his training? We long to hear where he is billeted. I sent my Sunday letter to him via Peter at school.

It was good to get news for Kay's husband Charles, first from his cable from Port Elizabeth, and the next day a letter posted at Freetown. He seems to have gone out on an American destroyer, so the talk about a roundabout route was all eye-wash, as he couldn't have gone more direct, or more quickly, by war-time travelling.

Jane got this telegramme from Ted on Saturday evening, 'Going leave 22 Feb. Intend Khartoum, 2 March, Cairo 8 March, Jerusalem 20 March and Wau 16 May. Presume no chance you sailing meanwhile. Hope wangle short leave when you come.' It is good that he will be getting away from malarial country, though hard for Jane to feel he's getting practically three months holiday which they can't have together. If only she could get a passage.

Monier to E.C.F.B., 30 January   *Chiddingstone*
John is happily settled at Rugby, and he is trying to get furniture for his men from the school. Two houses are closed, one of these is Steel's, which is a women's hostel! What would Mr Steel have thought of that? He may have Charles's old motor bike up there to help him get about locally. Part of his training is learning to ride one, and the bike is not getting any better standing here in our stable, so Kay says he may have it. He is a very careful rider, I am glad to say.

It is such a relief to know that Charles has arrived in Ceylon, he only took five ~~weeks~~ over the journey. Tony will almost certainly be on a slow troop ship.

Shall we save Singapore, I wonder? I am sure reinforcements must be on the point of arriving now. Once we can give the Japanese a defeat, they will not fight so well.

February

Geoffrey to E.C.F.B., 1 February   *Aberdeen*

This is the heaviest fall of snow and the longest continued spell of snowy weather we have had in Aberdeen since the winter of 1895, which I remember well as Port Meadow was frozen in Oxford, and there were weeks of skating. What would be useful here now are skis (if I knew how to use them), for everything is buried deep under snow, and labour is short to help clear it away. Moreover, no sooner is it cleared away than more falls. The tramways are kept open, but few motor cars venture on the street. Except under compulsion to go out for shopping or lectures, all of us have clung to the fireside this week and wondered how on earth they manage to fight in Russia in a winter many times more severe. I thought Churchill managed his parliamentary crisis with extraordinary skill.[1] His first speech was admirable, and the concessions he made to his critics in his second speech were exactly those, and conceded at precisely the right moment, to ensure his getting his vote of confidence, which he thoroughly deserved.

Now all eyes will be on Singapore (if they are not on Benghazi), and I think we ought to be able to hold it all right, while Wavell collects his army in Bengal for attacking the Japanese flanks through Siam. I ask myself whether that will be Tony's destination.

J.B.B. to E.C.F.B., 1 February   *H.Q. Canadian Corps*

I am so sorry that the illness of your maid made it necessary for you to move temporarily from Galen Lodge, as I know you had got used to the place.

---

[1] On 30 January 1942, in a three-day House of Commons debate on the war situation. That MPs should have declared their near unanimous support for Churchill was as predictable as the ILP member, Maxton, casting his vote against the government. There were, however, some 25 abstentions.

But I am glad that you appear to have got comfortable quarters in the Mount Craig Hotel.

We have made our move to Wakehurst Place, which is a really lovely Elizabethan house built around 1590 by John Culpeper. However, for the first two days there was no heating upstairs, and the water had all gone wrong. The first night was one of the iciest experiences I can remember for a long time. We have things more or less under control now, but it is still very cold.

I made a longish trip on Saturday, starting at 9.15 and going by Horsham to visit various units. On our way back I spent time with a unit of gunners encamped on the racecourse near Goodwood Park. They were most depressed. The camp was muddy and unfinished - no electric light, inadequate water-supply and lots of rats. It can't be helped, as many of these camps being erected all over this area for the constantly increasing number of troops could not be got ready in time, and yet the troops had to be housed somewhere. I suppose before the rest of the Canadian troops arrive, more English troops will have left the country and we shall enlarge our area, which is huge already. Julian and I are fully familiar with the conditions I saw yesterday - we lived for months together in such surroundings from 1915-18, but we were fighting. What the fellows yesterday found hard was to be asked to face such hardships, when in many ways we are really living under peacetime conditions.

You will have read that General McNaughton is now in Canada. I have known for many weeks that he was going there, and that was the reason I had to do so many memoranda for him. I had tea with him and Mrs McNaughton to say goodbye on 16 January, but then the boat was delayed and he did not actually sail until 23 January. We were beginning to get a bit anxious about his arrival. When he returns I think his Corps command will be dissolved and he will form an Army staff.[1] I hear that George Grant is returning to Canada as soon as he can get a ship, and that Lionel Massey is in a hospital attached to a Stalag five miles from Darmstadt.

Last night I rang up the Vicar of Ardingly (the village is one and-a-half-miles to the south of us) and found that Holy Communion was at 8.30. I shall not go, but will wait till it is at 8 a.m. again - from 15 February - as it makes everything too late. Unless one has breakfast before the service, which I don't like.

---

[1] It was. The 1st. Canadian Army came into official existence on 6 April 1942.

Monier to E.C.F.B., 3 February   *Chiddingstone*

I had quite a difficult time at a funeral yesterday, and now have a second one on Thursday. But in both cases I got the RE men from the Castle to dig the graves. They did so quite well.

John writes happily from Rugby, and has been very busy as it is the first time his unit has taken over billets as gunners. But he has been able to give Peter tea and see several of his master friends to fix up a running match between his men and the school. It seems to his fond father that he is proving a pretty efficient officer.

Our celery has turned out well, and we are much enjoying it. But the land girls did not earth it up quite well enough, and some of the thawed snow has got into it so it won't keep going as long as it did last year. But we are still eating leeks and sprouts, and of course our own potatoes.

Mary to E.C.F.B., 6 February   *Chiddingstone*

The Kent Red Cross Committee is going to pay Jane and me now for our connection with the county's 'Penny a Week' fund. This is to enable us to be able to say that we are paid when we are summoned to an interview about this conscription business. Voluntary jobs are very frowned on, we hear. We shall pay the bulk of both salaries back to the county, as it is much nicer to work voluntarily, and we should not have accepted the salaries at all if it had not been for the calling-up of women. I'm afraid I'm not a 'patriotic woman'. If I was a Russian I should have been in a munitions factory long ago, no doubt!

Geoffrey to E.C.F.B., 8 February   *Aberdeen*

It is astonishing how bravely people endure the hardships and partings and bereavements of war. One lady we know, who lives in a lovely country house outside Aberdeen, and has a husband of 84 and two grandchildren under her sole care, has no servants at all but manages somehow to keep the household and the garden - a big one - going by her own efforts. One son is seriously wounded and a prisoner in Paris. He has lost one eye, and she hardly ever hears from him. Another is in Shanghai, and she never hears from him at all now that the Japanese are in occupation (her letters to him are returned). His wife escaped to Australia, where she has been very ill with a nervous breakdown: their two children are the grandchildren, which the lady looks after and brings to school herself in this dreadful weather. Yet, she carries on, and though looking aged and weary, refuses to despair. And she is typical.

We have not yet heard from Tony and do not now (from what we have heard in similar cases) expect to get a cable except from his port of arrival. He may post letters *en route*, but not cable.

But, hard though it is to endure this complete silence, it's no use yielding to one's feelings. Moods of depression one must have, especially when, as now, the war does not seem to be going well for us (except of course in Russia), and when one reflects on the unmitigated sufferings of millions of innocent people. But the human mind has been so constructed, that it is, or ought to be, able to deal with its own moods. One was given one's reason to control one's moods (i.e. feelings), and the power of faith to control one's reason, and the power of prayer to fortify one's faith. One can't blame God if one won't use the weapons He has placed in one's hand. Moreover, I now feel about this war, even more than I did about the last one, that it has become far too big to be under human control. The main point is that a little hard thinking plus a modicum of faith in a loving God as controller of this war, ought to enable one to tackle with success one's inevitable moods of depression. One would not be human if one did not have them, nor English if one did not vent them in an occasional outburst of grumbling. But at bottom one knows in one's heart that the universe is being run exactly as it ought to be, and that against a background of eternity, the war itself and still more its effects on oneself individually look very small indeed.

Notes by E.C.F.B., 9 February

Yesterday it was announced that we had vacated our naval base at Singapore, because it could be reached by Japanese artillery at Jahore. No ships were left there, everything possible was removed from stores and repair shops, and the floating and graving docks were flooded. Overwhelming numbers of Japanese troops have landed in Singapore having repaired the causeway; our troops are retreating towards the city.

John to E.C.F.B., 13 February   *Newbold Grange, Rugby*

It is an amazing coincidence turning up here I must say. I have not seen much of the school, but I get a lot of exercise walking round the sites, which I am glad to have, as I have missed it since I left the infantry. I was able to invite several of the staff to a party we had a week ago, and as a result, I have even been asked help umpire a Field Day for the OTC next week, which might be amusing. As I have been given several things I would not otherwise have been able to get for the troops, I felt accepting the invitation was the least I could do.

Peter flourishes, and is larger than ever.

Geoffrey to E.C.F.B., 15 February   *Aberdeen*

Julian is home. He arrived in time for breakfast yesterday, looking very well, and admired by us all in his uniform of a subaltern in his famous regiment, the 60th. Rifles, to which he is so proud to belong.

Good as it was to have Julian back, it was even more welcome, perhaps, to have received the evening before five letters from Tony, three to Jean and me, one to Julian and one to Ursula.

When he wrote his last letter, he was sailing in perfect summer weather, in calm tropical seas, and so hot that he wore nothing but a shirt and shorts. They are fed with full peacetime food, enormous meals. Life on board is very lazy, practically no military duties, except to take it in turn to watch for submarines, and physical training for an hour a day. He is also learning Hindustani, under the tuition of some officers who know it. He thinks the voyage will become boring long before it is over, but at present is greatly enjoying the novelty of southern seas and skies. The transport (a big liner in peacetime) is tremendously over-crowded. He is glad he is not going out in the ranks, as the men are most uncomfortably quartered and not nearly so well fed. He thinks they have just cause for complaint, as better organisation would improve their lot considerably. I imagine his next letters will be posted from a South African port.

Our cook is shortly to be called up. She was interviewed last week, and they wouldn't let her stay with us. She may therefore go at any moment. We must try and get someone else, difficult though it is.

As for the war, we are (apart from Russia) decidedly in the trough of the wave at present, and the government is evidently going to catch it hot over the escape of the German warships from Cherbourg, or was it Brest?[1] Churchill will

---

[1] It was Brest. This was the famous 'Channel Dash' of 11-13 February 1942, in which the *Scharnhorst, Gneisenau* and *Prinz Eugen*, defying the Royal Navy and RAF, passed through the English Channel to take refuge in German ports.

have to continue as PM, but he will be compelled, I think, to satisfy the country in some way that he is not trying to run the war by himself, but is prepared to share his responsibility with others. I doubt if Singapore can hold out many days, perhaps hours longer.[1] On the other hand, these Japanese successes are ensuring that the USA shall take the war seriously. It is better for us that we should have reverses. Victory seems to demoralise us.

Ralph to E.C.F.B., 19 February   *Lombard Street*

We have seen a house on the outskirts of East Grinstead which, apparently, fulfils everything we require. Everything being all right we shall, I hope, buy it. It is about five minutes from the town, faces south, stands 350 feet above sea level, and all views are of the Ashdown Forest. The house really is a lovely one, built by an architect in 1904. It is not too big and could, at a pinch, be worked by two maids, although three would be better. It has three sitting rooms and nine bedrooms, with a large playroom at the top of the house in the attic. There is also a hard tennis-court. The train service is reasonably good, and the chief asset is that we are near the town for shopping, yet we are sufficiently far from the road to be quiet, in fact looking from the house you really cannot any other house at all. We also have central heating.

If everything goes to plan, we shall hope to move in about 1 May.

Notes by E.C.F.B., 20-23 February

It is announced today that Sir Stafford Cripps has been given a place in the War Cabinet, and been made Lord Privy Seal and Leader of the House of Commons. Attlee is being made Deputy Prime Minister.

On 23 February it was announced that Churchill had bent to the popular desire and made changes in the Cabinet, appointing younger men. Margesson has left, and for the first time in history a permanent secretary has been appointed as a minister, Sir James Grigg, whom Burgon has met through Tom Jones. Lord Reith,

---

[1] Lt-Gen. Percival, the GOC Singapore, surrendered to the Japanse on 15 February 1942. Different sources offer different figures, but at least 90,000 British and Empire prisoners were taken in what Churchill described as 'the worst disaster and largest capitulation in British history.'

has been shelved, with his place taken by Lord Portal,[1] while 'Jay' Llewellin[2] has been made Minister of Aircraft Production.

J.B.B. to E.C.F.B., 22 February   *H.Q. Canadian Forces*

I had a longish day on Wednesday - once again it was perishing cold - in Essex, which Sanders and I reached via the Gravesend -Tilbury ferry. After tea in the station restaurant, so chilled to the bone were we, I visited an AA regiment, then went on to Sir Francis Whitmore's[3] place. I called at the house, and as I was explaining to the butler who I was, Whitmore himself came through the hall and we almost fell on each others' necks. We had not seen each other since 1919. He and his wife absolutely insisted I stay for lunch, and so I telephoned to the CO of the Heavy AA regiment and arranged to see him at one of the battery sites at 2.30. All lunch we talked of old times.

On Friday, a group of American journalists came to lunch. They assured us that the Americans fully understand the difficulty of sending Canadians overseas under present conditions, but that British propaganda in the USA is still lamentably ineffective. Isolationism is by no means dormant, though in general the American people are determined to go all-out in defeating the Japanese. All their plans are based on a five-year war from the time the USA came into it!

Mary to E.C.F.B., 22 February   *Chiddingstone*

All went well in Tonbridge on Wednesday last. I arrived at the very poky little Labour Exchange for my appointment a few minutes early. When my turn came, I must say the girl was perfectly charming. She had my card filled in from when I registered and a letter attached to it in which I had said I couldn't possibly get to Westerham for an interview and could they possibly arrange it in Tonbridge. The girl began by saying, 'Now you do voluntary work for the Red Cross, don't

---

[1] Rt Hon. Lord Wyndham Portal, DSO (1885-1949). Min. of Works and Planning, 1st Comm. of Works and Public Buildings, 1942-44. PC (1942), Cr. Vt. (1945). President of Olympic Games, 1948.

[2] Rt Hon. John Jestyn Llewellin, MC (1893-1957). MP (Con) Uxbridge, 1929-45; Parl. Sec. Min. of Supply, 1939-40; Parl. Sec. Min. of Aircraft Production, 1940-41; Parl. Sec. Min. of War Transport, 1941-42; Min. of Aircraft Production, 1942; Minister Res. in Washington for Supply, 1942-43; Min. of Food, 1943-45. PC (1941), Cr. Baron (1945). Gov-Gen. and C-in-C, Rhodesia and Nyasaland, 1953-57.

[3] Col. Sir Francis Whitmore (1872-1962). Ld. Lieut. of Essex, 1936-58; Hon. Comdr. Essex Group AA Coys, 1942-45; Hon. Comdr. Essex Home Guard, 1940-44. KCB (1941), Cr. 1st Bart. (1954).

you?' Whereupon I replied, 'The position has now changed, and I'm paid.' Her answer was, 'Oh, that will make a lot of difference to your case.' She took down copious particulars about Daddy, and how I'd done some nursing training and was a member of the local women's AFS, and then she said, 'I don't expect you will hear anything else, but if something of national importance was set up in your district, you might be asked to transfer, but you would not be asked to leave home.' And as she said, it's highly unlikely that anything of such a nature should be set up in Chiddingstone. We then had a discussion on whether she got bored with interviewing people, and we agreed the women of Britain aren't a patch on the Russian women, and parted the best of friends. So that was that, and I don't expect I shall hear anything more for some time to come.

Jean to E.C.F.B., 26 February   *Aberdeen*

The snowstorms did not affect Aberdeen quite so badly as some smaller places. Fraserburgh, for instance, was without railway services for three weeks. Each time the line was cleared, which took several days, there was a fresh fall and it had to be done again. Aberdeen got its milk all right, but some dairies made customers call for it. We couldn't get bacon, and potatoes were another difficulty; they couldn't be got out of the pits, and then they couldn't bring them to town. Whenever I went out I took a large stout paper bag and a thick piece of string to collect potatoes whenever I could. Then there were the days when I had to hunt fish all over the town; fancy, a fish-less Aberdeen! Salt herring and cod were all that could be found, and the family having tried each of them said 'never again'. As this necessary food-hunting took a long time, and I couldn't bicycle owing to the snow, I had simply to fly through the housework and neglect a good deal - it was no use putting off shopping till afternoon, as all the food would be gone by then.

Notes by J.B.B., 28 February

It is known that Stafford Cripps never saw Stalin once, nor indeed many of the Commissars, during the period he was ambassador before Russia was invaded. The forecasts he gave were not particularly accurate. He took the view that Stalin would not fight and that, if he did, Russia could not last for three weeks.

The Beaverbrook-Harriman mission to Moscow was, to say the least, unconventional. On arrival, Beaverbrook refused to go near the British Embassy, took a suite of rooms at an hotel, hired a gipsy band and gave parties to which the

Commissars came and drank a good deal. He by-passed all the usual committees
and sub-committees, and demanded a plenary session. This was held. Stalin said, 'I
want so many tanks a month.' 'Agreed,' cried the Beaver. 'I want so many
aeroplanes a month.' 'Agreed,' cried the Beaver, and so on through the list. Stalin
was delighted. A great dinner, with the Empress Catherine's gold plate in use, was
held. On returning to England, Beaverbrook had great tussles with the WO and
Air Ministry and won. His argument was, 'Either the Russians will beat the
Germans; in which case we should give them everything we can to help: or the
Russians will be defeated, and we shan't have to send the equipment.' He had
always intended to conduct the conference at Moscow in the way he did. He
realised that government in Russia is not conducted by a number of
communistically-minded idealists, but by an Eastern despot who, as a sort of
Ghenghis Khan, loved oriental splendour and negotiations carried out on a lavish
scale. The approach was more successful than the Communist prattling and
correct diplomatic language of a Stafford Cripps.

James Stuart,[1] the chief whip, on whose shoulders the king-maker's mantle,
so long worn by David Margesson, has fallen, had much to do with the PM's
decision to ask Stafford Cripps to become Leader of the House. Fred (Stafford's
brother), who is a strong Conservative, assures everybody that Stafford will be 'all
right.' Actually, at the meeting of MPs which he recently addressed, Stafford was
so discreet as almost to be dull. The Tories left much reassured. In his speech to
the Anglo-Soviet youth in London he recently emphasised that any changes that
would come must be carried out in a British way.

Beaverbrook's departure from the government was by no means entirely
owing to bad health. He demanded the formation of a super-ministry of
production with himself at its head. The ministries of Supply, Shipping, Aircraft
Production and, of course Labour, were all to come under him. Even the PM
thought the suggestion was a bit too drastic. Besides, Bevin and Morrison both
dislike Beaverbrook - indeed, he is widely unpopular. The PM refused to approve,
and the Beaver left the government and departed for the USA. Cripps, with whom
the Beaver does not see eye-to-eye, rides to success on the military successes of

[1]   Rt Hon. James Gray Stuart, MC (1897-1971). MP (Con) Moray and Nairn, 1923-59; Govt.
Chief Whip, 1941-44; Chief Opposition Whip, 1945-48; Sec. of State for Scotland, 1951-57. PC
(1939), CH (1957), cr. Vt. Stuart of Findhorn (1959).

the Russian armies, and Beaverbrook goes out.[1] Some people are saying that Stafford might even end up as a Conservative PM. I don't believe this, though he is unquestionably a future PM.

The surrender of Singapore almost broke Churchill's heart. It was not a good show. The 18 Division, commanded by Beckwith-Smith,[2] who was at Christ Church with me, arrived after a four month voyage when the Japanese were already on the island, and went into action two days after disembarking. They did not do well, nor did the Australians. The Japs on several occasions drove them back with the bayonet. Of the Indians, the Gurkhas were the most effective fighters, not minding the jungle. The Pathans were accustomed to fighting in the open and were useless in enclosed country. In the last war, we had plenty of time to acclimatise ourselves. Divisions in France were first sent to some quiet sector to gain proficiency in trench fighting, and when open warfare came, it took us a little time to get used to that. We are bad starters.

Reith is heartbroken at losing his job as Minister of Works and Planning. He looked on himself as the saviour of the nation, and would gladly have taken on the job of Prime Minister had he been offered it. During the last reorganisation of the government, he literally camped in the outer hall of 10 Downing Street. Churchill did not really know him, and every time he passed through the hall he saw Reith sitting there. Churchill dubbed him 'Wuthering Heights'.

For the first time in 200 years the so-called 'governing classes' seem to have lost confidence in themselves. Throughout the nineteenth century and the great era of imperial expansion, they controlled the affairs of the country and, for as long as things went well, the supremacy of the 'old school tie' was unquestioned. Now, however, the people, looking on the war of 1914-18 and the failure of the last 25 years, realise their rulers are not infallible, and the significant thing is that the ruling classes are showing every sign of hesitancy. This uncertainty as to policy is clearly seen in their attitude towards India, Burma, Ceylon and other parts of the Empire during the last five years. They decided to grant measures of self-government, but retained control of what were considered essential areas, thus giving satisfaction to nobody.

---

[1] For a no less ironic account of Beaverbrook's resignation from the government in February 1942, see A.J.P. Taylor, *Beaverbrook* (Hamish Hamilton, 1972), pp. 506-20.
[2] Maj-Gen. Merton Beckwith-Smith, DSO, MC (1890-1942). Comdr. 1st Guards Brigade, 1939-40, and 18 Div., 1941-42. Died in captivity.

March

Geoffrey to E.C.F.B., 1 March   *Aberdeen*

We have not heard again from Tony, and I am afraid you are wrong if you think we are ever likely to hear from him regularly, even after he arrives in India. The means of transport are far too uncertain. Moreover, as soon as the Japanese capture Rangoon, which may happen at any moment now,[1] they will try and get raiders out into the Indian Ocean which will further complicate the smooth passage of mails.

The pressure on us in this country to start an offensive on the continent (Norway, France or Holland) this spring is growing; and we may be planning to do so. The recent parachute assault on the French coast shows that we could invade France if we wanted to.[2] If so, Julian may get to the fighting even before Tony. This war has been fertile in the unexpected, only I wish we could spring a surprise for a change, and not let it always be the enemy who dictates when and where we are to fight. I hope much myself from Sir Stafford Cripps.

Ralph to E.C.F.B., 5 March   *Lombard Street*

We had a good weekend at Rugby, although it was bitterly cold. Peter was taking part in a Warship Week march, as a member of the Home Guard. David Margesson took the salute and made a speech. Peter was not, therefore, available until tea time; naturally he was anxious to hear all about the new house. He seems to be getting on well, and I had a long discussion with his housemaster as to his going to Oxford in October. Apparently, everything is very much in the air still, so I have written to the Dean of Christ Church, but have not yet had his reply.

Geoffrey to E.C.F.B., 8 March   *Aberdeen*

At the end of last week, the coldest we have experienced so far during this exceptionally cold winter, we had a cable from Tony consisting of the four words, 'Well, all my love'. It was undated, so we do not know when it was dispatched or

---

[1] Rangoon, the capital of Burma, was occupied by Japanese forces on 8 March 1942.
[2] A reference to the successful Commando raid on Bruneval, near Le Havre, on 28 February 1942, in which a German radar installation was attacked, and the parts retrieved taken back to Britain for evaluation.

how long it may have been in transit; and with no indication of its place of origin. It is now just over eight weeks since he left England. Of course, the cable may mean he has already reached India. But if so, I think he would have been allowed to say so. The censorship seems to me, as it does to people generally who have relatives on active service abroad, needlessly strict. To be quite sure of being on the safe side, it is over-secretive. And the one extreme often does as much harm as the other.

There are all kinds of inefficiencies in the war effort. Take the case of the conscription of women. One would not mind if only they were making proper use of the girls they do call up. There is much resentment here about Aberdeen girls who had been sent to England to work for £4 a week in a factory where everyone was idling. They protested at being given no work to do and, though the foreman begged them to stay on doing nothing on full wages, they refused and came home at their own expense. Now no one can employ them, for they are still officially working for the factory in England. And this is not an uncommon case. Our cook is invaluable to us, but in a week or two's time she is quite likely to find herself engaged by the government to waste her time and the public's money in idling. This is all because the PM won't appoint any single authority to co-ordinate labour supply and munition works. I am glad to see that the very first step of the new secretary of state for war has been to order a comb-out of men holding high rank in regiments of the army. It was high time. This is a young man's war, and the battalion commanders and majors should all be men who have fought in this war; for our tactics, still based on those of the last war, are obviously quite out of date, first in France and now in Malaya and Burma. Moreover, it always takes a disaster to make the WO get a move on.

Notes by E.C.F.B., 8 March

The Prime Minister announced in the House of Commons today a bold step which the government is taking towards solving the Indian problem. Sir Stafford Cripps has offered to go out to India and lay before the Congress leaders a policy of 'constructive contributions to aid India in the realisation of full self-government'.[1] The loss of Sir Stafford, when he has just taken on the leadership of

---

[1]   News of this decision 'was greeted with some bewilderment in political circles'. From Churchill's point of view, however, Cripps agreeing to go to India was probably welcome. Better to have a rival abroad than at home. Better still if that rival could be seen to fail in his allotted

the House, is serious, but he is the one man in public life at the moment who commands sufficient confidence in India to heal the widening breach with Britain.

Monier to E.C.F.B., 10 March   *Chiddingstone*

John's leave was a very happy one. He is very well, and thoroughly enjoyed working in the garden and mending things. This took him right away from the war. He returned from leave to Rugby, but is now at Stow-on-the-Wold, and expects to be there for three or four weeks.

Archdeacon Hardcastle[1] to E.C.F.B, 10 March   *Brighton*

Cosmo Lang has been a real friend to all of us and he will be missed by many. But he is right to go now, and I do not think, owing to old age, he was leading our Church anywhere. In fact, I think Willie Temple has been given a great chance to steer a drifting boat through whirlpools and rocks which might easily wreck it - just like the river Wye - so tortuous and with dangerous rapids, it wants a good man at the helm.

J.B.B. to E.C.F.B., 10 March   *H.Q. Canadian Corps*

I had such a delightful time with Ralph and Alison on Sunday. I got to Groombridge about 1.15 (it is only about 35 minutes from here) and Ralph had just come in from Home Guard duties - they had been practising battle stations. He was very happy about his work, hard though it is to carry on with such short staff, but he likes Wingfield[2] immensely. As for the new house at East Grinstead, clearly it is a source of great interest and amusement, and seems to offer all that they want, given the fact that it really is not practical to go deep into the country, because the servant problem becomes impossible.

On Monday afternoon I was in London at the National Portrait Gallery where the Canadian exhibits were in their own room. It made quite a brave show and Will Ogilvie[3] (a professional artist, now a subaltern) did a good job in hanging

---

task. See. K. Jeffreys, *The Churchill Coalition and Wartime Politics* (Manchester UP, 1991), pp. 94-5.

[1] Ven. Edward Hoare Hardcastle (1862-1945). Vicar of Maidstone, 1904-24; Archdeacon of Canterbury and Canon Residentiary, 1924-39; Archdeacon Emeritus, 1939-45.

[2] Maj-Gen. Hon. Maurice Wingfield, DSO (1883-1956) Resigned from Army, 1926, having commanded Rifle Brigade; Chm. of A.W. Bain and Sons Ltd.; Pres. Corporation of Insurance Brokers, 1925-55.

[3] W.A. Ogilvie. War artist; attained rank of Major and was awarded the MBE.

such a heterogenous collection so cleverly.[1] Vincent Massey turned up and we looked at the pictures together. There was no formal opening but next day I was there again having been asked to be present while the King and Queen visited the exhibition. The visit was entirely informal, and neither the High Commissioner nor the Corps Commander were expected to be present. Our room was, in fact, the last they visited, and they spent some 20 minutes there. I told the King that Ogilvie had done several of the pictures, and the Queen said to me, 'You are not connected with the gallery in any way are you? I thought you were with the Canadians.' The King answered for me, 'Yes, my dear, he's been with McNaughton for a long time. McNaughton would not let him go back to Canada - obviously sensible, as all his boys are over here, aren't they Bickersteth?'

They showed commendable interest in the pictures, though it must have been a great strain, and a bore going round endless rooms and being faced with thousands of exhibits while constantly trying to say the right thing. They were photographed looking at a wooden statuette of a soldier with a Tommy gun, and were much amused at a torso of Gen. McNaughton made out of soap. 'You'd better keep it under lock and key these days,' said the King. Later, I bumped into 'Pug' Ismay, who had just the information Kay wanted about Charles, which I passed on to her. Charles should have arrived at Ceylon two days ago, and she can cable him c/o *HMS Lance* at Colombo.

Geoffrey to E.C.F.B., 15 March   *Aberdeen*

Tony has arrived safely in Bombay. He sent us a cable from there. It was put into my hand at King's College this morning, just after the Chapel service which I attended to hear Dr. Barbour[2] give the Myrtle lecture.

I think he must have arrived in Bombay on Wednesday or Thursday last; exactly nine weeks after he left the Clyde, and nine weeks on one ship without, I expect, once landing during the whole voyage. He must have become terribly tired of it long before the end.

The Far Eastern situation still seems to go from bad to worse. But I think we shall hold Australia. Our offensive when it begins will be, I predict, from

---

[1] Herbert Read's review of the Exhibition in *The Listener* (26 March 1942) concluded memorably: '...taste and talent descend to levels never before thought worthy of public display'.
[2] George Freeland Barbour (1882-1946) Author; Hon. Sec. Scottish Temperance Legislation Bd.; contested numerous parliamentary seats as a Liberal; worked for LNU, 1919-39, and for Perth and Kinross CC, Ed. Cttee., 1939-45.

several directions simultaneously. The USA is heart and soul in this war now, and really beginning to get a move on. And she will certainly not stop till she has wiped out Japan as a first class power. Nor shall we; and, if we can fix this matter of the Russian *post bellum* western frontiers, I think Russia will before long join us against the Japanese. She would like us to land another expeditionary force in Europe (France or Norway), but I hope we do nothing rash.

The snow up here is at last disappearing, though some still remains in the front garden. But it is mild and springlike today, such a relief to have it warmer.

J.B.B. to E.C.F.B., 15 March   *H.Q. Canadian Corps*

On Thursday - a long day - I had an interesting talk with a young lad from Toronto who is YMCA supervisor at the Martinique Barracks. He has been holding exhibitions of various kinds for some time, and finds them much appreciated. But he is concerned that so few of the tens of thousands of the young Canadians over here ever catch an idea of the life and culture of England. They hardly know it exists. Some men, it is true, are taken to see the usual places of historical interest in London or in the neighbourhood of their billeting areas, but no more than a few hundred. The vast majority do their training during the day, and then go to the local pub (if there is one handy) or attend the concert arranged by the Salvation Army or YMCA in the evening, and that is the end of it. I am thinking of making a large map and marking on it the chief places of interest, and then posting it up in some prominent place. Of course, there is no transport for the men, but they are very clever at hitch-hiking. But what about English life? If one arranges lectures the attendance is not good, and then one is faced with seeming discourtesy towards the lecturer. If we had one man on our staff doing nothing else but arranging good music, lectures on local history, art exhibitions and so forth, we might be able to do something. But I simply have not the time.

Last night, the Army Commander, Lt-General Montgomery came to our guest night, and I had a long talk with him after dinner. He knew Canterbury very well, having been for a year at the King's School, and when he was GOC 12 Corps he got Cosmo Lang to dine and speak to the men. About a month ago he got Hewlett Johnson to do the same thing. He said the Dean was put through a pretty severe cross-examination by members of 'A' mess after dinner, but came through it with flying colours!

He asked about my work and whether it was an advantage being a civilian. I said it was, and he, I think, agreed. I then asked him about educational work in his army, not telling him that I knew a considerable amount about it. He said he thought it had made a real contribution to the contentment of the men, and that last winter in the 12 Corps area there had been a real 'boom' in education. It was, under the circumstances, a most useful talk for me.

Notes by E.C.F.B., 20 March

Ralph, on a recent visit to Rugby, decided that, if possible, Peter should be sent to Oxford for a year, but it has just been announced that those born in 1924 are not allowed to go to a university unless scientists or brilliant classical scholars. Peter will, therefore, have to go into the Rifle Brigade in September, but they are having his name entered on the books of Christ Church, so that, after the war, we can get him out of the army quickly and give him two or three years there.

Coal and petrol are now being strictly rationed, and there are restrictions on clothing. Shopping is very difficult - deliveries may only be made three times a week: purchases may not be wrapped in paper except greasy articles, and if possible must be carried home by the buyer. As an amusing instance of this, General Sir Sidney Clive[1] was seen returning from Gloucester sitting in a bus (having no petrol for his car) clasping in one hand a joint of raw meat, wrapped in newspaper, and in the other, a bulging bag full of groceries, unwrapped and exposed to view.

Monier to E.C.F.B., 20 March   *Chiddingstone*

John tells me his course at Stow-on-the-Wold finishes next Sunday and that it has been very intensive. He has enjoyed his time there and loves the country round about. He moves shortly by train to a regiment stationed in Somerset or Wiltshire.

Last Sunday we had both RE and RAF to Church. On Palm Sunday, the National Day of Prayer, they both mean to come in force, and I hope the Home Guard also. Edward is now on leave in Jerusalem, and attended Pam Wavell's wedding (General Wavell's daughter).

---

[1] Lt-Gen. Sir (George) Sidney Clive, DSO (1874-1959). Retired, 1934; DL Herefordshire; a director of Royal Acad. of Music; President Union Jack Club and Hostel, 1944-55.

J.B.B. to E.C.F.B., 25 March   *H.Q. Canadian Forces*

Yesterday I was out all day in the Aldershot-Farnborough area. I lunched with the Assistant-Director Ordnance Services in the Canadian Armoured Division. Owing to age - he is 51 - he is being returned to Canada, and is very sad about it. As you have seen in the press, they are being pretty ruthless about this age business. Later I went to Deepcut and Blackdown. How drab and unimaginative are these barrack towns - set in the most perfect country, the beauty of which they effectively destroy.

My leave is settled all right. I mentioned it to General Crerar. I only hope 'Andy' McNaughton will not arrive home just then. We expect him almost any day.

Ralph to E.C.F.B., 27 March   *Lombard Street*

It is something of a shock to find that the house we are buying is in a defence area. I have got to go there tomorrow morning as the military are proposing to cover a good deal of the garden with barbed wire and slit trenches. I shall try and get this obviated, or at any rate altered to cause as little inconvenience as possible.

J.B.B. to E.C.F.B., 29 March   *Lavington Park*

I had a full day yesterday visiting units, but after visiting a camp at Petworth, my week was finished and I called to stay with Barbie Wallace at about 5 p.m. To my surprise I found Duff and Diana Cooper there. We had some extremely interesting talk. Duff, as you know, left Singapore before the final débâcle, so he could not tell me much about that. But he was extremely interesting about the general situation as he found it on arriving there. Diana was extremely funny about some of their experiences, especially in the Andaman Islands and India.

Next morning we all four went to church at Graffham, then, back at Lavington, Barbie, her son David and I went for a long walk up on to the Downs. It was too glorious for words, not really warm but there was a glorious sun and cloudless sky. It quite made one forget about the war. I sent Sanders off to stay at a neighbouring Brigade HQ, as one could not have a hungry soldier here in these days of rationing.

I have been invited to the enthronement of William Temple in Canterbury on 23 April. I shall try and go.

Geoffrey to E.C.F.B., 29 March   *Aberdeen*

Our cook leaves us on Tuesday to be married. At least this way she will
not be directed to work far from Aberdeen. For the present, Jean and Elfride will
have to run the kitchen, and seem confident that they can do so. Fortunately, it's
the vacation and we're all available to lend a hand. It is a blessing that we have
come through this cruelly long and cold winter without any illness. So long as we
remain well, we ought - or else be ashamed of ourselves - to be able to run the
household between us quite easily. For we have reduced to its utmost simplicity
the whole business of living. It is clear that the government intends to ration the
country more severely. Even so, we shall still be better fed than any other country
in Europe.

We share, of course, in the impending sense of epoch-making events on
the verge of happening. We hear plenty about the enemy's preparations for this
offensive or that, but, quite rightly, nothing about ours. So there is nothing to do
but sit tight, work hard at one's job, and keep calm. And I am sure the country
does not need all the advice being showered on it to do this. One gets sick of such
preaching.

J.B.B. to E.C.F.B., 31 March   *H.Q. Canadian Corps*

When I got back to Corps HQ from Lavington on Sunday evening, I
found, to my surprise, that General McNaughton had returned. He is established
once again in his house at Headley, but came down on the Sunday evening to dine
with us in 'A' Mess. The four divisional generals were invited, and the Commander
of the Tank Brigade. After dinner we continued to sit round the table and 'Andy'
gave us a most fascinating account of his visit to Canada. The general impression I
got, from what was essentially a confidential report, was that he was profoundly
struck with the work being done in Canada in the training of the fighting services
and in the production of munitions.

After dinner we went into the ante-room and continued our informal talk. I
got a word with him about the WO offer and he at once said, 'I think you ought to
go, though I had proposed that you should be with me at the new Army HQ.'[1]

---

[1] The first mention in the War Diary that J.B.B. had considered, still less intended, leaving the
Canadian forces and take up the post of Director of Army Education.

April

J.B.B. to E.C.F.B., 1 April   *H.Q.Canadian Forces*

I had a good talk with General McNaughton yesterday at his house. He is quite clear I must go, though he said some very kind things about missing me. A letter to the WO, stating he is prepared to let me go, is being dispatched today, but he has pointed out in it that it will be necessary to cable the governors of Toronto University before a final answer can be given. This was my suggestion. I reminded General McNaughton that the governors had lent me to him for a specific job, and that he therefore could not farm me out for another job with the English without asking their permission. Vincent Massey has mentioned the salary, and I think McNaughton has too, though I have not as yet seen copies of their letters. I do not want any announcement made till I get back from leave, as I want to tell people here before the news appears in the press. It is though a very trivial matter in itself at such a time as this.

I cannot find any of my margarine coupons, and I think somebody must have stolen them. It is really a hat and a medium weight overcoat I want most, and perhaps you have enough coupons for those which you could let me have? But I must not denude your supply. If I have to get more suits eventually, they will have to be according to the new rationed variety!

I join Julian in Oxford for my leave tomorrow. Sanders will drive me there via the Hospital at Cliveden, where I need to see some people.

Notes by E.C.F.B, 4 April   *Chiddingstone*

The Good Friday services (yesterday) arranged by the BBC were remarkable - they commenced at 8 a.m., followed by Matins and Ante-Communion at 10, and part of the three-hour service from 2-3, taken by Dom. Bernard Clements.[1] Children had their share in the services, followed by good and suitable music. The day ended with an Address by Archbishop Temple.

Notes by J.B.B., 7 April

The former professor of Economics of Rangoon University lunched with Julian and me at the Mitre Hotel today. He was very enlightening about our

---

[1] Bernard Clements (1880-1942). Benedictine Monk (Anglican) and broadcaster; Vicar of All Saints, Margaret St., W.1, 1934-42.

administration in Burma, which has for years been ineffective and unimaginative. *Thakin* (the nationalist revolutionary body) has for long been working against the British who, says the professor, failed completely to understand Burmese civilisation. They sent ICS personnel to man administrative posts, and, still worse, ICS police. At the university, the head was quite incapable of dealing with revolutionary tendencies, and the lower class Buddhist monks were a thoroughly subversive influence. It seems they plotted with Japanese Buddhist monks, even with Sinn Fein and the Nazis.

Geoffrey to E.C.F.B., 12 April   *Aberdeen*

Our household is solving all its little problems very happily so far, thank you; and I have nothing really to grumble about, owing to the splendid way - liberty, equality and fraternity all combining - in which my wife and family are facing our servant-less condition. It means a lot of extra hard work, of course, especially for Jean and Elfride. But they are vindicating the worth of a truly useful education by turning out the most appetising food. Ursula, assisted by David, is making scones this afternoon. The former cooked us delicious pancakes last night for supper, and Elfride made some delicious rock cakes for tea. It's a splendid education for the children to turn from getting up scenes from Shakespeare's plays, to making beds, washing up and cooking meals. It teaches them that life isn't just pressing buttons and getting food served as if by magic.

I must say I hope Tony does not have to go to Burma, partly because of the climate (damp heat) and even more because of the Japanese bestial habit of torturing and killing their prisoners (if they don't starve them). The British, of course, never retaliate, but it was clear from what Elmer Davis[1] said on the wireless last night, that the Americans will render tit for tat, and that they will regard it as God's service not merely to win victories over the Japanese, but to exterminate them.

Julian to E.C.F.B., 12 April   *Felsted*

I arrived in London for lunch, after which I went to my tailors and ordered a suit - not a very suitable material, but stocks are low and all the good stuff has

---

[1] Elmer (Holmes) Davis (1890-1958). Radio news analyst for American broadcasting companies; Dir-Gen. of War Information, US govt., 1942-45.

long since been used up. The cost is 15 guineas, which is a scandal, but what can one do?

I caught the 4.45 from Liverpool Street to Felsted via Bishop's Stortford, with a taxi waiting there to get me to the school. I got past the guards into my own house, where I found everything in excellent order. Of the school itself I am less than sure. The whole place is certainly being tidied up tremendously, but they are laying an enormous amount of asphalt for the innumerable staff cars of the huge Corps staff. It will take months taking up all this asphalt after the war - for we certainly neither want it, nor could we afford to keep it up - but I very much doubt if the government would pay for its removal. The buildings will all need to be painted from top to bottom, and most of the rooms re-plastered throughout the whole school. The grounds will require more attention still, and will cost an immense sum to put right. Huge huts are everywhere. On the cricket ground there is a great series of them linked together, where full course meals are served for the men. I had travelled to Bishop's Stortford on the train with the manageress of this NAAFI. She told me that very few of the men eat the meals provided from rations, they come to the NAAFI instead. She admitted this was a shame, as the excellent ration food was spoiled by the bad standard of cooking and too often wasted. If only the army could hand these fine rations over to the civilian population and live on the plentiful NAAFI supplies, it would be much fairer. If these men were fighting, one would not begrudge it them, but for all at Corps, as far as I could see, it is a very good war. The luxury these officers are living in is far higher than that which I saw when visiting Canadian troops with Burgon.

Bathrooms, lavatories, kitchens and heating plants have been put in. I have no doubt many of the officers connected with the Corps of Signals hope the war will go on for a very long time. Each of these officers has a batman, and in some cases an ATS girl as well. A whole village street of huts for these women has been built, and goodness knows what they do. They seem to get an awful lot of leave, and then, when they are away, there are batmen there to do their jobs for them. There were no fewer than seven of these sitting around my kitchen when I came to the house on the Saturday of my arrival.

I went in my first evening and sat in my own drawing-room chatting with the Colonel and six or so other officers. They had managed to secure easy chairs (not mine) and made the room quite comfortable. They were friendly, so I laid myself out to be pleasant to them. But oh! If Miss Anderson saw my kitchens -

dirt everywhere, and the independent boiler kept at 220°, with a reckless use of coke and the damper out all day. The engineers who put the boiler in told me that it should never be allowed to show more than 140° on the gauge - but the officers must have boiling water for hot baths available day and night, so the cooks pile on the fuel, keep the damper out, and do not mind if the whole caboodle blows up, which it probably will do! It won't last long with this use.

However, I must not run on in this strain. I suppose all these good fellows are doing their best to win the war, but certainly all the host of clerks and camp-followers who swarm over Corps HQ do not look very tough to me. I doubt if they'ld stand much of a fight. What really saddens me is the tremendous trouble all ranks from the GOC downwards are taking to secure their own comfort. The wife of an officer billeted nearby came down the other day to visit him and was, apparently, quite piqued to find her husband waited on hand and foot. 'He never had such luxuries in civil life as he has now,' she said. 'He used to clean his own boots and brush his own clothes, etc., etc.'

J.B.B. to E.C.F.B., 14 April   *'A' Mess, Canadian Army H.Q, England*

Here is my first letter from Army HQ. I moved up yesterday afternoon. Sanders and I moved here from Wakehurst yesterday afternoon. My personal belongings and files completely filled the little car. My bicycle we tied on in front of the bonnet. It was curious to be back at Headley, and to compare my initial arrival here in September 1940 with my return yesterday. My new room at Headley Court is only two doors off the room I had before, and is entirely satisfactory.

Notes by E.C.F.B., 18 April

The Chancellor of the Exchequer presented his budget to Parliament on 14 April. To everyone's relief there was no increase in Income Tax or Super Tax, but there are extra taxes on wines, beer, tobacco and entertainments.

There is no doubt that our collaboration with America is the greatest ever accomplished between any two nations. American troops are landing in large numbers in England and Northern Ireland. One batch of 2,500 arrived in Harrogate and were much disgruntled to find no there were no cigarettes on sale in the shops.

J.B.B. to E.C.F.B., 21 April   *H.Q. First Canadian Army*

They have sent me a ticket for the enthronement on Thursday. I am in the front row of the block just east of the Choir on the south side. There is a printed list, and I see that Mrs Gardiner is directly opposite me. One block opposite the throne is for William Temple's friends. The Mayor and officials are also there of course. It looks well arranged. I do wish you were going to be there, but at least Julian and I will do our best to represent Father and you.

General McNaughton willingly gave me permission to go to Canterbury and use the car. He told me, 'I think it important that you should go there in view of your new job.'

I met Alice Massey in town who helped me buy a new overcoat. It cost £19, and, I am afraid, it required 18 of your coupons. I am so grateful to you for letting me have them. I have still heard nothing about replacements for my coupons which were stolen. Then she showed me the flat which is Eaton House, 39-40 Upper Grosvenor Street, W.1.

It is very up-to-date with a strong concrete construction. There is a kitchen, a large bedroom (and a smaller one for David Johnson), as well as a sitting-room with a large window. The whole is very comfortably furnished, with modern equipment - pile carpet everywhere - and good armchairs. It was only a hasty look round, but everything was obviously in good taste and thoroughly comfortable.

After tea I went round to the WO and had a talk with Major-General Willans and Maude,[1] who came in later. Willans said that the WO does not like announcing things too far ahead, and it is not the practice of any government department to do so. The announcement of my appointment in the press will therefore not be made before the middle of May, but there is no reason why it should not be mentioned to anyone to whom one should wish to tell it. This seems a foolish arrangement, but it does not matter much one way or the other. I shall feel perfectly free to talk about the matter to William Temple or anyone else I choose at Canterbury, and you can say what you like to whosoever you please. Willans is going to tell Bendall tomorrow that I am to be his successor, although I should think Bendall knows it already. I shall write to him tactfully in a week or so when I get back from Canterbury suggesting we meet and talk. Meanwhile,

---

[1] Brig. Christian Maude, DSO (1884-1971). Inspector Army Education Corps, 1937; Controller AEC, 1943-4; retired, 1945.

Willans asked Maude to send me copies of the Army Educational Journal, as well as other articles and reports, so that I can begin to 'get the hang of things.' There is an awful lot of reading to do,

Peter to E.C.F.B., 21 April   *Groombridge*

I go back to Rugby for my last term on 11 May. I must say I am very sad about leaving and not going to Oxford, but privately I'm rather longing to get in this show and do my bit. I join up on 15 August, so will only have a fortnight's holiday at the new house - a very great pity, as the house is simply marvellous! Still, I've been accepted for the Rifle Brigade, which is the great thing.

I must admit I find it very sad that we are leaving so many friends here at Groombridge, especially the Home Guard men, who are most awfully nice. In fact they are staging a big battle on Monday week, in which the whole company is taking part.

Notes by E.C.F.B., 27 April

On Saturday we met a Felsted boy's mother, who gave a piteous account of her escape from Singapore, leaving her home and all her possessions at half an hour's notice. She went on board the *Empress of Japan*, a vessel of 27,000 tons. They were so packed that hundreds had to sleep on deck and submit to many other inconveniences until they reached Cape Town. The voyage took nine weeks. Her husband is safe, though still in the Pacific. She had not seen her son for four years.

On Thursday last, 23 April, William Temple was enthroned in Canterbury Cathedral. Julian and Burgon said it was a wonderful service, full of colour and devotion, and the singing really beautiful. It was a fitting climax for all that had taken place previously.

J.B.B. to E.C.F.B., 29 April

The ceremony in Canterbury Cathedral was intensely moving, set as it was against a background of ruthless war so few miles from where it was taking place. The pageantry and dignity were unforgettable. There can be few finer choirs in England now than that of Canterbury. Everyone, even the American bishops, were immensely impressed with the ceremony. It never became a 'show', but was permeated throughout with a deeply spiritual and other-worldly atmosphere.

Nevertheless, the enthronement service was not announced in the press. In the original invitation I received we were particularly told not to communicate the date to anybody. After all, it is only a few minutes from the German aerodromes (grouped in the St Omer area) to Canterbury.

Afterwards, over tea, I had a long talk with Albert Mansbridge[1] who was particularly interested in my new job as naturally he would be, being the founder of the WEA. I also talked with Lawrence Irving,[2] who is with RAF Intelligence attached to Army HQ, South Eastern Command, about his work. We are near neighbours here and must meet.

At about 9.30, Julian and I went round to see the Dean. We found him just about to listen to the broadcast of the service. This came through admirably. He explained that it was his prerogative to install the Archbishop in St Augustine's chair, but Sopwith was very anxious to do so, and so he gave up. The Deanery is a wilderness. After the broadcast we went to the kitchen for tea and toast. The walls round us were Norman, and it was comic to see Hewlett Johnson, who a few hours before dressed in all his glory escorting the Archbishop around the Cathedral before all the notables, now engaged in putting on the kettle and fetching dishes from the next room. We talked solidly till 12.45. He is still boycotted by the BBC and the press, but is addressing large meetings all over the country. The real hostility towards him comes from Bevin, Morrison and the Trade Unionists. The great block of population known as the lower middle class will prove to be, in his opinion, the power against making any really radical changes. He considers this class has a wonderful opportunity of helping in the economic changes that must come. It is in their own interests to move to the Left. If they do so, the changes will be sensible, reasonable, and carried out in an English way - no slavish imitation of the Soviets. If they move to the Right, then there may be bloodshed. He regards the public ownership of productive machinery as absolutely fundamental, that is not only banks, public utilities, land, transportation, coal, but also the chief industries, such as steel and the other heavy industries, clothing, boots and so forth. He said again what he has often said before, that in his opinion Russia has stumbled on something Godlike; an

---

[1] Albert Mansbridge (1876-1952). Founder of the Workers' Educational Association in England, 1903; worked on numerous commissions and co-founder of the National Central Library. CH (1931).

[2] Lawrence Irving (1897-1988). Theatrical Art Director; wartime service with the RAF; grandson of Sir Henry Irving, the first actor ever knighted.

economic system not for private profit but for public good. The Russians lack awareness of the 'little animal', the amoeba - groping, weak and defenceless, but always seeking and dissatisfied, and therefore progressing. That is the Christian man. Russia is obsessed at present with material development and lacks awareness of the Spiritual. She is in danger of being a specialist, and a satisfied specialist. That is where Christian nations, if true to themselves, can show Russia the way. At the moment the real danger is that the success of Russian arms is so great, that the Soviets will say, 'Look what we have been able to do without God. Why should we seek him?'

Julian and I walked back through the Precincts past the dark, silent Meister Omers, and out into Burgate (all the gates are permanently open night and day), and so home. What a strange world it is.

Abbreviations

AA	....	Anti-aircraft
ABCA	....	Army Bureau of Current Affairs
ADC	....	Aide-de-Camp
AFS	....	Auxiliary Fire Service
ARP	....	Air Raid Precautions
ATS	....	Auxiliary Territorial Service
Bn.	....	Battalion
Bde.	....	Brigade
BBC	....	British Broadcasting Corporation
BEF	....	British Expeditionary Force
BGS	....	Brigade General Staff
Brig.	....	Brigadier
BWP	....	*British Way and Purpose*
CAO	....	Canadian Army Overseas
Capt.	....	Captain
CD	....	Civil Defence
CEMA	....	Council for the Encouragement of Music and the Arts
CFLN	....	Comité Français pour la Liberation Nationale
CID	....	Committee of Imperial Defence
CIGS	....	Chief of the Imperial General Staff
C-in-C	....	Commander in Chief
CO	....	Commanding Officer
Col.	....	Colonel
Cpl.	....	Corporal
CPR	....	Canadian Pacific Railway
Coy.	....	Company
DAG	....	Deputy Adjutant General
Div.	....	Division
DIM	....	Director(ate) of Military Intelligence
DSO	....	Member of the Distinguished Service Order
ENSA	....	Entertainments National Service Association
Gen.	....	General

GHQ	....	General Headquarters
GOC	....	General Officer Commanding
GSO	....	General Staff Officer
ICS	....	Indian Civil Service
ITC	....	Infantry Training Centre
HMS	....	His Majesty's Ship (Royal Navy)
Hon.	....	Honourable
KRRC	....	King's Royal Rifle Corps
LCC	....	London County Council
LDV	....	Local Defence Volunteers
Lt.	....	Lieutenant
Maj.	....	Major
MC	....	Military Cross
MT(O)	....	Motor Transport (Officer)
MTB	....	Motor Torpedo Boat
NAAFI	....	Navy, Army and Air Force Institute
NUT	....	National Union of Teachers
OBLI	....	Oxfordshire and Buckinghamshire Light Infantry
OCTU	....	Officer Cadet Training Unit
ORTU	....	Officer Recruit Training Unit
OTC	....	Officer Cadet Corps
POW	....	Prisoner of War
Pte.	....	Private
RA	....	Royal Artillery
RAMC	....	Royal Army Medical Corps
RAOC	....	Royal Army Ordnance Corps
RNVR	....	Royal Navy Volunteer Reserve
RSM	....	Regimental Sergeant Major
Sgt.	....	Sergeant
UAB	....	Unemployed Assistance Board
VC	....	Victoria Cross
WVS	....	Women's Voluntary Service
WAAF	....	Women's Auxiliary Air Force

Index

ABCA (Army Bureau of Current Affairs),
xxi, 335, 336, 344, 355, 356

Aberdeen, xvii, 5, 17, 28, 72, 135-6, 146-7,
385, 389, 391, 396, 400, 406

Bishop of, 134, 168

raids on, 143

University, 16

Abyssinia, 296, 303

Adam, Lt-Gen. Sir Robert, 371, 384

Addison, Sir Joseph, 337

Admiralty, the, 7, 15, 21, 53, 103, 113-4,
140, 169, 179, 223

air raids, 17, 22, 31, 49, 50, 143, 170, 171-
2, 173-4, 175, 182, 183, 186, 190, 196
200, 257, 285

on Firth of Forth, 36, 43

ARP (Air Raid Precautions), 7, 13, 14, 21,
22, 27, 39, 40, 43, 49, 92, 110, 111,
127, 138, 148, 154, 174, 181, 182, 186,
196, 209, 212, 219, 230, 245, 291, 299
306, 313, 317, 342, 351, 353, 387

air raid shelters, 195, 205, 206, 212, 223

Abbey Factories, 280, 281-84

Millers, 281, 314, 333

Stayners, 281-4

61 Arch, 283, 285

air raid warnings, 92, 124, 148, 170, 173,
198, 202, 217, 225, 254, 289, 311

Albania, 287

Alderson, Ralph, 165-6

Aldershot (Hants.), 232, 302, 344

Alexander, A.V. (Hillsborough), 265

Alexandria, 251, 360

American:

Embassy, 102

Labour Movement, 310,

people, 15, 38, 127, 190, 296, 304, 350
395

Manhattan, 35

Reuben James, 360, 388

rifles, 216

soldiers, xxii, 341,

transistor radios, 325

see also USA

Amery, Leo, 330, 350

Amiens, Treaty of, 103-4

Anderson, Miss, 16, 18, 25, 27, 410

Anderson, Sir John, 55, 92, 94, 304

Andover (Hants.), 351

anti-aircraft guns (AA), 133, 135, 146, 152,
166, 195, 206, 209, 212, 213, 216, 219,
227, 233, 235, 238, 245, 268, 273, 345,
360-1, 368, 395

and shrapnel, 257

Argles, Major, 274

Artillery, 142, 155, 209, 306

Arundel (Sussex), 322

Ascot (Berks.), 219

Astor, Lady Nancy, 65, 67, 75, 272, 321

Astor, Lady Violet, 51, 290, 321

Astor, Lord Waldorf, 272

Athenæum, the, 352

Athlone, Lord, 83, 90

Atlantic Ocean, xxv, 258, 363

battle of, 300, 310

Attlee, Clement, 94,

as deputy PM, 394

418

Auchinleck, Gen. Claude, 329

Australia, xviii, 353, 375, 376, 388, 392
  troops, 70, 193-5, 197, 302, 305-5, 378,
  and fall of Singapore, 398

Australian Navy, 375

Australian Politics, 348

Austria, 225

Ayer, A.J. 'Freddie', 200

Babington, Miss, 29, 73, 215

Bain, A.W., Ltd., xvii,

Bain, Sir Ernest, 23, 26

Baldwin, Stanley, xviii, 47, 49, 84, 96, 100,
  130, 228, 243, 353,

Baldwin, Lady, 75

Balfour, Harold, 76

Balkans, the, 237, 279, 286, 291, 295, 297
  300

balloon barrage, 211-12, 221, 245, 246-7,
  290

Bank of England, 151

Barbour, Dr. George, 402

Barlow, Wing Co., 308

Barratt, Air Chief Marshal, Sir Arthur, 141

Barrington-Ward, Robert, 6

Barry, Rt. Rev. Russell, 307

Bartlett, Vernon, 350

Beaverbrook, Lord, 8, 65, 95, 341, 345, 382
  397, 398

  Beaverbrook-Harriman mission, 363, 384

Beckwith-Smith, Maj-Gen. Merton, 398

Bekesbourne (Kent), 170

Belgium, 5, 28, 45, 81, 85, 86, 89, 99, 100,
  103, 105, 113, 119-20, 140, 142, 155,
  159

Belgian Army, 88, 105, 113, 119-20, 122

  Brussels, 105

  Fort Eben Emael, 165

  Louvain, 86, 105, 119

Bell, Rt. Rev. George, 372

Bendall, Col. Francis, 205, 229, 412

Benes, Edvard, 362

Bennett, R.B., 288, 344

Beresford, John, 301

Berk, Sgt., 167

Bernays, Robert, 54

Betteshanger (Kent), 154, 338

Beveridge, Charles and Kay, xvii, 5, 8, 13,
  29, 98, 130, 171-2, 183-4, 361, 365,
  370, 372, 375, 377, 388, 389, 402

  and birth of their son, Robert, 349

'Beveridgism', xxi,

Bevin, Ernest, 115, 267, 294, 319, 397, 413

Bickersteth Family, xi, xv, xxiv, xxvi,

  Alison, xvii, 4, 5, 10, 13, 14, 24, 51, 89,
    90, 189, 192, 242, 260, 285, 401

  Burgon (JBB), xv, xvii, xviii, xix, xx, xxi,
    xxii, xxiii, xxiv, xxv, xxvi, xxvii, 3, 13,
    73, 86, 118, 132, 137, 147-8, 179, 187,
    189, 208, 223, 241, 256, 268, 277-80,
    291, 293, 317, 325, 337, 349, 363, 376,
    377, 378, 381, 382, 386, 394, 395, 408,
    409, 412, 414

    and art exhibition, 402

    and broadcast, 343

    and fifth column work, 321

    as Dir.of Army Ed., xxi

    and WO offer, 407

  David, 5, 17, 71, 79, 263, 408

  Edward (Ted), xvii, xxvii, 3, 5, 30, 47,

68, 89, 90, 219, 226-7, 278, 313, 363,
374, 386, 388, 405
and 'This Paper War', 250-53
Elfride, 5, 17, 23, 354, 386, 406, 408
Ella (ECFB), xvi, xvii, xviii, xxiii, xxiv,
xxv, xxvi, 3, 13, 65, 89, 90, 92-3, 127,
148, 166, 174-5, 182, 187, 189, 195,
202, 208, 209, 214, 344, 377, 390, 411
and evacuated from Canterbury, 210
Geoffrey, xvii, xviii, xxii, xxiv, xxvii, 5,
16, 22, 33, 71, 224, 240, 255, 361, 377,
381, 393
on the food situation, 340
fire-watching, 361
on the conscription of women, 400
Jean, 5, 18, 23, 43, 135, 168, 240, 255,
340, 361, 377, 393, 406, 408
John, (Rt. Rev.) xvi, xvii, 3, 5, 17, 25, 30,
37, 68, 176, 203, 227, 259, 277-8, 318
328, 334, 366, 368, 388, 391, 401, 404
commissioned in The Buffs 311
as editor of *The Bickersteth Diaries,
1914-1918*, xi, xii,
Julian, xv, xvi, xviii, xix, xx, xxi, xxiv,
xxvii, 3, 4,13, 14, 59, 60, 114-5, 186,
206, 208, 210, 214, 249, 253, 270, 287,
305, 325, 349, 353, 356, 361, 376, 377,
378, 381, 382, 407, 408, 411, 412, 414
as Archdeacon of Maidstone, xxi,
[Young] Julian, xvii, 3, 5, 17, 168, 242,
258, 351, 354, 393, 399
cadet in the KRRC, 351
Kitty, xvi,
Mary, xvii, 5, 30, 36, 89, 148, 184, 259
277, 338, 363, 368, 372, 377

and POW parcels fund, 290
and AFS work, 396
Monier, xvi, xxvii, 5, 17, 89, 90, 183,
185, 203, 227-8, 241, 265, 277, 288,
290, 311, 336, 361, 363, 370, 377, 386,
396
Morris, xvi, xviii, 329, 366
Peter, xviii, xxvii, 4, 10, 12, 13, 14, 24,
165, 183, 189, 214, 250, 260, 279, 296,
366, 376, 385, 388, 391, 399, 403
Ralph, xvi, xvii, xviii, xxvii, 4, 5, 10, 13,
16, 18, 21, 24, 27, 51, 52, 89, 90, 189,
229, 242, 260, 264, 279, 292, 296, 302,
352, 372, 385, 401, 403
Samuel, xvi, 412
Tony, xvii, xxii, xxiv, 3, 5, 16, 17, 33, 71,
72, 163, 168, 176, 242, 263, 294, 315,
334, 358, 359, 368, 377, 386, 387, 392,
393, 399, 402, 408
and Coventry blitz, 245-7
and views on ABCA, 356
Ursula, 5, 17, 79, 136, 263, 353, 393, 408
Bingham, Lt-Col. Ralph, 264, 269, 274
Birmingham, 189, 201, 233, 263, 339
Blacker, Col. Stewart, 310
blackout, the, 8-9, 22, 24, 28, 52, 80, 89,
93
and road accidents, 54-5
and immorality, 71
Blackshirts, 108-9, 274, 283, 330
Blenheim Palace, 273
Blitzkrieg, 42, 90, 106, 160, 192
Blore, Willie, 205, 269-70
Board of Education, 204, 332, 348
Board of Trade, 44, 60, 64, 267

420

bombs, 195, 197, 202, 205, 217, 220, 222,
    235, 268
    duds, 162, 170, 174
    high explosive, 175, 227, 282, 307
    incendiary, 93, 256, 307, 314
    land mines, 166, 171, 181, 231
    Molotovs, 162, 171, 181, 231
    random dropping, 161, 184
bomb blast, 175, 242, 245, 281, 282, 299,
    314
books:
    The Battle of Britain, 337
    Life of Neville Chamberlain,352(n)
    On England, 73
    Reaching for the Stars, 250
    Science and the War, 173
    The Socialist Sixth of the World, xix, 61,
        296, 318, 334
    Who Was Who, xxiv.
Bourdillon, Sir Bernard, 30
Bosche(s), the, 46, 132, 144, 150, 166,
    216, 304
    Bosche planes, 208, 213
Boyd, Air Vice Marshal Owen, 220
Bracken, Brendan, 97, 100, 140, 332, 337
Bradfield, Canon Harold, 209, 213, 216
Brand, Bob, 273
Bridge (Kent), 61, 63, 91, 127, 182, 200,
    201, 276, 306
Bristol, 65, 192, 254, 293
Britain, xviii, 5, 7, 9, 87, 102, 103-4, 107,
    147, 160, 186, 223, 265, 273, 325, 341,
    349, 363-4, 396, 400
British Army, xix, 5, 52, 69, 86, 142, 156-
    7, 164, 169, 249, 253, 257, 390, 404

Territorials, 87, 237
    humiliation of, 145
    evacuation from St Nazaire, 158
    and ATS 'girls', 410
    tanks, 173, 335
BBC (British Broadcasting Corp.), xxii,
    xxiii, 4, 43, 204, 250, 341, 343, 344,
    350, 363, 407, 413
    and White Russian influence, 346
British Commandos, 197, 287, 399
British Empire, xiii, 19, 96, 308, 325-6,
    351, 384, 397
BEF (British Expeditionary Force), 3, 45,
    46, 60-1, 76, 88, 113, 114, 120, 123-4,
    142, 162
    and evacuation, 89-90
British Propaganda, 78, 134
British Restaurants, 342
British Ships:
    Athenia, xix, 10, 15
    Aquitania, 194
    Canterbury, 12
    Duchess of Richmond, 25
    Duchess of York, 86, 88
    Empress of Britain, 5, 8, 9, 353
    Empress of Japan, 412
    Lancastria, 158
    Oronsay, 89
    Queen Mary, 194, 353
    Sepoy, 220
BWP (*British Way and Purpose*), xxi
Broadstairs (Kent), 216
Brockington, Leonard, 381
Brown, Lt-Gen Sir John, 204
Brown, Teresa, 144, 359

Buckingham Palace, 343, 357

Buckley, Brig. William, 342, 347

The Buffs, 32, 106, 168, 209, 223, 265,
    294, 311, 334

Bulgaria, 237

Burgin, Leslie, 80

Burma, vii, 359, 399, 400,
    and Buddhist monks, 407
    Rangoon, 370, 399, 407

Burrows, Leonard, 37

Butler (Sir) Neville, 264

Butler, J.R.M., 292

Butler, R.A., 'Rab', 4, 75, 95, 332
    and education policy, 347

Cabinet, the, 6, 19, 48, 49, 64, 273, 362,
    393
    War Cabinet, 46, 53, 75, 76, 325, 348,
    394

Cadogan, Sir Alexander, 64, 78

Calne (Wilts.), 254

Cambridge, 112

Cambridgeshire, 198

Cambridge University, 17, 177, 187, 234,
    245, 248, 328
    Colleges:
    Caius, 248
    Churchill , xxii, xxiii.
    Downing, 248
    King's, 56
    Magdalene, 189
    Pembroke, 189
    Trinity Hall, 189

Campbell, Sir Gerald, 264, 267, 350

Canada, xviii, xix, xxiii, xxv, 5, 6, 9, 17-
19, 30, 47, 59, 73, 87-8, 91, 96, 111,
    118, 130, 132, 148, 191, 205, 233, 243,
    264, 291, 304, 308-9, 314, 337, 343-4,
    349, 353, 354, 373, 376, 387, 390, 395,
    402, 406
    and evacuation to, 116-17, 127-8
    reception of evacuees, 215-6
    and art exhibits, 402
    Alberta, 151
    Montreal, 25, 191
    Nova Scotia, 151
    Halifax, 25, 32
    Ontario, 169
    Ottawa, 18, 83, 87, 238, 243, 264, 304,
    352, 355, 377
    Quebec, 88, 151, 377
    Toronto, 6, 73, 117, 130, 249, 270, 302,
    309, 334, 403, 407
    Toronto Univresity, xviii, xix, xx, 270,
    309

Canadian Convalescent Depot, 357

Canada House, 8, 9, 230, 332

Canadian Forces Overseas, xxi, xxii, xxv,
    171, 172, 194, 197, 224, 229, 230, 231,
    238, 249, 265, 293, 300, 302, 317, 321,
    324, 336, 346, 383, 388-9, 403, 409
    and ABCA, 344
    and wildness of, 190
    1st. Canadian Army, 390
    1st. Canadian Corps, xx, 264, 341, 354,
    358, 367, 373-4, 376, 406
    1st. Canadian Div., 61, 73, 89, 159, 205,
    and 'Brest Bust', 149-50
    2nd. Canadian Div., 62, 159, 224, 232
    3rd. Canadian Div., 336

in Hong Kong, 375

Canadian Tank Brigade (Div.), 334-5, 405

Sappers, 151, 162,

RCAF (Royal Canadian Air Force) 38(n), 87

Canadian Armed Forces - Education - 239, 242, 267, 270, 291, 293, 302, 337, 352, 360-1, 384, 403

Canadian General Hospital (Taplow), 272, 374 (Brixham), 357

Canadian Legion, 230, 232-3, 238-9, 243-4, 249

Canterbury, xvi, xvii, xix, xx, xxiii, 4, 5, 7, 15, 20, 65, 73, 85, 89, 90, 91-2, 98, 106, 109, 110-1, 114-5, 132, 133, 149, 153, 162, 169-70, 173-4, 185, 190, 195, 198, 200, 206-7, 208, 209-10, 212, 216, 218-9, 225, 226, 229, 231-2, 235-6, 277, 278, 286, 311, 318, 375

and raids on, 186, 205, 269, 275-6

and evacuation from, 213

Broad Street, 235

Burgate, 70, 174, 235-6, 239, 277

Canterbury East Station, 200

Canterbury West Station, 195, 205, 209, 215

Dane John, 118, 196

Greyfriars, 202

High Street, 174, 197, 209, 235

Mercery Lane, 168, 197, 209, 235

No. 16, New Dover Road, xxii, 111, 190, 195, 202, 212

Westgate, 92

Canterbury Cathedral, xix, xxii, 7, 15, 22,

23, 27, 29, 33, 67, 70, 73, 75, 78, 91, 108, 139, 168, 174, 190, 216-18, 223, 237, 239, 244, 274, 331, 358

and desecration of, 33

and gloom of, 142-3

and enthronement ceremony, 412-3

Angel Tower, 202, 207

Beckett's Crown, 277

Crypt, 239, 277

Deanery, xxii, 239, 413

Meister Omers, 142-3, 224, 414

Precincts, xxii, 70, 78, 118, 142, 174-5, 201, 209, 224, 235, 275, 277, 414

St Augustine's Chapel, 277

Carroll, Lewis, xvi, 225

Castlerosse, Vt., 8

Catterick (Yorks.), 172

Cecil, Lord Robert, 272

CEMA (Council for Encouragement of Music and the Arts), xxi, 293, 303, 332

Chamberlain, Lady Austen, 274

Chamberlain, Neville, xix, 4, 6, 8, 9, 28, 33, 36, 42, 53, 60, 76, 78, 80, 93, 96, 100, 101, 243, 254, 303, 352

and domination over cabinet, 75

death of, 243

Chamberlain, Mrs Neville, 75

Chappell (Julian's chauffeur) 3, 212

Charterhouse, xiv, 320, 369

Chartham (Kent), 148

Chatham. 7, 34, 201, 290, 321

Chatham House (Royal Inst. of Int. Affairs) 335, 336

Chatwin, Dr., 238, 243-4, 291, 353, 375

Chevenix-Trench, Brig. Ralph, 32, 265

Chequers, 140

Chelmsford (Essex), 212

Cheltenham (Gloucs.), 148, 376

Chiddingstone (Kent), xvi, 5, 31, 51, 86,
    89, 112, 148, 172, 185, 242, 244, 258,
    265, 336, 361, 375, 396
  and air raids, 175
  bomb damage, 176
  as 'Dornier bus route', 227

China, 73, 279, 326, 384
  Shanghai, 391

Cholmondeley, Lady Ti, 337

Chrystal, Sir George, 362

Church of England, xix, 51, 73, 115, 278,
    340, 348, 372
  and bell-ringing upon invasion, 161, 323
  and condition of, 320

Churchill, (Lady) Clementine, 361, 382

Churchill, Randolph, 383

Churchill, Sarah, 382

Churchill, W.S., xiv, 45, 49, 61, 66, 80, 83,
    93, 96, 97, 100, 107, 115, 137, 139-40,
    198, 213, 219, 249, 256, 273, 288, 302,
    310, 311, 315, 326, 330, 332, 335, 339,
    348, 350, 365, 374, 377, 383, 389, 397
    400
  as First Lord, 53
  meetings with Reynaud, 303-4
  and Atlantic Charter, 342
  and surrender of Singapore, 398

CID (Committee of Imperial Defence), 6,
    46, 139, 140

Cirencester (Gloucs.), 193

Clark, (Lord) Kenneth, 8

Clerk, Sir George, 274

Clive, Lt-Gen. Sir Sidney, 404

Cliveden, 67, 272, 352, 373, 407

Clydesdale, Lord (Hamilton), 311

Cody, Dr. Henry, 86, 304

Cohen, Sir Waley, 59, 69

Colchester (Essex), 200, 293, 360, 377

Colman, Jeremiah, 190

Communism, 294, 325, 326, 327, 340, 365

Communist Party (CPGB), 70, 283

Conservative Party, 95, 397

Cooper, Alfred Duff, 35, 36, 55, 65, 78, 79,
    95, 100, 134, 159, 325, 332, 336, 405
  Lady Diana, 35, 55, 65, 78, 79, 405

Corap, Gen. André, 160

Cornwall, 108, 137, 209

Coulter, Robert, 332

Courtauld, Sam, 111, 347

Coventry, 233, 245, 246-7, 250
  and blitz, 244
  and smoke generators, 256-7

Coward, Noël, 314-5

Cranborne, Lord 'Bobbety', 267, 363

Crerar, Lt-Gen. Henry, 73, 238, 373, 377,
    384, 387, 405

Crete, xiii, 311, 312, 313, 315, 316, 329,
    349, 381

Cripps, Lady Isobel, 44, 191

Cripps, John, 44, 191

Cripps, Sir Stafford, xix, 44, 83, 130, 137,
    142, 191, 273, 325, 396, 398, 399, 400
  and 'Communist prattlings', 397
  as Ld. Privy Seal, 394

Crombie, Minna, 178, 305

Crookshank, Harry, 226

Cross, Colin, 96

Crum, Canon John, 67, 70, 142, 143, 174, 245, 259

Crump, Mrs, 316

Czechoslovakia, 52, 243, 362

  Czech troops, 247

Daladier, Edouard, 74, 80, 83

Dakar, 179, 237, 304

  and fiasco of, 228

Dalrymple, Sir Hew, 139

Dante Alighieri, xvii, 79, 320, 354

Danzig, 4

D'Arcy Cooper, Sir Francis, 273

Darlan, Admiral François, 304, 341

Davis, Elmer, 409

Davies, Sir Walford, 293

Dawnay, Col. Alan, 363

Dawson, Geoffrey, 6, 161, 288

Dawson of Penn, Lord, 23, 47

Deal (Kent) 132, 167, 170

de Courcy, Kenneth, 103

de Gaulle, Gen. Charles, 141, 160, 178, 360

Dempsey, Maj-Gen. Miles, 322

Denmark, 81, 82

Dighton, Sgt. 273

Dill, Gen. Sir John, 88, 97, 331, 344

Dillwyn, Colin, 196

Dixon, Prof. Arthur, 301

Dominions Office, 267

Don, Alan, 222-3

Donovan, Col. William, 291

Dorchester, the (hotel), 89, 90, 228, 264, 301, 302, 325, 362, 371, 373, 381

Dover (Kent), 5, 13, 61, 90, 106, 114, 132, 137-8, 166, 199, 201, 209, 212, 220, 221-2, 286, 317-8, 344

  and attacks on, 161, 213

Dover Castle, 169, 221, 317, 345, 366

Downing Street, 23, 370, 382-3, 398

Draper, Ruth, 273

Drax, Admiral Sir Reginald, 6

Drew, Lt-Col. George, 354-5

Droitwich (Cheshire), 263

Duff, Sir Patrick, 7, 49, 67, 100, 115, 304

Dukes, Sir Paul, 352

Duncan, Sir Andrew, 60, 64, 96

Duncannon, Eric (Bessborough), xxv, 118, 166, 224, 235, 299, 315, 355

Dundas of Dundas, Adam, 200

Dunkirk, see under France

Dymchurch (Kent), 217

Eady, Sir Wilfrid, 49

East Anglia, 92-3

East Grinstead (Sussex), 394, 401

Eaton, Sybil, 293-4, 303

Eden, Anthony, 59, 74, 100-1, 116, 159, 242, 267, 285, 363, 384-5

Edenbridge (Kent), 216, 369, 371

Edinburgh, 203

Edward VIII, 84

Egypt, 70, 195, 220, 234, 237, 285, 296, 297, 300, 386

  Cairo, 251, 349, 388

  Suez, 194

Elliot, Walter, 80

Elmhirst, Dorothy, 357-8

Emptage, Ted, 205

England, Robert, 205, 244

ENSA (Entertainments Nat. Serv. Assoc.)

244

Epsom (Surrey), 237-8

evacuation, xiii, 6, 14, 21, 38, 44, 50, 89,
    92, 127, 138, 283, 309
    of Canterbury, 209, 213

evacuees, 18, 20, 21, 27, 29, 50, 90, 241,
    332, 341

exercises, 338-9
    'Binge', 322-4
    'Bumper' 357-358

Exeter, 357

Far East, the, xxii, 332, 359, 370, 372, 376,
    383

Farjeon's Diversions, 253

Farnham (Surrey), 267-8

Fascism, 294

Faversham (Kent), 7, 108, 199, 201

Feiling, Keith, 352

Felsted (Essex), xvi, xviii, xx, xxi, 4, 13,
    18, 21, 34, 111, 114, 115, 132, 147,
    208, 210, 212, 287, 332, 342, 347, 370,
    377, 381, 412
    and wartime occupants, 409-10

Fielden, Maj. Edward, 269

Films:
    Convoy, 240
    49th Parallel, 325
    24 Hours in Soviet Russia, 354

fifth column(ists), xx, 92, 100-1, 102, 104,
    128, 142, 152, 178, 185, 190, 198, 206,
    375

Finland, xx, 28, 54, 59, 72, 74, 76, 80, 349,
    353
    and Winter War, 51-2

Fisher, Sir Warren, 48

Fitzgerald, Helen, 219

Fleming, Peter, 331

Folkestone (Kent), 132, 137, 344

Foreign Office, 6, 116, 129, 198, 228, 386

Forster, Lt-Gen. Alfred, 114, 168

France, xiii, xvii, xix, 3, 4, 5, 6, 9, 11, 13,
    28, 60, 61, 74, 85, 96, 97, 103-4, 106,
    116-117, 129, 134, 146, 152, 159, 162,
    178, 190, 192, 194, 228, 235, 249, 255,
    276, 278, 293, 303, 304, 310, 341, 360,
    363, 398, 399, 400

Amiens, 4

Alsace Lorraine, 45

and armistice, 107

Arras, 3, 12, 88, 89, 106

Beauvais, 5

Boulogne, 4, 61, 88, 104, 106, 108, 114
    150, 217

and unlikely commando raid on, 287

Bordeaux, 160, 303

Brest, 149, 165, 394

Brittany, 160, 191, 241, 360

Calais, 3, 12, 74, 88, 92, 114, 217, 222,
    345

Cambrai, 12, 88

Cherbourg, 9, 235, 394

Colmar, 3

Compiègne, 107

Dunkirk, xxv, 88, 89, 91, 92, 98, 105-6,
    112, 113, 114, 118-24, 125, 146, 150,
    162, 164, 166, 193, 384, 388

Fontainbleau, 3

German invasion of, xx, 154

Laon, 12, 88

Le Havre, 160

Le Touquet, 12

Maginot Line, 3, 11, 81, 97, 153, 360

  criticisms of, 160

Marseilles, 160

Orleans, 141, 160

Paris, 4, 102, 103, 141, 162, 255, 351,
  360. 391

Quiberon, 144-6

Rheims, 11, 12, 155

Rouen, 160

St Malo, 150

St Nazaire, 144, 146, 150, 153

Sedan, 3, 120, 155, 160

Strasbourg, 3

Tours, 160

Troyes, 155-6

Verdun, 3

Vichy regime, 368, 377

Freetown (Sierra Leone), 180

French:

  army, 19, 61, 85, 88, 98, 144, 155, 160,
    363

  corruption, 146, 153

  enthusiasm for war, 13

  fleet, 107, 116, 129, 140, 299, 304

  general staff. 6, 142

  looting, 158

  mobilization, 5, 46

  tanks, 159

Fry, Sir Geoffrey, 49

Fuller, Miss, 222

Fyfe, William Hamilton, 16, 17, 254

Game, Sir Philip, 55, 101

Gamelin, Gen. Maurice, 60, 80, 83, 85, 86
  102, 103, 160

  and dismissal of, 88

Gardiner, Mrs, 15, 61, 99, 182, 202, 285,
  317, 411

  and Canon Gardiner, 278

Garland, Don, 155

Geddes, Aukland, 209

George VI, 9, 98, 102, 128, 137, 230, 244,
  259, 344, 357, 361, 373, 402

  and Queen, 102, 128, 230, 244, 344, 373,
  402

Georges, Gen. Joseph, 102

Germany, xviii, 3, 4, 7, 9, 13, 14, 15, 28,
  39, 41, 44, 45, 46, 66, 68, 72, 82, 83,
  96, 100, 103-4, 106, 107, 117, 165,
  177-8, 185, 206, 235, 237, 250, 254-5,
  257, 273, 276, 283, 295, 298-9, 300,
  309-310, 318, 320, 325, 327, 330-1,
  336, 341, 346, 349, 357, 359-60, 363,
  364-5, 370, 384, 387, 397, 399

  and expected invasion of Britain, 142

  and morale of, 239

  and invasion of Greece, 292

  and conquest of Yugoslavia, 297

  and invasion of Russia, 326

  and offensive in the west, 119-26

  and Siegfried Line, 3, 42, 66

German aircraft:

  aircraft losses, 201

  aircrew, 172, 175, 185, 199, 217-8, 225
  286, 327, 332

  dive bombers, 311

  Dornier, 175, 185, 199, 200, 225

  Heinkel, 158

Messerschmitt, 110, 170, 200, 217, 242

German army, 5, 84, 171, 217, 229-30, 288, 316, 368

  parachutists, xx, 90, 93, 108, 142, 155, 166, 203, 245-6, 315, 329

  prisoners, 305, 386

  tanks, 87, 99, 114, 149, 155, 181, 352, 386

German bombers, xxii, 63, 77, 91, 97, 113, 119, 135-6, 146, 155, 158, 170-1, 174-5, 181, 182-3, 190, 194, 197, 199, 200, 202-3, 216, 218, 227, 237, 240, 245, 257, 275, 277, 285, 291, 298, 311, 332, 359, 413

German cities, 214, 297

  Berlin, 4, 206, 213, 225, 351, 352, 362

German cross-Channel guns, 213, 317

German propaganda, 42, 62, 134

German ships:

  Altmark, 68(n), 69

  Bismarck, 312-3, 315, 367

  E-boats, 53

  Gneisenau, 394 (n)

  Graf Spee, 53

  pocket battleships, 240

  Prinz Eugen, 394 (n)

  Scharnhorst, 394 (n)

  surface raiders, 219-20

  U-boats, 258, 286, 316, 386

Gestapo, 67, 159, 316, 353

Gibbs, Sir Philip, 162

Gibraltar, 74, 89, 151, 367

Giraud, Gen. Henri, 119

Glasgow, xvii, 17, 28, 43, 197, 256, 258, 301, 328, 353, 370, 383

Gloucester, 193, 259

Gloucester, Duke of, 285

Goebbels, Josef, 41,42

Gollancz, Victor, 319

Goodrich Court, 112, 114-5, 193, 195, 208, 212, 214, 235-6, 270, 287, 323, 327, 349, 356, 377

Göring, Hermann, 40, 48, 307

Gort, Gen. Lord, 61, 83, 88, 102, 112

Gough, Gen. Hubert, 204

Gower, Sir Robert, 51

Grace, Raymond, 32

Grant, George, 313-4, 333, 371, 390

  and Oxford Bermondsey Club, 280-85, 332

Gravesend (Kent) 241, 395

Gray, Eric, 200

Gray, Miss, 15, 20, 37, 63, 89

Greece, 63, 78, 237, 260, 285, 292, 295, 297, 300, 309, 331, 349

  Athens, 34, 302, 309, 349, 371

  German conquest of, 302

Greenly, John, 87, 89

Greenwood, Arthur, 71, 94, 362

Grenfell, Joyce, 273

Greville, Mrs Ronnie, 274, 275, 330, 373

Grigg, Sir Edward 'Ned', 53, 64

Grigg, Sir James, xx, xxi, 97, 204, 394

Guards' Club, 226

Guildford (Surrey), 271

Gurkhas, xvii, 398

Hahn, Kurt, 69

Haig, Sylvia and Diana, 146

Haldenby, Eric, 149-50

Halifax, Lord, 6, 64, 71, 75, 80, 198, 264, 267, 348-9
  and failings as Ambassador to US, 345-6
Hankey, Lord, xix, 18-19, 48, 75, 142, 159-60, 161, 272, 332
Hardcastle, Ven. Edward, 401
Hardcastle, Mary, 232
Hardinge, Alexander, 103
Harker, Michael, 370
Harrod, Roy, 196, 355
Hart House (Toronto), xviii, xx, xxiii, 3, 86, 196, 224, 302, 332, 363, 376
Haslam. Major, 264
Headley (Surrey), 224, 323, 351, 369, 406, 410
Heeney, Arnold, 82
Henderson, Sir Neville, 4, 5
Herefordshire, xvi, xx,
Herne Bay (Kent), 174
Hertzberg, Brig. Charles, 324
Hess, Rudolf, 308-9, 310, 316, 320, 325, 341
  and flight to Scotland, 307
Hever Castle (Kent), 176, 258, 291, 336, 370, 377, 391
Hewlett, Mrs, 202, 212, 298
Heyworth, Lt-Col. Reginald, 387
Hignall (Ralph's butler), 13, 25
Hitler, Adolf, 5, 6, 20, 28, 33, 39, 41-2, 45, 66, 69, 73, 74, 77, 81-2, 85, 96, 97, 102-3, 104, 107, 116, 129, 132, 143, 219, 223, 225, 239, 243, 254, 260, 266, 276, 281, 286, 295, 298, 307, 308-9, 310, 314, 316, 320, 326, 341-2, 352, 374, 377

Hoare, Sir Samuel (Templewood), 75, 80, 93, 100
  as Ambassador in Madrid, 350
Hodgson, Patrick, 37, 60, 79, 101, 103, 116, 204
Holland, 28, 63, 74, 81, 85-86, 89, 119, 140, 142, 207, 295, 360, 399
  and Queen of, 102
Home Guard, xiv, xx, 148, 166, 171-2, 187, 200, 203, 205, 207, 209, 213, 215-16, 227, 231, 277, 289, 291, 292-3, 295, 306, 319, 323, 366, 375-6, 399, 401, 405, 412,
  and Ralph's membership of, 279
  and Osterley Park school, 161, 202, 203, 227, 230
  and technical school, 311,
Hopkins, Harry, 275
Hopkins, see under Norah
Hore-Belisha, Leslie, xv, 16, 62, 64, 65, 67, 75, 87, 102, 242
  and resignation, 60
House of Commons, 7, 28, 54, 60, 76, 94, 159, 348, 374, 400
  and Norway debate, 93
  and destruction of, 307
House of Lords, 255, 307, 348
Houston-Boswall, Jock, 378
Howe, Clarence, 264-5, 266
Howe, Major, 274, 318
Howes, Brig. Sidney 'Puggy', 107
Howorth, Sir Rupert, 49
Hudson, Robert, 96
Hull (Yorks.), 90
Hulton, Edward, 161, 204, 352

Hungary, 81, 97

Humphreys, Maj. George, xxiv, 224, 226
   230, 291

Huxley, Julian, xxi, 352

Hythe (Kent), 132, 137, 153, 161

Iceland, 168, 360, 365

Ignatieff, George, 332, 335

Ignatieff, Nick, 151, 185, 203, 343-4

Iliffe, Lord, 382

India (and Ceylon) 234, 328, 346-7, 350,
   358, 372, 383, 386, 398, 399, 400,
   402, 405, 408

   Andaman Islands, 405

   Bangalore, 234

   Bengal, 389

   Bombay, 402

   Colombo, 194

   Hindustani, 393

   Pathans, 398

Indian Army, 330, 359

Indian Ocean, 376, 399

ITC (Infantry Training Centre), 242, 265,
   292, 297

Inglis, Brig. Lindsay, 329-30

Inverness, 301

Iraq, 315-16

Ireland, 25, 116, 219, 234, 241, 316, 359

   Dublin, 359

Ironside, Gen. Sir Edmond, 61, 65, 83, 88,
   101, 102, 116,

   and fifth columnists, 128

Irving, Lawrence, 413

Isle of Man, 353

Isle of Wight, 365

Ismay (Lord) Hastings, 'Pug', xix, 5, 7, 45,
   139, 303-4, 365, 384, 402

   views on strategy, 140-2

   and Moscow mission, 363-4

Italy, xviii, 4, 6, 18, 61, 62, 68, 78, 85, 97,
   117, 129, 141, 157, 178, 194, 258, 279
   287, 295, 331, 368

Italian Airforce, 218

Italian Army, 286, 297, 305, 386

Italian Navy, 129, 161, 244, 304,

   Naples, 287

   Rome, 62, 107, 235

   Sicily, 220

   Taranto, 161, 244, 304

Jacques, Reginald, 303

Japan, 68, 82, 85, 116, 191, 225, 279,
   295, 300, 310, 327, 331, 342, 348,
   351, 359, 373, 385, 387, 389, 391,
   394

Japanese Airforce, 373

Japanese Army, 375, 376, 385, 392, 398,
   408

Japanese Navy, 370

Jerusalem, 388, 405

Jews, 33, 70, 75, 211, 282, 299, 309, 310
   353, 356

   and Richborough refugee camp, 59, 69

Joad, C.E.M., 352

Johnson, Hewlett, xix, xxii, 20, 29, 33, 37,
   51-52, 70-1, 73, 75, 78, 91, 137, 143,
   168, 216, 217-8, 237, 245, 318-9, 326,
   334, 340, 346, 349, 404

   and his book on Russia, 61

   and new haircut, 341

430

foretells the future, 413-4

Jones, Tom, xix, xxi, 47, 67, 73, 95-7, 161,
  272-3, 293, 394

Kaiser, the (Wilhelm II), 316

Keeble, Major Robert, 189

Kennedy, Joseph, 73

Kent, xx, 103, 108, 140, 152, 161, 170,
  174, 189, 198, 200, 201, 205, 249, 276-
  7, 290, 312, 331, 334, 342, 361, 391

Kenya, 366

Kerr, (Sir) Howard, 285

Kerr, Dr Munro, 181

Keynes, John Maynard, 228

King, Mackenzie, xix, 47, 82, 315, 335,
  344, 381, 387

King-Hall, William, 63, 74, 92

King's School Canterbury, 37, 73, 109, 209,
  245, 403

Knox, Franklin, 276

Labour Party, 5, 51, 53-4, 72, 100, 101-2,
  115, 267, 294, 319
  and dislike of Chamberlain, 80
  and attitude towards coalition govt., 95

Lambeth Palace, xix, 139, 222,
  and bomb damage to, 320

Land Army, the, 66, 291, 371, 391

Lang, Most Rev. Cosmo Gordon, xix, 37,
  78, 115, 137, 139, 210, 217-8, 222-3,
  224, 277, 320, 348, 401, 403
  and resignation, 386

Lascelles, Sir Alan, 'Tommy', 128, 288,
  343-4, 361

Laval, Pierre, 104

Lavington (Sussex), 24, 35-6, 54, 76, 79,
  219, 278, 301, 310, 330, 349, 405-6

LNU (League of Nations' Union), 53, 101

Leamington (Warwicks.), 176, 187, 233,
  247

Leatherhead (Surrey), 315, 351, 373

Lechlade (Gloucs.), 194

Lee, Brig-Gen. John, 310

Leeds (Yorks.), 140, 370, 377, 383

Leeson, Spencer, 127

Leicester, 231

Lenin, V.I., 354

Leopold, King of the Belgians, 88, 105,
  113, 119

Lester, Major G, 204

Libya, 285, 297, 300, 316, 356, 368, 370,
  370, 387
  Bardia, 265
  Benghazi, 389
  Sidi Rezegh, 370
  Tobruk, 305
  Tripolitania, 279, 368

Lichfield (Staffs.), 294, 328

Lindbergh, Charles, 48, 341, 375

Lindemann, Prof. Frederick, 97, 100, 140,
  196

Linlithgow, Lord, 350

Linnell, Miss, xxiii, xxv, 167

Lisbon, 62

Liverpool, 25, 87, 89, 194, 197, 204, 327
  364
  and blitz, 306
  and Bishop of, 324-5

Llewellin, John, 'Jay', 394

Lloyd George, David, 45, 84

and gloomy view of the war, 75

LDV (Local Defence Volunteers), xx, 90, 92, 101-2, 104, 108-9, 116, 131, 136-7, 139

London, xx, 5, 6, 13, 17, 21, 23-4, 25-6, 34, 38, 44, 52, 54, 55, 72, 89, 93, 95, 101, 107, 130, 138, 146, 174, 178, 194, 197, 200, 213-14, 219, 223-4, 226-7, 228-9, 233, 235, 238, 248, 256, 299, 300-1, 303-4, 307, 313, 324, 332, 337, 344, 351-2, 355, 370, 372, 384, 397, 402-3, 409

blitz, xvii, 208, 260, 289, 298, 306,

City of, xvii, 198, 214, 263, 268, 295, 298

and destruction of, 302

and Hart Massey's memo., 38-42

and looting, 304, 313

LCC (London County Council), 30-1, 39, 86, 282, 284

London landmarks/streets:

All Hallows Barking, 256, 264

Bank of England, 214

Bow Church, 214

Café de Paris, 289

Elephant and Castle, 313

Green Park, 229

Hyde Park, 38

Hyde Park Square, 14, 89, 307

London Bridge, 214

Mile End Road, 211

National Gallery, 293

Old Vic, the, 313

Pall Mall, 229, 299

Piccadilly, 8, 229, 299, 282

St Katharine's Dock, 214, 219

St James's Palace, 229

St Paul's, 22, 382

Strand, the, 381, 382

Tate Gallery, 222

Tower of London, 220, 264

Tower Bridge, 210

Trinity House, 264

Waterloo Bridge, 313

Trafalgar Square, 23

Westminster Abbey, 22, 23, 161, 307, 308, 313, 320

Westminster Bridge, 23, 280

Westminster Cathedral, 23

Westminster Hall, 307

Whitehall, 7, 46, 48, 62, 103, 107, 138

parts of London:

Aldgate, 211

Bermondsey, xxvi, 21, 50, 210, 274, 280 281, 283, 289, 313, 332

Chelsea, 198

East End, 210, 214, 232

Harrow, 204

Lambeth, 222

Poplar, 219

Southwark, 239, 313

Stepney, 211, 219

Westminster, 198

London stations:

Euston, 89, 370

Cannon St., 214, 281

Liverpool St., 210, 212, 409

London Bridge, 210, 263, 281

Paddington, 195

Victoria, xvii, 51, 89, 161, 178, 192

432

Lothian, Lord (Kerr), 345

Low, David, 41-2

Lowe, Rev. John, 139, 196, 204, 399

Lucas, Dr, 144-6, 190

Lunt, Rev. Francis, 248

Luxemburg, 28

Lydd, (Kent), 148, 207

Lyminge (Kent), 127

Lyttelton, Hon. George, 35

Lyttelton, Oliver (Chandos), 267

Macadam, Ivison, 336

MacAlpine, John, 343

MacDonald, James Ramsay, 243

MacDonald, Malcom, 75, 288, 304

MacDonell, Angus, 350

McKie, William, 193-4

Macmillan, Lord, 47, 52, 64, 159

Macmillan, Rt. Rev. John, 268, 383

MacKenzie, Eric, 78

McNaughton, Lt-Gen. Andrew, xx, xxi,
    150, 159, 205, 224, 226, 230, 231, 235-
    6, 238-9, 241-2, 249, 266, 270, 294,
    309-10, 322, 324, 343, 346, 354, 361,
    367, 373, 383-4, 390, 402, 405, 406-7

McNaughton, Mrs, 235-6, 390

McNutt, Canon, 15, 29, 142, 208, 245

Maidstone (Kent), 200, 205, 210, 218, 331

Maisky, Ivan, 137, 273, 346, 349, 383

Maisky, Mme., 382

Malaya, 359, 373, 385, 400

  Penang, 376

  Johore, 392

Malta, 287

Manchester, 231

Manchuria, 191

Mansbridge, Albert, 413

Margate (Kent), 111, 132, 137-8, 199, 202

Margesson, David, 76, 79, 266, 274, 275,
    349, 394, 397, 399

  and reasons for no second front, 330-1

Marlborough, xiv, 5, 17, 188, 254,

  Old Malburians, 176, 187, 189

Martin, Kingsley, 352

Mason-Macfarlane, Gen. Noel, 319, 330,
    364

Massey, Alice, 8, 89-90, 226, 228, 264,
    302, 309, 325, 411

Massey, Hart, 8, 228

Massey, Lionel, 8, 198, 371

  as prisoner, 309, 390

Massey, Vincent, xviii (n), xx, 8, 9, 89-90,
    103, 161, 198, 224, 226, 228, 264, 287,
    302, 309, 325, 332, 362, 371, 381-2,
    402, 407

Masterman, J.C., 42, 139, 196, 206

Mathew, Mr (and daughters), 21, 30, 89,
    90, 172, 184, 227, 237, 259, 377

Maude, Brig. Christian, 411-12

Maxton, Jimmy, 319

Meade-Waldo, Edmund, 184

Meade-Waldo, Jane, 30, 184, 203, 279,
    289, 321, 361, 365, 368, 372, 383, 386,
    388

Meade-Waldo, Colonel, 90, 176, 184, 203,
    228, 289

Mediterranean, the, 6, 81, 116, 129, 141,
    237, 275, 286, 304, 310, 367, 368

Melchett, Lord, 310

Menzies, Sir Robert, 48, 348

Middle East, xxii, 146, 178, 205, 310, 348, 365, 383

Miles, Eric, 174

Mills, Mary and Dorothy, 209

Ministry of Aircraft Production, 394, 397

Ministry of Defence, 304

Ministry of Economic Warfare, 97

Ministry of Food, xvii, 14, 24, 26, 299

Ministry of Information, xiii, 28-9, 34, 36, 40, 52-3, 64, 74, 134, 159, 332, 336

    as 'popular joke', 48

Ministry of Labour, 62, 267, 294, 397

MI6, xx, 204

Ministry of Transport, xix, 54, 64, 77-8, 95 96

Mitford, Unity, 103

Mollie (ECFB's maid), 15, 61, 63, 89, 182, 202, 226, 317

Monckton, (Sir) Walter, 272, 273, 318

Monier-Williams, Roy, 27

Montague, Maj-Gen. Percival, 226, 291,

Montgomery, Gen. Bernard (Alamein), 312, 363, 369, 387, 403

Moore-Brabazon (Lord), John, 364

Morrison, Herbert, 94, 397, 413

Morrison, W.S., 'Shakes', 94

Morshead, Brig. Leslie, 306

Mortimer, Robert, 196

Morton, Desmond, 97, 100, 140

Munich agreement, 63, 87, 103, 208, 243, 253

Murray, Gilbert, 272

Mussolini, Benito, 97, 281

    as 'top wop', 256

NAAFI (Navy, Army and Air Force Inst.) 258, 409

Napoleon, 103, 129, 257, 326, 352, 369

Nazis (ism), 81, 99, 105, 205, 272, 309, 326, 331, 340, 351, 357, 373, 407

Newbury (Berks.), 218

Newcastle, 201, 298

New Forest, 144, 154

New Guinea, 388

Newman, Fred, 174, 187, 201

Newport (Mon.), 154

Newspapers/Peridicals

    The Countryman, 192

    Daily Express, 38(n)

    Daily Telegraph, 137, 213

    Evening Standard, 41

    The Listener, 402(n)

    Manchester Guardian, 48

    Sunday Times, 129

    The Times, 10, 33, 37, 52, 62, 67, 73, 84, 96, 127, 128, 161, 165, 225, 237, 269, 274, 387

    Tribune, 44

New Zealand, 173, 223

    troops in Greece and Crete, 311, 349

'Ninny' - Miss Peters, 294

Norah Hopkins (ECFB's maid), 15, 89, 98, 127, 182, 202, 212, 278

North, Lord, 199

North Africa, 117, 141, 169, 178, 256, 260, 279, 310, 368, 386

Norton, Jean, 341

Norton, Maj-Gen. Edward, 375

Norway, 69, 74, 81-2, 85, 93, 237, 285, 295, 399

Narvick, 81

Stavanger, 82

Norwich, 328

Nye, Lt-Gen. Archibald, 384

OTC (Officer Training Corps), 16, 30, 163, 242, 395

OCTU (Officer Cadet Training Unit), xxiii, 169, 242, 256, 263-4, 265, 274, 292, 294, 351, 369

Ogilvie, Sir Frederick, 343

Ogilvie, Will, 402

Onslow, Capt. R.F.J., 179

Oppenheim, Hans, 357

Oran (Algeria), 179, 341

Orkneys, the, 74, 78, 134, 168

ORTU (Officer Recruit Traing Corps), 263

Ottley, Canon Fielding, 15, 215, 244

Oxford (City of), 69, 71, 74, 193, 196, 273, 299, 389

Mitre Hotel, 299, 408

Randolph Hotel, 299

Oxford University, 16-17, 30, 32-3, 37, 42, 62, 104, 139, 177, 187, 219, 225, 234, 249, 334, 399, 403, 407, 411

Colleges:

Balliol, 43, 62, 78-9

Brasenose, 43

Christ Church, xiv, xvii, 5, 17, 72, 100, 104, 140, 189, 273, 334, 398, 403

Exeter, 189

Hertford, 43

Magdalen, 193, 299, 300

New, 37

Oriel, 43, 299

Pembroke, 43, 189

Queen's, 189, 300

St Edmund's Hall, 189

St John's, 37, 299, 369

Trinity, 43, 189

Paddockhurst (Sussex), 367

Page, Brig. Lionel, 291, 303

Paget, Gen. Sir Bernard, xix, 292

Pakenham, Frank (Longford), 139, 200

Palestine, 75, 81, 194, 220

Pape, Joan, 9

Parliament, 8, 186, 308, 342

Paterson, Alexander, 280

Patterson, Jack, 8

Patrixbourne (Kent), 133, 170

Pawson, Guy and Helen, 342

People's Convention, 319

Pearkes, Maj-Gen. Georege, 367, 373

Pearl Harbor, 373

Pearson, Mike, 204, 224, 226

Peat, Sir Harry, 26

Pereira, Maj-Gen. Sir Cecil, 101

Pétain, Marshal Philippe, 160, 260, 360, 364, 377

Phelan, Brig. Frederick, 337

Phillips, Admiral Sir Tom, 374

Philippines, the, 373

Pick, Frank, 337

Pilgrim Trust, the, 47, 161, 243

Plymouth, 149

Poison Gas, 207-8

Poland, 3, 7, 18, 42, 46, 52, 65, 67, 358

and British guarantee, 3, 5

Cracow University, 317

and dismemberment of, 26
Polish airmen, 248, 358
Polish Officers, 317, 334, 358
Polish Forces, 243
Warsaw, 66
Pollitt, Harry, 319
Poole, Mr, 15
Poole, Canon Joseph, 143, 245
Portal, Lord, 394
Portsmouth, 140, 145, 201
and raids on, 171, 261, 297, 353
Pownall, Maj-Gen. Sir Henry, 116
Price, Maj-Gen, Basil, 336
Priestley, J.B., xiv, 134, 352
Pritt, D.N., 319
public schools, xiii, 69, 115, 192, 347-8
Bedford, 188
Eton, 35, 219, 255, 267
Charterhouse, xix, 320, 369
Christ's Hospital, 255
Clifton, 254
Harrow, 255
Malvern, 188
Radley, 188
Winchester, 255
Purvis, Arthur, 87, 345

Quisling, Vidkum, 303

Ramsay, Capt. Archibald, MP, 102
Ramsbotham, Herewald, 332
Ramsgate (Kent), 132, 137-8, 161, 190,
199, 201, 206, 221, 277
Reading (Berks.), 90, 218, 307
Reading, Lord, 60, 69

Reading University, 267, 270-1
Red Cross, 290, 329, 396
and 'penny a week fund', 391
and St John Ambulance, 290
Reith, Sir (Lord), John, 60, 64, 94, 363,
394, 398
Reynaud, Paul, 74, 80, 141, 303-4,
Reynolds, Quentin, 341
Riding, George, 69
Roberts, Sgt. (RSM), 133, 190-1, 202-3,
212, 277, 295
Rochester (Kent), 132, 174, 210
Roman Catholicism, 272
Romania, 61, 81, 97, 107, 237
Rommel, Gen. Erwin, 386
Roosevelt, F.D., 55, 74, 275, 286, 291, 342,
369, 370
and 'day of infamy', 373
Rose, Rt. Rev. Alfred, 59, 137, 152, 206,
213, 220, 318
Royal Air Force (RAF), 7, 19, 46, 91, 97,
141, 156, 164, 175, 177-8, 197-8, 199,
210, 216, 217, 219, 233, 248, 253-4,
267, 272, 278, 308, 316, 331, 350, 362,
404, 413
RAF aircraft:
Battle, 151
Blenheim. 329
Hurricane, 177, 200, 242
Spitfire, 35, 143, 170, 174, 177, 182, 199,
200, 202, 209, 217, 242
Tornado, 254
Typhoon, 254
RAF stations:
Bekesbourne, 123, 170, 327

436

Bembridge, 171

Croydon, 174

Detling, 174, 199, 205

Dyce, 143

Lympne, 170

Manston, 34

Mildenhall, 287

Northwood, 138

Penshurst, 90

Waddington, 351

Royal Army Medical Corps (RAMC)
145, 336

Royal Army Service Corps (RASC), 248

Royal Navy, 19, 46, 69, 81, 108, 156, 164,
168, 177, 217, 242-3, 258, 275, 279,
287, 315, 359, 364

Fleet Air Arm, 244

Royal Navy ships:

Ark Royal, 367-8

Barham, 304

Cossack, 68

Dorsetshire, 145

Hood, 312-3, 315

Lance, 402

MTBs, 217

Prince of Wales, 374

Repulse, 374

Royal Oak, 34

Royal Empire Society, 204, 381

Rugby, xiv, xvii, 24, 31, 60, 176, 188, 245,
250, 311, 366, 388, 391, 393, 401, 403,
411

Russia, xiii, xxii, 4, 6, 7, 26, 44, 46, 51, 52,
54, 75-6, 97, 116, 129, 137, 185, 225,
272, 273, 296, 300, 310, 318, 325-6,

327, 330, 334-5, 340-1, 346, 347, 349,
350, 352, 358, 361, 374, 384, 387, 389,
391, 397, 414

Caucasus, 359

German invasion of, xiii, 327

invasion of Finland, xx, 51

Kiev, 336

Leningrad, 336, 352

Moscow, 6, 74, 191, 325, 330, 336, 346
351, 370, 377, 382, 384, 397

Rostov, 368, 370

Siberia, 199, 342

Ukraine, 319

Russian armed forces, 327, 331, 346, 351,
352, 363, 365, 368, 370, 375, 384

Ryle, Gilbert, 196, 200

St Austell (Cornwall), 92

St Edmund's School (Canterbury), 92, 181,
200

St Margaret's Bay (Kent), 334, 339

Salisbury Cathedral, 292, 335, 357

Salisbury Plain, xxvi, 193, 194-5, 233, 292,
334

Salter, Arthur, 48

Salvation Army, the, 403

Sanders, Cpl. (JBB's driver), xxv, 249, 270,
317, 322, 332, 343, 367, 376, 395, 406,
407, 410

Sandhurst, 67, 69, 292

Sandwich (Kent), 338

Sargeant, Canon Alec, 209, 213

Sarre (Kent), 151

Saunders, Hilary, 337

Savoy, the (hotel), 288, 355

Scarlett, Maj-Gen. Gerald, 265

Scotland, 134, 168, 229, 301, 307, 325, 353 381

Scott, Sir Harold, 197, 371

servants, 25, 361

Sheppey, Isle of, 201, 209

Shirley, Rev. Dr John, 37, 73, 91, 142, 245

Shrewsbury, 131

Sibly, Sir Frank, 271

Simon, Sir John, 24(n), 49, 54, 75, 80, 84, 93, 101, 288

Simonds, Brig. Guy, 288-9, 367

Singapore, 373, 376, 385, 389, 392, 394, 405, 412

and surrender of, 378

Sinclair, Archibald (Thurso), 6

Sinclair, Brig. John, 369

Sinn Fein, 408

Sittingbourne (Kent), 7, 218

Skam (Taxi Service), 209, 212, 214

Sopwith, Ven. Thomas, 154, 341, 369, 413

South Africa, 83, 370, 386, 388, 393, 412

South America, 195, 287

Southampton, 9, 90, 146, 150, 172, 268, 353

Spain, 73, 129

Spanish Civil War, 152, 161, 173

and International Brigade, 204

and irregular warfare, 231

Spender Clay, Herbert, 288

Spears, Maj-Gen. Sir Edward, 160

Stalin, Joseph, 137, 142, 185, 327, 349, 353, 363-4, 384-5, 396

as Genghiz Khan, 397

Stamp, Lord, 47, 54

Stanhope, Lord, 80

Stainforth, Miss, 235

Stanley, Maureen, 55, 76

Stanley, Oliver, 26, 53, 55, 60, 64-5, 66-7, 76

Stanstead (Essex), 126, 166

Steele, Canon, 210

Stewart, Brig. Stewart

Stoke-on-Trent, 201

Stonewall, 90, 173, 176, 184, 203, 290

Storrs, Ronald, 8, 9

Stonehenge, 292

Stow-on-the-Wold (Gloucs.), 401, 404

Strang, William, 7

Strathcona, Lord, 228, 288

Streatfeild, Col., 172, 177

Streatfeild, Dick, 30, 172, 241

Stuart, James (Findhorn), 397

Stuart-King, Brig. Charles, 112-14

Surrey, xx, 152, 216, 224, 243, 317

Sudan, xvii, xxvii, 3, 30, 47, 89, 313, 386

and Sudan Defence Force, 226

Khartoum, 251-2, 388

Swanage (Dorset), 200

Swansea, 195

Sweden, 74, 81

Switzerland, xix, 3, 35, 85, 97

Basle, 3

Berne, 4, 11

Geneva, 3, 10

Locarno, 4, 10

Lucerne, 11

Syria, 310, 316

Tassall, Mr, 199

Taunton (Somerset), 234

Temple, Most Rev. William, xxii, 115, 277, 320, 386, 401
  and future of public schools, 255
  and enthronement ceremony, 406, 411-12

Thailand, 342, 389

Thames, river, 16, 23, 61, 111, 132, 223

Thesiger, Tony, 273

Thetford (Norfolk), 334, 335

Thomas, Sir Godfrey, 78

Thorne, Miss, 241, 289

Thorne, Maj-Gen. André 'Bulgy', 135, 312

Timoshenko, Marshal Semion, 370

Tonbridge (Kent), 210, 216, 376, 395

Torquay (Devon), 357

Tots and Quots Club, 355

Tower, Sir Reginald, 15

Travellers', the, xx, 6, 8, 128, 204, 224, 229 313, 332, 387
  and bomb damage, 298

Trenchard, Air Marshal Lord, 254, 272

Trevelyan, Charles, 129

Tryon, George, 64

Tunbridge Wells (Kent), 51, 172, 189, 258, 312

Turf, the, 230

Turkey, 81, 300

Turner, Brig. Guy, 291

Tweedsmuir, Lord, 67, 75, 78, 83

UAB (Unemployment Assistance Board), 161

United Services Club, 159

United States of America, 19, 36, 41, 55, 65, 87, 96, 104, 116-7, 118, 129, 142, 162, 207, 225, 235, 254, 264, 279, 296, 300, 310, 318-9, 325-6, 334, 341-2, 343, 345, 349, 350, 356, 363, 373, 375, 384, 386, 394-5, 408, 411
  and isolationism, 75
  and lend lease, 286
  New York, 36, 65, 86, 87, 350, 374
  Washington D.C., 264, 267, 349-50, 370

Wales, 7, 108, 153, 203

Wallace, Barbie, 35, 54, 65, 75, 89, 139, 219, 301, 325, 330, 349, 405
  and possible future political career, 292

Wallace, David, 34, 63, 78, 278, 349, 363 405

Wallace, Euan, xix, xx, 6, 9, 26, 34, 52, 67, 76, 89, 93-94, 96, 138-9, 159, 197-8, 219, 230, 278, 285, 292

Wallace, John, 78-9

Waller, Deaconess, 240

Walmer (Kent), 218

War Office (WO), xvii, xx, xxii, 7, 60, 62, 76, 97, 103, 115, 128, 147, 163-4, 173, 195, 198, 204, 223, 335, 340, 344, 355, 364, 368, 371, 378, 384, 397, 406, 411

Warminster (Wilts.), 166

Warren, Max, 248

Warrington (Ches.), 328

War Weapons Week (1941), 279, 285, 314

Warwick, 163, 169, 176, 187-8, 233, 246-7, 248

Watchet (Somerset), 368

Waugh, Evelyn, xiv

Wavell, Gen. Archibald, 279, 330, 359, 389, 405

compared with Marlborough, 285

Weir, Lord, 96

Weir, Sir John, 102

Westerham (Kent), 175

West Indies, 346-7

Weygand, Gen. Maxime, 88, 141

Weymouth (Dorset), 130, 140

White, Col. Archibald, 335

White-Thomson, Ian, 210, 217, 222, 275

Whitmore, Sir Francis, 395

Whitstable (Kent), 108, 132, 170, 186, 358

Wickhambreaux (Kent), 175, 225

Willans, Maj-Gen., Harry, xxiv, 288, 333, 336, 411

Williams, Rt. Rev. Alwyn, 320

Williams, W.E., xxi, 302, 330, 336, 344, 355

Willingdon, Lord, 288

Wilson, Sir Charles (Moran), 382

Wilson, Sir Horace, xx, 93, 96, 100, 204

Wimperis, Harry, 253-4

Winant, John G., 310, 343, 355, 363, 381

Winchester (Hants.), 363

Wingfield, Maj-Gen. Maurice, 401

Wintringham, Tom, 161, 204

Wiseman, Sir William, 36

Wodehouse, P.G., 134

Women's Voluntary Service (WVS), 342

Wood, Mr, 20

Wood, Sir Kingsley, 35, 96, 288, 410

Wood, R.S., 204-5

Woodruff, Commander Douglas, 242

Woolley, Sir Leonard, 381

Woolton, Lord, 96

Workers' Education Authority (WEA), 205

Worthing (Sussex), 322

Worthington, Brig. Frederick, 334, 335

Wrong, Hume, 82, 224, 226, 229

Gt Yarmouth (Norfolk), 315, 328, 339, 368, 372

Yeovil (Somerset), 368

YMCA (Young Men's Christ. Assoc.), xvi, 51, 90, 192-3, 215, 315, 303

Younghusband, Frank and Violet, 179-181

Yorkshire, 92, 93, 108, 161, 233

Yugoslavia, 81, 296-7, 300

Belgrage, 297, 302

and coup d'état, 295

King Peter, 296

Zuckerman, (Sir) Zolly, 355

STUDIES IN BRITISH HISTORY

1. Richard S. Tompson, **The Atlantic Archipelago: A Political History of the British Isles**

2. Edward C. Metzger, **Ralph, First Duke of Montagu, 1638-1709**

3. Robert Munter and Clyde L. Grose, **Englishmen Abroad: Being an Account of Their Travels in the Seventeenth Century**

4. Earl A. Reitan (ed.), **The Best of the Gentleman's Magazine, 1731-1754**

5. Peter Penner, **Robert Needham Cust, 1821-1909: A Personal Biography**

6. Narasingha P. Sil, **William Lord Herbert of Pembroke (c.1507 - 1570): Politique and Patriot**

7. Juanita Kruse, **John Buchan (1875-1940) and the Idea of Empire: Popular Literature and Political Ideology**

8. Ronald K. Huch, **Henry, Lord Brougham: The Later Years, 1830-1868**

9. C.W.S. Hartley, **A Biography of Sir Charles Hartley, Civil Engineer (1825-1915): The Father of the Danube**

10. Jeanie Watson and Philip McM. Pittman (eds.), **The Portrayal of Life Stages in English Literature, 1500-1800; Infancy, Youth, Marriage, Aging, Death, Martyrdom: Essays in Honor of Warren Wooden**

11. Carole Levin, **Propaganda in the English Reformation: Heroic and Villainous Images of King John**

12. Harvey B. Tress, **British Strategic Bombing Policy Through 1940: Politics, Attitudes, and the Formation of a Lasting Pattern**

13. Barbara J. Blaszak, **George Jacob Holyoake (1817-1906) and the Development of the British Cooperative Movement**

14. Karl W. Schweizer, **England, Prussia and the Seven Years War: Studies in Alliance Policies and Diplomacy**

15. Rex A. Barrell, **Anthony Ashley Cooper, Earl of Shaftesbury (1671-1713) and `Le Refuge Français'- Correspondence**

16. John Butler, **Lord Herbert of Chirbury (1582-1648): An Intellectual Biography**

17. William Blake, **William Maitland of Lethington, 1528-1573: A Study of the Policy of Moderation in the Scottish Reformation**

18. William Calvin Dickinson, **Sidney Godolphin, Lord Treasurer, 1702-1710**

19. Rex A. Barrell (ed.), **Francis Atterbury (1662-1732), Bishop of Rochester, and His French Correspondents**

20. Alan G. R. Smith (ed.), **The Anonymous Life of William Cecil, Lord Burghley**

21. Jeremy Caple, **The Bristol Riots of 1831 and Social Reform in Britain**

22. Gerald W. Morton, **A Biography of Mildmay Fane, Second Earl of Westmorland 1601-1666: The Unknown Cavalier**

23. Keith M. Wilson, **A Study in the History and Politics of the** *Morning Post* **1905-1926**

24. Rex A. Barrell, **George Augustus Selwyn (1719-1791) and France: Unpublished Correspondence**

25. Thomas Twining, **A Selection of Thomas Twining's Letters (1734-1804): The Record of a Tranquil Life**, Ralph S. Walker (ed.)

26. Rex A. Barrell, **Horace Walpole (1717 - 1797) and France**

27. Stephen Roberts, **Radical Politicians and Poets in Early Victorian Britain: The Voices of Six Chartist Leaders**

28. Joseph Green, **A Social History of the Jewish East End in London, 1914-1939: A Study of Life, Labour and Liturgy**

29. Christopher Robbins, **The Earl of Wharton and Whig Party Politics, 1679-1715**

30. Barry M. Gough, **British Mercantile Interests in the Making of the Peace of Paris, 1763**

31. P. E. H. Hair and J. D. Alsop, **English Seamen and Traders in Guinea, 1553-1565: The New Evidence of Their Wills**

32. Kenneth Warren, **John Meade Falkner, 1858-1932: A Paradoxical Life**

33. John A. Butler, **A Biography of Richard Cromwell, 1626-1712, the Second Protector**

34. Alan O'Day, **Government and Institutions in the Post-1832 United Kingdom**

35. David Franklin, **The Scottish Regency of Earl of Arran: A Study in the Failure of Anglo-Scottish Relations**

36. Terence M. Freeman, **Dramatic Representations of British Soldier and Sailors on the Lodon Stage, 1660-1800: Britons, Strike Home**

37. Clive E. Hill, **Understanding the** *Fabian Essays in Socialism* **(1889)**

38. Rex A. Barrell (complier), **The French Correspondence of James, 1st Earl Waldegrave (1684-1741)**

39. Peter Rowland, **The Life and Times of Thomas Day, 1748-1789 – English Philanthropist and Author**

40. Robert Bernays, **The Diaries and Letters of Robert Bernays, 1932-1939: An Insider's Account of the House of Commons**, edited by Nick Smart

41. Roger North, **Life of the Lord Keeper North by Roger North**, edited with introduction, notes and appendices by Mary Chan

42. Roger Lee Brown, **A History of the Fleet Prison, London: The Anatomy of the Fleet**

43. Elisabeth A. Cawthon, **Job Accidents and the Law in England's Early Railway Age: Origins of Employer Liability and Workmen's Compensation**

44. Arthur Sherbo, **Letters to Mr. Urban of the** *Gentleman's Magazine*, **1751-1811**

45. Michael Quill (ed.), *Revolution by Reason* and Other Essays by Oswald Mosley

46. Ian Sellers, **Early Modern Warrington 1520-1847: A Definitive History**

47. Brian P. Farrell, **The Basis and Making of British Grand Strategy, 1940-1943: Was There a Plan?** (2 volumes)

48. Edward Corp (ed.), **Lord Burlington–The Man and His Politics: Questions of Loyalty**

49. Norbert C. Soldon, **John Wilkinson (1728-1808), English Ironmaster and Inventor**

50. Norman A. Coles, **John Ashton's Case for James II as Rightful King of England: Rebellion or Revolution**

51. Pamela M. Gross, **Jane, the Quene, Third Consort of King Henry VIII**

52a. James H. Thomas, **The East India Company and the Provinces in the Eighteenth Century;** Volume I, **Portsmouth and the East India Company 1700-1815**

53. William T. Harper, **Origins and Rise of the British Distillery**

54. Eric Hopkins, **Charles Masterman (1873-1927), Politician and Journalist: The Splendid Failure**

55. D. Ben Rees, **Local and Parliamentary Politics in Liverpool From 1800 to 1911**

56. Priscilla Scott Cady,**The English Royal Messengers Service, 1685-1750: An Institutional Study**, assisted by Henry L. Cady

57. Peter T. Bradley, **British Maritime Enterprise in the New World: From the Late Fifteenth to the Mid-Eighteenth Century**

58. Nick Smart (ed.), **The Bickersteth Family World War II Diary: Dear Grandmother, Volume I: 1939-1942**

59. Kurt von S. Kynell, **Saxon and Medieval Antecedents of the English Common Law**

60. G.H. Bennett and Marion Gibson, **The Later Life of Lord Curzon of Kedleston–Aristocrat, Writer, Politician, Statesman: An Experiment in Political Biography**